# About Pearson

*Pearson is the world's learning company, with presence across 70 countries worldwide. Our unique insights and world-class expertise comes from a long history of working closely with renowned teachers, authors and thought leaders, as a result of which, we have emerged as the preferred choice for millions of teachers and learners across the world.*

*We believe learning opens up opportunities, creates fulfilling careers and hence better lives. We hence collaborate with the best of minds to deliver you class-leading products, spread across the Higher Education and K12 spectrum.*

*Superior learning experience and improved outcomes are at the heart of everything we do. This product is the result of one such effort.*

*Your feedback plays a critical role in the evolution of our products and you can contact us at reachus@pearson.com. We look forward to it.*

# Business Law

Third Edition

Tejpal Sheth

Pearson

*Editor—Acquisitions:* Varun Goenka
*Editor—Production:* Sakshi Kansal



ISBN 978-93-325-8615-4

First Impression, 2017
Eleventh Impression, 2024
**Twelfth Impression**



Published by Pearson India Education Services Pvt. Ltd, CIN: U72200TN2005PTC057128,

**Head Office:** 1st Floor, Berger Tower, Plot No. C-001A/2, Sector 16B,
Noida – 201 301, Uttar Pradesh, India.
**Registered Office:** Featherlite, 'The Address' 5th Floor, Survey No 203/10B,
200 Ft MMRD Road, Zamin Pallavaram, Chennai - 600044
Website: in.pearson.com, Email: companysecretary.india@pearson.com

*Printed in India at Sai Printo Pack Pvt Ltd*

# Brief Contents

# Contents

# Preface to the Third Edition

I am glad to present third edition of Business Law. It will aid commerce and management students to learn business law or legal aspect of business. This book also serves the students pursuing CWA (Inter) from ICAI.

Like previous edition, an attempt is made to cover the subject widely in a lucid way without compromising on technical details.

The book is divided in to 27 chapters. Each chapter is designed in four segment:

1. Theory supported with necessary example and case study;
2. Land mark judgements;
3. Questions—Test your knowledge; and
4. Multiple Choice Questions.

Chapters on Contract Act are made more concise. Basic concept of Indian Constitution is included as introduction. Now a days, company and LLP have become popular format of business and therefore provisions on Limited Liability Partnership Act, 2008 are explained in detail. Brief introduction on Constitution of India and fundamental rights are included. All applicable amendments in topics of Companies Act, 2013, Foreign Exchange Management Act, 1999 and Payment of Bonus Act, 1965 are incorporated at suitable places.

## About Book

This book covers syllables of "business law" for B.Com, B.B.A., BBM, and M.B.A. of all major universities of India. Also useful for CWA Intermediate.

Effort has been made to present the complicated provisions in simple manner so that students can easily grasp.

Law stated in this book is as amended upto 1st Jan 2015.
Book includes **250+** case study.
Book includes **800+** of questions under the 'test your knowledge' segment with hint answer.
Includes **900+** MCQ with answer.
Covers **360+** landmark judgements.
Each paragraph has been arranged under suitable heading for easy retention of concepts.

Each chapters has been uniformly organised under four heading:

1. Theory supported with necessary example and case study;
2. Land mark judgements;
3. Questions—Test your knowledge;
4. Multiple Choice Questions.

Although every efforts has been made to offer the most authentic position on subject, claiming cent per cent accuracy will be too tall claim. Moreover, there may be difference in interpretation. I shall be happy to receive suggestions and comments from readers.

I would like to thank publisher, Pearson Education, especially Mr. Varun Goenka for their commitment to the project. I would also like to thank the faculties of various business school and universities, students and reader for their continuous appreciation and creative suggestions.

Happy reading.

**Tejpal Sheth**

# Preface to the Second Edition

I am glad to present this second edition of *Business Law*. It will aid commerce and management students to learn business law or legal aspect of business. This book also serves the students pursing CWA (Inter) from ICAI.

Like the previous edition, an attempt is made to cover the subject widely in a lucid way without compromising on the technical details.

The book is divided into 27 chapters. Each chapter is designed in four segments: 1) theory supported with necessary example and case study; 2) landmark judgements; 3) Questions—Test your knowledge; and 4) Multiple-choice Questions.

Chapters on Contract Act have been framed more concisely. Nowadays, company and LLP have become popular format of business, and therefore, provisions on Limited Liability Partnership Act, 2008 have been explained in detail. Following three new topics have been included in this edition:

1. Provident Fund and Miscellaneous Provisions Act, 1952;
2. Limited Liability Partnership Act, 2008; and
3. Employees' State Insurance Act, 1948.

The Companies Act, 2013 has repealed old Companies Act, 1956 during the year 2013 by Ministry of Corporate Affair (MCA) and it has become fully functional by 2014. Chapters 18 to 22 contain applicable provisions of Companies Act, 2013. Likewise, all applicable amendments in topics of Foreign Exchange Management Act, 1999 and Information Technology Act, 2000 have been incorporated at suitable places.

Although every effort has been made on the accuracy of the content, there could always be some glitches. Moreover, there may be differences in interpretations also. I shall be happy to receive suggestions and comments from readers.

I would like to thank the publisher, Pearson Education, especially Vipin Kumar and Varun Goenka for their commitment to the project. I would also like to thank the faculties of various business schools and universities, students and readers for their continuous appreciation and creative suggestions.

**Tejpal Sheth**

# Preface to the First Edition

Business law has day-to-day application in any kind of business. Since managers and executives are sometimes required to plead in front of the court, they need to have a good understanding of the legal aspect of business. However, the requirements of a commerce student are different from law students. This book adopts a fresh approach to study and read business law. It will also be useful for candidates appearing for B.Com., BBA, BBM and MBA examinations. It is written in a student-friendly language without compromising on the technical details.

This book is divided into 24 chapters. It covers various topics of business law, namely, Contract Act, Partnership Act, Sales of Goods Act, Consumer Protection Act, Negotiable Instrument Act, Bonus Act, Gratuity Act, Information Technology Act, Foreign Exchange Management Act and Companies Act. Each chapter consists of 4 elements. (i) Theory supported with necessary examples and case studies; (ii) landmark judgements; (iii) test your knowledge, and (iv) multiple-choice questions. The book is supported with interpretations, explanations and illustrations to help students understand provisions in a better way. A small case study is also given after the completion of the subject–matter to test the understanding of students. Case studies include questions asked in CA and CS examinations in the recent past. Questions under Test Your Knowledge segment are prepared with reference answers by highlighting relevant paragraph number. A large number of multiple choice questions along with answers will encourage both the student and the teacher to test their knowledge and take tests, respectively. Although every effort has been made to make the information provided on the laws as authentic as possible, claiming absolute accuracy will be too tall a claim. Moreover, there may be differences in interpretation.

I would like to thank CA M. N. Mone, CA Sandeep Kamdar, CS Hitesh Buch, CS Umesh Ved, CS Upen Shah, Professor Milan Shah, Professor Ashish Dholakia and Professor Charu Dholakia. I would also like to express my gratitude to Dhiraj Pandey and Ruchi Sachdev of Pearson Education for their interest and support in this project. They have been meticulous, prompt and a pleasure to work with. Last but not the least, I would like to thank my wife, parents and daughter for their sacrifice and cooperation for providing the necessary environment. I would be happy to receive any suggestions or comments for the improvement of the book and students may also reach me on my face book id, Tejpal Sheth.

**Tejpal Sheth**

# About the Author

**Tejpal Sheth** is an associate member of Institute of Company Secretaries of India. He holds an MBA in International Business and Diploma in Pharmacy. Apart from Practising Company Secretary, he is dynamic and well-known educator in the professional stream. He is a visiting faculty in many reputed MBA colleges and professional institutes, ICSI, ICAI, ICWAI, Nirma Institute of Management, BSE Training Institute and Amity Global Business School, for more than 18 years. He has taught innumerable students of CA, CS, CWA, BBA and MBA programme on various topics like business law, mercantile law, corporate law, business ethics and communication. He has served as a member of various committees of Ahmedabad Chapter of ICSI in past. He is on expert panel of calubindia.com.

# Introduction to Constitution of India

**Learning Objectives**

*After reading introduction, you will be able to understand:*

- What is Preamble?
- Characteristics of Indian Constitution
- Fundamental rights, duties and directive principles of state

## CONSTITUTION OF INDIA

### 1. PREAMBLE

Almost in every constitution, there is a preamble, which provides the objectives, purposes, nature and scope of the constitution. The Preamble is an introduction of the Indian constitution and therefore, it is treated as a part of the Constitution. The Preamble is used to interpret the provisions of the constitution in case of disputes. Preamble to the Constitution of India is a brief introductory statement that sets out the guiding purpose and principles of the document. These are the opening words of the preamble of the Indian Constitution.

"We, the people of India, having solemnly resolved to constitute India into a sovereign, socialist, secular, democratic republic and to secure to all its citizens:

- **Justice:** social, economic and political
- **Liberty:** of thought, expression, belief, faith and worship
- **Equality:** of status and of opportunity; and to promote among them all
- **Fraternity:** assuring the dignity of the individual and the unity and integrity of the Nation

In our constituent assembly this twenty-sixth day of November 1949, do hereby adopt, enact and give to ourselves this constitution."

According to the Preamble, the "People of India" are only the supreme and on them, there is no hold of any other authority. Therefore, it is a republic state, wherein any king or dictator does not have any place; wherein the supremacy of the people is everything. The people elect the rulers and they are the representatives of the people.

## 2. CHARACTERISTICS OF INDIAN CONSTITUTION

The Constitution of India is largest and most detailed Constitution in world. It originally consisted of 395 Articles divided into 22 parts and 8 schedules. Indian Constitution has borrowed Parliamentary system of Government from British Constitution. Framers of Indian Constitution incorporated provisions of "Fundamental Rights" from the Constitution of United States of America, "Directive Principles of State Policy" from Ireland; Power of Judicial Review to the Supreme Court has been taken from the Constitution of United States of America.

The chief characteristics of Indian Constitution are as follows:

### Largest Constitution

The Indian Constitution is lengthiest and most detailed of all written Constitutions of the world. The Indian Constitution lays down the structure not only of Central Government but also of the States. The American Constitution on the other hand leaves the States to draw up their own Constitution. Because of peculiar problem of India like population, minorities, schedule class, Schedule tribe community peoples it had to incorporate many provisions.

### Democratic Form of Government

The Constitution of India constitutes India into a sovereign democratic republic. It thus provides for the establishment of a democratic form of government in the country. Justice, Liberty, Equality and Fraternity, which are essential characteristics of a democracy, are declared in the Preamble as the very objectives of the constitution. In a democracy, the Government derives all its authority from the will of the people. Our rulers are elected representatives of the people and are responsible to the people.

### Parliamentary Form of Government

The Indian Constitution establishes a parliamentary form of Government of India both at the Centre and in the States as distinguished from the presidential form of the Government in America.

### Fundamental Rights

The Constitution of India contains a long list of fundamental rights of citizens. The legislature and the executive cannot take away these rights unless it is necessary to do so in the public interest. These rights are, however, not absolute rights. They are restricted rights and can be restricted, abridged and taken away, when it is necessary in the public interest.

### Directive Principles

The Directive Principles of State Policy contained in Part IV of the Constitution. It set out the aims and objectives to be followed by the State in the governance of the country. The idea of the welfare state can be achieved only by implementing the various directive principles contained in the Constitution.

### Fundamental Duties

The 42nd Amendment Act, 1976, has added 10 Fundamental Duties in the Indian Constitution. It shall be the duty of every citizen of India to abide by all the fundamental duties.

## Distribution of Legislative Powers

The Indian Constitution contains three lists under Seventh Schedule:

- Union List—For subjects specified under union list, parliament has exclusive power to make laws.
- State List—For subjects specified under state list, the legislative of any State has exclusive power to make laws.
- Concurrent List—For subjects specified under concurrent list parliament and legislature of any state both have power to make laws.

Under Article 248 of the Indian Constitution, residuary powers are vested in the Centre. Articles 249, 250, 252 and 253 provide that Parliament can make laws on a matter specified in the State List in circumstances mentioned in these Arts.

## Single citizenship

Indian Constitution provides for single citizenship i.e., citizen of India.

## Independent Judiciary

Indian Constitution provides independence and impartiality of Judiciary. President makes appointment of Judges of the Supreme Court and High Court after consultation with judicial authorities. The Supreme Court and High Court recruit their own staff and frame rules regarding conditions of service.

# 3. FUNDAMENTAL RIGHTS

The fundamental rights as incorporated in the constitution can be classified under the following six groups:

## Right to equality

Right to equality includes equality before law, prohibition of discrimination on grounds of religion, race, caste, gender or place of birth, and equality of opportunity in matters of employment, abolition of untouchability and abolition of titles. Right to equality is provided from Article 14 to Article 18 of Indian constitution.

## Right to freedom

Right to freedom includes freedom of speech and expression, assembly, association or union or cooperatives, movement, residence, and right to practice any profession or occupation, right to life and liberty, protection in respect to conviction in offences and protection against arrest and detention in certain cases. Right to freedom is provided from Article 19 to 22 of constitution.

## Right against exploitation

Right against exploitation prohibits all forms of forced labour, child labour and traffic of human beings. It is provided under Articles 23 and 24 of Indian constitution.

## Right to freedom of religion

Right to freedom of religion includes freedom of conscience and free profession, practice, and propagation of religion, freedom to manage religious affairs, freedom from certain taxes and freedom from religious instructions in certain educational institutes. Article 25 to 28 enumerates the right to freedom of religion.

### Cultural and Educational rights

Preserve the right of any section of citizens to conserve their culture, language or script, and right of minorities to establish and administer educational institutions of their choice. Article 29 and Article 30 of Indian constitution provides for cultural and educational rights.

### Right to constitutional remedies

Right to constitutional remedies is present for enforcement of Fundamental Rights. It is provided under Article 32 of Indian constitution.

## 4. DIRECTIVE PRINCIPLES OF STATE POLICY

According to Dr. Ambedkar the directive principles are instruments of instructions to the legislature and the executives. Dr. Ambedkar said:

> "Whoever captures the power, will not be free to do what he likes with it. In the exercise of it, he will have to respect these instruments, which are called 'Directive-Principles'. He cannot ignore them."

Directive Principles are merely guidelines to Government in action. Following are the directive Principle:

- Principles of Internal State Policies
- The principles of International Policy
- To secure the right of all men and women to an adequate means of livelihood
- To ensure equal pay for equal work
- To make effective provision for securing the right to work, education and to public assistance in the event of unemployment old age, sickness and disablement
- To secure to workers a living wage, humane conditions of work, a decent standard of life, etc.
- To ensure that the operation of the economic system does not result in the concentration of wealth
- To provide opportunities and facilities for children to develop in a healthy manner
- To provide free and compulsory education for all children up to 14 years of age
- To promote educational and economic interest of scheduled castes, scheduled tribes and other weaker sections
- To organize village panchayats
- To separate judiciary from the executive
- To promulgate a uniform civil code for the whole country
- To protect national monuments
- To promote justice on a basis of equal opportunity
- To provide free legal aid
- To protect and improve environment and forests and wildlife
- To promote international peace and security

- To promulgate a uniform civil code for the whole country
- To settle international disputes by arbitration
- To take steps to maintenance of international peace and security
- To maintain friendly relationship with all the countries
- To give respect to the international law
- The Constitution (42nd Amendment) Act, 1976, has amended Article 39 (f). The new clause provides that children are given opportunities and facilities to develop in a healthy manner and in condition of freedom and dignity and that childhood and youth are protected against exploitation and against moral and material abandonment.

## 5. FUNDAMENTAL DUTIES

It shall be the duty of every citizen of India:

- To abide by the Constitution and respect its ideals and institutions, the National Anthem
- To cherish and follow the noble ideals which inspired our national struggle for freedom
- To uphold and protect the sovereignty, unity and integrity of India
- To defend the country and render national service when called upon to do so
- To promote harmony and spirit of common brotherhood amongst all the people of India transcending religious, linguistic and regional or sectional diversities; to renounce practices derogatory to the dignity of women
- To value and preserve the rich heritage of our composite culture
- To protect and improve the natural environment including forests, lakes, rivers and wild life, and to have compassion for living creatures
- To develop the scientific temper, humanism and the spirit of enquiry and reform
- To safeguard public property and to abjure violence
- To strive towards excellence in all spheres of individual and collective, so that the nation constantly rises to higher levels of endeavor and achievements
- To provide opportunities for education to his child or as the case be, ward between the age of 6 to 14 years by parent or guardian

# 1

# The Indian Contract Act, 1872: Nature and Kind of Contracts

**Learning Objectives**

*After reading this chapter, you will be able to understand:*

- What is an agreement and a contract?
- What are the essential elements of a contract?
- Types of contracts

## 1.1 SCOPE OF THE ACT

The Indian Contract Act was passed and implemented to control various kinds of commercial and business contracts. The preamble of the Contract Act states where it is expedient to define and amend certain parts of the law relating to contracts. Therefore, this act is not a complete code of contracts. It deals with general principles of the Law of Contract and Special Contract. The Contract Act is divided into 10 chapters.

The Contract Act came into force on 1 September 1872. The act is applicable to the whole of India except for the state of Jammu and Kashmir. The law of contract creates *jus in personam* and not *jus in rem*. *Jus in personam* means personal rights—the rights against a person or a party with whom you have entered into a contract. Therefore, it can be said that *jus in personam* provides the right to a contracting party to claim against another.

The Contract Act only provides rules and regulations for the purpose of contract. It does not list any rights and liabilities between parties to the contract. Rights and liabilities and their manner of performance are decided by the parties themselves under the contract but it is within the purview of the act.

***Examples***

1. A sells his car to B for ₹ 1 lakh. A has a right to recover the price of the car from B. The right of A is a right in personam, i.e., against a particular person B. This is *jus in personam.*
2. B buys a car and becomes the owner of the car. He has a right to have a quiet possession of the car and enjoy it against the whole world. Nobody in the world can disturb him in his right. The right of B is *jus in rem,* i.e., the right against the whole world.

**Case Study**

A and B of Srinagar entered into a contract on 1 September 2006 as per the provisions of the Indian Contract Act. Can they enforce the contract?

## 1.2 WHAT IS A CONTRACT?

### 1.2.1 Contract

In the words of Pollock, 'every agreement and promises enforceable by law is contract'. Section 2(h) of the Indian Contract Act, 1872 states that 'an agreement enforceable by law is contract'. This definition gives us two ingredients—an agreement and 'enforceable by law'. We can summarize it as under.

Contract = An agreement + enforceable by law

### 1.2.2 Agreement

An agreement means a promise and a reciprocal set of promises forming consideration for each other—Section 2(e). This definition gives us three ingredients—promise and a consideration. We can summarize it as under.

Agreement = Promise + reciprocal promise + consideration

### 1.2.3 Promise

As per Section 2(b) of the Contract Act, a proposal when accepted becomes a promise.

Promise = Proposal by one person + its acceptance by another person

### 1.2.4 Proposal

Section 2(a) states that 'when one person signifies another person his willingness to do or abstain from doing anything with a view to obtaining the assent of that other to such an act or abstinence, he is said to make a proposal'. A Proposal is also known as an offer.

### 1.2.5 Parties to an Agreement/a Contract

*Promisor:* A person making the proposal (offer) is known as a promisor. He is also known as an offeror. We can also recognize him as a proposor.

*Promisee:* A person accepting the proposal (offer) is known as a promisee. He is also known as an offeree. We can also recognize him as an acceptor.

### 1.2.6 Enforceability of an Agreement

It means an agreement which creates some legal obligation; if this agreement is not followed by any party to contract, he can be sued.

**Case Study**

A promises to deliver his watch to B and, in return, B promises to pay a sum of ₹ 2000. Is it an agreement or a contract?

## 1.3 ESSENTIAL ELEMENTS OF VALID CONTRACTS—SECTION 10

In order to determine whether an agreement is a contract or not, one has to see whether all the essentials, as required under the Indian Contract Act, are present in the agreement. The essentials required to be satisfied for a valid contract are as under.

### 1.3.1 Offer and Acceptance

There must be an offer and its acceptance. An offer is a starting point for any contract. No valid contract can come into existence without an offer. The offer is considered as the first step in the contract. The offer should be accepted to form a valid contract.

### 1.3.2 Intention to Create Legal Relation

There must be an intention to create a legal relation. In all social, domestic, moral, religious or political agreements, the usual presumption is that the parties do not intend to create the legal obligations. However, in business agreements, the usual presumption is that the parties intend to create the legal obligations.

***Example***

A invites B to a dinner and B accepts it. If A fails to serve the dinner, B cannot go to court. The invitation for dinner is a social agreement.

### 1.3.3 Lawful Consideration

The lawful consideration means something in return. As a contract contains the reciprocal set of promises, a consideration is necessary. The consideration must be lawful and should have a commercial value.

***Example***

A promises to pay ₹ 50,000 on a certain date to B without any promise in exchange. This is not a valid contract.

### 1.3.4 Free Consent

A contract is made when one person makes an offer while another person accepts the offer. This acceptance of the offer should be made without any force or threat. It means that a consent given should be free and genuine.

***Example***

A has two cars—one black and the other white. He offers to sell one of his cars to B. A intends to sell the black one while B accepts the offer believing that it is for the white car. Here, A and B are not thinking in the same sense of a particular thing. In this situation, there is a mistake, so it cannot be said to be a free consent.

### 1.3.5 Lawful Object

Every agreement has some objects or purposes. The object of an agreement should not be illegal, immoral or opposed to the public policy. In simple words, we can say that the object of an agreement must be lawful.

***Example***

A promised to pay ₹ 1 lakh to B to kill C. The killing of a person is punishable under the IPC. Therefore, the promise is unlawful and void.

### 1.3.6 Capacity of Parties

Every person is not competent to enter into a contract. Person who has attained the age of majority with a sound mind and not disqualified under any act is competent to enter into a contract.

### 1.3.7 Agreement Must Not Be Expressly Declared Void or Illegal

If a certain agreement is expressly declared to be void by the law of country then such an agreement, if entered into, shall not be enforceable by the court.

### 1.3.8 Certainty of Meaning

An agreement contains terms as decided by the parties. The terms of agreement must be certain and unambiguous. If the terms of an agreement are uncertain, it is not a valid contract.

***Example***

A agreed to pay ₹ 5 lakh to B for an ultra-modern decoration of his drawing room. The agreement is void because the meaning of the term 'ultra-modern' is not certain.

### 1.3.9 Possibility to Perform

Every agreement contains reciprocal promises. The promises under the contract must be possible to perform. If the parties have agreed on the contract which contains any promise not possible to perform in real life, the contract will not be considered as a valid contract.

***Example***

A agrees to discover treasure by magic for B. The agreement is void because the act in itself is impossible to be performed from the very beginning.

### 1.3.10 Legal Formalities

In some cases, the document in which the contract is incorporated has to be stamped. In some other cases, a contract, besides being a written one, has to be registered. Thus, where there is a statutory requirement that the contract should either be made in writing or registered, the required formalities must be complied with.

Therefore, we can say that an agreement will become a contract when it satisfies all the essentials of a valid contract. If any one of the elements of a valid contract is missing, it is treated as an invalid contract. All the agreements may or may not be a contract but all the contracts are basically agreements. All agreements are contracts if they are made by the free consent of the parties competent to contract, for a lawful consideration and with a lawful object, and are not hereby expressly declared to be void. Nothing herein contained shall affect any law in force in India and not hereby expressly repealed, by which any contract is required to be made in writing or in the presence of witnesses, or any law relating to the registration of the documents.

**Case Study**

A promised to pay his son B a sum of ₹ 1 lakh if B passed CA exams in the first attempt. B passed the examination on his first attempt but A failed to pay the amount as promised. B filed a suit for the recovery of the amount. State whether B can recover the amount under the Indian Contract Act, 1872.

**Case Study**

Salman promises Katrina to give a real pearl necklace at the time of his marriage. Salman fails to give it at the time of marriage. Can Katrina complain about the non-fulfillment of the promise against Salman at any court?

**Case Study**

State with reason, in brief, whether any contract is made in the following cases.

1. You have invited your business partner for a lunch.
2. When you eat meals at a restaurant.
3. When you board a public bus.
4. When you call a taxi on telephone.
5. When you put a coin in the slot of a weighing machine.

## 1.4 DISTINGUISH BETWEEN AN AGREEMENT AND A CONTRACT

| Matter | Agreement | Contract |
|---|---|---|
| Meaning | Every promise or a set of promises forming consideration for each other is an agreement. | Agreement enforceable by law is a contract. |
| One in another | All agreements are not contracts. | All contracts are agreements. |
| Enforceable at law | May or may not be enforceable. | Always enforceable by law. |
| Rights to parties | It does not always grant right. | It always grants rights. |

## 1.5 TYPES OF CONTRACT OR CLASSIFICATION OF CONTRACT

| On the Basis of the Mode of Formation | On the Basis of Performance | On the Basis of Validity or Enforceability |
|---|---|---|
| Express contract | Executed contract | Valid contract |
| Implied contract | Executory contract | Void contract |
| Quasi-contract | Partly executed and partly executory | Voidable contract |
| E-contract | Unilateral contract | Illegal agreement |
| | Bilateral contract | Unenforceable contract |
| | | Certain contract in writing |

### 1.5.1 Express Contract

An express contract is a contract made by the use of words spoken or written.

***Example***

A says to B 'Will you purchase my bike for ₹ 20,000?' B says 'Yes' to A.

### 1.5.2 Implied Contract

An implied contract is a contract which is made otherwise than by the words spoken or written. It came into existence on account of an act or conduct of the parties.

***Examples***

1. A stops a taxi by waving his hand and boards it. There is an implied contract that A will pay the prescribed fare on reaching his destination.
2. Withdrawal of cash from the ATM of a bank.

### 1.5.3 Quasi-contract

The quasi-contract is explained in detail in Chapter 8.

### 1.5.4 E-contract

An e-contract is a contract made through the electronic mode.

### 1.5.5 Executed Contract

In an executed contract both the parties have performed their promises under a contract. It is a contract where, under the terms of contract, nothing remains to be done by the parties.

***Example***

A sells his car to B for ₹ 1 lakh. A delivered the car and B paid the price. This is an executed contract.

### 1.5.6 Executory Contract

In an executory contract both the parties are yet to perform their promises. In other words, it is a contract where parties have to still perform their obligation in the future.

***Example***

A sells his car to B for ₹ 1 lakh. If A is still to deliver the car and B is yet to pay the price, it is an executory contract.

### 1.5.7 Partly Executed and Partly Executory Contract

In a partly executed and partly executory contract, one party has already performed his promise and the other party has yet to execute his promise.

***Example***

A sells his car to B. Though A has delivered the car, B has yet to pay the price. For A it is an executed contract, whereas it is an executory contract on the part of B since the price has yet to be paid.

### 1.5.8 Unilateral Contract

A unilateral contract is also known as a one-sided contract. It is a contract where only one party has to perform his promise. In such a contract, the promise on one side is exchanged for an act on the other side. After the formation of a unilateral contract, only one party remains liable to perform his obligation because the other party has already performed his obligation.

***Example***

Alap promises to pay ₹ 1000 to anyone who finds his lost cellphone. Bansi finds and returns it to Alap. From the time Bansi found the cell phone, the contract came into existence. Now Alap has to perform his promise, i.e., the payment of ₹ 1000.

### 1.5.9 Bilateral Contract

In a bilateral contract both the parties have to perform their respective promises. It is also known as a two-sided contract. Here, the obligation is outstanding on the part of both the parties.

***Example***

A promises to sell his car to B for ₹ 1 lakh and agrees to deliver the car on the receipt of the payment by the end of the week. The contract is bilateral as both the parties have exchanged a promise to be performed within a stipulated time.

### 1.5.10 Valid Contract

If the contract entered into by the parties and satisfies all the elements of a valid contract as per the act, it is said to be a valid contract.

### 1.5.11 Void Contract

A contract which ceases to be enforceable by law is known as a void contract. A void contract is not enforceable by the court. Generally, a valid contract ceases to be enforceable on the change in circumstances or on the change of provisions of an act.

### 1.5.12 Voidable Contract

When the contract is entered into without the free consent of party, it is considerate as a voidable contract. The definition of the act states that a voidable contract is enforceable by law at the option of one or more parties but not at option of the other parties. Voidable contract will be considered as valid if it is not cancelled by the aggrieved party within a reasonable time.

### 1.5.13 Illegal Agreement

An illegal agreement is one which is forbidden by law. All illegal agreements are void *ab initio*. It cannot be enforced by any court. Not only that any associated or collateral transaction to an illegal agreement is also void. No action is allowed on an illegal agreement. No action can be taken for the recovery of the money paid under illegal agreement or for the breach of the illegal agreement. The parties to an illegal agreement cannot get help from the court. No suit can be filled or any action taken in respect of the illegal agreement.

### 1.5.14 Unenforceable Contract

A contract which satisfies all the requirements of the contract but has technical defects is called an unenforceable contract. A contract is said to have a technical defect when it does not fulfil the legal formalities required by some other act. When such legal formalities are complied with later on, the act becomes enforceable.

### 1.5.15 Certain Contracts in Writing

The Contract Act never specifies that the contract to be valid should be in writing. It means an oral contract or a contract without any kind of writing is also valid. However, it is difficult to prove before the courtroom when the dispute arises.

The contracts are required to be in writing only if any other act specifically requires it to be so. Like the hire-purchase act requires that the hire-purchase agreement should be in writing.

**Case Study**

A, a tradesman, left certain goods at B's house by mistake. B treated and used the goods as his own. Can the tradesman recover the money of the goods used by B?

**Case Study**

Mohan agrees to pay Sohandada ₹ 50,000 to kill a business competitor. Mohan has borrowed this money from his friend but now refuses to pay him back. Can his friend claim it by approaching the court? Would your answer be different in any manner if his friend does not have the knowledge about the purpose of borrowing?

**Case Study**

A agrees to sell his DVD player to B promising to deliver it on the date of payment. B promises to pay the amount within one month. What kind of contract is it?

## 1.6 DISTINGUISH BETWEEN VOID AND VOIDABLE CONTRACT

| Matter | Void Contract | Voidable Contract |
|---|---|---|
| Definition | It means contract which ceases to be enforceable. | It means an agreement enforceable by law, by one or more parties. |
| Nature | Valid when made but subsequently becomes unenforceable. | It remains as voidable until cancelled by the party. |
| Rights or remedy | No legal remedy is available for the void contract. | Aggrieved party has a remedy to cancel the contract. |
| Performance of contract | Party cannot demand the performance of contract. | If aggrieved party does not cancel it within a reasonable time, performance can be demanded. |
| Reason | Contract becomes void due to change in law or circumstances. | If consent is not obtained freely then it is regarded as a voidable contract. |
| Damages | Party cannot claim damages. | Party can demand damages in certain cases. |

## 1.7 DISTINGUISH BETWEEN VOID AND ILLEGAL AGREEMENT

| Matter | Void Agreement | Illegal Agreement |
|---|---|---|
| What | Void agreement is not prohibited by law. | It is prohibited by law. |
| Effect on collateral transaction | Any agreement which is collateral to the void agreement is enforceable. | Any agreement or transaction which is collateral to illegal agreement is not enforceable. |
| Punishment | It is not punishable. | It is punishable. |
| Void *ab initio* | May not void *ab initio*. | Always void *ab initio*. |

## 1.8 SIMILARITIES BETWEEN VOID AND ILLEGAL AGREEMENTS

Both the void and the illegal agreements are unenforceable agreements, hence void. Restitution (restoration of benefits) is not possible in either of the two agreements.

### LIST OF LANDMARK JUDGEMENTS

1. ***Balfour vs Balfour (1919)***
   A husband agreed to pay 30 pound to his wife every month while he was abroad. As he failed to pay the promised amount, his wife sued him for the recovery of the amount. Here she could not recover it as it was a social agreement and the parties did not intend to create legal relations.

2. ***Rose and Frank vs J. R. Cromption & Bros (1923)***
When an agreement states that it is not a formal agreement, it shall not be subject to legal jurisdiction of any court. It was held that it is not a binding contract as there is no intention to create a legal relation.
3. ***Punjab National Bank vs Arura Lal Durga Das (1960)***
The Contract Act applies to all the contracts in India.
4. ***Taylor vs Porting (1855)***
An agreement the meaning of which is not capable to being made certain is void.
5. ***Jyoti Brothers vs Shree Durga Mining Co. (1956)***
An agreement to agree in future always remains only an agreement not enforceable by law.
6. ***Thawardas Pherumal vs UOI (1955)***
No contract is created where an offeree says that he would accept the proposal after it is reduced in writing.

## TEST YOUR KNOWLEDGE

1. Define agreement. **(Ref. Para-1.2)**
2. Define contract and distinguish between agreement and contract. **(Ref. Para-1.2,1.4)**
3. Enumerate the essentials of a valid contract. **(Ref. Para-1.3)**
4. All contracts are agreements but all agreements are not contract. Comment on the statement. **(Ref. Para-1.4)**
5. What is an express contract? Give a suitable example. **(Ref. Para-1.5)**
6. Explain in brief the implied contract with an example. **(Ref. Para-1.5)**
7. Explain in brief the executor and the executed contract. **(Ref. Para-1.5)**
8. Define void contract. **(Ref. Para-1.5)**
9. Define voidable contract. **(Ref. Para-1.5)**
10. What is the main difference between void and voidable contract? **(Ref. Para-1.6)**
11. What is an illegal agreement? Is illegal agreement always void? **(Ref. Para-1.5)**
12. Distinguish between void and illegal agreements. **(Ref. Para-1.7)**
13. What are similarities between void and illegal agreements? **(Ref. Para-1.8)**

## MULTIPLE-CHOICE QUESTIONS

1. The Law of Contract is nothing but
   (i) a child of commercial dealing.
   (ii) a child of religion.
   (iii) a child of day-to-day politics.
   (iv) a child of economics.
2. An agreement consists of reciprocal promises between at least
   (i) four parties.
   (ii) six parties.
   (iii) three parties.
   (iv) two parties.
3. In India, the express provisions of the Contract Act applies to
   (i) Hindus.
   (ii) female.
   (iii) businessman.
   (iv) all of the above.

4. Every promise and every set of promise forming the consideration for each other is a/an
   (i) contract.
   (ii) agreement.
   (iii) offer.
   (iv) acceptance.
5. A contract creates
   (i) rights in personam.
   (ii) rights in rem.
   (iii) no obligations.
   (iv) only obligations and no rights.
6. Valid contracts
   (i) are made by free consent.
   (ii) are made by competent parties.
   (iii) have lawful consideration and lawful object.
   (iv) all of the above.
7. Agreement to murder a person
   (i) cannot be enforceable by law.
   (ii) is valid in law.
   (iii) is invalid for want of consideration.
   (iv) has no consensus ad idem.
8. A invites B for coffee in Coffe day Restaurant and B accepts the invitation. On the appointed date, B goes there but A is does not come. In this case
   (i) B has no remedy against A.
   (ii) B has to wait for another invitation from A.
   (iii) B can sue A for not honouring his words.
   (iv) A has to invite B again, to keep the promise.
9. A promise to give ₹ 5000 per month pocket money to his son B. If A does not give the pocket money
   (i) B can sue his father.
   (ii) B has no remedy against A.
   (iii) B can accept a lower pocket money also.
   (iv) B has to give ₹ 5000 to his father.
10. An agreement is valid
   (i) which creates legal and social obligations of the parties.
   (ii) which creates rights of a party.
   (iii) which is written on a piece of paper and signed by the parties.
   (iv) which creates legally binding right and obligations of the parties to it.
11. When the contract is perfectly valid but cannot be enforced because of certain technical defects. This is called
   (i) unilateral contract.
   (ii) bilateral contract.
   (iii) unenforceable contract.
   (iv) void contract.
12. …………… is without any legal effect and cannot be enforced in a Court of Law.
   (i) Valid contract
   (ii) Void contract
   (iii) Voidable contract
   (iv) Unenforceable contract
13. A and B enter into a contract to marry each other. Before the time fixed for the marriage, A goes mad. The contract becomes
   (i) void.
   (ii) illegal.
   (iii) valid.
   (iv) voidable.
14. A makes a contract with B to beat his business competitor. This is an example of
   (i) valid contract.
   (ii) illegal agreement.
   (iii) voidable contract.
   (iv) unenforceable contract.
15. ……………… is made by words spoken.
   (i) Express contract
   (ii) Implied contract
   (iii) Tacit contract
   (iv) Unlawful contract

16. ................. is made by words written.
    (i) Express contract
    (ii) Implied contract
    (iii) Tacit contract
    (iv) Unlawful contract
17. A appoints B as his agent, by way of a power of attorney. This is an example of
    (i) express contract.
    (ii) implied contract.
    (iii) tacit contract.
    (iv) unlawful contract.
18. ................ implies a contract though the parties never expressed their intention to enter into a contract.
    (i) Express contract
    (ii) Implied contract
    (iii) Electronic contract
    (iv) Unlawful contract
19. ................ is a one-sided contract in which only one party has to perform his promise or obligation.
    (i) Void contract
    (ii) Illegal agreement
    (iii) Unilateral contract
    (iv) Bilateral contract
20. All illegal agreements are void; but all void agreements are not illegal.
    (i) True
    (ii) Partly true
    (iii) False
    (iv) None of the above
21. According to enforceability, the contracts may be classified as
    (i) valid contracts.
    (ii) void contracts.
    (iii) voidable contracts.
    (iv) all of the above.
22. A contract in which, under the terms of a contract, nothing remains to be done by either party is known as
    (i) executed contract.
    (ii) executory contract.
    (iii) unilateral contract.
    (iv) none of the above.
23. A contract in which, under the terms of a contract, one or both the parties have still to perform their obligations in future is known as
    (i) executed contract.
    (ii) executory contract.
    (iii) unilateral contract.
    (iv) none of the above.
24. Contracts classified on the basis of performance are
    (i) executed contracts.
    (ii) executory contracts.
    (iii) partly executed or partly executory contracts.
    (iv) all of the above.
25. Express contract means a contract made by
    (i) words either spoken or written.
    (ii) documents.
    (iii) both words and documents.
    (iv) all of the above.

## ANSWER KEYS

| | | | | |
|---|---|---|---|---|
| **1.** (i) | **6.** (iv) | **11.** (iii) | **16.** (i) | **21.** (iv) |
| **2.** (iv) | **7.** (i) | **12.** (ii) | **17.** (i) | **22.** (i) |
| **3.** (iv) | **8.** (i) | **13.** (i) | **18.** (ii) | **23.** (ii) |
| **4.** (ii) | **9.** (ii) | **14.** (ii) | **19.** (iii) | **24.** (iv) |
| **5.** (i) | **10.** (iv) | **15.** (i) | **20.** (i) | **25.** (iv) |

# 2

# The Indian Contract Act, 1872: Offer and Acceptance of an Offer

## Learning Objectives

*After reading this chapter, you will be able to understand:*

- Offer and its essential elements
- Kind of offer
- Lapse of offer
- Acceptance of an offer and its requirements
- Rule of communication for an offer and acceptance

An offer is the first step in the formation of a contract. An offer is a proposal by one person to another to enter into a contract. The term offer is defined under Section 2(a) as under:

'When one person signifies to another, his willingness to do or abstain from doing anything with a view to obtaining the assent of the other, to such an act or abstinence, he is said to make a proposal'.

## 2.1 ESSENTIAL ELEMENTS OF AN OFFER (PROPOSAL)

From the above definition, we can understand the following elements of an offer.

### 2.1.1 Two Parties

For a valid offer, there must be two parties. A person cannot make an offer to himself.

### 2.1.2 Communication

The offer must be communicated to the offeree. If it is never communicated to the offeree, it cannot be accepted and no valid contract comes into existence.

### 2.1.3 Willingness

The offer must show willingness of the offeror. Mere telling or sharing a plan is not an offer. Sharing the idea or the feelings is not willingness. If the party proposes certain terms on which he is willing to negotiate, in such a case, he is not making an offer because he is not expressing his willingness to enter into a contract.

### 2.1.4 With Intention of Obtaining Assent

The offer must be made with a view to obtaining the assent of the offeree. The offer made out of a prank or as a joke is not a valid offer, and therefore if accepted, it can never make the valid contract.

### 2.1.5 Offer May Be Positive or Negative

The offer may involve doing something or not doing something—Section 2(o). The offer to do something is a positive offer or not to do something is a negative offer.

***Examples***

1. A proposes to B to make a TV serial. The proposal is to do something, i.e., to make a serial. It is a positive proposal.
2. A proposes to B, 'If you do not file a suit against me for defamation, I shall give you ₹ 1 lakh'. The proposal is to abstain from doing something. It is a negative proposal.

## 2.2 LEGAL RULES AS TO OFFER

The offer is the first step in a valid contract. If the offer itself is not valid, the contract can never be valid. Following are the legal rules of an offer.

### 2.2.1 Offer Should Not Bind the Other Party to Reply

The offer should not bind the other party to reply. In the same way, if the offer should not contain terms, non-compliance of which may be assumed as acceptance.

***Example***

A writes a letter to B. I offer to sell my house for ₹ 10,00,000. If I do not receive your reply by next week, I will assume that you have accepted offer. If B does not reply, it means non-acceptance of the offer.

### 2.2.2 Offer Must Be Definite, Unambiguous and Certain

The terms of an offer must be definite, clear and certain. If the terms are vague and uncertain, contract cannot come into existence.

***Example***

A made a contract with B and promised that if he was satisfied as a customer, he would favorably consider his case for the renewal of the contract. The promise is too vague to create a legal relationship.

### 2.2.3 Offer Must Be Made to Create Legal Relationship

A social invitation is not regarded as an offer because if it is accepted it does not give rise to any legal relationship.

***Example***

Amar invites Bansi for dinner. It is social invitation.

### 2.2.4 Invitation to Offer is Not an Offer

An invitation to an offer or an intention to put a proposal does not amount to an offer. A catalogue or price list of goods or services for sale is not a proposal but the invitation of proposal. Hence, no business house is bound to sell its goods for the price stated in it. Price-tags attached with the goods displayed in any showroom or supermarket is also an invitation to proposal. If the salesman or the cashier does not accept the price, the interested buyer cannot compel him to sell. If he wants to buy it, he must make a proposal. The menu card of a restaurant is an invitation to put an offer. A job or tender advertizement inviting applications for a job or inviting tenders is an invitation to the offer. A prospectus inviting public to apply for shares in a company is an invitation to put the offer to buy shares. However, the offer for the right shares or for shares from a reserve quota to its existing members is the offer.

***Examples***

1. A, father, wrote to his intended son-in-law that his daughter would have a share of what he left after his death. Held, statement was merely an intention to put a proposal.
2. A sent a letter to B stating the terms on which he is ready to do business as an agent. It was not an offer but only a statement on intention.
3. An advertizement for auction sale is merely an invitation to make an offer, and not an offer for sale. Therefore, an advertizement of an auction can be withdrawn without any notice. The persons going to the auction cannot claim for the loss of time and expenses, if the advertisement for auction is withdrawn.

### 2.2.5 Terms and Conditions Communicated Along with an Offer

The terms and conditions of the offer must be communicated with the offer. If the terms and conditions are communicated or informed before or at the time of making an offer, it gives an opportunity to the offeree to decide about the acceptance of the offer. But if the terms and conditions are informed after the offer is made or after the contract is made, it is not binding to the offeree.

***Example***

A and his wife booked a room in a hotel, and paid rent in advance. When they entered into the room, they found a notice exempting the proprietor of hotel from the liability for loss or theft of articles of clients, staying therein. Due to negligence of hotel staff, their articles were stolen. A filed a suit on the proprietor for compensation of damages. Held, the proprietor was liable to pay compensation, since the terms of proposal were communicated after the acceptance. Hence, the terms were not a part of the contract and A was not bound by them.

A ticket purchased for entrance into places of amusement, ticket issued by railway or bus companies and many other contracts set out in printed documents contain numerous terms. Many of which the party receiving the ticket or document is ignorant of. If a passenger on a railway train receives a ticket on the face which is printed 'this ticket is issued subject to the notices, regulations and conditions contained in current time-tables of railways', the regulations and conditions referred to are deemed to be communicated to him, and he is bound by them whether or not he has read them. He is bound, even if he is illiterate and unable to read them. But the notice of the conditions must be given at the time of making a contract and not after the contract is made.

**Case Study**

A asks B, the shopkeeper—'What is the price of apples'? B says, '₹ 10 per kg'. Is there any valid contract between A and B?

**Case Study**

A offered to take a house on lease for a period of three years, if the house was handsomely decorated. Is it valid offer? Why?

**Case Study**

An auctioneer advertised in a newspaper that a sale of office furniture would be held on a certain date. A person, with the intention to buy furniture, came from a distant place for the auction but the auction was cancelled. Can he file a suit against the auctioneer for his loss of time and expenses?

**Case Study**

SBI Bank has communicated voluntary Retirement Scheme to all its employees. One of the managers has applied under it but the bank has refused his application. Does the bank manager has any right against the Bank? Why?

## 2.3 DISTINGUISH BETWEEN INVITATION TO OFFER AND AN OFFER

| Basis | Invitation to Offer | An Offer |
|---|---|---|
| Meaning | A person proposes certain terms on which he is willing to negotiate, and invites the other party to make an offer on those terms. | A person, expresses his willingness to be bound by the terms of his offer if the other party to whom he is making it, accepts it. |
| Willingness | It expresses initial intention. | It expresses final willingness. |
| Lead towards | Invitation to offer leads towards offer. There is a possibility to get many offers. | Offer lead towards acceptance and contract. |
| Binding | Intends to do some other/further act, before becoming bound by his act. | Shows or intends to be bound by the acceptance of invitation by the other. |

## 2.4 CLASSIFICATION OF OFFERS OR KINDS OF OFFERS

An offer or a proposal can be classified on a number of different bases. We can summarize the kinds of offer in the following manner.

### 2.4.1 Express Offer

The offer made by using words spoken or written is known as an express offer.

***Example***

A says to B—'Will you purchase my car for ₹ 2,00,000'?

### 2.4.2 Implied Offer

The offer which could be understood by a conduct of parties or circumstances of case is called the implied offer.

***Example***

Withdrawal of money from the card holder from the ATM. It creates an implied contract between the card holder and the bank.

### 2.4.3 Specific Offer

The offer made to a specific person or a particular person or two or more than two specific persons. The specific offer is made to an ascertained person.

***Example***

A says to B—'Will you purchase my house for ₹ 2 lakhs'? It is a specific offer as it is made to B. Only B can accept it.

### 2.4.4 General Offer

It is not necessary that the offer should be made to a specific person. The offer can be made to the world at large. If the offer is made to the world at large, it is known as the general or public offer. The general offer is one which is not made to a specific person. The general offer can be accepted by any one.

***Example***

An advertisment in a newspaper, 'Any one who will find my lost dog will be rewarded with ₹ 2000'.

### 2.4.5 Cross Offer

If two parties made offer to one another in ignorance of the offer made by other party, and terms-conditions in both the offers are same. Two cross offers do not conclude a contract.

***Example***

A offers by a letter to sell 100 tons of steel at ₹ 1000 per ton. On the same day B also writes to A offering to buy 100 tons of steel at ₹ 1000 per ton.

### 2.4.6 Continuous Offer

It is the offer which is open for a continuous period of time, it is also known as the open offer or the standing offer.

***Example***

A tender to supply goods as and when required, amounts to a standing offer.

### 2.4.7 Counter Offer

The offer made by the offeree in return of the original offer is called as the counter offer.

***Example***

A offered to sell his pen to B for ₹ 1000. B replied, 'I am ready to pay ₹ 950'. On A's refusal to sell at this price, B agreed to pay ₹ 1000. Held, there was not contract, as the acceptance to buy it for ₹ 950 was a counter offer, i.e. rejection of the offer of A. the subsequent acceptance to pay ₹ 1000 is a fresh offer from B to which A was not bound to give his acceptance.

### 2.4.8 Legal Effects of Counter Offer

It amounts as a rejection of the original offer. In the above example, when the counter offer of ₹950 is made by B, it amounts as a rejection of the original offer (i.e., ₹ 1000) made by A.

When the counter officer is made, the original offer is lapsed. It means when the counter offer of ₹950 is made, and not accepted by A, B cannot accept the original offer of ₹ 1000.

The counter offer results in a new offer which may be accepted or rejected by the other party. If he accepts it, the contract is said to be concluded.

**Case Study**

A says to B—'I offer to sell my car to you for ₹ 2 lakhs and B accepts the offer by saying clearly 'I accept your offer'. Is it a valid offer? If so, which kind of offer it is?

**Case Study**

B makes to memorise a proposal to his parrot and sends him to A to recite the proposal. The parrot does so. Is it valid proposal?

**Case Study**

A advertizes in paper that any person who found his lost dog can get a reward of ₹ 5000. Can the advertizement be said as the general offer? Can any person who finds the lost dog claim the reward money?

## 2.5 DISTINGUISH BETWEEN GENERAL OFFER AND SPECIFIC OFFER

| Basis | General Offer | Specific Offer |
|---|---|---|
| Meaning | It is the offer made to the public at large. | It is the offer made to a specific person or a group of specific persons. |
| Continuation | It continues, until accepted by any person. | It continues up to reasonable time, or until it gets revocked. |
| Acceptance | It is accepted from any one from public who has knowledge of offer. | It can be accepted only by the person to whom it is made. |
| Method of acceptance | It can be accepted by performance of condition. | It can be performed by performance of condition or by giving an acceptance. |

## 2.6 LAPSE OF OFFER OR WHEN OFFER COMES TO AN END

The offer may come to an end in any of following ways.

### 2.6.1 Notice of Withdrawal

If a notice of withdrawal given by an offeror to the offeree before the acceptance of offer then the offer cannot be accepted by the offeree.

### 2.6.2 Lapse of Time

The offeree must accept the offer within the time prescribed in the offer, and if no time is prescribed, it must be accepted within a reasonable time. Thus, the offer lapses if it is not accepted within the time prescribed in the offer or within a reasonable time. What is a reasonable time that depends upon the circumstances in each case.

### 2.6.3 Non-fulfillment of Condition Attached with an Offer

When there is a condition in the offer which must be fulfilled before the acceptance of the offer, the offer lapses if the acceptance is given without fulfilling that condition.

### 2.6.4 Counter Offer

A counter offer means making a fresh offer instead of accepting the original offer. The counter offer amounts to rejection of the original offer. Hence, as soon as the counter offer is made, the original offer stands lapsed.

### 2.6.5 Acceptance Is Not Made in the Prescribed Mode or Usual Manner by the Offeree

Sometimes, the offeror prescribes the mode of acceptance. In such a situation the offer must be accepted in that very manner, and if it is not accepted in the prescribed mode, the offer stands lapsed.

### 2.6.6 Death or Insanity of an Offeror or Offeree

The offer lapses by the death or insanity of an offeror, if the fact of his death or insanity comes to the knowledge of the acceptor, before he makes his acceptance. But if the offer is accepted in ignorance of the death or insanity of the offeror, there will be a valid contract. The offer comes to an end on the death of the offerer also because the offer can be accepted only by the offeree and not by any other person. It cannot be accepted even by the legal heirs of the offeree.

### 2.6.7 Rejection of an Offer by the Offeree

The offer lapses as soon as it is rejected by the offeree. Once the offer is rejected, it cannot be received subsequently. The offer is said to be rejected, if the offeree expressly rejects it or accepts it, subject to certain conditions.

### 2.6.8 Destruction of Subject–Matter

The offer lapses if it becomes illegal before it is accepted, or the subject matter of the offer is destructed.

### 2.6.9 By Change in Provision of Act or Any Law

If there is a change in law, which makes the offer illegal or unlawful or impossible in terms of its performance, the offer comes to an end.

## 2.7 LEGAL RULES FOR THE ACCEPTANCE

The acceptance is the assent given by the offeree to an offer made to him. It is a communication of his intention to be bound by the terms of the offer. As per Section 2(b) 'when the person to whom the proposal is made signifies his assent thereto, the proposal is said to be accepted. The proposal when accepted, becomes a promise'.

Sir William Anson has explained the effect of acceptance while saying that 'acceptance is to an offer what a lighted match is to a train of gunpowder'.

When a lighted match stick comes in contact with gunpowder, it creates a blast. Thereafter it will not be possible to bring things in normal. In the same way on acceptance to the offer, it gives rise to an agreement. Once the acceptace is given, immediately the contract comes into effect, and then there is no possibility to go back. The parties to contract are bound by the terms and conditions of the contract.

### 2.7.1 Acceptance Must Be Absolute and Unqualified

To form a valid contract, the acceptance must be absolute and unqualified. Unqualified means unconditional. The acceptance must be for the whole offer including all its terms and conditions if any. It may be noted that conditional acceptance will result into a counter offer.

***Example***

A offers to sell his house to B for ₹ 2 lakhs. B accepts the offer and promises to pay the price in four installments. This is not a valid acceptance as the acceptance is with variation in the terms of the offer.

### 2.7.2 Acceptance Must Be Communicated

Mere mental acceptance is no acceptance. But there is no requirement of communication of acceptance of the general offer. The general offer can be accepted by the performance of a condition.

***Example***

The Manager of railway company received a draft agreement relating to the supply of coal. The manager marked the draft with the words 'Approved', and put the same in the drawer of his table and forgot all about it. Held, there was no contract between the parties as the acceptance was not communicated. It may, however, be pointed out that the Court construed a conduct of parties, as railway company was accepting the supplies of coal from time to time.

### 2.7.3 Manner of Acceptance

The general rule says that it must be as per manner prescribed by the offeror. If no mode is prescribed, it can be accepted by some usual and reasonable manner.

If there is a deviation in communication of the acceptance of offer, the offeror may reject such acceptance by sending a notice within a reasonable period of time. If the offeror does not send a notice of rejection, he has accepted the acceptance of offer.

***Example***

A offers B and indicates that the acceptance be given by telegram. B sends his acceptance by ordinary post. It is a valid acceptance unless A insists for acceptance in the prescribed manner.

### 2.7.4 Acceptance of Offer Must Be from Competent Person

For a valid contract, the acceptance must be given by the competent person or an authorized person. The acceptance given by any person who is not authorized will not create any contact.

***Example***

A applied for the headmastership of a school. He was selected by the appointing authority but the decision was not communicated to him. However, one of the members in his individual capacity informed him about the selection. Subsequently, the appointing authority cancelled its decision. A sued the authority for breach of contract. The Court rejected A's action and held that there was no notice of acceptance. 'Information by unauthorized person' is as insufficient as overhearing from behind the door.'

The acceptance of the specific offer must be made by the person to whom it is made. The general offer can be accepted by anyone who fulfills the terms and conditions of the offer and has knowledge of it. Communication to the offeror is not required.

### 2.7.5 Time Limit for Acceptance

If the offer prescribes the time limit, it must be accepted within a specified time. If the offer does not prescribe the time limit, it must be accepted within a reasonable time.

***Example***

A applied (offered) for shares in a company in early June. The allotment (acceptance) was made in late November. A refused to take the shares. Held, A was entitled to do so as the reasonable time for acceptance had elapsed.

### 2.7.6 Acceptance May Be Express or Implied

The acceptance of offer may be expressly (by words spoken or written) or impliedly (by the acceptance of consideration) or by performance of conditions (e.g., in case of the general offer). Implied acceptance is inferred from the conduct or activities of the party. Implied acceptance does not require any formal acceptance.

### 2.7.7 Mere Silence Is Not Acceptance of an Offer

Generally, silence is not amounted as the acceptance of an offer.

***Example***

A offers to B to buy his house for ₹ 5 lakhs and writes 'If I hear no more about it within a week, I shall presume the house is mine for ₹ 5 lakhs' B does not respond. Here, no contract is concluded between A and B.

However, following are two exceptions to the above rule. It means silence amounts as acceptance of offer.

1. Where the offeree agrees that non-refusal by him within a specified time shall amount to the acceptance of offer.
2. When there is a custom or usage of trade which specifies that silence shall amount for the acceptance.

### 2.7.8 Acceptance Subject to Contract Is No Acceptance

If the acceptance has been given 'subject to contract' or subject to approval by certain persons, it has no effect at all. Such an acceptance will not create a binding contract until a formal contract is prepared and signed by all the parties.

**Case Study**

A offers B to sell his house for ₹ 15 lakhs and directs him to send his acceptance only by e-mail. B sends a letter of acceptance by post. Is there the valid contract between parties? What would be your opinion if A does not reject the acceptance made by e-mail within a reasonable time?

**Case Study**

'A' invites tenders for the supply of 10 quintals of cotton. 'B', 'C' and 'D' submit their tenders. When the contract can be concluded?

**Case Study**

A offered a reward to anyone who has returned his lost dog. B brought the dog to A without having heard of the offer. Can B claim the reward from A?

## 2.8 GENERAL RULES AS TO COMMUNICATION OF ACCEPTANCE

The general rules relating to communication of acceptance are the following:

### 2.8.1 In Case of Acceptance by Post

Where the acceptance is given by post, the communication of the acceptance is complete as against the proposer, when the letter of the acceptance is posted. Thus, a mere posting of the letter of the acceptance is sufficient to conclude the contract. However, the letter must be properly addressed and stamped.

### 2.8.2 Delayed or No Delivery of Letter

Where the letter of acceptance is posted by the acceptor but it never reaches the offeror or it is delayed in transit, it will not affect the validity of acceptance. The offeror is bound by the acceptance.

### 2.8.3 Acceptance by Telephones, Telex or Fax

If communication of the acceptance is mady by telephone, teleprinter, telex and fax machines, it completes when the acceptance is received by the offeror. The contract is concluded as soon as the offeror receives or hears the acceptance.

### 2.8.4 Place of Contract

In case of the acceptance by post, the place where the letter is posted is the place of contract. Where the acceptance is given by instantaneous means of communication (telephone, fax, teleprinter and telex), the contract is made at the place where the acceptance is received.

### 2.8.5 Time of Contract

In case of acceptance by post, the time of posting the letter of acceptance is the time of contract. But in case of acceptance by instantaneous means of communication, the time of contract is the time when the offeror gets the communication of the acceptance.

### 2.8.6 Communication of Acceptance in Case of Agent

Where the offer has been made through an agent, the communication of the acceptance is completed, when the acceptance is given either to the agent or to the principal. In such a case, if the agent fails to convey the acceptance received from the offeree, still the principal is bound by the acceptance.

### 2.8.7 Acceptance on Loudspeakers

The acceptance given on loudspeaker is not a valid acceptance.

## 2.9 COMMUNICATION OF OFFER AND ACCEPTANCE—SECTIONS 4 AND 5

The rules relating to communication of the offer and its acceptance are the following.

### 2.9.1 Communication of Offer

The communication of the offer is complete when it comes to the knowledge of the offeree.

### 2.9.2 Communication of Acceptance—Against the Offeror

The communication of the acceptance is complete as against the offeror, when it is put in a course of transmission to him so as to be out of the power of the offeree. It means the offeror is bound by acceptance as soon as the letter of the acceptance is duly posted by the offeree.

### 2.9.3 Communication of Acceptance—Against the Offeree

The communication of the acceptance is complete against the offeree, when it comes to the knowledge of the offeror. It means the offeree is bound by the acceptance when the letter of the acceptance reaches the offeror.

### 2.9.4 Communication of Revocation of an Offer

In case of revocation of the offer, the offeror is bound by revocation of the offer as soon as he duly posts the letter of revocation of the offer. He cannot cancel the revocation made by him. But revocation of the offer is binding on the offeree only if the letter of revocation of the offer is received by the offeree before the letter of acceptance is duly posted by the offeree.

### 2.9.5 Communication of Revocation of an Acceptance

In the case of revocation of the acceptance, the offeree is bound by revocation of the acceptance as soon as he duly posts the letter of revocation of the acceptance. But revocation of the acceptance is binding on the offeror only if the letter of revocation of the acceptance is received by the offeror before the letter of the acceptance is received by the offeror.

**Case Study**

Amar Posts a letter of offer to Kamla on 1 January 2011, which is received by kamla on 5 January 2011. Kamla posts a letter of acceptance to Amar on 12 January 2011, which is received by Amar on 17 January 2011.

1. When is the communication of offer completed?
2. When is Amar bound by an acceptance?
3. When is Kamla bound by an acceptance?

Further assumes that Amar revokes his offer by posting a letter on 17 January 2011, which is received by kamla on 13 January 2011.

1. Is revocation of offer by Amar binding on Kamla?
2. Would your answer be different in any manner if Kamla has received the said letter on 11 January 2011?

Further assume that if Kamla revokes her acceptance by posting the letter on 14 January 2011, which is received by Amar on 16 January 2011.

1. Is revocation of letter of the acceptance binding on Amar?
2. Would your answer be different if Kamla revokes her acceptance by posting the letter on 18 January 2011?

## LIST OF LANDMARK JUDGEMENTS

1. ***Banwarilal vs Sukhdarshan Dayal (1973)***
   The promises made over loud speaker have no legal binding.
2. ***Felthouse vs Bindley (1863)***
   The acceptance of the offer cannot be presumed from silence.

3. ***Olley vs Marborough Court Ltd (1949)***
   No excluding or limiting term will be effective, unless it is brought to the notice of the party or to the attention of the party at the time of making a contract.
4. ***Carllic vs Cabolic Smoke Ball Co. (1893)***
   The offer could be made to public at large. The performance of the conditions in the offer is sufficient enough to be considered as the acceptance, and it need not to be communicated.
5. ***Ramsgate Hotel Co. vs Montefiore (1966)***
   The acceptance of the offer should be made within the prescribed time if the time limit is given. If no time limit is given, acceptance of the offer should be made within a reasonable time. The term 'reasonable time', depends on the facts and circumstances of each case.
6. ***Gopi vs Raghu (1949)***
   When the offeror says that the acceptance will be presumed if no reply is received, the absence of reply cannot mean the acceptance of an offer. Mere silence is not assent or acceptance.
7. ***Hajee vs Murugesa (1958)***
   The contract to enter into contract is not a valid contract.
8. ***Foley vs Classique Ltd (1934)***
   The agreement to agree in future is not a contract.
9. ***Khwaja Muhammed vs Hussaini Begam (1910)***
   The benefit can be given to the third party to a contract by creating a trust or charge in favour of such a person. The beneficiary under the trust or charge may enforce the contract. However, it must be noted that the stranger must be clearly designated as a beneficiary, and the trust or charge in his favour, must also be of some specific property.
10. ***Harris vs Nickerson (1973)***
    A mere statement of intention is not an offer.
11. ***Partodge vs Critterden (1968)***
    An invitation to receive an offer is not an offer.
12. ***U. P. State Electricity Board vs Goel Electric Store (1977)***
    The proposal gets revoked when the counter offer is made.
13. ***Bhagwandas vs Girdharilal (1966)***
    The acceptance of the offer can be made by conduct.
14. ***Sharad Trading Co. vs State (1980)***
    If a person agrees to keep open a proposal for a certain time and accepts certain considerations for keeping the proposal open, he cannot withdraw the proposal before that date.

## TEST YOUR KNOWLEDGE

1. Define the term offer.
2. What are the essential elements of a valid offer? **(Ref. Para-2.1)**
3. An offer may be positive but not negative. Comment. **(Ref. Para-2.1)**
4. An offer must show willingness of the offeree. Is it a correct statement? **(Ref. Para-2.1)**
5. What are the legal rules as to proposal? **(Ref. Para-2.2)**
6. A valid offer should bind the other party to reply compulsarily. Comment. **(Ref. Para-2.2)**

7. Can a proposer add terms and conditions after an offer is made? **(Ref. Para-2.2)**
8. Write a short note on the invitation to make an offer. **(Ref. Para-2.2)**
9. Distinguish between the offer and the invitation to make an offer. **(Ref. Para-2.3)**
10. Write a short note on kinds of offer. **(Ref. Para-2.4)**
11. Explain counter offer with suitable examples. **(Ref. Para-2.4)**
12. A counter offer to an offer lapses the offer. Comment. **(Ref. Para-2.4)**
13. What are the main difference between an express offer and an implied offer? Explain with suitable examples? **(Ref. Para-2.4)**
14. What are the effects of a counter offer? **(Ref. Para-2.4)**
15. Distinguish between a general offer and a specific offer. **(Ref. Para-2.5).**
16. When does an offer come to an end? **(Ref. Para-2.6)**
17. An acceptance must be made before the proposal lapses. Comment. **(Ref. Para-2.6)**
18. Define the term acceptance. **(Ref. Para-2.7)**
19. Who is competent to accept the offer? **(Ref. Para-2.7)**
20. State the rules relating to the acceptance of an offer. **(Ref. Para-2.7)**
21. Silence does not amount to the acceptance of an offer. Is it correct? **(Ref. Para-2.7)**
22. The acceptance subject to contract is no acceptance. **(Ref. Para-2.7)**
23. When can silence amount to acceptance? **(Ref. Para-2.7)**
24. Mere mental acceptance is no acceptance of an offer. Explain. **(Ref. Para-2.7)**
25. Explain the general rules as to the communication of the acceptance? **(Ref. Para-2.8)**
26. When is the communication of an offer and its acceptance complete? **(Ref. Para-2.9)**

## MULTIPLE-CHOICE QUESTIONS

1. An implied offer means an offer made
   (i) by spoken words.
   (ii) by SMS.
   (iii) by body language.
   (iv) by both (i) and (iii).
2. A proposal may consist of a promise for
   (i) doing an act.
   (ii) abstaining from doing an act.
   (iii) either (i) or (ii).
   (iv) returning the consideration.
3. An offer may be made
   (i) by words.
   (ii) by conduct.
   (iii) either (i) or (ii).
   (iv) neither (i) nor (ii).
4. An offer can be accepted by
   (i) offeror.
   (ii) offeree.
   (iii) promisor.
   (iv) either (i) or (ii).
5. A specific offer is one which is made
   (i) by A to B.
   (ii) by a father to his only son for the sale of his factory to him.
   (iii) by a father of a girl to the father of an only son for her marriage.
   (iv) by all of the above.

6. A offers to sell his car on internet, it is
   (i) an express offer. (iii) a particular offer.
   (ii) an implied offer. (iv) no offer.
7. The offer which is allowed to remain open for the acceptance over a period of time is known as a/an
   (i) standing offer. (iii) express offer.
   (ii) specific offer. (iv) implied offer.
8. The offer made to a specific person is known as a
   (i) standing offer. (iii) special offer.
   (ii) specific offer. (iv) separate offer.
9. Communication of the proposal is complete when it comes to the knowledge of
   (i) the person to whom it is made. (iii) either (i) or (ii).
   (ii) the Proposer. (iv) the Central government.
10. A proposes by letter, to sell his horse to B at ₹ 10,000. Communication of the proposal is complete when
    (i) A posts the letter.
    (ii) B receives the letter.
    (iii) B acknowledges to A that he has received the letter.
    (iv) either (ii) or (iii), whichever is earlier.
11. Terms of the offer must be
    (i) ambiguous. (iii) definite.
    (ii) uncertain. (iv) vague.
12. Which of the following conditions is not necessary for a valid offer?
    (i) The intention to create legal relation.
    (ii) The unconditional terms.
    (iii) The certainty of terms.
    (iv) The communication to the person to whom it is made.
13. Which of the following conditions is not necessary for a valid offer?
    (i) The intention to obtain consent of the offeree.
    (ii) The communication to the person to whom it is made.
    (iii) The intention to create legal obligation.
    (iv) Expressed in written form.
14. An application filled in by a prospective applicant to the company is an example of
    (i) an invitation to offer. (iii) bid.
    (ii) an offer. (iv) an acceptance.
15. The statement of lowest price at which the seller would sell his goods constitutes
    (i) a valid contract. (iii) an express contract.
    (ii) a implied contract. (iv) no contract.
16. Which of the following is an invitation to offer?
    (i) A tender to supply goods at a certain time. (iii) A bid in an auction sale.
    (ii) A request for a loan. (iv) A catalogue of goods for sale.
17. There is a counter-offer when
    (i) the offeree gives conditional acceptance. (iii) the offeree makes some query.
    (ii) the offerer makes a fresh offer. (iv) the offeree accepts it.

18. When the offers made by two persons to each other containing similar terms of bargain cross each other in post, they are known as
   (i) cross offers.
   (ii) implied offers.
   (iii) direct offers.
   (iv) express offers.
19. A offers to sell his car for ₹ 50,000 to B. B says he would buy it for ₹ 40,000. This is a case of
   (i) counter offers.
   (ii) implied offers.
   (iii) direct offers.
   (iv) express offers.
20. In which of the following circumstances, the offer comes to an end?
   (i) Lapse of time.
   (ii) Counter offer.
   (iii) Death of offerer or offeree before acceptance.
   (iv) All of the above.
21. An offer comes to an end after the expiry of
   (i) time stipulated for acceptance.
   (ii) a reasonable time.
   (iii) either (i) or (ii).
   (iv) neither (i) nor (ii).
22. An offer can be accepted by
   (i) a notice of acceptance.
   (ii) a performance of condition specified in the offer.
   (iii) an acceptance of consideration for a reciprocal promise.
   (iv) all of the above.
23. The acceptance may be
   (i) express.
   (ii) implied.
   (iii) neither (i) nor (ii).
   (iv) either (i) or (ii).
24. The specific offer can be accepted by
   (i) any person.
   (ii) any friend of the offerer.
   (iii) only the person to whom it is made.
   (iv) any friend of the offeree.
25. The general offer can be accepted by
   (i) sending a communication of acceptance.
   (ii) mental acceptance of offer.
   (iii) complying with the conditions of offer.
   (iv) making a counter offer.
26. In order to convert a proposal into a promise, the acceptance must be
   (i) absolute.
   (ii) unqualified.
   (iii) express.
   (iv) all of the above.
27. When no mode is prescribed by the offerer for the acceptance of his offer, such acceptance shall be made
   (i) By telephone.
   (ii) As desired by the offeree.
   (iii) In some usual and reasonable manner.
   (iv) None of the above.
28. Which of the following is incorrect?
   (i) A valid contract results from identical cross offers.
   (ii) Communication of the offer is complete when the letter of offer is posted though it has not reached the person to who the offer is made.

(iii) An offer and invitation to offer are the same.
(iv) All of the above.

29. Conditions on the reverse of a train ticket, air ticket, bill issued by service providers are examples of
(i) normal business policy.
(ii) space saving measure.
(iii) special conditions.
(iv) general rules of Contract Law.

30. The acceptance on telephone should be
(i) heard by the offerer.
(ii) audible to the offerer.
(iii) understood by the offerer.
(iv) all of the above.

31. When two persons agree to enter into an agreement in the future, there is ............. between them.
(i) a valid contract
(ii) no contract
(iii) an agreement
(iv) a consensus

32. The person making the offer is known as the 'offeror' or the 'promisor' and to whom it is made is known as
(i) acceptor.
(ii) acceptor for honour.
(iii) offeree or promisee.
(iv) contracting party.

33. The general offer made to the public at large is valid and a binding contract is made with person who having the knowledge of the offer
(i) comes forward and acts accordingly.
(ii) acts accordingly and his act is ratified by the offeror.
(iii) seeks the offeror's permission to accept the offer.
(iv) informs the public that he is willing to accept the offer.

34. Which of the following is the legal rule of the valid acceptance?
(i) An acceptance must be given within prescribed or reasonable time.
(ii) An acceptance must be given before the lapse of an offer.
(iii) An acceptance may be expressed or implied.
(iv) All of the above.

35. A proposes, by letter, to sell a house to B for ₹ 10,000. The communication of the proposal is complete
(i) when B receives the letter.
(ii) when A dispatches the letter.
(iii) when A signs the letter.
(iv) when B knows about the letter.

36. Which of the following statements is correct?
(i) The valid contract cannot result from identical cross offers.
(ii) The proposal when accepted becomes a promise.
(iii) The rejected offer cannot be accepted.
(iv) All of the above.

37. Which of the following is correct?
(i) The acceptance must precede an offer.
(ii) The acceptance may be given in any manner unless the offeror insists acceptance in the prescribed manner.
(iii) Silence always amounts to acceptance.
(iv) The acceptance may be valid even if the offeree adds certain conditions.

## ANSWER KEYS

| | | | | |
|---|---|---|---|---|
| **1.** (iii) | **9.** (i) | **17.** (i) | **25.** (iii) | **33.** (i) |
| **2.** (iii) | **10.** (ii) | **18.** (i) | **26.** (iv) | **34.** (iv) |
| **3.** (iii) | **11.** (iii) | **19.** (i) | **27.** (iii) | **35.** (i) |
| **4.** (ii) | **12.** (ii) | **20.** (iv) | **28.** (iv) | **36.** (iv) |
| **5.** (iv) | **13.** (iv) | **21.** (iii) | **29.** (iii) | **37.** (ii) |
| **6.** (i) | **14.** (ii) | **22.** (iv) | **30.** (iv) | |
| **7.** (i) | **15.** (iv) | **23.** (iv) | **31.** (ii) | |
| **8.** (ii) | **16.** (iv) | **24.** (iii) | **32.** (iii) | |

# 3

# The Indian Contract Act, 1872: Capacity of Parties and Consideration

**Learning Objectives**

*After reading this chapter, you will be able to understand:*

- Capacity of parties to enter into contract
- Effects of minor's agreement
- Person disqualified to enter into contract
- Consideration and its rules
- Valid contracts without consideration

## 3.1 CAPACITY OF PARTIES

As per Section 10, all agreements are contracts, if they are made by the parties competent to contract. The competency of parties is one of the essential elements of the valid contract. The capacity of parties to the contract means the legal ability of the parties to enter into a contract.

### 3.1.1 Who Are Competent to a Contract?

Section 11 specifies the persons who are competent to contract. It suggests that every person who is of the age of majority, sound mind and disqualified from entering into a contract is competent to contract.

In simple form we can understand that the following persons can enter into the contract:

1. Person who has attained age of majority.
2. Person who is of sound mind.
3. Person who is not disqualified by law.

Conversely, it can be said that minors, persons of unsound mind and persons disqualified by law are not competent to enter into a contract.

## 3.2 MINOR

According to the Majority Act 1875, a person who has not completed the age of 18 years is a minor. When guardian is appointed by the court, the person becomes a major when he attains the age of 21 years.

## 3.3 EFFECT OF MINOR'S AGREEMENT

Effects of minor's agreement are briefly discussed under the following heads:

### 3.3.1 Agreement Is Void *ab initio*

The agreement by a minor is void *ab initio*. It is nullity in the eye of law. An agreement with a minor can never be enforced by the other party. The law protects the minors as they are not capable to understand the terms of contracts, and the rights and liabilities under the contract. Landmark judgment of Mohribibi explains the effect of minor's agreement as under.

***Example***

*Mohiribibi versus Dharmodas*

D minor borrowed money from M by executing mortgage of his house in favour of M. Later on his failure to pay money. It was held that minor's agreement is void and money cannot be recovered. M was ordered to release his house from mortgage. Court has explained that minor cannot be promisor but he can be promisee.

### 3.3.2 Minor Can Be a Promisee or Beneficiary

An agreement for the benefit of a minor is enforceable by the minor. It means if a major borrows money from a minor and later refuses to pay it, the minor can sue him and recover the same.

### 3.3.3 No Ratification

Ratification by the minor is not valid. The ratification means the acceptance of a transaction already done. However, on attaining majority, he can enter into a fresh contract having the same terms and conditions.

Again, it is worth noting that where a minor had not completed a transaction during his minority and continues to complete the same on majority, he will be liable for the whole transaction. Therefore, the services are rendered at the desire of the minor during his minority (to the minor) and are continued to be rendered at his request after his majority. If he makes a promise to pay for the whole, the promise is enforceable.

***Example***

A, a minor, borrowed ₹ 2000 from B. A executed a promissory note (P/N) in favour of B. This is void P/N. On attaining majority, A replaces a fresh P/N for the old one. Still this is void because ratification of void agreement is also void.

### 3.3.4 No Specific Performance

No specific performance order can be granted against a minor. A specific performance order is the order granted by the court against the defaulting party to contract to perform, the promise as per the terms and conditions of the contract. As a minor cannot be a promisor, a minor cannot be forced to perform a promise.

### 3.3.5 Restitution Order

A restitution order can be granted against a minor. The restitution order means restoring the things to its proper owner. The restitution order is granted subject to the following conditions:

1. The power of court to order restitution is discretionary.
2. It is generally allowed by the court when a minor had misrepresentation to the other party about his age.
3. The court considers all facts and circumstances.
4. If money paid to the minor is in same form, the minor may be ordered to pay it back.
5. If money is used to purchase property, property purchased by the minor shall be used in paying off money.

### 3.3.6 Contract by Parent or Guardian

Under certain circumstances, the guardian can enter into a contract on behalf of the minor. For the contract entered by the guardian on behalf of the minor is valid if:

1. It is the benefit of the minor.
2. The guardian is authorized to enter the contract.

***Example***

The guardian is not authorized to enter into the contract for the purchase of immovable property.

For the contract entered by the guardian on behalf of minor neither the guardian nor the minor is personally liable. But the assets or property of the minor is liable. It means money can be recovered by the other party from the asset or estate of the minor.

**Case Study**

A, a minor, entered into a contract for borrowing a sum of ₹ 40,000 out of which the lender paid him a sum of ₹ 18,000 A executed mortgage of property in favour of the lender. Is mortgage of property valid? Can the lender enforce the contract?

**Case Study**

A is a minor, B approaches A for a loan on the basis of a mortgage of the house owned by B. Hence, A advances the money and B executes a mortgage in favour of A, the minor. Is the mortgage of property valid? Can a minor enforce the contract against B?

**Case Study**

A, a minor, draws a cheque in favour of B. On attaining majority, A makes out a fresh cheque in lieu of the old one. Which cheque issued by the minor is valid? Explain reason.

## 3.4 DIFFERENT POSITION OF A MINOR

A minor cannot be a promisor but a minor can be a promisee or a beneficiary. Based upon this understanding, we can discuss the following different position of the minor.

### 3.4.1 Minor Agent

A minor cannot appoint an agent because only a person competent to contract can appoint the agent. However, the minor can be appointed as an agent.

### 3.4.2 Guarantee for and by a Minor

The contract of guarantee in favour of the minor is valid. However, the minor cannot be a surety in the contract of guarantee. This is because the surety is ultimately liable under the contract of guarantee, whereas the minor can never be held personally liable.

### 3.4.3 Minor and Insolvency

The minor can never enter into a contract and cannot create personal liability. Therefore, he cannot be declared insolvent.

### 3.4.4 Minor as a Joint Promisor

The minor can be a joint promisor with a major but the minor cannot be held liable under the contract as well as to his co-promisor. But the major promisor is liable.

### 3.4.5 Minor Shareholder

The minor cannot apply for the allotment of shares in a company as he is not competent to contract. However, the minor can apply to the transfer of fully paid shares in the company through his guardian.

### 3.4.6 Minor and Negotiable Instruments Act

The minor can draw, make, negotiate or endorse any negotiable instrument (i.e. cheque, P/N and B/E) but will not be personally liable under any such instruments. However, any negotiable instrument executed or endorsed in favour of the minor can be enforced by him.

### 3.4.7 Service Contract

The minor cannot be a promisee and therefore the contract of personal service by the minor is void.

### 3.4.8 Minor as Trade Union Member

Any person who has attained the age of 15 years may be a member for the registered trade union, provided the rules of the trade union allows so. Such a member will enjoy all the rights of a member.

### 3.4.9 Liability for Tort

The minor is liable for a tort, i.e. civil wrong committed by him.

***Example***

A 14-year-old boy drives a car carelessly and injures B. He is liable for the accident, i.e. tort.

## 3.5 MINOR'S LIABILITY FOR NECESSITIES

In any contract for supplying necessities to the minor or his dependent neither the minor nor his guardian is liable. But the property of the minor is liable**.** The things supplied must be necessities of life. It may be noted that necessities of life are those things without which an individual cannot reasonably exist. The minor is not already in possession of such necessities, otherwise it is not considered as necessities.

Food, clothes, bed, shelter, shoes, medicines and similar other things required for the maintenance of his life or for the life of his dependents, expenses for instruction in grades or arts; expenses for moral, religous or intellectual education, funeral expenses of his deceased family members, marriage expenses of a dependent female member in the family; expenses incurred in the protection of his property or personal liberty, Diwali pooja expenses, etc. have been held by the courts to be necessaries of life. However, the things like earrings for a male, spectacles for a blind person or a wild animal cannot be considered as necessaries.

### 3.5.1 Things Must Be Suitable to the Conditions in Life of the Minor

The things supplied must be suitable to the conditions in life to the minor. They must be according to the status in life of the minor. While deciding the things of necessity, one should not forget that 'what is necessity for a duchess is luxury for a farmer's wife'. Necessary is different from person to person.

***Example***

A minor was supplied a pair of pearl and diamond buttons. Held it could not be considered as necessaries in this case.

### 3.5.2 The Minor Must Be in Need of Such Things

The minor must be in need of the things supplied. If the minor is already having a sufficient supply of the things supplied and does not need them any more, further supply of them will not be considered to be necessary.

***Example***

A, a minor, purchased 11 fancy waist coats and other clothes. While he was already having sufficient clothes to wear. Held the 11 waist coats and other clothes purchased were not necessaries and the price was irrecoverable.

**Case Study**

Teji, a minor, broke his right leg in a football match. He engaged Curewell, a doctor to set it. Does the doctor have a valid claim for his services? Give reasons.

**Case Study**

Amit, 16 years of age, fractures his leg while playing cricket. He goes to a doctor and gets his leg plastered. The doctor demands a fees of ₹ 1000 but Amit refuses to pay on the ground that he is a minor. The doctor files a suit against Amit. Will the doctor succeed? Give reason.

## 3.6 PERSON OF UNSOUND MIND

At the time of entering into a contract, a person must be of sound mind. The law presumes that every person is of sound mind unless otherwise it is proved before the court. An agreement by a person of unsound mind is void. Following are the categories of persons considered as persons of unsound mind.

### 3.6.1 An Idiot

An idiot is a person who is congenital (by birth) unsound mind. His incapacity is permanent, and therefore he can never understand the contract, and makes a rational judgment as to its effects upon his interest. Consequently, the agreement of the idiot is absolutely void *ab initio*. He is not personally liable even for the payment of necessaries of life supplied to him.

### 3.6.2 Delirious Persons

A person delirious from fever is also not capable of understanding the nature and implications of an agreement. Therefore, he cannot enter into the contract so long as delirium lasts.

### 3.6.3 Hypnotized Persons

Hypnotism produces temporary incapacity till a person is under the effect of artificial induced sleep.

### 3.6.4 Mental Decay

There may be a mental decay or senile mind due to old age or poor health. When such person is not capable of understanding the contract and its effect upon his interest, he cannot enter into contract.

A lunatic is not permanently of unsound mind. He can enter into a contract during lucid intervals, i.e. during a period when he is of sound mind.

### 3.6.5 Drunken Person

An agreement by the drunken person, or by a person in a state of drunkenness, who is not capable to understand the terms and conditions of a contract is void. An agreement made by an intoxicated person is void.

## 3.7 PERSON DISQUALIFIED BY LAW

Following categories of persons are disqualified by law to enter into a contract or a specific type of contract.

### 3.7.1 Body Corporate or Company or Corporation

The contractual capacity of a company is determined by the object clause of its memorandum of association. Any act done in excess of power given is ultra-vires, and hence void. A company cannot enter into any contract which is beyond its memorandum or which is personal in nature as it is an artificial person.

### 3.7.2 Alien Enemy

An alien means a person who belongs to a foreign state. An alien can be an enemy or a friend. When he is a citizen of any country which was against India in war, he is known as alien enemy. If any contract is entered into with the alien enemy and the war breaks out with that country, the contract is suspended until the war is over. During the war, the contract can be entered into with the alien enemy with the permission of the central government.

### 3.7.3 Convict

A convict cannot enter into a contract while he is undergoing imprisonment. But he can enter into a contract with the permission of central government while undergoing imprisonment. However a convict can enter into a contract when is released from jail or he has been granted bail.

### 3.7.4 Insolvent

When any person is declared as an insolvent his property vests in the receiver and therefore, he cannot enter into a contract relating to his property. Again he becomes capable to enter into a contract when he is discharged by the court.

The foreign sovereigns, diplomatic staff and representative of foreign staff can enter into valid contract.

***Note:***

A person can enter into a contract with Foreign Sovereigns, their Diplomatic Staff and Representatives of Foreign States, who have a special privilege in the sense that they cannot be sued upon by others without a special permission of the central government.

## 3.8 WHAT IS CONSIDERATION?

In latin, consideration is known as 'quid pro quo'. It means something in return. It is the benefit received by a party to the contract in return of the promise made by him.

***Example***

A, a coolie, lifts B's luggage and B pays him remuneration. Lifting luggage is causing detriment to the coolie but a benefit to the passenger, i.e. promisor.

Consideration may be doing of some act or not doing an act. It means right, benefit, interest avoidance of loss or profit received by one party.

A contract is valid if supported by a consideration. A consideration is moving from both the parties. No consideration, no contract. A promise without consideration is not an agreement and hence it is not a contract. Ex nudo pacto, non oritur action—out of a naked pact, no cause of action arises. Pact means promise.

### 3.8.1 Consideration is Defined Under Section 2(d)

When, at the desire of the promisor, the promisee or any other person has done or abstained from doing, or does or abstains from doing, or promises to do or to abstain from doing, something, such act or abstinence or promise is called the consideration for the promise.

## 3.9 TYPE OF CONSIDERATION

We can understand the different types of consideration as under.

### 3.9.1 Past Consideration

It is also known as executed consideration. One party to contract has received the benefit before formation of contract.

***Example***

A requests B to find out his lost cow. B found out and delivered the cow to A. Thereafter, A promised to pay B ₹ 500 as a reward. Here, the efforts of B at the request of A constitute a valid past consideration for the promise by A to pay ₹ 500 to B. The consideration by B was given before the promise to pay is made by A.

### 3.9.2 Present Consideration

It is received at the time of formation of the contract. It is in process of execution.

***Example***

A buys a TV set from B's shop and pays the price immediately. The act of both the parties constitutes a present or executed consideration.

### 3.9.3 Future Consideration

It will be received by a party after the formation of the contract. It is also called as executory consideration.

***Example***

A agrees to sell a TV set to B for ₹ 10,000 on first of the next month and B agrees to pay the price 10 days after the date of delivery. In this contract, consideration for both the parties is future or executory.

## 3.10 ESSENTIALS OF VALID CONSIDERATION

We can summarize the following essentials of the valid consideration.

### 3.10.1 Consideration Means Doing or Not Doing Something

The consideration is some act or abstinence. Some act means doing something while abstinence means not to do something. Thus, a consideration can be positive or negative. To do something is known as positive consideration while not to do something is known as negative consideration.

### 3.10.2 Consideration Must Move at the Desire of Promisor

The consideration must move at the desire of the promisor. However, it is not necessary that it must be for the benefit of the promisor. It can be for the benefit of a third person also.

***Example***

A is employed by an institute to teach 'Mercantile Law' but A teaches 'Economics'. A is not entitled to claim the remuneration because he has done nothing at the desire of the promisor.

### 3.10.3 Consideration May Move from Promisee or Other Person

The consideration may move from a promisee or any other person. If the consideration is moved from the promisee or any other person, it is valid.

### 3.10.4 Consideration May Be Inadequate

The consideration may be inadequate. The act only says that there should be a consideration and consideration means something in return. It means if a person sells a book worth ₹ 2000 in ₹ 200, it is a valid consideration and a valid contract. However, the consideration should be certain. It means mutually agreed upon by both the parties.

### 3.10.5 Consideration May Be Past, Present or Future

The consideration may be past, present or future. A past consideration is valid in India while it is not regarded as valid in many other countries.

### 3.10.6 Act Promisor Bound to Do Is Not Consideration

If the promisor is legally bound or required to perform something as a part of his duty, and he agrees to do so, it is not a valid consideration. The consideration must be something different from a promisor's existing obligation.

***Example***

A promises to pay to B, a lawyer, an additional sum of money if the suit was decided in his (A's) favour. Held there was no consideration for this promise and hence void. The lawyer once accepted to defend the case was under contractual duty to render the best of his services.

### 3.10.7 Consideration Must Be Lawful

The consideration must be lawful. Lawful means as per the provisions of an act. An unlawful act or benefit received in an unlawful manner is not regarded as the consideration.

### 3.10.8 Consideration Should Be Possible to Perform

The consideration must be real and not illusory. It means the consideration should not be impossible to perform. An act does not recognize impossible performance. It may be physically impossible or can be legal impossible.

***Example***

A promises to discover treasure by magic if B pays him ₹ 1000. Consideration from A is void because it is impossible to perform the promise.

**Case Study**

A promises to pay an existing debt punctually, if B, the creditor, gives him a discount. Is this consideration valid?

## 3.11 STRANGER TO CONTRACT AND STRANGER TO CONSIDERATION

As a general rule, there should be 'a privity of contract' to enable the party to contract to sue against the other party to contract or for enforcement of contract against the other party. As a part of a general rule, a stranger to contract cannot sue. The stranger to contract and stranger to consideration are explained in brief after this example.

***Example***

If the contract is between A and B, D will be known as stranger to contract. D cannot sue either A or B as D is not party to contract. Here A can sue B or B can sue A.

### 3.11.1 Stranger to Consideration

The consideration can be supplied by any person, and it need not to be supplied by the promisee only. If it is supplied by any other person other than promisor, then the person who is supplying is known as stranger to the consideration.

### 3.11.2 Stranger to Contract

The stranger to contract means the person who is not party to contract. The stranger to contract is also known as third party. The stranger to contract cannot bring suit except in recognized cases.

## 3.12 EXCEPTION TO THE RULE OF STRANGER TO CONTRACT

The stranger to contract has the right to sue in the following cases.

### 3.12.1 Beneficiary

In case of trust, the beneficiary may enforce the contract. The beneficiary of a trust or other interest in specific immovable property can enforce it even if he is not a party named in the trust deed.

### 3.12.2 Family Settlement or Marriage Settlement

In case of family settlement, marriage settlement or any other agreement for such purpose, any person can sue even though he is not a party to the contract. But family settlement or marriage settlement should be reduced to writing.

***Example***

A partition deed between the male members of a family made a provision for the expenses of marriage of a female member. Accordingly, the expenses of the marriage were to be contributed by her father and brothers but they refused. Held she was entitled to the amount even though she was not a party to the contract.

### 3.12.3 Assignment of Contract

In case of an assignment of contract, when the benefit under a contract has been assigned, the assignee can enforce the contract. The assignment of the contract can take place by the act of parties. The contract requiring personal skill cannot be assigned.

### 3.12.4 Agency

When a contract entered into through an agent. Here the stranger can sue even party to contract when the agent has acted within his authority and in the name of principal.

## 3.13 EXCEPTION TO RULE 'NO CONSIDERATION NO CONTRACT'—SECTION 25

The essentials of a valid contract suggest that the contract is valid if it is supported by a consideration. The contract or agreement without a consideration is void. Latin maxim says that 'Ex Nudo pacto non oritur action', i.e. an agreement without a consideration is void. In layman language, we can say that no consideration, no contract. However following agreements and contracts entered into without consideration are valid.

### 3.13.1 Agreement on Account of Natural Love and Affection

If an agreement is made on account of natural love and affection, it is valid even if it is without the consideration if following conditions satisfied:

1. Agreement should be in writing.
2. Agreement should be registered as per the law.
3. Parties to agreement must fall within blood relation. Mere nearness of relation does not necessarily imply natural love and affection.

### 3.13.2 Voluntary Past Services

A promise made without a consideration is valid if it is the promise to compensate a person who has already voluntarily done something for the promise. But voluntary past services rendered should be lawful. In order that the promise to pay for the past voluntary services is binding, the following essential factors must exist:

1. The services should have been rendered voluntarily.
2. The services must have been rendered for the promisor.
3. The promisor must be in existence at the time when services were rendered.
4. The Promisor must have intended to compensate to the promisee.

***Example***

A finds B's purse and gives it to him. B promises to give A ₹ 50. This is a contract to compensate some voluntary service.

### 3.13.3 Bailment

No consideration requires for gratuitous bailment of goods. A bailment is a special contract.

### 3.13.4 Agreement to Pay Time Barred Debt

An agreement or promise to pay time barred debt is valid if:

1. It is made in writing signed by the debtor.
2. It relates to the debt which could not be enforced by the creditor because limitation period is over.

### 3.13.5 Gift

Rule of no consideration no contract is not applicable to completed gift. A gift is completed when it is accepted by donee. However, an agreement to make a gift is not enforceable. Same way a promise to make a gift is not enforceable.

### 3.13.6 Contract of Agency

No consideration requires for contract of agency.

### 3.13.7 Promise to Charities

A mere promise to contribute to charity is not enforceable by law because it is without a consideration.

However, if a person promises to contribute to charity and on this faith, the promisee undertakes a liability to the extent not exceeding the promised subscription, the contract shall be valid and enforceable.

***Example***

A person promised ₹ 500 to a fund started to rebuild a mosque. The secretary of the Mosque Committee filed a suit to recover the amount. Held, the subscriber was liable as neither the promisor gained nor the promisee (the secretary) suffered from the promise.

**Case Study**

Anurag promises to pay ₹ 11,000 to the management committee of a school by way of donation. The management committee on the basis of Anurag's promise, gets a water purifier system installed in the school at the cost of ₹ 8000 on credit. Now Anurag refuses to pay the donation. What is the remedy available to management committee of the school? Give reason.

**Case Study**

X transferred his house to his daughter M by way of gift. The gift deed, executed by X, contained a direction that M shall pay a sum of ₹ 5000 per month to N (the sister of the executants). Consequently M executed on instrument in favour of N agreeing to pay the said sum. Afterwards, M refused to pay the sum to N saying that she is not liable to N because no consideration had moved from her. Decide with reasons under the provisions of the Indian Contract Act, 1872 whether M is liable to pay the said sum to N.

## LIST OF LANDMARK JUDGEMENTS

1. ***Mohari Bibee vs Dharmodas Ghose (1903)***
   The minor is imcompetent to a contract and an agreement with him is void.
2. ***Suraj Narain vs Sukhu Aahir (1928)***
   The minor cannot ratify the contract after attaining majority.
3. ***Roberts vs Gray (1913)***
   The minor's estate is liable not only for the necessary goods but also for the necessary services rendered to him.
4. ***Inder Singh vs Parmeshwardhari Singh (1957)***
   The agreement by a person of unsound mind is absolutely void.
5. ***Leslie vs Sheill (1914)***
   If minor enters into the agreement by misrepresenting his age, he cannot be sued for fraud.

6. ***Raghava Chariar vs Srinivasa (1916)***
   The minor can be a beneficiary or a promisee.
7. ***Currie vs Misa (1875)***
   The consideration defined as 'some right, interest, profit or benefit accruing to one party for some forbearance, detriment, loss or responsibility given, suffered or undertaken by the other'.
8. ***Fazaluddin Mandal vs Panchannan Das (1957)***
   A single consideration may support more than one promise and may move from the promisee or any other person.
9. ***Bhoori vs Thakur Gulab Singh (1958)***
   The forbearance to sue an old contract or a fresh contract is a good consideration for dispensing with performance of a prior contract.
10. ***Raj Rani vs Prem Adib (1949)***
    The stranger to consideration cannot be a minor. As a minor cannot enter into a contract. The minor cannot be a promisor, he can be a promisee.
11. ***Dunlop Tyre Co. vs Selfridges Ltd (1915)***
    In general third party cannot sue for the carrying out of promises made by the parties to the contract.
12. ***Shadwell vs Shadwell (1960)***
    The consideration must be something more than the promisee is already bound to do for the promisor.
13. ***Chappell vs Nestle (1960)***
    The consideration need not be adequate but must have some value, however, slight.

## TEST YOUR KNOWLEDGE

1. Who is competent to enter into a contract? **(Ref. Para-3.1)**
2. Discuss briefly the position of a minor with regard to the contracts entered into by him. **(Ref. Para-3.2,3.3)**
3. Write a short note on the capacity of parties to enter into a contract. **(Ref. Para-3.1,3.2,3.6,3.7)**
4. A minor cannot recover the price of goods sold on credit to a major. Evaluate the correctness of the statement. **(Ref. Para-3.2)**
5. Ratification by a minor's agreement is not allowed after attaining the majority by him. **(Ref. Para-3.3)**
6. A minor can be a promisee. Comment. **(Ref. Para-3.3)**
7. What are necessaries for minor as per the contract act? Give few examples of necessaries. **(Ref. Para-3.5)**
8. A minor is personally liable for the necessaries supplied to him. Comment. **(Ref. Para-3.5)**
9. Who are treated as persons of unsound mind? **(Ref. Para-3.6)**
10. Who are treated as persons disqualified by law? **(Ref. Para-3.7)**
11. Insolvent person can enter into a contract. Comment. **(Ref. Para-3.7)**
12. Define consideration. **(Ref. Para-3.8)**

13. What are the essential elements of a valid consideration? **(Ref. Para-3.10)**
14. Write a short note on the adequacy of a consideration. **(Ref. Para-3.10)**
15. What do you understand by a stranger to consideration? **(Ref. Para-3.11)**
16. A stranger to contract cannot sue. Comment. **(Ref. Para-3.11)**
17. Explain—A stranger can perform a contract. **(Ref. Para-3.11)**
18. In what circumstances can a stranger to contract bring suit? **(Ref. Para-3.12)**
19. Explain the rule 'no consideration, no contract'. Are there any exceptions to this rule? **(Ref. Para-3.13)**
20. A promise to pay a time barred debt is not enforceable. Comment. **(Ref. Para-3.13)**

## MULTIPLE-CHOICE QUESTIONS

1. Capacity to contract means
   (i) the parties are financially sound to make contracts.
   (ii) the parties are physically able to enter into contracts.
   (iii) the parties are legally competent to enter into contracts.
   (iv) all of the above.
2. Competence to contract means
   (i) age of the parties.
   (ii) soundness of the mind of the parties.
   (iii) both (i) and (ii).
   (iv) intelligence of the parties.
3. A convict when undergoing an imprisonment
   (i) is capable of entering into a contract.
   (ii) is incapable of entering into a contract.
   (iii) is capable of entering into a contract, if it is permitted by the court.
   (iv) is capable of passing on a consideration.
4. A corporation cannot enter into contracts that are
   (i) ultra vires its Memorandum of Association.
   (ii) strictly of a personal nature as it is only an artificial person.
   (iii) either (i) or (ii).
   (iv) neither (i) nor (ii).
5. On attaining the age of majority, a minor's agreement
   (i) is void.
   (ii) cannot be ratified.
   (iii) becomes void.
   (iv) can be ratified.
6. A guardian shall .............. for breach of contact by the minor.
   (i) be held liable
   (ii) not be held liable
   (iii) be imprisoned
   (iv) not be questioned
7. A minor can be
   (i) a partner in a firm.
   (ii) an agent.
   (iii) an employer.
   (iv) all of the above.
8. A contract to take a loan by a boy 17 years of age from a money lender of 34 years is
   (i) valid contract.
   (ii) void contract.
   (iii) quasi contract.
   (iv) void agreement.

9. A minor, by misrepresenting his age, borrows some money. He
   (i) can be sued for fraud.
   (ii) cannot be sued for fraud.
   (iii) is liable to return the money.
   (iv) is liable to return the money on attaining majority.
10. A minor enters into a contract for the purchase of certain necessaries. In such a case
   (i) he is liable to return the necessaries.
   (ii) he is liable to pay.
   (iii) his estate is liable to pay.
   (iv) his guardian is liable to pay.
11. Which of these has not been held as a 'necessary'?
   (i) Food
   (ii) Clothing
   (iii) Shelter
   (iv) Mobile phone
12. Which of these is a not a 'necessary' for a minor?
   (i) Provision of education.
   (ii) Provision of medical and legal advice.
   (iii) Provision of a house on rent for the purpose of living and continuing his studies.
   (iv) Provision of alcoholic drinks.
13. Which of the following are the persons of unsound mind?
   (i) An idiot
   (ii) A lunatic
   (iii) A drunken person
   (iv) All of the above
14. Which of the following persons are not competent to the contract being the persons disqualified by law?
   (i) Alien enemies
   (ii) Insolvents
   (iii) Convicts
   (iv) All of the above
15. Which of the following persons do not fall in the category of persons of unsound mind
   (i) idiots.
   (ii) lunatics.
   (iii) aliens.
   (iv) drunken persons.
16. In a case where a lunatic enters into a contract for the purpose of 'necessaries,' then
   (i) a lunatic is personally liable to pay.
   (ii) a lunatic's guardian is liable to pay.
   (iii) a lunatic's estate is liable to pay.
   (iv) the guardian's estate is liable to pay.
17. A contracts with an alien enemy before the declaration of war, which are against the national interest, are
   (i) terminated.
   (ii) not affected at all.
   (iii) suspended and revived after war.
   (iv) none of the above.
18. A consideration means
   (i) *quid pro lo.*
   (ii) *quid pro quo.*
   (iii) *qui pro quo.*
   (iv) *quid pro quod.*
19. A consideration in a contract
   (i) may be any thing.
   (ii) nothing in return.
   (iii) something in return.
   (iv) may be illusory.

20. An essential feature of a consideration is that
    (i) it must be cash.
    (ii) it must be given by the promisee alone.
    (iii) it must be at the request of the promisor.
    (iv) it must be in kind.
21. A consideration may be
    (i) past.
    (ii) present.
    (iii) future.
    (iv) either (i) or (ii) or (iii).
22. A consideration must be something which the promisor
    (i) is already bound to do.
    (ii) is not already bound to do.
    (iii) may voluntarily do.
    (iv) must not do.
23. An executory consideration can be
    (i) positive.
    (ii) negative.
    (iii) neither (i) nor (ii).
    (iv) either (i) or (ii).
24. An executed consideration
    (i) can be positive or negative.
    (ii) the liability is outstanding on one side only.
    (iii) is an act against, future promise.
    (iv) all of the above.
25. A consideration may be
    (i) executory.
    (ii) executed.
    (iii) either (i) or (ii).
    (iv) both (i) and (ii).
26. A for natural love and affection, promises to give his son B ₹ 1000. A puts his promise to B into writing and registers it. This is a
    (i) contract.
    (ii) agreement.
    (iii) promise.
    (iv) offer.
27. A husband, by a registered agreement promised to pay his wife ₹ 5000 per month. There was no consideration moving from the wife to the husband. The agreement is ............
    (i) void.
    (ii) illegal.
    (iii) valid.
    (iv) unenforceable.
28. A consideration must move at the desire of
    (i) a promisor.
    (ii) a promisee.
    (iii) a stranger.
    (iv) either (ii) or (iii).
29. A consideration may move from
    (i) a promisor.
    (ii) a promisee.
    (iii) either (i) or (ii).
    (iv) both (i) and (ii).
30. Under the Indian Contract Act, a third person
    (i) beneficiary under the contract can sue.
    (ii) from whom the consideration has proceeded can sue.
    (iii) cannot sue even if the consideration has proceeded from him.
    (iv) cannot sue at all for want of privity of contract.

31. A stranger to contract means
    (i) first party to contract.
    (ii) second party to contract.
    (iii) third party to contract.
    (iv) either (i) or (ii).
32. The term privity of contract means
    (i) stranger to contract.
    (ii) contract is private.
    (iii) first party to contract.
    (iv) second party to contract.
33. A promises to pay ₹ 1000 to B if he brings a star from sky to earth and B agrees to bring the star to earth. In this case, contract is
    (i) valid.
    (ii) void as consideration is illusory.
    (iii) illegal.
    (iv) contingent.
34. A promises, for no consideration, to give to B ₹ 1000.
    (i) This is a void agreement.
    (ii) This is a valid agreement.
    (iii) This is a voidable agreement.
    (iv) None of the above.

## ANSWER KEYS

| | | | | |
|---|---|---|---|---|
| **1.** (iii) | **8.** (ii) | **15.** (iii) | **22.** (ii) | **29.** (ii) |
| **2.** (iii) | **9.** (ii) | **16.** (iii) | **23.** (iv) | **30.** (i) |
| **3.** (iv) | **10.** (iii) | **17.** (i) | **24.** (iv) | **31.** (iii) |
| **4.** (iii) | **11.** (iv) | **18.** (ii) | **25.** (iii) | **32.** (i) |
| **5.** (ii) | **12.** (iv) | **19.** (iii) | **26.** (i) | **33.** (ii) |
| **6.** (ii) | **13.** (iv) | **20.** (iii) | **27.** (iii) | **34.** (i) |
| **7.** (ii) | **14.** (iv) | **21.** (iv) | **28.** (i) | |

# 4

# The Indian Contract Act, 1872: Free Consent

**Learning Objectives**

*After reading this chapter, you will be able to understand:*

- Minute difference between consent and free consent
- Contract under coercion and undue influence
- Fraud and its elements
- Difference between fraud and misrepresentation
- Types of mistake and its effect on contract

One of the essential conditions of a valid contract is that it should be made out of free consent of the parties. It means free consent if important to determine the validity of a contract. First we will understand consent and thereafter free consent.

## 4.1 MEANING OF A CONSENT—SECTION 13

Two persons are said to consent, when they agree upon the same thing in the same sense. It is also known as consensus-ad-idem, which means identity of mind. Salmond describes it as an error in consensus. Absence of consent means agreement is void.

## 4.2 FREE CONSENT—SECTION 14

A consent is said to be free, when it is not obtained by

1. Coercion—Section 15
2. Undue influence—Section 16

3. Fraud—Section 17
4. Misrepresentation—Section 18
5. Mistake—Sections 20, 21 and 22

When the consent is there but it is not free, Salmond describes it as error in causa. In such a case, the contract is voidable at the option of one party.

## 4.3 COERCION

It means any act forbidden (prohibited) by the Indian Penal Code (IPS) or the detention or threat to detain the property. It may be noted that killing or beating another person and interfering in the personal freedom of another person are forbidden by the IPC. The English law uses the term 'duress' for coercion.

The threat to commit suicide is coercion. As per the IPC, attempt to commit suicide is offence but committing suicide is not an offence.

### *Examples*

1. A threatens to kill B, if B does not agree to sell his property to A. B's consent is obtained by coercion.
2. D threatens to kill A if he does not sell his house to B at a very low price. Even if D is a stranger to the transaction between A and B, the agreement is caused by coercion.
3. A Hindu gentleman died leaving his young wife. The relatives of the deceased threatened the widow that they would not allow to remove the dead body for cremation unless she adopted a boy to her husband. The widow signed the adoption papers. Held, the threat amounted to coercion and the consent was not free.

The IPC need not to be in force in the place where coercion is done. If A threats B on high seas, where the IPC is not applicable, it is still regarded as the coercion. The purpose of coercion is to compel a person to enter into a contract forcefully.

It is not necessary that a threat is given by the party to the contract only. The coercion may be exercised by the party to contract or by any third person.

### *Example*

If A wants to enter into contract with B but he engage D to give threat to B. It is also case of coercion if D gives threat to B.

The coercion may be directed against the party to contract or against the other person. Threat of life or any other threat creating danger to life, if given to a family member or relative or friend of the party also amounts as the coercion.

### *Example*

A gives threat to B that if he will not enter into contract with him, he will kill B's wife. It is also coercion.

When the coercion is employed, a contract becomes voidable at the option of the aggrieved party, and any benefit received by the other party under the contract must be paid back. If the aggrieved party has suffered from any loss, he can recover the loss from the defaulting party.

## 4.4 CERTAIN THREATS DO NOT AMOUNT TO COERCION

Every kind of threat is not regarded or said as coercion. The only threat which is an offence is considered as the coercion. Therefore, the following threats do not amount to the coercion.

### 4.4.1 Threat to Sue Does Not Amount to Coercion

Threat to prosecute a person or file a suit against the person is not coercion. Approaching court and seeking appropriate remedy by filing suit is the fundamental right of every person. Refusing to renew a contract will not amount to coercion. Similarly, a threat not to withdraw the pending criminal proceedings, unless a bond is executed, cannot be regarded as coercion.

### 4.4.2 Statutory Compulsions

Where the law requires that a contract be made by the parties, the consent in such a contract will not be deemed to be caused by the coercion, or undue influence. In the same way, if anything is done at the instance of the order of court, it is not coercion.

### 4.4.3 Threat to Strike

A threat to strike by the employees in support of their demands is not regarded as coercion. This is because the threat to strike is not an offence under the IPC. It is a right given under the Industrial Disputes Act.

### 4.4.4 Detaining Property Under Mortgage

Detention of property by a mortgage, until the payment of the loan, does not amount to coercion.

## 4.5 UNDUE INFLUENCE

Lord Halsbury has defined that 'undue influence is the unconscientions use, by one person, of the power possessed by him over another, in order to induce the other party to enter into a contract'.

A contract is entered on undue influence when relations that exist between the parties are such that one of them is in a position to dominate the will of the other, and the dominant party uses his position to obtain unfair advantage over the other. Thus, mere being in a position to be dominant is not enough but the party should have obtained unfair advantage by using dominant position. When a contract is made with undue influence, the contract is voidable. The aggrieved party can recover the damages, if he has suffered from any loss because of undue influence. When the contract is challenged in a court of law on the ground of undue influence, the burden of proof lies upon the weaker party.

## 4.6 WHEN A PERSON IS DEEMED TO BE IN POSITION TO DOMINANCE OF WILL OF OTHERS?

Generally, in the following situation or circumstances, a person is deemed to be in a position to dominate the will of others.

### 4.6.1 When a Person Holds Real or Apparent Authority Over Other

If one person holds real or apparent authority over the other, and uses his authority in an appropriate manner while entering into a contract with the other person, he is said to have obtained unfair advantage. Following are the relationships, where one party is enjoying authority over the other:

1. Master and servant
2. Parent and child

***Example***

A applied for a long leave to his offer the Registrar of a Court where A was working. The registrar proposed to grant the leave only if he promised in writing that he would not return to is job and be treated as retired. After completion of leave period, A returned to him job but the Registrar refused to accept him on the job. Held, the registrar used undue influence and the plaintiff be treated on the job.

### 4.6.2 When He Stands in Fiduciary Relationship Over Other

When one party stands in a fiduciary position or a relationship towards the other party, he should be in the position of dominance of the will as the other party keeps faith on him. Following are the relationships where one party stands in fiduciary relationship with the other:

1. Guardian and child
2. Guru and disciples
3. Doctor and patient
4. Solicitor and client
5. Trustee and beneficiary

### 4.6.3 When Contract Is Made with Mentally Weak Person

This is a contract that is made with a person whose mental capacity is temporarily or permanently affected by the reason of age, illness or bodily distress.

### 4.6.4 Contract with Pardanashin Woman

A pardanashin woman is one who observes complete seclusion because of the customs of her community to which she belongs. A contract with her is presumed to have been induced by undue influence.

### 4.6.5 No Presumption of Dominance of Will

However, in the following relationship, there is no presumption of dominance of will by one party over the other party:

1. Landlord and tenant
2. Creditor and debtor
3. Husband and wife
4. Principal and agent

***Example***

A applies to a Banker for a loan when the money market is very stringent. Banker says that loan could be provided only at 30% rate of interest. A accepts to such high interest. A's consent is not obtained by way of undue influence. A could have obtained the loan from any other bank or person. Moreover banker has not obtained any unfair advantage.

**Case Study**

An illiterate old woman made a gift deed of her entire property to her nephew who managed her affairs. Can a gift be set aside by an illiterate old woman? Explain.

## 4.7 DISTINGUISH BETWEEN COERCION AND UNDUE INFLUENCES

| Matter | Coercion | Undue Influences |
|---|---|---|
| Kind of force | Use of physical force. | Use of moral force/mental force. |
| Intention | Intention is to obtain consent for contract. | Intention is to obtain unfair advantage from weak party. |
| Punishment | It is criminally liable-IPC | No criminally liability arises. |
| Parties | Coercion can be employed by parties or by outsider. | Undue influences can be exercise by party to the contract. There must be relation exist between parties. |
| Relationship | Relation between parties are immaterial. | Relation between parties are material. |
| Consequences | Contract is Voidable at the option of aggrieved party. | Contract is voidable or court may set it aside on application of party. |

## 4.8 FRAUD

Fraud may be defined as an intentional, deliberate or willful mis-statement of facts, which are material for the formation of a contract.

The fraud means and includes the following acts:

1. Suggestion of facts which is not true by one person who does not believe it to be true.
2. Active concealment of the fact.

***Example***

Furniture dealer conceals the cracks in furniture by polish work.

3. A promise made without any intention of performing it.
4. Any act or omission, specifically declared as fraudulent by law.
5. Any other act to deceive.

The fraud is any of the above acts, if committed by the party to contract or with his consent, or by his agent with the intent to deceive another party to contract.

## 4.9 ESSENTIAL ELEMENTS OF FRAUD

The elements of fraud are the following:

### 4.9.1 False Representation

There must be a representation and the representation should be false. Alternatively, it can be said that false representation should be knowingly or without belief in its truth. Mere puffing like 'This product is No. 1 in market' is not fraud.

***Example***

A, a shopkeeper, while selling ghee represents the buyer that it is 'pure deshi ghee' although he knows that it is adulterated. A commits a fraud with the buyer by deliberate misrepresentation of facts.

### 4.9.2 Material Fact

Representation should be related to material facts.

### 4.9.3 Rely Upon the False Representation

One party makes false representation with the intention that the other party acts upon it. The other party should have relied on representation without knowledge. Only false statement is not sufficient to prove fraud.

### 4.9.4 Silence Is Not Fraud

Mere silence is not fraud unless it was the duty of the person to speak or to provide any information as per the act.

***Example***

A sells, by auction, to B a horse which A knows to be unsound. A says nothing to B about the horse's unsoundness. There is no fraud on the part of A because no deliberate misrepresentation of facts was made by him.

## 4.10 EXCEPTION TO THE RULE—SILENCE IS NOT FRAUD

In the following circumstances, silence is considered as fraud.

### 4.10.1 It Is Duty of a Person to Speak in Circumstances

In the following three situations, it is the duty of the person to speak and represent in full:

1. Where parties stand in fiduciary relationship.
2. Where a contract is contract of ubberimae fidei.
3. Where duty is imposed by act.

### 4.10.2 Silence Is Equivalent to Speech

The silence amounts to fraud, when it is the duty of a person to speak or to inform, where a person keeps silent knowing that his silence is going to be deceptive, he is responsible for fraud.

## 4.11 CONTRACT OF UBBERIMAE FIDEI

In some contracts all material facts should be disclosed compulsorily, whether it is asked by the party or not. This kind of a contract, where all material information should be provided, is known as a contract of *ubberimae fidei*. Following are the examples of contract of *ubberimae fidei*.

### 4.11.1 Contract of Insurance

Insurance contracts are founded upon the principle of utmost good faith. The proposer, therefore, is under a duty to disclose all the facts known or ought to be known to him, which are likely to affect the acceptance of the proposal.

### 4.11.2 Contracts for Sale of Immovable Property

In such contracts, the buyer as well as the seller is under a duty to disclose all the material facts. All material facts with regard to defect or limitation in the title of property and any charge or pledge in favour of the third party should be disclosed to the buyer.

### 4.11.3 Contracts of Marriage

Every party in a marriage contract is under a duty to disclose all the material facts.

### 4.11.4 Contracts of Family Settlement

Each member of family is under a duty to disclose all the material facts (i.e. as to property etc.) at the time of family settlement.

### 4.11.5 Contract of Partnership

All partners have a duty to consult and inform other partners. All partners must be faithful to one another.

## 4.12 EFFECTS OF FRAUD

A contract is voidable at the option of the party who is defrauded. It means a party can cancel a contract. However following are exceptions to the above rule, where a contract is not voidable:

1. If party could discover the truth with ordinary effort.

***Examples***

1. A by a fraudulent act induced B to believe that 500 TV. Sets per day are assembled in A's factory. He also produced accounts and other records of the factory but B bought the factory without verifying the fact. Later on, he found that factory was assembling only 400 TV sets per day and the accounts and records also showed the same. B is not entitled to rescind the contract because he was having the means of discovering the truth.
2. A candidate for the L.L.B. examination was short of attendance, did not mention the fact in his examination form. The university authorities did not proper scrutiny to discover the truth. Held, there was no fraud by the candidate because the university authorities had means of discovering the truth by ordinary diligence.

2. Fraud did not cause the consent of party.
3. Party has entered into a contract in ignorance of fraud. Alternatively, it can be said that if a false statement does not come to the notice of the party, there is no fraud.

***Example***

A bought shares in a Company on the faith of a prospectus that contained an untrue statement as to the Directorship of B. A had never heard of B and hence such statement was immaterial from his view point. A claimed damage for fraud. His claim for damage is dismissed on the ground that there was no fraud.

The aggrieved party can ask for a specific performance. The aggrieved party can sue for damage, if he has suffered a loss.

**Case Study**

A, fraudulently, sold his car to B. Afterwards, B came to know about the fraud but instead of complaining, he further sold the car to C. Now B wants to claim damage from A. Will he succeed? Advice.

**Case Study**

Sohan induced Suraj to buy his motorcycle saying that it was in a very good condition. After taking the motorcycle, Suraj complained that there were many defects in the motorcycle. Sohan proposed to get it repaired and promised to pay 40% cost of repairs after a few days, the motorcycle did not work at all. Now Suraj wants to file case of fraud against the Sohan. Advise Sohan. Can he recover damage from Sohan?

## 4.13 MISREPRESENTATION

It means false representation of the fact made innocently which is a material fact of contract. The misrepsentation includes:

1. A positive false statement made without any basis of information.
2. A breach of duty which brings advantages to the person committing it.
3. The inducement of mistake about subject matter.

### 4.13.1 Consequences of Misrepresentation

The aggrieved party can cancel the contract. It means a contract is voidable at the option of the aggrieved party but he cannot sue for damages.

## 4.14 ESSENTIAL ELEMENTS OF MISREPRESENTATION

All elements of fraud are equally applicable to misrepresentation except the knowledge of false facts. Following are the essential elements of misrepresentation:

1. The party makes a representation of facts which are false.
2. The misrepresentation should be related to the material facts of contract.
3. The misrepresentation should be with an intention that the other party should act upon it.
4. The representation should have been acted upon.
5. The misrepresentation was made innocently.
6. Other party actually acted believing misrepresentation to be true.

## 4.15 DISTINGUISH BETWEEN FRAUD AND MISREPRESENTATION

| Matter | Fraud | Misrepsentation |
|---|---|---|
| Meaning | It is deliberate mis-statement or active concealment of the fact. | It means incorrect or false statement made without innocently. |
| Party making statement believe in truth | Party making statement do not believe in truth. | Party making statement believe in truth. |
| Intention to deceive | Intention is to deceive other party. | Intention is not to deceive other party. |
| Action | Aggrieved party can avoid the contract and recover damages. | Aggrieved party can avoid the contract but cannot ask for damage. |
| Means for discovery of truth | Contract is voidable if party has means of discovering truth with normal effort. | Contract is not voidable if party has means of discovering truth with normal effort. |

## 4.16 SIMILARITIES BETWEEN FRAUD AND MISREPRESENTATION

Similarities between fraud and misrepresentation can be summarized as under.

1. Both of these result from misstatements made by a party.
2. The contract caused by both these factors is voidable at the option of the aggrieved party.

## 4.17 MISTAKE

It means an erroneous belief about some facts. A mistake can either be (a) mistake of law and (b) mistake of fact.

### 4.17.1 Mistake of Law

A mistake of law does not mean mistake in provisions of any law but it means there is mistake in understanding the provision of any law by the party to contract.

A mistake of law can be further classified either as mistake of Indian law or mistake of foreign law.

**4.17.1.1 Mistake of Indian Law** Everyone is supposed to know the law of land. In the latin maxim it is said that 'Ignoranlia juris non excusa'. Ignorance of law is no excuse. Therefore, if there is a mistake of Indian law, the contract is not void or voidable.

***Example***

A, a widow, was entitled to certain occupancy rights on the land of B. She remarried and believing that she has lost her occupancy rights by reason of her second marriage, agreed to take the land on lease from B, on an increased rent. Both A and B honestly believed that A had lost her occupancy rights. The contract for higher rent is valid and not voidable although they made the contract in ignorance of law.

**4.17.1.2 Mistake of Foreign Law** Everyone can be supposed to know the law of the foreign country. A mistake of foreign law is treated, as if it were a mistake of facts, because person cannot be expected to know the law of the other country.

### 4.17.2 Mistake of Fact

A mistake of facts can be classified either as a bilateral mistake or a unilateral mistake.

**4.17.2.1 Bilateral Mistake** It means both the parties are at mistake related to the essential part of agreement. If an agreement is entered into on the ground of bilateral mistake, the agreement is void. An erroneous opinion, as to the value of the thing which forms the subject-matter of agreement, is not deemed to be a mistake as to the matter of fact.

***Example***

A buys a painting from B at a price of ₹ 20,000. Both A and B believed it to be the work of a known artist by B did not make any representation or warranty about it. Later A comes to know that it was a new one and worth only ₹ 1000. A is bound by the contract.

The bilateral mistake can be further classified as:

1. Mistake of quantity
2. Mistake of price
3. Mistake as to possibility of performance

- *Mistake as to quantity*

If both the parties are under a mistake as to the quantity of the subject matter of the agreement, the agreement is void. Such a mistake may even be caused by the negligence of a third party but the agreement would be void.

***Example***

A agreed to buy 100 sewing thread reels from B. Both believed that each reel contains 500 metres of thread but, in fact, the length of thread was only 300 metres. Held, the agreement was void as there was a bilateral mistake as to quantity of subject-matter.

- *Mistake as to price*

If both the parties are working under a mistake as to the price, the agreement is void.

***Example***

A agreed with B to let out his house for a monthly rent of ₹ 520. However, in the lease deed it was written as ₹ 350. Held, the agreement was void.

- *Mistake as to possibility of performance*

***Example***

A agrees to sell 100 units of a particular product. Later, it is discovered that there was a ban on sale of the product even at the time of making the contract. The contract is void.

**4.17.2.2 Unilateral Mistake** A unilateral mistake means one party is at mistake. A contract is neither void nor voidable except that it is mistake as to the nature of the contract or a mistake with regard to the identity of the person.

***Examples***

1. Submitted a tender to B for construction of a number of houses. A made a mistake in calculating the cost therefore his offer was lower than other tenderers. A's tender was accepted. Held, it was a binding contract although it was an erroneous estimate based on unilateral mistake.
2. A intends to enter into contract with B but enters into contract with C believing him to be B. The contract is void if identity of person is a material factor.

**Case Study**

A agrees to sell his horse to B. But unknown to both the parties, the horse had already died at the time of making of the contract. Is it a valid contract? Why?

**Case Study**

A wrote to B inquiring price of rifles suggesting that he might buy as many as 50. On receipt of information, he telegraphed, 'Send three rifles'. Due to telegraphic mistake, message was transmitted as 'Send the rifles'. B dispatched 50 rifles. A rejected the 50 rifles and claim of B to pay for 50 rifles. Is contention of A valid? If so, on what grounds?

**Case Study**

A contracted to take on rent, a property for viewing the coronation procession of the King. Unknown to the parties, the procession had already been cancelled. Is it a valid contract between the parties?

**Case Study**

A had two scooters one black and the other white, and offered to sell his black scooter to B for ₹ 12,000. B accepted the offer believing it to be for white. Is there any contract between parties? Explain.

## 4.18 DISTINGUISH BETWEEN UNILATERAL MISTAKE AND BILATERAL MISTAKE

| Matter | Unilateral Mistake | Bilateral Mistake |
|---|---|---|
| Meaning | One party is at mistake. | Both parties to contract is at mistake. |
| Effect | Contract is not void or voidable. | Both parties to an agreement are under mistake of facts, agreement is void. |
| Provision applicable | Section 22 | Section 20 |

## LIST OF LANDMARK JUDGEMENTS

1. ***Ranganyakamma vs Alwar Setti (1889)***
   The consent obtained from wife by detaining corpse of her husband is coercion.
2. ***Purabi Banerjee vs Basudev Mukherjee (1969)***
   The consent obtained by threat to commit suicide is coercion. An attempt to commit suicide is an offence under the Indian Penal Code (IPC).
3. ***V. Srinivasa Pillai vs LIC (1977)***
   A contract of insurance is the contract of *'uberrimae fidei'* and an insured person and insurer, must disclose all material facts on their own, even if the other party does not specifically ask them.
4. ***Shri Krishna vs Kurukshetra University (1976)***
   A candidate failed to mention the fact of shortage of attendance in the examination form. It was held that mere silence is not fraud.
5. ***Resee River Silver Mining Co. vs Smith (1869)***
   The representation or statement which is made with knowledge of its falsity is fraud.
6. ***Horsefull vs Thomas (1862)***
   The fraud must have actually deceived the other party.
7. ***Shireen Mall vs John James Taylor (1952)***
   If at the time of entering into a contract, a party has no intention to perform his promise, if will be considered as fraud.
8. ***Ningawa vs B. S. Hire Kurabar (1968)***
   Every act done with the intention of deceiving a party will be considered as fraud.
9. ***Griffith vs Brymer (1903)***
   If an agreement is impossible to perform but the fact of impossibility is unknown to both the parties, the agreement is void.

**10.** ***Couturier vs Hastie (1856)***

Where both the parties to an agreement are under a mistake, as to the matter of fact essential to the agreement, the agreement is void.

**11.** ***Foster vs Mackinnon (1869)***

Unilateral mistake as regard to the nature of an agreement makes the agreement void.

## TEST YOUR KNOWLEDGE

1. Define Consent. When is consent said to be free? **(Ref. Para-4.1,4.2)**
2. What is coercion? State the effects of coercion on the validity of a contract. **(Ref. Para-4.3)**
3. A threat to commit suicide amounts to coercion. Comment **(Ref. Para-4.3)**
4. Which threats do not amount to coercion? **(Ref. Para-4.4)**
5. A threat to lodge a criminal prosecution on a false charge amounts to coercion. Comment. **(Ref. Para-4.4)**
6. What is undue influence? State the effects of undue influence. **(Ref. Para-4.5)**
7. When is the party said to be in a position to dominate the will of others? **(Ref. Para-4.6)**
8. Distinguish between coercion and undue influence. **(Ref. Para-4.7)**
9. Define fraud. Give its suitable example. **(Ref. Para-4.8)**
10. What are the elements of fraud? **(Ref. Para-4.9)**
11. Mere puffing is not fraud. Comment. **(Ref. Para-4.9)**
12. Does silence always amount to fraud? **(Ref. Para-4.10)**
13. What do you understand by contract of *'uberrimae fidei?'* **(Ref. Para-4.11)**
14. In which circumstances, the right of aggrieved party to cancel a contract on the basis of fraud is lost? **(Ref. Para-4.12)**
15. A deceit which does not deceive is no fraud. Explain. **(Ref. Para-4.12)**
16. Explain the effects of fraud? **(Ref. Para-4.12)**
17. Write a short note on misrepresentation. **(Ref. Para-4.13,4.14)**
18. What will be the effect of misrepresentation on a contract? **(Ref. Para-4.13)**
19. Distinguish between fraud and misrepresentation. **(Ref. Para-4.15)**
20. What are the similarities between fraud and misrepresentation. **(Ref. Para-4.16)**
21. Explain various kinds of mistakes with suitable examples. **(Ref. Para-4.17)**
22. Unilateral mistake means the contract is valid. Critically evaluate this statement. **(Ref. Para-4.17)**
23. Write a short note on bilateral mistake. **(Ref. Para-4.17)**
24. Distinguish between unilateral mistake and bilateral mistake. **(Ref. Para-4.18)**

## MULTIPLE-CHOICE QUESTIONS

1. Consent means parties agreeing on
   (i) the terms of contract.
   (ii) some terms of contract.
   (iii) the same thing in the same sense.
   (iv) any matter of contract.

2. Two persons are said to consent
   (i) when they agree on any thing.
   (ii) when they agree upon the same thing in their own way.
   (iii) when they agree upon the same thing in the same sense.
   (iv) when they agree upto the same thing in different sense.
3. ................ means forcibly compelling a person to enter into a contract.
   (i) Intimidation (ii) Fraud (iii) Mistake (iv) Coercion
4. Coercion includes
   (i) threat to life.
   (ii) threat to detain property.
   (iii) detain goods unlawfully.
   (iv) all of the above.
5. A threatens to kill B, if B does not agree to sell his property to A. B's consent is obtained by
   (i) fraud. (ii) undue influence. (iii) coercion. (iv) misrepresentation.
6. Duress under English contract law is similar to
   (i) undue influence. (ii) coercion. (iii) fraud. (iv) misrepresentation.
7. ................ means unfair use of one's superior power in order to obtain the consent of a person, who is in a weaker position.
   (i) Coercion (ii) Undue influence (iii) Fraud (iv) Misrepresentation
8. The agreement entered into without free consent is
   (i) valid. (ii) void. (iii) voidable. (iv) illegal.
9. Which of the following relationships raise presumption of undue influence?
   (i) Parent and child
   (ii) Guardian and ward
   (iii) Spiritual guru and disciple
   (iv) All of the above
10. Which of the following relationships raise presumption of undue influence?
    (i) Doctor and patient.
    (ii) Solicitor and client.
    (iii) Trustee and beneficiary.
    (iv) All of the above.
11. To employ 'Undue Influence,' relationship between the parties is
    (i) necessary. (ii) not necessary. (iii) required. (iv) presumed.
12. Fraud means
    (i) suggestion as a fact, of something which is not true, by a person who does not believe it to be true.
    (ii) active concealment of a fact.
    (iii) promise made without any intention of performing it.
    (iv) all of the above.
13. Which of these does not constitute fraud?
    (i) Suggestion as a fact, of something which is not true, by a person who does not believe it to be true.
    (ii) Active concealment of a fact.
    (iii) Innocent statement, honestly believing the same to be true.
    (iv) Promise made without any intention of performing it.

14. In which of the following situations. silence is regarded as fraud?
    (i) Having regard to the circumstances, if it is the duty of the person to speak.
    (ii) In cases where silence by itself is equivalent to speech.
    (iii) Both (i) and (ii).
    (iv) Neither (i) nor (ii).
15. When the contract is entered into by fraud, it is
    (i) void. (ii) valid. (iii) invalid. (iv) voidable.
16. In cases of silence amounting to fraud, where the other party had the means of discovering truth with ordinary diligence, the contract is
    (i) void. (ii) voidable. (iii) not voidable. (iv) conditional.
17. The important element which distinguishes mispresentation from fraud is that the misrepresentation is an
    (i) intentional statement.
    (ii) innocent statement.
    (iii) important statement.
    (iv) irrelevant statement.
18. For a marriage contract, the relatives speaking for the girl failed to disclose that she was suffering from epileptic fits. In this case, engagement is voidable on account of
    (i) fraud.
    (ii) misrepresentation.
    (iii) undue influence.
    (iv) none of the above.
19. Which of the following are essential features of misrepresentation?
    (i) Representation should be of a material fact.
    (ii) It must be made before the conclusion of the contract.
    (iii) There should not be an intention to deceive the other party.
    (iv) All of the above.
20. .......... is an erroneous belief about something.
    (i) Representation (ii) Mistake (iii) Fraud (iv) Misrepresentation
21. When one of the parties is under a mistake as to a matter of fact essential to the agreement, it is called
    (i) unilateral mistake.
    (ii) bilateral mistake.
    (iii) partial mistake.
    (iv) incomplete mistake.
22. An old illiterate man was made to sign a bill of exchange, by means of a false representation that it was a guarantee. The contract is
    (i) illegal. (ii) valid. (iii) void. (iv) voidable.
23. Bilateral mistake may relate to
    (i) subject matter.
    (ii) possibility of performance.
    (iii) neither (i) nor (ii).
    (iv) both (i) and (ii).
24. Threat to commit suicide amounts to
    i. fraud
    ii. coercion
    iii. undue influence
    iv. offence under IPC.
    (i) i and ii (ii) ii and iii (iii) iii and iv (iv) ii and iv
25. Threat to detain property in unlawful manner amount as
    (i) fraud. (ii) coercion. (iii) mistake. (iv) all of the above.

26. Undue influence is a kind of
   (i) mental coercion.
   (ii) physical coercion.
   (iii) both (i) and (ii).
   (iv) none of the above.
27. The fiduciary relations means the relationship of
   (i) trust and confidence.
   (ii) master and servant.
   (iii) none of the above.
   (iv) both (i) and (ii).
28. A, intending to deceive B, falsely represents that 500 bags are made daily at his factory, and thereby induces B to buy the factory. The contract is
   (i) voidable at the option of B.
   (ii) voidable at the option of A.
   (iii) void.
   (iv) none of the above.
29. The husband asks his wife that he would commit suicide, if she does not give him her ornaments. The wife gives the ornaments.
   (i) The contract can be avoided by the wife.
   (ii) The contract is void.
   (iii) The husband can enforce the contract.
   (iv) Both (ii) and (iii).

## ANSWER KEYS

| | | | | |
|---|---|---|---|---|
| **1.** (iii) | **7.** (ii) | **13.** (iii) | **19.** (iv) | **25.** (ii) |
| **2.** (iii) | **8.** (iii) | **14.** (iii) | **20.** (ii) | **26.** (i) |
| **3.** (iv) | **9.** (iv) | **15.** (iv) | **21.** (i) | **27.** (i) |
| **4.** (iv) | **10.** (iv) | **16.** (iii) | **22.** (iii) | **28.** (i) |
| **5.** (iii) | **11.** (i) | **17.** (ii) | **23.** (iv) | **29.** (i) |
| **6.** (ii) | **12.** (iv) | **18.** (i) | **24.** (iv) | |

# 5

# The Indian Contract Act, 1872: Void Agreement and Contingent Contract

**Learning Objectives**

*After reading this chapter, you will be able to understand:*

- When an object or a consideration is regarded as unlawful?
- Agreements against public policy and its effect
- Illegal agreements and its effect
- Wagering agreement and its effect
- Contingent contract

The legality of the object and consideration is an important requirement for a valid contract. Every agreement of which the object or consideration is unlawful is void.

## 5.1 WHEN AN OBJECT OR A CONSIDERATION IS UNLAWFUL?—SECTION 23

The object or consideration of an agreement is unlawful in following cases:

### 5.1.1 If It Is Forbidden (Prohibited) by Law

The agreement is unlawful if it involves doing of an act which is forbidden by any law for the time being in force. An act forbidden by a law is punishable by the criminal law or by a special act. The agreement to give bribe if some work will be performed is unlawful and hence unenforceable.

***Example***

A sold liquor without license to B. The sale is unlawful as the sale of liquor without license is forbidden by the law, i.e. The Excise Act. Hence, A cannot recover the price.

### 5.1.2 An Act Which Would Defeat the Provisions of Any Law

The agreement is unlawful if it is of such a nature that if permitted, it would defeat the provisions of any law.

***Example***

A and B agreed to carry on business in partnership with a view to evading of Income Tax and Sales Tax. One of the partners brought an action against the other for recovery of the amount due to him. Held, the agreement aimed at defeating the provisions of Tax laws and therefore, the same was not enforceable.

### 5.1.3 If It Creates Injury to Any Person or Property of Person

The agreement if it is made for creating an injury to a person or to the property of a person is unlawful. The agreement with such an object or consideration is void.

***Example***

A agrees to blast a bomb at railway station for ₹ 10,000.

### 5.1.4 Object or Consideration of an Agreement Is Fraudulent

The agreement is unlawful if it is made to make a fraud on any person. The agreement with such an object or consideration is void.

***Example***

A, B and C enter into an agreement for the division of gains acquired or to be acquired by them by fraud. The agreement is void as its object is unlawful.

### 5.1.5 Where Court Consider It As Immoral or Against Public Policy

The agreement is unlawful if the court considers that the object or consideration of such agreement is immoral or against public policy.

**Case Study**

A enters into an agreement on the behalf of her minor daughter that her daughter will act in an adult movie. Is agreement valid? Why?

**Case Study**

A borrows money from B to purchase smuggled cameras from C. B knows the purpose. Is agreement between A and B valid? Why?

**Case Study**

A agrees to pay ₹ 20,000 to B, if he produces false evidence in his favour. Is it enforceable agreement? Why?

**Case Study**

A agrees to sell his mobile phone to B, if B pays ₹ 30,000. Is it enforceable agreement? Why?

## 5.2 AN AGREEMENT OPPOSED TO PUBLIC POLICY

No person is allowed to act in such a way which is injurious to the public. Therefore, any agreement against the public policy or public welfare is unlawful and void. There is no definition of the public or public policy. If the court holds a consideration or an object as against the public policy, such agreement will be void. Following agreements have been treated as against 'public policy' through the various court judgments.

### 5.2.1 Trading with an Enemy

The agreement to trade or deal with the enemy of the nation is against the public policy as it would give benefit to the enemy and create a danger or threat to the public.

### 5.2.2 Agreement to Commit Crime

The agreement to commit any kind of crime is against the public policy as public or any part of the public will have damage or loss. The court will not enforce this kind of agreements.

***Example***

A promises to pay ₹ 10,000 in consideration of his killing C.

### 5.2.3 Agreement Interfering Course of Justice

The agreement interfering with the course of justice is opposed to the public policy. Every person has the fundamental right to get justice. Creating hurdles in the process of justice, to manipulate with the witness, are considered as interfering course of justice. However, a compromise and a settlement in a civil case is not regarded as interference with the course of justice. Similarly, an agreement to refer to present or future disputes to arbitration is also not void.

### 5.2.4 Agreement Interfering Admistration

The agreement interfering with the administration or administrative duties is opposed to public policy.

### 5.2.5 Stifling Prosecution

The agreement for stifling prosecution means to release any criminal or drop any prosecution against any person unreasonably. Public interest requires that criminals should be prosecuted and punished. The agreement to stifle is void.

***Example***

Promise to restore the stolen property if prosecution is dropped. It is void.

### 5.2.6 Maintenance Agreement

It is promotion of litigation in which one has no interest but gives money to another to assist in the matter of litigation. However, if the object is to help a needy person to establish his claim or recover damage, it is a valid agreement. In the same manner, helping relatives or friends or guidance by lawyer to his client will not be considered as the maintenance agreement.

***Example***

A unduly induces B to file a suit against C and A promises B to give ₹ 5000 to maintain in the suit although he has no legal interest in the suit. The agreement between A and B is maintenance agreement and is void.

### 5.2.7 Champerty Agreement

It is the agreement where one party agrees to assist the other in receiving property with an object of sharing the profit out of litigation. This is a sort of gambling on litigation, and treated as against public policy, the champerty agreement is void.

***Example***

A agrees to advance ₹ 40,000 to B to enable him to file a suit against D for recovery of his property. B in turn agrees to give one-third share in the property, if recovered. This is a champertous agreement.

### 5.2.8 Agreement in Restraint of Legal Proceeding

The agreement which curtails or restrains the legal proceeding is void. It is explained in detail in the later part.

### 5.2.9 Agreement in Restraint of Parental Rights

Parents are natural guardians of the child. They have the rights and duties of guardianship. Any agreement which takes away the right of a guardian for a child is void.

***Example***

A father having two minor sons agreed to transfer their guardianship in favour of B and agreed not to revoke it. Subsequently, he filed suit for the recovery of boys and the declaration that he was the rightful guardian. Held, that he had the right to revoke his authority and get back the children.

### 5.2.10 Agreement in Restraint of Personal Freedom

Every person has the right of personal freedom with reference to speech, expression and behaviour. If any agreement takes away the freedom of a person then such agreement is against the public policy and void.

***Example***

A, debtor, promised with a money lender B that he will not change his residence or his employment or dispose off his property without B's consent. Held, the agreement was void on the ground of public policy.

### 5.2.11 Agreement in Restraint of Marriage

Every person has the right to marry a person of his/her choice. Therefore, any agreement which restrains a major person from marriage is void. But an agreement in restraint of marriage of the minor is valid—Section 26.

The agreement in restraint of marriage is void if the restraint is complete or partial. The agreement which prevents a person from marrying a particular person is partial restrain, and thus void. If a person agrees not to marry any person, it is said as complete restraint and it is also void. Every major person has the right to marry a person of his/her choice.

***Example***

Amar promised to marry no one else except Ms. Bina and in default pay her a sum of ₹ 1,00,000. Amar married some one else and Bina sued Amar for the recovery of the sum. Held, the agreement was in restraint of marriage and as such void.

### 5.2.12 Marriage Brokerage

It is the agreement whereby one person receives money or money's worth, in consideration of the negotiating marriage. Such kind of an agreement is against the public policy, and hence void. But marriage will not be void.

### 5.2.13 Agreements for Sale of Public Offices and Titles

It is also known as trafficking public office. An agreement of trafficking (i.e. to buy, sell, or procure) in public office or title is against the public policy. Hence, such an agreement is unlawful and void. Following agreements have been held to be against the public policy, since they are tantamount to the sale of public offices.

1. An agreement to provide money to a Member of Parliament or Assembly or Minister to influence his opinion and judgment.
2. An agreement intended to induce a public officer to act corruptly.
3. An agreement to procure a public title like 'Bharat Ratna' and 'Padma Vibhushan' for reward.
4. An agreement for procuring votes in election for consideration.
5. An agreement to sell seat in a medical or an engineering college (except payment seat).

An agreement to create monopolies or eliminate or reduce competition is void on the ground of public policy.

**Case Study**

Point out with reasons whether the following agreements are valid or void:

(i) Kamala promises Ramesh to lend ₹ 50,000 in *lieu* of consideration that Ramesh gets Kamala's marriage dissolved and he himself marries her.

(ii) Sohan agrees with Mohan to sell his black horse. Unknown to both the parties, the horse was dead at the time of agreement.

(iii) Ram sells the goodwill of his shop to Shyam for ₹ 4,00,000 and promises not to carry on such business forever and anywhere in India.

(iv) In an agreement between Prakash and Girish, there is a condition that they will not institute legal proceeding against each other without consent.

(v) Ramamurthy, who is a citizen of India, enters into an agreement with an alien friend.

**Case Study**

An agreement between the ice manufacturers not to sell ice below a stated price and to divide the profits in a certain proportion. Discuss about the validity of the agreement.

**Case Study**

An agreement among the members of a co-operative society to deliver all the crops grown by them to the society. The society sells it and divides the profit amongst its members. Is it valid agreement between members of co-operative society? Why?

**Case Study**

A agrees to pay B ₹ 15,000 for suing C and in turn seeking 50% share in the proceeds received by B in the suit. B win case but refuse to Pay 50% share in proceed. Can A recover the amount as decided under agreement?

**Case Study**

A promises to pay B ₹ 50,000, if B secures him an employment in the public service. Decide about the validity of the agreement between A and B.

**Case Study**

A promises to pay B ₹ 30,000, if B procure for him the title 'Padma Shri'. After payment B fails to procure the award. Can A enforce agreement?

**Case Study**

Amit promises to procure an employment for Bimal in a government department, and Bimal promises to pay ₹ 5000 to Amit for the same. Amit gets the said job for Bimal. However, Bimal refuses to pay the promised money to Amit who files a suit in the court of law to recover ₹ 5000 from Bimal. Will Amit succeed? Give reasons.

## 5.3 AGREEMENTS IN RESTRAINT OF TRADE—SECTION 27

Every person has the right to carry on any trade, profession occupation or business activities so far as it is lawful and allowed by law. An agreement which is restrained from doing lawful profession, trade or business of any kind is void to that extent.

### 5.3.1 Exceptions to the Rule

In the following cases, restraints are considered valid:

1. When the goodwill of the business is sold, the seller may be restrained from carrying on a similar business within specified local limit. But when the seller of the goodwill of a business agrees not to carry on a similar business, the limits and conditions imposed have to be reasonable having regard to the nature of business.
2. The partners' agreement—restraint on the partner of a firm from carrying on any business is allowed under the Partnership Act. Reasonable restriction can be placed on the outgoing partner by way of agreement.
3. The service agreement may restrain the employees from working elsewhere during the period of employment. But any agreement which prohibits a person not to engage anywhere else, after he has left the employment is not valid.
4. The sole selling agreements are held valid by court.
5. The agreement between the members of a trade union.
6. Regulation, as to the opening and closing of business in the market, licensing of traders, supervision and control of deals are not void. A joint venture agreement, entered into by two companies or two persons are valid as it is not an agreement in restraint of trade. It is the agreement to work and carry on the business with the joint effort.
7. The law relating to the copyright, trade mark, design and patent permit restrictions while entering into the agreement to protect the intellectual property right.

**Case Study**

'X' agreed to become an assistant for five years to 'Y' who was a Doctor practising at Ludhiana. It was also agreed that during the term of agreement 'X' will not practise on his own account in Ludhiana. At the end of one year, 'X' left the assistantship of 'Y' and began to practise on his own account. Referring to the provisions of the Indian Contract Act, 1872, decide whether 'X' could be restrained from doing so?

## 5.4 AGREEMENT IN RESTRAINT OF LEGAL PROCEEDINGS—SECTION 28

It means any agreement, which stops a person from taking a legal action or enforcing his right under any contract. It also includes any agreement which reduces the time for taking the legal action. It is void. But an agreement between the two persons to refer to any dispute to arbitration is not void.

***Examples***

1. An employee agreed with his employer not to sue for his wrongful dismissal. Held, the agreement was in restraint of legal proceedings and void.

2. A clause in an agreement between the parties provided that all the disputes shall be subject to Mumbai Jurisdiction only. A party filed a suit at Varanasi. The suit was dismissed. The Supreme Court of India held the agreement was not opposed to public policy and therefore, the suit filed at Varanasi was rightly dismissed.

**Case Study**

Mr. Seth, an industrialist, has been fighting a long drawn litigation with Mr. Raman, another industrialist. To support his legal campaign Mr. Seth enlists the services of Mr. X, a legal expert, slating that an amount of ₹ 5 lakhs would be paid, if Mr. X does not take up the brief of Mr. Raman. Mr. X agrees but at the end of the litigation Mr. Seth refuses to pay. Decide whether Mr. X can recover the amount promised by Mr. Seth under the provisions of the Indian Contract Act, 1872?

**Case Study**

A and B entered into an agreement that A can enforce his rights at Bombay only. Is it a valid agreement? Why?

## 5.5 AGREEMENTS UNLAWFUL IN PARTS

### 5.5.1 Where Lawful Part Can Be Separated from the Unlawful Part

If a part of the consideration or the object which is unlawful can be separated from the other lawful part, the court will enforce that part which is lawful.

***Example***

A promises B to maintain accounts of his legal and illegal businesses or a total monthly remuneration of ₹ 3000, being ₹ 1000 for the legal, and ₹ 2000 for illegal business. Here, both the parts of consideration are separable, hence the former is enforceable where as the later is not.

### 5.5.2 Where Lawful and Unlawful Parts Cannot Be Separated

Where the lawful and unlawful parts of consideration or object cannot be separated, the whole agreement is void.

***Example***

A promises to superintend on behalf of B, a legal manufacture of Indigo, and an illegal traffic in the other articles. B promises to pay to A, a salary of ₹ 10,000 a year. The agreement is void, the object of A's promise, the consideration for B's promise, being in part unlawful but the two cannot be separated.

### 5.5.3 Reciprocal Promise to Do Things Legal and Also Other Things Illegal

Where persons reciprocally promise, firstly to do certain things which are legal and secondly, under specified circumstances, to do certain other things which are illegal, the first set of promises is a contract but the second is a void agreement.

***Example***

A and B agree that A shall sell B a house for ₹ 10,000 but that, if B uses it as a gambling house, he shall pay A ₹ 50,000 for it. The first set of reciprocal promises, namely to sell the house and to pay ₹ 10,000 for it, is a contract. The second set is for an unlawful object, namely that B may use the house as a gambling house, and is a void agreement.

### 5.5.4 Alternative Promise, One Branch Being Illegal

In the case of an alternative promise, one branch of which is legal and the other illegal, the legal branch alone can be enforced.

***Example***

A and B agree that A shall pay B ₹ 1000 for which B shall afterwards deliver to A either rice or smuggled opium. This is a valid contract to deliver rice and a void agreement as to the opium.

## 5.6 WAGERING AGREEMENT—SECTION 30

'A wagering agreement is a promise to give money or money's worth upon the determination of an uncertain event'—Sir William Anson'. Wager means gambling or betting.

An agreement between two persons is the wagering agreement, if money or money's worth is payable by one person to another on the happening or non-happening of an uncertain event.

The agreement to pay a prize of ₹ 500 or more to the winner of horse race is also the wagering agreement. It means if the agreement is to pay or the award prize money is less than ₹ 500, it is not wagering agreement. The lottery conducted by the state government is not illegal but the wager and therefore the claim to recover the winning money is not maintainable.

***Example***

X agrees to pay Y ₹ 500 if it does not rain on 15 August 2011. Y promises to pay ₹ 500 to X if it rains on 15 August 2011.

## 5.7 ESSENTIALS OF WAGERING AGREEMENT

A wagering agreement has the following features:

### 5.7.1 Promise to Pay Money or Money's Worth

There must be a promise to pay money or money's worth. If the agreement between a party is without a promise to pay money, it is not a wagering agreement. There must be an intention to play a gamble on the part of both the parties. If the intention is only on part of one person, it is not a wagering agreement.

### 5.7.2 Performance Depend Upon Event

The performance of a promise must depend upon the determination of an uncertain event. An event, on which the performance of a promise is depending, could be related to the past or future. It might have already happened but the parties are not aware about it.

### 5.7.3 Change of Win or Loss

There must be a chance of win or lose. If both the parties win, or if both the parties lose, it is not a wagering agreement. One party has to win and one party has to lose.

### 5.7.4 No Interest or Control Over an Event

Neither party should have any control or interest over an event other than the sum or stake he will win or lose. Insurance is not a wagering agreement because the person who obtains insurance has interest in his life or goods covered under the insurance.

If any party can control the event, then the event cannot be considered as uncertain. If any activity where the party can exercise his skill, it is controllable and hence cannot be said as the wagering agreement.

***Example***

A lottery is a wagering agreement. Therefore, an agreement to buy and sell lottery tickets is a wagering agreement. Section 294 (A) of the Indian Penal Code declares that drawing of lottery is an offence. However, the government may authorize the lotteries. The persons authorized to conduct lotteries are exempt from the punishment. But the lotteries still remain a wagering transaction.

It may be noted that as per the Prize Competition Act, 1955, the prize competitions in the games of skill are enforceable, if the amount of prize does not exceed ₹ 1000.

***Examples***

1. ***Crossword competition with entry fees***
   Crossword competition involving skill for its solution. If skill plays an important role in the result of a competition, and prizes depend upon the result, the competition is not a lottery and wager. The literary competitions involve applications of skill, and prizes are awarded to the participants on the basis of merit of their solutions, and not on chance. Therefore, such competitions are valid and are not wagers. However, if the crossword puzzle prizes depend upon sameness of the competitor's solution with a previously prepared solution kept with the organizer or newspaper editor is a lottery and, therefore, a wagering transaction.
2. ***Share market transaction***
   A commercial transaction is done with an intention of the delivery of goods (commodity or security) and the payment of price. Therefore, it is not a wagering agreement. However, when any transaction in any commodity or in shares, with an intention of paying or getting the difference in price, the agreement is a wager.
3. ***Athletic competitions***
   The athletic competitions also fall in the category of games of skill. Therefore, these are also not wagers.
4. A tells B that Wrestler No. 1 will win. B challenges the statement of A. They bet with each other over the result. It is not a wagering agreement, as here the money or money's worth is not involved.
5. A and B, two wrestlers, agreed to enter into a wrestling contest in Ahmedabad, on a certain day. They further agreed that a party failing to appear on the fixed day was to forfeit ₹ 500 and the winning party will receive a sum of ₹ 1000. Held, it was not a wagering agreement.

## 5.8 EFFECTS OF WAGERING AGREEMENT

A wagering agreement is void but not illegal. No suit can be filled for any recovery of the amount won on any wager. However, any agreement collateral to the wagering agreement is valid.

However, the wagering agreement is illegal in the state of Maharashtra and Gujarat.

**Case Study**

A, in Ahmedabad, bets with B and loses. A applies to C for a loan in order to pay B. C gives the loan to A to enable him to pay B. In this case C can recover loan from A?

## 5.9 DISTINGUISH BETWEEN A WAGERING AGREEMENT AND AN INSURANCE CONTRACT

| Matter | Wagering Agreement | Insurance Contract |
|---|---|---|
| Meaning | If money or money's worth is payable by one person to another person, on the happening or non-happening of an uncertain event. | It is a contract to compensate the loss. |
| Legal effect | It is a void contract and not enforceable. | It is a valid contract and can be enforced. |
| Insurable interest | No party has any insurable interest. | Insurable interest in the property insured. |
| Amount payable | In a wagering agreement, the amount to be payable is fixed. | The amount to be payable depends upon the loss, and the terms and conditions of the insurance. |
| Premium | It is not based upon scientific calculation. | It is based upon scientific calculation. |
| Purpose | The purpose of a wagering agreement is to make profit. | The purpose of an insurance is not to make profit but to safeguard the loss. |
| Public interest | A wagering agreement is not in public interest. | An insurance is beneficial to public. |

## 5.10 DISTINGUISH BETWEEN A WAGERING AGREEMENT AND A CONTINGENT CONTRACT

| Basis | Wagering Agreement | Contingent Contract |
|---|---|---|
| Meaning | If money or money's worth is payable by one person to another person, on the happening or non-happening of an uncertain event. The party may win or lose, depending upon an uncertain event. | The performance of a contract depends upon the future uncertain event, collateral to the main contract. |
| Nature of uncertain event | The uncertain event may be past or future. | An uncertain event must be related to future. |
| Legal effect | A wagering agreement is void. | The contingent contract is valid. |
| Example | Betting on a cricket match. | An insurance contract. |

## 5.11 ILLEGAL AGREEMENT

An agreement which is prohibited by law is an illegal agreement.

***Example***

Agreement to commit crime.

### 5.11.1 Effects of Illegal Agreement

1. The illegal agreement is always void. It is void *ab initio*. It is to be noted here that all void agreements may not be illegal.
2. Any collateral transaction to the illegal agreement is also void.
3. No action is allowed on the illegal agreement. No action or complaint can be made by any party for breach of the illegal agreement by the other party. If a complaint is made for the illegal agreement, the court will not help any party.
4. No restitution can be granted by the court in the illegal agreement.

***Example***

If Raja pays ₹ 50,000 to Prem to beat Tarun. The money cannot be recovered if Prem does not beat Tarun.

## 5.12 CONTINGENT CONTRACT—SECTION 31

A contract may be absolute or contingent. The contract is said to be absolute when the promisor binds himself to the performance in any event. While a contingent contract is the contract to do or not to do something, if some event collateral to such contract does or does not happen.

The contingent contract is defined as the contract in which the promisor undertakes to perform the contract upon the happening or non-happening of a specified future uncertain event, which is collateral to the contract.

The contingent contract contains a conditional promise. The contract of insurance, contract of guarantee and contract of indemnity are good examples of the contingent contract.

***Examples***

1. A contracts to pay B ₹ 10,000 if B's house is burnt.
2. A agrees to sell 20 computers to B for ₹ 20 lakhs if the ship fetching them reaches safely. The contrast is contingent on happening of the event.

## 5.13 ESSENTIAL FEATURES OF CONTINGENT CONTRACT

The essential features of a contingent contract are as under:

### 5.13.1 Event in Future

The performance of the contingent contract depends upon the happening or non-happening of some future events. The liability to perform a promise in the case of contingent contract depends upon the happening or non-happening of an event. This event is specified and agreed in advance by the party at the time of entering into a contract.

### 5.13.2 Event Must Be Uncertain

The contingent contract is based upon the uncertainty of an event. If the event has already taken place, it is not uncertain. In the same way, if the event is bound to happen or impossible then it is not uncertain.

### 5.13.3 Event Must Be Collateral

***Example***

A agrees to deliver 100 TV sets and B agrees to pay the price only after the delivery. These are reciprocal promises. It is not a contingent contract because the event on which B's promise depends is a part of the promise or consideration of the contract, and not a collateral event.

### 5.13.4 Event Must Not Depend Upon Act of Party

The contingent contract is a contract to do or not to do something. The contingent event or act must not be the mere will of the promisor. It must not rest upon the pleasure and sweet will of the promisor. However, if the event is within the promisor's will or control, (not merely at will) it may be a contingent contract.

***Example***

A agrees to do some work for B if he would feel pleasure in doing so. It is not a contract at all.

## 5.14 RULES REGARDING ENFORCEMENT OF CONTINGENT CONTRACT

A contingent contract is perfectly valid and can be enforced by the parties on the happening or non-happening of an uncertain event, as the case may be. The rules regarding the enforcement of the contingent contract contained under Sections 32–36 of the Indian Contract Act, which may be discussed as under:

### 5.14.1 Contingent Contract Dependent on the Happening of Future Uncertain Event

The contingent contract dependent on the happening of a future uncertain event can be enforced only when that uncertain event has happened. However, if the event becomes impossible then such a contract becomes void and cannot be enforced.

***Examples***

1. A makes a contract with B to sell a horse to B at a specified price, if C, to whom the horse has been offered, refuses to buy him. The contract cannot be enforced by law, unless and until C refuses to buy the horse.
2. A contracts to pay B a sum of money when B marries C. C dies without being married to B. The contract becomes void.

### 5.14.2 Contingent Contract Dependent on the Non-happening of Future Uncertain Event

The contingent contract dependent on the non-happening of a future uncertain event can be enforced only when that uncertain event becomes impossible as then that event cannot happen.

***Example***

A agrees to pay B a sum of money if a certain ship does not return. This ship is sunk. The contract can be enforced when the ship sinks.

### 5.14.3 Contingent Contract Dependent on Happening of Specified Uncertain Event Within Fixed Time

The contingent contract dependent on the happening of a specified uncertain event within a fixed time can be enforced if that event happened within a fixed time. It means if the event does not take place or does not happen within a fixed time or if it becomes impossible then such a contract become void and cannot be enforced.

### 5.14.4 Contingent Contract Dependent on Non-happening of Specified Uncertain Event Within Fixed Time

The contingent contract dependent on the non-happening of a specified uncertain event within a fixed time can be enforced, if that event does not happen within a fixed time or if it becomes certain that such event will not happen.

***Examples***

1. A promises to pay B a sum of money if a certain ship returns within a year. The contract may be enforced if the ship returns within the year and becomes void if the ship is burnt within the year.
2. A promises to pay B a sum of money if a certain ship does not return within a year. The contract may be enforced if the ship does not return within the year or is burnt within the year.

### 5.14.5 Contingent Contract Dependent Upon Impossible Events

The contingent contract dependent upon the happening of an impossible event is void and cannot be enforced. The contract is void because it can never be enforced as the impossible event will never happen.

***Examples***

1. A agrees to pay B ₹ 1000 if two-straight lines should enclose a space. The agreement is void.
2. A agrees to pay B ₹ 1000 if B will marry A's daughter C. C was dead at the time of the agreement. The agreement is void.

## 5.15 UNCERTAIN AGREEMENT

It means an agreement meaning of which is not certain or capable of being made certain. An uncertain agreement is void.

***Examples***

1. A agrees to sell to B 'a 100 ton of oil'. It is uncertain agreement as it does not specify which type of oil. In market various types of oils are available.
2. A agrees to sell to B 'all the grain in my granary at Ahmedabad'. There is no uncertainty here to make the agreement void.

**Case Study**

Whether following are uncertain agreement?

1. A agrees to sell to B '100 tons of oil of specified description known as an article of commerce'.
2. A, who is a dealer in coconut oil, agrees to sell to B '100 tons of oil'.
3. A agrees to sell to B 1000 ton of rice at the price fixed by C.
4. A agrees to sell to B 'my white horse for ₹ 500 or 1000.
5. A agrees to sell to B 10 tons of Punjab wheat. But the price is not indicated.
6. X agreed to buy a horse from Y for ₹ 5000 and to pay ₹ 100 more if the horse proved lucky.
7. X agreed to pay ₹ 10,000 when he will be able to pay.
8. X agrees to agree in future.

## 5.16 DISTINGUISH BETWEEN A VOID AGREEMENT AND A VOID CONTRACT

| Matter | Void Agreement | Void Contract |
|---|---|---|
| Meaning | A void agreement is not enforceable by law. | A contract which ceases to be enforceable by law is known as a void contract. |
| Status at the time of formation | All essentials of the contract are not satisfied in the case of a void agreement. | All the essentials of a contract are satisfied at the time of formation of the contract. |
| Restitution | A restitution is not allowed in the case of a void agreement. | A restitution is allowed in the case of a void contract. |
| Legal obligation | A void agreement does not create any legal obligation. | In case of a void contract, the legal obligation created under a contract becomes come to end subsequently. |

## LIST OF LANDMARK JUDGEMENTS

1. ***Charles vs Mcdonald (1899)***
   The agreement of service by which a person binds himself during the terms of the agreement not to take service with anyone else is valid.
2. ***Subba Naidu vs Haj Badsha (1902)***
   The sole selling agreement or exclusive dealing agreement which restrains to deal with any other product is valid.
3. ***K. M. Kamath vs K. R. Baliga and Co. (1959)***
   The object or consideration of an agreement is unlawful where it is forbidden by law.
4. ***Baivijli vs Hamda Nagar (1885)***
   The object or consideration of an agreement is unlawful, where it is regarded immoral or opposed to the public policy.

5. ***Venktaramananya vs J. M. Lobo (1953)***
The agreements which adversely affect the normal working of the government officers are void as they are opposed to the public policy.
6. ***Kalavanguta vs Laxmi Narain (1909)***
The marriage brokerage contract, being against the public policy is void.
7. ***Lower vs Peers (1918)***
The agreement in restraint of marriage is void.
8. ***District Board of Jhelum vs Harichand (1934)***
The agreement which creates monopoly is void.
9. ***Madhub Chander vs Raj Coomar (1874)***
The agreement which restrains a person from carrying an any lawful business is void.
10. ***Harward vs Miller's Timber and Trading Company (1917)***
The agreement, which restricts the personal liberty of an individual, is void as being opposed to the public policy.
11. ***Niranjan Shankar vs Century Spinning and Mfg. Co. (1967)***
The service agreement which restrains an employee from working elsewhere during the period of an employment is valid.
12. ***Uphill vs Wright (1911)***
The illegal agreement is void and does not confer any right and obligation on the parties.
13. ***Giddue Narayanish vs Annie Besant (1915)***
The agreement in restraint of parental rights is void.
14. ***Babalateb vs Rajaram (1931)***
The cross word competition is not a wager since it involves skills.
15. ***H. Anand Raj vs Govt. of Tamil Nadu (1986)***
The lotteries with prior permission of the government are legal, and it confers right upon the winner of the lottery to receive the prize money.
16. ***Brij Mohan vs MPSRT Corporation (1987)***
The agreement to transfer the permit against the provisions of a motor vehicle act was held as not enforceable.

## TEST YOUR KNOWLEDGE

1. Under what circumstances an object or a consideration of a contract deemed unlawful? Give examples. **(Ref. Para-5.1)**
2. Enumerate the agreements which have been expressly declared void by the Indian Contract Act. **(Ref. Para-5.1,5.2)**
3. Explain in brief-maintenance agreement and champerty agreement. **(Ref. Para-5.2)**
4. Every agreement in restraint of marriage of any person is void. Discuss. **(Ref. Para-5.2)**
5. What do you understand by the term 'trafficking public office'. **(Ref. Para-5.2)**
6. What is public policy? Write any seven agreements that are considered opposed to public policy? **(Ref. Para-5.3)**
7. Explain the exceptions of an agreement in restraint of trade. **(Ref. Para-5.3)**
8. When is an agreement in restraint of trade valid? **(Ref. Para-5.3)**

9. An agreement in restraint of legal proceedings is altogether void. Comment. **(Ref. Para-5.4)**
10. How will you decide about the enforceability of agreements which are unlawful in parts? **(Ref. Para-5.5)**
11. Write a short note on wagering agreement. **(Ref. Para-5.6,5.7,5.8)**
12. What are the effects of a wagering agreement? Where a wagering agreement is considered illegal? **(Ref. Para-5.8)**
13. Transactions incidental to wagering agreements are not void. Comment. **(Ref. Para-5.8)**
14. Distinguish between a wagering agreement and an insurance contract. **(Ref. Para-5.9)**
15. Wagering agreements do not cover insurance contracts. Comment. **(Ref. Para-5.9)**
16. What is the difference between a wagering agreement and a contingent contract? **(Ref. Para-5.10)**
17. What is an illegal agreement? **(Ref. Para-5.11)**
18. What are the effects of an illegal agreement? **(Ref. Para-5.11)**
19. No action is allowed on an illegal agreement. Comment. **(Ref. Para-5.11)**
20. Collateral transaction to an illegal agreement also becomes illegal. Explain. **(Ref. Para-5.11)**
21. What is a contingent contract? Give suitable example. **(Ref. Para-5.12)**
22. What are the essential elements of a contingent contract? **(Ref. Para-5.13)**
23. What are the rules regarding the enforcement of a contingent contract. **(Ref. Para-5.14)**
24. Write a short note on an uncertain agreement. **(Ref. Para-5.15)**
25. An uncertain agreement is neither valid nor void. Comment. **(Ref. Para-5.15)**

## MULTIPLE-CHOICE QUESTIONS

1. Consideration and object of an agreement is unlawful if it
   (i) is forbidden by law.
   (ii) would defeat the provisions of any law.
   (iii) either (i) or (ii).
   (iv) neither (i) nor (ii).
2. Consideration and object of an agreement is unlawful if it
   (i) would defeat the provisions of any law.
   (ii) creates injury to the person
   (iii) is fraudulent.
   (iv) all of the above.
3. Which of the following is incorrect?
   (i) An agreement to create monopoly is void.
   (ii) An agreement to defraud others is unlawful.
   (iii) Both of the above.
   (iv) None of the above.
4. Consideration and object of an agreement is unlawful if it
   (i) is fraudulent.
   (ii) is possible.
   (iii) is impossible.
   (iv) all of the above.
5. A, B and C enter into an agreement for sharing the money obtained by fraud. This agreement is
   (i) valid.
   (ii) wagering.
   (iii) void.
   (iv) voidable.
6. Which of the following agreements are valid?
   (i) Uncertain agreements.
   (ii) Wagering agreements.
   (iii) Agreements to do impossible events.
   (iv) None of the above.

7. Which of the following agreements are void?
   (i) Agreements to do impossible acts.
   (ii) Illegal agreements.
   (iii) Both (i) or (ii).
   (iv) Neither (i) nor (ii).
8. The agreement to create monopoly is
   (i) valid.
   (ii) void.
   (iii) illegal.
   (iv) wagering.
9. In which of the following agreements, restraint of trade is valid?
   (i) Agreement with buyer of goodwill.
   (ii) Trade combinations not opposed to public policy.
   (iii) Partnership agreements.
   (iv) All of the above.
10. Trade combination agreements like opening and closing of business ventures, licensing of traders, supervision and control of dealers are
    (i) void.
    (ii) valid.
    (iii) voidable.
    (iv) immoral.
11. When two companies enter into a joint venture agreement, the agreement is
    (i) opposed to public policy.
    (ii) void.
    (iii) either (i) or (ii).
    (iv) neither (i) nor (ii).
12. A service agreement where an employee agrees that he will not service anybody else during service period is a
    (i) valid agreement.
    (ii) void agreement.
    (iii) illegal agreement.
    (iv) unlawful agreement.
13. An agreement with the employees to serve the organization for a few years after training is
    (i) voidable.
    (ii) void.
    (iii) unenforceable.
    (iv) valid.
14. An agreement not to enforce any legal remedy or enforce the right is
    (i) valid.
    (ii) void.
    (iii) voidable.
    (iv) unenforceable.
15. An agreement between two parties to refer to arbitration for any dispute between them is valid
    (i) if any party wishes so.
    (ii) if it is in writing.
    (iii) either (i) or (ii).
    (iv) neither (i) nor (ii).
16. An agreement is void, if the meaning of such agreement is
    (i) not certain.
    (ii) not capable of being made certain.
    (iii) either (i) or (ii).
    (iv) neither (i) nor (ii).
17. A promised to pay an extra ₹ 5000 to B if the horse he purchased from B proved to be lucky. The promise is
    (i) valid.
    (ii) void.
    (iii) voidable.
    (iv) enforceable.
18. All illegal agreements are
    (i) void *ab initio*.
    (ii) valid.
    (iii) voidable.
    (iv) enforceable.
19. All void agreements are always
    (i) illegal.
    (ii) valid.
    (iii) enforceable.
    (iv) none of the above.

20. A void agreement is
    (i) not punishable.
    (ii) punishable.
    (iii) prohibited.
    (iv) illegal.
21. Which of the following is not a feature of a wagering agreement?
    (i) Chances of gain or loss.
    (ii) Uncertainty of future event.
    (iii) Neither party have control over future event.
    (iv) Neither parties should have an interest in the event.
22. An athletic competitions are valid because they are
    (i) games of skill.
    (ii) just games.
    (iii) game of luck.
    (iv) all of the above.
23. Any agreements to solve picture puzzles are
    (i) wagering agreements.
    (ii) not wagering agreements.
    (iii) void agreements.
    (iv) voidable agreements.
24. Which of these are not opposed to public policy?
    (i) Trading with enemy.
    (ii) Stifling prosecution.
    (iii) Compromise of compoundable offences.
    (iv) Agreement to commit a crime.
25. Which of these are opposed to public policy?
    (i) Restraint of marriage.
    (ii) Restraint of personal freedom.
    (iii) Interference with course of justice.
    (iv) All of the above.
26. Marriage brokerage contracts are
    (i) enforceable.
    (ii) valid.
    (iii) void.
    (iv) voidable.
27. An agreement intended to defraud income tax authorities is
    (i) contrary to public policy.
    (ii) void.
    (iii) both (i) and (ii).
    (iv) neither (i) nor (ii).
28. An agreement to remain unmarried is
    (i) valid.
    (ii) void.
    (iii) voidable.
    (iv) enforceable.
29. A contigent contract is
    (i) illegal.
    (ii) not contract at all.
    (iii) wagering in nature.
    (iv) none of the above.
30. A contract based on the happening or non-happening of a future event is called
    (i) a wagering contract.
    (ii) uncertain agreement.
    (iii) a contingent contract.
    (iv) voidable contract.
31. Which of the following is a contingent contract?
    (i) Contract of insurance.
    (ii) Contract for doing impossible acts.
    (iii) Marriage contract.
    (iv) Wagering agreements.
32. If A promises to pay B ₹ 10,000 if he so chooses, it is a contingent contract.
    (i) True
    (ii) Partly true
    (iii) False
    (iv) None of the above

33. A agrees to pay B ₹ 50,000 if a titanic ship does not return. The ship is sunk. The contract can be enforced
    (i) when the ship sinks.
    (ii) before the ship sinks.
    (iii) when the ship returns.
    (iv) when ship does not start its journey.
34. The performance of contingent contract depends upon.
    (i) Main event.
    (ii) Collateral event.
    (iii) Both (i) and (ii).
    (iv) Either (i) or (ii).
35. An agreement is said to be opposed to public policy when it
    (i) against the welfare of the society.
    (ii) prejudical to the public interest or public policy.
    (iii) either (i) and (ii).
    (iv) is against provision of any law.
36. A agrees to pay ₹ 30,000 to B, a rival shopkeeper, if he closes his business in A's locality only. This agreement is
    (i) valid.
    (ii) voidable.
    (iii) void.
    (iv) none of the above.
37. A partner of a firm, so long as he is partner, can be restrained from carrying on
    (i) any business.
    (ii) similar business.
    (iii) both of the above.
    (iv) none of the above.
38. A promises to pay ₹ 500 to B if it rains on the first Monday of the next. It is a
    (i) wagering agreement.
    (ii) contingent contract.
    (iii) void contract.
    (iv) voidable contract.
39. A agrees to pay ₹ 5000 to B, if B's car is burnt. It is
    (i) void.
    (ii) voidable contract.
    (iii) wagering agreement.
    (iv) contingent contract.
40. B agrees to sell to A '1 kg of gram at a price to be fixed by C'.
    (i) the agreement is valid.
    (ii) the agreement is void.
    (iii) the agreement is voidable.
    (iv) the agreement is illegal.

## ANSWER KEYS

| | | | | |
|---|---|---|---|---|
| **1.** (iii) | **9.** (iv) | **17.** (ii) | **25.** (iv) | **33.** (i) |
| **2.** (iv) | **10.** (ii) | **18.** (i) | **26.** (iii) | **34.** (ii) |
| **3.** (iii) | **11.** (iv) | **19.** (iv) | **27.** (iii) | **35.** (iii) |
| **4.** (i) | **12.** (i) | **20.** (i) | **28.** (ii) | **36.** (iii) |
| **5.** (iii) | **13.** (iv) | **21.** (iv) | **29.** (iv) | **37.** (iii) |
| **6.** (iv) | **14.** (ii) | **22.** (i) | **30.** (iii) | **38.** (ii) |
| **7.** (iii) | **15.** (ii) | **23.** (ii) | **31.** (i) | **39.** (iv) |
| **8.** (ii) | **16.** (iii) | **24.** (iii) | **32.** (iii) | **40.** (i) |

# 6

# The Indian Contract Act, 1872: Performance of Contract

## Learning Objectives

*After reading this chapter, you will be able to understand:*

- Performance of a contract and its type
- What is a valid tender and its effect on a contract?
- Contracts which need not to perform
- Who can perform the promise under contract?
- Rules regarding performance of a joint promise
- Rules regarding appropriation of a payment

Performance of a contract is one of the methods of discharge of a contract. The performance may be of two types: (a) actual performance and (b) attempted performance.

An actual performance of a contract means performing all the promises and fulfilling all the liabilities by all the parties. The actual performance discharges the contract and also discharges the parties. It is known as the natural method of discharge of the contract.

An attempted performance means the promisor has made an offer to perform a promise to the promisee but it has not been accepted. The attempted performance is known as tenders. If there is a valid tender, it discharges the party who is not at fault. Let us understand in detail, when a tender is said to be a valid tender.

## 6.1 ESSENTIALS OF A VALID TENDER

An attempt to perform a promise by a promisor is regarded as a valid tender, when it fulfills all of the following conditions.

### 6.1.1 It Must Be Unconditional

An unconditional means without condition. It means the promisor shall perform the promise as per the terms of contract as decided between the parties of contract. If the promise is not performed as per the condition, it is known as the conditional tender.

*Example*

A owes B ₹ 5000 and has fallen due. A offers to pay in five installment and tenders the first installment. This is a conditional tender.

### 6.1.2 It Must Be at Proper Place

The tender must be made at a proper place as specified in the contract. If no place is specified in the contract, the tender must be made at a place fixed by the promisee. Once a valid tender of goods is made at the specified or fixed place, the promisor is under no further responsibility of the performance even if the tender is not accepted.

*Example*

A contracts to deliver cotton to B at his warehouse. A must bring the cotton to B's warehouse only and tender the performance.

### 6.1.3 For Whole Obligation

It must be for the whole obligation and not in part. However, a minor deviation from the terms do not make a tender invalid.

*Example*

A agreed with B to sell 10,000 kg of rice but A delivered 22 kg less than that. Held, the buyer could not refuse to take delivery because the deficiency is negligible.

### 6.1.4 In Legal Tender Money

In case of a tender of money, the tender must be in legal tender money. Legal tender money means current currency notes or coins. The tender of money in the form of foreign currency is not a valid tender, unless it is agreed between the parties. A payment by a cheque is the valid tender, if the person to whom it is made is ready and willing to accept it.

### 6.1.5 It Must Be Made at Proper Time and to a Proper Person

The tender must be at a proper time i.e. at a stipulated time or during business hours. The tender of performance must be made to a proper person. The promisee or his authorized agent is considered as a proper person.

### 6.1.6 Reasonable Opportunity to Promisee

The tender must give a reasonable opportunity to the promisee to verify or examine the goods. The promisee has a right to examine, verify and check the goods or money tendered.

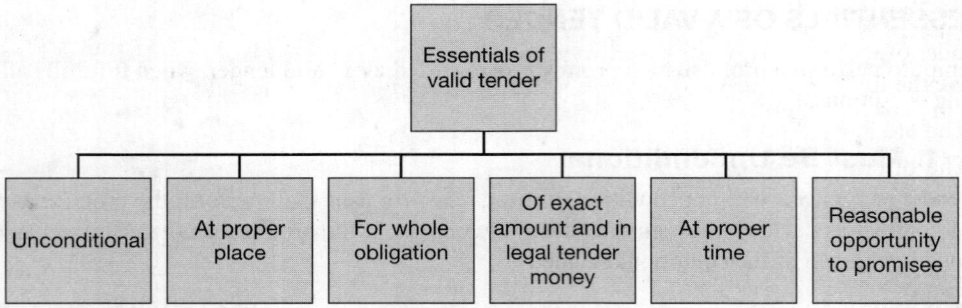


**Figure 6.1** Essentials of a valid tender.

**Case Study**

A contracts to deliver 100 bales of cotton, of a particular quality, to B at his warehouse on 1 March 2011. In order to make a valid tender what A should do?

## 6.2 EFFECTS OF A VALID TENDER

On making a valid tender of performance by the promisor, it becomes the duty of the promisee to accept the performance. If the promisee does not accept the valid tender, the promisor is not required to perform his promise again. The promisor is discharged from his obligation. At the same time, the promisor is not responsible for the non-performance because the promisee has not accepted the valid performance. However, the promisor does not lose his right under the contract.

***Example***

A agreed to deliver goods, at a specified place of B, for consideration of ₹ 5000. As per the agreement, A takes goods and delivered to B at the specified place but B rejects the deliver of goods. Here, A can recover his money or damage he has sustained.

## 6.3 TYPES OF TENDERS

There are two types of tenders (a) tender of goods and services and (b) tender of money. The rules for both the tenders are given here under:

### 6.3.1 Tender of Goods and Services

When a promisor offers the delivery of goods or services to the promisee it is said to be the tender of goods or services. If the promisee does not accept a valid tender, it will have the following effects:

1. The promisor is not responsible for the non-performance of the contract.
2. The promisor is discharged from his obligation under the contract. Therefore, he need not to offer again.
3. The promisor does not lose his right under the contract. Therefore, he can sue the promisee.

### 6.3.2 Tender of Money

The tender of money is an offer to make a payment. In case a valid tender of money is not accepted, it will have the following effects:

1. The offeror is not discharged from his obligation to pay the amount.
2. The offeror is discharged from his liability for the payment of interest from the date of the tender of money.

**Case Study**

A entered into a contract with B to deliver certain goods to B. A offered the goods to B at a proper time and place but B refused to accept the goods. In this case, what are the rights available to both the parties as per Contract Act, 1872?

## 6.4 CONTRACTS WHICH NEED NOT TO PERFORM

The purpose of a contract is its performance. However, the following contracts are not required to be performed:

### 6.4.1 Performance Becomes Impossible

When the performance of the contract becomes impossible, it is not required to perform. In the same manner, if the subject matter for which the contract or promise is made is destroyed, the promisor gets discharged from the performance.

***Example***

A agrees to dance in B's theatre for a month. A falls ill and becomes too weak to dance. The contract is void for impossibility and performance is excused by the law.

### 6.4.2 New Contract in Place of Old Contract

When the parties to contract agree to change, rescind or enter into a new contract, the old contract is not required to be performed. The promise under the old contract is not required to be performed.

### 6.4.3 Waiver by Promisee

When the promisee waives the promisor from the performance of the promise, the promisor is not required to perform his promise. Here, waiver means a sacrifice of right to get performance.

***Example***

A promises to paint a picture for B. B afterwards forbids him to do so. A is no longer bound to perform the promise.

### 6.4.4 Promise Becomes Illegal

When the performance of the promise becomes illegal, the promise is not required to be performed. An illegal thing or an object is not required to be pursued.

### 6.4.5 Rejection of Valid Tender

When a promisee rejects the valid tender of performance, the promisor is not liable to perform it again.

*Example*

A sold 100 tons of sugar to B. A tenders the delivery on Monday but B refused to accept. A is free from the obligation of performance of contract.

### 6.4.6 No Reasonable Facility

When a promisee does not provide a reasonable facility to a promisor to perform the promise, he gets a discharge from the performance.

*Example*

A contracts with B to repair B's house. B does not point out to A, the places in the house require to be repaired. A is excused for the non-performance of the contract.

## 6.5 WHO CAN PERFORM CONTRACT?

At the first instance, a contract should be performed by the promisor himself. However in certain cases, the contract may also be performed by persons other than the promisor.

### 6.5.1 Promisor

Generally, the contract shall be performed by the promisor himself. The contract shall be specifically performed by the promisor only, when it is the intention of the promise. The contract involving personal skill or personal trust and confidence must be performed by the promisor himself.

*Examples*

1. A promises to paint a picture for B by a certain day at a certain price. A dies before the day. The contract cannot be enforced either by A's representatives or by B.
2. A promises to paint a picture for B. A must perform this promise personally. Painting picture is a personal skill.

### 6.5.2 Legal Representative

The contract which does not involve any personal skill, may be performed by the legal representative of the promisor, on the death of the promisor. However, the liability of the legal representative under the contract is limited to the value of the property inherited. The legal representative does not have any liability under the contract, if the terms and conditions of the contract provide so.

*Example*

A promises to deliver goods to B on a certain day, on payment of ₹ 1000. A dies before that day. A's representatives are bound to deliver the goods to B and B is bound to pay ₹ 1000 to A's representatives.

### 6.5.3 Third Party

The third party may perform the promise if the promisee accepts the performance. When the promisee accepts the performance of the promise from a third person, he cannot afterwards enforce it against the promisor.

**Case Study**

A promises to paint a picture for B. A dies before painting the picture. Can B ask legal representative of A to paint picture as per the contract? What is correct legal position here?

**Case Study**

A owes ₹ 60,000 to B. Before clearing his liability, a dies leaving behind an estate worth ₹ 40,000. In this case, A's legal representatives are liable for what amount? Explain the rule in this regard.

## 6.6 PERFORMANCE OF JOINT PROMISE—SECTIONS 42–45

When two or more persons enter into a joint agreement with one or more persons, in such a case, the promise is known as a joint promise. The rules relating to the performance of the joint promises are contained in Sections 42–45 of the Contract Act, 1872, and may be discussed under the following heads.

### 6.6.1 Promisee May Compell to Perform Any One of Joint Promisor

In the absence of any express agreement to the contrary, the promisee may compel any one or more of the joint promisors to perform the whole joint promise.

*Example*

A, B and C jointly promise to pay D a sum of ₹ 3000. D may compel either A or B or C to pay him ₹ 3000.

### 6.6.2 The Joint Promisors Are Liable to Contribute Equally

Each of the joint promisors may compel every other joint promisor to contribute equally with himself and to the performance of the promise, unless a contrary intention appears from the contract.

*Example*

A, B and C jointly promise to pay D a sum of ₹ 3000. C is compelled to pay the whole. C is entitled to receive ₹ 1000 each from A and B, unless a contrary intention appears from the contract among them.

### 6.6.3 Joint Promisors Liable to Share Loss Equally

In case, a joint promisor has been compelled to pay more than his share of liability, he can claim contribution from the other joint promisors. But if any of the joint promisors makes a default (e.g. due to insolvency) in such a contribution, the remaining joint promisors must bear the loss arising from such a default in equal shares.

***Example***

A, B and C are under joint promise to pay D a sum of ₹ 3000. C is unable to pay anything and A is compelled to pay the whole. A is entitled to receive ₹ 1500 from B. This amount includes ₹ 1000 as normal contribution plus equal share of the sum under default.

### 6.6.4 Effect of Release of Joint Promisor

A release of one of the joint promisors by the promisee does not discharge the other joint promisor or promisors and their liability continues as before.

**Case Study**

'A', 'B' and 'C' are partners in a firm. They jointly promise to pay ₹ 1,50,000 to 'P'. C became insolvent and his private assets are sufficient to pay only 1/5 of his share of debts. A is compelled to pay the whole amount to P. Examining the provisions of the Indian Contract Act, 1872, decide the extent to which A can recover the amount from B.

**Case Study**

X, Y and Z jointly borrowed ₹ 50,000 from A. The whole amount was repaid to A by Y. Decide in the light of the Indian Contract Act, 1872 whether:

(i) Y can recover the contribution from X and Z,
(ii) legal representatives of X are liable in case of death of X,
(iii) Y can recover the contribution from the assets, in case Z becomes insolvent.

**Case Study**

A, B and C jointly promise to pay D a sum of ₹ 6000. C is compelled to pay the whole. A is insolvent but his assets are sufficient to pay one-half of his debts. What amount C can recover from B?

## 6.7 TIME AND PLACE FOR PERFORMANCE OF PROMISE—SECTIONS 46–50

The rules relating to the time and place of performance are contained in Sections 46–50 of Contract Act, 1872, which may be discussed under the following heads:

### 6.7.1 Time for Performance of Promise Where No Application Is to Be Made and No Time Is Specified

Where, by the contract, a promisor is to perform his promise without an application by the promisee, and if no time for performance is specified, the engagement must be performed within a reasonable time. The question 'What is a reasonable time' is in each particular case, a question of fact.

### 6.7.2 Time and Place for Performance of Promise Where Time Is Specified and No Application to Be Made

When a promise is to be performed on a certain day and the promisor has undertaken to perform it without an application by the promisee, the promisor may perform it at any time during the usual hours of business on such a day and at the place at which the promise ought to be performed.

***Example***

A promises to deliver goods at B's warehouse on the 1st January. On that day, A brings the goods to B's warehouse but after the usual hour for closing it they are not received. A has not performed his promise.

### 6.7.3 Application for Performance on Certain Day to Be at Proper Time and Place

When a promise is to be performed on a certain day and the promisor has not undertaken to perform it without an application by the promisee, it is the duty of the promisee to apply for the performance at a proper place, and within the usual hours of business. The question 'What is a proper time and place' is, in each particular case, a question of fact.

### 6.7.4 Place for Performance of Promise Where No Application to Be Made and No Place Fixed for Performance

When a promise is to be performed without an application by the promisee, and no place is fixed for the performance of it, it is the duty of the promisor to apply to the promisee, to appoint a reasonable place for the performance of the promise and to perform it at such place.

***Example***

A undertakes to deliver a 1000 kg of jute to B on a fixed day. A must apply to B to appoint a reasonable place for the purpose of receiving it, and must deliver it to him at such place.

### 6.7.5 Performance in Manner or at Time Prescribed or Sanctioned by Promisee

The performance of any promise may be made in any manner, or at any time, which the promisee prescribes or sanctions.

***Examples***

1. B owes A ₹ 2000. A desires B to pay the amount to A's account with C, a banker. B, who also banks with C, orders the amount to be transferred from his account to A's credit, and this is done by C. Afterwards, and before A knows of the transfer, C fails. There has been a good payment by B.
2. A and B are mutually indebted. A and B settle an account by setting off one item against another, and B pays A the balance found to be due from him upon such settlement. This amounts to a payment by A and B, respectively, of the sums which they owed to each other.
3. A owes B ₹ 2000. B accepts some of A's goods in deduction of the debt. The delivery of the goods operates as a part payment.

4. A desires B, who owes him ₹ 100, to send him a note for ₹ 100 by post. The debt is discharged as soon as B puts, into the post, a letter containing the note duly addressed to A.

## 6.8 WHO CAN DEMAND PERFORMANCE OF PROMISE?

The performance of a promise can be demanded by the promisee only. The rules in this regard are discussed as under:

### 6.8.1 Promisee

A promisee can demand the performance of a promise under the contract.

### 6.8.2 Legal Representative of Promisee

On the death of the promisee, his legal representative can demand a performance of promise except:

1. Where an agreement provides the contrary.
2. Where a contract is of a personal nature.

### 6.8.3 Third Party

Generally, the third party (stranger) cannot demand the performance of a promise under the contract as he is not the party to the contract. However, the third party can demand the performance of the contract in some exceptional cases like in the case of trust, the beneficiary can enforce the contract.

### 6.8.4 Demand by Joint Promisees

In the case of joint promisees, the demand to perform can be made based upon the circumstances as under:

1. If all the promisees are alive then all the promisees must jointly demand performance of the promise.
2. If there is a death of any of the joint promisees, the representative of the deceased promisee along with the surviving promisees can demand performance of the promise.
3. If there is death of all the joint promisees, the legal representatives of all of them can jointly demand performance of the promise.

## 6.9 KINDS OF RECIPROCAL PROMISE

The promise exchange for a promise is known as a reciprocal promise. In the case of a reciprocal promise, each party to contract is the promisor as well as the promisee. Lord Mansfied in the case of *Jones vs Barkley* classified reciprocal promises as under:

### 6.9.1 Mutual and Independent

When the promises are to be performed by each party independently without waiting for the other party to perform his promise, it is called as it mutual and independent reciprocal promises.

***Example***

A agrees to deliver goods to B. B agrees to pay ₹ 1000 for goods. Here, both parties can perform their respective promises anytime.

### 6.9.2 Mutual and Dependent

When the performance of one party depends on the prior performance of the other party, it is known as the mutual and dependent reciprocal promises.

***Example***

A agrees to deliver goods to B on advance payment of ₹ 1000. Here, A's performance of promise is depend upon the performance of promise by B.

### 6.9.3 Mutual and Concurrent

When the promises are to be performed by both the parties simultaneously, it is the mutual and concurrent reciprocal promises.

***Example***

A agrees to deliver goods to B against cash payment of ₹ 1000 by B.

## 6.10 RULES REGARDING PERFORMANCE OF RECIPROCAL PROMISES

The rules regarding the performance of reciprocal promises are as follows:

### 6.10.1 Simultaneous Performance of Reciprocal Promise—Section 51

When a contract requires simultaneous performance of the reciprocal promise, the promisor need not perform his promise unless the promisee is ready and willing to perform his reciprocal promise.

***Example***

A and B contract that A shall deliver goods to B to be paid for by B on delivery. A need not deliver the goods unless B is ready and willing to pay for the goods on delivery. B need not pay for the goods unless A is ready and willing to deliver them on payment.

### 6.10.2 Order of Reciprocal Promise Is Fixed—Section 52

Where the order of performance of the reciprocal promise is fixed in the contract, the promise should be performed according to the order specified under the contract. If no order of performance of the promise is fixed, then it should be performed according to the nature of transaction.

***Examples***

1. A and B contract that A shall build a house for B at a fixed price. A's promise to build the house must be performed before B's promise to pay for it.
2. A and B contract that A shall make over his stock-in-trade to B at a fixed price, and B promises to give security for the payment of the money. A's promise need not be performed until the security is given for the nature of the transaction requires that A should have security before he delivers up his stock.

### 6.10.3 Effect of Preventing Performance—Section 53

When one party to contract prevents the other from performing his promise, the contract becomes voidable at the option of the party so prevented and the compensation can be claimed.

***Example***

A and B contract that B shall execute certain work for A for ₹ 1000. B is ready and willing to execute the work accordingly but A prevents him from doing so. The contract is voidable at the option of B, and if he elects to rescind it, he is entitled to recover a compensation, from A, for any loss which he has incurred by its non-performance.

### 6.10.4 Effect of Default As to Promise to Be Performed First Under Contract—Section 54

If a party, who is liable to perform first, fails, he cannot demand performance from the other party and compensation. The person, who is at fault, cannot demand the performance against the other party. The defaulting party can be held liable for the payment damage, if the other party has suffered loss as a result of his failure to perform.

***Examples***

1. A contacts with B to execute certain builder's work for a fixed price, B supplying the scaffolding and timber necessary for the work. B refuses to furnish and scaffolding or timber, and the work cannot be executed. A need not execute the work, and B is bound to make compensation to A for any loss caused to him by the non-performance of the contract.
2. A contracts with B to deliver to him, at a specified price, certain merchandise on board a ship which cannot arrive for a month, and B engages to pay for the merchandise within a week from the date of the contract. B does not pay within the week. A's promise to deliver need not be performed, and B must make compensation.
3. A promises B, to sell him 100 bales of merchandise, to be delivered next day, and B promises A to pay for them within a month. A does not deliver according to his promise. B's promise to pay need not be performed and A must make compensation.

### 6.10.5 Effect of Promise to Do Legal and Illegal Things—Section 57

If one contract contains two promises, out of which one is legal and the other is illegal, the first part is the contract while the second part is the void agreement if the legal promise and the illegal promise are separable from each other. But if both the promises cannot be separated from each other, the entire agreement is void.

***Example***

A and B agree that A shall sell a house to B for ₹ 10,000 but if B uses it as a gambling house, he shall pay A ₹ 50,000 for it. The first set of reciprocal promises, namely, to sell the house and to pay ₹ 10,000 for it is a contract. The second set is for an unlawful object, namely that B may use the house as a gambling house and is a void agreement.

**Case Study**

A hires B's ship to take in and convey from Calcutta to Mauritius, a cargo to be provided by A, B receiving a certain freight for its conveyance. A does not provide any cargo for the ship. Advise on parties' right to claim damage.

## 6.11 TIME IS THE ESSENCE OF A CONTRACT

When a party to the contract promises to do a certain thing at or before a specified time or certain things at or before specified times, and fails to do any such thing at or before the specified time, the contract or so much of it as has not been performed becomes voidable at the option of the promisee, if the intention of the parties was that time should be of the essence of the contract.

### 6.11.1 Effect of Such Failure When Time Is Not Essential

If it was not the intention of the parties that time should be of the essence of the contract, the contract does not become voidable by the failure to do such thing at or before the specified time but the promisee is entitled to compensation from the promisor for any loss occasioned to him by such failure.

### 6.11.2 Effect of Acceptance of Performance at Time Other Than That Agreed Upon

If in case of a contract voidable on account of the promisor's failure to perform his promise at the time agreed, the promisee accepts the performance of such a promise at any time other than that agreed, the promisee cannot claim compensation for any loss occasioned by the non-performance of the promise at the time agreed unless, at the time of such acceptance, he gives a notice to the promisor of his intention to do so.

## 6.12 APPROPRIATION OF PAYMENTS—SECTIONS 59–61

Sometimes, a debtor owes several distinct debts to the same creditor and he makes a payment which is insufficient to satisfy all the debts. In such a case, a question arises as to which particular debt the payment is to be appropriated. Sections 59–61 of the act, lay down the following rules as to the appropriation of payments which provide an answer to this question.

### 6.12.1 Appropriation As per Express Instructions

Every debtor, who owes several debts to the creditor, has a right to instruct his creditor to which particular debt the payment is to be appropriated or adjusted. Therefore, where the debtor expressly states that the payment is to be applied to the discharge of a particular debt, the payment must be applied accordingly.

***Example***

A owes B three distinct debts of ₹ 20,000, ₹ 30,000 and ₹ 50,000. A sends ₹ 50,000 and instructs B that the payment should be appropriated against the third debt. He is bound to appropriate the payment against the third debt only.

### 6.12.2 Appropriation As per Circumstances Implying

Sometimes, the debtor makes a payment to his creditor without any express instructions as to which particular debt the payment is to be appropriated. In such a case, the creditor must appropriate the payment towards the debt to which under the implying circumstances the debtor intended to do so.

***Example***

A owes to B, among other debts, the sum of ₹ 520. B writes to A and demands payment of this sum. A sends to B ₹ 520. This payment is to be applied to the discharge of the debt of which B had demanded payment.

### 6.12.3 Appropriation of Payment Where No Express Instructions or Implying Circumstances Are There

Sometimes neither the debtor sends express instructions nor the circumstances imply as to which debt the payment is to be applied. In such a case, the creditor may apply it at his discretion to any lawful debt, actually due and payable to him from the debtor. He cannot, however, apply the payment to unlawful or disputed debt. It may also be noted that the creditor also has a right to first appropriate the payment to the interest due and then to the principal sum.

### 6.12.4 Appropriation in Chronological Order, i.e., in Order of Time

Sometimes neither the debtor nor the creditor makes any appropriation of the payment. In such a case, the payment shall be applied in discharge of the debts due, in order of time, whether they are, or not barred by the Law of Limitations. If the debts are of equal standing (i.e., of the same debt or time barred), the payment shall be applied in discharge of each such debt proportionately.

***Example***

A owes B the following debts:

| Amount of the Debt | Position of the Debt |
|---|---|
| ₹ 4000 | Time barred. |
| ₹ 2000 | Time barred. |
| ₹ 2000 | Due on 10 June 2009 |
| ₹ 3000 | Due on 20 July 2010 |

A sends ₹ 3000 in the month of June. He neither expressly intimates, nor circumstances of the case imply as to which debt the amount is to be applied. Moreover, B also does not appropriate the payment at his own discretion. Therefore, the payment will be appropriated in order of time. However, here in this case two debts are of equal standing. The payment will, therefore, be appropriated in order of time but to all equal standing debts. In this case, ₹ 3000 will be appropriated towards the first two debts of equal standing proportionately, i.e., in the ratio of 2:1.

### 6.12.5 Appropriation in Case of Current Account

In case of a current account, first debit entry is set-off against first credit entry.

### 6.12.6 In Case Interest is Also Due

Sometimes the debt is due with interest and the debtor makes payment of a certain sum of money. In such a case, the general rule is that the payment should be applied at the first instance to the whole interest due and thereafter to the principal, provided the parties have no contract to the contrary.

### 6.12.7 Payment Received in Demand for Various Debts

Sometimes, the creditor makes a demand for the payment of various debts due from the debtor and the debtor pays a part of the amount due. In such a case, the payment will be appropriated to the each debt due, proportionately.

### 6.12.8 Appropriation in Case of Trust Fund

Sometimes, the man keeps one bank account and makes a series of deposits and withdrawals in it of his own money as well as the money of which he is a trustee. In the course of transaction, sometimes trust funds are misappropriated. In such a case, the withdrawals are to be debited to his own money at the first instance and then to the trust fund and deposits are to be credited first to the trust fund and next to his own fund, whatever be the actual order of withdrawals and deposits.

**Case Study**

A owes B, a total amount of ₹ 25,000. He sends a cheque for ₹ 10,000 stating that it shall be appropriated towards his first sum of ₹ 10,000, he took from B. Against which sum B shall appropriate it?

## 6.13 ASSIGNMENT AND SUCCESSION OF A CONTRACT

The assignment of contracts means voluntary transfer of rights, title, interest or benefit under the contract to the third party. While succession to the contract is the process where one person succeeds in another person's right, interest, benefit and obligation in the contract by the process of law. Only contracts which are impersonal in nature can be assigned or succeeded. The contract which is based upon the use of personal skill is a personal contract which cannot be assigned or succeeded.

The succession of the contract takes place in the following two situations:

1. In the case of death of the party to contract his legal heir succeeds to the rights and liabilities under the contract. However, he is liable for non-personal contract and liable to the extent of property inherited by him.
2. In the case of insolvency of the party to contract, his rights and liabilities under the contract are acquired by the official liquidator.

## LIST OF LANDMARK JUDGEMENTS

1. ***Kirti Chunder vs Strathers (1878)***
   Where two or more persons have made the joint promise, a release of one of such joint promisor by the promisee does not discharge the other joint promisors.
2. ***Taylor vs Caldwell (1863)***
   If the subject matter of the contract is destroyed after the formation of the contract, without the fault of either party, the contract becomes void.
3. ***K. S. Vidyanandan vs Vairavan (1997)***
   When time is not the essence of a contract, the promisor must perform his part of the contract within a reasonable time, and a reasonable time should be determined by looking at all surrounding circumstances, including the express terms of the contract and the nature of property.
4. ***Rulia Devi vs Raghunath Prasad (1979)***
   Unless there is a contract to the contrary, the payment should be first appropriated towards the interest, and after the interest is fully paid off, to the principal.

5. ***Suresh Kumar Rajendra Kumar vs K. Assan Koya and Sons (1990)***
The tender must be for the performance of the whole obligation. But where the quantity is large, the buyer could not refuse to take the delivery of goods because the deficiency is negligible.
6. ***New India Motors (P) Ltd vs Smt. S. P. Duggal (1982)***
The liabilities of the legal representative under the contract is limited to the extent of the value of property inherited by them from the deceased.
7. ***Harikrishan Das vs Nariman (1927)***
Where there is only one debt, although payable in installments, the debtor has no right to appropriate payment to a particular installment.
8. ***Hind Construction Contractors vs State of Maharashtra (1979)***
If the contract includes clauses for the extension of time in certain contingencies or for the payment of fine or penalty for delay, such clauses indicate that time is not the essence of the contract.
9. ***Kapurchand Godha vs Nawabhimyat Ali (1963)***
The performance by the third person is also effective, if the promisee accepts for the same. Once the promisee accepts the performance from the third person, he cannot compel the promisor to perform the contract again.
10. ***Shirten Anderson and Co. vs Weil Bros and Co. (1972)***
The valid tender of performance must be of the whole obligation.
11. ***Municipal Corporation of Delhi vs Jagan Nath Ashok Kumar (1987)***
Whether time is the essence of the contract or not can be gathered from the intention of the parties and from the terms of the contract.
12. ***Gomathninayatam Pilla vs Palaniswani Nadan (1967)***
In the contract for sale of land or immovable property, time is not considered to be the essence of the contract.

## TEST YOUR KNOWLEDGE

1. What do you understand by the performance of a contract? **(Ref. Beginning of the chapter)**
2. Write a short note on the performance of the contract. **(Ref. Beginning of the chapter)**
3. Distinguish between the actual performance of the contract, and the attempted performance of the contract. **(Ref. Beginning of the chapter)**
4. What are the requisites of the valid tender of performance? **(Ref. Para-6.1)**
5. What are the effects of refusal by the promisee, to accept valid tender of goods and services? **(Ref. Para-6.2)**
6. The tender must be conditional. Comment. **(Ref. para-6.2)**
7. The tender can be performed at any place. Comment. **(Ref. para-6.2)**
8. Write a short note on the types of tender. **(Ref. para-6.3)**
9. Is there any difference between the tender of services and the tender of money? **(Ref. para-6.3)**
10. In which circumstances the contract is not required to be performed? **(Ref. Para-6.4)**
11. The contract involving personal skill can be performed by the promisor himself. Comment. **(Ref. Para-6.5)**
12. When is the legal representative of a promisor not required to perform the promise under a contract? **(Ref. Para-6.5)**

13. When should the contract be compulsorily performed by the promisor himself? **(Ref. Para-6.5)**
14. Who can perform the promise under a contract? **(Ref. Para-6.5)**
15. Discuss the law relating to the rights and liabilities of joint promisors in the contract. **(Ref. Para-6.6)**
16. The joint promisors are liable to share losses equally. Comment. **(Ref. para-6.6)**
17. What are the rules relating to time and place of the performance of a contract? **(Ref. Para-6.7)**
18. Who can demand the performance of promise? **(Ref. Para-6.8)**
19. Explain rules with regard to demand of promise by the joint promisors. **(Ref. para-6.8)**
20. In what different ways can reciprocal promises be classified? **(Ref. Para-6.9)**
21. Reciprocal promises are always performed simultaneously. Comment. **(Ref. para-6.9)**
22. State the provisions relating to the performance of reciprocal promises. **(Ref. Para-6.10)**
23. What will be the effect, if one party to the contract prevents the other party from performing a promise? **(Ref. Para-6.10)**
24. When is time the essence of a contract? **(Ref. para-6.11)**
25. Explain the rules relating to the appropriation of a payment with suitable examples. **(Ref. Para-6.12)**
26. Write a short note on the assignment and succession of the contract. **(Ref. para-6.13)**

## MULTIPLE-CHOICE QUESTIONS

1. Performance of a contract may be in the form of
   (i) actual.
   (ii) attempted.
   (iii) either (i) or (ii).
   (iv) both (i) and (ii).
2. When the parties under the contract fulfill their respective promises, the contract is said to be discharged
   (i) by breach of contract.
   (ii) by impossibility of performance.
   (iii) by agreement and novation.
   (iv) by performance of contract.
3. Which are the essentials of a valid tender?
   (i) Tender must be unconditional.
   (ii) Tender must be made at a proper place.
   (iii) Tender must be to a proper person.
   (iv) All of the above.
4. The parties to a contract need not perform when the performance is
   (i) dispensed with.
   (ii) excused under the provisions of any law.
   (iii) either (i) or (ii).
   (iv) neither (i) nor (ii).
5. A promises to deliver goods to B for ₹ 20,000. A dies before before performance of promise.
   (i) The contract becomes void.
   (ii) The contract becomes impossible.
   (iii) The contract can be enforced against A's representatives and B is bound to pay ₹ 20,000 to A's representatives.
   (iv) The contract is void.

6. Who cannot demand performance of promise?
   (i) Promisee.
   (ii) Any of the joint promisees.
   (iii) Legal representative on death of promisee.
   (iv) Stranger to the contract.
7. 'A' promises to act in a movie for 'B'. In this case
   (i) legal representative of A can perform the promise.
   (ii) A's agent can perform the promise.
   (iii) A's employer can perform the promise.
   (iv) A must perform this promise personally.
8. It is not always required of the parties to perform the contract ....
   (i) in time.
   (ii) before time.
   (iii) personally.
   (iv) both (ii) and (iii).
9. When two or more persons have made a joint promise, then, unless a contrary intention appears from the contract, the promise shall be performed, during their joint lives
   (i) by any one of them.
   (ii) by a majority of the joint promisors.
   (iii) by all of the joint promisors.
   (iv) all of the above.
10. The liability of joint promisors is
   (i) joint.
   (ii) several.
   (iii) joint or several.
   (iv) joint and several.
11. A, B, and C jointly promise to pay ₹ 1000 to D. D files a suit to recover the amount against A
   (i) D must sue all of them.
   (ii) D can recover ₹ 100 only from A.
   (iii) D can recover the amount from any one of them.
   (iv) D cannot sue any of them.
12. If any one of joint promisors makes default in such contribution, remaining joint promisors must share the loss arising from such default
   (i) equally.
   (ii) not equally.
   (iii) in the ratio of their properties.
   (iv) either (i) or (ii).
13. In case of a joint promise, release of one of joint promisors by the promisee
   (i) discharges all promisors.
   (ii) discharges the other joint promisors.
   (iii) does not discharge the other joint promisors.
   (iv) discharge the promisee.
14. In a contract where time is not specified for performance, the promisor can perform the contract
   (i) at any time he wishes.
   (ii) within the shortest time.
   (iii) within a reasonable time.
   (iv) within the latest time.
15. If a contract provides for the order of performance of reciprocal promises, the promises shall be performed
   (i) in the order mentioned.
   (ii) in any reasonable order.
   (iii) in any appropriate order.
   (iv) in any order whatsoever.
16. The promises forming consideration for each other are called
   (i) reciprocal promises.
   (ii) mutual promises.
   (iii) independent promises.
   (iv) none of the above.

17. The promises which are to be performed simultaneously are known as
    (i) mutual and concurrent.
    (ii) conditional and dependent.
    (iii) mutual and independent.
    (iv) none of these.
18. Where the performance of a promise by one party depends upon the prior performance of promise by the other, the promise is known as
    (i) mutual and concurrent.
    (ii) conditional and dependent.
    (iii) mutual and independent.
    (iv) concurrent and dependent.
19. A promises to deliver goods at B's godown. A delivers the goods during business hours to B's house.
    (i) A has not performed his promise.
    (ii) A has performed his promise.
    (iii) B has not performed his promise.
    (iv) both (ii) and (iii).
20. A contracts to act at a theatre for 6 months in a consideration of a sum paid in advance by B. On several occasions A is too ill to act.
    (i) The contract becomes void.
    (ii) The contract becomes voidable.
    (iii) The contract becomes illegal.
    (iv) Any one of the above.
21. A hired a music hall to B for performing concerts. The hall accidentally burnt before beginning of the concert. The contract become
    (i) void.
    (ii) voidable.
    (iii) illegal.
    (iv) any of the above.
22. A contracted to supply certain quantity of timber to B. Before the supply of any timber, a war broke out, resulting in disruption of supply of the timber.
    (i) A was discharged from performing the contract.
    (ii) A was not discharged from performing the contract.
    (iii) A has to pay compensation.
    (iv) A has to pay penalty.

## ANSWER KEYS

| | | | |
|---|---|---|---|
| **1.** (iii) | **7.** (iv) | **13.** (iii) | **19.** (i) |
| **2.** (iv) | **8.** (iii) | **14.** (iii) | **20.** (i) |
| **3.** (iv) | **9.** (iii) | **15.** (i) | **21.** (i) |
| **4.** (iii) | **10.** (iv) | **16.** (i) | **22.** (ii) |
| **5.** (iii) | **11.** (iii) | **17.** (i) | |
| **6.** (iv) | **12.** (i) | **18.** (ii) | |

# 7

# The Indian Contract Act, 1872: Discharge of a Contract

**Learning Objectives**

*After reading this chapter, you will be able to understand:*

- What is discharge of a contract?
- Various methods of discharge of a contract
- Initial and supervening impossibility of a performance
- Breach of a contract and its consequences

## 7.1 DISCHARGE OF A CONTRACT

Discharge of a contract means termination of the contractual relations between the parties to the contract. The contract may be discharged in the following six modes as shown in Figure 7.1.

## 7.2 DISCHARGE OF A CONTRACT ON PERFORMANCE

A contract can be discharged by performance in any of the following ways.

### 7.2.1 By an Actual Performance

It means the parties to contract have performed their respective promises under the contract.

### 7.2.2 By an Attempted Performance or a Tender

It means the promisor has made an offer of the performance of promise but it has not been accepted by the promisee.

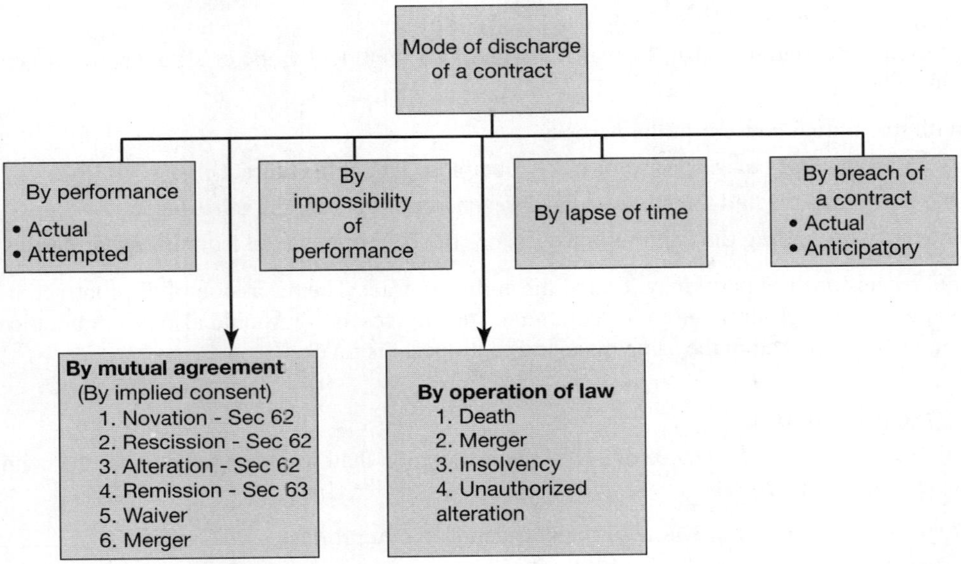


**Figure 7.1** Mode of discharge of a contract.

## 7.3 DISCHARGE OF A CONTRACT BY A MUTUAL AGREEMENT OR BY AN IMPLIED CONSENT

A contract can be discharged by mutual agreement in any of the following ways.

### 7.3.1 Novation

The novation means a new contract is entered into in consideration of the old contract. The new contract is entered into between the same parties or the new parties. The novation is valid when all the parties must consent it. The new contract must be valid and enforceable, otherwise the old contract will continue valid.

***Example***

A owed ₹ 100 to B, under contract. B owed ₹ 100 to C. It was agreed among A, B and C that A would pay ₹ 100 to C.

### 7.3.2 Alteration

An alteration of a contract means a change in one or more terms of the contract with the mutual consent of the parties. The alteration discharges the original contract and creates a new contract. However, the parties to the new contract remain the same. In case of alteration of the contract, the old terms and conditions need not to be performed while the new terms and conditions must be performed.

***Example***

A agreed with B to supply 100 TV sets at a certain price by the end of October. Subsequently, A and B mutually agree that the supply be made by the end of November. This is an altercation in the terms of the contract by consent of both the parties.

### 7.3.3 Rescission

The rescission of a contract means the cancellation of the contract by one or all the parties to contract. It may take place:

1. With the mutual consent of the parties.
2. By a party whose consent was not freely obtained (voidable contract).
3. One party may rescind the contract, if a breach of contract by the other party.
4. The party rescinding the contract must restore the benefit received from the other party.

No partial rescission. The party may rescind the entire contract. The rescission of the contract in part is not possible. Just as a proposal has to be communicated, the rescission should also be communicated. A rescission may be revoked in the same manner as a proposal is revoked.

### 7.3.4 Remission

The remission means the acceptance of a lesser consideration than what is agreed under the contract. It takes place when the promisee:

1. Dispenses with a part or whole of the performance of a promise.
2. Extends the time for a performance by the promisor.
3. Accepts a lesser sum.
4. Accepts any other consideration, than agreed in the contract.

***Example***

A owes B ₹ 5000. A pays ₹ 2000 to B and B accepts the amount in satisfaction of the whole debt. The whole debt is discharged.

It may be noted that when a party accepts a lesser sum in satisfaction of a larger sum due under the contract it is called 'accord and satisfaction' in the English Law. The promisee accepts a lesser sum than what is due under the contract is known as 'Accord' and the actual payment is the satisfaction. This is a valid contract.

### 7.3.5 Waiver

It means the abandonment (i.e., giving up) of right by the party under the contract. No consideration is necessary for the waiver.

***Example***

A promises to supply goods to Y. Later on, Y exempts A from carrying out the promise. It amount as waiver of right of performance on part of Y.

### 7.3.6 Merger

The conversion of the inferior right into superior right is called as merger. It is also called as vesting of rights and liabilities in the same person.

***Example***

A person holds property under lease, purchases the property. On purchase, his lease agreement is discharged.

**Case Study**

A bill of exchange which was accepted by B, reaches B's hands after being negotiated and endorsed through several other parties. Is it a valid contract? Is B require to make payment on bill?

**Case Study**

A took a house on rent from B. During tenancy, A purchases that house. Now does he requires to pay the rent? Why?

## 7.4 DISTINGUISH BETWEEN A NOVATION AND AN ALTERATION

| Matter | Novation | Alteration |
|---|---|---|
| Meaning | It means a new contract is entered into in the place of the old contract. | Alteration means a change in one or more terms of the contract with the consent of all the parties. |
| Different Parties | Novation may involve different parties. | In the case of alteration, parties are the same. |
| Change in terms and Conditions | Novation may or may not involve changes in the terms and conditions. Generally, novation includes alteration. | Alteration always requires changes in one or more terms and conditions of the contract. |

## 7.5 DISTINGUISH BETWEEN A RESCISSION AND AN ALTERATION

| Matter | Rescission | Alteration |
|---|---|---|
| Meaning | It means cancellation of the contract. | It means change in one or more terms of the contract with the consent of all the parties. |
| Mutual consent | Novation takes place with the mutual consent or by aggrieved party or a party whose consent is not free. | Alteration cannot take place without mutual consent. |
| Effect | On cancellation, the contract comes to an end. | The parties are legally bound to each other under the altered contract. |

## 7.6 DISCHARGE OF A CONTRACT BY IMPOSSIBILITY OF PERFORMANCE

Sometimes, the performance of a contract is impossible. In such a case, the contract is discharged. This is based on the principle that law does not recognize what is impossible. The impossibility of performance may be of two types, namely (a) the initial impossibility and (b) the subsequent impossibility.

### 7.6.1 Initial Impossibility or Pre-contractual Impossibility

It means impossibility exists at the time of making a contract. The initial impossibility may be (i) known or (ii) unknown to the parties at the time of making the agreement.

### 7.6.2 Known Impossibility

It means one or both the parties have a knowledge that a promise is impossible to perform even though they enter into an agreement.

***Example***

A agrees with B to bring a dead man to life. It is known to the parties at the time of making the agreement that the performance is impossible. The agreement is void *ab initio.*

### 7.6.3 Unknown Impossibility

It means both the parties genuinely believe that the performance of a promise is possible but it is impossible to perform. It can also be said here that there is a bilateral mistake of parties.

***Example***

A agrees to sell certain goods to B, supposed to be on their way from Mumbai to Kolkata in a certain ship. Unknown to both the parties, the ship had already sunk in the deep sea, and the goods ceased to exist at the time of contract. The contract becomes void when the impossibility of performance is discovered.

### 7.6.4 Supervening Impossibility or Post-contractual Impossibility

The contract becomes void on account of the subsequent impossibility only if the following conditions are satisfied.

1. The act should have become impossible after the formation of the contract.
2. The impossibility should have been caused by a reason of some event which was beyond the control of the promisor.
3. The impossibility must not be the result of some act or negligence of the promisor himself.

***Example***

A and B contract to marry each other. Before the time fixed for the marriage, A becomes mad. The contract becomes void.

**Case Study**

A, a Hindu, who was already married, contracts to marry B, a Hindu girl. Is it a valid contract? Why?

## 7.7 SPECIFIC GROUNDS OF SUBSEQUENT IMPOSSIBILITIES

It is also known as the doctrine of frustration under the English law. In the following cases, the contract is discharged on the ground of the supervening impossibility.

### 7.7.1 Destruction of Subject–Matter

The destruction of the subject–matter after a contract is made without the fault of any party discharge the contract. But if the destruction of the subject matter is due to the fault of any party, he is liable for the damage to the other party.

***Example***

A music hall and a garden was let out by A to B for a series of concerts on four different days. The hall was burnt-down before the date of the first concert. Held, the contract became void by the supervening impossibility.

### 7.7.2 Incapacity or Death

Incapacity or death of the promisor and the contract is for personal service or skill. The contracts involving the use of personal skill or ability of the promisor are discharged on the illness, death, or incapacity of the promisor.

***Example***

A piano player agreed to perform a concert on a particular day. She was not able to give her performance due to her illness. Held, the contract was discharged due to her illness.

### 7.7.3 Change in Law or Circumstances

Sometimes, certain circumstances arise subsequent to the formation of a contract, which makes the performance of the contract impossible, as contemplated by the parties. In such circumstances, the contract is discharged.

***Example***

A agreed to sell his land to B. Subsequently, the land was acquired by the government. Held, the contract was discharged.

### 7.7.4 Declaration of War

The pending contract at the time of declaration of a war is either suspended or declared void. Generally, the contract at the time of the declaration of a war is void, when the government declares it against the public interest or national interest.

***Example***

A contracts to take in a cargo for B at a foreign port. A's government, afterwards, declares a war against the country in which the port is situated. The contract becomes void when war is declared.

**Case Study**

A contracts with the Indian Cricket Board to play for IPL-4 at South Africa. A falls ill and is advised by the doctor to rest. What will be the impact on the contract?

**Case Study**

A musical hall was agreed to be let out on certain dates but before those dates the hall was destroyed by fire. What will be the status of the contract?

## 7.8 CASES WHERE A CONTRACT IS NOT DISCHARGED ON THE GROUND OF SUPERVENING IMPOSSIBILITY

In the following cases, the contract is not discharged on the ground of supervening impossibility. Such excuses are not recognized by the law.

### 7.8.1 Performance Becomes Difficult

When the performance of the contract becomes difficult, the contract is not discharged. Difficulty is not impossibility. A party can perform it with more effort or hardship.

### 7.8.2 Commercial Impossibility

The party is not discharged from the performance on the ground that it will be non-profitable for him to perform the contract.

***Example***

A agreed to sell to B, dhotis manufactured in a particular mill. The mill got into repairs and so, dhotis did not manufacture. Held, the contract was not frustrated as the stipulation as to delivery did not make the delivery by the mills, a condition precedent. It was a breach of the contract.

### 7.8.3 Impossibility Due to the Conduct of Third Party

If a promisor could not perform the promise because of default of the third party, he cannot make an excuse and claims that it is impossible to perform the promise. The third party's fault or conduct has nothing to do with the contract. The contract is not discharged because of third party's default.

***Example***

A agreed with B to supply certain cloth manufactured by a specified mill. The terms of the agreement stipulated that A could supply goods as soon as they are supplied to him by the mill. The mill failed to supply the goods to A. Held, A was liable to supply as the terms only indicated the process of delivery.

### 7.8.4 Strikes, Riots or Civil Disturbances

Strikes, riots, or civil disturbances do not discharge the contract. When such an event takes place, the performance of a promise under the contract becomes impossible for the time being. Once a strike is called off or life becomes normal, it is possible to perform the promise.

***Example***

A agreed to supply certain goods to B which were to be imported from Algeria. The goods could not be imported due to the riots and civil disturbances in that country. Held, A cannot be excused for the non-performance of the contract.

### 7.8.5 Self-induced Impossibility

If the performance of the contract becomes impossible due to the act of the omission of a party, it is called as self induced impossibility. In such cases, the contract is not discharged.

### 7.8.6 Failure of Object

The failure of one of the object out of many objects, do not discharge the contract. But, if all the objects of the contract fail, the contract becomes discharged.

**Case Study**

A entered into a contract with B for supply of 100 bicycles manufactured by C. C did not manufacture it. Can A discharge from the contract?

**Case Study**

A agreed to supply certain goods to B. As a result of an increase in the raw material costs, it is no longer profitable for A to supply them at the agreed rate. A refused to perform the contract on the argument of impossibility. Is argument of A justifiable? Why?

**Case Study**

Akhilesh entered into an agreement with Shekhar to deliver him (Shekhar) 5000 bags, to be manufactured in his factory. The bags could not be manufactured because of the strike by the workers, and Akhilesh failed to supply the said bags to Shekhar. Decide whether Akhilesh can be exempted from liability under the provisions of the Indian Contract Act, 1872.

**Case Study**

'A' promised to 'B' that he would arrange for 'B's marriage with his daughter. 'A' could not persuade his daughter to marry 'B.' 'B' sued 'A', who pleaded on the ground of impossibility that he is not liable for any damages. Is he liable to B? On what ground?

## 7.9 DISCHARGE OF A CONTRACT BY LAPSE OF TIME

Every contract and promise under the contract should be performed within a time limit. The contract is discharged, if it is not performed or enforced within a specified period called as the period of limitation.

***Example***

The period of limitation for recovering the debt is 3 years and 12 years for the recovery of immovable property.

## 7.10 DISCHARGE OF A CONTRACT BY OPERATION OF LAW

In the following circumstances, the contract is discharged by the operation of law.

### 7.10.1 Death

The contract that requires personal skill is discharged on the death of the promisors. However, any benefit received before the performance shall be returned by the legal representative of the deceased party.

### 7.10.2 Merger

The conversion of the inferior right into superior right is called as merger. It is also called as vesting of rights and liabilities in the same person.

### 7.10.3 Insolvency

The insolvent is discharged from all the liabilities on all the contracts, entered into, up to the date of insolvency.

### 7.10.4 Unauthorized Material Alteration

The alteration which changes the nature of the contract is material alteration. If one party makes any material alteration in the terms of the contract without the approval of the other party, the contract comes to an end.

***Example***

One of the parties without the consent of the other party changes the date of payment or the place of delivery.

## 7.11 DISCHARGE OF A CONTRACT BY BREACH OF CONTRACT

It means the failure of a party to fulfill his obligation or promise under the contract. When there is a breach of contract, certain remedy or consequences are available to the aggrieved party. The aggrieved party means a party who is not at a fault.

### 7.11.1 Consequences of Breach of Contract

The aggrieved party is not required to perform his part of the promise. The aggrieved party is having various remedies depending upon the type of breach. The breach of contract is of the following two types:

1. Actual breach
2. Anticipatory breach

### 7.11.2 Actual Breach of Contract

An actual breach of contract means any party to contract refuses or fails to perform his promise on the due date of performance, or during the performance. The actual breach of contract may take place expressly or impliedly.

***Examples***

1. A agreed with B to sell 500 TV sets on 21 January. A refuses to deliver the TV sets on the due date. This is a breach of contract on the due date.
2. A agreed with B to supply 3000 computers at a certain price to be delivered in three installments of 1000 each. After 2000 computers had been supplied, B informs A to deliver no more. This is the actual breach of contract during the performance by express refusing, and B can claim damages for the breach.

Following are the consequences of the actual breach of contract:

(i) If time is the essence of the contract
  (a) The contract is voidable at the option of the aggrieved party.
  (b) The aggrieved party can claim the compensation for the loss for non-performance.
  (c) The aggrieved party cannot claim compensation when he accepts delayed performance.
(ii) If time is not the essence of the contract

If time is not the essence, the contract is not voidable but the aggrieved party can claim compensation for any loss caused for non-performance.

### 7.11.3 Anticipatory Breach of Contract

When any party declares his intention of not performing the contract before the performance is due, it is called as anticipatory breach of contract.

***Example***

A agrees with B to sell his car on 21 January. Before this date he informs B that he will not sell it. This is an anticipatory breach of contract.

There are two modes of anticipatory breach (a) express repudiation and (b) implied repudiation. The express repudiation means when the party refuses expressly to perform his obligation before the performance due. The implied repudiation means the party acts in such manner that it becomes impossible for him to fulfill his obligation under the contract. In the case of implied repudiation, the party does something which indicates his unwillingness to perform the contract.

Following are the consequence of anticipatory breach.

1. The aggrieved party may treat the contract as alive.
2. The aggrieved party can rescind the contract and claim damages.

Here, the damage will be equal to the difference between the contract price and the price as on the date of communication.

***Note:***

When a contract becomes void, any benefit received under such contract is bound to restore such benefit or to make compensation for such benefit to the person from whom he received it.

**Case Study**

A contracts with B to deliver goods to B on 10 July. A fails to deliver goods on 10 July. Is it anticipatory breach of contract? Why?

**Case Study**

A contracted to supply 200 bags of rice to B on 30 December 2010. After supply of 20 bags of rice, A informed B that he will not supply remaining the bags of rice to B. What will be consequences for this contract? Explain.

**Case Study**

Mr. Dubious textile enters into a contract with a Retail Garments Show Room for supply of 1000 pieces of cotton shirts at ₹ 300 per shirt to be supplied on or before 31 December 2004. However, on 1 November 2004 Dubious Textiles informs the Retail Garments Show Room that he is not willing to supply the goods as the price of cotton shirts in the meantime has gone upto ₹ 350 per shirt. Examine the rights of the Retail Garments Show Room in this regard.

## LIST OF LANDMARK JUDGEMENTS

1. ***Cort vs Ambergate Rly. Co. (1851)***

   The actual breach of contract also occurs when during the performance; the party fails to perform his obligation.

2. ***Krell vs Henri (1903)***

   The failure of the object due to non-occurrence of the contemplated event discharges the contract.

3. ***Shiam Sunder vs Durga (1966)***

   The contract is discharged if the performance becomes impossible due to a change of law or a change in the government policy after the formation of the contract.

4. ***Jacob vs Credit Lyonnais (1884)***

   The strikes lock-out and civil disturbances is not the impossibility for the performance of a contract and therefore, the contract is not discharged.

5. ***Shankar Lal Damodar vs A. Ajaipal (1946)***

   In the case of novation of a contract if the new contract is not enforceable by law the existing contract is received and the parties are bound by it.

6. ***Manohar Koyal vs Thakur Dass Naker (1888)***

   The novation must take place before the breach of the original contract.

7. ***Loonkaran Sethia vs Ivan E. John (1977)***

   Where one party, without the consent of the other party, changes the date of payment or delivery of goods or substitutes, such words which change the meaning and affect the contract, such changes are material alterations to the contract.

8. ***Robinson vs Davidson (1871)***

   The contract involving the use of personal skill or ability of the promisor is discharged on the illness, death or incapacity of the promisor.

9. ***Shanty Vijay and Co. vs Princess Fatima Fouzia (1980)***

   The injunction order or stay order is in force, the performance of a contract may be stayed. The contract cannot be enforced.

10. ***Blackburn Bobbin Co. vs T. W. Allen and Sons (1918)***

    If the performance of a contract becomes difficult, in such a case, the contract is not discharged.

11. ***H. B. Steamboat Co. vs Hutton (1903)***

    Where there are several objects for which a contract is entered into, the failure of one of the objects will not discharge the contract.

## TEST YOUR KNOWLEDGE

1. State the various methods of termination of a contract. **(Ref. Para-7.1)**
2. How is the contract discharged on the performance of a promise? **(Ref. Para-7.2)**
3. Explain with examples, the principle of novation, alteration and rescission, where the contract need not to be performed. **(Ref. Para-7.3)**
4. Novation means entering into a new contract in place of the old contract. Explain. **(Ref. Para-7.3)**
5. Write a short note on the novation of the contract. **(Ref. Para-7.3)**
6. Write a short note on the alteration of the contract. **(Ref. Para-7.3)**
7. What do you understand by 'accord' and 'satisfaction'? Write a short note on the novation of a contract. **(Ref. Para-7.3)**
8. Explain the meaning of the term 'remission'. Write a short note on the novation of a contract. **(Ref. Para-7.3)**
9. Remission may be part or full. Is it correct statement? **(Ref. Para-7.3)**
10. Distinguish between a novation and an alteration. **(Ref. Para-7.4)**
11. Distinguish between a rescission and an alteration. **(Ref. Para-7.5)**
12. The law does not compel the impossible. Comment. **(Ref. Para-7.6)**
13. Discuss the impossibility of performance as the mode of discharge of a contract, stating the difference between the initial and supervening impossibility. **(Ref. Para-7.6)**

14. Does the frustration discharge the contract in all cases? If not, then specify the circumstances in which the contract is not discharged on the ground of frustration. **(Ref. Para-7.7,7.8)**
15. When may a contract be discharged by the operation of law? **(Ref. Para-7.10)**
16. Explain the meaning of the breach of contract. **(Ref. Para-7.11)**
17. Write a short note on the breach of contract. **(Ref. Para-7.11)**
18. Write the difference between the actual breach and the anticipatory breach of contract. **(Ref. Para-7.11)**
19. What remedy is available to party on the breach of contract? **(Ref. Para-7.11)**
20. What are the consequences for the actual breach of contract? **(Ref. Para-7.11)**
21. Write a short note on the anticipatory breach of contract. **(Ref. Para-7.11)**

## MULTIPLE-CHOICE QUESTIONS

1. A contract is discharged by the breach when a party to a contract
   (i) refuses to perform his promise.
   (ii) fails to perform his promise.
   (iii) disables himself from performing his part of the promise.
   (iv) all of the above.
2. A agrees with B to bring back the life of the dead patient for ₹ 50,000. The agreement is
   (i) void.
   (ii) voidable.
   (iii) unenforceable.
   (iv) illegal.
3. The breach of a contract may be
   (i) an actual breach.
   (ii) an anticipatory breach.
   (iii) either (i) or (ii).
   (iv) neither (i) nor (ii).
4. The doctrine of impossibility of performance, rendering a contract void, is based on
   (i) a commercial impossibility.
   (ii) a supervening impossibility.
   (iii) just and reasonable ground.
   (iv) an unjust enrichment.
5. The third party's failure to perform a promise, on whose performance your performance of promise depends upon. In this case, the contract
   (i) is not discharged.
   (ii) is discharged.
   (iii) becomes void.
   (iv) becomes voidable.
6. When the contract is made for several purposes, a failure of one of them
   (i) terminates the entire contract.
   (ii) does not terminate the entire contract.
   (iii) makes the contract unlawful.
   (iv) renders the object illegal.
7. Which of the following is incorrect?
   (i) Contracts are discharged by lapse of time.
   (ii) The discharge of a party and the discharge of a contract are one and the same thing.
   (iii) The cancellation of contract discharges the contract.
   (iv) All of the above.

8. Where performance has become more difficult than estimated at the time of entering into a contract, the contract
   (i) is not discharged.
   (ii) is discharged.
   (iii) becomes void.
   (iv) becomes voidable.

9. An obligation under a contract stands discharged by
   (i) dispensing with the performance.
   (ii) impossibility of performance.
   (iii) death of the party and contract is personal in nature.
   (iv) all of the above.

10. A contract stands discharged
   (i) by performance of the contract.
   (ii) by breach of the contract.
   (iii) by agreement.
   (iv) all of the above.

11. In which of the ways can a contract be discharged by the operation of law?
   (i) Death of the promisor.
   (ii) Insolvency of the promisor.
   (iii) Merger of rights.
   (iv) All of the above.

12. In which of the ways can a contract be discharged by the operation of law?
   (i) Unauthorized material alteration contract.
   (ii) Vesting of rights and liabilities in the same person.
   (iii) Neither (i) nor (ii).
   (iv) Both (i) and (ii).

13. In which of the ways can a contract be discharged by agreement between the parties?
   (i) Novation.
   (ii) Rescission.
   (iii) Alteration.
   (iv) All of the above.

14. The original contract need not to be performed, if there is
   (i) rescission of contract.
   (ii) novation of contract.
   (iii) alteration of contract.
   (iv) all of the above.

15. If a new contract is substituted in the place of an existing contract, it is called
   (i) alteration.
   (ii) rescission.
   (iii) novation.
   (iv) waiver.

16. For a valid novation, a new contract must be made
   (i) before making of the original contract.
   (ii) during the continuance of the original contract.
   (iii) after the conclusion of the original contract.
   (iv) all of the above.

17. Rescission of a contract means
   (i) the termination of the contract.
   (ii) the renewal of the contract.
   (iii) the alteration of the contract.
   (iv) the substitution of the new contract in the place of the earlier one.

18. A contracts with B to deliver goods to B on 1st July. A does not deliver goods on 1st July. B may rescind the contract. The contract is rescinded due to
    (i) mutual decision.
    (ii) A's failure to perform.
    (iii) impossibility of performance.
    (iv) revocation of proposal.
19. If a person accepts a lesser sum of money, than what was contracted for, in the discharge of the whole debt, it is known as
    (i) a waiver.
    (ii) a remission.
    (iii) an alteration.
    (iv) a rescission.
20. A owes B ₹ 50,000. Due date for the payment is 25th March. A pays to B ₹ 30,000 on 25th March, who accepts it in full satisfaction of the debt. The debt is discharged on account of
    (i) remission.
    (ii) extension time of performance.
    (iii) novation.
    (iv) all of the above.
21. In case of novation, there is
    (i) a change to some of the terms and conditions of the original contract.
    (ii) a substitution of an existing contract with the new one.
    (iii) either (i) or (ii).
    (iv) neither (i) nor (ii).
22. In case of alteration,
    (i) old terms and conditions need not to be performed.
    (ii) new terms and conditions must be performed.
    (iii) both (i) and (ii).
    (iv) neither (i) nor (ii).
23. Actual breach may take place
    (i) expressly.
    (ii) impliedly.
    (iii) either (i) or (ii).
    (iv) neither (i) nor (ii).
24. A agreed to supply certain goods to B, which were to be imported by C. But C failed to import the goods. In this case, the contract is
    (i) discharged.
    (ii) not discharged.
    (iii) voidable.
    (iv) impossible to perform.
25. In case of an anticipatory breach, the promisee can
    (i) put an end to the contract.
    (ii) elect to keep the contract alive till the date of performance.
    (iii) either (i) or (ii).
    (iv) neither (i) nor (ii).
26. Where a party to contract transfers his rights under the contract to another person, it is legally known as
    (i) novation of a contract.
    (ii) rescisson of a contract.
    (iii) waiver of a contract.
    (iv) assignment of a contract.
27. A contracts to buy B's scooter for ₹ 10,000 but breaks the promise. What compensation must A pay to B?
    (i) The excess amount of the contract price, over the price which B can obtain for the scooter at the time of breach of promise.
    (ii) The contract price of ₹ 10,000.
    (iii) The price which B demands.
    (iv) None of the above.

## ANSWER KEYS

| | | | | | |
|---|---|---|---|---|---|
| **1.** (iv) | **6.** (ii) | **11.** (iv) | **16.** (ii) | **21.** (ii) | **26.** (iv) |
| **2.** (i) | **7.** (ii) | **12.** (iv) | **17.** (i) | **22.** (iii) | **27.** (i) |
| **3.** (iii) | **8.** (i) | **13.** (iv) | **18.** (ii) | **23.** (iii) | |
| **4.** (ii) | **9.** (iv) | **14.** (iv) | **19.** (ii) | **24.** (ii) | |
| **5.** (i) | **10.** (iv) | **15.** (iii) | **20.** (i) | **25.** (iii) | |

# 8

# The Indian Contract Act, 1872: Remedies for Breach of Contract and Quasi-contract

**Learning Objectives**

*After reading this chapter, you will be able to understand:*

- Various remedies for breach of contract
- When particular remedy is appropriate?
- Types of damages
- Quantum meruit
- Quasi-contract

Remedy means a course of action available to an aggrieved party when the other party breaches the contract. When one party to contract breaches the contract, the other party who is not at fault has certain remedy available to him. These remedies available are as shown in the chart below. But all the remedies are not available at the proper time. The aggrieved party has one or more remedies available, depending upon the facts and circumstances of each such case.

## 8.1 RESCISSION OF A CONTRACT—SECTION 39

The rescission of a contract means the right to the party to cancel the contract. In case of breach of contract, the other party may rescind the contract.

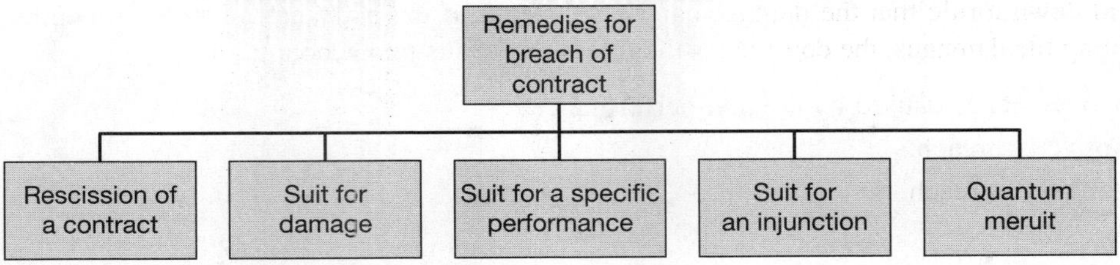


**Figure 8.1** Remedies for breach of contract.

### 8.1.1 Effects of Rescission of a Contract

When the contract is rescind by the aggrieved party as a result of the breach of contract, it has the following effects:

1. The aggrieved party is not required to perform his part of obligation under the contract.
2. The aggrieved party can claim compensation for any loss.
3. The party is liable to restore benefit, if any.

In certain circumstances, on the application of any party to the contract, the court may also rescind the contract. If the court rescinds the contract, it is said that the court has set aside the contract. Generally, the court may set aside the contract when:

1. The contract is voidable.
2. The contract is unlawful.

**Case Study**

A agrees to sell a land to B for ₹ 40,000. B pays to A ₹ 4000 as a deposit at the time of the contract, the amount to be forfeited to A if B does not complete the sale within a specified period. B fails to complete the sale within the specified period, nor is he ready and willing to complete the sale within a reasonable time after the expiry of that period. Can A rescind the contract and at the same time retain the deposit?

## 8.2 SUIT FOR DAMAGES

It means the monetary compensation allowed for a loss. The purpose is to compensate the aggrieved party and not to punish the party at fault. In India, the rules relating to the damages are based on the English judgment of *Hadley vs Baxendale*. This case is a leading case on the remoteness of damage. The facts of case were—H's mill was stopped due to the breakdown of the shaft. He delivered the shaft to a common carrier to repair it, and agreed to pay a certain sum of money for doing this work. H has not informed B that the delay would result into a loss of profit. B delivered the shaft a reasonable time after the repair. H filed a suit for the loss of profit. It was held that B is not liable for the loss of profit. The court laid down a rule that the damage can be recovered, if the party has a breach of contract. While determining the damages, the court takes the following points into account:

1. Inconvenience caused by the non-performance.
2. Motive of breach.
3. Manner of breach.

## 8.3 KINDS OF DAMAGES

Following are the different kinds of damages:

### 8.3.1 Ordinary Damages

These are the damages which are payable for the loss arising naturally and directly as a result of the breach of contract. The purpose of ordinary damage is that the injured party is to be put in the same financial position as he would have been, if the contract had been performed according to the terms of the contract. Ordinary damage is also known as the proximate damage or natural damage. It is also known as a general damage.

*Example*

Amar has agreed to give his car on lease to Aalap for a period of 1 year for ₹ 30,000. Amar later on refuses to give the car on lease and breaches the contract, and therefore, Aalap has to enter in lease for taking the car on lease for ₹ 40,000. In this case, Amar is liable to pay Aalap ₹ 10,000, the difference between the contract price and the price. Aalap pays for the lease of the car from some other person. Here, ₹ 10,000 is ordinary damage.

### 8.3.2 Special Damages

These are damages which are payable for the loss arising due to some special circumstances. It can be recovered only if the special circumstances which result in a special loss in the case of breach of contract and the party has a notice of such damage. If the defaulting party has no knowledge of the special circumstances, he will not be liable for the special damages.

***Example***

A sent a sample of his products for exhibition to an agent of a railway company for carriage to 'New Delhi' for an exhibition. The consignment note stated: 'Must be at New Delhi Monday Certain'. Due to the negligence of the company, the goods reached only after the exhibition was over. Held, the company was liable for the loss caused by the late arrival of the products because the company's agent was aware of the special circumstances.

### 8.3.3 Exemplary or Punitive or Vindictive Damages

These damages are a sum awarded beyond the pecuniary loss sustained by the injured party. Ordinarily, the damages for the breach of contract are intended to compensate the plaintiff and not to punish the defendant. But the exemplary damages are allowed not to compensate the party but as a means of punishment to the defaulting party. The courts generally do not award vindictive damage but it may award these damages in the case of:

1. Breach of contract to marry—loss based on mental injury.
2. Wrongful dishonor of the cheque-smaller the amount, larger the damage.

### 8.3.4 Nominal Damages

Where the party suffers no loss, the court may allow nominal damages, simply to establish that the party has proved his case and won. The nominal damage is very small in amount. The nominal damages are awarded only at the discretion of the court. The aggrieved party cannot claim the nominal damages as a matter of right.

### 8.3.5 Damages for Inconvenience

If the party has suffered physical inconvenience, discomfort, or mental agony as a result of the breach of contract, the party can recover the damage for such inconvenience.

***Example***

A photographer agreed to take photographs at a wedding ceremony but failed to do so. The bride brought an action for the breach of contract. Held, she was entitled to the damages for her injured feelings.

### 8.3.6 Liquidated Damages and Penalty

The party may specify an amount at the time of entering into a contract. The amount so specified may be (a) a liquidated damage or (b) a penalty. If the specified sum represents fair and genuine pre-estimate damages, likely to result due to breach, it is called as a liquidated damage. But if the specified sum is disproportionate to damages, it is called as a penalty. As regards the payment of the liquidated damages and the penalty, the court cannot increase the amount of damages beyond the amount specified in the contract. The penalty is imposed by a way of punishment for the breach of contract. While the intention for fixing the liquidated damages is to recover the damages that might arise due to breach.

***Example***

A gives B, a bond for the repayment of ₹ 1000 with interest at 12%, at the end of six months, with a stipulation that in case of default, the interest shall be payable at the rate of 75% from the date of default. This is a stipulation by a way of penalty, and B is only entitled to recover from A such compensation as the court considers reasonable.

### 8.3.7 Forfeiture of Security Deposit

This means, if there is any clause in the contract, entitling the aggrieved party to forfeit the security deposit in the nature of penalty. The court has held in the case of *Chiranjit Singh versus Har Swarup* that there is a difference between the security deposit and the earnest money. The earnest money is a part of the purchase price and is paid in advance. After the contract is completed, the earnest money is adjusted towards the purchase price. It means that if the party paying the earnest money fails to perform the contract, the other party can cancel the contract and retain the earnest money. It means the earnest money can be forfeited. The security deposit is for the performance of the contract. After the contract is completed, the security deposit is not adjusted towards the purchase price. And if the party fails to perform the contract, it cannot be forfeited as its forfeiture will amount to a penalty. Thus, the security deposit is not liable to be forfeited.

### 8.3.8 Payment of Interest

It is permissible when the contract provides that the payment of money is to be made on a particular date and the failure by a party will attract the payment of a specified percentage of interest. If the interest is in the nature of the penalty, the court may grant relief. If no rate of interest is specified in the contract, the party shall be liable to pay as per the law in force or as per the custom or usage of trade.

### 8.3.9 Cost of Suit or Decree

The court has also the discretion to award the cost of suit for damages, in addition to the damages for the breach of contract. This damage or remedy is available to the party who has won the case.

**Case Study**

A contracts to deliver 1000 bags of rice at ₹ 100 per bag on a future date. On the due date he refuses to deliver. Market price on that day is ₹ 120 per bag. What amount of damage can be recovered from A?

**Case Study**

M Ltd contracts with Shanti Traders to make and deliver a certain machinery to them by 30 June 2004 for ₹ 11.50 lakhs. Due to the labour strike, M Ltd could not manufacture and deliver the machinery to Shanti Traders. Later, Shanti Traders procured the machinery from another manufacturer for ₹ 12.75 lakhs. Shanti Traders was also prevented from performing a contract which it had made with Zenith Traders, at the time of their contract with M Ltd, and were compelled to pay a compensation for the breach of contract. Advise Shanti Traders the amount of compensation which it can claim from M Ltd, referring to the legal provisions of the Indian Contract Act.

**Case Study**

A contracted with B to supply him (B) 500 tons of iron-steel at ₹ 5000 per ton, to be delivered at a specified time. Thereafter, A contracts with C for the purchase of 500 tons of iron-steel at ₹ 4800 per ton, and at the same time told 'C' that he did so for the purpose of performing his contract entered into with B. C failed to perform his contract in due course. Consequently, A could not procure any iron-steel and B rescinded the contract. What would be the amount of damages which A could claim from C in the circumstances? Explain with reference to the provisions of the Indian Contract, 1872.

## 8.4 SUIT FOR A SPECIFIC PERFORMANCE

It means demanding an order from the court that the promise agreed in a contract shall be carried out. And the court may direct the defaulting party to carry out his obligation according to the terms of the contract. The party cannot demand a specific performance as a matter of right. The courts at their discretion grant specific relief.

### 8.4.1 When a Specific Performance Is Allowed?

The specific performance of a contract may be allowed by the court, where the subject matter of the contract is not an ordinary article of commerce or where the goods are not easily available in the market. The specific performance may be ordered by the court in the following situations:

1. Where the actual damages arising from the breach are not measurable.
2. Where the monetary compensation is not an adequate remedy.

### 8.4.2 When a Specific Performance Is Not Allowed?

In the following cases, specific performance is not allowed:

1. When the damages are an adequate remedy.
2. Where the performance of a contract requires a number of minute details and therefore, not possible for the court to supervise.
3. Where the contract is personal in nature.
4. Where the contract made by the company is beyond its power. (ultra-vires)
5. Where one party to contract is minor.
6. Where the contract is inequitable to either party.

*Example*

A agrees to sell B, an artist painting for ₹ 30,000. Later on, he refused to sell it. Here, B can file a suit against A for the specific performance of the contract.

## 8.5 SUIT FOR INJUNCTION

The injunction may be defined as an order of the courts restraining a person from doing something which he promised not to do. It means a stay order granted by the court. This order prohibits a person to do a particular act. Where there is a breach of contract by one party and the order of a specific performance is not granted by the court, the injunction may be granted. The injunction is granted by the courts at their discretion.

*Example*

Film actress agreed to act exclusively for W for one year and for no one else. During the year, she contracted to act for Z.

**Case Study**

A, a singer, agreed with B to perform at his theatre for two months, on a condition that during that period, he would not perform anywhere else. When A performs somewhere else, what remedy B would have available to him?

## 8.6 QUANTUM MERUIT

Quantum meruit is a Latin phrase. It means 'as much as is earned' i.e., in proportion to the extent of work done. It is right to claim compensation for the work already done. The quantum meruit arises only when the original contract is discharged. The claim on quantum meruit can be claimed by the party at fault and by the party at default.

### 8.6.1 Claim on Quantum Meruit by a Party Not at Fault

Following are the cases in which a claim on quantum meruit may arise:

1. When one party prevents the other from a completion of the contract.
2. Where the contract has become void before the completion of the contract.
3. Where an agreement is discovered to be void.

### 8.6.2 Claim on Quantum Meruit by a Party at Fault

Following are the cases in which a claim on quantum meruit may arise, even by the party at fault:

If a divisible contract is partly performed and refuses to perform a part of work, in such a case, the party in default may sue on quantum meruit, if the other party has enjoyed the benefits of the part of performance.

*Example*

A agreed with B to supply 500 units of TV before a particular date. A supplied 400 units only, before the date, and declared his intention not to deliver the remaining units. B retained the 400 units. A, therefore, is entitled to recover the price of 400 units on quantum meruit.

Sometimes, an indivisible contract is performed completely but badly. In such a case, the person who has performed the contract is entitled to claim the lump-sum, less a deduction for the work of poor quality.

*Example*

A agreed to paint and decorate B's house for lump-sum of ₹ 1 lakh. The work was done but in a defective manner. The cost of remedy the defect was ₹ 15,000. Held, A could recover from B ₹ 1 lakh less ₹ 15,000.

**Case Study**

A, a businessman, leaves his goods at B's place by mistake. B treats the same as his own and uses it. Is B bound to compensate A for the same? On what ground?

## 8.7 QUASI-CONTRACT—SECTIONS 68–72

'Quasi-contracts' are known as 'constructive contracts' in English law. The Indian Contract Act describes such contracts as, 'certain relations resembling those created by contracts'.

It is not a real or a true contract at all in the sense of law. The quasi-contract is created by law without any enforceable agreement. It is not based on the express or implied intentions of the parties. It is not based upon the offer and acceptance rule. It means a contract which lacks one or more of the essentials of the contract. It does not arise from any formal agreement but is imposed by law.

It is based upon the principle of equity. In other words, it is based upon the maxim of *'nemo debet locuplat ex liene justlia'* i.e., no one should grow rich out of another person's cost. It is also known as the contracts implied by law or implied contracts. The quasi-contracts give rise to obligations similar to that of a true contract.

### 8.7.1 Cases of Quasi-contract

In the following circumstances quasi-contractual obligations arise:

**8.7.1.1 Supply of Necessaries to Incompetent Persons** This is the supply of necessaries to a minor or a person of unsound mind. Here, the minor or the person of unsound mind is not personally liable. The property of the incapable person is liable. And where the incapable person does not own any property, nothing shall be payable.

**8.7.1.2 Payment by a Person Who Is Interested in Transaction** An interested person who makes the payment is entitled to recover the money from the person who was legally bound to make the payment.

***Example***

A supplies to B, a lunatic, the necessaries for maintaining his life. Here, A is entitled to recover the amount from B's property.

**8.7.1.3 Obligation of a Person Enjoying Benefit of Non-gratuitous Act** A non-gratuitous act means the act which is not done free. The person who does some non-gratuitous acts for another is entitled to recover the compensation for such acts. The obligation of a person enjoying the benefit or the non-gratuitous act arises in respect of the lawful acts only.

***Example***

A pizza boy delivers a pizza at your door step by mistake instead of your neighbour who ordered it. You eat it having knowledge that it was ordered by your neighbour. You are required to pay for the same. You enjoyed something which was a non-gratuitous act.

**8.7.1.4 Finder of Goods** A finder of goods means a person who finds the goods belonging to another and takes them into his custody. A person who finds the goods belonging to another and takes them into his custody is subject to the same responsibility as a bailee. A finder of goods has the duty to find the real owner and return the goods. He can reimburse the expense, he has incurred in preserving and maintains the goods from the original owner.

**8.7.1.5 Money Paid Under the Mistake or Delivery of Goods Under Mistake** If certain amount of money is paid or goods delivered to a person under a mistake, the person receiving the money or goods must repay it.

*Example*

A and B jointly owe ₹ 100 to C. A pays the amount to C, and B, not knowing this fact, also pays ₹ 100 to C. C is bound to repay ₹ 100 to B.

**Case Study**

A supplies, the wife and children of B, a lunatic with necessaries suitable to their condition in life. Is A entitled to reimburse the expenses? Is so, from whom?

**Case Study**

Y holds an agricultural land in Gujarat on a lease granted by X, the owner. The land revenue payable by X to the Government being in arrear, his land is advertized for sale by the Government. Under the Revenue Law, the consequence of such a sale will be the termination of Y's lease. Y, in order to prevent the sale and the consequent termination of his own lease, pays the Government, the sum due from X. Referring to the provisions of the Indian Contract Act, 1872, decide whether X is liable to make good to Y, the amount so paid?

## 8.8 DISTINGUISH BETWEEN A QUASI-CONTRACT AND A CONTRACT

| Matter | Quasi-contract | Contract |
|---|---|---|
| Intentionally Form | It is not intentionally formed but law-imposes upon the parties. | It is intentionally formed by the parties. |
| Essentials of contract | A quasi-contract does not posses all the essentials of a valid contract. | A contract possesses all the essentials of a valid contract. |
| Obligations | Obligations are implied upon by the law. | Obligations are mutually created by the parties. |
| Foundation | It is founded upon the principle of equity. | It is founded upon general principles of law of contracts. |

## LIST OF LANDMARK JUDGEMENTS

1. ***Hadley vs Baxandale (1854)***

   The ordinary damages are recoverable, which arise due to the natural and probable consequences of breach.

2. ***Sunder Koer vs Rai Sham Krishan (1907)***

   The stipulation to pay a compound interest at a higher rate of interest than the ordinary rate of interest may be regarded as a penalty.

3. ***Lumely vs Wagner (1852)***

   The injunction is a mode of securing the performance in negative terms in the contract.

4. ***Trojan vs Nagappa (1953)***

   The damages should be ascertained as on the date of breach, and any risk of profit or loss arising from a subsequent increase or decrease is entirely the vendor's and has nothing to do with the other party.

5. ***Smith vs Green (1876)***

   The damages may also be claimed from a breach of warranty or condition (Refer Sales of Goods Act—condition and warranty).

6. ***Union of India vs Vasudeo Agarwal (1960)***

   If the amount fixed is a genuine pre-estimate of the loss in case of breach, it is the liquidated damages and will be allowed. But if the amount fixed is without any regard to the probable loss, it is a penalty and will not be allowed.

7. ***Tayya vs Gangayya (1927)***

   Where the contract provides for the payment in a number of instalment but on failure to pay any instalment, the whole amount is to be paid forthwith, such stipulation is not a penalty and the contract can be enforced according to its terms.

8. ***Pudi Lazarus vs Johnson Edward (1976)***

   The party to contract who seeks specific performance must in his turn, performs all the terms of the contract which he ought to have performed at the date of action.

9. ***UOI vs Tribhuwan Das Lalji Pate (1971)***

   The party is not entitled to recover the damages, unless he has actually suffered some loss as a result of the breach of contract.

10. ***Planche vs Cocburn (1831)***

    When one party abandons or refuses to perform the whole conduct, the compensation for the work done, may be recovered on the basis of quantum meruit.

11. ***Murlidhar vs Harishchandra (1962)***

    If a person does not take steps to mitigate the loss subsequent on breach, he cannot claim the damages which are due to his neglect to take such steps.

12. ***Dakin and Co. vs Lee (1961)***

    An indivisible contract for a lump-sum is completely performed but of a poor quality. In such cases, the person who has performed the contract is entitled to claim the lump-sum less a deduction for the work of a poor quality.

## TEST YOUR KNOWLEDGE

1. What are the remedies available to an aggrieved party on the breach of contract? **(Ref. Para-8.1,8.2,8.3,8.4,8.5,8.6)**
2. Comment—The damages for the breach of contract are granted by a way of compensation, and not by a way of punishment. **(Ref. Para-8.2)**
3. Explain the case of *Hadely versus Baxendale* on which the damages are assessed for the breach of contract. **(Ref. Para-8.2)**
4. The damage for the breach of contract is awarded by the court for the purpose of punishing the defaulting party. **(Ref. Para-8.2)**
5. What kind of damage may be awarded in case of the breach of contract under the law of contract? **(Ref. Para-8.3)**
6. Explain the type of damages awarded in the case of a breach of contract. **(Ref. Para-8.3)**
7. Explain the ordinary damage with a suitable example. **(Ref. Para-8.3)**
8. What do you understand by special damages? When special damages are granted? **(Ref. Para-8.3)**
9. Distinguish between the ordinary and special damages. **(Ref. Para-8.3)**

10. Explain the vindictive damage. **(Ref. Para-8.3)**
11. Distinguish between the liquidated damages and a penalty. **(Ref. Para-8.3)**
12. Distinguish between the ordinary damages and liquidated damages. **(Ref. Para-8.3)**
13. What do you understand by a specific performance? When can a specific performance be granted by the court? **(Ref. Para-8.4)**
14. When can a specific performance not be granted by the court? **(Ref. Para-8.4)**
15. When can a court grant injunction order? Give its one suitable example. **(Ref. Para-8.5)**
16. Write a short note on quantum meruit. **(Ref. Para-8.6)**
17. When can the party to contract claim on quantum meruit? Explain. **(Ref. Para-8.6)**
18. Write a short note on quasi-contract. **(Ref. Para-8.7)**
19. Quasi-contract is based upon the principle of equity. Comment. **(Ref. Para-8.7)**
20. Explain any three examples or cases of quasi-contract. **(Ref. Para-8.7)**

## MULTIPLE-CHOICE QUESTIONS

1. The remedies available to a person, suffering from the breach of contract are
   (i) suit for damages. (iii) quantum meruit
   (ii) suit for injunction. (iv) all of the above.
2. The court may grant rescission where the contract is
   (i) voidable. (iii) unenforceable.
   (ii) void. (iv) all of the above.
3. A specific performance may be ordered by the court when
   (i) the contract is voidable (iii) the damages are not an adequate remedy.
   (ii) the damages are an adequate remedy (iv) the quantum meruit is not possible.
4. In case of breach of contract of sale of some antique goods, the court may grant a/an
   (i) quantum meruit. (iii) specific performance.
   (ii) rescission. (iv) injunction.
5. In which of the following situations is specific performance not granted?
   (i) Where the monetary compensation is an adequate relief.
   (ii) Where the contract is of a personal skill.
   (iii) Either (i) or (ii).
   (iv) Neither (i) nor (ii).
6. .............means an order of the court restraining a person from doing what he promised not to do.
   (i) Quantum meruit (iii) Injunction
   (ii) Rescission (iv) Specific performance
7. When a person has done some work under a contract and the other party repudiates the contract, then the party who performed the work can claim remuneration for the work done. This is based on the principle of
   (i) rescission. (iii) injunction.
   (ii) quantum meruit. (iv) specific performance.
8. Remedy under the quantum meruit is available to a
   (i) party at the fault. (iii) either (i) or (ii).
   (ii) party not at the fault. (iv) both (i) and (ii).

9. In case of the breach of contract, the compensation can be claimed for the
   (i) remote consequences of the breach.
   (ii) the natural consequences of breach.
   (iii) indirect consequences of the breach.
   (iv) all of the above.
10. In case of a breach of contract, the Indian Law awards the damages
    (i) for the loss of profit which may have been earned.
    (ii) which arose naturally.
    (iii) as matter of a penalty.
    (iv) to compensate party from physical loss.
11. A contracts to deliver 1000 bags of rice at ₹ 100 per bag on a future date. On the due date, he refuses to deliver. The market price on that day is ₹ 120 per bag. Which damages can be granted by the court?
    (i) Ordinary damage
    (ii) Special damage
    (iii) Remote damage
    (iv) Vindicative damage
12. When there is a breach of contract, special damages are awarded
    (i) when there are special circumstances.
    (ii) when there is a special loss.
    (iii) when there is a notice of the likely special loss.
    (iv) all of the above.
13. H's mill stopped due to the breakdown of a shaft, which was delivered to B, a common carrier to be taken to the manufacturer for the repairs. H did not communicate to B that a delay in the delivery would cause a loss of the profits. For some reason, the delivery was delayed by B beyond a reasonable time. Here,
    (i) H can rescind the contract.
    (ii) H cannot claim the loss of profits from B.
    (iii) H can claim the loss of profits from B.
    (iv) H can claim the loss of profits from the manufacturer.
14. The damages awarded by a way of punishment are called as
    (i) special damages.
    (ii) ordinary damages.
    (iii) exemplary damages.
    (iv) nominal damages.
15. Nominal damages are awarded to indicate that the party has .....
    (i) won the case.
    (ii) actually suffered the loss.
    (iii) suffered huge loss.
    (iv) suffered unusual loss.
16. Exemplary damage is also known as
    (i) a vindictive damage.
    (ii) a punitive damage.
    (iii) a direct damage.
    (iv) either (i) or (ii).
17. Vindictive damages have been awarded
    (i) for a breach of the promise to marry.
    (ii) for a wrongful dishonour of a cheque.
    (iii) either (i) or (ii).
    (iv) neither (i) nor (ii).
18. Nominal damages can be
    (i) claimed by the aggrieved party as a matter of right.
    (ii) awarded only at the discretion of the court.
    (iii) claim by the aggrieved party for loss.
    (iv) all of the above.

19. Liquidated damages means an amount of the ..... that may result from the breach of contract.
    (i) actual loss
    (ii) loss suffered
    (iii) pre-estimated probable loss
    (iv) pre-estimated actual loss
20. Liquidated damages are calculated .... a contract.
    (i) at the time of making
    (ii) after making
    (iii) at the time of performance of
    (iv) either (ii) or (iii).
21. A stipulation for increased interest from the date of default is known as
    (i) a compensation.
    (ii) a penalty.
    (iii) liquidated damages.
    (iv) damages.
22. A quasi-contract
    (i) is a contract.
    (ii) is an agreement.
    (iii) has only a legal obligation.
    (iv) is not any of these.
23. Which of the following is incorrect?
    (i) In a quasi-contract, the promise to pay is always an implication of law and not of facts.
    (ii) Quasi-contracts are not contracts at all.
    (iii) A quasi-contract is implied in law.
    (iv) A quasi-contract is not a real contract.
24. A quasi-contract is ...... law.
    (i) entered by
    (ii) creature of
    (iii) made by
    (iv) both (i) and (iii).
25. A saves B's goods from fire.
    (i) A is not entitled to compensation from B.
    (ii) A is entitled to compensation from B.
    (iii) B must compensate A.
    (iv) None of the above.
26. A finder of goods
    (i) has no responsibility for the goods.
    (ii) is subject to the same responsibility as a bailee.
    (iii) is the owner of the goods.
    (iv) none of the above.
27. A and B jointly owe ₹ 10 lakhs to C. A pays the amount to C and B, not knowing this fact, B pays ₹ 10 lakhs over again to C.
    (i) C is bound to repay the amount to B.
    (ii) C is bound to repay the amount to B and A jointly.
    (iii) C is bound to repay the amount to A and B equally.
    (iv) C is not bound to repay the amount to B.
28. In which of the following cases, specific performance can be allowed?
    (i) Contract to sing a song.
    (ii) Contract to paint a picture.
    (iii) Contract to enter into partnership at will.
    (iv) None of the above.

29. Where the banker wrongfully dishonors a customer's cheque, the court may award
    (i) ordinary damages.
    (ii) special damages.
    (iii) exemplary damages.
    (iv) none of the above.

30. A contracts to repair B's house and receives payment in advance. A repairs the house but not according to the contract.
    (i) B is entitled to recover from A, the additional cost of making the repairs as per the contract.
    (ii) B is not entitled to recover any cost from A.
    (iii) B is entitled to recover a penalty from A for the non-performance of the contract.
    (iv) None of the above.

## ANSWER KEYS

| | | | | |
|---|---|---|---|---|
| **1.** (iv) | **7.** (ii) | **13.** (ii) | **19.** (iii) | **25.** (i) |
| **2.** (i) | **8.** (iii) | **14.** (iii) | **20.** (i) | **26.** (ii) |
| **3.** (iii) | **9.** (ii) | **15.** (i) | **21.** (iv) | **27.** (i) |
| **4.** (iii) | **10.** (iv) | **16.** (iv) | **22.** (iv) | **28.** (iv) |
| **5.** (iii) | **11.** (i) | **17.** (iii) | **23.** (ii) | **29.** (iii) |
| **6.** (iii) | **12.** (iv) | **18.** (ii) | **24.** (ii) | **30.** (i) |

# 9

# The Indian Contract Act, 1872: Indemnity and Guarantee

### Learning Objectives

*After reading this chapter, you will be able to understand:*

- Meaning of a contract of indemnity and contract of guarantee
- Rights of an indemnity holder
- Difference between a contract of indemnity and a contract of guarantee
- Different types of guarantees
- Right of surety

## 9.1 INDEMNITY CONTRACT

A contract of indemnity is a special contract. All the general principles of the contract are equally applicable to it.

The contract by which one party promises to save the other from the loss caused to him by the conduct of the promisor himself or by the conduct of any other person is called a 'contract of indemnity'—Section 124.

The person who promises to make good the loss is called the indemnifier (Promisor) and the person whose loss is to be made good is called the indemnified or indemnity holder (Promisee). A contract of indemnity is really a class of contingent contracts.

***Example***

A contracts to indemnify B against the consequences of any proceedings which C may take against B in respect of a certain sum of ₹ 200. This is a contract of indemnity. A is an indemnifier or a promisor while B is an indemnity holder or a promisee.

## 9.2 ESSENTIAL ELEMENTS OF AN INDEMNITY CONTRACT

All the essentials of a valid contract must also be present in the contract of indemnity. The contract of indemnity is possible by the express or implied manner. It is a class of contingent contract. Following are the essential elements of the indemnity contract:

### 9.2.1 Loss to One Party

A person can indemnify another person, only if such other person incurs some loss or is about to incur some loss. Therefore, a contract of indemnity can be performed only when the loss has incurred to the promisee or the loss to the promisee has become certain.

### 9.2.2 Indemnity by the Promisor

The purpose of the contract of indemnity is to protect the indemnity holder from any loss that may be caused to the indemnity holder in future (i.e., such a loss has not already been caused to the indemnity holder).

### 9.2.3 Reason for Loss

The contract of indemnity may specify that the indemnity holder shall be protected from the loss caused due to the action of the promisor, or the action of any other person or any act, event or accident, which is not in the control of the parties.

## 9.3 RIGHT OF AN INDEMNITY HOLDER—SECTION 125

The indemnity holder has the right to recover the following from the indemnifier by the way of compensation:

### 9.3.1 Right to Recover Damages

The indemnity holder is entitled to recover from the indemnifier all the damages which he is compelled to pay in any suit in respect of any matter covered by the contract of indemnity.

### 9.3.2 Right to Recover Costs

The indemnity holder is entitled to recover from the indemnifier all the costs which he is compelled to pay in bringing or defending such suit. It may be noted that the indemnity holder must act within the scope of his authority and while bringing or defending the suit, he must act as a prudent person.

### 9.3.3 Right to Recover Sums Paid in Compromise

The indemnity holder is entitled to recover from the indemnifier all the amount which he has paid under the terms of a compromise of the suit. However, he must act within the scope of his authority. While in a compromise, he must act like a prudent man.

## 9.4 GUARANTEE

A 'contract of guarantee' is a contract to perform the promise, or discharge the liability of a third person in case of his default.

The person who gives the guarantee is called the 'surety', the person in respect of whose default the guarantee is given is called the 'principal debtor' and the person to whom the guarantee is given is called the 'creditor'.

A guarantee may be either oral, or written (Section 126). The contract of guarantee may be express, or implied, and may even be inferred from the course of conduct of the parties concerned.

**Example**

Sagar requests Chetan to lend ₹ 500 to Paresh and guarantees that if Paresh fails to pay the amount, he will pay. This is a contract of guarantee. Sagar, in this case, is the surety, Chetan, the creditor and Paresh, the principal debtor.

The contract of guarantee is a tripartite agreement which contemplates the principal debtor, the creditor, and the surety. Here, the following three collateral contracts may be distinguished:

1. As between the creditor and the principal debtor, there is a contract out of which the guaranteed debt arises.
2. As between the surety and the creditor, there is a contract by which the surety guarantees to pay to the creditor, the principal debtor's debt, in case of his debtor's default.
3. As between the surety and the principal debtor, there is a contract that the debtor shall indemnify the surety, in case the surety pays, in the event of a default by the principal debtor. This contract if it is not expressed between the parties is always implied.

**Case Study**

A obtains a housing loan from LIC Housing, and, if B promises to repay. What is the nature of the contract?

## 9.5 ESSENTIAL ELEMENTS OF CONTRACT OF GUARANTEE

The essential elements of the contract of guarantee are discussed as under:

### 9.5.1 Concurrence

A contract of guarantee requires the concurrence of all the three parties to it *viz.*, the principal debtor, the creditor and the surety.

### 9.5.2 Primary Liability in Some Person

There must be a primary liability in some person other than the surety. The word 'liability', as used in the definition of guarantee, means a liability which is enforceable at law. If that liability does not exist, there cannot be a contract of guarantee. But a guarantee given for the debt of a minor is an exception to this rule.

### 9.5.3 Essentials of a Valid Contract

A contract of guarantee must have all the essential elements of a valid contract like free consent, capacity of parties, lawful object and consideration. But the following two points should be noted:

1. All the parties must be capable of entering into a valid contract though the principal debtor may be a person suffering from the incapacity to contract. In such a case, the surety is regarded as the principal debtor and is liable to pay personally, even though the principal debtor (e.g., a minor) is not liable to pay.
2. A consideration received by the principal debtor is sufficient for the surety and it is not necessary that it must necessarily result in some benefit to the surety himself. It is sufficient if something is done or some promise is made for the benefit of the principal debtor.

### 9.5.4 Writing Not Necessary

A guarantee may be either oral or written. It may be express or implied. The implied guarantee may be inferred from the course of conduct of the parties concerned.

## 9.6 KINDS OF GUARANTEE

A guarantee may either be prospective or retrospective guarantee.

### 9.6.1 Retrospective Guarantee

A guarantee given for an existing debt or obligation is called the 'retrospective guarantee'.

### 9.6.2 Prospective Guarantee

A guarantee given for a future debt or obligation is called the 'prospective guarantee'.

A guarantee may be classified either as a specific guarantee, or a continuing guarantee.

### 9.6.3 Specific Guarantee

When a guarantee extends to a single transaction or debt, it is called the specific guarantee. The specific guarantee is also known as a simple guarantee. On the completion of a specific transaction, the guarantee is discharged.

### 9.6.4 Continuing Guarantee—Section 129

When a guarantee extends to a series of transactions, it is called the continuing guarantee. The continuing guarantee does not come to an end on the performance of a single transaction, or the discharge of debt but it will be enforceable for the subsequent transactions also. At the time of giving a continuing guarantee, the surety can either fix the amount of time.

**Examples**

1. A, in consideration that B will employ C in collection the rents of B's Zamindari, promises B to be responsible to the amount of ₹ 5000 for the due collection and payment by C of those rents. This is a continuing guarantee.
2. 'A' becomes the surety of 'C' for B's conduct as a manager in C's bank, and 'B' is appointed on the faith of this guarantee. 'A' is precluded from annulling the guarantee so long as B acts as a manager in C's bank.

A guarantee for the faithful discharge of his duties by a person appointed to a place of trust in a bank is not a continuing guarantee. It is a guarantee of appointment.

A guarantee for payment of a certain sum by installments, within a definite time, is not a continuing guarantee. It is a guarantee of loan.

## 9.7 REVOCATION OF A CONTINUING GUARANTEE

On the revocation of a continuing guarantee, the surety's liability comes to an end for the future transactions. However, the surety is liable for the previous transactions. A continuing guarantee can be cancelled in the following manner:

### 9.7.1 By Notice—Section 130

The surety may cancel the continuing guarantee for further transaction at any time.

### 9.7.2 By Death of Surety—Section 131

A continuing guarantee is cancelled on the death of the surety. In such case, no notice is required to be given to the creditor. However, the contract may provide contrary to the above rule. On the death of the surety, the guarantee is cancelled but for the future transaction. For the past transaction which has already taken place, the surety's estate will be liable.

### 9.7.3 On Discharge of Surety

A continuing guarantee is revoked when the surety is discharged from the liability.

**Case Study**

Ravi becomes a guarantor for Ashok for the amount which may be given to him by Nalin within 6 months. The maximum limit of the said amount is ₹ 1 lakh. After 2 months, Ravi withdraws his guarantee. Up to the time of revocation of the guarantee, Nalim had given to Ashok ₹ 20,000.

(i) Whether Ravi is discharged from his liabilities to Nalin for any subsequent loan?

(ii) Whether Ravi is liable, if Ashok fails to pay the amount of ₹ 20,000 to Nalin?

## 9.8 SURETY'S LIABILITY—SECTION 128

Section 128 of Contract Act, 1872 explains about the surety's liability as under:

### 9.8.1 Liability Is Secondary and Conditional

The liability of the principal debtor is primary. However, the surety's liability is secondary and conditional. The surety is liable to the creditor only when a default is made by the principal debtor. The creditor can sue the surety without suing the principal debtor. As soon as the debtor has made a default in the payment of a debt, the surety is immediately liable. But until the default, the creditor cannot call upon the surety to pay. In this way, the nature of the surety's liability is secondary.

If the principal debtor performs the contract in part, the surety shall be liable only in the respect of that part of the contract, which has not been performed by the principal.

### 9.8.2 Liability Is Coextensive with Liability of Principal Debtor

The liability of the surety is co-extensive with that of the principal debtor. It means the surety is liable for all the debts, payable by the principal debtor to the creditor. Accordingly, the interest, damages and costs which may be recovered from the principal debtor may also be recovered from the surety. Thus, ordinarily, the liability of the surety shall be the same as that of the principal debtor. However, the contract of guarantee may provide otherwise, i.e., the surety has a right to limit his liability.

**Example**

Amar guarantees to Balram, the payment of a bill of exchange by Chetan, the acceptor. The bill is dishonored by Chetan. Amar is liable not only for the amount of the bills but also for any interest and charges which may have become due on it.

The principal debtor and the surety are jointly and severally liable. If the principal debtor is not liable on the principal debt, the surety also shall not be liable. If the principal debt is illegal or is unenforceable, the principal debtor as well as the surety shall not be liable. If the principal debtor is discharged by the creditor's breach, the surety shall also be discharged.

### 9.8.3 Surety's Liability May Be Limited

Generally, the liability of the surety is the same as that of the principal debtor. However, the surety may limit his liability by the express provision in the contract of guarantee. Thus, the contract of guarantee may provide that the surety shall not be liable—

1. Beyond a fixed amount (where the guarantee is fixed on amount)
2. For any amount due after a fixed date (where the guarantee given with reference to the time period may be fixed during which the guarantee shall remain effective).

## 9.9 RIGHTS OF SURETY

The surety has certain rights against the creditors, the principal debtor and the co-sureties. These rights may be discussed as under:

### 9.9.1 Against the Principal Debtor—Sections 140 and 145

**9.9.1.1 Right of Subrogation** A subrogation means substitution of one person for another. According to this right, when the surety has paid the debt or discharged the performance of the debtor to the creditor, he is vested with all the rights which the creditor had against the principal debtor. The right of the surety is known as the right of the subrogation, namely the right to stand in the shoes of the creditor.

The surety is entitled to the benefit of all the security made available to the creditor by the principal debtor, whether the surety was aware of its existence or not.

**9.9.1.2 Right of Indemnify** The surety is entitled to recover from the principal debtor, whatever sums he has rightfully paid. The amount includes loan, interest and other costs, if any, paid to the creditor.

The surety can also claim indemnity for any special damages, which he has suffered, while discharging his duties. The surety can claim, even if he has paid a time barred debt, as it is a rightful payment, though there are contrary views on this issue.

Where the surety becomes a surety without the knowledge of the principal debtor, he is entitled for all the rights against the principal debtor but not the right to claim an indemnity against the principal debtor. However, the amount wrongfully paid cannot be recovered.

### 9.9.2 Against the Creditor

The rights of sureties against the creditor are the following:

**9.9.2.1 Right to Claim Securities** The surety is entitled for all the securities which the debtor has provided to the creditor, whether the surety is aware of it or not, on the payment of debt or discharge of the payment to the creditor.

Where the creditor loses any of the securities by the default or negligence, the liability of the surety reduces proportionately. If the creditor does not hand over the securities to the surety, he can be compelled to do so.

**Example**

C advances to B, his tenant, ₹ 2000 on the guarantee of A. C has also a further security for the ₹ 2000 by a mortgage of B's furniture. C cancels the mortgage. B becomes insolvent, and C sues A on his guarantee. A is discharged from the liability to the amount of the value of the furniture.

**9.9.2.2 Right of Set Off** Set off means the deductions from the amount of loan. The surety has a right of set off against the principal debtor exactly as a creditor would have.

### 9.9.3 Against Co-sureties

When two or more persons give a guarantee for the same debt, they are termed as a co-sureties. All the co-sureties are equally liable to the creditor in the absence of any contrary contract. The rights of the co-sureties are discussed as under:

**9.9.3.1 Right to Contribution** When one co-surety pays the debt or discharges the entire obligation, he can recover equal contribution from the other co-surety. This rule is applicable whether the sureties are liable jointly or severally and whether their liability is under the same contract or a different contract. However, if the co-sureties fix their liability by an agreement, then they are liable to contribute as agreed among themselves.

**Examples**

1. A, B and C are sureties to D for the sum of ₹ 3000 lent to E. E makes default in payment. A, B and C are liable as between themselves, to pay ₹ 1000 each.
2. Amar has borrowed ₹ 1000 from a bank. Ram and Balram guaranteed for the repayment of the loan in the ration of 3:1. On default of Amar, Ram is liable to pay ₹ 750 and Balram is liable to pay ₹ 250.

It is important to note that where the co-sureties have agreed to guarantee different sums of one single debt to the principal debtor, even then they are liable to contribute equally, subject to the maximum limit fixed by them. Thus, within the maximum limit fixed by the co-sureties, they are liable to contribute an equal amount.

**Examples**

1. A, B and C, as sureties for D, enter into three several bonds, each in a different penalty, namely, A in the penalty of ₹ 10,000, B in that of ₹ 20,000 and C in that of ₹ 40,000, conditioned for D's duty accounting to E. D makes default to the extent of ₹ 30,000. A, B and C are each liable to pay ₹ 10,000.
2. A, B and C, as sureties for D, enter into three several bonds, each in a different penalty, namely, A in the penalty of ₹ 10,000, B in that of ₹ 20,000 and C in that of ₹ 40,000, conditioned for D's duly accounting to E. D makes default to the extent of ₹ 40,000. A is liable to pay ₹ 10,000, and B and C ₹ 15,000 each.
3. A, B and C, as sureties for D, enter into three several bonds, each in a different penalty, namely, A in the penalty of ₹ 10,000, B in that of ₹ 20,000 and C in that of ₹ 40,000, conditioned for D's duly accounting to E. D makes default to the extent of ₹ 70,000. A, B and C each have to pay the fully penalty of his bond.

**9.9.3.2 Right to Share the Benefit of Securities** If the one co-surety receives any security from the principal debtor at the time of guarantee or from the creditor on the discharge of debt or obligation of the principal debtor, other co-sureties are entitled to share the benefit of the securities.

## 9.10 DISCHARGE OF A SURETY

A surety may be discharged from the liability under the following circumstances:

### 9.10.1 By Notice of Revocation—Section 130

On the revocation of a continuing guarantee, the surety's liability comes to an end for the future transactions. However, the surety is liable for previous transactions. A continuing guarantee can be cancelled in the following manner.

### 9.10.2 By Death of Surety—Section 131

On the revocation of a continuing guarantee, the surety's liability comes to an end for the future transactions. However, the surety is liable for previous transactions. A continuing guarantee can be cancelled in the following manner:

### 9.10.3 By Variance in Terms of Contract—Section 133

Any variance, made without the surety's consent, in the terms of the contract between the principal (debtor) and the creditor discharges the surety as to the transactions subsequent to the variance.

**Examples**

1. A becomes the surety to C for B's conduct as a manager in C's bank. Afterwards, B and C contract, without A's consent that B's salary shall be raised, and that he shall become liable for one-fourth of the losses on overdrafts. B allows a customer to overdraw, and the bank loses a sum of money. A is discharged from his suretyship by the variance made without his consent, and is not liable to make good this loss.
2. A guarantees C against the misconduct of B in an office, to which B is appointed by C, and of which the duties are defined by an Act of the Legislature. By a subsequent Act, the nature of the office is materially altered. Afterwards, B misconducts himself. A is discharged by the change from future liability under his guarantee though the misconduct of B is in the respect of a duty is not affected by the later Act.

### 9.10.4 By Release or Discharge of Principal Debtor—Section 134

The surety is discharged by any contract between the creditor and the principal debtor by which the principal debtor is released or by any act or omission of the creditor, the legal consequence of which is the discharge of the principal debtor.

**Example**

A contracts with B for a fixed price to build a house for B within a stipulated time, B supplying the necessary timber. C guarantees A's performance of the contract. B omits to supply the timber. C is discharged from his suretyship.

But where the creditor fails to sue the principal debtor within the limitation period, the surety is not discharged.

### 9.10.5 When Creditor Compound or Give Time to Debtor—Section 135

A contract between the creditor and the principal debtor is discharged when the creditor makes a composition with, or promises to give time to, or not to sue, the principal debtor without the consent of the surety.

### 9.10.6 By Creditor's Act—Section 139

If the creditor does any act which is inconsistent with the rights of the surety or omits to do any act which his duty to the surety requires him to do, and the eventual remedy of the surety himself against the principal debtor is thereby impaired, the surety is discharged.

**Examples**

1. B contracts to build a ship for C for a given sum, to be paid by instalments as the work reaches certain stages. A becomes the surety to C for B's due performance of the contract. C, without the knowledge of A, prepays to B, the last two instalments. A is discharged by this prepayment.
2. 'A' puts 'M' as the cashier under 'B' and agrees to stand as the surety, provided 'B' checks the cash every month. 'M' embezzles cash. 'A' was not held to be responsible as B failed to verify the cash every month.

### 9.10.7 By Release or Lose of Security by Creditor—Section 141

If the creditor loses or parts with any security given by the debtor at the time of entering into the contract of guarantee, the surety is discharged to the extent of the value of the security, unless the surety consented to the release of the security. It is immaterial whether the surety was or is aware of such a security or not.

### 9.10.8 By Invalidation of Contract of Guarantee

The surety is liable under the contract of guarantee, if the contract is valid. But in the following circumstances, the guarantee contract is treated as invalid:

1. When the guarantee has been obtained by the means of mis-representation.
2. When the guarantee is obtained by the concealment of facts or by remaining silent as to the material circumstances.
3. When the guarantee is given by the surety on the condition that the creditor shall not act until the co-surety join. And the co-surety fails to join.

**Example**

A engages B as a clerk to collect money for him and B fails to account for some of his receipts. There upon, A calls upon B to furnish security for his duly accounting the receipts. C gives the required guarantee. A does not inform C of the fact of a previous defalcation by B and thereafter, B again makes a default. The guarantee would be invalid.

**Case Study**

B owes C, a debt guaranteed by A. C does not sue B for a year after the debt has become payable. In the meantime, B becomes insolvent. Is A discharged? Decide with reference to the provisions of the Indian Contract Act, 1872.

**Case Study**

Explaining the provisions of the Indian Contract Act, 1872, answer the following:

(i) A contracts with B for a fixed price, to construct a house for B within a stipulated time. B would supply the necessary material to be used in the construction. C guarantees A's performance of the contract. B does not supply the material as per the agreement. Is C discharged from his liability?

Business 1.18 and Corporate Laws

(ii) C, the holder of an over due bill of exchange drawn by A as the surety for B, and accepted by B, contracts with X to give time to B. Is A discharged from his liability?

**Case Study**

If A becomes a surety to C for the payment of rent by B under a lease, and B and C contract, without 'A' consent, that 'B' will pay a higher rent. What would be the liability of 'A' as a surety?

## 9.11 DIFFERENCE BETWEEN A CONTRACT OF INDEMNITY AND A CONTRACT OF GUARANTEE

| Contract of Indemnity | Contract of Guarantee |
|---|---|
| There are two parties to the contract viz., the indemnifier (promisor) and the indemnified (promise). | There are three parties to the contract *viz.*, the creditor, the principal debtor and the surety. |
| Liability of the indemnifier to the indemnified is primary and independent. | Liability of the surety to the creditor is collateral or secondary, the primary liability being that of the principal debtor. |
| There is only one contract in the case of a contract of indemnity, i.e., between the indemnifier and the indemnified. | In a contract of guarantee, there are three contracts, between the principal debtor and the creditor, between the creditor and the surety, and between the surety and the principal debtor. |
| It is not necessary for the indemnifier to act at the request of the indemnified. | It is necessary that the surety should give the guarantee at the request of the debtor. |
| The liability of the indemnifier arises only on the happening of a contingency. | There is usually an existing debt or duty, the performance of which is guaranteed by the surety. |
| An indemnifier cannot sue a third party for the loss in his own name because there is no privity of contract. He can do so only if there is an assignment in his favour. | A surety, on discharging the debt due by the principal debtor, steps into the shoes of the creditor. He can proceed against the principal debtor in his own right. |

## LIST OF LANDMARK JUDGEMENTS

1. ***Osman Jamal and Sons vs Gopal Purshottam (1928)***

   The disability of the indemnifier commences as soon as the liability of the indemnity holder becomes absolute.

2. ***Kashiba vs Shripat (1895)***

   The contract of guarantee must be made by the parties, competent to the contract.

3. ***PN Bandak vs Sri Vikram Cotton Mills (1970)***

   The liability of the surety should arise, only when the principal debtor makes a default.

4. ***Eastern Bank Ltd vs Parts Services of India (1986)***

   The guarantee which is given for a series of transactions of continuing nature is a continuing guarantee.

5. ***Kanlu Bibi vs Abdullah (1880)***

   If without the consent of the surety, the creditor makes any material change in the nature or terms of his contract with the principal debtor, the surety is discharged from the liability.

6. ***Midland Motors vs Newman (1929)***

   When the creditors give more time to the principal debtor for the repayment without the consent of surety, he is discharged.

7. ***Gajanan Moreshwar vs Moreshwar Madan (1942)***

   The indemnifier is to make the payment as soon as the liability arises. It is not that the indemnity holder should first pay, and then claim the reimbursement from the indemnifier.

8. ***Subramanian vs Narayanswami (1951)***

   If the liability of principal debtor is reduced by the operation of law, the liability of surety is also reduced as liability is co-extensive with that of the principal debtor.

9. ***London General Omnibus Co. vs Holloway (1912)***

   The continuing guarantee is uberrimaefidea. If material facts are concealed, the guarantee is invalid.

## TEST YOUR KNOWLEDGE

1. Define the contract of indemnity. **(Ref. Para-9.1)**
2. What are the essentials of the contract of indemnity? **(Ref. Para-9.2)**
3. What are the legal rules for the contract of indemnity? **(Ref. Para-9.2)**
4. What are the rights of the indemnity holder? **(Ref. Para-9.3)**
5. Define the contract of guarantee. **(Ref. Para-9.4)**
6. What are the essentials for a valid contract of guarantee? **(Ref. Para-9.5)**
7. There is no consideration in case of the contract of guarantee. Comment. **(Ref. Para-9.5)**
8. The contract of guarantee may be oral or in writing. Comment. **(Ref. Para-9.5)**
9. What are the various kinds of guarantee? **(Ref. Para-9.6)**
10. What is a continuing guarantee? How it can be revoked? **(Ref. Para-9.6,9.7)**
11. A continuing guarantee can never be revoked. Comment. **(Ref. Para-9.7)**
12. The death of the surety operates as a revocation of the continuing guarantee and not of the specific guarantee. Comment. **(Ref. Para-9.7)**

13. State the nature and extent of the surety's liability. **(Ref. Para-9.8)**
14. Liability of the surety is primary and independent. Comment. **(Ref. Para-9.8)**
15. In the contract of guarantee, the primary liability is of the surety. Comment. **(Ref. Para-9.8)**
16. What are the surety's rights against the principal debtor and the creditor? Does he have any right against the co-sureties? **(Ref. Para-9.9)**
17. What are the rights of surety against the other co-surety? **(Ref. Para-9.9)**
18. What are the rights of surety against the principal debtor? **(Ref. Para-9.9)**
19. What are the rights of surety against the creditor? **(Ref. Para-9.9)**
20. How, and in what circumstances, is the surety discharged from his liability? **(Ref. Para-9.10)**
21. In what circumstances is the contract of guarantee regarded as invalid? **(Ref. Para-9.10)**
22. Variance in the terms of contract of guarantee do not affect contract. Comment. **(Ref. Para-9.10)**
23. When does the creditor's act discharge surety? **(Ref. Para-9.10)**
24. Loss of security by the surety means the loss of surety. Explain. **(Ref. Para-9.10)**
25. Explain the difference between the contract of indemnity and the contract of guarantee. **(Ref. Para-9.11)**

## MULTIPLE-CHOICE QUESTIONS

1. The number of contracts in the contract of guarantee are
   (i) two.
   (ii) three.
   (iii) four.
   (iv) none of the above.
2. Liability of the surety is
   (i) coextensive with the principal debtor.
   (ii) primary with the principal debtor.
   (iii) secondary to the principal debtor.
   (iv) all of these.
3. A contract in which one person promises to compensate the other for the loss suffered by him, due to the conduct of the promisor or of any other person, is known as a
   (i) contract of indemnity.
   (ii) contract of guarantee.
   (iii) quasi-contract.
   (iv) none of the above.
4. The party who gives the indemnity is known as
   (i) the indemnity-holder.
   (ii) the indemnifier.
   (iii) the surety.
   (iv) the principal debtor.
5. Section 124 defines the contract of indemnity in a wider sense as it also covers all the contracts of insurance, whereas the English Law defines this term in a narrower sense as it does not cover the insurance contracts.
   (i) True
   (ii) False
6. One of the following is not an essential of a valid contract of indemnity, which states that it must
   (i) have requisites of a valid contract.
   (ii) be to save a party from some loss.
   (iii) be in writing and signed.
   (iv) be lawful in nature.
7. Co-sureties bound in different sums are liable to pay
   (i) equally, as far as the limits of their respective obligation permit.
   (ii) proportionally, according to their respective obligation.
   (iii) none of the above.

8. On making the payment of the loss suffered by the indemnity-holder, the indemnifier's rights are not provided in any section of the Contract Act, thus he gets
   (i) the right of surety.
   (ii) the moral right.
   (iii) the fundamental rights.
   (iv) none of the above.
9. The liability of the indemnifier to compensate the indemnity-holder commences when
   (i) the indemnity-holder has suffered actual loss.
   (ii) the liability of the indemnity-holder becomes clear and certain.
   (iii) he is called upon to pay.
   (iv) he fixes the date for the same.
10. A contract in which a person promises to discharge the liability of another person, in case of default by such person, is known as a
    (i) quasi-contract.
    (ii) contract of indemnity.
    (iii) contract of guarantee.
    (iv) none of the above.
11. In a contract of guarantee, a person who promises to discharge another's liability is known as
    (i) the principal debtor.
    (ii) the creditor.
    (iii) the indemnified.
    (iv) the surety.
12. A guarantee given for the minor's debts is
    (i) valid.
    (ii) void.
    (iii) voidable.
    (iv) illegal.
13. The liability of a surety is
    (i) more than that of the principal debtor.
    (ii) less than that of the principal debtor.
    (iii) same as that of the principal debtor.
    (iv) dependent on the court's discretion.
14. The liability of a surety arises when
    (i) the principal debtor commits a default in payment.
    (ii) the creditor fails to recovery anything from the principal debtor.
    (iii) the surety is reimbursed by the principal debtor.
    (iv) the court directs him to pay.
15. On default of the principal debtor, the creditor cannot proceed against the surety, until he exhausts all the remedies against the principal debtor.
    (i) True
    (ii) False
16. A surety is discharged from the liability by
    (i) revocation notice by surety.
    (ii) material alteration in terms.
    (iii) discharge of principal by the creditor.
    (iv) all of the above.
17. Two parties, namely the 'indemnifier' and the 'indemnity-holder', are involved in a contract of indemnity. And the parties in a contract of guarantee are
    (i) three, the creditor, the principal debtor and the surety.
    (ii) two, the creditor and the principal debtor, as surety is simply a guarantor not a party.

18. A contract of insurance is also a contract of indemnity.
    (i) True
    (ii) False
19. The liability of the indemnifier is the primary liability.
    (i) True
    (ii) False
20. The discharge of the principal debtor will discharge the surety also.
    (i) True
    (ii) False
21. The death of the surety brings an end to a continuing guarantee.
    (i) True
    (ii) False
22. The guarantee given for a person incompetent to enter into a contract is not enforceable?
    (i) True
    (ii) False
23. The rights of surety may be discussed under the
    (i) rights against the principal debtor.
    (ii) rights against the creditor.
    (iii) rights against the co-sureties.
    (iv) all of the above.
24. A surety is discharge from the liability
    (i) on the death of the surety.
    (ii) on the notice of revocation by the surety.
    (iii) on composition with the principal debtor.
    (iv) all of the above.
25. A surety is discharged from the liability
    (i) by giving more time to the principal debtor.
    (ii) by impairing the surety's remedy.
    (iii) all of the above.
    (iv) none of the above.

## ANSWER KEYS

| | | | | |
|---|---|---|---|---|
| **1.** (i) | **6.** (iii) | **11.** (iv) | **16.** (iv) | **21.** (i) |
| **2.** (i) | **7.** (i) | **12.** (i) | **17.** (i) | **22.** (ii) |
| **3.** (i) | **8.** (i) | **13.** (iii) | **18.** (i) | **23.** (iv) |
| **4.** (ii) | **9.** (ii) | **14.** (i) | **19.** (i) | **24.** (iv) |
| **5.** (ii) | **10.** (iii) | **15.** (ii) | **20.** (ii) | **25.** (iii) |

# 10

# The Indian Contract Act, 1872: Bailment and Pledge

**Learning Objectives**

*After reading this chapter, you will be able to understand:*

- What is a bailment and pledge of goods?
- Types of bailment
- Duties and rights of a bailee
- Duties and rights of a bailor
- Termination of a bailment
- Lien
- Pledge
- Rights of a pwanor and a pledgee

## 10.1 WHAT IS A BAILMENT?

The term 'bailment' is derived from the French word 'bailer' which means to deliver a thing under a contract. The delivery of goods by one person to another person for a specific purpose with a condition to return the goods when the purpose is over or otherwise disposed off according to the direction of the person.

The person who delivers the goods is known as the 'Bailor' and the person who receives the goods is known as the 'Bailee' and the transaction is known as the 'Bailment'.

***Example***

Arun gives a cloth to his tailor for stitching. It is a bailment of the cloth. As soon as the cloth is stitched, it will be returned to Arun.

## 10.2 ESSENTIALS OF A VALID BAILMENT

The essential features of a valid bailment are as under:

### 10.2.1 Delivery of Possession

Under the bailment, the possession of goods is delivered by the bailor to the bailee. If the possession is not delivered, it is not a bailment. If the ownership is transferred to other person, it is not a bailment.

The delivery of goods may take place either by a way of an actual delivery or by a constructive delivery. An actual delivery means the bailor hands over the physical possession of goods to the bailee. A constructive delivery means some act on the part of the bailor, which has the effect of putting the goods in the possession of the bailee. The bailment is not possible with an immovable property.

***Example***

The deposit of money in a bank is not a bailment, since the money returned by the bank would not be the identical currency notes. Moreover, money is not goods.

### 10.2.2 Contract Between the Parties

There must be a contract between the parties. The contract must be provided for the transfer of the possession of goods from one person to another. The contract may be expressed or implied. Sometimes, the bailment may arise even without the contract, i.e., a finder of goods is treated as a bailee.

### 10.2.3 Delivery for Some Purpose

The delivery of goods must be for some purpose. The purpose could be the safe custody of the goods or the transportation of goods. The purpose may be expressly specified in the contract or may be implied from the circumstances.

### 10.2.4 Return or Disposal of Goods

The goods must be delivered to the bailee for some purpose and subject to the condition that when the purpose is achieved, the goods shall be returned to the bailor or disposed off according to his direction. The return of goods may be in the original or altered form.

**Case Study**

Examine whether the following constitute a contract of 'Bailment' under the provisions of the Indian Contract Act, 1872:

(i) V parks his car at a parking lot, locks it and keeps the keys with himself.

(ii) The seizure of goods by the customs authorities.

## 10.3 TYPES OF BAILMENT

A bailment can be classified either on the basis of reward or on the basis of benefits. The bailment on the basis of reward can be classified as (i) a gratuitous bailment or (ii) a non-gratuitous bailment.

### 10.3.1 Gratuitous Bailment

It is the bailment of goods without any charges or reward. The bailee is not required to pay any charges for the bailment.

### 10.3.2 Non-gratuitous Bailment

It is the bailment for some charges or reward. The bailee is required to pay some charges to the bailor.

The bailment on the basis of benefit may be classified in the following three manners:

### 10.3.3 Bailment for the Exclusive Benefit of a Bailor

It is the bailment in which the goods are delivered by the bailor to the bailee only for the exclusive benefit of the bailor himself.

### 10.3.4 Bailment for the Exclusive Benefit of a Bailee

It is the bailment in which the goods are delivered by the bailor to the bailee only for the exclusive benefit of the bailee.

### 10.3.5 Bailment for Mutual Benefit of Both Bailor and Bailee

It is the bailment in which the goods are delivered by the bailor to the bailee for the benefit of both the parties.

## 10.4 DUTIES OF A BAILEE

Duties of the bailee in the bailment are grouped as under.

### 10.4.1 Duty of Care—Sections 151 and 152

The bailee should take reasonable care of the goods which are in his possession. The degree of care required by the bailee is similar to that of a man of ordinary prudence would take of his own goods under the similar circumstances. If he has taken such care, he is not liable, even if the goods are lost or damaged. He is also not liable for the destruction or the loss of goods due to an act of God.

***Example***

If X bails his ornaments to 'Y' and 'Y' keeps these ornaments in his own locker at his house along with his own ornaments and if all the ornaments are lost/stolen in a riot, 'Y' will not be responsible for the loss to 'X'.

### 10.4.2 Compensation for an Unauthorized Use—Section 154

The bailee should not use the goods for an unauthorized purpose. He can use the goods as per the terms of the bailment.

If the bailee makes any unauthorized use of goods, he shall be liable for any loss or destruction of the goods even if he was not negligent. On any unauthorized use of goods, the bailor may terminate the contract of bailment. In other words, the contract of bailment becomes voidable.

### 10.4.3 Duty Not to Mix—Sections 155–157

The bailee should not mix the bailor's goods with his own goods. If the bailee mixes his own goods with the bailor's goods with the bailor's consent, the bailor and the bailee shall have an interest in the proportion to their respective shares in the mixture thus produced. It must be remembered that if the mixture has taken place by an act of God, the bailee is not liable for such mixture.

When the bailee mixes the bailor's goods with his own without a consent and the goods are separable, the bailee is required to pay the cost of separation but if it cannot be separated, the bailor entitled to be compensated.

***Examples***

1. A bails a barrel of Cape flour worth ₹ 45 to B. B, without A's consent, mixes the flour with a country flour of his own worth only ₹ 25 a barrel. B must compensate A for the loss of his flour.
2. A bails 100 bales of cotton marked with a particular mark to B. B, without A's consent, mixes the 100 bales with other bales of his own bearing a different mark. A is entitled to have his 100 bales returned and B is bound to bear all the expenses incurred in the separation of the bales and any other incidental damage.

### 10.4.4 Duty to Return Goods—Sections 160 and 161

On the achievement of the object or completion of the purpose or expiry of the contract period, the bailee should return the goods to the bailor. When the bailor gives direction to the bailee for the return of the delivery of goods, in such a case, the bailee should deliver the goods as per the direction. The bailee should return or deliver the goods without waiting for the demand from the bailor. In case, if the bailee fails to return the goods to the bailor, the goods will be at his risk even though the loss has been created due to an act of God.

### 10.4.5 Duty to Return Increase or Profit—Section 163

If the goods which are bailed due to any circumstances get an accretion, the goods should be returned back along with such addition. If some profit arises from the goods, the bailee is bound to return the profit of the bailor. This is, however, subject to any contract to the contrary.

***Example***

A leaves a cow in the custody of B to be taken care of. The cow has a calf and B is bound to deliver the calf as well as the cow to A.

### 10.4.6 Duty Not to Set Up Adverse Title

The bailee should not use the goods in such a way that it impairs the right of the bailor. The bailee, as such, can apply the goods only for the purpose of bailment and thus he cannot create the adverse title.

**Case Study**

Sunil delivered his car to Mahesh for repairs. Mahesh completed the work but did not return the car to Sunil within the reasonable time, though Sunil repeatedly reminded Mahesh for the return of car. In the meantime, a big fire occurred in the neighbourhood and the car was destroyed. Decide whether Mahesh can be held liable under the provisions of the Indian Contract Act, 1872?

**Case Study**

M lends a sum of ₹ 5000 to B on the security of two shares of a Limited Company on 1 April 2007. On 15 June 2007, the company issued two bonus shares. B returns the loan amount of ₹ 5000 with an interest but M returns only two shares which were pledged and refuses to give the two bonus shares. Advise B in the light of the provisions of the Indian Contract Act, 1872.

## 10.5 DUTIES OF A BAILOR

The following are the duties of a bailor.

### 10.5.1 Duty to Disclose Fault—Section 150

It is the duty of the bailor to disclose the known defects in the goods. The bailor should compensate the bailee for such a loss if the bailer fails to disclose such defects and as a result, if the bailee suffers from any loss. But these provisions are applicable only for the known defects.

However, it must be noted that a non-gratuitous bailer would be liable for known as well as unknown defects.

***Example***

A lends a horse, which he knows to be vicious, to B. He does not disclose the fact that the horse is vicious. The horse runs away. B is thrown and injured. A is responsible to B for the damage sustained.

### 10.5.2 Duty to Bear Extraordinary Expenses—Section 158

The bailor is liable to reimburse, to the bailee, all the necessary and extraordinary expenses incurred by the bailee in case of a gratuitous bailment. But in case of non-gratuitous bailment, the bailor is liable to reimburse the extra-ordinary expenses incurred by the bailee.

### 10.5.3 Duty to Indemnify Loss for Permanent Termination of Bailment—Section 159

In case of a gratuitous bailment, the bailer may prematurely terminate the bailment. If the loss caused to the bailee due to the premature termination is more than the benefit obtained by the bailee, it is the duty of the bailer to compensate the bailee for such an excess loss.

### 10.5.4 Duty to Indemnify the Bailee for Any Loss—Section 164

If the bailor does not have any title to deliver the goods on the bailment, he would be liable to indemnity to the bailee for any loss which the bailee has paid to the original owner.

### 10.5.5 Duty to Receive Back the Goods—Section 164

If the bailor wrongfully refuses to take the custody of the goods, he is liable to pay to the bailee, the necessary expenses of the custody.

### 10.5.6 Duty to Bear a Loss—Section 162

If the goods are destroyed or lost while in possession of the bailee without his fault, the bailor is required to bear the loss.

**Case Study**

A hire a carriage of B and agrees to pay ₹ 500 as hire charges. The carriage is unsafe though B is unaware of it. A is injured and claims compensation for the injuries suffered by him. B refuses to pay. Discuss the liability of B.

## 10.6 BAILEE'S RIGHTS

The duties of the bailor are the rights of the bailee. In addition to these rights, the bailee has the following rights:

### 10.6.1 Return/Delivery of Goods—Section 165

The bailee has a right to return the goods to anyone of the several joint bailors. It is not necessary that the goods should be delivered in the presence of all the bailors. However, if any agreement provides the contrary then the goods should be returned accordingly.

### 10.6.2 File Suit to Court

If the bailee gets the ownership claims of the goods from more than one person, he has a right to request the court to decide the real ownership of the goods. Until the final decision comes, the bailee can keep the goods with himself.

If the third person or the wrong doer prevents the bailee to use the goods under the bailment, he has the right to file a suit and can ask for compensation from the third party.

### 10.6.3 To Recover Charges

The bailee has the right to recover the charges as agreed. The bailee has the right to recover the expenses incurred by him.

### 10.6.4 Right of Lien

To recover his due, the bailee can exercise his right of lien. However, the bailee gets only a particular lien and not the general lien.

## 10.7 BAILOR'S RIGHTS

The duties of the bailee are the rights of the bailor. In addition, the bailor has the following rights:

### 10.7.1 Enforcement

The bailor has a right to force the bailee to perform his duties. The bailor can compel the bailee to take proper care of the goods. If the bailee neglects his duties, the bailor has the right to enforce by filing a suit to the court.

### 10.7.2 Termination of Bailment—Section 153

If the bailee uses the goods in an unauthorized manner, the bailor can terminate the bailment before the completion of the bailment. A contract of bailment is regarded as a voidable contract. In such an event, the bailee cannot suit the bailor for a breach of contract.

***Example***

'A' lets on hire his horse to 'B' for his own riding but 'B' uses the horse for driving his carriage. 'A' has a right to terminate the contract of bailment.

### 10.7.3 File Suit Against a Wrong Doer

To protect his goods, the bailor has a right to take a legal action against any person who has caused any loss or damage to the goods.

### 10.7.4 To Demand Goods at Any Time—Section 159

In gratuitous bailment, the bailor has a right to demand the return of goods even before time.

## 10.8 TERMINATION OF A BAILMENT

The bailment is terminated in the following circumstances:

### 10.8.1 Efflux of Time

If the bailment contract is made for a specific period, it terminates on the expiry of the specific period.

### 10.8.2 Fulfillment of Purpose

If the bailment contract is made for a specific purpose, it terminates as soon as the purpose is achieved.

### 10.8.3 Inconsistent Use of Goods

If the bailee makes unauthorized use of the goods, in such a case, the contract of bailment becomes voidable at the option of the bailor. If the bailor does so, the contract is terminated.

### 10.8.4 Destruction of the Subject-Matter

On the destruction of the goods which is the subject-matter, the bailment is terminated.

### 10.8.5 Death of Any Party

A gratuitous bailment is terminated on the death of the bailor or the bailee.

### 10.8.6 Termination by a Bailor

A gratuitous bailment may be terminated by the bailor at any time. The bailor may terminate the gratuitous bailment even if it was for a specific purpose or for a specified time.

## 10.9 LIEN

A lien means the right to retain the possession of goods till the bailee is paid for his charges for services or any other amount. The lien of goods can be either a general lien or a particular lien. The lien can be either the general lien or the particular lien.

### 10.9.1 General Lien

A certain bailee entitled to retain any goods for any amount due. It is known as a general lien. The bankers, factors, wharfingers, attorneys of a High Court and policy-brokers may, in the absence of a contract to the contrary, retain as a security for a general balance of account any goods bailed to them.

***Example***

The chartered accountants have a general lien against the books of their clients, which come into their possession against the professional fees, not paid to them by those clients.

### 10.9.2 Particular Lien

Where the bailee has, in accordance with the purpose of the bailment, rendered any service involving the exercise of labour or skill in respect of the goods bailed, he has, in the absence of a contract to the contrary, a right to retain such goods until he receives the due remuneration for the services he has rendered in respect of them.

***Examples***

1. A delivers a rough diamond to B, a jeweller, to be cut and polished, which is accordingly done. B is entitled to retain the stone till he is paid for the services he has rendered.
2. A gives a cloth to B, a tailor, to make into a coat. B promises A to deliver the coat as soon as it is finished and to give a three months credit for the price. B is not entitled to retain the coat until he is paid.

Finder of goods, Pawnee's lien, Agent's lien and Unpaid-seller's lien have particular lien.

## 10.10 DIFFERENCE BETWEEN A GENERAL LIEN AND A PARTICULAR LIEN

The difference between a general lien and a particular lien can be summarized as follows:

1. A particular lien is exercisable only on such goods in respect of which charges are due. A general lien is a right to detain/retain any goods of the bailor for the general balance of an account outstanding.
2. A particular lien is automatic. A general lien is not automatic but is recognized through an agreement. It is exercised by the bailee only by name.
3. Particular lien comes into play only when there is some labour or skill is involved. A general lien can be exercised against the goods even without involvement of labour or skill.

## 10.11 FINDER OF GOODS

The person who finds the goods belonging to some other person and takes them in his possession is known as the finder of goods. The finder of goods is in the position of the bailee and therefore, all the duties of the bailee are equally applicable to the finder of goods. Following are the duties of the finder of goods:

1. The finder of goods must take the reasonable care of goods.
2. The finder of goods must return the goods to the owner when found.
3. The finder of goods must not use the goods for his own purpose.
4. The finder of goods must not mix the goods with his goods.
5. The finder of goods must return any increase in goods along with the goods.
6. The finder of goods must make a reasonable effort to find the owner.

## 10.12 PLEDGE

A pledge is a special kind of bailment. Here, the goods are delivered as a security for the payment of debt or for the performance of a promise. The person who delivers the goods is known as the Pledger or Pawner and the person who receives the goods is known as the Pledgee or Pawnee. In the pledge, there is no change in the ownership of the property.

## 10.13 RIGHTS OF A PAWNEE

Following are the rights of a pawnee with reference to the goods pledged:

### 10.13.1 Right of a Retainer—Sections 173 and 174

The pawnee can retain the goods pledged with him until he is paid:

1. Money in advance by him
2. Necessary expenses
3. Interest paid on debt

But the pawnee has no right to retain the goods even for subsequent advance.

***Example***

Malav pledges stock of goods for certain loan from a bank, the bank has a right to retain the stock not only for adjustment of the loan but also for payment of interest.

### 10.13.2 Extraordinary Expenses—Section 175

The pawnee has a right to retain the extra ordinary expenses related to the goods from the pawner for the preservation of the goods pledged with him.

### 10.13.3 When a Pawnor Defaults—Section 176

If the pawner makes a default, the pawnee has a right to sell the goods after giving notice of his intention to sell goods. Even if the title of the pawnor is defective, the pawnee gets valid title. If sale proceeds of goods by the pawnee are less than the amount of debt, the pawnee can recover such deficit from the pawnor.

On default by the pawnor, the pawnee has the right to file a recovery suit for the recovery of money due, interest due on the money lent, the necessary expenses and the extraordinary expenses.

### 10.13.4 To Sell Goods

The pawnee can sell the goods if the pawnor makes a default after giving a reasonable notice. The contract may exclude this right. If the sale is made by the pawnee without notice is void.

**Case Study**

Ravi sent a consignment of goods worth ₹ 60,000 by railway and got a railway receipt. He obtained an advance of ₹ 30,000 from the bank and endorsed and delivered the railway receipt in favour of the bank by a way of security. The railway failed to deliver the goods at the destination. The bank filed a suit against the railway for ₹ 60,000. Decide in the light of provisions of the Indian Contract Act, 1872, whether the bank would succeed in the said suit?

## 10.14 RIGHTS OF A PAWNOR

Following are the rights of the pawnor under the contract of pledge:

### 10.14.1 Redeem Goods Pledged

The pawner has a right to redeem his goods on the payment of debt or other charges. The right to redeem means get back his goods.

The pawner gets all the protection that is available to the ordinary debtor under any law which is for the time being enforced in India. The pawner has a right to recover the extraordinary expenses related to the goods from the pawnee.

### 10.14.2 Surplus on Sale

The pawnor has the right to take back any increase alone with the goods. But the pawnor can get it back only on the payment of debt or other charges.

## 10.15 PLEDGE BY A NON-OWNER

An owner of goods can create a pledge. However, this is subject to certain exceptions as under:

### 10.15.1 Mercantile Agent

A mercantile agent means an agent who has the authority to sell the goods in the ordinary course of business. At the time of creation of pledge, the pawnee has no notice of the fact that the mercantile agent had no authority to pledge the goods.

### 10.15.2 Possession Under a Voidable Contract

The person possessing the goods under a voidable contract can make a valid pledge on the satisfaction of following conditions:

1. The voidable contract has not been declared as void.
2. The pawnee must act in good faith. He should not have any notice of pawnor's defective title.

### 10.15.3 Person with Limited Interest

When a person pledges the goods in which he has only limited interest, the pledge is valid only to the extent of such limited interest.

### 10.15.4 Seller in Possession After Sale

When the seller continues to be in possession of goods ever after sale, he can make a valid pledge of goods. The pledge is valid only if the pawnee acts in good faith and had no notice of previous sale.

## 10.16 DISTINGUISH BETWEEN A BAILMENT AND A PLEDGE

The main distinctions between a bailment and a pledge are as under:

1. The pledge is a variety of bailment. Under a pledge, the goods are bailed as a security for a loan or a performance of a promise. In a regular bailment, the goods are bailed for other purpose than the two referred above. The bailee takes them for repairs and safe custody.

2. The pledge enjoys the right to sell only on default by the pledgor to repay the debt or perform his promise after giving due notice. In a bailment, the bailee, generally, cannot sell the goods. He can either retain or sue for the non-payment of dues.
3. The pledgee has a right to use the goods. A bailee can if the terms so provide use the goods.

## LIST OF LANDMARK JUDGEMENTS

1. ***State of Gujrat vs Haji Hassan (1967)***
If the goods are seized by the tax authority, it is not a bailment as there is no contract. However, the tax authority is in the position of the bailee after the goods are seized by them.
2. ***Standard Chartered Bank vs Custodian (2000)***
If the shares are transferred to the bank as a security and if the bank gets dividend or bonus shares, these can be retained by the bank (as bailee) but must be returned to the bailor after the purpose of bailment is over.
3. ***Purshottamdas vs UOI (1967)***
If a person takes a delivery of goods against a forged railway receipt, railways (bailee) can file a suit against him.
4. ***R. D. Saxena vs Balram Prasad (2000)***
An advocate has no lien over litigation files for his unpaid fees. The files must be returned to the client even if the fees not paid. The client's file is not the goods bailed.
5. ***Revenue Authority vs Sundersanam Pictures (1968)***
The bailment requires a physical or a constructive delivery. Hence, mere agreement to deliver the goods in future when ready for security is not a pledge.
6. ***Houghland vs R. R. Luxury Coaches (1962)***
If the bailee is negligent in taking the care of the goods bailed then he is liable to pay damages for the loss or destruction of the goods.
7. ***Shaw and Co. vs Symmons and Sons (1917)***
The bailee should return the goods without waiting for the demand from the bailor. If he fails to do so, he will keep the goods at his own risk and will be liable for the loss of destruction.
8. ***Chand Mal vs Ganda Singh (1855)***
The bailee can retain only such goods in respect of which he has exercised his labour and skill.
9. ***PNB vs Satya Pal (1956)***
The acceptance of goods and securities for a special purpose excludes a general lien.
10. ***GubaxRai vs PNB (1984)***
The bank cannot exercise lien on the goods belonging to the firm against the partners' individual accounts.
11. ***SBI vs J. A. Hussain (1993)***
A lending branch of a bank can exercise lien for the loans given by it but not for the loans given by another branch of the same bank.
12. ***Morvi Mercantile Bank vs UOI (1965)***
The delivery of the documents of titles which enables the pawnee to obtain the possession is the constructive delivery of goods and therefore, a valid pledge.

**13.** ***Blundell Leigh vs Atten-Borough (1921)***
The delivery of goods should be made in the pursuance of contract of pledge. The delivery of goods may be made before or after the advance of money.

**14.** ***M. R. Dhawan vs Madan Mohan (1969)***
If there is an increase in the pledged goods, the pawnor has the right to take back the increase along with the goods.

**15.** ***Prabhat Bank vs Babu Ram (1966)***
In case of a default made by the pawnor, the pawnee may sell the goods pledged with him after giving a reasonable notice.

## TEST YOUR KNOWLEDGE

1. Define a bailment. **(Ref. Para-10.1)**
2. What is a bailment? What are the essentials of a valid bailment? **(Ref. Para-10.1,10.2)**
3. In a bailment there is a transfer of possessory right forever. Comment. **(Ref. Para-10.2)**
4. A bailment can be made of both movable and immovable goods. Comment. **(Ref. Para-10.2)**
5. A bailment is the delivery of goods by one person to another for some purpose. Comment. **(Ref. Para-10.2)**
6. A bailment of goods without any charges to be paid to the bailee is invalid. Comment. **(Ref. Para-10.3)**
7. How can a bailment contract be classified? **(Ref. Para-10.3)**
8. What are the legal provisions when the bailee mixes the goods bailed to him with his own goods? **(Ref. Para-10.4)**
9. What are the provisions under the Contract Act, 1872, when the bailee mixes the goods bailed to him with his own goods? **(Ref. Para-10.4)**
10. What is the liability of a bailor in case of defect in goods? **(Ref. Para-10.5)**
11. Write a short note on the bailor's liability in case of defect in goods. **(Ref. Para-10.5)**
12. Explain the rights and duties of the bailee. **(Ref. Para-10.4,10.6)**
13. Discuss the right and duties of the bailor. **(Ref. Para-10.5,10.7)**
14. What are the rights of a bailor. **(Ref. Para-10.7)**
15. When will a bailment be terminated? **(Ref. Para-10.8)**
16. What is a lien? Explain a general lien. **(Ref. Para-10.9)**
17. Write a short note on a particular lien. **(Ref. Para-10.9)**
18. Distinguish between a general lien and a particular lien. **(Ref. Para-10.10)**
19. The position of a finder of goods is exactly that of a bailee. Comment. **(Ref. Para-10.11)**
20. What are the duties of the finder of goods? **(Ref. Para-10.11)**
21. What are the rights of the pawnee under pledge? **(Ref. Para-10.13)**
22. What are the rights of the pawnor under pledge? **(Ref. Para-10.14)**
23. When the non-owner can create a pledge? **(Ref. Para-10.15)**
24. Distinguish between a bailment and a pledge. **(Ref. Para-10.16)**

## MULTIPLE-CHOICE QUESTIONS

1. The transfer of the ownership of goods by one person to another for some specific purpose is known as a
   (i) bailment. (iii) hypothecation.
   (ii) pledge. (iv) none of these.
2. The delivery of goods by one person to another for some specific purpose is known as a
   (i) bailment. (iii) hypothecation.
   (ii) pledge. (iv) mortgage.
3. The bailment of goods can be made by its owner of
   (i) movable goods only. (iii) both of these.
   (ii) immovable goods only. (iv) none of these.
4. A lent his car to his friend B for two days without any charges. It is a
   (i) non-gratuitous bailment. (iii) hypothecation.
   (ii) gratuitous bailment. (iv) beneficial bailment.
5. In which of the following ways, the bailment is not terminated?
   (i) Expiry of a specified period. (iii) Bailor's insolvency.
   (ii) Fulfillment of an object. (iv) Death of a bailor or a bailee.
6. Which of the following persons does not have a right of general lien?
   (i) Bankers. (iii) Finder of goods.
   (ii) Wharfingers. (iv) Factors and policy brokers.
7. Which of the following statements is true?
   (i) The lien can be exercised for the realization of time-barred debt.
   (ii) The lien also gives a right to sell the goods for the recovery of lawful charges.
   (iii) The bank cannot exercise lien on the goods belonging to the firm, against the partner's individual account.
   (iv) The bank cannot exercise lien for loans given by another branch of the same bank.
8. The delivery of goods by one person to another as a security for the repayment of a debt is known as a
   (i) bailment. (iii) pledge.
   (ii) hypothecation. (iv) mortgage.
9. In case of a default made by the pawnor in repaying the loan, the pawnee may sell the goods after giving a notice of such sale.
   (i) True, as it is pawnee's right.
   (ii) False, as pawnee can only exercise lien.
10. 'X' delivers his car to 'Y' for repair. It is the case of a ________
    (i) sale. (iii) pledge.
    (ii) bailment. (iv) mortgage.
11. 'X' delivers his car to 'Y' for repair. Here X is a
    (i) bailor. (iii) pledgee.
    (ii) bailee. (iv) pawnor.
12. 'X' delivers his car to 'Y' for repair. Here Y is a
    (i) bailor. (iii) pledgee.
    (ii) bailee. (iv) pawnor.

13. Out of following which is/are not an example of a bailment?
    (i) Immovable goods
    (ii) Money
    (iii) Movable goods
    (iv) Both (i) and (ii)
14. 'A' lets on hire his horse to 'B' for his own riding. 'B' uses the horse for driving his carriage. Here, which of the following is most appropriate?
    (i) A should terminate the bailment.
    (ii) A may terminate the bailment.
    (iii) A will not allow any other goods for use to B.
    (iv) Both (i) and (iii).
15. Under the pledge the person who pledges is known as a.........
    (i) bailor.
    (ii) bailee.
    (iii) pledgee.
    (iv) pledgor.
16. Under the pledge the person who pledges is known as a pledgor and the bailee is known as a ..........
    (i) bailor.
    (ii) bailee.
    (iii) pledgee.
    (iv) pledgor.
17. In a bailment the bailee ______________________ for the non-payment of dues.
    (i) cannot sell the goods
    (ii) retains the goods
    (iii) sue for non-payment
    (iv) all of the above
18. Is the deposit of money in a bank is a bailment?
    (i) Yes
    (ii) No
    (iii) May be
19. Whether depositing of ornaments in a bank locker is a bailment?
    (i) Yes
    (ii) No
    (iii) Yes—as it is in possession of bank
    (iv) No—as it is in possession of owner
20. Any increase of profit from the goods bailed belongs to
    (i) bailor.
    (ii) bailee.
    (iii) both.
21. The bailor is responsible for the loss caused to the bailee on account of defects in the goods bailed but unknown to him in the case of a
    (i) gratuitous bailment.
    (ii) non-gratuitous bailment.
    (iii) bailment for mutual benefit.
22. Out of following, which statement is/are correct?
    (i) Bailment may arise without a contract also.
    (ii) Bailment must be for mutual benefits of both the parties.
    (iii) Both (i) and (ii).
    (iv) None of the above.
23. Out of following which statement is/are correct?
    (i) Bailee has the right of specific lien.
    (ii) Pledge is a type of bailment.
    (iii) Both (i) and (ii).
    (iv) None of the above.

24. Out of following, which is/are duty of a bailee?
    (i) To take care.
    (ii) To take a reasonable care.
    (iii) To sell the goods.
    (iv) To retain the goods.
25. Out of following, which is/are rights of a bailee?
    (i) To indemnity.
    (ii) To claim necessary expenses.
    (iii) To delivery of goods to any one of the joint bailor of the goods.
    (iv) All of the above.

## ANSWER KEYS

| | | | | |
|---|---|---|---|---|
| **1.** (iv) | **6.** (iii) | **11.** (i) | **16.** (iii) | **21.** (ii) |
| **2.** (i) | **7.** (ii) | **12.** (ii) | **17.** (iv) | **22.** (i) |
| **3.** (i) | **8.** (iii) | **13.** (iv) | **18.** (iv) | **23.** (iii) |
| **4.** (ii) | **9.** (i) | **14.** (i) | **19.** (iv) | **24.** (ii) |
| **5.** (iii) | **10.** (ii) | **15.** (iv) | **20.** (i) | **25.** (iv) |

# 11

# The Indian Contract Act, 1872: Agency

**Learning Objectives**

*After reading this chapter, you will be able to understand:*

- What is a contract of agency-agent-principal?
- Requirement of a valid agency contract
- Difference between an agent, a sub-agent and a substituted agent
- Types of agents
- Mode of creation of an agency
- Rights and duties of an agent and a principal
- Termination of an agency

## 11.1 CONTRACT OF AGENCY

A person cannot do every business transaction by himself because of time constraint and business complexity. Therefore, business people perform many activities through another person. The person who carried out the transaction on behalf of another is known as an agent. This arrangement is known as contract of agency.

### 11.1.1 Agent

A person employed to do any act for another or to represent another in dealings with a third person is known as an agent.

### 11.1.2 Principal

The person for whom such an act is done or who is so represented is called the principal.

***Example***

Devdas appoints Paro to buy liquor on his behalf. Devdas is the principal and Paro is the agent. The relationship between Devdas and Paro is called 'an agency'.

There are two important rules on which the agency is based—

1. Whatever a person can do personally, he can do through the agent.
2. He, who does an act through another, does by himself. Consequently, all the acts of the agent are the acts of the principal.

The function of the agent is thus to bring his principal into contractual relation with the third parties. In other words, the agent is merely a connecting link between the principal and the third parties.

## 11.2 ESSENTIALS FOR A VALID AGENCY

The essentials for a valid agency or feature of an agency are discussed as under:

### 11.2.1 Agreement Between the Principal and the Agent

An agency is created by an agreement between the principal and the agent. The agency may be express or implied.

### 11.2.2 Agent Must Act in a Representative Capacity

An agent must represent his principal and act on his behalf. The agent must have the power to create a legal relationship of his principal with the third person. Thus, the agent need not be a competent person. Even a minor or a lunatic can act as the agent.

### 11.2.3 Consideration

The contract of agency can be created without consideration. The fact that the principal has agreed to be represented by the agent is a sufficient 'detriment' to the principal to support the contract of agency.

### 11.2.4 Capacity of a Party

For a valid contract of agency, the principal must be a competent person to enter into a contract. Thus, a minor or a person of unsound mind cannot appoint the agent. A major and a competent agent, working for an incompetent principal, will be personally liable for his act to the third party.

On the other hand, any person may become the agent and he need not to be competent to contract. It means even a minor or a person of unsound mind may be appointed as the agent. An incompetent agent is not liable to the principal.

## 11.3 TEST OF AN AGENCY

To determine whether a person is or is not the agent, one should ask—'Has that person the capacity to bind the principal and make him answerable to a third person by bringing him into legal relations with that third person and thus establish a privity of contract between that party and the principal?'

If the answer is yes, he is the agent otherwise not.

## 11.4 DIFFERENCE BETWEEN AN AGENT AND A SERVANT

| Agent | Servant |
|---|---|
| An agent has the authority to act on behalf of the principal and to create contractual relations between the principal and third persons. | A servant does not have the authority to bind and create contractual relations between his master and third persons. The servant acts under the authority of the master. |
| An agent, though bound to exercise his authority in accordance with all lawful instructions, which may be given to him by his principal, is not subject to the direct control and supervision of the principal. | The servant acts under the control and supervision of the master and is bound to conform to all reasonable orders given to him in course of his work. |
| An agent receives commission on the basis of work done. | A servant is paid salary or wages. |
| The principal is liable for the wrongs of his agent if they are done within the 'scope of the authority'. | A master is liable for the wrongs of his servant if they are committed in the ordinary course of the servant's employment. |
| An agent may work for several principals at the same time. | A servant usually serves only one master. |

## 11.5 DIFFERENCE BETWEEN AN AGENT AND AN INDEPENDENT CONTRACTOR

An independent contractor is to exercise his own discretion, as to the mode and time of doing work, for which he is engaged. The agent, on the other hand, is one who acts according to the instructions of the principal.

The independent contractor does not represent his employer, in dealing with the other persons, whereas the agent represents his principal in dealings with the third persons and can bind the principal by entering into contracts with other persons within the scope of his authority.

## 11.6 DIFFERENT KINDS OF AGENTS

Various kinds of agents are enumerated below.

### 11.6.1 General Agent

A general agent is one, who has the authority to do all the acts connected with a particular trade, business or employment, e.g., solicitors, brokers. The authority of the general agent is continuous unless it is terminated.

### 11.6.2 Particular Agent

A particular or a special agent is one who has the authority only to do particular transactions.

***Example***

An agent appointed to sell a particular house or to sell a particular piece of land.

### 11.6.3 Universal Agent

A universal agent is one whose authority to do all the acts which the principal can lawfully do. He has unlimited authority to bind the principal.

### 11.6.4 Mercantile Agent

A mercantile agent is one, who is authorized to sell or buy goods of the principal, in the customary course of his business as such an agent. He has the authority to consign goods for the purpose of sale or to buy goods or to raise money on the security of the goods.

### 11.6.5 Factor

A factor is the mercantile agent, entrusted with the possession of goods, who has the authority to buy, sell or otherwise deal with goods or to raise money on their security.

### 11.6.6 Broker

A broker is the mercantile agent who is employed to negotiate and make contracts for sale or purchase or goods on behalf of the principal. He is not given the possession of goods. He has no lien on goods.

### 11.6.7 Commission Agent

A commission agent is one who secures buyers for a seller of goods and sellers for a buyer of goods in return for a commission on the transaction for his labour and trouble. He buys goods in the market on behalf of his employer in his own name and on the best available terms. He may have the possession of goods or not. His position is more or less similar to that of a broker. The duties and responsibilities of the commission agent depend upon his agreement with his principal.

### 11.6.8 Auctioneer

An auctioneer is the mercantile agent who is appointed to sell goods at the public auction. He has the authority to receive the auctioned price. He has a particular lien on the goods for his charges.

### 11.6.9 Del Credere Agent

A del credere agent, also called Dubash in Madras, or Banian in North India, is an agent, who, in consideration of an extra remuneration, guarantees the solvency of the parties with whom he brings the principal into contractual relations and undertakes to indemnify the principal against any damage that may be caused by the party's failure to perform the contract. His liability like that of surety is secondary and arises only on the insolvency of the other party or other similar grounds.

## 11.7 MODE OF CREATING AN AGENCY

The relationship of the principal and the agent may be created in anyone of the following ways:

### 11.7.1 Agency by an Express Agreement—Sections 186 and 187

Normally, a contract of agency is created by an express agreement, i.e., the authority is expressly given by the principal to his agent. Such an agreement may be oral or in writing. No particular form or words is required for the appointment of the agent.

***Example***

Contract of agency created by power of attorney.

### 11.7.2 Agency by an Implied Agreement—Section 187

An agency agreement may be implied under certain circumstances from the conduct situation or relationship of the parties. The agency by implied agreement includes the following agencies also:

1. Agency by estoppel
2. Agency by holding out
3. Agency by necessity

**11.7.2.1 Agency by Estoppel** 'Estoppel' means that a person is stopped or prevented from denying the truth of a statement, which he has made. Thus, where a person by his conduct or words spoken or written leads wilfully to another person to believe that a certain person is his agent, he is estopped from denying subsequently the fact of agency. Thus, agency is created by the implication of law.

**11.7.2.2 Agency by Holding Out** An agency by holding out is a kind of agency by estoppel. In this case, there is some prior positive or affirmative conduct of the principal which indicates that a certain person has already become his agent.

**11.7.2.3 Agency of Necessity** It is some extraordinary situation that compels a person to act as the agent of some person without his consent or authority of that person. Such an agency is created as an agency by necessity.

To constitute a valid agency by necessity, the following conditions must be satisfied:

1. There must be an emergency.
2. There was a necessity to act on behalf of the principal.
3. The agent was not in a position to communicate with the principal.
4. The agent has acted honestly and in the interest of the principal.

### 11.7.3 Agency by Ratification—Sections 196 and 197

A ratification means confirmation of the acts already done. When a person does some acts on behalf of another person without his knowledge or authority. Later on, if the other person ratifies the acts done on his behalf. In such a case, an agency is created by the ratification. It is also known as an ex post facto agency. On the ratification, the principal is bound by the acts done by the agent. The ratification may be express or implied.

## 11.8 REQUISITES OF A VALID RATIFICATION—SECTIONS 198–200

To be valid, the ratification must fulfil the following conditions:

### 11.8.1 The Agent Must Expressly Contract Agent

In other words, a person must purport to act as the agent for a principal, who is in contemplation and at the time of the contract such a principal must be identifiable. If the agent acts for himself, such act cannot be ratified by the principal.

***Example***

A, without B's authority, lends B's money to C. Afterwards B accepts interest on the money from C. B's conduct implies a ratification of the loan.

### 11.8.2 The Principal Must Be in Existence at the Time of the Contract

Thus, a company cannot ratify the contracts entered into by the promoters on its behalf before its incorporation.

### 11.8.3 The Principal Must Have Contractual Capacity Both at the Time of the Contract and at the Time of the Ratification

The principle is that since ratification tantamount to prior authority, the principal must be a person competent to have authorized the transaction at its inception.

### 11.8.4 Ratification must be with Full Knowledge of Facts

No valid ratification can be made by a person whose knowledge of facts of the case is materially defective.

### 11.8.5 The Act to be Ratified Must Be Lawful and Not Void or Illegal

There can be no ratification of an illegal act or an act which is void. The act to be ratified must be valid in itself and not illegal.

***Example***

A holds a lease from B terminable on three months' notice. C, an unauthorized person, gives notice of termination to A. The notice cannot be ratified by B so as to be binding on A.

### 11.8.6 Ratification Must Be Done Within a Reasonable Time

If it is made after the expiry of a reasonable time, it will not be valid.

### 11.8.7 The Whole Act to Be Ratified

A person, ratifying any unauthorized act done on his behalf, ratifies the whole of the transaction of which such act formed a part.

### 11.8.8 Ratification Must Be Communicated

For the ratification to be effective, it must be proved that there was a communication of the ratification to the party who is sought to be bound by the act by the agent.

### 11.8.9 Ratification Can Be of the Acts Which the Principal had the Power to do

The act which the principal himself is incapable of doing cannot be ratified. Thus, a minor is not competent to act and hence minor's act cannot be ratified.

### 11.8.10 Ratification Should Not Put a Third Party to Damages

An act done by one person on behalf of another without such other person's authority which, if done with the authority, would have the effect of subjecting a third person to damages or of terminating any right or interest of a third person cannot, by ratification, be made to have such an effect.

## 11.9 HUSBAND AND WIFE

The relationship between a husband and his wife is also that of a principal and the agent. The husband is treated as a principal and the wife as his agent. The agency relation between the husband and his wife may be discussed under the following two heads:

### 11.9.1 Wife Living with Her Husband

When the wife is living with her husband, she has implied an authority to buy the articles of household necessaries. The following conditions should be satisfied for treating the wife as an agent of the husband:

1. The husband and wife are living together in a domestic establishment of their own.
2. The wife should be in charge of the domestic establishment.
3. The wife must have purchased articles or goods suitable to the style in which the husband chooses to live.

However, the husband can escape his liability if he proves that:

1. He has forbidden his wife expressly to buy goods on credit. The tradesman is also expressly forbidden to supply goods on credit to his wife.
2. The wife was supplied with sufficient articles or goods.
3. The wife was supplied necessary funds to purchase the necessaries.
4. The goods purchased were not necessaries.

### 11.9.2 Wife Living Apart from Her Husband

Where the wife is living apart without any fault on her part then she is legally entitled to receive maintenance from her husband. If the husband does not provide her maintenance, the wife has implied an authority to purchase the necessaries of her life and the husband is bound to pay for the same.

**Case Study**

R is the wife of P. She purchased some sarees on credit from Q. Q demanded the amount from P. P refused. Q filed a suit against P for the said amount. Decide in the light of provisions of the Indian Contract Act, 1872, whether Q would succeed?

## 11.10 EXTENT OF AN AGENT'S AUTHORITY

An agent's authority means the capacity of the agent to bind his principal. The acts of the agent, done within the scope of his authority, bind the principal.

Such an authority of the agent to bind the principal may be:

1. Actual or real authority.
2. Ostensible or apparent authority.
3. Authority in an emergency.

### 11.10.1 Actual Authority—Section 186

An actual authority means that authority which has been really delegated to the agent. The authority of the agent may be express or implied.

An authority is said to be express when it is given by words spoken or written. An authority is said to be implied when it is to be inferred from the circumstances of the case or the ordinary course of dealing between the parties.

The principal is bound by the act of the agent done within his express or implied authority.

***Example***

A owns a shop in Dhanbad, living himself in Calcutta and visiting the shop occasionally. The shop is managed by B and he is in the habit of ordering goods from in the name of A for the purposes of the shop and of paying for them out of A's funds with A's knowledge. B has an implied authority from A to order goods from C in the name of A for the purpose of the shop.

### 11.10.2 Ostensible or Apparent Authority

When the agent is employed for a particular business, persons dealing with him can presume that he has the authority to do all such acts as are necessary for such a business. Such an authority of the agent is called an ostensible or an apparent authority. The ostensible or an apparent authority is the authority of the agent as it appears to others. It often coincides with the actual authority.

### 11.10.3 Authority in Emergency—Section 189

The agent has an authority, in an emergency, to do all such acts for the purpose of protecting his principal from loss as would be done by a person of ordinary prudence in his own case under the similar circumstances. When the agent has acted beyond the authority in emergency, the principal is bound by the act of the agent.

### 11.10.4 When the Agent Exceeds His Authority

When the agent acts beyond the scope of his authority, he will be personally liable and the principal cannot be held liable.

***Example***

A consigns goods to B at Calcutta, with directions to send them immediately to C at Cuttack. B may sell the goods at Calcutta if they will not bear the journey to Cuttack without spoiling.

## 11.11 DELEGATION OF AUTHORITY BY AN AGENT

### 11.11.1 Delegation of Authority—Section 190

The rule is that the agent who has obtained power from the principal to act must act himself. He is not entitled to delegate his authority to another person without the consent of his principal. The rule is expressed in Latin maxim—*'Delegatus non-protest delegare'*, i.e., a delegate cannot further delegate. It simply means that delegated powers cannot further be delegated. One cannot delegate that which one has himself undertaken to do. So, the agent cannot, without the permission of the principal, delegate his authority and ask some other person to do the thing.

The agent cannot lawfully employ another to perform acts which he has expressly or impliedly undertaken to perform personally.

### 11.11.2 Exceptions to the Rule of '*Delegatus Non-protest Delegare*'

In the following exceptional cases, the agent can delegate his authority:

1. Where the principal is aware of the intention of the agent.
2. Where there is an emergency, or unforseen circumstances.
3. Where the nature of the authority requires it.
4. Where the act is purely ministerial.
5. Where the power of the agent to delegate can be inferred.
6. Where the principal permits the appointment of a sub-agent.
7. Where the custom of trade permits delegation.

## 11.12 SUB-AGENT—SECTION 191

A 'sub-agent' is a person employed by and acting under the control of the original agent in the business of the agency. The sub-agent is the agent of the original agent. As between the original agent and the sub-agent, the relationship is that of the principal and the agent.

### 11.12.1 Where a Sub-agent Is Properly Appointed—Section 192

Where the sub-agent is properly appointed, the principal is, so far as regards the third persons, represented by the sub-agent as is bound by and responsible for the acts as if he were the agent originally appointed by the principal.

The agent is responsible to the principal for the acts of the sub-agent. The sub-agent is responsible for his acts to the agent but not to the principal except in case of fraud or wilful wrong.

### 11.12.2 Where a Sub-agent Is Not Properly Appointed—Section 193

Where an agent, without having an authority to do so, has appointed a person to act as a sub-agent stands towards such person in the relation of a principal to the agent and is responsible for his acts both to the principal and to third persons; the principal is not represented by or responsible for the acts of the person so employed, nor is that person responsible to the principal.

## 11.13 SUBSTITUTED AGENT OR CO-AGENT—SECTION 194

A substituted agent is an agent named by the original agent to act on behalf of principal. Thus, the substituted agent is the agent appointed by the original agent to act for the principal. The substituted agent acts under the direct control of the principal and not under the original agent.

The agent is not concerned with the efficiency of the substitute.

***Example***

A directs B, his solicitor, to sell his estate by auction and to employ an auctioneer for the purpose. B names C, an auctioneer, to conduct the sale. C is not a sub-agent but is A's agent for the conduct of the sale.

In selecting a co-agent for his principal, an agent is bound to exercise the same amount of discretion as a man of ordinary prudence would exercise in his own case; and if he does this, he is not responsible to the principal for the act or negligence of the co-agent.

## 11.14 DIFFERENCE BETWEEN A SUB-AGENT AND A SUBSTITUTED AGENT

1. The sub-agent does the work under the direct control of the agent whereas the substituted agent works under the instructions of the principal.
2. There is no privity of contract between the sub-agent and the principal and therefore:
   a. the sub-agent cannot sue the principal for his remuneration and
   b. the sub-agent is not directly answerable to the principal but both the principal and the sub agent can sue the agent.
3. It is the agent who is responsible to the principal for the acts of the sub-agent but the agent is not responsible to the principal for any act or negligence of the substituted agent.
4. The original agent, who names the substituted agent, drops out completely from the transactions, whereas the agent, who appoints the sub-agent, still continues to function and is still answerable.

## 11.15 DUTIES OF AN AGENT

Duties of an agent are the rights of the principal. The duties of an agent may be broadly classified under the following heads:

### 11.15.1 Duty to Follow the Instruction of Principal—Section 211

The agent is bound to conduct the business of his principal according to the directions given by the principal. In the absence of any such directions according to the custom which prevails at the place where the agent conducts such a business. When the agent acts otherwise, if any loss be sustained, he must make it good to his principal and if any profit accrues, he must account for.

***Example***

B, a broker in whose business it is not the custom to sell on credit, sells goods of A on credit to C, whose credit at the time was very high. C, before payment, becomes insolvent. B must make good the loss to A.

### 11.15.2 Duty to Carry Work with Care and Skill—Section 211

The agent is bound to conduct the business of the agency with reasonable care and skill. The standard of reasonable care required from the agent depends upon the nature of the business and the circumstances of each case. The agent is required to make compensations to his principal in respect of the direct consequences of his own neglect, want of skill or misconduct but not in respect of loss or damage which is indirectly or remotely caused by such neglect, want of skill or misconduct.

***Example***

A, air agent for the sale of goods, having authority to sell on credit, sells to B on credit without making the proper and usual enquiries as to the solvency of B. B at the time of such sale is insolvent. A must make compensation to his principal in respect of any loss thereby sustained.

### 11.15.3 Duty to Render Accounts to the Principal—Section 213

The agent is bound to render the proper account to his principal on demand. It is the absolute duty of the agent.

### 11.15.4 Duty to Communicate with the Principal—Section 214

It is the duty of the agent in cases of difficulty to make reasonable efforts to communicate with his principal and to obtain his instruction.

### 11.15.5 Duty Not to Deal on His Own Account—Section 215

The role of the agent is fiduciary in nature and therefore the agent must conduct his business in good faith. He should not deal on his own account. If the agent deals on his account without the principal's consent or without full disclosure, the principal may cancel the contract.

***Example***

A directs B to sell A's estate. B, on looking over the estate before selling it, finds a mine on the estate which is unknown to A. B informs A that he wishes to buy the estate for himself but conceals the discovery of the mine. A allows B to buy, in ignorance of the existence of the mine. A, on discovering that B knew of the mine at the time he bought the estate, may either repudiate or adopt the sale at his option.

### 11.15.6 Duty Not to Make Secret Profit—Section 216

If the agent, without the knowledge of his principal, deals in the business of the agency on his own account, instead of on account of his principal, the principal is entitled to claim from the agent, any benefit which may have resulted to him from the transaction.

### 11.15.7 Duty to Pay Sums Received for the Principal—Sections 217 and 218

It is the duty of the agent to his principal, all monies received on his behalf. However, the agent can deduct lawful expenses he has incurred for the agency work and the commission from this amount.

### 11.15.8 Duty to Protect Interests of the Principal in Case of His Death or Insolvency—Section 209

On the death or insanity of the principal, the agent is terminated. However, in such a case it becomes the duty of the agent to take all the reasonable steps to protect the interest of the principal.

### 11.15.9 Duty Not to Delegate—Section 190

The agent cannot delegate his authority to perform his act in express or implied manner unless the custom of trade or the nature of the agency so requires.

**Case Study**

P appoints A as his agent to sell his estate. A, on looking over the estate before selling it, finds the existence of a good quality Granite-Mine on the estate, which is unknown to P. A buys the estate himself after informing P that he (A) wishes to buy the estate for himself but conceals the existence of Granite-Mine. P allows A to buy the estate in ignorance of the existence of Granite-Mine. State, giving reasons in brief, the rights of P and the principal against A, the agent.

What would be your answer if A had informed P about the existence of Granite-Mine before he purchased the estate but after 2 months, he sold the estate at a profit of ₹ 1 lac?

**Case Study**

Mr. Ahuja of Delhi engaged Mr. Singh as his agent to buy a house in west extension area. Mr. Singh bought a house for ₹ 20 lakhs in the name of a nominee and then purchased it himself for ₹ 24 lakhs. He then sold the same house to Mr. Ahuja for ₹ 26 lakhs. Mr. Ahuja later comes to know the mischief of Mr. Singh and tries to recover the excess amount paid to Mr. Singh. Is he entitled to recover any amount from Mr. Singh? If so, how much can he recover? Explain.

## 11.16 RIGHTS OF AN AGENT

Rights of the agent are the duties of the principal. The rights of the agent may be discussed under the following heads:

### 11.16.1 Right to a Retainer—Section 217

The agent may retain out of any sums received on account of the principal in the business of the agency, all money due to him in respect of the advances made or the expenses properly incurred by him in conducting such business and also such remuneration as may be payable to him for acting as the agent.

### 11.16.2 Right to Receive the Remuneration—Sections 219 and 220

The agent has the right to receive the agreed remuneration from the principal. If the remuneration is not fixed, the agent is entitled to receive reasonable remuneration. The agent is entitled to receive the remuneration only when it becomes due. Usually, the remuneration becomes due when the agent completes the work undertaken.

The agent who is guilty of misconduct in the business of the agency is not entitled to any remuneration in respect of that part of the business, which he has misconducted.

### 11.16.3 Right of Lien—Section 221

In the absence of any contract to the contrary, the agent is entitled to retain the goods, papers and other property, whether movable or immovable, of the principal received by him, until the amount due to himself for commission, disbursements and services in respect of the same has been paid or accounted for, to him.

### 11.16.4 Right to Be Indemnified—Section 222

The principal is bound to indemnify the agent against the consequences of all the lawful acts within his authority.

***Example***

A employs B to beat C and agrees to indemnify him against all consequences of the act. B thereupon beats C and has to pay damages to C for so doing. A is not liable to indemnify B for those damages.

### 11.16.5 Right of Compensation—Section 225

The agent has the right to receive compensation for the loss suffered due to the principal's negligence or want of skill.

## 11.17 POSITION OF A PRINCIPAL AND AN AGENT IN RELATION TO THIRD PARTIES

If the agent acts within the scope of his authority, the principal is bound by the act of the agent. The position of the principal as regards the contracts made by the agent with the third party may be discussed under following heads:

1. Where the agent contracts for the named principal.
2. Where the agent contracts for the unnamed principal.
3. Where the agent contracts for the undisclosed principal.

## 11.18 PRINCIPAL RELATIONSHIP WHERE AN AGENT CONTRACTS FOR A NAMED PRINCIPAL

The position of the principal for the acts of the agents where the name and existence of the principal are disclosed is as follows:

### 11.18.1 Acts of the Agents Are Within His Authority—Section 226

The principal is bound by all lawful acts of the agent, which are done within the scope of his authority. It means the act of the agent is the act of the principal.

### 11.18.2 Agent Act in Excess His Authority—Section 227

The principal is liable only for the acts done within the authority. The principal's liability for the work done by the agent beyond his authority may be discussed under the following two points:

**11.18.2.1 When Work of an Agent Is Separable** When the agent does some work beyond the authority, which is separable from the authorized work, the principal is bound by the authorized work of the agent.

**11.18.2.2 When Work is Not Separable—Section 228** When the agent does some work beyond the authority, which is not separable from the authorized work, the principal is not bound by whole of the work. He may cancel the whole transaction.

### 11.18.3 Consequences of Notice Given to Agent—Section 229

Any notice given to or information obtained by the agent shall have the same legal consequences as if it had been given to or obtained by the principal. This means that the knowledge of the agent is the knowledge of the principal.

### 11.18.4 Principal Inducing Belief that Agent's Unauthorized Acts Are Authorized—Section 237

The principal is liable for the unauthorized acts of the agent if the principal, by his conduct, has created an impression on the third party that the agent has the authority to do such an act.

### 11.18.5 Misrepresentation or Fraud by an Agent—Section 238

The principal is liable for the misrepresentation or fraud committed by his agent while acting in the course of his business. However, the principal is not liable for any misrepresentation or fraud of the agent which does not fall within the agent's authority.

## 11.19 PRINCIPAL'S RELATION WHERE AN AGENT CONTRACTS FOR AN UNNAMED PRINCIPAL

When the agent contracts with the third party after disclosing the fact that he is the agent but does not disclose the name of the principal, in such a case, the principal is known as unnamed principal. The position of the agent contracting for and on behalf of an unnamed principal is as under:

1. In case of the agent contracting for a principal is still liable for the contract of the agents unless, of course, there is a trade custom or a term of express or implied to the effect which makes the agent personally liable.
2. In such a case, where the name of the principal is not disclosed, the third party who contracts with the agent, knowing that there is a principal, cannot sue the agent.
3. If the agent declines to disclose the identity of the principal, when asked by the third party, he will become personally liable on the contract.

## 11.20 PRINCIPAL'S RELATION WHERE AN AGENT CONTRACTS FOR AN UNDISCLOSED PRINCIPAL

In certain cases, the agent not only conceals the name of the principal but also the fact that he is the agent. This is known as the 'doctrine of undisclosed principal'. In such cases, the agent conveys to a third person an impression that he is contracting as a principal himself, i.e., independent party.

In such a case, the relationship between the principal, agent and third party may be discussed as under:

### 11.20.1 Position of an Agent

As the agent has contracted in his own name, he is personally liable to the third party. He has all the rights of the agent as against the principal. He can be sued by the third party. He can sue the third party.

### 11.20.2 Position of a Principal

The principal may obtain performance of the contract, subject to the rights and obligations, subsisting between the agent and the third party. He can be sued by the third party. An undisclosed principal cannot intervene if some express or implied terms of the contract exclude him from doing so.

### 11.20.3 Position of a Third Party

On discovery of the fact that there is a principal, the third party may file a suit either against the principal or agent or both. If the third party decides to file a suit against the principal, he must allow the principal, the benefit of all the payments received by him from the agent.

## 11.21 PERSONAL LIABILIES OF AN AGENT

Usually, the agent cannot personably be liable for the contract entered into by him on behalf of the principal. However, the agent is personally responsible in the following cases.

### 11.21.1 When the Agent Acts for a Foreign Principal—Section 230

Where the contract is made by the agent for the sale or purchase of goods for the principal residing abroad, in such a case, it is presumed that the agent is personally liable.

### 11.21.2 When the Agent Acts for an Undisclosed Principal—Section 230

Where the agent acts for an undisclosed principal, he is personally liable, though the principal, on being discovered by the third party is also liable.

### 11.21.3 When Agent Acts for an Incompetent Principal—Section 230

When the principal is incompetent to enter into the contract, e.g., in the case where the principal is a minor or where the principal cannot be sued, e.g., where he is a foreign sovereign, the agent is personally liable as the credit is presumed to have been given to the agent and not to the principal.

### 11.21.4 When the Contract Expressly Provides

In case the agent agrees to do, he becomes personally responsible.

### 11.21.5 When the Agent Acts for a Principal Not in Existence

When the agent contracts for the principal who is fictitious or non-existent, in such a case, the agent is personally liable. For example—The promoters of a company, yet to be incorporated, enter into the contract on behalf of the company. In such cases, the company, i.e., the principal is not in existence till it is finally incorporated.

### 11.21.6 When the Agent Signs a Contract in His Own Name

The agent when he signs the contract in his own name but without any qualifications, though he may be known to be the agent, is taken to contract personally.

### 11.21.7 When the Agent Acts Beyond His Authority

When the agent exceeds his authority and the principal does not ratify such acts of the agent, the agent in such cases is personally responsible to the third parties.

### 11.21.8 Where There Is a Misrepresentation or Fraud by Agent

The agent is personally responsible if he makes misrepresentations or frauds acting in the course of the business of the principal.

### 11.21.9 Where the Trade, Usage or Custom Makes the Agent Personally Liable

If a trade, usage or custom make the agent personally liable, he is so liable unless there is the contract to the contrary.

### 11.21.10 Where Authority Is Coupled with an Interest

The agent has *locus standi* to sue in his own name in all cases where he has interest in the subject matter of the agency.

### 11.21.11 Pretended Agent—Sections 235 and 236

A person who untruly represents himself to be the authorized agent of another and induces a third person to enter into the contract or otherwise deals with him is called a pretended agent.

If the pretended agent includes the third party to enter into the contract with him then he is personally liable to the third party for the loss of damage suffered due to such dealing.

However, if the principal ratifies the acts of the agent then he will not be personally liable. Again if the third party already knew about the truth then the agent is not liable.

In cases where the agent is personally liable, a person dealing with him may hold either him or his principal or both of them liable.

## 11.22 TERMINATION OF AN AGENCY

A termination of an agency means the end of a relationship of the principal and his agent. The termination of the agency may broadly be discussed under the following two heads:

1. The termination of the agency by the act of parties.
2. The termination of the agency by the operation of law.

## 11.23 TERMINATION OF AN AGENCY BY THE ACT OF PARTIES

The agency relationship may be terminated by the act of parties. The agency can be terminated by either the principal or the agent in the following manner:

### 11.23.1 By an Agreement

The agency can be created by an agreement in the same way it can be terminated by the agreement.

### 11.23.2 By Revocation of an Authority

The principal may revoke the authority given to his agent at any time before the authority has been exercised so as to bind the principal. The principal cannot revoke the authority given to his agent after the authority has been partly exercised.

### 11.23.3 By Renunciation of Agency by Agent

The agency is terminated if the agent renounces the business of the agency. A renunciation means giving up.

***Note:***

For a revocation and renunciation of an agency—Sections 205–207

1. A reasonable notice must be given of such revocation or renunciation otherwise the damage thereby must be made good to the one by the other.
2. The revocation and renunciation may be express or may be implied in the conduct of the principal or the agent, respectively.
3. Where there is an express or in implied contract that the agency should be continued for any period of time, the principal must make compensation to the agent or the agent to the principal as the case may be for any previous revocation or renunciation of the agency without a sufficient cause (Section 205).

## 11.24 TERMINATION OF AN AGENCY BY THE OPERATION OF LAW

The agency relationship may be terminated by the operation of law in the following manner:

### 11.24.1 By Performance

When the transaction is completed, the agency terminates automatically.

### 11.24.2 By Efflux of Time

Where the agency is for a fixed period of time, it terminates on the expiry of that time. It is not important whether the work is completed or not.

### 11.24.3 By Death or Insanity

Death or insanity of the principal or the agent terminates the agency.

### 11.24.4 By Insolvency

The agency is terminated when the principal is declared insolvent. An insolvent cannot enter into the contract.

### 11.24.5 On Destruction of Subject Matter

The agency is terminated when the subject matter of the contract of agency is destroyed.

### 11.24.6 On Winding Up of Company

The agency is also terminated when the principal or agent is the company and it goes in winding up.

### 11.24.7 On Principal Becoming an Alien Enemy

The agency is terminated when the principal and the agent are citizens of two different countries and war breaks out between these two countries.

## 11.25 IRREVOCABLE AGENCY

An irrevocable agency means an agency which cannot be revoked by the principal. The agency is considered as the irrevocable in the following cases.

### 11.25.1 Where the Agency Is Coupled with an Interest

Where the agency is coupled with interest which is a case where the agent has interest in the subject matter of the agency. In this case, the agency cannot be terminated except where there is an express provision. The agency coupled with an interest does not come to an end on the death, insanity or the insolvency of the principal.

The interest of the agent must exist at the time of creation of the agency. Moreover, the interest of the agent must be substantial and not ordinary. It must be over and above his remuneration as the agent.

### 11.25.2 Where an Agent Has Incurred a Personal Liability

Where the agent contracts in his own name and makes himself a personal liability for his act. In such case, the agency becomes irrevocable.

***Example***

'A' appoints 'B' as his agent and 'B' purchases, as per the orders of 'A', 'rice' in his personal name. A cannot revoke the authority.

### 11.25.3 Where an Agent Has Partly Exercised an Authority

Where the agent has partly exercised the authority, the authority cannot be revoked.

***Example***

'A' appoints 'B' as his agent to procure 10 bags of rice and 'B' procures in the name of 'A' then 'A' cannot revoke his authority.

## LIST OF LANDMARK JUDGEMENTS

1. ***Grover and Grover vs Mathews (1910)***
   The principal should be competent to contract at the time of the act of the agent. If it is so then a valid ratification can take place.
2. ***Mulchand vs State of M. P. (1968)***
   The ratification by the principal is possible where the act must be lawful and void. The act *void-ab-initio* cannot be ratified.
3. ***Badriprasad vs State of M. P. (1966)***
   Once the action of the agent is ratified by the principal, it relates back to the date of action of the agent and not from the date of ratification, i.e., it tantamount to prior authority.
4. ***Debenham vs Mellon (1880)***
   The married woman living with her husband is presumed to have powers to pledge credit of her husband for necessaries.
5. ***Green vs Barlett (1863)***
   The agent is entitled to commission as long as the work is done due to his efforts.
6. ***Ryan vs Pilkington (1969)***
   The principal is bound by the agent's acts done within his implied authority.
7. ***Bawdwn vs London Insurance Co. (1892)***
   A knowledge of the agent is the knowledge of the principal.
8. ***London County Freehold and Leasehold Properties Ltd vs Bakerlay Property and Insurance Co. (1936)***
   The principal is liable for the misrepresentation or fraud committed by his agent while acting in the course of his business.
9. ***United Commercial Bank vs Hem Chandra Sarkar (1990)***
   The important distinction between the bailee and the agent is that the bailee does not represent the bailor. The bailee has no power to make contracts on the bailor's behalf. While the agent represents the principal.
10. ***Swarswati Devi vs Moti Lal (1982)***
    Where the commission was payable to an estate agent as and when he introduces a ready and willing customer, the agent becomes entitled to his commission when such a customer was introduced even if the principal refused to sign the contract.
11. ***Armstrong vs Jackson (1977)***
    If the agent deals on his account without the principal's consent and without disclosing full facts to the principal, the principal may cancel the contract.
12. ***Timblo Irmaos Ltd vs Jorge A. M. Sequeira (1977)***
    The power to sell will not authorize the agent to borrow money or to pledge goods unless clear authority in this regard is granted to the agent.

13. ***Smart vs Sandars (1948)***
For the creation of the agency coupled with interest, the interest of the agent must be existing at the time of creation of the agency.
14. ***Debenham vs Mellon (1880)***
The husband is bound to pay for the credit purchase made by his wife, only if husband and wife are living together in a domestic establishment of their own and the wife should be in charge of the domestic establishment.
15. ***Lilley vs Double Day (1881)***
If the agent fails to act according to the direction or customs then he is liable to the principal for any loss suffered by the principal due to such an act of the agent.
16. ***Williams vs North China Insurance Co. (1876)***
On the ratification, the principal is bound by the acts already done by the agent.
17. ***Keighley Maxted and Co. vs Durant (1901)***
The ratification is valid and effective when the agent has acted on behalf of the principal.
18. ***Kelner vs Baxter (1866)***
For a valid ratification, the principal must be competent to contract and in existence at the time of contract by the agent.
19. ***Anderson vs Ramsay and Co. (1903)***
It is the duty of an agent not to make secret profit. If the agent makes secret profit, the principal can claim such a benefit from the agent.

## TEST YOUR KNOWLEDGE

1. Every person has the right to employ an agent lawfully. Comment. **(Ref. Para-11.1)**
2. What are the essentials of a valid contract of an agency? **(Ref. Para-11.2)**
3. Consideration is not required for creating a contract of agency. Comment. **(Ref. Para-11.2)**
4. What is the real test of an agency? **(Ref. Para-11.3)**
5. Distinguish between an agent and an independent contract. **(Ref. Para-11.5)**
6. Distinguish between a special agent and a general agent. **(Ref. Para-11.6)**
7. Write a short note on different kinds of agents. **(Ref. Para-11.6)**
8. Explain the various modes of creation of agency. **(Ref. Para-11.7)**
9. Write a short note on the doctrine of 'holding out'. **(Ref. Para-11.7)**
10. Write a short note on the agency by ratification. **(Ref. Para-11.7)**
11. What do you understand by the agency by ratification? What is the effect of ratification? **(Ref. Para-11.7,11.8)**
12. The ratification of agency is valid even if the knowledge of the principal is materially defective. Comment. **(Ref. Para-11.8)**
13. The wife is always assumed to be an agent of her husband. Is it a correct statement? **(Ref. Para-11.9)**
14. Comment. He, who acts through an agent is himself acting. **(Ref. Para-11.10)**
15. *'Delegatus non-protest delegare'*. Explain the Latin maxim. **(Ref. Para-11.10)**
16. Distinguish between an agent and a servant. **(Ref. Para-11.4)**
17. Discuss the nature and extent of the authority of an agent. **(Ref. Para-11.10)**
18. Write a short note on a sub-agent. **(Ref. Para-11.12)**

19. An agent cannot appoint a sub-agent. Comment. **(Ref. Para-11.12)**
20. Write a short note on a substituted agent. **(Ref. Para-11.13)**
21. Distinguish between a sub-agent and a substituted agent. **(Ref. Para-11.14)**
22. State the duties of an agent to his principal. **(Ref. Para-11.15)**
23. What are the rights of an agent? **(Ref. Para-11.16)**
24. Discuss the provisions in respect of remuneration of the agent. **(Ref. Para-11.16)**
25. What will be the position of the principal where the agent contracts for the named principal? **(Ref. Para-11.18)**
26. What will be the position of the principal where the agent contracts for the unnamed principal? **(Ref. Para-11.19)**
27. Write a short note on an undisclosed principal. **(Ref. Para-11.20)**
28. When will an agent be personally liable? **(Ref. Para-11.21)**
29. Describe the various modes by which the authority of an agent may be terminated? **(Ref. Para-11.22,11.23,11.24)**
30. Write a short note on an irrevocable agency. **(Ref. Para-11.25)**

## MULTIPLE-CHOICE QUESTIONS

1. A person appointed to contract on behalf of another person is known as a/an
   (i) principal.
   (ii) agent.
   (iii) independent contractor.
   (iv) servant.
2. A person who appoints another person to do work on his behalf is known as a/an
   (i) principal.
   (ii) agent.
   (iii) independent contractor.
   (iv) servant.
3. Which of the following is not an essential element of a valid agency?
   (i) Principal must be competent to contract.
   (ii) Agent must be competent to contract.
   (iii) Both of above.
   (iv) None of the above.
4. Which of the following is not an essential element of a valid agency?
   (i) Agent must act in representative capacity.
   (ii) There must be express or implied agreement.
   (iii) Both of above.
   (iv) None of the above.
5. A single agent can be appointed by more than one person by a power of attorney signed jointly by all the principals.
   (i) True
   (ii) False
6. The wife is considered to be an implied agent of the husband for the purpose of buying household necessaries on credit.
   (i) True
   (ii) False

7. A mercantile agent to whom the possession of the goods is given for the purpose of selling the same is known as a/an
   (i) broker.
   (ii) factor.
   (iii) commission agent.
   (iv) insurance agent.
8. Which of the following agents cannot exercise a right of general lien?
   (i) A factor.
   (ii) A banker.
   (iii) An auctioneer.
   (iv) All of these.
9. Which of the following statements is not true?
   (i) An agent is not personally liable for the acts done by him within the scope of his authority.
   (ii) Principal is liable for wrongful acts of his agent, done within the scope of his authority.
   (iii) Both of above.
   (iv) None of the above.
10. Which of the following statements is not true?
   (i) An independent contractor is personally liable for the acts done by him while working for his employer.
   (ii) A bailor is personally liable for the acts of a bailee, done during the period of bailment.
   (iii) Both of above.
   (iv) None of the above.
11. Which of the following statements is not true?
   (i) An agent should conduct business according to his principals's instructions.
   (ii) An agent is liable to account for any secret profit made by him.
   (iii) Both of above.
   (iv) None of the above.
12. Which of the following statements is not true?
   (i) An agent is not liable for any misinformation given to the principal.
   (ii) An agent should not deal on his own account.
   (iii) Both of above.
   (iv) None of the above.
13. The agent becomes entitled to receive his remuneration on the fulfillment of which of the following conditions?
   (i) When the act undertaken by the agent is completed.
   (ii) When the concluded transaction is the result of the agent's services and efforts.
   (iii) Both (i) and (ii) above.
   (iv) None of these, as remuneration is payable without any condition.
14. Which of the following is not a right of the agent?
   (i) Right of lien.
   (ii) Right to be indemnified.
   (iii) Right to remuneration.
   (iv) Right to make secret profits.
15. A person appointed by the original agent to act in the business of the agency but under the control of the original agent is known as a/an
   (i) agent.
   (ii) sub-agent.
   (iii) substituted agent.
   (iv) del credere agent.

16. A person, appointed by the original agent, to act for and under the control of the principal, is known
    (i) agent.
    (ii) sub-agent.
    (iii) substituted agent.
    (iv) del credere agent.
17. A power of attorney, executed by several persons jointly, in favour of one person is valid.
    (i) True, as there can be more than one principals of one agent.
    (ii) False, as there can be only one principal of one agent at a time.
18. Where one person allows another person to assume an appearance of authority, to act on his behalf, such a position is known as
    (i) express authority.
    (ii) implied authority.
    (iii) ostensible authority.
    (iv) none of these.
19. Which of the following statements is not true?
    (i) Principal is liable for fraud committed by his agent, acting in the course of his business.
    (ii) Principal is bound by the agent's acts done in the scope of his authority.
    (iii) Both of above.
    (iv) None of the above.
20. Which of the following statements is not true?
    (i) Authority given to sell goods, also authorizes the agent to borrow money and pledge the goods.
    (ii) Authority given to borrow money makes the principal liable, even if the agent borrows beyond the authorized limits.
    (iii) Both of above.
    (iv) None of the above.
21. Where the agent contracts with a third party, without disclosing the name and existence of his principal, in such a case on knowing about the principal, the third party may file a suit against the
    (i) principal alone.
    (ii) agent alone.
    (iii) both of them jointly.
    (iv) either the agent or the principal or both.
22. Where the agent contracts for a principal, who is not competent to contract, in such a case the agent is
    (i) personally liable.
    (ii) not personally liable.
    (iii) exceeding authority.
    (iv) none of these.
23. In which of the following cases, the agency is not terminated?
    (i) Completion of agency business.
    (ii) Death of the principal or agent.
    (iii) Insolvency of the principal.
    (iv) Agent exceeding the given authority.
24. In case, the principal revokes the agency, he
    (i) remains bound by the agent's acts, done prior to revocation.
    (ii) is not bound by the agent's acts, done prior to revocation.
    (iii) is bound by the agent's subsequent acts also.
    (iv) liable to punishment, as revocation is illegal.
25. The third party, who contracts with an agent without any knowledge of termination of the agent's authority, can enforce the contract against the principal.
    (i) True
    (ii) False

26. Which of the following agency is irrevocable?
    (i) Agency for a fixed period.
    (ii) Agency for a single transaction.
    (iii) Agency coupled with an interest.
    (iv) Continuing agency.
27. 'A' owns a shop. 'B' manages the shop. 'A' as owner orders purchases. 'B' also as the
    (i) Yes
    (ii) No
    (iii) Cannot say.
28. What is the name given to an agency which cannot be terminated?
    (i) Revocable agency.
    (ii) Agency for a single transaction.
    (iii) Irrevocable agency.
    (iv) Agency created in necessity.
29. Substituted agent is appointed by whom?
    (i) Government.
    (ii) Court.
    (iii) Principal.
    (iv) Agent.
30. A person appointed by the original agent to act in the business of the agency but under the control of the original agent is known as a/an
    (i) agent.
    (ii) sub-agent.
    (iii) *del credere* agent.
    (iv) substituted agent.

## ANSWER KEYS

| | | | | | |
|---|---|---|---|---|---|
| **1.** (ii) | **6.** (i) | **11.** (iv) | **16.** (iii) | **21.** (iv) | **26.** (iii) |
| **2.** (i) | **7.** (ii) | **12.** (i) | **17.** (i) | **22.** (i) | **27.** (i) |
| **3.** (ii) | **8.** (iii) | **13.** (iii) | **18.** (iii) | **23.** (iv) | **28.** (iii) |
| **4.** (iv) | **9.** (iv) | **14.** (iv) | **19.** (iv) | **24.** (i) | **29.** (iii) |
| **5.** (i) | **10.** (ii) | **15.** (ii) | **20.** (i) | **25.** (i) | **30.** (ii) |

# 12

# The Partnership Act, 1932

**Learning Objectives**

*After reading this chapter, you will be able to understand:*

- What is partnership and how it is different from other forms of business organization?
- Procedure for registration of partnership
- Types of partner
- Rights and duties of a partner
- Re-constitution and dissolution of a firm and formalities related thereto

## 12.1 APPLICABILITY OF THE ACT

This act extends to the whole of India except the State of Jammu and Kashmir. It came into force w.e.f. 1 October 1932.

## 12.2 DEFINITION OF PARTNERSHIP—SECTION 4

A partnership is the relation between two or more persons who have agreed to share the profits of a business, carried out by all or any of them acting for all.

Persons who have entered into the partnership with one another are called individually 'partner' and collectively 'firm', and the name under which their business is carried on is called 'firm name'.

## 12.3 ESSENTIAL CHARACTERISTICS OF PARTNERSHIP

### 12.3.1 Agreement

The relation between the partners is created by an agreement. As per Section 5, the relation of partnership arises from a contract and not from status. If the agreement between the partners is in writing, it is called as partnership deed. It may be expressing (i.e., oral or written) or implied. The agreement must be lawful. The partnership agreement should not necessarily be in writing. Prior to the Indian Partnership Act, 1932, the provisions relating to partnership were contained in the Indian Contract Act, 1872 and therefore, all the elements of the contract are applicable to the partnership agreement.

### 12.3.2 Number of Persons

There must be at least two persons. All the persons must be competent to enter into a contract. A minor cannot become a partner of the firm. A person of unsound mind cannot become a partner in the firm.

***Example***

A, minor, and B, major, agree to carry on a cloth business in partnership. It is not a valid partnership. Since A is a minor, not capable to entering in to contract.

### 12.3.3 Maximum Number of Persons

In case of a banking business, the maximum number of partners is 10. In case of other business, the maximum number of partners is 20. If the number of partners exceeds this limit, the partnership will become an illegal association (as per Companies Act 1956).

### 12.3.4 Business

The partnership can be formed to carry on business and not for social welfare or charitable activity. The business includes every lawful trade, occupation and profession. If no business is carried on, there is no partnership. The word ‘carry on business’ implies to the presence of a series of business transactions. Single or isolated activity cannot be considered within the meaning of a business.

### 12.3.5 Sharing or Profit

There must be a sharing of profits. The requirement of the sharing of profits does not require that all the partners must share the profits equally. It is possible for the partners to agree to share the profits in such a ratio as they may mutually agree. However, in the absence of an agreement between the partners, all the partners shall share the profit equally. The sharing of profit also includes sharing of losses.

### 12.3.6 Mutual Agency

There must be a mutual agency. The mutual agency means the principle—agent relation. It means any one partner can act for the others and bind them as well as to the firm by his act. The partner of a firm is not an employee or officer of the firm.

***Example***

A and B are partners. A purchased the raw material for the business of a firm in the ordinary course of business. Here, B is bound by the act of A as well as the firm is also liable for the purchased made by A.

**Case Study**

The partners of two banking firms, each having six partners, combine by an agreement into one firm. Is it an illegal association?

**Case Study**

20 individuals form an association to which each person contributes ₹ 1000. The purpose is to distribute food for free to poor children. Is it a valid partnership? Why?

## 12.4 TRUE TEST OF PARTNERSHIP

Whether an association of persons is a partnership or not, shall depend upon various factors. No single factor can determine the existence of a partnership.

The principle of the true test of partnership was held in the case of *Cox vs Hickman*. A mutual agency is a fundamental test of partnership. Sharing of profit is not a true test of partnership. There is a chance that the person is getting a profit but not able to bind the other for his act. When he cannot bind others by his act, it is simply said that there is no mutual agency. This mutual agency distinguishes a partnership from co-ownership, HUF and Company.

**Case Study**

A and B entered into an agreement to carry on a business of manufacturing and selling toys. Each one of them contributed ₹ 35 lacs as their capital with a condition that A and B will share the profits equally but the loss, if any, is to be borne by A alone. Referring to the provisions of the Indian Partnership Act, 1932, decide whether there exists a partnership between A and B?

## 12.5 CASES WHERE NO PARTNERSHIP EXISTS—SECTION 6

One of the essentials of a partnership is the sharing of profits. However, mere sharing of the profits does not necessarily mean that the association is the partnership. Similarly, even the person who gets a share in the profits of the firm may not always be a person. In the following cases, there is the sharing of profit but there is no partnership:

1. The joint owners of a property sharing the profits or gross returns arising from the property, do not become partners. Mere owning a joint property does not mean that some business is carried on. Also there is no mutual agency, i.e., one joint owner cannot make the other joint owner liable for the acts done by him.

***Example***

X and Y are the co-owners of a house, let out to a tenant. X and Y divide the net rents between themselves. It is not a partnership.

2. The lender of a firm who receives a share in the profit.

***Example***

The bank has provided the loan to the firm and the firm has agreed to pay 4% of its profit as interest. Here the bank does not become a partner, just for the reason that it is getting percentage of profit.

3. The servant or employee engaged in a business receives his remuneration as a share of the profit. The mere fact that an employee gets a share of profits does not make him a partner.
4. The widow or the child of a deceased partner receives a portion of the profits. In such a case the legal representative does not become the partner even though he is paid a certain share of the profits.
5. Where a person has sold his business along with its goodwill and receives a portion of the profits in consideration of the sale. In this case, although the old partners receive the profits, they cannot be called as the partners of the new firm.
6. The members of the HUF carrying the family business are not partners and HUF is not a partnership firm.

**Case Study**

A is employed by a partnership firm entitled to the remuneration of ₹ 5000 per month plus 7% on the profits of the firm if profits exceed ₹ 1 lakh. Is he a partner of the firm If so, what kind of partner he is?

**Case Study**

A and B purchase a factory jointly. They purchased the equipments and other things contributing equally. They let out the factory and shared the rent equally. Is it a partnership?

**Case Study**

A and B agreed to act together in one movie and share the profits of the film with the producer of the film. Is it a partnership?

**Case Study**

A and B enter into an agreement for preparing Ahmedabad Bombay Express Highway. Is this arrangement is a partnership?

## 12.6 DISTINGUISH BETWEEN A PARTNERSHIP AND A HINDU UNDIVIDED FAMILY

| Matter | Partnership | H.U.F. |
|---|---|---|
| Applicable law | Partnership Act 1932 | Hindu Law |
| Made of creation | It is created by an agreement. | It is created by status. |
| Mutual agency | Mutual agency present in the partnership. | No mutual agency among the family members of HUF. |
| Right to carry on business | Yes, every partner can carry on business on behalf of the firm. | Only Karta can manage business. |
| Nature of liability | Every partner's liability is joint and severally. | The liability of Karta is unlimited. Every member is liable up to his share. |
| Right to inspect accounts | Every partner has the right to inspect the accounts. | Every member of the family has no right to inspect the accounts. |
| Minor | A minor can be admitted to partnership. | A minor cannot be admitted to family. |
| Maximum number | 10 for banking business and 20 for other business. | No limit for the number of members. |
| Admission of new partner | A new partner can be admitted with the consent of all the partners. | A new person gets entry in the family on birth, marriage and adoption. |

## 12.7 DISTINGUISH BETWEEN A PARTNERSHIP AND AN ASSOCIATION

| Matter | Partnership | Association |
|---|---|---|
| Meaning | It is the relation between persons who agreed to share the profit for business carried out by all of them or anyone of them on behalf of all. | Is the body of a person gathered for some mutual benefit. |
| Business | A parternership cannot exist without business. | The association may exist without business. |
| Sharing of profit | The partners of a firm share the profit. | It is not to earn profit. |
| Nature of liability | Every partner is jointly and severally liable | A member is liable for his act only. |
| Mutual agency | A mutual agency among the partners of a firm. | No mutual agency among the members of an association. |
| Dissolution on death or insolvency | The partnership comes to an end on the death or insolvency of the partner unless otherwise agreed | The association is not automatically dissolved on the death or insolvency of any member. |
| Maximum number of persons | 10 for banking business and 20 for the other business. | No limit for the number of members. |

## 12.8 DISTINGUISH BETWEEN A PARTNERSHIP AND A CO-OWNERSHIP

| Matter | Partnership | Co-Ownership |
|---|---|---|
| Creation | The partnership is created by an agreement. | Co-ownership is created by an agreement or the operation of the law or status. |
| Mutual agency | Mutual agency among the partners of the firm. | No mutual agency among the co-owners. |
| Business | The partnership is created for business. | Co-ownership may or may not be created for business. |
| Right of partition | The partner cannot demand the partition of property. | Yes, the co-owner can demand partition. |
| Maximum number of members | 10 for banking business and 20 for other business. | No limit for the number of members. |
| Lien for expenses | Yes, the partners have lien on partnership property. | The co-owner does not have lien on the property. |

## 12.9 DISTINGUISH BETWEEN A PARTNERSHIP AND A CLUB

| Matter | Partnership | Club |
|---|---|---|
| Meaning | The partnership is a relationship between the partners who have agreed to share the profit of the business carried out by any one of them or all of them. | It is an association of the person with the object of the promotion of interest of the members. |
| Business | The partnership cannot exist without business. | The club is not created for business. |
| Sharing of profit | The partnership is created for earning and sharing profit. | The club is not to earn profit. |
| Mutual agency | A mutual agency among the partners of firm. | No mutual agency among the members of the club. |
| Nature of liability | Every partner is jointly and severally liable. | The member is liable for his act only. |
| Periodical subscription | The capital is contributed once by every partner. | Yes. The annual fee is paid each year. |
| Dissolution | The partnership firm can be dissolved easily. | The club cannot be dissolved without certain formalities. |
| Maximum number | 10 for banking business and 20 for other business. | No limit for the number of members. |

## 12.10 REGISTRATION OF FIRM—SECTIONS 56–71

A registration of partnership firm is not compulsory. It is optional. Therefore, the registration of the firm can be affected at any time. It can be affected at the time of commencing the partnership or at any time after the firm has started its business.

### 12.10.1 Procedure for Registration of Firm—Sections 58 and 59

An application for the registration is required to be made in the prescribed format to the Registrar of Firms with the prescribed fees and shall contain the following particulars:

1. The firm name.
2. The place or principal place of business of the firm.
3. The names of any other places where the firm carries on business.
4. The date when each partner joined the firm.
5. The names in full and permanent addresses of the partners.
6. The duration of the firm, if any.

The application shall be accompanied with the partnership agreement, if any. The application may be sent to the registrar of the firm by hand or by registered post.

Generally, the firm can select any name but the name should not be familiar with the name of any existing firm. A firm name shall not contain any of the following words without the consent of the State Government, namely Crown, Emperor, Empress, Empire, Imperial, King, Queen, Royal or words implying the patronage of Government. The application shall be signed by all the partners.

When the Registrar is satisfied that the above provisions have been duly complied with, he shall make an entry in the Register of Firms and he shall then issue under his hands, a certificate of registration. The registration is effective from the date when the Registrar files the statement and makes entries in the register. *(CIT vs Jaylakshmi Rice and Oil Mill)*.

## 12.11 REGISTRATION OF ALTERATIONS—SECTIONS 60–63

If any changes occur in the constitution of a firm, it is to be informed to the Registrar of firm. The following changes are required to be registered with the Registrar:

1. Alteration in the firm's name.
2. Alteration in the location of the principal place of business of a registered firm.
3. When a branch is closed or a new one is opened.
4. Changes in the names and address of the partners.
5. Changes in the constitution of a registered firm due to the admission and retirement of the partners. Dissolution of a firm should also be reported.
6. Withdrawal or continuation by a minor on attaining the majority.

If a registered firm changes its name or location of the principal place of business, a new application form is sent to the Registrar of firm. Thus, a change in the firm name and the principal place of business requires almost a new registration. If the change is made in any other particulars, the firm shall send a notice of change to the Registrar of firm. The notice shall be accompanied with the prescribed fees.

## 12.12 TIME FOR REGISTRATION

The act does not provide any time for the registration of the firm. It is possible at any time. The act has not prescribed any penalty for the non-registration of the firm. No suit can be filed in any court by the firm against any third party unless the firm is registered. This means before any suit is filed in a court, the registration must be affected. The subsequent registration does not cure the initial defect at the time of the institution of the suit.

## 12.13 EFFECTS OF NON-REGISTRATION—SECTION 69

The non-registration of the firm does not affect the validity of any act, dealing, transaction or any contract entered into by the firm. Mere non-registration of the firm does not make the business of the firm illegal. However, if the firm is not registered, following disabilities are created:

1. An unregistered firm or its partners cannot file a suit against the other partners or the firm to enforce a right arising out of a contract.
2. An unregistered firm or its partners cannot file a suit against the third parties.
3. An unregistered firm or its partners cannot claim the set-off in a suit filed against the firm by a third party except for a sum not exceeding ₹ 100.

The non-registration of the firm, however, does not affect the followings:

1. The right of the third parties to sue the firm or its partners.
2. The partner of the unregistered firm can file a suit for the three matters as under:
   (a) For the dissolution of firm.
   (b) For the accounts of a dissolved firm.
   (c) For the realization of the property of a dissolved firm.
3. The power of an official assignee or receiver to realize the property of an insolvent partner.
4. The rights of the firms or the partners of the firms having no place of business in India.
5. Right to set off where the claim does not exceed ₹ 100.
6. The right of an unregistered firm to enforce any other right arising otherwise than out of a partnership contract.

**Case Study**

Abhinav buys certain goods worth ₹ 50,000 from an unregistered firm Ram and Sons. Ram and Sons has to pay ₹ 60,000 to Abhinav for the goods purchased by the firm in the past. Referring to the provisions of the Indian Partnership Act, 1932, decide whether Ram and Sons can compel Abhinav to accept ₹ 10,000, i.e., the difference between ₹ 60,000 and ₹ 50,000 as the final settlement?

**Case Study**

Anil and Sunil purchased a lorry to ply it in the partnership. They plied the lorry for about two years when Anil, without the consent of Sunil, disposed of the lorry. Sunil brought an action to recover his share in the sale proceeds. Anil resisted Sunil's claim on the plea that the firm was not registered. Will Sunil succeed in his claim? Decide with reference to the provisions of the Indian Partnership Act, 1932.

## 12.14 TYPES OF PARTNERS

### 12.14.1 Actual or Active Partner

He is also known as the ostensible partner. He takes active part into the business of the firm. He is liable for all the acts of the firm. He must give a public notice of his retirement from the firm. His insolvency or permanent incapacity to perform his duties may be ground for the dissolution of the firm.

### 12.14.2 Sleeping or Dormant Partner

He does not take part in the business but is liable for all the acts of the firm. He need not give public notice of his retirement from the firm because the public does not have any idea that he is a partner. His insolvency or permanent incapacity to perform his duties is not the ground for the dissolution of the firm.

### 12.14.3 Nominal Partner

He lends his name to the firm. He does not take part in the business of the firm but is liable for all the acts of the firm. He does not contribute any capital to the firm and does not share any profits from the firm. The purpose of admitting a partner as the nominal partner is to use the name of such person. He must give public notice of his retirement from the firm. His insolvency or permanent incapacity to perform his duties is not the ground for the dissolution of the firm.

### 12.14.4 Partner in Profit

The partners may lawfully agree that one or more of them shall not be liable for the losses. In such a case, the partner who is entitled to share the profit but is not liable for the losses is called as the partner in profit. He is like any other normal active partner. He is liable for all the acts of the firm. He requires giving public notice of his retirement. His insolvency or permanent incapacity to perform his duties may be ground for the dissolution of the firm.

### 12.14.5 Sub-partner

He is one who shares the profits of another partner. The sub partner is not a partner in the original firm. He is not liable for the act of the firm. He does not require giving public notice. His insolvency or permanent incapacity to perform his duties is not the ground for the dissolution of the firm. The sub-partner is excluded while counting the total number of partners of the firm. A sub-partner is a transferee.

### 12.14.6 Partner by Estoppel or Holding Out

Sometimes, a person is not a partner in a firm. But he may be liable for the debts of the firm as if he were a partner. Such a partner is called a partner by estoppel or holding out. For this, the following conditions must be fulfilled:

1. He must have expressly or impliedly represented himself to be a partner or he must have knowingly permitted himself to be represented as a partner to the other person.
2. The other person must have acted on the faith of such representation and given credit to the firm. This rule is based on the principle of equity and natural justice.

### 12.14.7 A Minor Partner

The minor may be admitted to the benefits of a partnership with the consent of all the partners. The liability of the minor partner is confined only to the extent of his share in the profits and the property of the firm. Over and above this, he is neither personally liable nor is his private estate liable. He cannot be declared insolvent but if the firm is declared insolvent, his share in the firm vests in the official receiver or official assignee.

**Case Study**

A introduces B to C as a partner in his business. B, in fact, was not a partner but he did not deny the statement. C advanced a loan to A. A could not repay the loan. Can C hold B responsible for the repayment of loan?

**Case Study**

A, B and C are partners in a firm. A introduces D to X as a partner in the business. D, infact, was not a partner in the firm's business. D did not deny this statement. X advanced a loan of ₹ 20 lakhs to the firm. Firm's failure to repay the loan, X wants to hold D responsible for the repayment of the above loan. Referring to the provisions of the Indian Partnership Act, 1932, decide whether X would succeed in recovering the loan from D?

## 12.15 POSITION OF A MINOR PARTNER AFTER ATTAINING MAJORITY

On attaining a majority, the minor partner has to decide whether he shall continue in the firm or leave it. He has to decide within six months:

- From the date of his attaining majority.
- From the date when he first comes to know that he had been admitted to the benefits of partnership.

The minor has to give a public notice of his choice within the above period. If he fails to give a public notice, he is deemed to have become a partner after the expiry of the above period.

### 12.15.1 Where a Minor Elects to Become a Full Fledged Partner

He becomes personally liable to the third parties for all the acts of the firm done, since he was admitted to the benefit of the partnership and not from the date he becomes a major. When the minor elects to become a full fledged partner, his share in the property and the profits of the firm remains the same as before.

### 12.15.2 Where He Elects Not to Become a Partner

He continues to be liable as before, until the date of public notice. His share shall not be liable for any acts of the firm done after the date of the notice. He shall be entitled to sue the partners for his share of the property and the profits.

## 12.16 WHO CAN BE A PARTNER IN THE FIRM?

A person, if competent to enter into a contract can be a partner in the firm. One person can be a partner in any number of firms. A minor can not be a partner in the firm but he can be admitted to the benefit of the partnership firm. A company, or a corporation or a body corporate can become a partner in the partnership firm. A partnership firm cannot enter into a partnership with another partnership firm. The HUF cannot be a partner in the partnership firm. However, Karta of HUF can become a partner in the partnership firm in his individual capacity. Trust cannot become a partner in the partnership firm.

The foreigner or NRI can become a partner in the parternship firm.

## 12.17 RIGHTS OF A PARTNER

### 12.17.1 Right to Take Part in Business

In the absence of any agreement between the partners, every partner has a right to take part in the conduct of the business.

### 12.17.2 Right to Be Consulted

The ordinary matters of the business may be decided by the majority. But no change can be made in the nature of the business without the consent of all the partners. Every partner has a right to be consulted for the admission of any new partner to the firm.

### 12.17.3 Right to Access the Books of Account

Every partner has a right to access and inspect and take copy of the books of the firm. The minor partner has a right to inspect and copy the accounts of the firm but not the books.

### 12.17.4 Right to Share Profit

All the partners are entitled to share the profit equally. The agreement between the partners may provide otherwise also.

### 12.17.5 Right to Interest

A partner is entitled to claim interest on the capital out of the profit if the agreement provides so. The partner is entitled to claim interest on any loan or advances he has made to firm at the rate of 6% per annum. The interest on the loan is payable whether or not firm makes profit.

### 12.17.6 Right to Be Indemnified

Every partner has the right to be indemnified by the firm in respect of the payment and liability incurred by him in the ordinary course of business.

### 12.17.7 Right to the Use the Firm's Property

Every partner has the right to use partnership property for the purpose of the business of the firm. However, a partner may use the partnership property for his personal purpose if the agreement provides so.

### 12.17.8 Right to Retire from Partnership

Every partner has the right to retire from the partnership either by giving a notice in writing to the other partners or as per the method agreed under the partnership agreement. The retired partner has the right to carry on the competition business and also has the right to advertise his new business. Every retiring partner has the right to receive a proportionate profit from the firm.

### 12.17.9 Right to Receive Remuneration

No partner is entitled to receive any salary or remuneration for taking part into conduct of business. However, the agreement between partners may expressly provide for payment to remuneration to working partners.

### 12.17.10 Right Not to Be Expelled from Partnership

Every partner is entitled to continue as a partner until death or retirement. No partner shall be expelled.

**Case Study**

A and B entered into an agreement to carry on a business of manufacturing and selling toys. Each one of them contributed ₹ 35 lakhs as their capital with a condition that A and B will share the profits equally but the loss, if any, is to be borne by A alone. Referring to the provisions of the Indian Partnership Act, 1932, decide whether there exists a partnership between A and B.

## 12.18 PARTNER'S OPTIONAL DUTIES

The duties which can be modified by an agreement are known as optional duties. They are also known as the general duties of the partner. Unless otherwise agreed by the partner, every partner has the following duties.

### 12.18.1 Duty to Share Losses Equally

Every partner is liable to contribute equally to the losses of the firm. However, an agreement between the partners may provide otherwise.

### 12.18.2 Duty Not to Act for Individual Benefit

All the partners are duty bound to carry on the firm's business to the greatest common advantage and not for their individual benefit.

### 12.18.3 Duty Not to Carry on Any Other Business

If any personal profit is made by any partner from the partnership transactions or from any use of the partnership property, name or business connection, he must account for it and pay it to the firm.

In the absence of any agreement, a partner cannot carry on the competing business. If he does, he is bound to account for and pay to the firm all the profits made by him in that business.

***Example***

A and B are partners in a firm, which consists of supplying meat to the Government. Subsequently, it is found out that A is engaged with C in the supplying of meat to the same Government. Held, A is bound to account to the firm for the profits so made by him. *(Loch vs Lynam)*

### 12.18.4 Duty to Indemnify the Firm from Loss Cause Due to Willful Neglect

The partner has to indemnity (compensate) the firm for any loss caused to the firm by his willful neglect. However, this duty may be excluded by an agreement between the partners.

### 12.18.5 Duty to Make Proper Use of Property of Firm

The partner must use the firm's property for the purpose of the business of the firm. No partner should use the partnership property for his personal benefit otherwise he is liable for the profit he has made by using the property. However, this duty may be excluded by an agreement between the partners.

## 12.19 PARTNER'S COMPULSORY DUTIES

Compulsory duties are the duties which cannot modify by an agreement or otherwise.They are also known as mandatory duties. The mandatory duties are as follows.

### 12.19.1 Duty of Good Faith

This is the primary and the most important duty of every partner. Every partner is duty bound to act in good faith. It means to remain faithful to one another.

### 12.19.2 Duty to Carry on Business to the Greatest Common Advantage

Every partner must conduct the business of the firm in such a manner which is most beneficial to the firm. No partner should make any personal profit at the expenses of firm.

### 12.19.3 Duty to Render True Accounts of Firm

Every partner should keep proper accounts of all the money transactions relating to the business of the firm. Every partner should explain all the accounts to the other partners.

### 12.19.4 Duty to Give Full Information

No partner should hide or conceal any material facts and information affecting the business of the firm from any other partner.

### 12.19.5 Duty to Indemnify for Loss Caused by Fraud

If any fraud is committed by any partner in the conduct of the business of the firm, he shall be liable to indemnify the firm from loss caused to it.

### 12.19.6 Duty to Act Within Authority

Every partner is duty bound to act within the scope of his authority, expressed and implied. Where he exceeds the authority conferred on him and the firm suffers a loss, he shall have to compensate the firm such loss.

### 12.19.7 Duty to be Liable Jointly and Severally

Every partner is liable jointly and severally for the acts of the firm while he was partner.

***Note:***

The mutual rights and duties of partners are governed by the Partnership Agreement and Partnership Act.

## 12.20 PARTNERSHIP PROPERTY—SECTION 14

A property originally brought in the common stock of the firm by the partner while at the time of joining the firm is the property of the firm. The property acquired for the purpose of business of the firm also belongs to the firm. The property acquired with the firm's money is also the partnership property. The goodwill created or developed over a period of time is the property of the firm.

## 12.21 AUTHORITY OF PARTNER—SECTIONS 19 AND 22

The authority of the partner may be express or implied. Any act of the partner done within his express authority or implied authority shall be the act of the firm and consequently the firm shall be bound by it.

### 12.21.1 Express Authority

An express authority is given to a partner by an agreement.

***Example***

One of the partners may be authorized to operate the bank account on behalf of the firm.

### 12.21.2 Implied Authority

This is an authority which is not given to a partner by an agreement but by the law. It flows from the legal relations of the partners and is based on the law of agency. It is also known as the apparent, ostensible and ordinary authority.

The act of the partner will be within the implied authority of the partner if the following conditions are satisfied:

1. The act must be done in the ordinary course of business.
2. The act must be done in the usual way. 'What is a usual way?' It is a question of facts and circumstances.
3. The act must be done in the firm's name.

**Case Study**

A and B are partners in a firm dealing in cloth. A placed an order on the firm's letter pad for 10 bags of wheat to be supplied at his residence. Is firm liable for A's order?

## 12.22 ACTS WITHIN THE IMPLIED AUTHORITY OF A PARTNER

If the following activities are performed or done by the partner then it is considered as an act within the meaning of the implied authority:

1. To purchase and sell the goods on behalf of the firm in which the firm deals.
2. To receive payments from the debtors of the firm and give receipts for same.
3. To settle accounts with the persons dealing with the firm.
4. To engage servants for the partnership business.
5. To borrow money on the credit of the firm.
6. To draw, accept indorse negotiable instruments in the name of the firm.
7. Pledge any goods of the firm for the purpose of borrowing money.
8. To employ a lawyer to defend an action against the firm.

## 12.23 ACTS OUTSIDE THE IMPLIED AUTHORITY OF A PARTNER

In the absence of any usage or custom of trade to the contrary, the implied authority of a partner does not empower him to do the following acts:

1. To submit a dispute relating to the business of the firm to arbitration.
2. To open a bank account on behalf of the firm in his own name.
3. To compromise any claim or a portion of a claim by the firm.
4. To withdraw a suit or proceeding filed on behalf of the firm.
5. To admit any liability in a suit or proceeding against the firm.
6. To acquire immovable property on behalf of the firm.
7. To transfer immovable property belonging to the firm.
8. To enter into a partnership on behalf of the firm.

A partner has no implied authority to bind the firm by giving a guarantee which is apparently unconnected with the partnership trade. He cannot accept the shares of a company against the debt due to the firm. He has no right to set off his own separate debts against the debt due to the firm.

**Case Study**

A, B and C are the partners in a firm called the ABC Firm. A has the intention of deceiving D, a supplier of office stationery, buys certain stationery on behalf of the ABC Firm. The stationery is of use in the ordinary course of the firm's business. A does not give the stationery to the firm, instead brings it to his own use. The supplier D, who is unaware of the private use of the stationery by A, claims the price from the firm. The firm refuses to pay for the price on the ground that the stationery was never received by it (firm). Referring to the provisions of the Indian Partnership Act, 1932, decide:

(i) Whether the Firm's contention shall be tenable?

(ii) What would be your answer if a part of the stationery so purchased by A was delivered to the firm by him and the rest of the stationery was used by him for private use, about which neither the firm nor the supplier D was aware?

**Case Study**

Mahesh, Suresh and Dinesh are partners in a trading firm. Mahesh, without the knowledge or consent of Suresh and Dinesh, borrows himself ₹ 50,000 from Ramesh, a customer of the firm, in the name of the firm. Mahesh then buys some goods for his personal use with that borrowed money. Can Mr. Ramesh hold Mr. Suresh and Mr. Dinesh liable for the loan? Explain the relevant provisions of the Indian Partnership Act,1932.

## 12.24 RESTRICTION ON AN IMPLIED AUTHORITY

A restrictions on the implied authority of a partner may be imposed by the partnership agreement.

## 12.25 LIABILITY OF A PARTNER

Every partner is liable jointly with all the other partners and also severally for all the acts of the firm done while he is a partner. The firm is liable for any loss caused to a third party by the wrongful act or omission of a partner, while acting in the ordinary course of the business or with the authority of his partner.

In the ordinary course of the business of the firm, the money or property belonging to the third party is received by the firm or its partner. If the partner misapplies it to his own use, the firm is liable for same as per following rules:

1. Where a partner acting within his apparent authority receives money or property from a third party and misapplies it.
2. Where a firm in the course of its business receives money or property from a third party and the money or property is misapplied by any of the partners while it is in the custody of the firm.

***Example***

A appointed a firm of B and C to buy and sell wine for him on commission. A left money with the firm for the purpose. B, the active partner, rendered false accounts of purchase and sale to A and misappropriated the money. Held, the firm was liable. *(Mellors vs Shaw)*

## 12.26 PARTNER'S AUTHORITY IN EMERGENCY

Generally, the partner cannot act beyond his authority. However, the firm is liable if the partner has acted beyond his authority in case of an emergency. The following conditions must be satisfied:

1. There was an emergency.
2. The partner has exceeded his authority to save the firm from loss.
3. The partner has acted prudently.

## 12.27 RECONSTITUTION OF A FIRM

The reconstitution of the firm means a change in the constitution of the firm. It means the old partnership ends up and a new partnership commences. The reconstitution of the firm can take place in the following manner:

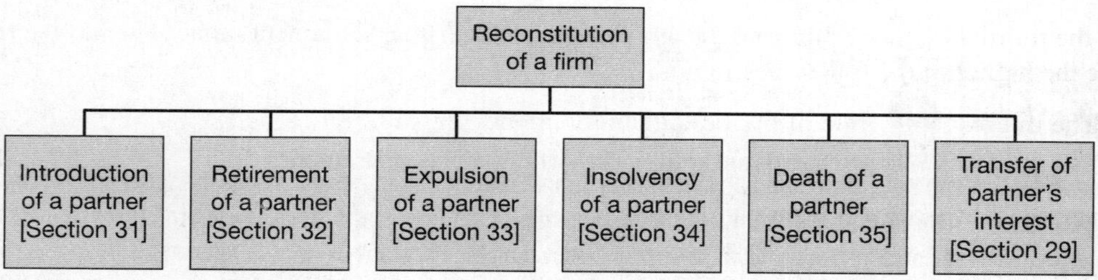


**Figure 12.1** Reconstitution of firm.

### 12.27.1 Admission of a Partner—Section 31

A person may be admitted as a new partner either in accordance with the partnership deed or with the consent of all the existing partners.

### 12.27.2 Liability of an Incoming Partner

A new partner is not liable for any act of the firm done before his admission. However, an incoming partner may, by an agreement, agree to become liable for the acts done before his admission, provided:

1. The newly constituted firm has agreed to pay the debts.
2. The creditors have agreed to accept the new firm as their debtor and discharge the old firm form its liability.

If a minor on attaining the majority elects to become the partner, he will be liable for all the acts of the firm done since he was admitted to the benefit of the partnership and not from the date he becomes a major.

### 12.27.3 Retirement of a Partner—Section 32

A partner may retire in accordance with the partnership deed or with the consent of all the other partners or where the partnership is at will, by giving a notice in writing to all the other partners of his intention to retire.

### 12.27.4 Liability of a Retired Partner

A retired partner is not liable for any act of the firm done after his retirement. However, he is liable for the act of the firm done before his retirement unless he is discharged. He is liable for all the transaction which had began but remained unfinished on the date of retirement. He is liable as per the principle of holding out if after retirement no notice is given. If no notice is given of retirement, the firm shall be liable for the act of the retired partner.

### 12.27.5 Rights of a Retired Partner

A retired partner may carry on a business competing with the firm and he may advertise such business but he cannot:

1. Use the firm's name.
2. Represent himself as carrying on the business of the firm.
3. Solicit the old customer of the firm.

When the retiring partner is not paid the amount due to him (final settlement money) he has the right to receive the higher of the following amount:

1. The interest at the rate of 6% per annum on money unpaid.
2. The proportion of the profit earned by the firm after his retirement.

However, the partnership agreement may provide otherwise.

### 12.27.6 Expulsion of a Partner—Section 33

The general rule suggests that the partner cannot be expelled from the partnership. However, the partner may be expelled, subject to the following conditions:

1. The power of expulsion of a partner should be conferred by the partnership deed.
2. The power should be exercised by a majority of the partners.
3. The power should be exercised in good faith.

### 12.27.7 Test of Good Faith for Expulsion

The following are the three criteria for the test of good faith:

1. The expulsion must be in the interest of the partnership.
2. A proper notice is served to the expelled partner.
3. He is given an opportunity of being heard.

If a partner is expelled without complying with the above conditions, the expulsion is called irregular. In such a case, the expelled partner may claim re-instatement as a partner or sue for the refund of his share of capital and profits in the firm but he cannot claim damages. The rights and liabilities of an expelled partner is the same as the retired partner. The expelled partner has to give public notice otherwise he is liable for the act of the firm after his expulsion. The firm is also liable for the act of the expelled partner if no notice is given.

### 12.27.8 Insolvency of a Partner—Section 34

He ceases to be a partner on the date on which the order of insolvency is made.

The firm is also dissolved on the date of the order except the agreement that provides the contrary. The estate of the insolvent-partner is not liable for the acts of the firm done after the date of the order of insolvency. A public notice to the effect that a partner has been adjudicated insolvent is not required. The firm is also not liable for any act of the insolvent partner after the date of the order of adjudication.

### 12.27.9 Death of a Partner—Section 35

The death of any one partner results into the dissolution of the partnership. The firm is dissolved unless otherwise agreed in the partnership agreement. No requirement of the public notice. The estate of the deceased partner is not liable for act of firm after his death.

***Example***

M was a partner in a firm. The firm ordered goods in M's lifetime but the delivery was made after M's death. Held, M's estate was not liable for the price for goods sold and delivered. *(Bagel vs Miller)*

On the death of the partner, his legal representative has the right to get the final settlement money. If the firm makes a delay in the payment of the final settlement amount, the legal representative is entitled to receive the higher of following amount:

1. The interest at the rate of 6% per annum on the money unpaid to the retiring partner or
2. The proportion of the profit earned by the firm after his retirement.

However, the agreement may provide otherwise. Upon the death of a partner, the legal heir does become the partner. If they want to become partners, a fresh contract has to be made as the partnership is created by a contract.

### 12.27.10 Transfer of Partner's Interest—Section 29

When a partner agrees to shares his own share in the profits and assets with an outsider, it is called as sub-partnership and the outsider is called the sub-partner. The transfer of interest may be made by a way of absolute sale, creation or charge or otherwise. The transfer of interest may be absolute or in part. A partner can assign his share of the profit and his share in the assets of the firm to the outsider. In that case, the transferee does not entitle:

1. To participate into the business of the firm.
2. To require the accounts of the firm.
3. To inspect the books of the firm.

But such a transferee is entitled:

1. To receive the share of the profit of the transferring partner. He is bound to accept the account of the profit agreed to by the partners.
2. In the case of dissolution, to receive the transferring partner's share in the assets of the firm.

Where a partner has transferred the whole of his interest in the firm to a third party or where his share has been attached under a decree or sold in the recovery of the arrears of the land revenue, the court may dissolve the firm at the instance of any other partner.

### 12.27.11 Rights and Duties of a Partner After Re-constitution—Section 17

The mutual rights and duties of the partners in the reconstituted firm remain the same as they were before the change.

### Case Study

Ram, Mohan and Gopal were partners in a firm. During the course of partnership, the firm ordered Sunrise Ltd to supply a machine to the firm. Before the machine was delivered, Ram expired. The machine, however, was later delivered to the firm. Thereafter, the remaining partners became insolvent and the firm failed to pay the price of machine to Sunrise Ltd. Explain with reasons:

1. Whether Ram's private estate is liable for the price of the machine purchased by the firm?
2. Against whom can the creditor obtain a decree for the recovery of the price?

### Case Study

Ram and Co., a firm consists of three partners A, B and C having one third share each in the firm. According to A and B, the activities of C are not in the interest of the partnership and thus want to expel C from the firm. Advise A and B whether they can do so quoting the relevant provisions of the Indian Partnership Act.

### Case Study

A, B, C are partners. Can A and C continue the firm's business on the death of B?

### Case Study

A, B and C are in partnership. A is adjudicated insolvent but B and C agree to continue the firm. Advise.

### Case Study

A, B and C are partners in a firm. As per the terms of the partnership deed, A is entitled to 20% of the partnership property and profits. A retires from the firm and dies after 15 days. B and C continue business of the firm without settling accounts. What are the rights of A's legal representatives against the firm under the Indian Partnership Act, 1932?

**Case Study**

Ram, Shyam and Gopal are partners in a firm. Ram retires. Shyam and Gopal continue to carry on firm's business in the same 'firm name'. Do you agree that in this situation change in the relationship between partners is involved but this is not extinguishment of the existence of the firm itself? Give reasons.

## 12.28 DISTINGUISH BETWEEN DISSOLUTION OF A PARTNERSHIP AND DISSOLUTION OF A FIRM

| Basis of Distinction | Dissolution of Partnership | Dissolution of Firm |
|---|---|---|
| Termination of the old partnership and formation of a new partnership. | The old partnership comes to an end and a new partnership comes into existence. | The old partnership comes to an end but no new partnership comes into existence. |
| Continuation of the business under the firm's name. | The business continues under the firm's name. | The business does not continue under the firm's name. |
| Which type of account is prepared? | The revaluation account is prepared. | Under the firm's dissolution realization account is prepared. |

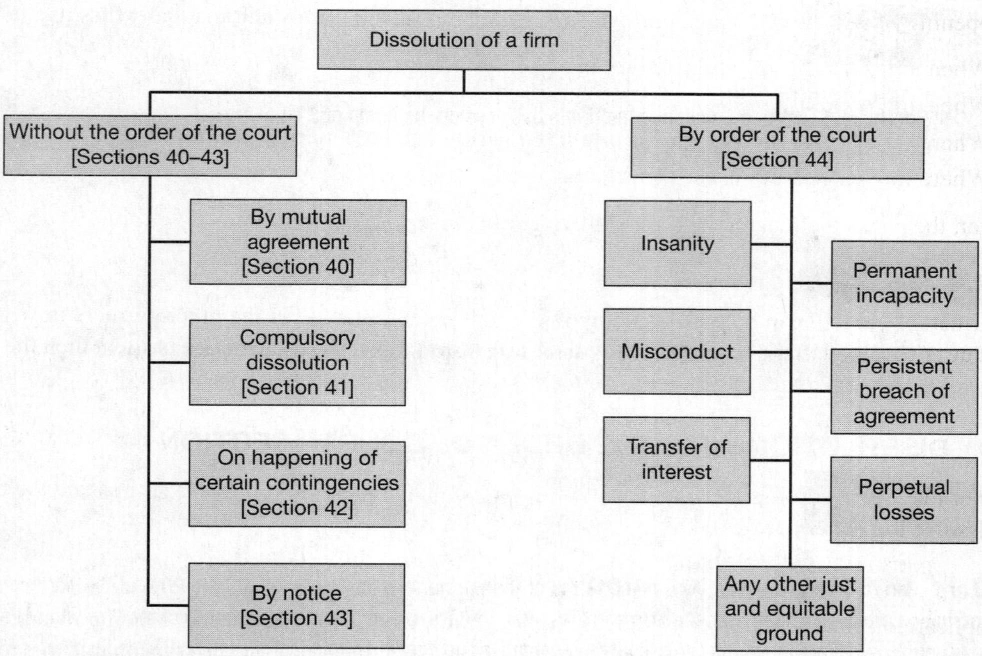


**Figure 12.2** Dissolution of firms.

The dissolution of a partnership between all the partners of a firm is called the 'dissolution of the firm'. It means closing business of the firm.

## 12.29 DISSOLUTION WITHOUT THE ORDER OF COURT—SECTIONS 40–43

The dissolution of the firm without order of the court may take place in any of the following ways:

### 12.29.1 Dissolution by Mutual Agreement

It is also called as dissolution with the consent of all the partners. The partnership can be brought to an end by entering the agreement. It is applied in all the cases:

1. The partnership is for a fixed period.
2. The partnership is for a particular venture.
3. The partnership is at will.

### 12.29.2 Compulsory Dissolution

It is also known as dissolution by the operation of law. The compulsory dissolution of the firm takes place in the following circumstances:

1. All the partners die.
2. All the partners except one die.
3. All the business of the firm becomes unlawful.

### 12.29.3 Dissolution on Happening of Certain Contingencies

On happening of any of following contingencies (i.e., events), the firm is automatically dissolved:

1. When any partner is adjudicated as an insolvent.
2. When any partner dies.
3. Where the partnership is formed for a fixed period and such period is expired.
4. Where the partnership is for a particular venture and such venture is completed.

However, the partnership agreement may provide otherwise.

### 12.29.4 Dissolution by Notice

The partnership at will can be dissolved anytime by giving a notice to all the other partners in writing. If the date is specified in the notice then it will dissolve from that date. If the notice is silent then the firm will dissolve from the date on which the notice is served.

## 12.30 DISSOLUTION WITH THE ORDER OF COURT—SECTION 44

A partner may file a suit for the dissolution of the firm on anyone of the following groups and the court may dissolve the firm on the following grounds:

### 12.30.1 Unsoundness of Mind

The application for dissolution can be made by his next friend if the partner has become insane or of unsound mind. The court may dissolve the firm if due to unsoundness of mind he is incapable to perform his duties as a partner.

### 12.30.2 Permanent Incapacity

If the partner becomes permanently incapable to perform his duties as a partner, any other partner may apply to the court to dissolve the firm. The incapacity may be due to the illness, mental or physical disability of any kind but it should be permanent in nature. This is not applicable to the sleeping partner.

***Example***

The partner becomes blind or is paralyzed due to polio.

### 12.30.3 Misconduct

If the partner is guilty of misconduct, the application to dissolve the firm can be made by the other partner. It is not necessary that misconduct should be connected with the business but misconduct should be likely to affect carrying on the business.

***Example***

Traveling on railway by a partner without a ticket.

### 12.30.4 Persistent Breach of Agreement

If any partner continuously and willfully breaches the partnership agreement, the application to dissolve the firm can be made by the other partner.

***Example***

A partner having the keys of the shop continuously fails to come to the shop in time.

### 12.30.5 Transfer of Interest

When a partner agrees to shares his own share in the profits and assets with an outsider, it is called as sub-partnership and the outsider is called the sub-partner. The transfer of interest may be made by a way of absolute sale, creation or charge or otherwise. The transfer of interest may be absolute or in part. A partner can assign his share of the profit and his share in the assets of the firm to the outsider.

### 12.30.6 Perpetual Losses

The business of the firm cannot be carried on except the loss; the court may allow the dissolution of the firm on the application of any partner.

### 12.30.7 Just and Equitable Ground

The firm may also be dissolved by the court on 'just and equitable' ground. The just and equitable ground means any ground which is fair and reasonable according to the opinion of the court. The just and equitable grounds may be continued quarrelling, deadlock in the management etc.

## 12.31 RIGHTS OF PARTNERS ON DISSOLUTION

On the dissolution of a firm, every partner is entitled to have the property of the firm applied in the payment of the outside debts and the liabilities of the firm and have the surplus distributed among the partners in accordance with their rights. This right of a partner is called 'Partner's Lien'. The debts of the firm shall be paid first out of property of the firm and if there is any surplus, it shall be distributed among the partners. If the firm is dissolved due the death of a partner and the surviving partners or the representatives of the deceased partner have earned any personal profit from the use of the firm's property or firm's name or firm's business connections before the firm have been completely wound up, a partner has a right to a share in such personal profits. Where a partner has paid a premium on entering into the partnership for a fixed term and the firm is dissolved before the expiry of the term, he is entitled to the repayment of the whole or part of the premium. However, no refund can be claimed where the dissolution:

1. Is due to the death of a partner or
2. Is due to the misconduct of the partner who had paid the premium or
3. Is in pursuance of an agreement, which contains no provisions for the refund of the premium or any part thereof.

After the firm is dissolved, every partner may restrain any other partner from carrying on a similar business in the firm's name or from using any of the property of the firm for his own benefit, until the affairs of the firm have been completely wound up. However, it is to be noted that this restriction does not apply in the following two conditions:

1. When there is a contract between the partners to the contrary.
2. When a partner has bought the goodwill of the firm.

## 12.32 LIABILITIES OF PARTNERS ON DISSOLUTION

If the public notice for the dissolution is not given, the partners continue to be liable to the third party for any act done by it after the dissolution. After the dissolution of a firm, the authority of each partner to bind the firm and the other mutual rights and obligations of the partners continue so far as may be necessary for the following purposes:

1. To wind up the firm.
2. To complete the transactions begun but unfinished at the time of the dissolution.

## 12.33 SETTLEMENT OF ACCOUNTS

The partners are free to lay down the modes in which the accounts will be settled on the dissolution of the firm. In the absence of any specific agreement, the provisions of partnership will apply, which are as follows:

### 12.33.1 Sale of Goodwill

In settling the account, the goodwill shall be included in the assets and it may be sold either separately or along with the other property of the firm.

### 12.33.2 Sharing of Deficiency

If at the time of settlement, any deficiency arises, the partners shall bear such deficiency in the profit sharing ratio. Thus, the losses shall be paid in the following order:

1. First out of profits.
2. Next out of capital.
3. Lastly, if necessary, by the partners, individually in the profit sharing ratio.

### 12.33.3 Application of Assets

The assets of the firm shall be applied in the following order:

1. In paying the debts of the firm to the third party.
2. In paying to each partner's for advances.
3. In paying to each partner's capital.
4. The surplus, if any, shall be divided among the partners in the profit sharing ratio.
5. If the assets are sufficient to pay the outside debts and the advance of the partner but insufficient to repay to each partner his full capital, the deficiency in the capital shall be borne by the partners in the proportion in which they are entitled to share the profits.

## 12.34 GARNER VERSUS MURRAY RULE

G, M and W were partners in a firm on the terms that the profits should be divided equally. The capital was contributed in unequal shares. The capital contributed by G was more than the capital contributed by M. On the dissolution of the firm, the assets were insufficient to repay the capital in full. W became the insolvent. The following decisions are given in this case:

1. The solvent partners should bring the share of their loss in cash.
2. The solvent partners shall bear the deficiency of the capital of the insolvent partner in the ratio of their capitals.

It is to be noted that the rule of *Garner vs Murray* is applicable only when there is no other agreement between the partners. Again, this rule is not strictly applied in India, in as much as, the solvent partners are not asked to bring the share of their loss in cash.

## 12.35 MODE OF GIVING A PUBLIC NOTICE

| In Case of a Registered Firm | In Case of The Unregistered Firm |
|---|---|
| Publication in the official gazette. | Publication in the official gazette. |
| At least one vernacular (regional) news paper. | At least one vernacular (regional) news paper. |
| Must be given to the Registrar of the firm. | — |

## LIST OF LANDMARK JUDGEMENTS

1. ***Malabar Fisheries Co. vs CIT (1979)***

   The partnership is not a separate legal entity, apart from the partners constituting it.
2. ***Sham Sunder vs State of Haryana (1989)***

   The partnership is not a legal entity but a mere association of persons.
3. ***Mahavir Cold Storage vs CIT (1991)***

   The partnership firm cannot enter into a partnership with another partnership firm, HUF or individual.
4. ***CIT vs Bhagyalakshmi and Co. (1965)***

   The partnership is a contract.

5. ***Surjitlal Chhabda vs CIT (1976)***
The HUF is a creature of law and cannot be created by the act of the parties, except to the extent to which a stranger may be affiliated to the family by an adoption.
6. ***Russel vs Russel (1980)***
The expelled partner must be given an opportunity of being heard.
7. ***Jiwan Singh vs Laxmi Chand (1935)***
An illegal expulsion of the partners does not put an end to the partnership.
8. ***Kotak vs Chawda (1998)***
In the case of the reconstitution of the firm, the existing firms continue and there is no need of getting fresh registration.
9. ***Cox vs Hickman (1860)***
The profit sharing is an essential element of a partnership but it is not the essence of partnership. The real test of a partnership is mutual agency among the partners.
10. ***CIT vs ST Phoolchand (1965)***
The minor is incompetent to contract. Hence, he cannot become a partner because he cannot contract.
11. ***Regional Director of ESIC vs Ramnuja Match Industries (1985)***
The partners of the firm are not considered its employees even if they are drawing a remuneration of their services.
12. ***Badri Prasad vs Nagarmal (1959)***
The partnership is illegal if it consists of more than 20 persons and if it is a banking partnership of more than 10 persons.
13. ***CIT vs Seth Govindram Sugar Mills (1965)***
If there are only two partners and one of them dies, the firm automatically dissolves.
14. ***CIT vs Jaylaxmi Rice and Oil Mills (1971)***
The firm becomes registered only when the entries are made in the register of the firms.

## TEST YOUR KNOWLEDGE

1. Define partnership. Explain the essential elements of a partnership. **(Ref. Para-12.2,12.3)**
2. Sharing of profit is a prima-facie evidence of the existence of partnership but it is not the conclusive evidence. Comment. **(Ref. Para-12.4)**
3. Distinguish between a partnership and a Hindu undivided family. **(Ref. Para-12.6)**
4. Distinguish between a partnership and a co-ownership. **(Ref. Para-12.8)**
5. Is it compulsory for the partnership firm to get itself registered? Explain briefly the procedure for the registration of the firm. **(Ref. Para-12.10)**
6. What are the consequences of non-registration of the firm? **(Ref. Para-12.13)**
7. Enumerate the difference types of partners and briefly explain the extent of their liabilities. **(Ref. Para-12.14)**
8. Can a minor be admitted to partnership? If so, what are the rights and liabilities to him? **(Ref. Para-12.14)**
9. Write a short note on the partner by estoppels. **(Ref. Para-12.14)**
10. Write a short note on the rights of the partners. **(Ref. Para-12.17)**

11. What are the mandatory duties of partners? **(Ref. Para-12.18)**
12. What is partnership property? **(Ref. Para-12.19)**
13. What is meant by the implied authority of a partner? **(Ref. Para-12.20)**
14. Write a short note on the partner's authority in an emergency. **(Ref. Para-12.25)**
15. How can a person be admitted in an existing firm? Is an incoming partner liable for the firm's acts done before his admission? **(Ref. Para-12.26)**
16. How can a partner retire from a firm? Is a retiring partner liable for the acts done before his retirement? **(Ref. Para-12.26)**
17. Explain the rights of the retiring partner. **(Ref. Para-12.26)**
18. Can a partner be expelled? If so, what are the conditions to be fulfilled for the expulsion? **(Ref. Para-12.26)**
19. What are the rights and liabilities of the expelled partners? **(Ref. Para-12.26)**
20. What are the rights available to the partner who has been wrongly expelled? **(Ref. Para-12.26)**
21. Write a short note on the insolvency of a person. **(Ref. Para-12.26)**
22. Does the death of a partner necessarily result in the dissolution of the firm? **(Ref. Para-12.26)**
23. What is meant by the dissolution of the firm? **(Ref. Para-12.27)**
24. Distinguish between dissolution of a partnership and dissolution of the firm. **(Ref. Para-12.27)**
25. Under what circumstances is a firm compulsorily dissolved? **(Ref. Para-12.28)**
26. Discuss the grounds on which the firm may be dissolved by the court? **(Ref. Para-12.29)**
27. Discuss the rights and liabilities of the partners on the dissolution of the firm. **(Ref. Para-12.30,12.31)**
28. Write a short note on the settlement of the accounts. **(Ref. Para-12.32)**
29. Explain the mode of giving public notice under the Indian Partnership Act, 1932? **(Ref. Para-12.34)**

## MULTIPLE-CHOICE QUESTIONS

1. Prior to the Indian Partnership Act, 1932, the provisions relating to partnerships were contained in
   (i) The Indian Contract Act, 1972.
   (ii) The Partnership Act, 1912.
   (iii) The Indian Contract Act, 1872.
   (iv) The English Partnership Act, 1845.
2. According to the Partnership Act, 'Business' includes
   (i) trade.
   (ii) occupation.
   (iii) profession.
   (iv) all of the above.
3. Which of the following constitutes partnership?
   (i) Family business of HUF.
   (ii) Persons who have inherited a house property jointly.
   (iii) Two parties carrying on a business for sharing the profits.
   (iv) A Burmese Buddhist husband and wife carrying on a business.
4. Which of these gives the correct definition of partnership?
   (i) It is a written agreement between the persons for sharing the profits of the business.
   (ii) It is an oral arrangement between the partners for sharing the profit.
   (iii) It is a relation between the persons who have agreed to share the profits of the business, carried on by all or any of them acting for all.
   (iv) All of the above.

5. A and B agree to share profits of a business in equal but if any loss, it will be borne by A alone. The partnership agreement is
   (i) valid.
   (ii) unlawful.
   (iii) illegal.
   (iv) voidable.
6. Which of this is not a valid partnership?
   (i) Minor admitted to benefits of the partnership.
   (ii) Company admitted as a partner.
   (iii) Partnership between Indian national and alien friend.
   (iv) Partnership between Indian national and alien enemies.
7. To form a partnership, the minimum capital contribution should be
   (i) ₹ 1 lakh.
   (ii) ₹ 5 lakhs.
   (iii) ₹ 10 lakhs.
   (iv) none of the above.
8. Partnership agreements may be
   (i) expressed.
   (ii) implied.
   (iii) neither (i) nor (ii).
   (iv) either (i) or (ii).
9. Which of these statements does not reflect the mutual agency principle in partnership?
   (i) The partner is both an agent and principal.
   (ii) A partner can, by his act bind other partners and is in turn bound by acts of other partners.
   (iii) All partners should actively participate in the business.
   (iv) Business may be managed by one or more partners.
10. A is employed by a partnership firm entitled to remuneration of ₹ 5000 per month plus 7% on the profits of the firm if profits exceed ₹ 1 lakh. Here,
    (i) A is not a partner in the firm.
    (ii) A is a partner in the firm.
    (iii) appointment of A is invalid.
    (iv) A can claim only ₹ 5000 per month but not the share of the profits.
11. Which of the following is correct?
    (i) Partnership arises by status.
    (ii) HUF is created by an agreement between the members.
    (iii) Partnership may arise from the conduct of the parties concerned.
    (iv) None of the above.
12. Which of the following is incorrect?
    (i) The partnership may be formed with two partnership firms as partners.
    (ii) A company can become partner in firm.
    (iii) A HUF can be created by an agreement of members.
    (iv) Both (i) and (iii).
13. In the HUF .......... is personally liable to the third party.
    (i) Karta and major members
    (ii) Karta
    (iii) all major members
    (iv) all the members
14. A person may become a partner with another person for particular adventures. This arrangement is called
    (i) partnership at will.
    (ii) particular partnership.
    (iii) undisclosed partnership.
    (iv) joint venture.

15. A and B enter into an agreement for preparing Ahmedabad to Bombay Express Highway. The partnership comes to an end after preparing of Highway. This arrangement is called
    (i) particular partnership.
    (ii) partnership at will.
    (iii) undisclosed partnership.
    (iv) joint venture.
16. A partner who is not partner but represents himself as a partner in a firm is called a
    (i) sleeping partner.
    (ii) partner by estoppels.
    (iii) working partner.
    (iv) sub-partner.
17. Active partner is also known as a
    (i) dormant partner.
    (ii) working partner.
    (iii) sub-partner.
    (iv) ostensible partner.
18. Partners are bound to carry on the business of the firm
    (i) to the advantage of the working partner.
    (ii) for his benefit.
    (iii) for the benefit of minor partners.
    (iv) to the greatest common advantage.
19. Which of the following is not covered by general duties of partners?
    (i) To carry on the business of the firm to the greatest common advantage of the firm.
    (ii) To be just and faithful to each other.
    (iii) To arrange for the audit of accounts of the firm.
    (iv) To render true accounts.
20. Ordinary matters of business may be decided by consent of
    (i) all the partners.
    (ii) majority partners.
    (iii) working partners.
    (iv) sleeping partners.
21. A change in nature of business can be effected only based on
    (i) unanimous consent of all the partners.
    (ii) consent of majority partners.
    (iii) consent of the working partners.
    (iv) consent of the sleeping partners.
22. When agreement is silent, rate of interest payable on advance by any partner is
    (i) 6%.
    (ii) 8%.
    (iii) 7%.
    (iv) 10%.
23. Which of the following conditions is not necessary for the exercise of implied authority?
    (i) The act must relate to the business of the firm.
    (ii) The act must be done in the firm's business name.
    (iii) The act must be done in the usual way of carrying on the firm's business.
    (iv) The act must be done in an emergency.
24. Which of the following is incorrect?
    (i) Maintain bank A/c of the firm by the partner is not within implied authority of a partner.
    (ii) A partner in a firm has a right to receive interest on advances at the rate of 12 per cent p.a.
    (iii) The irregular expulsion of a partner does not give any right to the expelled partner.
    (iv) All of the above.
25. Which of these acts falls outside the implied authority?
    (i) Purchase of goods on behalf of the firm.
    (ii) Sale of the goods of the firm.
    (iii) Receiving payments of debts due to the firm.
    (iv) Withdraw any suit filed on behalf of the firm.

26. Which of this falls outside the implied authority?
    (i) Pledging of the goods of the firm for loans.
    (ii) Drawing, accepting and endorsing the negotiable instruments on behalf of the firm.
    (iii) Acquire immovable property on behalf of the firm.
    (iv) Engage the lawyer to defend suit against the firm.
27. Which of these acts are within the implied authority?
    (i) Settlement of the accounts with the third party on behalf of the firm.
    (ii) Open a bank account on behalf of the firm in his name.
    (iii) Compromise any claim by the firm.
    (iv) Submit the dispute to arbitration.
28. For all acts of the firm done while he is a partner, every partner is
    (i) jointly liable only
    (ii) severally liable only
    (iii) jointly and severally liable.
    (iv) not liable at all.
29. Partner's duty of good faith ______ be excluded by an agreement to the contrary.
    (i) cannot
    (ii) can
    (iii) may
    (iv) may not.
30. It is the right of every partner to be consulted in
    (i) the matters affecting to him only.
    (ii) all matters relating to the business of the firm.
    (iii) both (i) and (ii).
    (iv) none of the above.
31. Which matter can be decided with the consent of all the partners?
    (i) Alteration of business.
    (ii) Addition to the business.
    (iii) Admission of a new partner.
    (iv) All of the above.
32. Which of the following is not covered by the term 'Property of the Firm'?
    (i) Property and rights and interest in property originally brought into the firm.
    (ii) Property acquired by the firm.
    (iii) Goodwill of the business.
    (iv) Property of the partners.
33. Which of the following person may be admitted as a partner?
    (i) Person of unsound mind.
    (ii) A minor.
    (iii) Alien enemy.
    (iv) An insolvent.
34. Which of the following is incorrect?
    (i) One major and another minor can form a partnership.
    (ii) One minor and another minor can form a partnership.
    (iii) One minor female with another major female can form partnership.
    (iv) All of the above.
35. On attaining majority, within how many months a minor may give public notice of his decision to continue or withdraw from the firm?
    (i) 3 months.
    (ii) 4 months.
    (iii) 6 months.
    (iv) 12 months.

36. New partner's liability commences from
    (i) the date of his admission.
    (ii) the financial year in which he was admitted.
    (iii) the day he start working for firm.
    (iv) either (i) or (ii) whichever is earlier.
37. In case of partnership at will, a retiring partner has to give a written notice
    (i) to the firm.
    (ii) to the working partners.
    (iii) to all the partners.
    (iv) to the state government.
38. Retiring partner continues to be liable for acts of the firm done
    (i) upto the date of admission of a new partner.
    (ii) upto the date of giving public notice of retirement.
    (iii) upto the end of the financial year in which he retires.
    (iv) all of the above.
39. Public notice of retirement should be given by
    (i) retiring partner only.
    (ii) any partner of firm only.
    (iii) by the retiring partner or any partner of the reconstituted firm.
    (iv) all the partners of the reconstituted firm.
40. Where a partner in a firm is declared as insolvent by court order
    (i) the firm is automatically dissolved.
    (ii) the firm is not automatically dissolved.
    (iii) the firm becomes illegal association.
    (iv) the firm is also considered as insolvent.
41. According to the Partnership Act, a partner can
    (i) transfer his interest in the firm.
    (ii) transfer his interest in the firm with consent of all the other partners.
    (iii) transfer his interest in the firm with consent of majority of partners.
    (iv) transfer his interest to any third party without the consent.
42. Which of the following statements is correct?
    (i) The estate of insolvent partner is not liable for the acts of the firm done after the order of insolvency.
    (ii) The public notice of insolvency of a partner is not necessary.
    (iii) The firm is not liable for any act of the insolvent partner done after the date of order of insolvency.
    (iv) All of the above.
43. Dissolution by agreement can be
    (i) with the consent of all the partners.
    (ii) in accordance with a contract between the partners.
    (iii) either (i) or (ii).
    (iv) both (i) and (ii).
44. Which of the following is correct?
    (i) The death of a partner automatically dissolves the firm.
    (ii) Any partner can dissolve the firm by giving notice if partnership is at will.
    (iii) All business of firm becomes unlawful.
    (iv) All of the above.

45. In partnership at will where no date has been mentioned in the notice, the firm is dissolved from
    (i) the date decided by the registrar of firms.
    (ii) the date as decided by the partners.
    (iii) the date when the notice is communicated.
    (iv) the date decided by majority of partners.
46. Which of the following do not constitute ground for dissolution by court?
    (i) Insanity of the partner.
    (ii) Incapacity of partner to perform his duties.
    (iii) Admission of minor to the benefits of partnership.
    (iv) Continuous losses of the firm.
47. Which of the following do not constitute a ground for dissolution by court?
    (i) Misconduct by partner.
    (ii) Transfer of interest by partner.
    (iii) Just and equitable grounds.
    (iv) Suit by the dormant partner.
48. Which of the following is incorrect?
    (i) The death of a partner automatically dissolves the firm.
    (ii) Any partner can dissolve the firm by given an oral notice if partnership is at will.
    (iii) Insolvency of a partner automatically dissolves a firm.
    (iv) All of the above.
49. Which of the following do not constitute just and equitable grounds for dissolution of firm?
    (i) Deadlock in management.
    (ii) Disappearance of the substratum of business.
    (iii) Partners not in talking terms.
    (iv) None of the above.
50. The estate of a partner who dies is not liable for acts done after the date on which he ceases to be a partner.
    (i) True
    (ii) Partly true
    (iii) False
    (iv) None of the above
51. No premium or part thereof shall be repaid if the dissolution is
    (i) due to the partner's own misconduct.
    (ii) in accordance with an agreement containing no provision as to return of premium.
    (iii) both (i) and (ii).
    (iv) either (i) or (ii).
52. Which of the following firm can be dissolved by a written notice of dissolution given by any partner?
    (i) General partnership.
    (ii) Particular partnership.
    (iii) Partnership at will.
    (iv) Both (i) and (ii).
53. In a firm where a partner has become permanently incapable of performing his duties, the firm
    (i) is automatically dissolved.
    (ii) may be dissolved by the court.
    (iii) cannot be dissolved.
    (iv) none of the above.
54. In a firm where a partner is guilty of misconduct which adversely affect the partnership business, the firm
    (i) is automatically dissolved.
    (ii) is compulsorily dissolved.
    (iii) may be dissolved by the court.
    (iv) cannot be dissolved.

55. Which of the following words are permissible in a Firm's name?
 (i) Associates.
 (ii) King.
 (iii) Royal.
 (iv) Empress.

56. Which of the following rights are not applicable for unregistered firms?
 (i) Right of partners to sue the firm for enforcing a right arising out of a contract.
 (ii) Right of partners to sue for dissolution of the firm.
 (iii) Right of partners to sue for settlement of accounts of a dissolved firm.
 (iv) Right of partners to sue for realizing the property of a dissolved firm.

57. If a firm is not-registered its business
 (i) does not become illegal.
 (ii) becomes illegal.
 (iii) becomes void.
 (iv) becomes voidable.

58. In the case of the registered firms, public notice is given in the following manner:
 (i) Serving a copy of the notice to the registrar of firms.
 (ii) Publishing the notice in the official gazette.
 (iii) Publishing the notice in one vernacular newspaper.
 (iv) All of the above.

59. The registration of a firm is made to the
 (i) Registrar of companies.
 (ii) Registrar of firms.
 (iii) Registrar of trust.
 (iv) High court.

60. A partner shall pay to the firm any profit derived by him
 (i) from any transaction of the firm.
 (ii) from the use of the property of the firm.
 (iii) from the business using the firm-name.
 (iv) all of the above.

61. The implied authority of any partner in a firm ..............................
 (i) restricted
 (ii) extended.
 (iii) either (i) or (ii).
 (iv) none of the above.

## ANSWER KEYS

| | | | | | |
|---|---|---|---|---|---|
| **1.** (iii) | **12.** (iv) | **23.** (iv) | **34.** (iv) | **45.** (iii) | **56.** (i) |
| **2.** (iv) | **13.** (ii) | **24.** (iv) | **35.** (iii) | **46.** (iii) | **57.** (i) |
| **3.** (iii) | **14.** (ii) | **25.** (iv) | **36.** (i) | **47.** (iv) | **58.** (iv) |
| **4.** (iii) | **15.** (i) | **26.** (iii) | **37.** (iii) | **48.** (ii) | **59.** (ii) |
| **5.** (i) | **16.** (ii) | **27.** (i) | **38.** (ii) | **49.** (iv) | **60.** (iv) |
| **6.** (iv) | **17.** (iv) | **28.** (iii) | **39.** (iii) | **50.** (i) | **61.** (iii) |
| **7.** (iv) | **18.** (iv) | **29.** (i) | **40.** (i) | **51.** (iv) | |
| **8.** (iv) | **19.** (iii) | **30.** (ii) | **41.** (iv) | **52.** (iii) | |
| **9.** (iii) | **20.** (ii) | **31.** (iv) | **42.** (iv) | **53.** (ii) | |
| **10.** (i) | **21.** (i) | **32.** (iv) | **43.** (iii) | **54.** (iii) | |
| **11.** (iii) | **22.** (i) | **33.** (ii) | **44.** (iv) | **55.** (i) | |

# 13

# Sales of Goods Act, 1930

## Learning Objectives

*After reading this chapter, you will be able to understand:*

- Concepts of sale and agreement to sell and definitions
- Condition and warranty
- Passing of the property from the seller to the buyer
- Performance of the contract of sale
- Rights of an unpaid seller
- Breach of contract to deliver specific or ascertained goods

## 13.1 APPLICABILITY

In trade and commerce, sales and purchase of goods are very common transactions. These transactions may appear to be very simple but the possibilities of complications are always there. Therefore, knowledge of basic principles of sale and purchase is very much essential for all the concerned parties as well as for the entire community. The Sale of Goods Act contains the basic principles as well as the legal framework of transactions of sale and purchase.

Earlier, the Sale of Goods Act was a part of the Indian Contract Act. A separate Act was framed in the year 1930. This act extends to the whole of India, except the State of Jammu and Kashmir. This act comes into force w.e.f. 1 July 1930.

## 13.2 DEFINITION

### 13.2.1 Buyer—Section 2(1)

Buyer means a person who buys or agrees to buy the goods.

### 13.2.2 Seller—Section 2(13)

Seller means a person who sells or agrees to sell the goods.

### 13.2.3 Delivery—Section 2(2)

Delivery means voluntary transfer of the possession of goods from one person to another. Usually, the goods are delivered from the seller to the buyer. Immediate delivery of goods is not necessary or mandatory.

### 13.2.4 Price—Section 2(10)

Price means the money consideration for the sale of goods. The money here means the currency in circulation. Remember any contract without consideration is usually not valid.

### 13.2.5 Goods—Section 2(7)

Goods means every kind of movable property other than actionable claims and money and includes stock and shares, growing crops, grass and things attached to or forming a part of the land, which are agreed to be severed before the sale or under the contract of sale.

***Example***

Shares, debentures, goodwill, water, fruit, sim card and newspaper are considered as goods.

### 13.2.6 Agreement to Sell

Where the transfer of property in goods takes place at a future date.

### 13.2.7 Sale

Where the transfer of property in goods takes place at the time of contract.

### 13.2.8 Document of Title—Section 2(4)

The document of title of goods includes the following documents:

1. The bill of lading
2. The dock-warrant
3. The warehouse keeper's certificate
4. The wharfinger's certificate
5. The railway receipt
6. The multimodal transport document
7. The warrant
8. The order for the delivery of goods.

In the ordinary course of business, it is a proof of the possession of goods or authorizing either by endorsement or delivery, the possessor of the document to transfer or receive the goods.

### 13.2.9 Property—Section 2(11)

Property means the general property in goods.

The property can be understood in two ways with reference to any goods; general property and special property. The general property in goods means ownership, while the special property means the possession or control of goods. Therefore, the transfer of property in goods is different from the delivery of goods. The delivery of goods means a transfer of special property in goods.

***Example***

When you pledge the jewelry with a bank as a matter of security for the repayment of the loan, you are only transferring the special property to the bank. Its general property (ownership) belongs to you.

## 13.3 ESSENTIALS OF VALID SALES

The essentials of a contract of sale are as under:

### 13.3.1 Two Parties

There must be two parties. One cannot sell to himself. The seller and the buyer must be different. A part owner can sell goods to another part owner.

### 13.3.2 Goods

The subject matter of the contract of sale is goods. The goods must be movable. Immovable things are out of the purview of the act. The goods may be present or future.

### 13.3.3 Transfer of Property

The seller transfers or agrees to transfer the property in goods. The transfer of property in goods means the transfer of general property.

### 13.3.4 Consideration

The price is the consideration for the contract of sale of goods. The exchange of goods for goods is barter. Exchange is partly for goods and partly for money in a sale. In case where the promissory note or the negotiable instrument is given in exchange of the transfer of goods, it will be a sale since a negotiable instrument is always paid in money.

### 13.3.5 Elements of Contract

All essential elements of a valid contract must be observed because basically it is a contract.

### 13.3.6 Form of Contract of Sale

No form of contract of sale is prescribed under the Sales of Goods Act. The contract of sale can be expressed or implied. The contract of sale may be in writing or by word of mouth. The contract of sale can be conditional or absolute.

### 13.3.7 Delivery of Goods

The contract of sale may provide any of the following methods for the delivery of goods:

1. Immediate delivery of goods.
2. Immediate payment of price but delivery at some future date.
3. Immediate payment of price and immediate delivery of goods.
4. Delivery or payment or both made in installments.
5. Delivery or payment or both will be made at future date.

**Case Study**

A agrees to deliver his old car valued at ₹ 90,000 to B, a car dealer, in exchange for a new car and agrees to pay the difference in cash. Is it a valid contract of sale? What would be your answer if he exchanges the car against the new car and does not pay any money?

## 13.4 DISTINGUISH BETWEEN A SALE AND AN AGREEMENT TO SELL

| Subject Matter | Sale | Agreement to Sell |
|---|---|---|
| Transfer of ownership | In a sale, the ownership of goods is transferred immediately. | In case of an agreement to sell, the ownership will be transferred in future. |
| Nature of contract | A sale is an executed contract. | An agreement to sell is an executor contract. |
| If price is not paid | A seller can sue for the price. He has all the rights of an unpaid seller. | A seller can sue for damages. |
| Risk | The buyer bears the risk. | The seller bears the risk. |
| Type of goods involved | A sale takes place in the case of existing goods usually. | An agreement to sell takes place in the case of future goods. |

## 13.5 DISTINGUISH BETWEEN A SALE AND A HIRE–PURCHASE

| Subject Matter | Sale | Hire–Purchase |
|---|---|---|
| Meaning | It is a transaction where the ownership of goods is transferred immediately to the buyer. | It is an agreement where the hirer uses the goods on the payment of the installment and he has the option to return the goods. The ownership transfers on the payment of the last installment. |
| Applicable Act | Sales of Goods Act, 1930. | Hire–Purchase Act, 1972. |
| Parties | A contract of sale involves two parties namely the seller and the buyer. | Hire–purchase agreement involves two parties, the hirer and the hire vendor. |
| Mode of forming contract | A contract of sale can be made orally or in writing. | The hire–purchase agreement should be in writing. |
| Risk | The risk of loss passes to the buyer. | The risk of loss does not pass to the hirer as the ownership is not transferred. It will pass to the hirer when the last installment is paid. |
| Return of goods | The buyer cannot return goods usually. | The hirer can return the goods. |
| Sales Tax | The sales tax is payable immediately. | The sales tax is payable when all the installments are paid. |

## 13.6 DISTINGUISH BETWEEN A SALE AND A BAILMENT

| Subject–Matter | Sale | Bailment |
|---|---|---|
| Meaning | It is the transfer of property in goods for price. | It is the transfer of special property in goods for some specific purpose where the goods are returned on the completion of the purpose. |
| Consideration | A contract of sale is always with consideration. | The bailment of goods can be without consideration. |
| Returning of goods | The goods are not returned by the buyer. | The goods are returned by the bailee after the purpose is over. |

## 13.7 CONTRACT FOR WORK AND SKILL

A contract for work and skill is a contract if it involves the exercise of skill and labour by one party on some goods or materials supplied by the other party or supplied by the party who exercises skill and labour for the price.

Following are the main features of contract for work and skill:

1. The main purpose of a contract is to exercise work and skill.
2. The supply of own goods is only subsidiary or supportive.
3. The intention of the parties is to transfer goods, only after the exercise of some skill and labour.

The Sales of Goods Act is not applicable to this category of transaction. As the Sales of Goods Act is not applicable, there is no liability of sales tax.

***Example***

An artist was asked to paint a portrait. The material was supplied by the party and not by the painter. It was held to be a contract for work and labour and not of sale.

## 13.8 TYPES OF GOODS

The goods forming the subject matter of the contract of sale may be classified as under:

### 13.8.1 Existing Goods

Existing goods are in actual existing at the time of the contract of sale. The existing goods are the goods which are owned and possessed by the seller at the time of sale. The existing goods may be of three types:

**13.8.1.1 Specific Goods** The goods which are identified and agreed upon by the parties at the time of the contract of sale are specific goods. It should be noted that the goods must be both identified and agreed upon.

**13.8.1.2 Ascertained Goods** Ascertained goods are the goods which are identified after the formation of the contract of sale. When the unascertained goods are identified and agreed upon by the parties, the goods are called as ascertained goods.

**13.8.1.3 Unascertained Goods** These are the goods which are not identified and agreed upon at the time of the contract of sale. These goods are merely described by the parties at the time of the contract of sale.

### 13.8.2 Future Goods

Future goods are those goods which do not exist at the time of the contract of sale. These goods are to be manufactured or acquired by the seller after the making of the contract of sale. The future goods cannot be sold but there can only be an agreement to sell.

### 13.8.3 Contingent Goods

It is a kind of future goods. These goods are those goods, the acquisition of which is contingent upon the happening or non-happening of an uncertain event.

***Example***

A agrees to sell the cargo loaded on the ship 'Victory', which is coming from London to Bombay. The ship may or may not arrive. So, these goods will be called as contingent goods.

**Case Study**

A, a farmer, agrees to sell B, mangoes, provided there is good rain during season. Is it sale or agreement to sell?

**Case Study**

A agrees to sell B, all crops to be grown in his farm during 2011 season. It is contract about which type of goods?

**Case Study**

A had 5 sofas. He agreed to sell one sofa to B. Is it contract for the sale of specific goods? If not, which type of goods?

## 13.9 PRICE OF GOODS—SECTIONS 9 AND 10

The modes of determining the price are following:

### 13.9.1 Method 1

The price is specified under the contract. It is the most common method of determining the price. Here, the parties decide the price in advance.

### 13.9.2 Method 2

The price may be determined as per the method specified in the contract. Here, the parties decide in advance, the method of determining the price.

***Example***

Delivery of rice on 1 December 2008 at the rate prevailing on that day.

### 13.9.3 Method 3

The price may be determined in accordance to the custom and the usage of the trade. This method is applicable if the parties regularly trade. Where the price is not fixed as above, the buyer shall pay the seller a reasonable price. 'What is a reasonable price' is a question of facts and circumstances. A reasonable price under the Sale of Goods Act means the market price.

### 13.9.4 Method 4

The price may be determined by the third party. If it is so, the contract shall specify the name of the third party. If the third party fails to specify, the contract is void but if the goods are delivered to the buyer and used by him, he is required to pay a reasonable price. If the third party is prevented from fixing the price, the defaulting party is liable for the damages.

**Case Study**

A agrees to sell his 100 bags of rice to B at a price to be fixed by C. But C failed to fix the price. Is it valid contract now?

## 13.10 CONSEQUENCES OF DESTRUCTION OF SPECIFIC GOODS—SECTIONS 7 AND 8

The consequences of the destruction of specific goods can be discussed under the following three heads:

### 13.10.1 If Goods Perish Before Making of Contract

The contract is *void-ab-initio.* due to the mistake as to the existence of the subject matter. It is to be noted that if the seller has knowledge about the destruction of goods, even then he enters into the contract of sale with the buyer then the seller is bound to compensate to the buyer.

### 13.10.2 Where a Part of the Goods Is Perished Before Making of Contract

If the goods were divisible then the contract can be enforced partly and if the goods were indivisible then the contract becomes *void-ab-initio*.

***Example***

A contracted to sell one wagon containing 700 bags of groundnut to B. Unknown to A, 109 bags had been stolen at the time of sale. Therefore, A made a delivery of 591 bags. Held, the sale was void.

### 13.10.3 If Goods Perish After the 'Agreement to Sell' But Before 'Sale'

The contract is void if subsequently the goods have perished and there is no fault on the part of the buyer or the seller in perishing the goods.

***Example***

A horse was delivered upon trial for 8 days. However, the horse died within 8 days without the fault of buyer or seller. Held, the seller must bear the loss as the contract was void.

However, the parties to the contract may provide otherwise also.

## 13.11 CONDITIONS AND WARRANTIES

Generally, at the time of sale, the seller makes some representations, statements or stipulations for the praise of his goods. Some of the representations are in nature of opinion, while others are in nature of facts. The representation as to the fact which becomes a part of the contract of sale is called as stipulation. The stipulation may be a condition or warranty depending upon its importance in relation to the contract. The stipulation which is essential to the main purpose of a contract is known as condition. The breach of condition gives the aggrieved party the right to terminate the contract.

The stipulation which is collateral to the main purpose of the contract is warranty. The breach of warranty gives rise to the aggrieved party the right to claim the damages but the contract cannot be terminated. The conditions and warranties may be expressed or implied.

The express conditions and warranties are those which the parties agree expressly, i.e., orally or in writing. The implied conditions are those which are implied by the law in the absence of any agreement to the contrary. The conditions and warranties in the contract of sale constitute stipulation with the reference to goods. In the case of a conflict between the express conditions and the implied conditions, express conditions shall prevail.

The breach of condition in a contract of sale of goods gives right to cancel the contract. If the party has suffered from any loss, he can also claim compensation for the breach of condition. But the breach of warranty in a contract of sale of goods gives the right to claim the damages only. However, the liability for the implied conditions and warranties may be excluded by the parties in the following situations:

1. If an express agreement between the parties provides so.
2. If the course of dealings between the parties suggests so.
3. If there is a custom or usages of a particular trade.

According to the Section 13 of the Sale of Goods Act, 1930, a breach of condition may be treated as a breach of warranty in the following circumstances:

1. Where a contract of sale is subject to any condition to be fulfilled by the seller, the buyer may waive the condition.
2. Where the buyer elects to treat the breach of condition as the breach of a warranty.
3. Where the contract of sale is non-severable and the buyer has accepted the whole goods or any part thereof.
4. Where the fulfilment of any condition or warranty is excused by law by the reason of impossibility or otherwise.

## 13.12 IMPLIED CONDITIONS

Following are the implied conditions which are contained in the Sales of Goods Act:

### 13.12.1 Conditions as to Title—Section 14(a)

There is an implied condition on the part of the seller that:

1. In the case of a sale, the seller has a right to sell the goods.
2. In the agreement to sell, the seller will have a right to sell the goods at the time of passing of the ownership in goods.

If the title of a seller turns out to be defective, the buyer must return the goods to the true owner and recover the price from the seller.

### 13.12.2 Conditions as to Description—Section 15

Where the goods are sold by description, there is an implied condition that the goods shall correspond to the description. If later on, the buyer finds that the goods are not as per description, he may reject the goods and claim a refund of the price.

***Example***

A machine was sold. The buyer has not seen the machine but the seller described it as a new one. However, it was found to be a very old one. Held, the machine was not according to the description.

### 13.12.3 Sale by Sample—Section 17

Where the goods are sold by the sample, followings are the implied conditions:

1. The bulk shall correspond to the sample in quality.
2. The buyer shall be given a reasonable opportunity to compare the goods with the sample.
3. The goods shall be free from any defect rendering them un-merchantable. It is to be noted that this implied condition applies only in the case of the latent defects, i.e., those defects which cannot be discovered by an ordinary inspection. In fact, such defects are discovered when the goods are put to use or by examination in the laboratories. The seller is not liable for any apparent or visible defects, which can be discovered by examination.

### 13.12.4 Sale by Description as well as Sample—Section 15

If the sale is by sample as well as description, both the conditions shall be satisfied. The goods must correspond with the sample as well as the description.

***Example***

A agreed to sell to C some oil described as 'Foreign refined oil' and warranted only equal to sample. The goods supplied were equal to sample but contained a mixture of hemp oil. Held, C could reject the goods.

### 13.12.5 Conditions as to Quality and Fitness for Buyer's Purpose—Section 16

Where the buyer, expressly or impliedly, tells the seller the particular purpose for which he needs the goods and relies on the skill or judgment of the seller, there is an implied condition that the goods shall be reasonably fit for such a purpose. It is not necessary that the purpose should be expressed in words. The purpose can also be ascertained from the nature or description of the goods.

When the article can be used only for one particular purpose, the buyer need not to inform the seller the purpose for which the goods are required.

***Example***

A purchased a hot water bottle from a chemist. While the bottle was being used by A's wife, it burst and injured A's wife. Held, the seller was liable for damages as the bottle was not fit for the purpose for which it was meant. *(Priest versus Last)*

**13.12.5.1 Exceptions to the Implied Condition as to Quality or Fitness** 'The conditions as to the quality or fitness' will not apply. If the buyer is suffering from an abnormality, which renders the goods unsuitable for a particular purpose and the buyer does not inform the seller about that abnormality.

***Example***

A purchased a coat. He had abnormally sensitive skin. By wearing the coat, he got a skin complaint. Held, there was no breach of condition as he had not disclosed the abnormality of his skin.

Where the goods can be used for a number of purposes, the buyer should inform the particular purpose for which such goods were required. If he does not disclose, there is no such condition of the quality or fitness.

### 13.12.6 Conditions as to Merchantability—Section 16

There is an implied condition that the goods shall be of merchantable quality, where the goods are bought by description from a seller who deals in the goods of that description.

'Merchantability' means that there is no defect in the goods, which renders them unfit for sale. Thus, a watch that will not keep time and a pen that will not write cannot be regarded as merchantable. In a contract for the sale of goods, the condition as to merchantability applies where the goods are bought by description or where the goods are sold under the trade mark.

***Example***

A radio set was sold to a layman. The set was defective. It did not work in spite of repairs. Held, the buyer could return the set and claim refund.

### 13.12.7 Condition as to Wholesomeness

In the case of eatables and food-stuff, there is an implied condition that the goods shall be wholesome, i.e., free from any defect which renders them unfit for human consumption. The implied condition as to the wholesomeness of the goods is applicable for every type of goods in the nature of food.

***Example***

A purchased milk from B, a milk dealer. The milk contained typhoid germs. A's wife on taking the milk got infected and died. Held, A was entitled to get damages. *(Frost vs Aylesbury Dairy Co. Ltd.)*

**Case Study**

For the purpose of making uniform for the employees, Bansi Bhaiya bought dark blue coloured cloth from Vivek but did not disclose to the seller the purpose of the said purchase. When uniforms were prepared and used by the employees, the cloth was found unfit. However, there was an evidence that the cloth was fit for caps, boots and carriage lining. Advise Bansi Bhaiya whether he is entitled to have any remedy under the Sale of Goods Act, 1930?

**Case Study**

A contracts to sell B, by showing sample, certain quantity of rape-seed oil described as 'foreign refined rape-seed-oil'. The oil when delivered, matches with the sample but is not foreign refined rape-seed oil. Referring to the provisions of the Sale of Goods Act, 1930, advise the remedy, if any, available to B.

**Case Study**

Mr. Amit was shopping in a self-service Super market. He picked up a bottle of cold drink from a shelf. While he was examining the bottle, it exploded in his hand and injured him. He files a suit for damages against the owner of the market on the ground of breach of condition. Decide, under the Sale of Goods Act, 1930, whether Mr. Amit would succeed in his claim?

**Case Study**

Jolly bought a second hand car from Yogesh for ₹ 85,000 and paid for it. After Jolly had used the car for six months, he was deprived of it because Yogesh had no title to it. Can Jolly recover the price of the car from Yogesh? Advise Jolly.

**Case Study**

A told B, a car dealer, that he wanted to purchase a car 'suitable for touring purposes', B suggested that a 'Maruti Alto' car would be fit for the purpose. Relying upon his statement, A bought a 'Alto' car which turned out to be unfit for touring purposes. What remedy is available to Mr. A?

## 13.13 IMPLIED WARRANTIES

Following are the implied warranties which are contained in the Sales of Goods Act:

### 13.13.1 Warranty as to Quiet Possession—Section 14

In the absence to any contract showing a contrary intention, there is an implied warranty that the buyer shall have and enjoy the quiet possession of the goods. If the buyer is disturbed in the enjoyment of the goods, he can claim the damages from the seller.

### 13.13.2 Warranty Against Encumbrances—Section 14

Unless the circumstances of the case are such as to show a contrary intention, there is an implied warranty that the goods shall be free from any charge or encumbrance in favour of any party not declared to the buyer before or at the time contract is made. However, there will not be any such warranty if the charge is declared to the buyer at the time of sale.

### 13.13.3 Warranty as to Quality and Fitness by Usage of Trade—Section 16

An implied warranty, as to the quality or fitness for a particular purpose, may be annexed by the usage of trade.

### 13.13.4 Warranty to Disclose the Dangerous Nature of Goods

In case of the sale of dangerous goods, the seller is under an obligation to warn the buyer about the probable danger. A failure to do so, will make the seller liable to pay the damages.

***Example***

A sold a tin of a disinfectant to B, knowing that it was likely to be dangerous to B if opened without special care. B opened the tin, whereupon the disinfectant powder went into her eyes causing an injury. Held, A was liable in damages to B as he failed to warn B of the probable danger.

### 13.13.5 Circumstances When a Condition Can Be Treated as Warranty

Section 13 of the act provides for the situations in which the condition can be treated as a warranty. These are:

1. If the buyer waives the condition.
2. If the buyer elects to treat the breach of condition as a breach of warranty.
3. If the condition becomes impossible or if the performance of the condition is otherwise excused.

**Case Study**

Aman borrows ₹ 200 from Bhuvan against the security of his wrist-watch. After a week's time, Aman obtains the watch from Bhuvan on some pretext and then sells the same watch to Chandan, an innocent buyer, who has no knowledge about Bhuvan's charge on the watch. Subsequently, Bhuvan disturbs Chandan's possession and gets the payment of ₹ 200 from him. Now Chandan files a suit against Aman for the recovery of ₹ 200 from him. Will Chandan succeed? Give reasons.

## 13.14 DISTINGUISH BETWEEN A CONDITION AND A WARRANTY

| Matter | Condition | Warranty |
|---|---|---|
| Stipulation | The condition is a stipulation essential to the main purpose of the contract. | The warranty is collateral (subsidiary) to the main purpose of the contract. |
| If breach? | The buyer has the right to cancel a contract on the breach of conditions. | The buyer has no right to cancel the contract on the breach of warranty. The buyer can claim the damages. |
| Treatment | The breach of condition may be treated as the breach of warranty. | The breach of warranty cannot be treated as the breach of condition. |

## 13.15 DOCTRINE OF CAVEAT EMPTOR

'Caveat Emptor' is a Latin word. It means 'let the buyer beware.' It is the buyer's duty to select the goods of his requirement and the seller is not bound to supply the goods which shall be fit for any particular purpose of the buyer. It suggests that the buyer, while purchasing the goods, must act with a 'third eye and ear,' i.e.:

1. He should be careful to see that the goods purchased will serve his purpose well.
2. If the buyer is not careful and he finds later on that the goods do not serve his purpose, he cannot hold the seller liable for it.

3. The seller is under no obligation to tell the defects of his articles.

If the buyer selects the goods as per his requirement and the goods are not satisfying his requirement, he cannot claim anything against the seller. However, in the following exceptions, the Doctrine of caveat emptor is not applicable:

1. Where the implied conditions as to the quality or fitness for the buyer's purpose is applicable. It means when the buyer has specified his purpose and relied on the skill of the seller, the doctrine of caveat emptor is not applicable.
2. When the goods are sold by description, it should be of merchantable quality. In such case, the doctrine of caveat emptor is not applicable.
3. In case of edible items, the implied condition of wholesomeness is applicable and the goods should be of merchantable quality. If the goods are not fit for human consumption then the buyer is not liable but the seller will be liable.
4. Custom may provide that a particular defect will amount to unfitness and the buyer can reject the goods. Here the doctrine of caveat emptor is not applicable. But the custom must be reasonable.
5. When the consent of the buyer is obtained by fraud, the provision of the doctrine of caveat emptor is not applicable.

**Case Study**

A goes to B's shop and purchases a silk saree, thinking that it is made of Banarsi Silk. The shopkeeper knows that A's thinking is wrong. He, however, does not correct A's impression. Later on, when A discovers that the saree is not made of Banarsi-silk he wants to avoid the contract. Would A succeed? Give reasons.

## 13.16 TRANSFER OF OWNERSHIP OF SPECIFIC GOODS—SECTIONS 20–22

In case of the sale of specific goods, the rules relating to the transfer of ownership are contained in Sections 20–22 of the Sale of Goods Act which may be discussed as under:

### 13.16.1 Ownership is Transferred at the Time of Making Contract

The ownership is transferred immediately at the time of making the contract if all the following conditions are satisfied:

1. The contract is for the specific goods.
2. The goods are in deliverable state.
3. The goods are not required to be weight or measured for determining price.

***Example***

A sold to B, 100 bales of cotton lying in his godown. Before the bales could be identified and separated, all the bales were destroyed in fire. Here, the seller is liable for damage because the ownership is not transferred.

### 13.16.2 Ownership Is Transferred When Goods Are Put in Deliverable State

If the goods are not ready in the deliverable state at the time of making the contract of sale, the ownership of goods is transferred after the formation of the contract of sale when the following conditions are satisfied:

1. The contract is for specific goods.
2. The goods are put in deliverable state by the seller.
3. The fact that the goods are put into a deliverable state, has come to the knowledge of the buyer.

***Example***

A certain quantity of oil was purchased by A. The oil was to be filled in tins. B filled up some of the tins and informed A to take the delivery. In the meantime, a fire destroyed the entire quantity of oil. Held, A will bear the loss of the oil which was filled in the tins and the seller must bear the loss of the balance.

### 13.16.3 Ownership Is Transferred When Goods in Deliverable State Put to Weighed or Measured to Ascertained Price

If the goods are not weighed or measured at the time of making a contract of sale, the ownership of the goods is transferred after the formation of a contract of sale when the following conditions are satisfied:

1. The contract is for the specific goods.
2. At the time of formation, the price is not determined. It is determined later by the weight or measurement.
3. The goods are put in deliverable state by the seller.
4. The fact that goods have been weighed or measured in order to determine the price has come to the knowledge of the buyer.

***Example***

A sold 10 kg of wheat. The wheat was to be weighed. Before the wheat was weighed, it was carried away by the flood. Held, the ownership of the wheat was left with the seller and it did not pass to the buyer.

**Case Study**

A certain quantity of oil was bought. The oil was to be filled into barrels by the seller and then taken away by the buyer. Some barrels were filled in the presence of the buyer but before the remainders could be filled, a fire broke out and the entire quantity of oil was destroyed. State the liabilities of the buyer and the seller.

## 13.17 TRANSFER OF OWNERSHIP IN THE CASE OF UNASCERTAINED GOODS—SECTIONS 18 AND 23

In the case of the unascertained goods, when both the parties came to know which particular goods shall be delivered, the ownership is transferred. Following conditions must be satisfied to transfer the ownership:

1. Ascertainment is the first step in the transfer of ownership. It means the process of identification and setting aside of the goods from a huge mass of goods.
2. Generally, it is made by the seller (unilateral act).
3. The contract to sell unascertained goods is not a complete sell. It is the agreement to sell.

**Example**

20 bags of sugar out of a bulk were agreed to be sold. 4 bags of sugar were filled up and taken away by the buyer. Subsequently, the seller filled up 16 bags and informed the buyer. The buyer replied that he will take the delivery as soon as possible. However, before the buyer could take their delivery, the goods were lost. Held, the buyer was responsible as the ownership had passed to the buyer.

## 13.18 TRANSFER OF OWNERSHIP IN CASE OF GOODS SALE ON APPROVAL OR ON SALE OR RETURN BASIS—SECTION 24

The term 'sale on approval' basis may be defined as the sale in which the buyer may return the goods within a reasonable time. This is also known as 'sale on return' basis. It means the buyer has the option either to return or retain the goods. Here, the property in goods does not pass from the seller to the buyer:

| Case | When Ownership Transferred |
|---|---|
| When the buyer gives his approval or acceptance. | The approval or acceptance is communicated to the seller. |
| When the buyer does some act adopting the transaction. | When the act of adoption is done. |
| When the buyer fails to return the goods. | |
| (a) If the time fixed for the return of goods. | The ownership of the goods transferred on the expiry of the fixed time. |
| (b) If no time is fixed. | The ownership of the goods transferred on the expiry of a reasonable time. |

**Example**

A certain jewellery was delivered to a buyer on sale or return basis. The buyer pledged the jewellery. Held, the buyer had adopted the transaction and as such the property had passed and the seller could not recover the jewellery from the Pawnee.

Where the railway receipt or the bill of lading is in the name of the buyer but is sent through the bank with the instructions that the same is to be delivered against the acceptance of the bill or payment of the price, the property in the goods shall not pass until the buyer makes a payment to the bank and obtain the documents.

**Case Study**

With a view to boost the sales Hanuman Automobiles sells a motorcar to Mr. A on trial basis for a period of three days with a condition that if Mr. A is not satisfied with the performance of the car, he can return back the car. However, the car was destroyed in a fire accident at the place of Mr. A before the expiry of three days. Decide whether Mr. A is liable for the loss suffered.

**Case Study**

Mr. S agreed to purchase 100 bales of cotton from V, out of his large stock and sent his men to take the delivery of the goods. They could pack only 60 bales. Later on, there was an accidental fire and the entire stock was destroyed including 60 bales that were already packed. Referring to the provisions of the Sale of Goods Act, 1930, explain as to who will bear the loss and to what extent?

**Case Study**

A delivers his watch to B on 'sale or return' basis. B delivers the same watch to C on 'sale or return' basis. C delivers it to D on 'sale or return' basis and D delivers the same watch to E on 'sale or return' basis. While in the possession of E, the watch is damaged. Who will bear the loss? Give reasons.

**Case Study**

Asha delivers some furniture to Bipasha on 'sale or return' basis. Bipasha then delivers the same furniture to Chitra and Chitra further delivers it to Divya on similar basis. Before Divya could give her acceptance, the furniture is suddenly destroyed by fire. Who is to bear the loss of furniture? Give reasons.

**Case Study**

Sanjay delivers some goods to Tarun on the 'sale or return' basis for seven days. State the legal position in each of the following different situations:

(i) Such goods-are destroyed by fire on the second day itself with no fault of Tarun.

(ii) Tarun informs the acceptance of the goods over phone to Sanjay and immediately thereafter, the goods are destroyed by fire.

(iii) These goods are further delivered by Tarun to Umesh on the fourth day and then by Umesh to Vivek on the same terms. The goods are stolen while in the custody of Vivek.

(iv) Tarun neither returns the goods nor gives any notice of rejection even after the expiry of the ninth day. The goods are destroyed by fire on the tenth day.

(v) Tarun retains the goods but gives the notice of rejection on the seventh day. The goods are destroyed by fire on the eighth day.

## 13.19 PASSING OF RISK

The general rule is that risk passes with the ownership. We can say that risk and ownership go together. However, express agreement between the parties may provide otherwise. It means risk and property may be separated by the term in agreement. The possession of goods is immaterial for the risk. When the delivery is delayed because of the fault of any party, he is liable for risk.

Sometimes the risk is based upon the custom or the usage of trade. Where the delivery of the goods has been delayed due to the fault of buyer/seller, the goods are at the risk of the party in fault.

**Case Study**

Aman contracted to erect machinery on Sapan's premises on the condition that the price shall be paid on the completion of work. During the progress of work, the premises and machinery were destroyed by an accidental fire. Referring to the provisions of the Sale of Goods Act, 1930, decide whether the parties are bound to perform their promises and can Aman recover the price of the work actually done?

## 13.20 RULES REGARDING DELIVERY OF GOODS—SECTIONS 32–39

The rules regarding the delivery of the goods are contained in Sections 32–39 of the sales of Goods Act which may be discussed as under:

### 13.20.1 Payment of Price

The general rule suggests that the delivery of the goods and the payment of the price are concurrent conditions. However, the parties may provide otherwise. It means if the contract of sale provides that the payment will be made in future or the payment will be made in instalments, it is a valid contract. The payment of price and the transfer of ownership has nothing to do with each other.

### 13.20.2 Buyer's Duty to Demand Goods

It is the seller's duty to be ready and willing to deliver the goods to the buyer. But he is not bound to deliver the goods, unless the buyer makes a demand for the delivery of the goods.

If the buyer fails to demand the delivery of goods, the seller is not liable for breach. The buyer must demand the delivery within a reasonable time. However, the contract may provide otherwise.

### 13.20.3 Types or Mode of Delivery

**13.20.3.1 Actual Delivery** It is the delivery where the goods are handed over to the buyer or his authorized agent. It means the goods are physically put in possession of the buyer.

**13.20.3.2 Symbolic Delivery** When the goods are not physically delivered to the buyer but some symbol of the real possession or control over the goods is handed over to the buyer. The symbolic delivery of goods is also known as attornment. The transfer of documents of title to the goods, i.e., the railway receipts, bill of lading and delivery orders are instances of symbolic delivery. Such delivery is made when the goods are bulky.

***Example***

Delivery of key of car.

**13.20.3.3 Constructive Delivery** Where the third party who is in possession of goods acknowledges to hold the goods on behalf of the buyer is known as constructive delivery.

***Example***

A sells 100 bags of cement lying in B's godown. B agrees to hold the 100 bags of cement on behalf of A.

### 13.20.4 Place of Delivery

Unless otherwise agreed anything contrary, the seller is required to make the delivery of goods at the place shown in the table below:

| Situation | Place Where Goods are to be Delivered |
|---|---|
| If the contract specified the place of delivery. | At the place specified. |
| Contract had not specified the place of delivery | |
| (a) In case of sale. | At a place at which the goods are at the time of sale. |
| (b) In case of agreement of sale. | |
| (i) In respect of the existing goods. | At a place at which the goods are at the time of agreement of sale. |
| (ii) In respect of the future goods. | At a place at which the goods are manufactured or produced. |

### 13.20.5 Time of Delivery

If the contract specified the time of delivery, the goods shall be delivered within such time. If no time is specified in the contract as to the time of the delivery of goods, it should be delivered within a reasonable time. A reasonable time is question of the fact depending upon the facts and circumstances of each particular case.

### 13.20.6 Expenses

All the expenses of making the delivery of goods shall be paid by the seller unless, otherwise, agreed and all the expenses of receiving the goods are paid by the buyer. However, the seller and the buyer may agree otherwise.

### 13.20.7 Delivery of Wrong Quantity

The delivery of wrong quantity means the seller has delivered the goods in excess or short.

If the seller has delivered excess quantity, the buyer has the following options:

1. To accept the whole of the goods delivered to him.
2. To reject the whole of the goods delivered to him.
3. To accept the contracted quantity and reject the excess.

If the seller has delivered a short quantity, the buyer has the following options:

1. To accept the goods delivered to him.
2. To reject the whole quantity delivered to him.

The right to reject the goods in excess of the contract does not apply where the variation is negligible.

Further, the right to reject the goods is not similar to the right to cancel the contract. If the buyer rejects the goods (either because they are less than or in excess of the quantity contracted for), the seller has a right to tender again the contract quantity and the buyer is bound to accept the same.

The buyer is not bound to return the rejected goods. It is sufficient if the buyer intimates the seller that he refuses to accept the goods.

### 13.20.8 Delivery of Mixed Quality–Quantity

The seller is bound to deliver the goods of exact quality–quantity otherwise the buyer may:

1. Reject the whole.
2. Reject the goods not complying with the quality or quantity and accept the rest.

### 13.20.9 Delivery by Instalment

The buyer is not bound to accept the goods delivered in instalment. The delivery by instalment is not valid except if the contract provides so or the buyer accepts the delivery in instalment.

### 13.20.10 Right to Examine—Section 41

In every contract for Sale of Goods, the buyer has the right to examine the goods unless, otherwise, agreed in the contract.

### 13.20.11 Delivery to Carrier or Wharfinger—Section 39

The delivery to the carrier or the wharfinger amounts as the delivery to the buyer if the following conditions satisfy:

1. The buyer has made a reasonable contract with the carrier.
2. The seller is required to give notice to the buyer to enable him to insure the goods.

### 13.20.12 Seller Duty on Valid Delivery of Goods

If the seller makes a valid delivery of the goods, the buyer has the following duties:

1. To accept the goods.
2. To pay the unpaid price.

### 13.20.13 Acceptance of Delivery—Section 42

The delivery of goods should be voluntary and lawful. The delivery of goods has the effect of putting the goods in the buyer's possession. The delivery does not mean the acceptance of goods. The buyer is deemed to have accepted the goods under the following circumstances:

1. When he intimates the seller about the acceptance of goods.
2. After the receipt of goods, he does some act of affirmation.
3. When he does not inform the seller about the rejection of goods with in a reasonable time.

### 13.20.14 Wrongful Refusal to Take Delivery

If the buyer wrongfully refuses to take the delivery of goods, he is liable for the damages and expenses like the storage cost and the transportation cost to the seller.

### 13.20.15 Goods Sent by Sea Route

Where the goods are sent by the sea route, the seller shall give a notice to the buyer to insure the goods, otherwise he will be liable for a loss.

**Case Study**

Amit sells to Sachin a specific horse which is to be delivered to Sachin the next week. Sachin is to pay the price on delivery. In the next week, Sachin was ready to pay the price for the horse but Amit was not in a position to deliver the horse to Sachin. Amit asks Sachin to take delivery of the horse after another week and pay the price then. During the second week, the horse dies before it is delivered and paid for. Who shall bear the loss? Explain.

## 13.21 UNPAID SELLER

The seller to whom the full price of the goods sold has not been paid the price is known as an unpaid seller. A seller of goods is deemed to be unpaid in the following cases:

1. The price must be due but not paid.
2. A negotiable instrument like cheque and bill of exchange was received but the same has been dishonoured.
3. The seller who has obtained a decree for the price of the goods will also be an unpaid seller if the decree has not been satisfied.
4. When the seller has been paid a large amount but small portion of the payment remains to be paid.
5. When the price has been paid but some other expenses which were payable to the seller has not been paid.
6. The seller must have an immediate right of action for the price.

However, the seller is not an unpaid seller if the buyer has tendered the price and the seller has refused to accept it.

***Example***

Z sells goods worth ₹ 50,000 to B on credit of five months. After five months, B did not pay the price. Z shall be regarded as an unpaid seller.

## 13.22 RIGHTS OF UNPAID SELLER

An unpaid seller has the right against the goods as well as against the the buyer:

### 13.22.1 Rights of Unpaid Seller Against the Goods When Ownership Is Transferred

Where the ownership of the goods is transferred, the seller has the following rights available to him, based upon the circumstances which can be discussed as under:

1. The right of lien—Sections 47–49
2. The right of stoppage in transit—Sections 50–52
3. The right to the resale of goods.

### 13.22.2 Rights of Unpaid Seller Against the Goods When Ownership Is Not Transferred

Where the ownership is not transferred to the buyer, the seller has the right to withhold the delivery of goods. In case where the ownership is not transferred to the buyer, the seller has no other right available to him.

### 13.22.3 Rights of Unpaid Seller Against Buyer

An unpaid seller has the following rights available against the defaulting buyer:

1. He may sue for the price—Section 55
2. He may sue for the damages for the non-acceptance of goods—Section 56
3. He may sue for the damages for the repudiation of the contract before the due date of the delivery of goods—Section 60
4. He has the right of interest for the delayed payment—Section 61.
5. He may sue the damages for the wrongful refusal to take the delivery.

## 13.23 RIGHT OF LIEN

Lien means the right to retain the possession of goods until the full price is received. The right of lien can be exercised on the goods. The seller can exercise his right of lien on the following two conditions:

1. He must be in possession of the goods.
2. He is an unpaid seller.

If the buyer has paid a part of the price, he cannot compel the seller to release the goods in proportion to the price paid. If the buyer becomes insolvent, the lien can be exercised by the unpaid seller. In the following circumstances, the unpaid seller's lien is lost:

1. When the seller waives his right of lien.
2. When the buyer disposes off the goods by sale with the consent of the seller.
3. When the goods are delivered to the buyer or his agent.
4. When the price is paid by the buyer.
5. The right of lien cannot be exercised where the right of lien has been expressly excluded.
6. When the goods are destroyed.

## 13.24 RIGHT OF STOPPAGE IN TRANSIT—SECTIONS 50–52

The right of stoppage in transit is an extension of the right of lien. The right of lien is a right to retain the possession, whereas the right of stoppage in transit is a right to regain the possession. The right of stoppage in transit can be exercised if the goods are in transit and the buyer has become insolvent in the meantime. The right of stoppage in transit can be exercise by the unpaid seller where he has lost his right of lien. The goods in transit can be stopped for the price. The unpaid seller has made a part delivery of the goods, he may exercise his right of stoppage in transit on the remaining part of the goods for the price.

### 13.24.1 Duration of Transit—Section 51

A carrier may hold the goods in three capacities:

**13.24.1.1 As Seller's Agent** In this case, the seller has lien on the goods, so the question of the right of stoppage in transit does not arise.

**13.24.1.2 As Buyer's Agent** In this case, the seller cannot exercise the right of stoppage in transit.

**13.24.1.3 In an Independent Capacity** In this case, the seller can exercise the right of stoppage in transit.

The goods are deemed to be in course of transit from the time they are delivered to a carrier for the purpose of transmission to the buyer until the buyer or his agent takes their delivery.

The goods are in transit even if the buyer asks the carrier to take them to some other destination, until they are delivered to the buyer at some other destination.

If the goods are rejected by the buyer and the goods are in the possession of the carrier, the transit is not at an end, even if the seller has also refused to take them back.

The right of stoppage of goods in transit can be exercise either:

1. By taking the actual possession of the goods.
2. By giving a notice of his claim to the carrier who holds the goods.
3. By a notice of his claim to the bailee who is in possession of the goods.

Where the unpaid seller exercises his right of stoppage in transit and regains the possession of goods his right of lien is revived.

**Case Study**

Ram sells 200 bales of cloth to Shyam and sends 100 bales by lorry and 100 bales by Railway. Shyam receives the delivery of 100 bales sent by lorry but before he receives the delivery of the bales sent by railway, he becomes bankrupt. Ram, who is still unpaid, stops the goods in transit. The official receiver, on Shyam's insolvency claims the goods. Decide the case with reference to the provisions of the Sale of Goods Act, 1930.

**Case Study**

A, who is an agent of a buyer, had obtained the goods from the Railway organization and loaded the goods on his truck. In the meantime, the Railway organization received a notice from B, a seller, for stopping the goods in transit as the buyer had become insolvent. Referring to the provisions of the Sale of Goods Act, 1930, decide whether the Railway organization can stop the goods in transit as instructed by the seller?

## 13.25 RIGHT OF RESALE

If the ownership of the goods is transferred to the buyer but the price is not paid and the goods are in possession of the seller, he can exercise the right of resale. In case of perishable goods, the unpaid seller can resale the goods if the buyer fails to pay the price within a reasonable time. The seller is not required to give notice of the re-sale in the case of perishable goods.

In case of the non-perishable goods, the unpaid seller can resell the goods if he has exercised his right of lien or stoppage of goods in transit. In the case of non-perishable goods, the seller is required to give a notice to the buyer to pay the price within a reasonable time and the buyer fails to pay the price. The seller can exercise his right of the re-sale of the goods when he expressly reserves this right. In such case, no separate notice is given.

Following will be the effects of the resale of goods:

| Rights | In Case of Resale After Notice | In Case of Resale Without Notice |
|---|---|---|
| The unpaid seller's right to recover the loss on sale. | Yes, the loss can be recovered. | No, the-loss cannot be recovered. |
| The original buyer's right to recover the profit on goods. | No, the profit cannot be recovered. | The profit can be recovered. |
| New buyer's right to acquire good title. | Acquire title. | Acquire title. |

## 13.26 RIGHT TO WITHHOLD DELIVERY OF GOODS

The right to withhold the delivery of goods means the seller refuses to deliver the goods to the buyer. The following conditions must be satisfied to exercise the right to withhold the delivery of goods:

1. The seller is an unpaid seller.
2. The ownership of goods has not been passed.

The right to withhold the delivery of goods is in addition to the other remedies available to the seller.

**Case Study**

Suraj sold his car to Sohan for ₹ 75,000. After inspection and satisfaction, Sohan paid ₹ 25,000 and took possession of the car and promised to pay the remaining amount within a month. Later on, Sohan refuses to give the remaining amount on the ground that the car was not in a good condition. Advise Suraj as to what remedy is available to him against Sohan.

## 13.27 DELIVERY TO CARRIER

A carrier means a transporter or a bailee to whom the goods are delivered by the seller for transportation to the buyer. When the goods are delivered to a carrier, it is deemed delivery of goods to the buyer if the following conditions are satisfied:

1. The seller delivers exactly the same goods as per the contract.
2. The buyer has informed the carrier name, address and the goods required to be delivered.
3. The seller delivers the goods for the purpose of delivery.

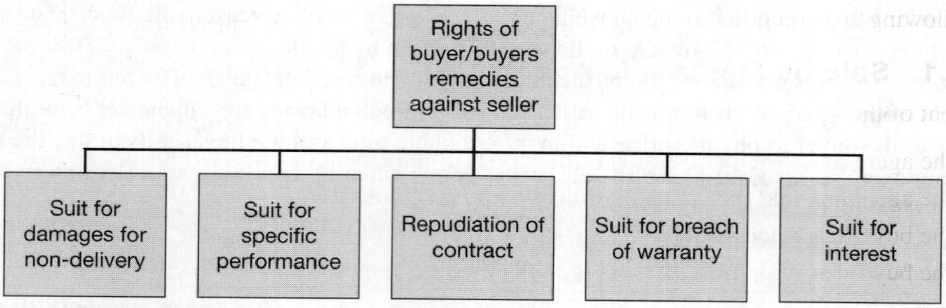


**Figure 13.1** Rights of buyer.

## 13.28 BUYER'S RIGHT AGAINST THE SELLER OR REMEDIES AGAINST SELLER—SECTIONS 55–61

The buyer has the following remedies against the seller:

### 13.28.1 Suit for Damage for Non-delivery

The buyer is ready and willing to take the delivery of goods but the seller wrongfully neglects or refuses the delivery of goods, the buyer may sue the seller for the damage for non-delivery.

### 13.28.2 Suit for Specific Performance

Where the seller's wrongful refusal to deliver specific or ascertained goods is seen, the court may direct a specific performance order.

### 13.28.3 Suit for Breach of Warranty

If there is breach of warranty, the buyer may claim the damages from the seller. The buyer may deduct the amount of damage from the price payable if the price is not paid. The buyer may recover the damages if the price is paid.

### 13.28.4 Right to Repudiate the Contract

If the seller declares his intention of the non-delivery of goods, the buyer may repudiate the contract and immediately sue for damages.

### 13.28.5 Suit for Interest

In the absence of any contract to the contrary, no interest shall be payable by the buyer on the delay payment. If there is no such agreement the seller may give notice to the buyer of his intention to charge interest on the delayed payment.

## 13.29 SALE BY NON-OWNERS OR TRANSFER OF TITLE BY NON-OWNERS—SECTIONS 27–30

The general rule is expressed by the maxim *'Namo dat quod non habet'* which means no one can give what he does not himself possess. If the seller's title is defective then the buyer's title will be defective. Alternatively, we can say that the seller cannot give a better title to the buyer than he himself has.

Following are exception to the above general rule:

### 13.29.1 Sale by Mercantile Agent

The agent of the seller can transfer the title if the following conditions are satisfied:

1. The agent must be in possession of the goods or document of title.
2. The agent has sold the goods in ordinary course of business.
3. The buyer has acted in good faith.
4. The buyer has no knowledge that the seller had no authority to sell.

**_Example_**

A entrusted his car to a mercantile agent to receive the offers and not to sell. A also delivered signed documents to the agent. On the basis of these documents, the agent pretended to the buyer that he had the authority to sell the car and thus, the car was sold. Held, the owner was stopped from denying the buyer's title.

### 13.29.2 Sale by One of the Joint Owners—Section 28

One of the joint owners can sell the goods if the following conditions are satisfied:

1. The goods are in sole possession of one of the joint owners.
2. The buyer has acted in good faith.
3. The buyer has no knowledge that the seller had no authority to sell.

**_Example_**

A and B jointly purchased a car. The car was in the possession of A with the consent of B. Later on, A sold the car to an innocent purchaser. The purchaser will get a good title.

### 13.29.3 Sale by Person in Possession Under Voidable Contract

1. The seller must be in possession of the goods under the contract voidable.
2. The goods must have been sold before the contract is rescinded.
3. The buyer has acted in good faith.
4. The buyer has no knowledge that the seller had no authority to sell.

**_Example_**

A purchased a watch from B under fraud. A sold the watch to C who bought it in good faith. C gets good title.

### 13.29.4 Sale by Seller in Possession After Sale—Section 30

The seller may sell the goods in possession after sale if the following conditions are satisfied:

1. The ownership of goods has been passed to the buyer.
2. The seller continues to be in possession of the goods even after sale.
3. The seller resells the goods to a new buyer.
4. The new buyer buys without any notice to prior sell.

**_Example_**

A sells certain goods to B and promises to deliver the goods the next day. Before the delivery, A sells and delivers the goods to C who buys them in good faith and without notice of the prior sale to B. C gets a good title to the goods, notwithstanding that the property had, before he purchased, passed to B.

### 13.29.5 Sale by Unpaid Seller

This is the sale by the unpaid seller after the exercise of his right of lien or the right of stoppage of goods in transit.

### 13.29.6 Sale by Liquidator

If the owner of the goods has declared insolvent and his goods are sold by the official receiver or assignee or liquidator. The liquidator has the authority to sell the goods as per the court order.

### 13.29.7 Sale by Finder of Goods

If the owner cannot be found or found but refuses to pay the lawful charges to the finder.

The finder of goods can sell the goods when the goods are perishable in nature or in danger without finding the true owner of goods to save the goods from loss.

The finder of the goods can sell the goods if the lawful charges of the finder amount as two-third of its original value.

### 13.29.8 Sale by Pawnee or Pledgee

If there is a default on the part of payment of price or performance within time after serving the notice of a reasonable time, the pawnee or pledge can sell the goods in public auction to recover his due.

**Case Study**

J the owner of a Fiat car wants to sell his car. For this purpose he hand over the car to P, a mercantile agent for sale at a price not less than ₹ 50,000. The agent sells the car for ₹ 40,000 to A who buys the car in good faith and without notice of any fraud. P misappropriated the money also. J sues A to recover the Car. Decide given reasons whether J would succeed.

**Case Study**

A, B and C were joint owners of a truck and the possession of the said truck was with B. X purchased the truck from B without knowing that A and C were also owners of the truck. Decide in the light of provisions of the Sale of Goods Act, 1930, whether the sale between B and X is valid or not?

**Case Study**

B buys goods from A on payment but leaves the goods in the possession of A. A then pledges the goods to C who has no notice of the sale to B. State whether the pledge is valid and whether C can enforce it. Decide with reference to the provisions of the Sale of Goods Act, 1930.

## 13.30 AUCTION SALE—SECTION 64

It means public sale. The seller invites the interested parties by advertisement to offer the price (i.e., bid). The seller may hire the service of the auctioneer. An auctioneer is an agent of the seller. The advertisement of the auction sale is not an offer but an invitation to make an offer and therefore if an auction sale is not held on the appointed day, the bidder cannot sue the auctioneer.

Every bid amounts as an offer and the acceptance is given by the auctioneer by some usual mode of acceptance e.g., fall of hammer, going-going-gone or one-two-three.

The auction sale starts with the placing of bids. The auctioneer accepts the highest bids but he may accept the lower bid without giving reason. When the bid is accepted, a valid contract is formed.

A bid once made can be withdrawn before the fall of hammer even if expressly prohibit. The seller can bid at an auction sale if the bidders are informed of the fact (Pretended bidding). If the seller makes use of the pretended bidding to raise the price, the sale is voidable at the option of the buyer. The bid is said to be pretended when it is made by the seller or someone on his behalf. Only one person can be appointed for bidding.

They auctioneer may set a reserve price or upset price. The bid lower than which is invalid.

In the case of Knockout agreement, the buyers join their hands to eliminate competition among themselves at an auction sale. They agree that they will not raise the bid against each other and only one of them will bid at the auction. When the goods have been purchased, they will share the profit. *Prima facie,* a knockout agreement is not illegal. However, if the intention of the parties to the agreement is to defraud a third party, this will be illegal.

Damping is an act by which an intending bidder is discouraged from bidding. Damping is an illegal. It includes:

1. Pointing out defects in the goods.
2. Misleading the purchaser or doing any other act so that he may not participate in the auction.

The damping empowers the auctioneer to withdraw the property from the auction.

## 13.31 DELIVERY OF GOODS IN CONTRACT BY SEAR ROUTE

It includes the following three categories of contracts:

### 13.31.1 CIF Contract

It means 'cost, insurance and freight'. Here the price of goods includes the cost of goods, insurance and freight expenses. In the CIF contract, the buyer pays the insurance and freight expenses.

The essential of the CIF contract is that the seller shall deliver the shipping documents to the buyer usually through the bank. If the seller fails to deliver the documents within a reasonable time, he is liable for breach of contract.

The ownership of goods is transferred to the buyer when he pays the price of the goods while receiving the shipping documents. If the buyer refuses to pay the price, the seller can claim the damages for the breach of contract.

### 13.31.2 F.O.B. Contract

It means free on board. Here, the seller is required to put the goods on the board of ship at his expenses. The buyer is liable for all the expenses and risk, once goods are loaded on the ship. The ownership of goods is transferred to the buyer as soon as the goods are loaded to the ship.

### 13.31.3 Ex-ship Contract

It means the contract in which the seller has to deliver the goods to the buyer at the port of destination. All the freight charges and risks during the voyage for the goods remain with the seller. The ownership of the goods is transferred to the buyer when the goods are actually delivered at the port of destination.

## LIST OF LANDMARK JUDGEMENTS

1. ***Commissioner of Sales Tax vs M. P. State Electricity Board (1970)***
   The electricity is goods since it is capable of being transferred, transmitted, delivered, stored and possessed.
2. ***Jabalpur Cable Network (P) Ltd vs ESPN Software Ind (P) Ltd (1999)***
   The electricity signals like cable tv signals is goods.
3. ***SBI vs Neela Naik (2000)***
   The bank fixed deposit receipt is goods.
4. ***H. Anurag vs Govt. of Tamil Nadu (1986)***
   The lottery Tickets are goods and not actionable claims.
5. ***Grant vs Australian Knitting Mills Ltd (1936)***
   In case of undergarments, if they are purchased, there is an implied condition that they shall not contain any chemicals which would cause harm to skin.
6. ***State of Gujrat vs Raman Lal and Co.***
   The distribution of goods among the partners on account of dissolution of the firm does not amount to the sale of goods because they cannot be both sellers and buyers.
7. ***K. J. Abraham vs Asst. STO (1960)***
   Animals and birds in captivity are goods.
8. ***R. D. Goyal vs Reliance Industries Ltd (2003)***
   After the allotment shares are goods.
9. ***Damodar Valley Corp. vs State of Bihar (1961)***
   In the case of hire-purchase, 'sale' takes place only when the purchaser exercises the option to purchase after paying all the agreed amount. Till then it is bailment.
10. ***Belsize Motor Supply Co. vs Cox (1914)***
    If a person had obtained goods on hire-purchase or lease, he has the option to buy the goods. In such a case, he has neither bought nor agreed to buy goods. Hence, he has no right to pledge or otherwise dispose of the goods. He cannot pass a better title to the third person and the owner can claim back the possession of goods.
11. ***Consolidated Coffee Ltd vs Coffee Board (1980)***
    The Property in auction sale passes to the purchaser on the acceptance of bid.
12. ***Zilla Parishad vs Udi Veer Singh (1989)***
    If the bidder withdraws the offer before acceptance, the security deposit paid by him cannot be forfeited.
13. ***Suresh Kumar Rajendra Kumar vs Assan Koya (1990)***
    The goods cannot be rejected by the buyer on account of the minor difference in the quantity.

**14.** ***Escorts JCB Ltd vs CCE (2000)***

The delivery of goods to the carrier is *prima facie* delivery of goods to the buyer.

**15.** ***Venkatu Lallaya vs Ramaswami and Co. (1964)***

The contract of sale may provide for the manner in which the price is to be fixed.

**16.** ***Geddling vs Marsh (1920)***

The implied condition as to fitness for the purpose goods also applies to the containers in which the goods are packed.

**17.** ***Philip Head and Sons Ltd vs Showfronts Ltd (1970)***

When there is a contract for the sale of specific goods not in deliverable state, the property does not pass until it is put in a deliverable state and the buyer has notice of it.

**18.** ***Lacis vs Cashmarts (1964)***

In a self service supermarket where the goods are picked up by the customers from the shelves and their prices are paid at the counter, no contract of sale is made until the price is actually paid and the property passes after the price is paid at the counter.

## TEST YOUR KNOWLEDGE

1. Define the goods. Explain it with suitable examples. **(Ref. Para-13.2)**
2. Which documents are included under the document of title? **(Ref. Para-13.2)**
3. Explain the concept of property with reference to goods. **(Ref. Para-13.2)**
4. State briefly the essential elements of a contract of sale under the Sale of Goods Act, 1930. **(Ref. Para-13.3)**
5. How is a contract of sale made? **(Ref. Para-13.3)**
6. Distinguish between a sale and an agreement to sell. **(Ref. Para-13.4)**
7. In what ways does a sale differ from hire-purchase? **(Ref. Para-13.5)**
8. Distinguish between a sale and a bailment. **(Ref. Para-13.6)**
9. The contract for work and skill are not included in the Sales of Goods Act. Explain. **(Ref. Para-13.7)**
10. What are the main features of the contract for work and skill? **(Ref. Para-13.7)**
11. Define goods. Explain in brief the meaning of the existing goods and future goods. **(Ref. Para-13.8)**
12. How is the price in the contract of sale of goods ascertained? **(Ref. Para-13.9)**
13. What do you understand by Goods? What are the rules in case the goods perish before and after making contract of sale of goods? **(Ref. Para-13.2,13.10)**
14. What do you understand by the conditions and warranties of a contract of the sale of goods? **(Ref. Para-13.11)**
15. What are the circumstances when a condition can be treated as warranty? **(Ref. Para-13.11)**
16. What are the implied warranties and conditions in a contract of sale of goods? **(Ref. Para-13.12,13.13)**
17. What are the implied warranties in a contract of sale under the Sales of Goods Act, 1930? **(Ref. Para-13.13)**
18. Point out the difference between the conditions and warranties under the Sales of Goods Act, 1930. **(Ref. Para-13.14)**
19. What do you understand by 'caveat emptor' under the Sale of Goods Act, 1930? What are the exceptions to this rule? **(Ref. Para-13.15)**
20. In the contract of sale, when does the property in goods passes on to the buyer? **(Ref. Para-13.16, 13.17,13.18)**

21. When is the ownership transferred in the case of goods sent on approval? **(Ref. Para-13.18)**
22. How does the risk pass in the contract for Sale of Goods Act? **(Ref. Para-13.19)**
23. Risk always passes with ownership. Comment. **(Ref. Para-13.19)**
24. What are the rules relating to the delivery of the goods in a contract of sale of goods? **(Ref. Para-13.20)**
25. Explain the modes of the delivery of goods. **(Ref. Para-13.20)**
26. The delivery of goods does not mean an acceptance of goods. Comment. **(Ref. Para-13.20)**
27. Who is an unpaid seller? What are his rights against the goods? **(Ref. Para-13.21)**
28. What types of suits can be preferred by the seller against the buyer in case of a breach of contract of sale? **(Ref. Para-13.22)**
29. Write a short note on an unpaid seller's lien. **(Ref. Para-13.23)**
30. Write a short note on the unpaid seller's right of the stoppage of goods in transit. **(Ref. Para-13.24)**
31. Write a short note on the right of the unpaid seller to re-sell the goods. **(Ref. Para-13.25)**
32. What do you understand by the right to withhold the delivery of goods? **(Ref. Para-13.26)**
33. Write a short note on the delivery to carrier. **(Ref. Para-13.27)**
34. What type of remedies are available to the buyer against the seller? **(Ref. Para-13.28)**
35. *'Nemo dat quod non habet'* explain. What are its exceptions? **(Ref. Para-13.29)**
36. What are the provisions relating to the auction sale? **(Ref. Para-13.30)**
37. Write a short note on the CIF, FOB and Ex-ship contract. **(Ref. Para-13.31)**

## MULTIPLE-CHOICE QUESTIONS

1. The Sale of Goods Act, 1930 deals with
   (i) bailment.
   (ii) gift.
   (iii) hire-purchase sales.
   (iv) sale of goods in general.
2. The Sale of Goods Acts applies to contracts of
   (i) sale of goods.
   (ii) sale of services.
   (iii) pledge of goods.
   (iv) hire-purchase.
3. A contract of sale may be
   (i) oral.
   (ii) written.
   (iii) always expressed.
   (iv) either (i) or (ii).
4. A agrees to deliver 1 kg of wheat to B in exchange of 2 kg of rice. It is a/an
   (i) contract of sale.
   (ii) agreement to sell.
   (iii) sale on approval.
   (iv) barter.
5. A agrees to deliver 1 kg of wheat to B in exchange of 500 gm of rice and 500 gm of sugar. It is a/an
   (i) contract of sale.
   (ii) agreement to sell.
   (iii) sale on approval.
   (iv) barter.
6. A agrees to deliver 1 kg of wheat to B in exchange of 500 gm of rice and ₹ 50. It is
   (i) contract of sale.
   (ii) hire purchase.
   (iii) sale on approval.
   (iv) barter.
7. Which of the following are not included in the term 'Goods' under the Sale of Goods Act.
   (i) Stock and shares.
   (ii) Actionable claims.
   (iii) Growing crops, grass etc.
   (iv) Personal use property.

8. According to Sale of Goods Act, the term 'Goods' includes
   (i) goodwill.
   (ii) patent.
   (iii) old coins and notes.
   (iv) all of the above.
9. According to Sale of Goods Act, the term 'Goods' includes
   (i) copy right.
   (ii) information.
   (iii) autograph.
   (iv) all of the above.
10. The word 'Property' in the Sale of Goods Act, 1930 means
    (i) ownership.
    (ii) transferor.
    (iii) purchaser.
    (iv) all of the above.
11. Under the Sale of Goods Act, 'Existing Goods' means
    (i) goods which are already manufactured before the contract made.
    (ii) goods which are to be manufactured after making the Contract of Sale.
    (iii) both (i) and (ii).
    (iv) goods which come into being, upon the happening of a contingency.
12. The term 'Contingent Goods' means
    (i) goods, the acquisition of which depends upon a contingency.
    (ii) goods which are not capable of identification.
    (iii) goods which may not be sold.
    (iv) goods the acquisition of which does not depend upon any contigency.
13. The goods which are to be produced by the seller after the contract of sale is made are known as
    (i) contingent goods.
    (ii) unascertained goods.
    (iii) future goods.
    (iv) none of the above.
14. The price of goods may be fixed
    (i) under the contract of sale.
    (ii) by manner provided in the contract of sale.
    (iii) by course of dealing between the parties.
    (iv) all of the above.
15. Gift of goods is not a sale as the following essential elements of sale is missing
    (i) capacity of party.
    (ii) lawful consideration.
    (iii) price.
    (iv) all of the above.
16. Which of the following is correct?
    (i) In a hire-purchase agreement, the buyer may either buy or return the goods.
    (ii) Hire-purchase agreement must be written.
    (iii) Hire-purchase agreement is governed by the Hire-purchase Act.
    (iv) all of the above.
17. A agreed to sell old rare coins to B at ₹ 300 per coin. It is a
    (i) void contract.
    (ii) valid contract.
    (iii) voidable contract.
    (iv) none of the above.
18. In a contract of sale where goods lie with the seller, the risk of loss of goods remains with the
    (i) insurance company.
    (ii) buyer only.
    (iii) seller only.
    (iv) buyer and seller equally.
19. A mechanic while repairing car supply of the spare parts required for such repairs. It is
    (i) a contract of sale.
    (ii) an agreement to sell.
    (iii) a contract for work and skill.
    (iv) hire-purchase.

20. Which of the following statements is incorrect?
    (i) A contract of sale may be implied.
    (ii) A contract of sale must be made in a particular mode, as prescribed by any law.
    (iii) A contract of sale cannot be partly in writing and orally.
    (iv) A contract of sale may be made in writing or orally.
21. If a price is not determined by the parties in a contract of sale, the buyer is bound to pay
    (i) the price demanded by the seller.
    (ii) a reasonable price.
    (iii) the price which the buyer thinks is reasonable.
    (iv) either (i) or (ii) or (iii) whichever is less.
22. Condition in a contract of sale, constitute stipulation with reference to
    (i) time.
    (ii) price.
    (iii) goods.
    (iv) delivery.
23. Warranty in a contract of sale, constitute stipulation with reference to
    (i) time.
    (ii) price.
    (iii) goods.
    (iv) delivery.
24. The breach of a 'Condition' in a contract of sale of goods gives the right to
    (i) cancel the contract.
    (ii) claim for damages.
    (iii) either (i) or (ii).
    (iv) both (i) and (ii).
25. Breach of a 'Warranty' in a contract of sale of goods, gives the right to
    (i) reject the goods.
    (ii) claim for damages.
    (iii) repudiate the contract.
    (iv) all of the above.
26. When the buyer's right of quiet possession of goods is affected by the seller's fault, the buyer can
    (i) reject the goods.
    (ii) claim for damages.
    (iii) repudiate the contract.
    (iv) all of the above.
27. There is an ______________ that the goods shall be free of any charge in favour of any third party.
    (i) implied warranty
    (ii) implied condition
    (iii) express condition
    (iv) express warranty
28. A agreed to sell 100 per cent cotton shirt by sample. The shirt delivered was equal to sample but not of cotton. What are the Buyer's rights?
    (i) Reject the goods.
    (ii) Claim for damages.
    (iii) Reclaim the price paid.
    (iv) All of the above.
29. In case of conflict between the express conditions and the implied conditions, which one of them shall prevail
    (i) implied conditions.
    (ii) express conditions.
    (iii) neither of them.
    (iv) new terms imposed by court.
30. A purchased a hot water bottle from a chemist. The bottle burst and injured his wife. The chemist is liable on account of
    (i) breach of express condition as to quality.
    (ii) breach of implied condition as to quality.
    (iii) personal injury caused to the buyer's wife.
    (iv) breach of implied warranty as to quality.

31. In a contract of sale of goods, the implied condition as to wholesomeness applied to ....
    (i) drug.
    (ii) food.
    (iii) clothes.
    (iv) jewelry.
32. Which of the following is correct?
    (i) Disclosure of dangerous nature of goods is an implied condition in a contract of sale.
    (ii) Generally, there is no implied condition as to quality or fitness of goods for any particular purpose of the buyer.
    (iii) A warranty may be treated as condition under certain cases.
    (iv) All of the above.
33. 'Caveat Emptor' means
    (i) buyer must take care.
    (ii) buyer must take a chance.
    (iii) seller must take care.
    (iv) seller must take a chance.
34. The process of identifying the goods and setting apart is called
    (i) identification.
    (ii) procurement.
    (iii) ascertainment.
    (iv) allocation.
35. For the passing of property in goods, the goods should be in a
    (i) deliverable state.
    (ii) non-deliverable state.
    (iii) consumable state.
    (iv) packed.
36. Where the specific goods are in a deliverable state but the seller has to do some act to ascertain the price, the property in the goods is transferred to the buyer when the
    (i) seller does that act.
    (ii) buyer comes to know about the same.
    (iii) both (i) and (ii).
    (iv) buyer takes the delivery of goods.
37. In case of sale on approval basis, property passes to the buyer when
    (i) buyer accepts the goods.
    (ii) buyer does any act adopting the transaction.
    (iii) buyer retains the goods beyond the stipulated time or reasonable time, without giving notice of rejection.
    (iv) all of the above.
38. Which of the following statements is incorrect in relation to 'sale on approval'?
    (i) The seller cannot ask for the return of the goods sold.
    (ii) The seller cannot recover the price, if the goods are not returned within a reasonable time.
    (iii) The seller can recover the price, if the goods are not returned without a reasonable time.
    (iv) The ownership of goods is transferred to the buyer, if he fails to return the goods within fixed time.
39. In case of sale on 'sale or return' basis, the property passes to the buyer when
    (i) buyer retains the goods for more than the contract-stipulated time.
    (ii) buyer rejects the goods with in a reasonable time.
    (iii) neither (i) nor (ii).
    (iv) both (i) and (ii).
40. Risk passes with
    (i) ownership.
    (ii) completed agreement.
    (iii) verification of goods.
    (iv) payment of price.

41. Where delivery has been delayed through the fault of either the buyer or the seller _____ is liable for any loss to goods.
(i) buyer.
(ii) seller.
(iii) party at fault.
(iv) party not in fault.

42. Which of the following is incorrect?
(i) Generally, the property in the ascertained goods is transferred to the buyer at such time as the parties intend it to be transferred.
(ii) Contingent goods are type of future goods.
(iii) All of the above.
(iv) None of the above.

43. Where the contract is for the sale of divisible lot of specific goods and only a part of the goods is destroyed, the contract ……
(i) becomes void.
(ii) is valid for remaining part.
(iii) becomes illegal.
(iv) becomes voidable.

44. A finder of goods has the power to sell the goods when
(i) the owner cannot be found out.
(ii) the owner can be found out.
(iii) the finder donot want to find the owner.
(iv) either (ii) or (iii).

45. A finder of goods has the power to sell the goods when lawful charges in preserving the goods amount to at least ...... of the value of the goods found.
(i) one-half.
(ii) one-third.
(iii) two-third.
(iv) three-fourth.

46. A general rule says that the delivery and the payment of price are ............ conditions.
(i) subsequent.
(ii) consequent.
(iii) concurrent.
(iv) relevant.

47. When the goods are physically handed over to the the buyer, it is a case of
(i) actual delivery.
(ii) constructive delivery.
(iii) symbolical delivery.
(iv) general delivery.

48. When the seller causes a change in the possession of goods without any actual change in their actual and visible custody, it is a case of
(i) actual delivery.
(ii) constructive delivery.
(iii) symbolical delivery.
(iv) forward delivery.

49. Delivery of the godown keys where the goods are lying to the buyer is an example of
(i) actual delivery.
(ii) constructive delivery.
(iii) symbolical delivery.
(iv) forward delivery.

50. Transfer of documents of title to the goods sold to the buyer amounts to
(i) actual delivery.
(ii) symbolic delivery.
(iii) constructive delivery.
(iv) none of the above.

51. The goods sold to the buyer should be delivered at
(i) the specified place.
(ii) the place of seller's choice.
(iii) the place of buyer's choice.
(iv) either (ii) or (iii).

52. In case of delivery of wrong quantity of goods, the buyer has a right to
    (i) accept the whole.
    (ii) reject the whole.
    (iii) accept the quantity contracted for and reject the rest.
    (iv) either (i) or (ii) or (iii).
53. In which of the following situations, the buyer is not deemed to have accepted the goods?
    (i) When he intimates to the seller that he has accepted them.
    (ii) When the goods are delivered to him, he does some action which is inconsistent with the ownership of the seller.
    (iii) When he does not return the goods after rejecting them.
    (iv) None of the above.
54. Buyer is not bound to return rejected goods. It is sufficient if the buyer
    (i) returns the goods to the carrier.
    (ii) returns the goods to the seller's agent.
    (iii) intimates the Seller that he refuses to accept the goods.
    (iv) dishonours the Bill of Exchange drawn.
55. A sold the goods to B for ₹ 20,000. B paid ₹ 5000 A is
    (i) an unpaid debtor.
    (ii) an unpaid seller.
    (iii) not a defaulter.
    (iv) none of the above.
56. Unpaid seller has right of
    (i) lien.
    (ii) stoppage of goods in transit.
    (iii) either (i) or (ii).
    (iv) neither (i) nor (ii).
57. Unpaid seller has right against buyer when
    (i) ownership of goods is transferred to buyer.
    (ii) ownership of goods is not transferred to buyer.
    (iii) either (i) or (ii).
    (iv) neither (i) nor (ii).
58. Unpaid seller can exercise his right of lien
    (i) even when property in goods has passed to the buyer.
    (ii) when general property in goods has passed to the buyer.
    (iii) either (i) or (ii).
    (iv) neither (i) nor (ii).
59. In which of the following situations, the right of lien is lost?
    (i) Where the goods have been delivered to the buyer.
    (ii) Where the goods have been delivered to the buyer's agent.
    (iii) Neither (i) nor (ii).
    (iv) Either (i) or (ii).
60. The unpaid seller does not lose his right of lien
    (i) when he delivers the goods to a carrier for the purpose of transmission to the buyer without reserving the right of disposal.
    (ii) when the buyer obtains possession of the goods.
    (iii) when the teller waives the right of lien.
    (iv) when the seller obtains a decree for the price of the goods.

61. The Right of Stoppage in transit can be exercised by the unpaid seller where he
    (i) has lost his right of lien.
    (ii) still enjoys his right of lien.
    (iii) both (i) and (ii).
    (iv) neither (i) nor (ii).
62. The Right of Stoppage in transit can be exercised by the unpaid seller where the buyer
    (i) is solvent.
    (ii) becomes insolvent.
    (iii) has become insane.
    (iv) neither (i) nor (ii).
63. The unpaid seller's right of lien is to
    (i) re-organize possession of goods.
    (ii) re-sell the goods.
    (iii) regain possession of goods.
    (iv) retain possession of goods.
64. The unpaid seller's right of stoppage in transit is to
    (i) re-organize the possession of goods.
    (ii) re-sell the goods lying with the carrier.
    (iii) regain the possession of goods.
    (iv) retain the possession of goods.
65. Which of the following rights are available to an unpaid seller against the buyer?
    (i) Suit for price.
    (ii) Suit for interest.
    (iii) Suit for repudiation.
    (iv) All of the above.
66. If no notice is given to original buyer of the intention to re-sell, the unpaid seller
    (i) cannot claim any damages.
    (ii) has to pay to the original buyer, the profits, if any, on re-sale.
    (iii) either (i) or (ii).
    (iv) both (i) and (ii).
67. Where the buyer wrongfully refuses to accept and pay for goods, the seller may sue him for
    (i) payment of price of goods.
    (ii) damages for non-acceptance of goods.
    (iii) payment of other expenses.
    (iv) all of the above.
68. Which of the following is correct?
    (i) Seller may file suit for specific performance.
    (ii) Seller may claim damages where buyer refuse to take delivery of the goods.
    (iii) Both (i) and (ii).
    (iv) None of the above.
69. Auction sale is also known as
    (i) public sale.
    (ii) private sale.
    (iii) cash sale.
    (iv) none of the above.
70. In the case of sale by auction, the seller of goods has a right to bid at the auction
    (i) with the permission of the auctioneer.
    (ii) only when the right to bid has been expressly reserved.
    (iii) even when the right to bid has been impliedly reserved.
    (iv) with the permission of the bidder.
71. In the case of sale by auction, contract is made
    (i) by strike of hammer third time.
    (ii) on payment.
    (iii) by bid.
    (iv) by delivery of goods.

72. In the case of an auction sale, contract is entered into by which of the following method?
   (i) On strike of hammer third time.
   (ii) By saying 1-2-3.
   (iii) By saying going-going and gone.
   (iv) All of the above.
73. In a contract through the sea route, the contract for the sale of goods at the price which include the cost of goods, insurance and freight charges, the contract is known as
   (i) C.I.F. contract.
   (ii) F.O.B contract.
   (iii) insurance obligatory contract.
   (iv) ex-ship contract.
74. In which of the following contracts, the seller is under an obligation is insure the goods?
   (i) Ex-ship contract.
   (ii) FOB contract.
   (iii) CIF contract.
   (iv) None of the above.
75. In case of ex-ship contract, during voyage the goods are at the risk of the
   (i) seller.
   (ii) buyer.
   (iii) caption of the ship.
   (iv) none of these.
76. In case of ex-ship contract, the ownership of the goods is transferred to the buyer when the
   (i) goods are loaded on board the ship.
   (ii) goods are actually delivered at the port of destination.
   (iii) shipping documents are delivered to the buyer.
   (iv) shipping documents are handed over to the captain of the ship.
77. The buyer has the right
   (i) to examine the goods before purchase.
   (ii) to have reasonable opportunity to examine the goods.
   (iii) to intimate defects in the goods to the seller.
   (iv) all of the above.

## ANSWER KEYS

| | | | | | |
|---|---|---|---|---|---|
| **1.** (iv) | **14.** (iv) | **27.** (i) | **40.** (i) | **53.** (iii) | **66.** (iv) |
| **2.** (i) | **15.** (iii) | **28.** (i) | **41.** (iii) | **54.** (iii) | **67.** (ii) |
| **3.** (iv) | **16.** (iv) | **29.** (ii) | **42.** (iv) | **55.** (ii) | **68.** (ii) |
| **4.** (iv) | **17.** (ii) | **30.** (ii) | **43.** (ii) | **56.** (iii) | **69.** (i) |
| **5.** (iv) | **18.** (ii) | **31.** (ii) | **44.** (i) | **57.** (iii) | **70.** (ii) |
| **6.** (i) | **19.** (iii) | **32.** (ii) | **45.** (iii) | **58.** (iii) | **71.** (i) |
| **7.** (ii) | **20.** (iii) | **33.** (i) | **46.** (iii) | **59.** (iv) | **72.** (iv) |
| **8.** (iv) | **21.** (ii) | **34.** (iii) | **47.** (i) | **60.** (iv) | **73.** (i) |
| **9.** (iv) | **22.** (iii) | **35.** (i) | **48.** (ii) | **61.** (i) | **74.** (iii) |
| **10.** (i) | **23.** (iii) | **36.** (iii) | **49.** (iii) | **62.** (ii) | **75.** (i) |
| **11.** (i) | **24.** (i) | **37.** (iv) | **50.** (ii) | **63.** (iv) | **76.** (ii) |
| **12.** (i) | **25.** (ii) | **38.** (ii) | **51.** (i) | **64.** (iii) | **77.** (iv) |
| **13.** (iii) | **26.** (ii) | **39.** (i) | **52.** (iv) | **65.** (iv) | |

# 14

# The Negotiable Instrument Act, 1881

**Learning Objectives**

*After reading this chapter, you will be able to understand:*

- Negotiable instruments like promissory note, bill of exchange and cheque
- Types of negotiable instrument
- Maturity period of negotiable instrument
- Negotiation, assignment of instrument
- Crossing of cheque
- Dishonour of instrument
- Noting and protesting
- Hundi

## 14.1 INTRODUCTION TO NEGOTIABLE INSTRUMENTS

In India, there is a reason to believe that instruments to exchange were in use from early times and we find that papers representing money were introduced into the country, by one of the Mohammedan sovereigns of Delhi in the early part of the fourteenth century.

The word 'hundi', a generic term used to denote instruments of exchange in vernacular is derived from the Sanskrit root 'hund', meaning 'to collect' and well expresses the purpose to which instruments were utilized in their origin. With the advent of British rule in India, commercial activities increased to a great extent. The growing demands for money could not be met by mere supply of coins; and the instrument of credit took the function of money which they represented.

Before the enactment of the Negotiable Instrument Act, 1881 the law of negotiable instruments as prevalent in England was applied by the courts in India when any question relating to such instruments arose between the Europeans. When the parties were Hindu or Mohammedans their personal law was held to apply. Though, neither the law books of the Hindus nor those of the Mohammedans, contain any reference to negotiable instruments such as, the customs prevailing among the merchants of the respective community were recognized by the courts and applied to the transactions among them. During the course of time, there had developed in the country a strong body of usage relating to hundis which even the Legislature could not, without hardship to Indian bankers and merchants, ignore. In fact the Legislature felt the strength of such local usages and though fit to exempt them from the operation of the Act, with a provision that such usage may be excluded altogether by appropriate words. In the absence of any such customary law, the principles derived from the English law were applied to the Indians, as rules of equity justice and good conscience.

The history of the present act is a long one. The act was originally drafted in 1866 by the India Law Commission and introduced in December 1867 in the Council and it was referred to a Select Committee. Objections were raised by the mercantile community to the numerous deviations from the English Law which it contained. The Bill had to be redrafted in 1877. After the lapse of a sufficient period for criticism by the Local Governments, the High Courts and the Chambers of Commerce, the Bill was revised by a Select Committee. In spite of this Bill could not reach the final stage. In 1880 by the Order of the Secretary of State, the Bill had to be referred to a new Law Commission. On the recommendation of the new Law Commission, the Bill was re-drafted and again it was sent to a Select Committee which adopted most of the additions recommended by the new Law Commission. The draft thus prepared for the fourth time was introduced in the Council and was passed into law in 1881, being the Negotiable Instruments Act, 1881.

Negotiable instrument means a promissory note or bill of exchange or cheque payable either to order or to the bearer.

An instrument, the property in which is acquired by anyone, who takes it bonafide and for value notwithstanding any defect in the title of any prior party is known as a negotiable instrument.

## 14.2 ESSENTIALS OR CHARACTERISTICS OF A NEGOTIABLE INSTRUMENT

The important characteristics of the negotiable instrument are the following:

1. Negotiable instrument must be payable either to order or to bearer.
2. Negotiable instruments are freely transferable from one person to another.
3. It is transferable infinitum (i.e., indefinitely). It means it can be transferred for any number of times.
4. The holder in due course gets a good title to negotiable instrument even though the title of transferor is defective.
5. The holder of the instrument is presumed to the owner of the property contained in it.
6. A negotiable instrument may name more than one payee, jointly or alternatively.

## 14.3 PRESUMPTIONS AS TO NEGOTIABLE INSTRUMENTS

A negotiable instrument is subject to certain presumptions. These have been recognized by the Negotiable Instrument Act under Sections 118 and 119, with a view to facilitate the business transactions. These are detailed below:

1. Every negotiable instrument was made, accepted and endorsed for consideration. Consideration is not required to be mentioned on the instrument.
2. Every negotiable instrument bearing a date was made or drawn on such date.

3. Every accepted bill was accepted within a reasonable time after its date and before maturity.
4. Every transfer of a negotiable instrument was made before its maturity.
5. A lost promissory note or bill was duly stamped and signed.
6. The holder of a negotiable instrument is a holder in due course.
7. Endorsement appearing upon negotiable instrument was made in the order in which they appear thereon.

However, these legal presumptions are rebuttable by evidence to the contrary.

## 14.4 PROMISSORY NOTE—SECTION 4

A 'promissory note' is an instrument in writing containing an unconditional undertaking signed by the maker to pay a certain sum of money only to—

(a) A certain person
(b) The order of a certain person

## 14.5 ESSENTIALS CHARACTERISTICS OF A PROMISSORY NOTE

To be a promissory note, an instrument must possess the following essentials.

### 14.5.1 In Writing

The promissory note should be in writing. It could be in hand writing or printing. An oral promise to pay is not sufficient.

### 14.5.2 Express Promise to Pay

The promissory note must contain express promise to pay. Mere acknowledgement of indebtedness is not sufficient.

***Example***

'Mr. B I.O.U ₹ 10,000'. There is no promise to pay and therefore this is not a valid promissory note.

### 14.5.3 Definite and Unconditional Promise

If a promise to pay is dependent upon an event which is certain to happen although the unconditional time of its happening is uncertain, the promise to pay is unconditional.

***Example***

'I promise to pay Bina ₹ 5,00,000 on D's death'. The promise is not conditional but definite since death of D is certain. Therefore, the promissory note is valid.

### 14.5.4 Signed by Maker

The promissory note must be signed by the maker. The signatures may be made on any part of the instrument. An agent of a trading firm can sign a promissory note on behalf of the firm.

### 14.5.5 Promise to Pay a Certain Sum

The promissory note should contain the promise to pay a certain sum of money. It should contain the promise to pay only money and nothing else.

***Examples***

1. 'I promise to pay Balwant ₹ 2500 and all other sums which shall be due to him'. Since the amount payable is not certain, it is not a valid promissory note.
2. 'I promise to pay Blawant ₹ 1200 and to deliver to him my rabbit on 1 March 2011'. It is not a valid promissory note since the promisor is required to deliver rabbit which is not 'money'.

### 14.5.6 Payee Must Be Certain

The name of the payee must be specified in the promissory note otherwise it will be invalid.

### 14.5.7 Stamped

The promissory note must be stamped. The stamp duty is paid as per the Stamp Act.

### 14.5.8 Parties

The person who makes the promissory note is called as maker. His liability is primary and unconditional. The person to whom money is to be paid, is called as payee.

**Case Study**

'I promise to pay Blawan ₹ 1200 after deducting there from any money which he owes me'. Is it valid promissory note? Why?

**Case Study**

'I promise to pay Balwant ₹ 100, 10 days after my marriage with C'. Is it valid promissory note? Why?

**Case Study**

'I promise to pay B ₹ 2000 on D's death, provided D leaves me enough to pay that sum'. Is it valid promissory note? Why?

**Case Study**

'I acknowledge myself to be indebted to B in ₹ 5000 to be paid on demand for value received'. Is it valid promissory note? Why?

**Case Study**

State giving reasons, whether the following instruments are valid promissory notes:

(i) X promises to pay Y by a promissory note, a sum of ₹ 5000, 15 days after the death of B.

(ii) X promises to pay Y by a promissory note, ₹ 5000 and all other sums which shall be due.

**Case Study**

Referring to the provisions of the Negotiable Instruments Act, 1881 examine the validity of the following promissory notes:

(i) I owe you a sum of ₹ 1000. 'A' tells 'B'.

(ii) 'X' promises to pay 'Y' a sum of ₹ 10,000, six months after 'Y's marriage with 'Z'.

## 14.6 BILL OF EXCHANGE—SECTION 5

A 'bill of exchange' is an instrument in writing containing an unconditional order signed by the maker, directing a certain person to pay a certain sum of money only to—

1. A certain person.
2. The order of a certain person.
3. The bearer of the instrument.

***Examples***

1. 'A' wrote and signed an instrument ordering 'B' to pay ₹ 500 to 'C' This is a bill of exchange.
2. 'On demand pay to 'A' or order the sum of ₹ 500 for value received'.

The characteristics of bill of exchange are almost similar to the promissory note. The essentials characteristics of a bill of exchange are following:

1. It must be in writing.
2. It must contain an express order to pay.
3. The order to pay must be definite and unconditional.
4. It must be signed by the drawer.
5. The sum contained in the order must be certain.
6. The order must be to pay money only.
7. Drawer, drawee and payee must be certain. The drawer and payee may be same person.
8. It must be stamped.

The person who draws or makes the bill is known as the drawer. His liability is secondary and conditional. The person on whom the bill is drawn is called as the drawee. On the acceptance of the bill, the drawee is called as the acceptor. He becomes liable for the payment of the bill and his liability is primary and unconditional. The person to whom the money is to be paid is known as the payee.

**Case Study**

An acceptor accepts a 'Bill of Exchange' but write on it 'Accepted but payment will be made when goods delivered to me is sold'. Decide the validity.

## 14.7 DIFFERENCE BETWEEN PROMISSORY NOTE AND BILL OF EXCHANGE

Following points highlight the main difference between a promissory note and a bill of exchange.

1. There are two parties in a Promissory Note—the maker and the payee. In a bill, there are three parties—the drawer, the drawee and the payee.
2. A promissory note contains an unconditional promise to pay. A billofexchange contains an unconditional order to pay.
3. The maker of a note is the debtor and he himself undertakes to pay. The drawer of a bill is the creditor who directs the drawee (his debtor) to pay.
4. The maker of a note corresponds in general to the acceptor of a bill. But the maker of the note cannot undertake to pay conditionally whereas the acceptor may accept the bill conditionally because he is not the originator of the bill.
5. The liability of a maker of a note is primary and absolute whereas the liability of the drawer of a bill is secondary and conditional.
6. A note cannot be made payable to the maker himself whereas in a bill, the drawer and the payee may be one and the same person.
7. A note requires no acceptance and it is signed by the person who is liable to pay. A bill, payable after sight or after a certain period must be accepted by the drawee before it is presented for payment.
8. A note cannot be drawn payable to bearer. A bill can be so drawn. But in no case can a note or bill be drawn 'payable to bearer on demand'.

## 14.8 CHEQUE—SECTION 7

A cheque is a bill of exchange, drawn on a specified banker and it includes 'the electronic image of truncated cheque' and 'a cheque in electronic form'. The cheque is always payable on demand.

A cheque must contain all the characteristics of a bill of exchange. The essentials characteristics of a cheque can be summarized as under—

1. It must be in writing.
2. It must contain an express order to pay.
3. The order to pay must be definite and unconditional.

4. It must be signed by the drawer.
5. The sum contained in the order must be certain.
6. The order must be to pay money only.
7. Drawer, drawee and payee must be certain.
8. It is always drawn upon a specified banker.
9. It is always payable on demand.

A cheque does not require stamping or acceptance.

The person, who draws or makes the cheque is called as drawer. His liability is primary and conditional. The bank on whom, the cheque is drawn is called as drawee. The bank makes the payment of the cheque. The person to whom money is to be paid is called as payee. The payee may be the drawer himself or a third party. A cheque is usually valid for 6 months. However, it is not invalid if it is post dated or antedated.

### 14.8.1 Truncated Cheque

A truncated cheque means a cheque which is truncated during the course of a clearing cycle either by the clearing house or bank whether paying or receiving payment immediately on generation of an electronic image for transmission, substituting the further physical movement of the cheque in writing.

### 14.8.2 Cheque in Electronic Form

A cheque in electronic form means a cheque which contains the exact mirror image of a paper cheque and is generated, written and signed in a secure system, ensuring the minimum safety standards with the use of digital signature (with or without biometric signature) and asymmetric crypto system.

### 14.8.3 Presentment of Truncated Cheque

In case of and reasonable suspicion about the genuineness of the electronic image of a truncated cheque (e.g., suspicion as to fraud, forgery, tampering or destruction of the instrument), the paying banker is entitled to demand any further information regarding the truncated cheque. The paying banker can also demand the presentment of truncated cheque itself for verification.

## 14.9 DIFFERENCE BETWEEN BILL OF EXCHANGE AND CHEQUE

| Bill of Exchange | Cheque |
|---|---|
| Bill of exchange can be drawn on any person. | Cheque is always drawn on the bank. |
| Bill of exchange need not always be payable on demand. | It is always payable on demand. |
| It cannot be payable to bearer on demand. | It can be drawn, payable on bearer on demand. |
| It require an acceptance of drawee. | It does not require an acceptance. |
| It requires stamp as per Stamp Act. | It does not require stamp. |
| It cannot be crossed. | It can be crossed. |
| Notice of dishonour is usually required. | Notice of dishonour is not required. |

## 14.10 DIFFERENCE BETWEEN ELECTRONIC CHEQUE AND TRANCATED CHEQUE

| Electronic Cheque | Truncated Cheque |
|---|---|
| Paper is not used at any stage in creation of an electronic cheque. | A truncated cheque is nothing but a paper cheque which is truncated during the clearing cycle. |
| Digital signatures must be used to create an electronic image of a cheque. Thus, an electronic cheque contains digital signature. | The paper cheque which is afterwards truncated, contains no digital signature. The signatures in ink appear on the truncated cheque. The original writing of a truncated cheque is on paper, duly signed in ink. |
| The electronic cheque is in electronic form. | Trancated cheque is in paper form. |

## 14.11 CAPACITY OF A PERSON TO BE A PARTY TO A NEGOTIABLE INSTRUMENT

A person, capable to enter into contract is capable to make or draw negotiable instrument. A person shall be liable on a negotiable instrument (by reason of making, drawing, accepting, endorsing, delivering or negotiating a negotiable instrument), only if he is capable of contracting, according to the law to which he is subject.

A minor may draw, endorse, deliver and negotiate any negotiable instrument. All the parties shall be bound on such negotiable instrument. However, the minor shall not be bound on such negotiable instrument.

An agent who signs in his name on a promissory note, bill of exchange or cheque without indicating thereon that he signs as an agent will be personally liable on instrument.

**Case Study**

X, a major and M, a minor, executed a promissory note in favour of P. Examine with reference to the provisions of the Negotiable Instruments Act, the validity of the promissory note and whether it is binding on X and M.

## 14.12 CLASSIFICATION OF NEGOTIABLE INSTRUMENTS

A negotiable instruments may be classified as under:

### 14.12.1 Order Instrument—Section 13

The negotiable instrument is payable to order—

1. Which is payable to a particular person.
2. Which is payable to a particular person or his order.
3. Which is payable to the order of a particular person.

### 14.12.2 Bearer Instrument—Section 13

The negotiable instrument is payable to bearer when—

1. It is expressed to be payable to bearer.
2. The last endorsement is in blank.

A promissory note cannot be made payable to bearer. The bill of exchange cannot be made payable to bearer on demand.

### 14.12.3 Demand Instrument—Sections 19–21

The negotiable instrument on which time for payment is not specified, is an instrument payable on demand. The negotiable instrument which is expressed to be payable on demand is also demand instrument.

A cheque is always payable on demand. A demand instrument may be presented for payment at anytime. The demand instrument is not entitled to any days of grace.

### 14.12.4 Time Instrument

An instrument in which the time for payment is specified is known as time instrument. The time instrument may be payable—

1. On a specific day or
2. After a specified period or
3. Certain period after sight or
4. On the happening of an event which is certain to happen.

### 14.12.5 Inland Instrument—Section 11

A negotiable instrument is an inland instrument if it is—

1. Drawn or made in India.
2. Payable in India or is drawn on a person resident in India.

***Example***

A bill drawn in India payable in Japan, upon a person in India is an inland instrument.

### 14.12.6 Foreign Instrument—Section 12

The negotiable instrument which is not an inland instrument is called as foreign instrument. The foreign instrument must be drawn outside India and made payable outside or inside India.

### 14.12.7 Ambigious Instrument—Section 17

An ambitious instrument means an instrument which can be constructed either as a promissory note or bill of exchange. Once the option is exercised, the instrument shall be treated accordingly.

### 14.12.8 Accommodation Bill

An accommodation bill means a bill which is drawn accepted without consideration. The person who becomes the holder of such a bill in good faith and for consideration after maturity may recover the amount from any party.

### 14.12.9 Fictitious Bill

A fictitious bill is a bill in which the name of the drawer or the payee or both is fictitious.

### 14.12.10 Documentary Bill

A documentary bill means a bill to which the documents of title of the goods are attached.

### 14.12.11 Clean Bill

A clean bill means a bill to which no document relating to the goods, is attached.

## 14.13 DISTINGUISH BETWEEN INLAND AND FOREIGN BILLS

An inland bills are drawn in India on a person residing in India, payable any where or drawn in India on a person residing outside India, payable in India, while a foreign bill is a bill which is not inland bill.

A foreign bills are drawn and are payable outside India, or drawn in India and payable outside India or drawn in India upon the persons resident outside India and made payable outside India.

The foreign bills may be of five kinds:

1. A bill drawn in India on a person resident outside India and made payable outside India.
2. A bill drawn outside India and made payable in India.
3. A bill drawn outside India on any person resident outside India.
4. A bill drawn outside India on a person resident in India.
5. A bill drawn outside India are made payable outside India.

The inland bills are drawn in a single copy but foreign bills are drawn in triplicate.

In the inland bills, dishonour requires noting. The protest is optional but in foreign bills, dishonour requires protesting.

## 14.14 INCOMPLETE INSTRUMENT OR INCHOATE INSTRUMENT—SECTION 20

Where one person signs and delivers to another, a paper stamped in accordance with the law relating to negotiable instruments then in force in India and either wholly blank or having written thereon an incomplete negotiable instrument, he thereby gives prima facie authority to the holder thereof to make or complete as the case may be, upon it a negotiable instrument for any amount specified therein; and not exceeding the amount covered by the stamp. Such instrument is called as inchoate instrument.

The person so signing shall be liable upon such instrument in the capacity in which he signed the same to any holder in due course for such amount; provided that no person other than a holder in due course shall recover from the person delivering the instrument anything in excess of the amount intended by him to be paid there under.

## 14.15 DISTINGUISH BETWEEN AMBIGUOUS INSTRUMENT AND INCHOATE INSTRUMENT

| Ambiguous Instrument | Inchoate Instrument |
|---|---|
| Ambiguous instrument can be negotiated. | Inchoate instrument is not a negotiable instrument. It can be negotiated only after amounts are filled in. |
| The holder of ambiguous instrument can sue on it after electing to treat it either as promissory note of bills of exchange. | The holder of inchoate instrument can sue only after amounts are filled in. |

## 14.16 MATURITY OF A NEGOTIABLE INSTRUMENT—SECTIONS 22–25

Cheques are always payable on demand but other instruments like bills and notes, may be made payable on specified date or after specified time. Maturity of a negotiable instrument means the date on which the negotiable instrument falls due for payment. The negotiable instrument which is payable otherwise than on demand is entitled to three days of grace.

### 14.16.1 Calculation of Days

| Type of Instrument | Date of Maturity |
|---|---|
| Negotiable instrument payable on a specified day. | Specified day + third day. |
| Negotiable instrument payable on a stated number of days after date. | Date on which negotiable instrument is drawn + stated number of days + third day. |
| Negotiable instrument payable on stated number of days after sight. | Date on which negotiable instrument is presented for sight + stated number of days + third day. |
| Negotiable instrument payable on stated number of days after happening of a certain event. | Date on which such event happens + stated number of days + third day. |
| Negotiable instrument payable on stated number of months after date. | Corresponding day of the relevant month* (i.e., Date on which negotiable instrument is drawn + stated number of months) + third day. |
| Negotiable instrument payable in installment. | Each installment is entitled to three days of grace. |

If the day of maturity of the negotiable instrument is a public holiday instrument is payable immediately preceding business day. But if the day of maturity of the negotiable instrument is an emergency or unforeseen public holiday, the instrument is payable immediately on the succeeding business day.

***Examples***

1. A negotiable instrument dated 29 January 1878 is made payable at one month after date. The instrument is at maturity on the third day after the 28 February 1878.
2. A negotiable instrument, dated 30 August 1878 is made payable three months after date. The instrument is at maturity on the 3 December 1878.
3. A promissory note or bill of exchange, dated 31 August 1878 is made payable three months after date. The instrument is at maturity on the 3 December 1878.

**Case Study**

As certain, the date of maturity of a bill payable 100 days after sight and which is presented for sight on 4 May 2000.

**Case Study**

Promissory note dated 1 February 2001 payable two months after dale was presented to the maker for payment 10 days after maturity. What is the date of maturity?

## 14.17 A NEGOTIABLE INSTRUMENT MADE WITHOUT CONSIDERATION

A negotiable instrument made, drawn, accepted, endorsed or transferred without consideration creates no obligation of payment between the parties to the transaction.

But if any such party has transferred the instrument to a holder for a consideration, such holder and every subsequent holder deriving title from him, may recover the amount due on such instrument from the transferor for consideration or any prior party thereto.

No party, for whose accommodation a negotiable instrument has been made, drawn, accepted or endorsed can, if he has paid the amount there of recover thereon such amount from any person who became a party to such instrument for his accommodation.

## 14.18 NEGOTIATION—SECTION 14

A negotiation means transfer of a negotiable instrument to any other person so as to constitute that person the holder of such negotiable instrument. When a negotiable instrument is transferred by negotiation, the rights of the transfree may rise higher than those of the transferor, depending upon the circumstances. When the transfer is made by assignment, the assignee has only those rights which the assignor possessed.

Two methods of the negotiation of instrument are follows:

### 14.18.1 Negotiation by Delivery

A bearer instrument may be negotiated by delivery. The delivery must be voluntary.

### 14.18.2 Negotiation by Endorsement and Delivery

An order instrument can be negotiated only by way of endorsement and delivery.

## 14.19 ENDORSEMENT—SECTIONS 15 AND 16

An endorsement means, signing on the face or back of a negotiable instrument or on a slip of paper annexed to the negotiable instrument by the holder of the negotiable instrument. The endorsement is made for the purpose of negotiating such negotiable instrument.

The endorsement must be in writing. The endorsement shall not be valid unless it is signed. The endorsement shall be valid only if the negotiable instrument is signed by the holder. The person to whom the instrument is endorsed is called the endoresee. In other words, 'endorsement' means and involves the writing of something on the back of an instrument for the purpose of transferring the right, title and interest therein to some other person.

## 14.20 KINDS OF ENDORSEMENTS—SECTIONS 16, 50, 52 and 56

Different kinds of possible endorsements are following:

### 14.20.1 Blank or General Endorsement

A general endorsement means an endorsement, made by the endorser without writing the name of the endorsee. It is also known as endorsement in blank. The general endorsements only contain a sign on the back of instrument. With the general endorsement, the order instrument is converted into a bearer instrument.

***Example***

Where bill is payable to 'Mohan or order' and he writes on its back 'Mohan,' it is an endorsement in black by Mohan and property in the bill can pass by mere delivery.

### 14.20.2 Special or Full Endorsement

A special endorsement means an endorsement made by a holder by signing his name and adding a direction to pay the amount to a specified person. It is also known as endorsement in full. A blank endorsement can be turned into special one by addition or an order making the bill payable to the transferee.

***Example***

A bill made payable to Mohan or order and endorsed 'pay to the order of Sohan' would be specially endorsed and Sohan endorses it further.

### 14.20.3 Restrictive Endorsement

An endorsement which restricts the right of further negotiation is called as restrictive endorsement.

***Examples***

1. 'Pay A only'.
2. 'Pay A on account of B'.

### 14.20.4 Partial Endorsement

An endorsement which purports to transfer only a part of the amount of the instrument is called as partial endorsement. The partial endorsement is not valid at law.

***Example***

A holds a bill for ₹ 10,000 and endorses it as 'pay B or order ₹ 500'. The endorsement is partial and invalid.

### 14.20.5 Conditional or Qualified Endorsement

An endorsement is conditional which limits the liability of the endorser. An endorser may limit his liability in any of following ways:

*Sans Recourse*—The endorser relieves himself from the liability to all subsequent endorsees. It is a type of endorsement on a negotiable instrument by which the endorser absolves himself or declines to accept any liability on the instrument of any subsequent party. The endorser signs the endorsement, putting his-signature along with the words, SANS RECOURSE.

*Facultative*—The endorser waives any of his rights.

*Contingent*—The endorser makes his liability dependent upon happening of some event.

***Example***

The holder of bill endorse it—'pay A or order on his marrying B'. In such case, the endorser will not be liable until A marry to B.

## 14.21 NEGOTIATION BACK

If a negotiable instrument is negotiated by the holder; but the endorser again becomes the holder of such negotiable instrument then it is called as negotiation back.

***Example***

A, holder of bill endorses it to B, B endorses it to C and C to D and D endorses it again to A.

### 14.21.1 Effects of Negotiation Back

The effects of negotiation back are following:

1. The holder cannot enforce the payment against an intermediate party to whom he was previously liable.
2. The holder can enforce the payment against all the parties to whom he was not previously liable.
3. However, the holder can sue all the prior parties (including all intermediate parties to whom he was previously liable) if he had made sans the recourse endorsement.

**Case Study**

A bill of exchange is drawn payable to X or order. X indorses it to Y, Y to Z, Z to A. A to B and B to X. State with reasons whether X can recover the amount of the bill from Y. Z, A and B if he has originally indorsed the bill to Y by adding the words 'Sans Recourse'.

## 14.22 DISTINCTION BETWEEN NEGOTIATION AND ASSIGNMENT

| Negotiation | Assignment |
|---|---|
| Negotiation means transfer of a negotiable instrument to any other person, so as to constitute that person the holder of such negotiable instrument. | Transfer of a right to receive the payment of a debt by one person (viz., assignor) to another person (viz., assignee) by way of a written document is called as assignment. |
| If a negotiable instrument is transferred by way of negotiation, Negotiable Instrument Act, 1881 applies. | Where any right is transferred by way of assignment, the Transfer of Property Act applies. |
| Negotiation can be made for transferring negotiable instruments only. | Assignment can be made of any right. |
| A bearer instrument can be negotiated merely by delivery and an order instrument can be negotiated by endorsement and delivery. | Assignment is valid only if it is made in writing, and is signed by the assignor. |
| Notice of negotiation is not required to be given to any party. | Notice of assignment must be given by the assignee to the debtor. |
| Every negotiable instrument is negotiated for consideration. | Assignment can be without consideration. |
| Negotiation does not require payment of stamp duty. | Assignment requires payment of stamp duty. |

## 14.23 CROSSING OF CHEQUE

A cheque is either 'open' or 'crossed'. An open cheque can be presented by the payee to the paying banker and is paid over the counter. A crossed cheque cannot be paid across the counter. Crossing means a direction given by the drawer of the cheque to the drawee bank, not to pay the cheque at the counter of the bank but to pay it to a person who presents it through a banker.

The crossing makes it possible to trace the person to whom the payment has been made. Thus, it makes the cheque safe and protects the holder of the cheque:

### 14.23.1 Modes or Types of Crossing—Sections 123–131(A)

**14.23.1.1 General Crossing** The cheque must contain two parallel transverse lines. The cheque must be paid only to a banker. In the case of general crossing, the holder cannot get payment over the counter of bank.

***Example***

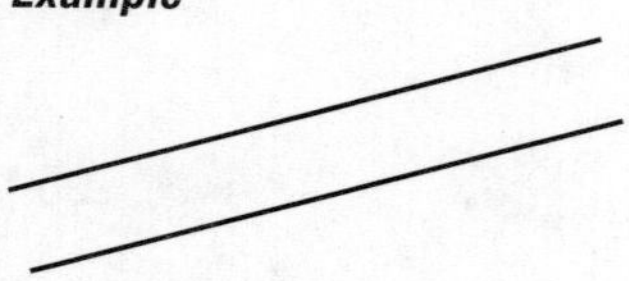

**14.23.1.2 Special Crossing** The cheque must contain the name of a banker. The cheque must be paid only to the banker to whom it is crossed. A special crossing may be made only once. The special crossing cannot be converted into general crossing. The paying banker will pay only to the banker whose name appears across the cheque or to his collecting agent.

***Example***

**Bank of baroda**

**14.23.1.3 Not Negotiable Crossing** The cheque must contain the words 'not negotiable'. The cheque must be crossed generally or specially. The title of the transferee shall not be better than the title of the transferor. Not negotiable crossing does not restrict transferability but restrict negotiability only.

***Example***

**Not negotiable**

**14.23.1.4 A/c Payee Crossing i.e., Restrictive Crossing** The cheque must contain the words 'A/c Payee' or 'A/c Payee only'. It is also known as restrictive crossing. The cheque does not remain negotiable anymore.

The cheque must be crossed generally or specially. It warns the collective banker that the proceeds are to be credited only to the account of the payee.

***Example***

**A/c payee**

## 14.24 BOUNCING OR DISHONOUR OF CHEQUES—SECTIONS 31 AND 138

A cheque is said to be bounced or dishonoured by non-payment when the drawee of cheque makes a default in payment in when cheque is presented to him for payment.

### 14.24.1 Liability of Drawee on Dishonour

In case of default by the drawee (i.e., Banker), the drawee shall compensate the drawer for loss caused to him. The liability of a drawee arises by non-payment, if the following three conditions are fulfilled on the dishonour of cheque:

1. The drawer has sufficient funds in the account; and
2. Such funds are properly applicable to payment of the cheque.
3. The drawee is duly required to pay the cheque.

### 14.24.2 Liability of Drawer on Dishonour

On the dishonour of the cheque, the drawer is punishable with imprisonment upto two years or fine not exceeding twice the amount of cheque or both if the following conditions are satisfied:

1. The cheque was issued to discharge a legally enforceable debt.
2. The cheque was returned or dishonoured for insufficiency of funds.

3. The cheque was presented within six months from which it was drawn or validity period of the cheque.
4. The payee or the holder in due course has made a demand from the drawer within 30 days of dishonour.
5. The drawer of cheque has failed to make a payment within 30 days of demand made.
6. A complaint can be made only by the payee or the holder within one month of expiry of 30 days of the receipt of notice by the drawer.

## 14.25 HOLDER—SECTION 8

### 14.25.1 Meaning of 'Holder'

A person is a holder of a negotiable instrument who is entitled in his own name:

1. To the possession of negotiable instrument in his own name.
2. To recover the amount due on a negotiable instrument from the parties liable on negotiable instrument.

It is not every person in possession of the instrument who is called a holder. To be a holder, the person must be naked in the instrument as the payee or the endorsee or he must be the bearer thereof. A person who has obtained the possession of instrument by theft or under forged instrument is not a holder.

### 14.25.2 Meaning of 'Holder in Due Course'—Section 9

1. He must be a holder.
2. He must have become the holder for consideration.
3. He must have obtained the possession of negotiable instrument before maturity.
4. He must have obtained the negotiable instrument in good faith i.e., without a sufficient cause to believe that any defect existed in the title of the person from whom he derived his title.

## 14.26 PRIVILEGES OF A HOLDER IN DUE COURSE

A holder in due course, is in a privileged position. He enjoys the following privileges:

1. Every prior party to a negotiable instrument is liable to a holder in due course (Section 36).
2. A holder who derives the title from a holder in due course, has the same rights as that of a holder in due course (Section 53).
3. No prior party can set up a defence that the negotiable instrument was drawn, made or endorsed by him without any consideration (Section 43).
4. No prior party can set up a defence that the negotiable instrument was lost or was obtained from him by an offence or fraud or for an unlawful consideration. Thus, a holder in due course gets a valid title to the negotiable instrument, even though the title of the transferor was defective (Section 58).
5. No prior party can allege that the negotiable instrument was delivered conditionally or for a special purpose only (Section 46).
6. A holder in due course can claim full amount of the negotiable instrument (but not exceeding the amount covered by the stamp) even though such amount is in excess of the amount authorized by the person delivering an inchoate negotiable instrument (Section 20).

**Case Study**

The drawer, 'D' is induced by 'A' to draw a cheque in favour of P who is an existing person. 'A' instead of sending the cheque to 'P' forgoes his name and pays the cheque into his own bank. Whether 'D' can recover the amount of the cheque from 'A's banker. Decide.

**Case Study**

A found a negotiable instrument lying on the road and transferred it to B who received it in good faith and for consideration. Can B recover the amount due on the instrument?

## 14.27 DIFFERENCE BETWEEN HOLDER AND HOLDER IN DUE COURSE

| Holder | Holder in Due Course |
|---|---|
| A person becomes a holder even if he obtains the negotiable instrument without any consideration. | A person becomes a holder in due course, only if he obtains the negotiable instrument for consideration. |
| A person becomes a holder, even if he does not the negotiable instrument in good faith. | For being a holder in due course, a person must obtain the negotiable instrument in good faith. |
| A person becomes a holder even if he obtains the negotiable instrument after the maturity of the negotiable instrument. | A person becomes a holder in due course only if he obtains the negotiable instrument before its maturity. |
| A holder is not entitled to the privileges which are available for HDC. | A holder in due course is entitled to various privileges as specified under the Negotiable Instruments Act, 1881. |
| A holder cannot sue all the prior parties. | A holder in due course can sue all the prior parties. |

## 14.28 PAYMENT IN DUE COURSE—SECTION 10

Any person liable to make payment under negotiable instrument must make the payment of amount due, there under in due course in order to obtain valid discharge against the holder. A payment in due course means payment in accordance with the apparent tenor of instrument in good faith to any person in possession thereof. The payment will be a payment in due course if—

1. Payment is made as per apparent tenor.
2. Payment is made in good faith.
3. Payment is made without negligence.

4. Payment is made to holder of negotiable instrument.
5. Payment is made in money only.

## 14.29 PROTECTION TO PAYING BANKER—SECTION 85

A paying banker is one who makes the payment of cheque on behalf of customer.

| Nature of cheque | Conditions subject to which protection is available to paying banker. |
|---|---|
| Cheque payable to order | Payment is made in due course. The protection shall be available notwithstanding, that any endorsement subsequently turns out to be a forgery. |
| Cheque originally payable to bearer | Payment is made in due course. Payment is made to the bearer of the cheque.<br>The protection shall be available notwithstanding that any endorsement appears on the cheque. |
| Cheques crossed generally | Payment is made in due course.<br>Payment is made to any banker. |
| Cheques crossed specially | Payment is made in due course.<br>Payment is made to the banker to whom the cheque is crossed. |

## 14.30 LIABILITY/DUTY OF THE PAYING BANKER AND COLLECTING BANKER—SECTION 129

The paying banker shall be liable to the true owner of the cheque for any loss sustained by him in the following two cases:

1. Where the paying banker pays a cheque crossed generally, otherwise than to a banker.
2. Where the paying banker pays a cheque crossed specially, otherwise than to the specified banker.

### 14.30.1 Duties of Collecting Banker

The collecting banker shall verify with due diligence and ordinary care:

1. The prima facie genuineness of the cheque to be truncated.
2. As to whether any fraud, forgery or tampering is apparent on the face of the instrument.

## 14.31 WHEN BANKER MUST REFUSE TO HONOUR A CUSTOMER'S CHEQUE

The authority of the banker to honour the customer's cheque comes to an end he must refuse to honour issued by the customer is in the following cases:

1. When a customer countermands payment i.e. stop payment.
2. When an order garnishee of court prohibits payment.
3. When the banker receives notice of death of the customer.
4. When the customer has been adjudged as insolvent.
5. When bank receives notice of customer's insanity.

6. When the customer has given notice of assignment of funds.
7. When the holder's title is defective and the banker comes to know about it.
8. When the customer has given a notice for closing of account.
9. When there is loss of cheque and the customer has informed the bank.
10. Materially altered cheque, mutilated cheque, cheque of doubtful validity and incomplete cheque.
11. When there is signatures mismatch.
12. When the banker has received an application for closure of account.
13. When there is irregular endorsement.

## 14.32 BANKER MAY REFUSE TO HONOUR A CUSTOMER'S CHEQUE

The banker may refuse to pay customer's cheque in the following cases:

1. Insufficient funds.
2. Funds not applicable.
3. Presentment at different branch.
4. Presentment after banking hours.
5. Stale cheque i.e., outdated cheque.
6. Post dated cheque.
7. Undated cheque.

## 14.33 EFFECT OF NON-PRESENTMENT OF CHEQUE WITHIN REASONABLE TIME

No liability of the drawer, if the bank fails conditions:

1. The drawer has sufficient balance when he issues the cheque and when the cheque ought to be presented for payment.
2. The holder fails to present the cheque within a reasonable time of issue of the cheque.
3. Meanwhile (i.e., after issue of the cheque but before presentation of the cheque by the holder) the bank fails and consequently the drawer suffers actual damages.

## 14.34 MATERIAL ALTERATION—SECTIONS 87–89

An alteration is called as material alteration if it alters the character or operation (i.e., the legal effect) of a negotiable instrument or the rights and liabilities of any of the parties to a negotiable instrument. The material alteration renders the instrument void but it alters only those persons who have already become parties at the date of alteration.

***Examples***

1. Alteration of the date of instrument.
2. Alteration of the amount payable.
3. Alteration in the time of payment.
4. Alteration in the place of payment.
5. Alteration in rate of interest.
6. Addition of new party to an instrument.

However, following are not considered as material alteration as it is authorized under act:

1. Filling blanks of an inchoate instrument (Section 20).
2. Conversion of a blank endorsement into an endorsement in full (Section 49).
3. Crossing of cheques (Section 125).
4. Conversion of general crossing into a special crossing or not negotiable crossing or A/c Payee Crossing (but not vice-versa).
5. Additional of the words 'on demand' to a note in which no time or payment is expressed.
6. Conversion of a bearer instrument into an order instrument by deleting the word 'Bearer'.
7. Correction of mistake in instrument.
8. An alteration made before the instrument is issued and made with the consent of parties.

### 14.34.1 Effect of Material Alteration—Sections 87 and 88

The effect of a material alteration of a negotiable instrument is only to discharge those who become parties, thereto prior to the alteration; But if an alteration is made in order to carry out the common intention of the original parties, it does not render the instrument void. Any material alteration if made by an indorsee, discharges his indorser from all liability to him in respect of the consideration thereof.

The alteration must be so material that it alters the character of the instrument to a great extent. In *Hongkong and Shanghai Bank versus Lee Shi (1928)*, it has been held that an accidental alteration will not render the instrument void. It is necessary to show that the alteration has been made improperly and intentionally. The effect of making the material alteration without the consent of the party bound is exactly the same as that of cancelling the deed.

In short, we can conclude that all the parties to the negotiable instrument not consenting to the material alteration are discharged.

## 14.35 ACCEPTANCE OF BILL

An acceptance means the drawee signs the bill and delivers it to the holder of the bill or gives a notice of acceptance to the holder of the bill. On the acceptance of a bill, the drawee becomes the acceptor.

### 14.35.1 Essentials of a Valid Acceptance

The acceptance on the bill should be in written. Writing may be either on the face or back of the bill. Valid acceptance is said when the drwaee sign the instrument. Writing the word 'Acceptance' is not necessary. It means, if the bill is signed with or without the word 'accepted' it is valid. After the signature delivery or intimation to the holder is given that the bill has been accepted.

### 14.35.2 Types of Acceptance

The acceptance may be either general or qualified. A general acceptance is absolute. It is an acceptance of bill without any qualification. A qualified acceptance of bill means acceptance of a bill subject with some qualification (e.g., accepting the bill subject to the condition that the payment of bill shall be made only on happening of an event specified therein).

### 14.35.3 Effect of Qualified Acceptance

The holder may object to the qualified acceptance. In such a case, it shall be treated that the bill is dishonoured due to non-acceptance.

He may give his consent to the qualified acceptance. In such a case, all the prior parties not consenting to it are discharged.

***Example***

Accepted payable on giving up bill of landing.

## 14.36 DISHONOUR BY NON-ACCEPTANCE

A bill is dishonoured by non-acceptance, if it is duly presented for acceptance but the bill is not accepted.

Following are cases where the bill is dishonoured by non-acceptance:

1. Where a bill is not accepted by the drawee within 48 hours of presentment of bill. If the holder allows to the drawee more than 48 hours for acceptance, all the prior parties not consenting to the same are discharged from liability to such holder.
2. In case, there are two or more drawees who are not partners, if the bill is not accepted by all the drawees.
3. Where the drawee is a fictitious person.
4. When the drawee cannot be found even after a reasonable search.
5. When the drawee is incompetent to contract.
6. Where the drawee gives a qualified acceptance and the holder does not give his consent to the qualified acceptance.

### 14.36.1 Effects

The holder gets an immediate right to sue all the prior parties without waiting for the maturity of the bill. A promissory note or a cheque cannot be dishonoured by non-acceptance since a promissory note or a cheque does not require any acceptance.

## 14.37 ACCEPTANCE FOR HONOUR

The person who accepts the bill for the honour of any other person is called as an 'acceptor for honour'.

### 14.37.1 Conditions for 'Acceptance for Honour'

The bill must have been noted for non-acceptance. The acceptance is given:

1. For the honour of any party, already liable under the bill;
2. By any person who is already not liable under the bill;
3. With the consent of the holder of the bill.

The acceptance must be made in writing on the bill.

### 14.37.2 Liability of Acceptor for Honour

He is liable to pay the amount of the bill if the drawee does not pay on maturity. He is liable only to the parties, subsequent to the party for whose honour the bill is accepted.

### 14.37.3 Rights of Acceptor for Honour

He is entitled to recover the amount paid by him from the party for whose honour the bill was accepted and from all the parties prior to such party.

## 14.38 PAYMENT FOR HONOUR

A person who pays a bill for honour of any other person is called as 'payer for honour'.

### 14.38.1 Conditions for 'Payment for Honour'

The bill must have been noted for non-payment. The payment for honour is made—

1. For the honour of any party, already liable under the bill;
2. By any person (whether or not he is already liable under the bill);
3. With the consent of the holder of the bill.

The payment must be recorded by Notary Public.

### 14.38.2 Rights of Payer for Honour

The payer for honour is entitled to all the rights of a holder. He can recover all the sums paid by him from the party for whose honour he pays and all the parties prior to such party.

## 14.39 DISHONOUR BY NON-PAYMENT

A negotiable instrument shall he dishonoured by non-payment if default in payment is made by the maker of a promissory note or acceptor of bill.

A bill which does not require acceptance shall be dishonoured by non-payment if default in payment is made by the drawer. A cheque shall be dishonoured by non-payment by the drawee.

## 14.40 NOTICE OF DISHONOUR

A notice of dishonour may be given by the holder or any party liable on the negotiable instrument. The notice of dishonour must be given to all the parties to whom the holder seeks to make liable. The notice of dishonour must disclose the fact of dishonour of negotiable instrument. A party (other than the party primarily liable on the negotiable instrument) to whom the notice of dishonour is not given is discharged from liability on the negotiable instrument. The notice may be oral or in writing. It must be given within reasonable time of dishonour.

### 14.40.1 When Notice of Dishonour Is Unnecessary or Excused?

In the following circumstances or situation, the notice of dishonour is not necessary:

1. When the notice of dishonour is dispensed with, by a party.
2. Where the drawer of the cheque has countermanded payment, notice to drawer is not required to be given.
3. When the party entitled to notice, cannot be found even after due search.
4. Where the party bound to give notice, is unable to give notice without any fault of his own.
5. When it is dispensed with or waived by the party.
6. When the party charged could not suffer damage for want to notice.
7. When the omission to give notice, is caused by unavoidable circumstances i.e. death.
8. Where the acceptor is also drawee e.g. where firm draws on its branch.

## 14.41 NOTING AND PROTESTING—SECTIONS 99–104(A)

Recording the fact of dishonour of a negotiable instrument on the negotiable instrument is known as noting. The notice or minute must be recorded by notary public within a reasonable time after dishonour and must contain the fact of dishonour, the date of dishonour, reason if any.

The dishonoured bill is handed over to a Notary Public. The Notary Public presents it again for acceptance/payment. If the drawee or acceptor refuses to accept or pay the bill, the Notary Public records the fact of dishonour on the bill. Noting is optional. It is not mandatory to get the feet of dishonour noted.

When the instrument is dishonoured and noting is carried out a certificate issued by the Notary Public, stating the fact of dishonour. This process is known as protesting.

## 14.42 DRAWEE IN CASE OF NEED

The name of any person may be given in a bill as 'drawee in case of need'. His liability arises on the bill, only when the bill is not accepted by the drawee named in the bill. The bill is not dishonoured until it has been dishonoured by the drawee in case of need.

## 14.43 DISCHARGE OF A NEGOTIABLE INSTRUMENT

The discharge in relation to a negotiable instrument may be either (i) discharge of instrument or (ii) discharge of one or more parties.

The negotiable instrument is discharged:

### 14.43.1 Payment in Due Course

The negotiable instrument is discharged if the party is primarily liable to the payment in due course. When the payment is made, the negotiable instrument must be cancelled or the fact of payment must be recorded on the negotiable instrument.

### 14.43.2 Cancellation

Where the holder cancels the name of the party primarily liable on the negotiable instrument with intent to discharge him, the negotiable instrument is discharged.

### 14.43.3 Release

Where the holder releases or renounces his rights against the party primarily liable on the negotiable instrument, the negotiable instrument is discharged.

### 14.43.4 Negotiation Back

Where a party primarily liable on a negotiable instrument becomes the holder of the negotiable instrument, the negotiable instrument is discharged.

## 14.44 DISCHARGE OF A PARTY

When any particular party is discharged, the instrument continues to be negotiable and the undischarged parties remain liable on it.

***Example***

Non-presentment of bill on due date discharge the endorsers from their liability but the acceptor remain liable on it.

The party may be discharge in following ways:

### 14.44.1 By Payment

A payment by a party who is secondarily liable on a negotiable instrument discharges the holder and all the parties, subsequent to the party, making payment of the negotiable instrument.

### 14.44.2 By Cancellation

Where the holder cancels the name of any party, liable on the negotiable instrument (other than the party primarily liable on the negotiable instrument), such a party and all parties subsequent to him are discharged.

### 14.44.3 By Release

Where the holder releases any party, liable on the negotiable instrument (other than the party primarily liable on the negotiable instrument) such a party and all parties subsequent to him are discharged.

### 14.44.4 By Allowing Drawee More Than 48 Hours to Accept

All prior parties not consenting to the same are discharged from liability to such holder.

### 14.44.5 By Qualified Acceptance

Where a holder of the bill consents to qualified acceptance, all the prior parties who did not consent to qualified acceptance are discharged.

### 14.44.6 By Material Alteration

Every party not consenting to a material alteration of a negotiable instrument is discharged.

### 14.44.7 By Negotiation Back

Where a party already liable on the negotiable instrument becomes the holder of negotiable instrument, such a party and all intermediate parties to whom such a party was previously liable shall be discharged.

### 14.44.8 By Operation of Law

A party is discharged if the negotiable instrument becomes time barred. A party is discharged if he is declared as an insolvent by the court.

## 14.45 HUNDI

A hundi means a bill of exchange drawn in local language. The Negotiable Instruments Act, 1881 applies to hundies if there is no local usage of trade or custom prevailing in the area in which hundi is drawn. However, if there is any custom or usage prevailing in such an area, the same will apply to the hundies and therefore Negotiable Instruments Act, 1881 shall not apply to hundies.

The different types of the hundies are following:

### 14.45.1 Nam Jog Hundi

It means the hundi payable to a party, named in the hundi or to his order.

### 14.45.2 Diiani Jog Hundi

It means the hundi payable to the dhani or the owner i.e., the bearer.

### 14.45.3 Darshani Hundi

It means the hundi payable at sight.

### 14.45.4 Miadi Hundi or Muddati Hundi

The hundi that is payable after a specified period of time.

### 14.45.5 Shahjog Hundi

The hundi that is payable to a Shah.

### 14.45.6 Jokhmi Hundi

The hundi drawn in respect of goods shipped on the vessel and is payable only when the goods reach their destination safely.

### 14.45.7 Peth

Duplicate copy of the hundi.

### 14.45.8 Perpeth

Triplicate copy of the hundi.

### 14.45.9 Khoka

The hundi which has already been paid or discharged.

## LIST OF LANDMARK JUDGEMENTS

1. ***M/s. Tailor Priya vs Gulab Chand (1965)***
   The negotiability involves two elements, namely transferability free from equities and transferability by delivery or endorsement.
2. ***Ashok Yeshwant Badave vs Surendra Madhavrao (2001)***
   Past dated cheque remains bills of exchange. It becomes a cheque on the date of cheque. Therefore period of 6 months should be calculated from the date of cheque and not from the date when the installment was handed over to drawee.
3. ***Great Western Rail Co. vs London and County Banking Co. (1901)***
   Everyone who takes a cheque marked 'not negotiable', takes it at his own risk.
4. ***National Bank vs Sil Ke (1891)***
   Writing word 'A/c Payee' does not make the chequenegotiable. An A/c payee cheque remains transferable.

5. ***Punjab National Bank vs BOB (1944)***

   In the case of cheque, liability is only of drawer. The holder of a cheque has no remedy against the banker.

6. ***United Bank of India vs Center Scientific Supplies Co. Ltd (1999)***

   The bank is liable if amount of cheque is increased by forgery.

7. ***Bank of Bihar vs Mahabir Lal (1964)***

   The bank is liable if it honours a forged cheque. But if such forgery was due to negligence of customers bank will not be liable.

8. ***Pooja Granites vs Ispat Finances (2004)***

   The cheque must be presented within six months to drawee bank.

9. ***NEPC Micon Ltd vs Magma Leasing Ltd (1999)***

   If a cheque is returned with remark 'A/c closed', it would be offence u/s 138.

10. ***Vinod Tanna vs Zaher Siddiqui (2002)***

    No prosecution if a cheque returned for signature difference.

11. ***Modi Cements Ltd vs Kuchil Kumar Nandi (1998)***

    Stop payment instructions to the banker in the case of cheque cannot stop prosecution of drawer.

12. ***SMS Pharmaceuticals Ltd vs Neeta Bhalla (2005)***

    The managing director of a company, deemed to be in charge and responsible to conduct of business of company. Therefore, if the offence is committed by company, its director in charge of affairs will be personally liable.

13. ***Sil Import, USA vs Exim Aides Silk Expoerters (1999)***

    Notice of dishonour of cheque to the drawer of cheque can be sent by fax.

14. ***Rajneesh Agrawal vs Amit J. Bhalla (2001)***

    Notice of dihonour of cheque to M.D., who has signed the cheque on behalf of company is sufficient. It is not necessary to send notice to company.

15. ***Sadanandan Bhadram vs Sunil Kumar (1998)***

    The drawee can deposit cheque any number of times but he can send notice only once he sends notice of dishonour of cheque he forfeits his right of presenting cheque again.

16. ***Sivaram vs Jayaram (1966)***

    Specified place means full address of exact location. Mere mentioning name of city is not specified place.

17. ***Braja Kishore Dikshit vs Purna Chandra Panda (1957)***

    The person who is holder of Negotiable instrument after paying valuable consideration and become possessor/payee/endoresee before date whom amount is payable and without knowledge and defect in the title of person, transferring the instrument in good faith is only holder in due course.

18. ***Dhanumal Parasmal vs P. Kuppura (1977)***

    Material alteration means it should change the character or identity of instrument.

19. ***SBI vs Kerala State Co-op. Marketing Federation (1995)***

    Change in name of party, dates sum payable, time of payment, place of payment, the signature of drawer, without the consent of drawer would be material alteration.

## TEST YOUR KNOWLEDGE

1. Explain the various characteristic of a Negotiable Instrument. **(Ref. Para-14.2)**
2. What are the presumptions applicable to all the negotiable instruments, as provided under the Negotiable Instrument Act, 1881? **(Ref. Para-14.3)**
3. What is a promissory note and what are its elements? **(Ref. Para-14.4,14.5)**
4. Define the bill of exchange and explain its salient features. **(Ref. Para-14.6)**
5. In what ways does a 'promissory note' differ from a 'bill of exchange'. **(Ref. Para-14.7)**
6. Define the cheque. Mention its character. **(Ref. Para-14.8)**
7. In what respect bill of exchange differ from a cheque? **(Ref. Para-14.9)**
8. Write down the difference between electronic cheque and truncated cheque. **(Ref. Para-14.10)**
9. Who can be party to negotiable instrument? **(Ref. Para-14.11)**
10. How can negotiable instrument be classified? **(Ref. Para-14.12)**
11. What is demand instrument? **(Ref. Para-14.12)**
12. What do you understand by time instrument? **(Ref. Para-14.12)**
13. What do you understand by ambiguous instrument? **(Ref. Para-14.12)**
14. Distinguish between 'inland bill' and 'foreign bill'. **Ref. Para-14.13)**
15. What is inchoate instrument? Explain the provisions relating to inchoate instrument. **(Ref. Para-14.14)**
16. What are the differences between an ambiguous instrument and inchoate instrument? **(Ref. Para-14.15)**
17. State briefly the rules laid down under Negotiable Instrument Act, 1881 for determining the date of maturity of bills of exchange. **(Ref. Para-14.16)**
18. Can a negotiable instrument be drawn without consideration? **(Ref. Para-14.17)**
19. Write a short note negotiation. **(Ref. Para-14.18)**
20. What do you understand by endorsement? Explain different kind of endorsement. **(Ref. Para-14.19,14.20)**
21. When the term 'negotiation back' used in Negotiable Instrument Act? What are the effects of negotiation back? **(Ref. Para-14.21)**
22. What are the difference between 'negotiability' and 'assignability'? **(Ref. Para-14.22)**
23. What do you understand by the crossing of cheque? What is object of crossing? **(Ref. Para-14.23)**
24. Explain clearly the meaning of 'general' and 'special crossing' of cheque. **(Ref. Para-14.23)**
25. Write short note on restrictive crossing. **(Ref. Para-14.23)**
26. Write short note on not-negotiable crossing. **(Ref. Para-14.23)**
27. A cheque marked 'not negotiable' is not tranferable. Comment. **(Ref. Para-14.23)**
28. Write a short note on crossing of cheque. **(Ref. Para-14.23)**
29. Explain the meaning of 'holder' and 'holder in due course'. **(Ref. Para-14.25)**
30. State the privileges of a 'holder in due course' under the Negotiable Instrument Act. **(Ref. Para-14.26)**
31. What are the main differences between a holder and a holder in due course? **(Ref. Para-14.27)**
32. When payment will be a payment in due course? **(Ref. Para-14.28)**
33. A paying banker is always protected. Comment. **(Ref. Para-14.29)**
34. State the cases in which a banker is justified or bound to dishonour cheque. **(Ref. Para-14.31)**
35. State the grounds on the basis of which a cheque may be dishonour by bank? **(Ref. Para-14.32)**
36. What will be effect of non-presentment of cheque within reasonable time? **(Ref. Para-14.33)**

37. When is an alteration of an instrument as material alteration under act? **(Ref. Para-14.34)**
38. Which kind of alteration to an instrument is allowed under the act and not regarded as material alteration? **(Ref. Para-14.34)**
39. Which are the essentials elements of a valid acceptance of bill of exchange? **(Ref. Para-14.35)**
40. When can a bill of exchange be dishonoured by 'non-acceptance' and 'non-payment' under the provisions of Negotiable Instrument Act, 1881? **(Ref. Para-14.36)**
41. Explain the meaning of 'acceptance for honour' under the Negotiable Instrument Act, 1881. **(Ref. Para-14.37)**
42. Explain the meaning of 'payment for honour' under the Negotiable Instrument Act, 1881. **(Ref. Para-14.38)**
43. When notice of dishonour is unnecessary? **(Ref. Para-14.40)**
44. Explain the provisions of negotiable Instrument Act, 1881 relating to 'notify' and 'protesting' of bill of exchange which has been dishonoured by the acceptor. **(Ref. Para-14.41)**
45. When the negotiable instrument is discharged? **(Ref. Para-14.43)**
46. When party to negotiable instrument is discharged? **(Ref. Para-14.44)**
47. Write a short note on 'hundi'. **(Ref. Para-14.45)**

## MULTIPLE-CHOICE QUESTIONS

1. The negotiable instruments includes
   (i) promissory note.
   (ii) bill of exchange.
   (iii) cheque.
   (iv) all of these.
2. The Negotiable Instruments Act includes cheque, bill of exchange and
   (i) promissory note.
   (ii) hundi.
   (iii) bank draft.
   (iv) customary note.
3. Which one of the following is not the characteristic of a negotiable instrument?
   (i) It must be in writing.
   (ii) It must be freely transferable.
   (iii) It must be registered.
   (iv) It must contain definite amount of money.
4. A person who receives a negotiable instrument in good faith and for valuable consideration is known as
   (i) holder for consideration.
   (ii) holder for value.
   (iii) holder in due course.
   (iv) holder in rights.
5. A negotiable instrument drawn in India on a person residing in India and payable outside India is known as
   (i) inland instrument.
   (ii) foreign instrument.
   (iii) incomplete instrument.
   (iv) none of these.
6. A negotiable instrument in which no time for payment is specified is payable
   (i) after acceptance.
   (ii) after sight.
   (iii) after one month.
   (iv) on demand.
7. A negotiable instrument may be drawn to be payable
   (i) on demand.
   (ii) after sight.
   (iii) after one month.
   (iv) either (i) or (ii) or (iii).

8. A cheque is always payable on demand
   (i) True
   (ii) False
9. A promissory note cannot be made payable to bearer.
   (i) True
   (ii) False
10. Which of the following is not an essential of a valid promissory note?
   (i) It must be signed by maker.
   (ii) It must be stamped.
   (iii) It must be in writing.
   (iv) It must be registered.
11. Which of the following is not an essential of a valid bill of exchange?
   (i) It must be signed.
   (ii) It must be stamped.
   (iii) It must be in writing.
   (iv) It must be registered.
12. Which of the following is not an essential of a valid cheque?
   (i) It must be signed.
   (ii) It must be drawn on bank.
   (iii) It must be in writing.
   (iv) It must be registered.
13. A bill of exchange payable to bearer on demand is
   (i) valid.
   (ii) voidable.
   (iii) invalid.
   (iv) conditional.
14. A person who is directed to pay the amount of bill of exchange is known as
   (i) drawer.
   (ii) drawee.
   (iii) payee.
   (iv) creditor.
15. Generally bill of exchange has _____ parties.
   (i) two
   (ii) three
   (iii) four
   (iv) any number
16. Generally promissory note has _____ parties.
   (i) two
   (ii) three
   (iii) four
   (iv) any number
17. A bill of exchange dishonoured due to non-acceptance by the drawee becomes
   (i) void.
   (ii) voidable.
   (iii) invalid.
   (iv) none of these.
18. All cheques are bills of exchange.
   (i) True
   (ii) False
19. All bills of exchange are not cheques.
   (i) True
   (ii) False
20. On acceptance of a bill of exchange by the drawee, he is legally known as
   (i) acceptor.
   (ii) acceptor for honour.
   (iii) drawee in case of need.
   (iv) none of these.

21. A negotiable instrument drawn in favour of a minor is
    (i) void.
    (ii) voidable.
    (iii) valid.
    (iv) invalid.
22. A negotiable instrument drawn by minor is
    (i) void.
    (ii) voidable.
    (iii) valid.
    (iv) invalid.
23. Which of the following is not competent to draw a valid negotiable instrument?
    (i) Insolvent.
    (ii) Company.
    (iii) Agent.
    (iv) Both (ii) and (iii).
24. A holder is a person who is entitle to the instrument in his own name and the term includes
    (i) payee of instrument.
    (ii) bearer of instrument.
    (iii) endorsee of instrument.
    (iv) all of these.
25. A person becomes a 'holder in due course' of a negotiable instrument, if he receives it
    (i) in good faith.
    (ii) for value.
    (iii) before maturity.
    (iv) all of these.
26. A holder in due course can recover the amount of the instrument irrespective of any defect in the title of prior parties.
    (i) True
    (ii) False
27. A negotiable instrument payable to order can be transferred by
    (i) simple deliver.
    (ii) endorsement.
    (iii) endorsement and delivery.
    (iv) registered post.
28. In case, a finder or a thief of a bearer negotiable instrument transfers it to a person who receives the same in good faith and for valuable consideration then such a transferee is
    (i) entitled to receive the payment.
    (ii) not entitled to receive the payment.
    (iii) punishable for helping a thief.
    (iv) conditional owner of the instrument.
29. A negotiable instrument is complete and operative when:
    (i) it is in writing.
    (ii) it is signed.
    (iii) it is delivered to the party concerned.
    (iv) all of the above.
30. A slip of paper attached to the back of instrument for signing endorsements is known as
    (i) allonge.
    (ii) escrow.
    (iii) zickri chit.
    (iv) peth.
31. An endorsement made by an endorser by signing his name and also by writing the name of the endorsee is known as
    (i) general endorsement.
    (ii) special endorsement.
    (iii) restrictive endorsement.
    (iv) none of these.
32. An endorsement by which the endorser excludes his liability by express words is known as
    (i) facultative endorsement.
    (ii) restrictive endorsement.
    (iii) sans recourse endorsement.
    (iv) contingent endorsement.
33. When during the course of negotiation, the negotiable instrument comes back to the original endorser, it is known as
    (i) negotiation back.
    (ii) reverse endorsement.
    (iii) facultative endorsement.
    (iv) back recourse endorsement.

34. The liability of the maker of a promissory note is
(i) primary.
(ii) secondary.
(iii) conditional.
(iv) none of these.

35. The liability of the acceptor of a bill of exchange is
(i) primary.
(ii) secondary.
(iii) conditional.
(iv) none of these.

36. On the acceptance of the bill of exchange by the drawee, the liability of the drawer becomes
(i) primary.
(ii) secondary.
(iii) extinct.
(iv) none of these.

37. The presentment for acceptance is required in case of a
(i) bill of exchange.
(ii) promissory note.
(iii) cheque.
(iv) both (i) and (ii).

38. The presentment for payment is required in case of a
(i) bill of exchange.
(ii) promissory note.
(iii) cheque.
(iv) all of these.

39. Which of the following bill of exchange must be presented for acceptance of the drawee?
(i) A bill payable on demand.
(ii) A bill payable on fixed date.
(iii) A bill payable 30 days after date.
(iv) None of these.

40. Which of the following note must be presented for sight?
(i) A note payable at sight.
(ii) A note payable after sight.
(iii) A note payable on demand.
(iv) All of the above.

41. A negotiable instrument should be presented for payment to the party who is
(i) primarily liable.
(ii) secondarily liable.
(iii) willing to make payment.
(iv) any person who can make payment.

42. A bill of exchange is treated as dishonoured due to non-acceptance where the drawee
(i) does not accept within 48 hours of presentment.
(ii) is incompetent to contract.
(iii) gives a conditional acceptance.
(iv) in all the above cases.

43. In case of dishonour of a cheque, the holder's remedy is against the
(i) drawee of cheque.
(ii) drawer of cheque.
(iii) indorsee of cheque.
(iv) both (i) and (iii).

44. With reference to negotiable instrument the 'noting' may be done in case of
(i) promissory note.
(ii) bill of exchange.
(iii) cheque.
(iv) both (i) and (ii).

45. The liability of which of the following parties comes to an end when negotiable instrument is discharged ?
(i) Primarily liable party.
(ii) Secondarily liable party.
(iii) Subsequent liable party.
(iv) None of the parties.

46. Material alteration of a negotiable instrument without the consent of the parties, discharge the parties who have become liable
(i) after such alteration.
(ii) prior to such alteration.
(iii) because of alteration.
(iv) without such alteration.

47. Which of the following is not a material alteration?
   (i) Alteration of date.
   (ii) Alteration of amount.
   (iii) Alteration of time of payment.
   (iv) Alteration correcting clerical mistake.
48. A cheque is said to contain a general crossing when two parallel lines are drawn across the face of the cheque
   (i) without any words.
   (ii) with words '& Co.'
   (iii) with words 'not negotiable'.
   (iv) in all the above cases.
49. A cheque is said to contain a special crossing when two parallel lines are drawn across the face of the cheque and by writing between the lines the
   (i) name of bank.
   (ii) name of bank and '& Co.'
   (iii) a/c payee only.
   (iv) in (i) and (ii) cases.
50. After receiving an uncrossed cheque its holder can make on it
   (i) general crossing.
   (ii) special crossing.
   (iii) either (i) or (ii).
   (iv) neither (i) nor (ii).
51. The payment of a crossed cheque can be obtained
   (i) at the counter.
   (ii) by depositing in account.
   (iii) by the payee only.
   (iv) both (i) and (iii).
52. The payment of a cheque containing special crossing can be obtained
   (i) by depositing in any bank.
   (ii) by depositing in named bank.
   (iii) at the counter of named bank.
   (iv) either (i) or (iii).
53. The payment of a negotiable instrument becomes due
   (i) at maturity.
   (ii) before maturity.
   (iii) after maturity.
   (iv) on third day of maturity.
54. The negotiable instruments payable on demand are due for payment
   (i) from third day of date of issue.
   (ii) from the date of issue.
   (iii) after 15 days of date of issue.
   (iv) after 30 days of date of issue.
55. The negotiable instruments payable on a specified date are due for payment
   (i) from the specified date.
   (ii) from the date of issue.
   (iii) from third day after specified date.
   (iv) after presentment for sight.
56. Which of the following negotiable instrument is not entitled to days of grace?
   (i) A bill of exchange payable on specified date.
   (ii) A promissory note payable on specified date.
   (iii) A promissory note payable 'after sight'.
   (iv) A cheque.
57. A negotiable instrument made without any consideration at all is
   (i) void between all parties.
   (ii) voidable between all parties.
   (iii) void between immediate parties.
   (iv) voidable between immediate parties.
58. In which of the following circumstances a banker may refuse to make the payment of his customer's cheque?
   (i) Where cheque is post dated.
   (ii) Where cheque is stale.
   (iii) Where funds are insufficient.
   (iv) In all the above cases.

59. A hundi is an indigeneous negotiable instrument, written in local language of people which may be in the form of either a bill of exchange or a promissory note.
   (i) True
   (ii) False

60. A hundi which is payable 'at sight' is known as
   (i) miadi hundi.
   (ii) zikri hundi.
   (iii) darshani hundi.
   (iv) none of these.

61. A hundi which is payable to the holder or bearer is known as
   (i) nam jog hundi.
   (ii) firman hundi.
   (iii) jawabi hundi.
   (iv) dhani jog hundi.

62. A letter of protection given by a drawer to the holder of a hundi which enables him to receive payment in case of dishonour is known as
   (i) zickri chit.
   (ii) perpeth.
   (iii) khoka.
   (iv) purja.

63. The duplicate of a hundi is known as
   (i) perpeth.
   (ii) peth.
   (iii) khoka.
   (iv) purja.

64. A hundi when paid up and cancelled is then called
   (i) perpeth.
   (ii) purja.
   (iii) khoka.
   (iv) none of these.

## ANSWER KEYS

| | | | | | |
|---|---|---|---|---|---|
| **1.** (iv) | **12.** (iv) | **23.** (i) | **34.** (i) | **45.** (i) | **56.** (iv) |
| **2.** (i) | **13.** (iii) | **24.** (iv) | **35.** (i) | **46.** (ii) | **57.** (iii) |
| **3.** (iii) | **14.** (ii) | **25.** (iv) | **36.** (ii) | **47.** (iv) | **58.** (iv) |
| **4.** (iii) | **15.** (ii) | **26.** (i) | **37.** (i) | **48.** (iv) | **59.** (i) |
| **5.** (i) | **16.** (i) | **27.** (iii) | **38.** (iv) | **49.** (iv) | **60.** (iii) |
| **6.** (iv) | **17.** (iv) | **28.** (i) | **39.** (iv) | **50.** (iii) | **61.** (ii) |
| **7.** (iv) | **18.** (i) | **29.** (iv) | **40.** (ii) | **51.** (ii) | **62.** (i) |
| **8.** (i) | **19.** (i) | **30.** (i) | **41.** (i) | **52.** (ii) | **63.** (ii) |
| **9.** (i) | **20.** (i) | **31.** (ii) | **42.** (iv) | **53.** (i) | **64.** (iii) |
| **10.** (iv) | **21.** (iii) | **32.** (iii) | **43.** (ii) | **54.** (ii) | |
| **11.** (iv) | **22.** (i) | **33.** (i) | **44.** (iv) | **55.** (iii) | |

15

# Consumer Protection Act, 1986

**Learning Objectives**

*After reading this chapter, you will be able to understand:*

- Object of the Consumer Protection Act
- Rights of consumer
- Meaning of certain terms expressed under the Act
- Consumer forum
- Requirement of complaint under the Act

## 15.1 OBJECT OF THE ACT

Let the buyer beware is a traditional concept which is no longer acceptable in open and competitive environment.

In India, we have the Indian Contract Act, the Sale of Goods Act, the Dangerous Drugs Act, the Agricultural Produce (Grading and Marketing) Act, the Indian Standards Institution (Certification Marks) Act, the Prevention of Food Adulteration Act, the Standards of Weights and Measures Act, and the Trade and Merchandise Marks Act which to some extent protect consumer interests.

However, these laws required the consumer to initiate action by way of a civil suit which involved a lengthy legal process proving to be too expensive and time consuming for lay consumers. Therefore, the need for a simpler and quicker access to redressal to the consumer grievances was felt and accordingly, it lead to the legislation of the Consumer Protection Act, 1986.

The main objective of the Act is to provide for the better protection of consumers. Unlike the existing laws which are punitive or preventive in nature the provisions of this Act are compensatory in nature. The Act is intended to provide simple, speedy and inexpensive redressal to the consumers' grievances and reliefs of a specific nature and award of compensation wherever appropriate to the consumer.

## 15.2 EXTENT AND COVERAGE OF THE ACT

The salient features of the Act are summed up as under:

1. The Act applies to all goods and services unless specifically exempted by the Central Government.
2. It covers all the sectors whether private, public or cooperative.
3. The provisions of the Act are compensatory in nature.
4. It enshrines the following rights of consumers.
5. The Act envisages the establishment of the Consumer Protection Councils at the central and state levels, whose main objects will be to promote and protect the rights of the consumers.
6. The CPA extends to the whole of India except the State of Jammu and Kashmir and applies to all the goods and services unless otherwise notified by the Central Government.
7. The provisions of this Act are in addition to and not in derogation of the provisions of any other law for the time being in force.

## 15.3 RIGHTS OF CONSUMER

The basic rights of the consumer as per the Consumer Protection Act are as under:

1. The right to be protected against the marketing of the goods and services which are hazardous to life and property.
2. The right to be informed about the quality, quantity, potency, purity, standard and the price of goods or services so as to protect the consumer against unfair trade practices.
3. The right to be assured wherever possible the access to a variety of goods and services at competitive prices.
4. The right to be heard and to be assured that the consumers' interests will receive due consideration at appropriate forums.
5. The right to seek redressal against unfair trade practices and unscrupulous exploitation of the consumers.
6. The right to consumer education.

## 15.4 DEFINITION

### 15.4.1 Appropriate Laboratory

An appropriate laboratory means a laboratory or organization recognized by the Central Government or by a State Government or any such laboratory or organization, established by or under any law for the time being in force which is maintained, financed or aided by the Central Government or a State Government for carrying out the analysis or test of any goods with a view to determining whether such goods suffer from any defect.

### 15.4.2 Complainant

A complainant means:

1. A consumer; or
2. Any voluntary consumer association registered under the Companies Act, 1956 or under any other law for the time being in force; or
3. The Central Government or any State Government who or which makes a complaint; or
4. One or more consumers where there are numerous consumers having the same interest.

### 15.4.3 Complaint

A complaint means any allegation in writing made by a complainant that:

1. An unfair trade practice or a restricted trade practice has been adopted by any trader.
2. The goods bought by him or agreed to be bought by him suffer from one more defects.
3. The services hired or availed of or agreed to be hired or availed of by him suffer from deficiency in any respect.
4. The trader has charged for the goods mentioned in the complaint a price excess of the price fixed by or under any law for the time being in force or displayed on the goods or any package, containing such goods.
5. The goods which will be hazardous to life and safety when used are being offered for sale to the public in contravention of the provisions of any law for the time being in force requiring the traders to display information in regard to the contents, manner and effect of use of such goods; with a view to obtaining any relief provided by the law under the CPA.

The complaint must be in writing and the complaint must be made to the appropriate consumer forum.

### 15.4.4 Consumer

A consumer means any person who buys or agrees to buy any goods or one who hires or avails any service for a consideration which has been paid or promised or partly paid and partly promised or under any system of deferred payment.

It also includes any user of such goods other than the person who actually buys goods and such use is made with the approval of the purchaser.

It includes any beneficiary of such service other than the one who actually hires or avails of the service for consideration and such services are availed with the approval of such a person.

A person is not a consumer if he purchases the goods for commercial or resale purposes. However, the word 'commercial' does not include use by the consumer of the goods bought and used by him exclusively for the purpose of earning his livelihood by means of self employment.

***Examples***

1. Mr. Amar purchased car for his personal use. He is consumer. But if he lets out his car as taxi he will not be regarded as consumer.
2. An applicant for ration card is not a consumer.
3. The beneficiaries of the municipal services have been held not to be in the category of consumers. (*Parab Chand Jain versus C.E.O. Nagar Palika*).

**Case Study**

Mr. Paras, chartered accountant in practice purchased a computer on instalments for being used in his office. Can he be said as consumer under the Act?

**Case Study**

Vishwa Jyoti printers supplied a warranty of free service for one year at the time of sale of printing machine to Manan. After a year, Vishwa Jyoti printers contended that since it was rendering free service for the maintenance of the machine for one year under the warranty, the buyer is not a consumer. Decide.

### 15.4.5 Service

A service is defined to mean service of any description which is made available to the potential users and includes the provision of facilities in connection with banking, financing, insurance, transport, processing, supply of electrical or other energy, board or lodging or both housing construction, entertainment, amusement or the purveying of news or other information but does not include the rendering of any service free of charge or under a contract of personal service.

The above definition can be divided in following points:

1. It means a service of any description. The service is not restricted only to the actual users but is also made applicable to the potential or prospective users, i.e., the persons who are likely to use the services in future.
2. It includes the provisions of facilities in connection with banking, financing, insurance, transport, processing, supply of electrical or other energy, boarding or lodging or both entertainment, amusement or the purveying of news or other information. The housing construction is also included in the definition of 'Service'.
3. The services which are rendered free of charge, and the personal service, e.g., master and servant have been excluded. Therefore, if services rendered in the hospital are totally free then no complaint under this Act is maintainable against the hospital.

***Examples***

1. The subscriber of telephone is availing the services from the telephone company.
2. The person who buys life insurance policy is availing service from the insurance company.

**Case Study**

An applicant for a passport who pays fees to obtain a passport is a consumer availing service.

### 15.4.6 Goods

The goods means goods as defined in the Sale of Goods Act, 1930.

Under that act goods means every kind of movable property other than the auctionable claims and money and includes stocks and shares, growing crops, grass and things attached to or forming part of the land which are agreed to be severed before the sale or under the contract of sale.

***Example***

Shares and debentures after the allotment are goods.

## 15.4.7 Consumer Dispute

A consumer dispute means a dispute where the person against whom a complaint has been made, denies or disputes the allegation contained in the complaint.

## 15.4.8 Restrictive Trade Practice

A restrictive trade practice means a trade practice which tends to bring about the manipulation of price or its conditions of delivery or to affect the flow of supplies in the market relating to the goods or service in such a manner as to impose on the consumers, unjustified the costs or restrictions.

Any trade practice which makes delay beyond the period agreed to be a trader in supply of such goods or in providing the services which has led or is likely to lead to rise in the price is also the restrictive trade practice.

The restrictive trade practice means any trade practice which requires a consumer to buy, hire or avail of any good or as the case may be services as a condition precedent for buying, hiring or availing of any other goods or services.

***Example***

Compelling a consumer to buy insurance while he purchases a vehicle from the same company.

**Case Study**

The gas company insists on the purchase of a gas stove from his shop only as a pre-condition to release gas connection to Mr. Amar. When Amar applied for the gas connection, he was not informed of any such condition. Neither was it disclosed in the application form he filled with the gas Company. Should Mr. Amar approach the consumer forum for the restrictive trade practice?

## 15.4.9 Unfair Trade Practice

An unfair trade practice means a trade practice which for the purpose of promoting the sale use or supply of any goods or for the provision of any service, adopts any unfair method or unfair or deceptive practice including any of the following practices:

1. False or misleading representation about quality, quantity and standard of goods.
2. Bargain price.
3. Offering of gifts, prize and contest.
4. Non-compliance of product safety standard.
5. Hoarding or destruction of goods.

6. Falsely represents any re-built, second-hand, renovated, reconditioned or old goods as new goods.
7. Represents that the goods or service have sponsorship, approval, performance, characteristics, accessories, uses or benefits which such goods or service do not have.
8. Makes a false or misleading representation, concerning the need for or the usefulness of any goods or service.
9. Gives to the public any warranty or guarantee of the performance, efficacy or length of life of a product or of any goods that is not based on an adequate or proper test thereof.

***Example***

Cure medical college, which is registered under the Societies Registration Act alleged and giving wrong impression in his publicity material that the college is authorized and equipped to impart medical education leading to M.B.B.S. degree. The college was actually neither recognized by the Medical Council of India nor affiliated to any university. It amounts as unfair trade practice.

**Case Study**

AB Ltd was manufacturing acupressure sandals which they claimed were designed to improve blood circulation and for keeping the users healthy by walking daily on the chappals for 8 minutes every morning and evening before meals. They also claimed that WHO has approved of this therapy. When the matter was referred to the All India Institute of Medical Sciences, it was very clearly stated by way of medical opinion that there was no proven evidence in modern medical literature that acupressure helps treat any ailment and that the science of acupressure was not accepted even in developed countries. Even the WHO disclaimed any approval having been granted to the use of such sandals. Further, on the box containing the chappals, it was mentioned that the sandals were not to be used for more than ten minutes and that heart and blood pressure patients should consult the doctor before using them but these facts were not mentioned in the advertisement. Can it be considered as an unfair trade practice?

**Case Study**

Miss Chandni has been buying Amul milk packet 500 ml from a retailer. The packet though gives only 400 ml. What action can she take against the company?

### 15.4.10 Defect

A defect means any fault, imperfection or shortcoming in the quality, quantity, potency, purity or standard which is required to be maintained by or under any law for the time being in force or under any contract, express or implied or as is claimed by the trade in any manner, whatsoever in relation to any goods. The defect is with regard to goods. However, it has been held that defect in the title of goods is not defect in goods.

***Example***

If the seller fails to deliver the goods which he agreed to sell it will be treated as a defect.

### 15.4.11 Deficiency

A deficiency means any fault, imperfection or shortcoming or inadequacy in the quality, nature and manner of performance which is required to be maintained by or under any law for the time being in force, or has been undertaken to be performed by a person in pursuance of a contract or otherwise in relation to any service. The deficiency is with regard to service. Any fault or negligence in setting the claim by the insurance company is deficiency in service.

***Examples***

1. The disconnection of electric supply on account of arbitrary and excessive billing and without giving notice is deficiency in service.
2. The bank dishonouring the bank draft or cheque despite sufficient funds in the account is deficiency in service.
3. The housing board fails to give possession of the flat after receiving the full price and after registering it in favour of the allottee. It is held as a deficiency on part of the housing board.

**Case Study**

A D.D. of ₹ 1,00,000, was issued by the state bank of Travankore on the SBI, Surat. When it is presented at the drawee branch, the payment is refunded on the ground that under the signature of one of the persons signing the draft (accountant of bank), the capacity to which he signed the same is not mentioned. Can the D.D. holder get the compensation?

**Case Study**

X had got a confirmed ticket on Jet Airways. The flight was later cancelled on account of technical snag. Is it a deficiency in service?

**Case Study**

X was allotted a Maruti car. There was a delay in the delivery of the car. Subsequently the dealer called upon X to make further payment as the price of the car had gone up. Is Mr. X liable to bear the price increase on account of delay caused by the dealer?

**Case Study**

The Sterling Hospital where Mr. Shah was treated, declined to give him the medical records pertaining to his treatment and operation for Ulcer. Can it be termed a deficiency in service on the part of the hospital?

**Case Study**

Miss Chandni had paid the telephone bill but inspite of that, the telephone department disconnected my telephone without any notice. Can the department disconnect the telephone without notice to the subscriber?

### 15.4.12 Spurious Goods and Services

The spurious goods and services mean, such goods and services which are claimed to be genuine but they are actually not so.

## 15.5 WHO CAN FILE A COMPLAINT

The following can file a complaint under the Act:

1. A consumer. When the consumer is a minor or a lunatic person on his behalf, his parent or guardian can file the complaint.
2. Any voluntary consumer organization registered under the Societies Registration Act, 1860 or under the Companies Act, 1956 or under any other law for the time being in force.
3. The Central Government.
4. The State Government or Union Territory Administrations.
5. One or more consumers on behalf of the numerous consumers who are having the same interest.

A consumer association cannot file a complaint on behalf of unspecified or unidentified number of consumers. In the Case of *Upbhokta Sanrakshan Samiti vs Winsard Foods Ltd*, the consumers association found that, the biscuit packets sold by a food company were less in weights. A complainant, demanding a compensation for the public of the State of Rajasthan was not maintainable.

The Act contemplates an identified consumer in order to make the application of its provisions or any consumer association to represent it. The Act also contemplates an action in the representative capacity, by providing that when there are numerous consumers having the same interest one or more consumers must file the complaint on behalf of others.

## 15.6 REDRESSAL MACHINERY UNDER THE ACT

To provide simple, speedy and inexpensive redressal of consumer grievances, the Act envisages three-tier quasijudicial machinery at the National, State and District levels.

- National Consumer Disputes Redressal Commission—known as 'National Commission'.
- Consumer Disputes Redressal Commissions—known as 'State Commission'.
- Consumer Disputes Redressal Forums—known as 'District Forum'.

### 15.6.1 District Forum

Under the CPA, the State Government has to set up a District Forum in each district of the state. The government may establish more than one District Forum in a district if it requires.

Every member of the District Forum holds office for five years or upto the age of 65 years, whichever is earlier and is not eligible for re-appointment.

The District Forum can entertain complaints where the value of goods or services and the compensation, if any claimed is less than ₹ 20 lakhs.

A complaint shall be instituted in the District Forum within the local limits of whose jurisdiction:

(a) The opposite party or the defendant actually and voluntarily resides or carries on the business or has a branch office or personally works for gain at the time of institution of the complaint; or

(b) Any one of the opposite parties (where there are more than one) actually and voluntarily resides or carries on business or has a branch office or personally works for gain at the time of institution of the complaint provided that the other opposite party/parties acquiescence in such institution or the permission of the Forum is obtained in respect of such opposite parties; or

(c) The cause of action arises wholly or in part.

### 16.6.2 State Commission

The Act provides for the establishment of the State Consumer Disputes Redressal Commission by the State Government in the state by notification. Each State Commission shall consist of:

Every appointment made under this shall be made by the State Government on the recommendation of a Selection Committee consisting of the president of the State Commission, Secretary—Law Department of the State and Secretary in charge of Consumer Affairs in the state.

Every member of the State Commission holds office for five years or upto the age of 65 years, whichever is earlier and is not eligible for re-appointment.

The State Commission can entertain complaints where the value of goods or services and the compensation, if any claimed exceeds ₹ 20 lakhs but does not exceed ₹ 1 Crore. Any person aggrieved by an order made by the District Forum may prefer an appeal to the State Commission within 30 days from the date of order. The State Commission also has the jurisdiction to entertain appeal against the orders of any District Forum within the state.

### 15.6.3 National Commission

Every member of the National Commission shall hold office for a term of five years or upto 70 years of age whichever is earlier and shall not be eligible for reappointment.

Any person, aggrieved by an order made by the State Commission may prefer an appeal to the National Commission within 30 days from the date of order. Any person aggrieved by any original order of the National Commission may prefer an appeal to the Supreme Court within 30 days.

## 15.7 HOW TO FILE A COMPLAINT

### 15.7.1 Requirements

The procedures for filing complaints and seeking redressal are simple. There is no fee for filing a complaint before the District Forum, the State Commission or the National Commission. There should be three to five copies of the complaint on plain paper. The complainant or his authorized agent can present the complaint in person. The complaint can be sent by post to the appropriate Forum/Commission. The complaint should be signed by the complainant or his authorized agent. The complaint is to be filed within two years from the date on which the cause of action has arisen.

### 15.7.2 Information Given

A complaint should contain the following information:

1. The name, description and the address of the complainant.
2. The name, description and address of the opposite party or parties as the case may be, as far as they can be ascertained.
3. The facts relating to the complaint and when and where it arose.
4. The documents, if any in support of the allegations contained in the complaint.
5. The relief which the complainant is seeking.

***Note:***

A specimen of the complaint file before the consumer forum is given as Annexure I to the chapter.

## 15.8 RELIEF AVAILABLE TO THE CONSUMERS

Depending on the nature of relief sought by the consumer and facts, the Redressal Forums may give orders for one or more of the following reliefs:

1. Removal of defects from the goods.
2. Replacement of the goods.
3. Refund of the price paid.
4. Award of compensation for the loss or injury suffered.
5. Removal of defects or deficiencies in the services.
6. Discontinuance of unfair trade practices or restrictive trade practices or direction not to repeat them.
7. Withdrawal of the hazardous goods from being offered to sale or award for adequate costs to parties.

## 15.9 PROCEDURE FOR FILING THE APPEAL

An appeal against the decision of a District Forum can be filed before the State Commission within a period of 30 days. The appeal against the decision of a State Commission can be filed before the National Commission within 30 days. The appeal against the orders of the National Commission can be filed before the Supreme Court within a period of 30 days.

There is no fee for filing an appeal before the State Commission or the National Commission.

The procedure for filing the appeal is the same as that of the complaint except the application should be accompanied by the orders of the District/State Commission as the case may be and the grounds for filing the appeal should be specified.

## 15.10 SPEEDY DISPOSAL

The thrust of the Act is to provide simple, speedy and inexpensive redressal to the consumers' grievances. To ensure the speedy disposal of consumers' grievances, the following provisions have been incorporated in the Act and the rules framed there under:

1. It is obligatory on the complainant or appellant or their authorized agents and the opposite party to appear before the Forum/Commission on the date of hearing or any other date to which hearing could be adjourned.
2. The National Commission, State Commission and District Forums are required to decide complaints as far as possible, within a period of three months from the date of notice received by the opposite party where complaint does not require analysis or testing of the commodities and within five months, if it requires analysis or testing of commodities.
3. The National Commission and State Commissions are required to decide the appeal as far as possible within 90 days from the first date of hearing.
4. On receipt of a complaint, a copy of the complaint is to be referred to the opposite party, directing him to give his version of the case within 21 days. This period may be extended by another 15 days. If the opposite party admits the allegations contained in the complaint the complaint will be decided on the basis of materials on the record. Where the opposite party denies or disputes the allegations or omits or fails to take any action to represent his case within the time provided, the dispute will be settled in the following manner.
5. In case of a dispute relating to any goods where the complaint alleges a defect in the goods which cannot be determined without proper analysis or test of the goods a sample of the goods shall be obtained from the complainant, sealed and authenticated in the manner, prescribed for referring to the appropriate laboratory for the purpose of any analysis or test whichever may be necessary, so as to find out whether such goods suffer from any other defect. The appropriate laboratory would be required to report its finding to the referring authority, i.e., the District Forum or the State Commission within a period of 45 days from the receipt of the reference or within such extended period as may be granted by these agencies.

**Case Study**

Mr. Mehra, a businessman, applies to ICICI Bank for grant of loan. The bank charges the application fee and refuses to grant loan on the ground of inadequacy of security. Can Mr. Mehra approach the consumer court?

**Case Study**

The transformer which was supplying electricity to Miss Bijli, got burnt and was replaced by the department after about two months. However, she was billed with consumption charges. Is she liable to pay any such charges when there was no consumption of electricity by her?

**Case Study**

Mr. Fast's car met with an accident. The insurance claim was rejected on the ground that his driver was not holding valid driving license. Should Mr. Fast approach a consumer court for seeking the insurance claim?

## 15.11 POWERS OF THE DISPUTE REDRESSAL AGENCIES

The District Forum, the State Commission and the National Commission are vested with the powers of a civil court under the Code of Civil Procedure while trying a suit in respect of the following matters:

1. The summoning and enforcing attendance of any defendant or witness, examining the witness on oath.
2. The discovery and production of any document or other material producible as evidence.
3. The reception of evidence on affidavits.
4. The requisitioning of the report of the concerned analysis or test from the appropriate laboratory or from any other relevant source.
5. Issuing of any commission for the examination of any witness.
6. Any other matter which may be prescribed.
7. To issue remedial orders against the opposite party.
8. To dismiss frivolous and vexatious complaints and to order the complainant to make payment of costs, not exceeding ₹ 10,000 to the opposite party.

## LIST OF LANDMARK JUDGEMENTS

1. ***Mahabubnagar Citizens Council vs District Consumer Disputes Redressal Forum (1997)***
   The consumer association can file complaint, even on behalf of non-member of the association.
2. ***Laxmi Engineering Works vs P. S. G. Industrial Institute (1995)***
   Any person buying goods for purpose of being used in any activity on a large scale for making profit is not consumer.
3. ***GM, South Eastern Railways vs Anand Prasad Sinha (1991)***
   Railway passenger travelling on payment of fare is consumer.

4. ***Spring Medow Hospital vs Harjot Ahluwalia (1998)***
   A consultant could be negligent when he delegates the responsibility to his junior with the knowledge that the junior was incapable of performing his duties properly.
5. ***Srimati vs UOI (1996)***
   Advocates are covered under the Consumer Protection Act.
6. ***Neela Vasant Raje vs Amogh Industries (1993)***
   Accepting the deposit from public agreeing to pay interest is 'service'. If the interest and principal is not paid on due dates, it is deficiency of service.
7. ***Cosmopolitan Hospitals vs V. P. Nair (1992)***
   The medical services are covered under the Consumer Protection Act.
8. ***Indian Airlines Ltd vs Dr V. J. Philip (1997)***
   The delay in flight, due to bad weather and poor visibility are unforeseen circumstances. There is no 'deficiency in service'.
9. ***Mahesh Enterprises vs Arum Kumar (2001)***
   Parking vehicle in parking lot on payment of parking charges is bailment. The person responsible for the management of parking area is liable to make a good the los due to theft.
10. ***Punjab and Sind Bank vs Manpreet Singh Sood (1994)***
    The dishonour of a cheque despite sufficient balance in the account is gross negligence and it is deficiency in service.
11. ***Consumer Unity Trust Society vs State of Rajathan (1991)***
    The patients availing medical treatment in the Government hospital are not consumers and the facility offered in the government hospitals cannot be regarded as service hired for consideration.
12. ***Raj Kumari Khurana vs Murablack India Ltd (1994)***
    Representing that the application money will be refunded if the allotment is not made and not refunding the money is held as unfair trade practice.
13. ***N. S. Ahluwalia vs Hindustan Motors (1997)***
    Puffing up, is not unfair trade practice but misleading about quality and standard can be UTP.
14. ***Nittie Education Trust vs UOI (1997)***
    The education is not a trade practice.
15. ***Murlidhar Sarangi vs The New India Assurance Co. Ltd (2000)***
    The claim can be denied if the particular risk is not covered under the policy. It is not the deficiency of service on part of insurance company.

## TEST YOUR KNOWLEDGE

1. Discuss in details the objects of Consumer Protection Act. **(Ref. Para-15.1)**
2. Briefly explain the salient features of the Consumer Protection Act. **(Ref. Para-15.2)**
3. What are the basic rights available to consumers? **(Ref. Para-15.3)**
4. What constitutes a complaint under the Consumer Protection Act? **(Ref. Para-15.4)**
5. Write a short note on commercial purpose under the Consumer Protection Act. **(Ref. Para-15.4)**
6. Write a short note on consumer. **(Ref. Para-15.4)**

7. Write a short note on deficiency in service. **(Ref. Para-15.4)**
8. Explain the word 'consumer' under the Consumer Protection Act with suitable examples. **(Ref. Para-15.4)**
9. What do you understand by unfair trade practices? **(Ref. Para-15.4)**
10. State whether a person purchasing of a sewing machine for earning her livelihood is a consumer? **(Ref. Para-15.4)**
11. Can an association of persons seek remedy under the Consumer Protection Act, 1986? **(Ref. Para-15.5)**
12. Complainant means any person. Comment. **(Ref. Para-15.5)**
13. Who can file a complaint? Can a parent or guardian of minor file complaint on his behalf? **(Ref. Para-15.5)**
14. Where an aggrieved consumer can file complaint under the Consumer Protection Act? **(Ref. Para-15.6)**
15. Write short note on District Forum and State Commission. **(Ref. Para-15.6)**
16. Explain the nature and scope of the remedies under the Act. **(Ref. Para-15.6,15.8)**
17. What is the limitation period for filing of complaint under the Act? **(Ref. Para-15.7)**
18. Explain reliefs available under the Consumer Protection Act, 1986. **(Ref. Para-15.8)**
19. What is the procedure to deal with a complaint made under the Consumer Protection Act? **(Ref. Para-15.9)**
20. What are the powers available by the dispute redressal agencies under Act? **(Ref. Para-15.11)**

## MULTIPLE-CHOICE QUESTIONS

1. The provisions of Consumer Protection Act is applicable to
   (i) goods.
   (ii) service.
   (iii) goods or service.
   (iv) goods and service.
2. Under the Consumer Protection Act, complainant means
   (i) consumer.
   (ii) Central Government.
   (iii) State Government.
   (iv) all of the above.
3. Under the Consumer Protection Act, complainant means
   (i) Central or State government.
   (ii) legal representative of the deceased consumer.
   (iii) both (i) and (ii).
   (iv) neither (i) nor (ii).
4. Under the Consumer Protection Act, complaint means
   (i) allegation in writing.
   (ii) oral allegation.
   (iii) claim in writing.
   (iv) oral claim for damage.
5. Under the Consumer Protection Act, service does not include
   (i) rendering service free of cost.
   (ii) rendering service under a contract of personal service.
   (iii) both (i) and (ii).
   (iv) neither (i) nor (ii).

6. Representation by the seller that he has sponsorship or approval which the seller does not have amount as
   (i) defect in goods.
   (ii) deficiency in service.
   (iii) restrictive trade practice.
   (iv) unfair trade practice.
7. Trade practice which tends to bring about manipulation of price amount as
   (i) fraud.
   (ii) unfair trade practice.
   (iii) restrictive trade practice.
   (iv) none of the above.
8. Trade practice which tends to bring about manipulation of conditions of delivery of goods amount as
   (i) fraud.
   (ii) unfair trade practice.
   (iii) restrictive trade practice.
   (iv) none of the above.
9. Under the Consumer Protection Act, ______ shall constitute central consumer protection council.
   (i) Central Government
   (ii) State Government
   (iii) President of India
   (iv) Supreme Court
10. Under the Consumer Protection Act, ______ shall constitute State consumer protection council.
    (i) Central Government
    (ii) State Government
    (iii) President of India
    (iv) Supreme Court
11. Consumer disputes redressal agencies include ______
    (i) District Forum.
    (ii) State Commission.
    (iii) National Commission.
    (iv) all of the above.
12. Every member of the District Forum, shall hold office for term of ______ years or up to age of 65 years.
    (i) 5
    (ii) 4
    (iii) 3
    (iv) 10
13. The District Forum shall have jurisdiction to entertain complaints where the value of the goods or services and the compensation claimed does not exceed ______
    (i) ₹ 20,00,000.
    (ii) ₹ 5,00,000.
    (iii) ₹ 25,00,000.
    (iv) ₹ 1,00,00,000.
14. The State Commission shall have jurisdiction to entertain complaints where the value of the goods or services and the compensation claimed does not exceed ______
    (i) ₹ 20,00,000.
    (ii) ₹ 5,00,000.
    (iii) ₹ 25,00,000.
    (iv) ₹ 1,00,00,000.
15. Any person, aggrieved by an order of the National Commission can appeal against order of the National Commission to the
    (i) High Court.
    (ii) Supreme Court.
    (iii) Magistrate Court.
    (iv) any of the above as per person's choice.
16. Any person aggrieved by an order of the National Commission can appeal against order of the National Commission to the Supreme Court within period of ______
    (i) 15 days.
    (ii) 30 days.
    (iii) 45 days.
    (iv) reasonable time.
17. An appeal filed with State or National Commission shall be heard as expeditiously as possible and efforts will be made to dispose an appeal with in period of ______ days.
    (i) 30
    (ii) 60
    (iii) 90
    (iv) reasonable time

18. District Forum shall have same power as are vested in the ______
    (i) civil court.
    (ii) criminal court.
    (iii) fast track court.
    (iv) special court.
19. Usually a complaint can be made to district forum, state commission or national commission within period of ______ years from the date on which the cause of action has arisen.
    (i) one
    (ii) two
    (iii) three
    (iv) five
20. Which relief can be obtained by consumers from commission?
    (i) To remove defects from goods.
    (ii) Not to offer the hazardous goods for sale.
    (iii) To stop manufacturing of hazardous goods.
    (iv) All of the above.
21. Which relief can not be obtained by consumers from commission?
    (i) Imprisonment for six months.
    (ii) Not to offer the hazardous goods for sale.
    (iii) To stop manufacturing of hazardous goods.
    (iv) All of the above.
22. State Commission and National Commission shall have same power as are vested in the ______
    (i) civil court.
    (ii) criminal court.
    (iii) fast track court.
    (iv) special court.
23. Any ______ can be consumer
    (i) natural person
    (ii) artificial person
    (iii) both (i) and (ii)
    (iv) none of the above
24. Defect under the Consumer Protection Act can be for ______
    (i) goods.
    (ii) services.
    (iii) both (i) and (ii).
    (iv) none of the above.

## ANSWER KEYS

| | | | | | |
|---|---|---|---|---|---|
| **1.** (iv) | **5.** (iii) | **9.** (i) | **13.** (i) | **17.** (iii) | **21.** (i) |
| **2.** (iv) | **6.** (iv) | **10.** (ii) | **14.** (i) | **18.** (i) | **22.** (i) |
| **3.** (iii) | **7.** (iii) | **11.** (iv) | **15.** (ii) | **19.** (ii) | **23.** (iii) |
| **4.** (i) | **8.** (iii) | **12.** (i) | **16.** (ii) | **20.** (iv) | **24.** (i) |

## ANNEXURE-I—SAMPLE NOTICE

(The notice may be prepared in the following style and sent by registered acknowledgement—due post)

Dated: 3-1-2003

The Managing Director
ABC Engineering Works
Gala No. 22, XYZ Compound
Gandhi Nagar
Mumbai 400602

**SUB: NOTICE BEFORE FILING CONSUMER COMPLAINT**

Dear Sir,

1. Give details of your purchase of product or service (cash memo number and date).
2. Give information about the warranty or guarantee received by you at the time of purchase.
3. Give details of the deficiency in the product or service.
4. Give the problems you are facing due to this deficiency.
5. Give the details about your efforts to inform about this grievance in the past to which the party has not responded.
6. Give a time limit of at least 15 to 30 days to settle your grievance by asking for refund of full amount with suitable interest (15%), or replacement of the product along with suitable compensation, else you will file a complaint with the Consumer Court as you are protected under the Consumer Protection Act of 1986.
7. Inform that the consumer complaint will be at his cost and expenses, and you will seek compensation for the mental agony caused due to his deficiency in services.

Yours truly,

Your signature,
name and address

# 16

# Foreign Exchange Management Act, 1999

**Learning Objectives**

*After reading this chapter, you will be able to understand:*

- Difference between FEMA and FERA
- Person resident in India and person resident out of India
- Authorized person
- Current account transaction and capital account transaction
- Export of goods and services
- Transfer of immovable property out of India
- Dealing in Foreign Exchange and foreign securities
- Penalty provisions and compounding of offences

## 16.1 APPLICATION OF ACT—SECTION 1

The act extends to the whole of India. It also applies to:

1. All branches, offices and agencies outside India owned or controlled by a person resident in India.
2. Any contravention committed outside India by any person to whom this act applies.

## 16.2 *FERA VS FEMA*

The authorized dealers and money changers have been clubbed together under the definition of 'Authorized Person'. In addition it also includes an 'offshore banking unit'.

The definitions of capital account transaction and current account transaction have been inserted keeping in mind the possibility of introduction of capital account convertibility.

The definitions of 'export' and 'import' have been inserted on similar lines as The Customs Act, 1962.

The definition of 'person' has been inserted and the definition of 'person resident in India' has been aligned with the Income Tax Act, 1961. This has probably been done considering the difficulties arising due to different definitions and different interpretations. All non-resident accounts with the banks were on the basis of the definition in the FERA. Now according to the FEMA definition, very few of them will be non-resident accounts. However, the EXIM policy definition still remains different.

The FEMA is a much smaller enactment—49 sections as against 81 sections of the FERA.

The theme of FERA was: 'everything that is specified is under control'. While the theme of the FEMA is: 'everything other than what is expressly covered is not controlled'. Thus, there is a lot of deregulation.

In the process of simplification many of the 'laid downs' of the erstwhile the FERA have been withdrawn.

Many provisions of the FERA like the ones relating to blocked accounts Indians taking up employment abroad employment of foreign technicians in India contracts in evasion of the act, vexatious search and culpable mental state have no appearance in the FEMA.

## 16.3 DEFINITION

### 16.3.1 Person—Section 2(u)

A person includes individual, HUF, company, firm, AOP whether incorporated or not and any agency, office or branch owned or controlled by such person.

### 16.3.2 Person Resident in India—Section 2(v)

A person residing in India for more than 182 days during the course of the preceding financial year but does not include—

1. A person who has gone out of India or who stays outside India in either case
   - (i) For or on taking up employment outside India.
   - (ii) For carrying on any business or vocation outside India.
   - (iii) For any other purpose in such circumstances as would indicate his intention to stay outside India for an uncertain period.
2. A person who has come to or stays in India in either case otherwise than
   - (i) For or on taking up employment in India.
   - (ii) For carrying on any business or vocation in India.
   - (iii) For any other purpose in such circumstances as would indicate his intention to stay in India for an uncertain period.

3. Any person or body corporate, registered or incorporated in India.
4. Any branch, office or agency in India owned or controlled by a person resident outside India.
5. Any branch, office or agency outside India owned or controlled by a person resident in India.

**Case Study**

'Printex Computer' is a Singapore based company having several business units all over the world. It has a unit for manufacturing computer printers with its headquarters in Pune. It has a branch in Dubai which is controlled by the headquarters in Pune. What would be the residential status under the FEMA, 1999 of printer units in Pune and that of Dubai branch?

**Case Study**

Mr. Ram had resided in India during the financial year 1999–2000, for less than 183 days. He again came to India on 1 May 2000 for higher studies and business and stayed up to 15 July 2001. State under the Foreign Exchange Management Act, 1999:

(i) If Mr. Ram can be considered 'person resident in India' during the financial year 2000–2001, and
(ii) Is the citizenship relevant for determining such a status?

**Case Study**

Examine whether the following branches can be considered as a 'person resident in India' under the Foreign Exchange Management Act, 1999:

(i) ABC Limited, a company incorporated in India established a branch at London on 1 January 2003.
(ii) M/s XYZ, a foreign company established a branch at New Delhi on 1 January 2003. The branch at New Delhi controls a branch at Colombo.

**Case Study**

Mr. Sekhar resided for a period of 150 days in India during the financial year 2003–2004 and thereafter went abroad. He came back to India on 1 April 2004 as an employee of a business organization. What would be his residential status during the financial year 2004–2005?

**Case Study**

Examine, with the reference to the provisions of the Foreign Exchange Management Act, 1999 the residential status of the branches mentioned below:

(i) MKP Limited, an Indian company having its Registered office at Mumbai, India established a branch at New York, U.S.A. on 1 April 2004.

(ii) WIP Ltd, a company incorporated and registered in London, established a branch at Chandigarh in India on 1 April 2004.

(iii) WIP Ltd's Singapore branch which is controlled by its Chandigarh branch.

### 16.3.3 Currency—Section 2(h)

It includes all the currency notes, postal notes, postal orders, money orders, cheques, drafts, travellers cheques, letters of credit, bills of exchange, promissory notes, credit cards or such other similar instruments as may be prescribed by the Reserve Bank of India (RBI).

The RBI has notified that debit cards, ATM cards or any other instrument which can be used to create a financial liability is currency.

### 16.3.4 Foreign Currency—Section 2(m)

A foreign currency is any currency other than the Indian currency, dollar, euro and yen are examples of foreign currency.

### 16.3.5 Foreign Exchange—Section 2(n)

Foreign exchange means foreign currency and includes the following:

1. Deposits, credits and balances payable in any foreign currency.
2. Demand drafts, travellers cheques, letters of credit or bills of exchange expressed or drawn in the Indian currency but payable in foreign currency.
3. Demand drafts, travellers cheques, letters of credit or bills of exchange drawn by person outside India but payable in Indian currency.

### 16.3.6 Foreign Security—Section 2(o)

Any security in the form of shares, stocks, bonds, debentures or any other instrument denominated or expressed in foreign currency and includes the securities expressed in foreign currency but where redemption or any form of return such as interest or dividend is payable in Indian currency.

### 16.3.7 Person Resident Outside India—Section 2(w)

This is for every person who is not a person resident in India.

## 16.4 AUTHORIZED PERSONS

The RBI cannot do all the transactions in Foreign Exchange itself. Hence the RBI delegates its powers to the 'authorized persons' with suitable guidelines.

### 16.4.1 Authorized Persons—Section 2(c)

An 'Authorized person' means an authorized dealer, money changer, off-shore banking unit or any other person authorized by the RBI to deal in Foreign Exchange and foreign securities.

Generally, all the nationalized banks and foreign banks are appointed as the 'authorized dealers' to deal in Foreign Exchange. 'Authorized dealers' can deal in all other transactions in Foreign Exchange like bill of exchange, cheques, letter of credit and deposits.

The 'authorized person' should deal in Foreign Exchange and foreign securities as per the guidelines issued by the RBI. They should submit reports to the RBI as prescribed. Their accounts can be inspected by the RBI.

### 16.4.2 Duties of Authorized Person

Every authorized person granted permission by the RBI shall follow certain guidelines as under:

1. To comply with the directions or orders of the RBI in all his dealings.
2. To deal only in those transactions for which the authorization has been received.
3. To accept the required undertaking and declaration from the person to satisfy himself that the transaction is not in violation of the FEMA. If he has doubts he should refuse the transaction in writing.
4. If the authorized person has a reason to believe that any such contravention or evasion is contemplated he should report the matter to the RBI.

### 16.4.3 Authorization and Its Revocation

The RBI can authorize any person as 'authorized person'. The authorization shall be in writing and subject to the conditions.

The authorization granted by the RBI may be revoked at any time if the RBI is satisfied that it is in public interest to do so the authorized person has failed to comply with the conditions or any provisions of the act. Such a revocation can be done only after the dealer has given an opportunity for making the representation. The RBI can issue directions to the authorized persons and ask them to furnish information.

The RBI can impose a penalty upto ₹ 10,000 for contravention of any direction. In case of continuing contravention a penalty upto ₹ 2000 per day can be imposed by the RBI (Section 11).

The RBI can inspect the accounts of an authorized person for verification, obtaining information and seeking compliance. The authorized person is duty bound to produce all the records books and accounts at the time of inspection (Section 12).

## 16.5 CURRENT ACCOUNT TRANSACTION

Any transaction other than capital account transaction is current account transaction. It includes the following:

1. Payments due in course of foreign trade, current business, services and other short term banking and credit facilities in the ordinary course of business.
2. Payments due as interests on loans.
3. Net income from investments.
4. Remittances for the living expenses of parents spouse and children residing abroad.
5. Expenses in connection with foreign travel, education and medical care of parents, spouse and children.

All the current account transactions are generally permitted. A person may sell or draw Foreign Exchange to or from an authorized person if there is such a sale or drawal in the current account transaction.

However, the Central Government may, in public interest and in consultation with the Reserve Bank impose such reasonable restrictions for the current account transactions.

The current account transactions are divided in to the following three categories:

1. Prohibited current account transactions.
2. Current account transactions with prior approval of the Central Government (CG).
3. Current account transactions with prior approval of the RBI.

### 16.5.1 Prohibited Current Account Transactions

Drawal of Foreign Exchange for the following transactions is prohibited:

1. Remittance out of lottery winnings.
2. Remittance of income from racing/riding or any other hobby.
3. Remittance for the purchase of lottery tickets, banned/prescribed magazines, football pools and sweepstakes.
4. Payment on commission on exports made towards equity investments in the joint venture/wholly owned subsidiary abroad of Indian company.
5. Remittance of the dividend by any company to which the requirement of dividend balancing is applicable.
6. Payment of commission on the exports under Rupee State Credit Route except the commission up to 10% of invoice value of the exports of tea and tobacco.
7. Payment related to the call back service of telephones.
8. Payment for travel to Nepal and Bhutan.
9. Any transaction with a person resident in Nepal and Bhutan.
10. Remittance of interest income on funds held in non-resident special rupee scheme account—NRSR ACCOUNT.

### 16.5.2 Current Account Transactions with Prior Approval of the CG

The prior approval of the Central Government shall be required for the drawal of Foreign Exchange (by any person) for the purposes listed below:

| Purpose of Remittance | Permission Granting Authority |
|---|---|
| 1. Cultural Tours | Ministry of HRD (Department of Education and Culture). |
| 2. Advertisement in foreign print media for the purposes other than the promotion of tourism, foreign investments and international bidding (exceeding US $10,000) by a State Government and its Public Sector Undertakings | Ministry of Finance, Department of Economic Affairs. |
| 3. Remittance of Freight of vessel chartered by a PSU | Ministry of Surface Transport (Chartering Wing). |
| 4. Payment of import through ocean transport by a Government Department or a PSU on c.i.f. basis (i.e. other than f.o.b. and f.a.s. basis) | Ministry of Surface Transport (Chartering Wing). |
| 5. Multi-modal transport operators making remittance to their agents abroad | Registration Certificate from the Director General of Shipping. |
| 6. Remittance of hiring charges of transponders by | |
| (a) TV Channels | Ministry of Information and Broadcasting. |
| (b) Internet service providers | Ministry of Communication and Information Technology. |
| 7. Remittance of container detention charges exceeding the rate prescribed by the Director General of Shipping | Ministry of Surface Transport (Director General of Shipping). |
| 8. Remittances under technical collaboration agreements, and payment of royalty | No Permission needed |
| 9. Remittance of prize money/sponsorship of the sports activity abroad by a person other than International/National/State Level sports bodies if the amount involved exceeds US $1,00,000 | Ministry of HRD (Department of Youth Affairs and Sports). |
| 10. Remittance for membership of P&L Club | Ministry of Finance (Insurance Division). |

Prior approval of the Central Government is not required where the payment is made out of funds held in the RFC/EEFC account of the remitter.

### 16.5.3 Current Account Transactions with Prior Approval of the RBI

Prior approval of the RBI shall be required for the drawal of Foreign Exchange by any person for the purposes listed below. A permission is required to be obtained when the drawal is in excess of the limit prescribed.

| | Purpose of Remittance or Release of Foreign Exchange for | Remittance Limit |
|---|---|---|
| | **Facilities for Individuals:** | |
| 1 | One or more private visits to any country except Nepal and Bhutan | US $ 2,50,000 per Financial Year |
| 2 | Gift or donation by any resident individual or entity (trust, company, partnership firm etc.) | US $ 2,50,000 per Financial Year to person resident out of India |
| 3 | Person going abroad for employment | US $ 2,50,000 per financial year |
| 4 | Emigration<br>**Note:** This remittance facility is not allowed for undertaking capital account transaction. | US $ 2,50,000 or amount prescribed by country of emigration |
| 5 | Business trip<br>**Note:** Above amount is available irrespective of period of stay. Business trip includes attending of an international conference, seminar, specialized training, apprentice training etc. | US $ 2,50,000 per financial year irrespective of number of visits |
| 6 | Medical treatment abroad or medical check up | US $ 2,50,000<br>For amount exceeding US $ 2,50,000 estimate from the doctor in India or hospital/doctor abroad, is required to be submitted with authorized dealer.<br>Authorised Dealer may release foreign exchange for medical treatment to person who has fallen sick after proceeding abroad. |
| 7 | Person accompanying as attendant to a patient going abroad for medical treatment or check-up | US $ 2,50,000 per financial year |
| 8 | Studies abroad | US $ 2,50,000<br>Remittance in excess of US $ 2,50,000 is allowed based on estimate from institution abroad. |
| 9 | Maintenance of close relative abroad | US $ 2,50,000 per financial year. |
| 10 | Any other current account transaction | US $ 2,50,000 |
| | **Facilities for Persons Other than Individuals:** | |
| 1 | Remittance for any consultancy services procured from outside India | US $ 1,00,00,000 per project for infrastructure project and US $ 10,00,000 for other consultancy project<br>Power, telecommunication, rail, ways, roads including bridges, seaport, airport, industrial parks and urban infrastructure (i.e. water supply, sanitation and sewage) are infrastructure project. |

| | | |
|---|---|---|
| 2 | Donations by corporate:<br>• To create chairs in reputed educational institutes<br>• To funds promoted by educational institutes<br>• To a technical institution or body or association in the field of activity of the donor company | 1% of foreign exchange earnings during the previous 3 financial years or US $ 50,00,000, whichever is less. |
| 3 | Commission to agents abroad for sale of residential flat or commercial plots in India | Commission exceeding 5% of the inward remittance or US $ 25,000 whichever is higher |
| 4 | Reimbursement of pre incorporation expenses by Indian entity to meet incorporation expenses out of India | 5% of the investment bought into India or US $ 1,00,000, whichever is higher. |

**Case Study**

Examine, whether the following transactions are permissible or not under the above act as the capital account transactions:

(i) Investment by a person resident in India in Foreign securities.

(ii) Foreign currency loans raised in India and abroad by a person resident in India.

(iii) Export, import and holding of currency/currency notes.

(iv) Trading in transferable development rights.

(v) Investment in a Nidhi Company.

**Case Study**

Mr. Basu desires to draw Foreign Exchange for the following purposes:

(i) Payment related to 'Call back services' of telephones.

(ii) US $1,20,000 for studies abroad on the basis of the estimates given by the foreign university.

(iii) US $25,000 for sending a cultural troupe on a tour of Europe.

Advise him whether he can get Foreign Exchange and if so, under what conditions.

**Case Study**

Mr. Atul, an Indian national desires to obtain Foreign Exchange for the following purposes:

(a) Remittance of US $10,000 for the payment for goods purchased from a party situated in Nepal.

(b) US $10,000 for remitting as commission to his agent in U.S.A. for the sale of commercial plots situated near Bangalore, consideration in respect of which was received by Mr. Atul by way of foreign currency inward remittance amounting to US $1,00,000. Advise him if he can get the Foreign Exchange and under what conditions.

**Case Study**

Mr. Sane, an Indian national desires to obtain Foreign Exchange for the following purposes:

(i) Remittance of US $50,000 out of winnings on a lottery ticket.

(ii) US $1,00,000 for sending a cultural troupe on a tour of U.S.A.

US $50,000 for meeting the expenses of his business tour to Europe. Advise him whether he can get Foreign Exchange and if so, under what conditions?

**Case Study**

State which kind of approval is required for the following transactions under the Foreign Exchange Management Act, 1999:

(i) X, a Film Star wants to perform along with his associates in New York on the occasion of Diwali for the Indians residing at New York. A Foreign Exchange drawal to the extent of US $20,000 is required for this purpose.

(ii) F International Ltd has purchased the trade mark from a Foreign company to establish a retail business chain in India as a joint venture at a consolidated price of US $500,000 which is to be paid in the foreign currency of that country.

(iii) R wants to get his heart surgery done at UK. Up to what limit Foreign Exchange can be drawn by him and what are the approvals required?

(iv) L wants to pursue a course in Fashion design in Paris. The Foreign Exchange drawal is US $20,000 towards the tuition fees and US $30,000 for the incidental and stay expenses for studying abroad.

## 16.6 EXPORT OF GOODS AND SERVICES

The export of goods and services is current account transaction. The RBI can direct any exporter to comply with the prescribed requirements to ensure that full export value of the goods or such reduced value of the goods as the RBI determines is received without delay.

Every exporter of goods or software in physical form or through any other form, either directly or indirectly to any place outside India, other than Nepal and Bhutan shall furnish to the specified authority, a declaration in one of the forms set out in the schedule. The declaration should be submitted within 21 days from the export.

The declaration should be supported by the evidence specified containing true and correct material particulars including the amount representing the full export value of the goods or services. If the full export value is not ascertainable at the time of export, the exporter shall indicate the amount he expects to receive.

In respect of the export of services to which none of the forms specified in these regulations apply, the exporter may export such services without furnishing any declaration but shall be liable to realize the amount of Foreign Exchange which becomes due or accrues on account of such export and to repatriate to India as per the act.

However, in the following cases, the export of goods or services may be made without furnishing the declaration:

1. Trade samples of goods and publicity material supplied free of payment.
2. Personal effects of travelers whether accompanied or un-accompanied.
3. Ship's stores, transshipment cargo and goods supplied under the orders of Central Government or of such officers as may be appointed by the Central Government in this behalf or of the military, naval or air force authorities in India for the military, naval or air force requirements.
4. Goods or software accompanied by a declaration by the exporter that they are not more than ₹ 25,000 in value.
5. By way of gift of goods accompanied by a declaration by the exporter that they are not more than ₹ 5,00,000 in value.
6. Aircrafts or aircraft engines and spare parts for overhauling and/or repairs abroad subject to their re-import into India after overhauling/repairs within a period 6 months from the date of their export.
7. Goods imported free of cost on re-export basis.
8. Replacement goods exported free of charge in accordance with the provisions of the Exim Policy in force for the time being.

### 16.6.1 Indication of Importer–Exporter Code Number (IEC)

The importer–exporter code number shall be indicated on all copies of the declaration forms submitted by the exporter to the specified authority and in all correspondence of the exporter with the authorized dealer or the Reserve Bank.

On realization of the export proceeds, the authorized dealer shall after due certification submit the duplicate of the EDF or as the case may be SOFTEX form to the nearest office of the Reserve Bank.

### 16.6.2 Period Within Which Export Value of Goods/Software to Be Realized

The amount representing the full export value of goods or software exported shall be realized and repatriated to India within 6 months from the date of export.

However, if the goods are exported to a warehouse established outside India with the permission of the Reserve Bank, the amount representing the full export value of the goods exported shall be paid to the authorized dealer, as soon as it is realized and in any case within 15 months from the date of the shipment of goods. This period of 6 months/15 months can be extended by the RBI or the authorized dealer as per the directions issued by the RBI for a sufficient and reasonable cause. The export on elongated credit terms beyond 6 months can be given only with the approval of the RBI.

### 16.6.3 Transfer of Documents

An authorized dealer may accept for negotiation or collection, shipping documents, including the invoice and the bill of exchange, covering the exports from his constituent. The person submitting the documents has to give declaration regarding full value of the export goods.

## 16.7 CAPITAL ACCOUNT TRANSACTIONS—SECTION 2(E)

A capital account transactions means, a transaction which alters the assets or liabilities positioned outside India of the persons resident in India or assets or liabilities in India of the persons resident outside India. The liabilities also include the contingent liabilities.

The term capital account transactions include the following:

1. Transfer or issue of foreign security by a person resident in India.
2. Transfer or issue of security by a person resident outside India.
3. Borrowing or lending in Foreign Exchange.
4. Borrowing or lending in rupees between a person resident in India and a person resident outside India.
5. Deposits between persons resident in India and persons resident outside India.
6. Export import or holding of currency.
7. Transfer of immovable property outside India other than a lease not exceeding 5 years by a person resident in India.
8. Acquisition or transfer of immovable property in India other than a lease not exceeding 5 years by a person resident outside India.
9. Guarantee or surety in respect of any debt by a person resident in India and owed to a person resident outside India or by a person resident outside India.

A person may sell or draw Foreign Exchange from an authorized person for a capital account transaction under an act within the limit.

The capital account transactions can be divided into the following two categories:

1. Permissible capital account transactions.
2. Prohibited capital account transactions.

### 16.7.1 Permissible Capital Account Transactions for Residents

1. Investment in foreign securities.
2. Foreign currency loans raised in India or abroad.
3. Transfer of immovable property outside India.
4. Guarantee in favour of a person resident outside India.
5. Export/import and holding of foreign currency notes.
6. Borrowings from a non-resident.
7. Maintenance of foreign currency account in India and abroad.
8. Purchase of insurance policy from a company outside India.
9. Lending to non-resident.

10. Remittance of capital assets outside India.
11. Sale and purchase of Foreign Exchange derivatives in India and abroad and commodity derivative abroad.

### 16.7.2 Permissible Capital Account Transactions for Non-residents

1. Issue of security in India.
2. Investment in securities if Indian companies or investment in firms and proprietorship concern or association.
3. Acquisition and transfer of the immovable property in India.
4. Guarantee in favour of a resident.
5. Import and export of the currency notes.
6. Deposits between a person resident and non-resident.
7. Foreign currency accounts in India.
8. Remittances outside India of the capital assets in India.

### 16.7.3 Prohibited Capital Account Transactions

Any person who is a resident outside India cannot make investment in India in any company or partnership firm or proprietary concern or any entity which is engaged:

1. In the business of chit fund.
2. As Nidhi company.
3. In agricultural or plantation activities.
4. In real estate business or construction of farm houses.
5. In trading in Transferable Development Rights (TDRs).

'Real estate business' shall not include development of townships construction of residential/commercial premises roads or bridges.

**Case Study**

State whether there are any restrictions in respect of the following transactions:

(i) The drawal of Foreign Exchange for payments due on account of amortization of loans in ordinary course of business.

(ii) Purchase by a person resident outside India, of shares of a company in India engaged in plantation activities.

## 16.8 ACQUISITION AND TRANSFER OF IMMOVABLE PROPERTY IN INDIA

A person resident outside India who is a citizen of India may acquire any immovable property in India other than agricultural/plantation/farm house subject to the following conditions:

1. He can transfer immovable property in India to a person resident in India.
2. He can transfer any immovable property other than agricultural/plantation property/farm house to a person resident outside India.

3. The asset is sold after three years.
4. An amount equivalent to the Foreign Exchange brought in can be repatriated.

### 16.8.1 Acquisition and Transfer of Property in India by a Person of Indian Origin (PIO)

A person of Indian origin resident outside India may acquire property other than agricultural/plant/farm from out of the funds received in India by way of inward remittance or the fund held in the NR Account on the following conditions:

1. He can acquire it by gift inheritance.
2. It can be transferred to the citizen of India.
3. If the asset is sold after three years, the amount equivalent to Foreign Exchange brought in can be repatriated.

### 16.8.2 Acquisition of Immovable Property for Carrying on Business

A person resident outside India who has established in India a branch/place of business in accordance with the RBI regulations can acquire any immovable property which is necessary for or incidental to carrying on such activity:

1. A person acquiring property should file with the RBI declaration from the NRI within 90 days.
2. The property can be transferred by way of mortgage to the authorized dealer as a security for any borrowing.
3. If the asset is sold, the sale proceeds can be repatriated only with prior permission of the RBI.

## 16.9 ACQUISITION AND TRANSFER OF IMMOVABLE PROPERTY OUTSIDE INDIA

A person resident in India can acquire/transfers any immovable property situated outside India as per the following conditions. In other cases general/special permission of the RBI will be required.

The restrictions do not apply to a property held by a person resident in India who is a national of a foreign state or was acquired on or before 1947 or had inherited from the person who was resident outside India.

The person resident in India acquires immovable property outside India by way of gift/inheritance from person resident in India.

The person resident of India also acquires property outside India by way of purchase out of Foreign Exchange held in the RFC account maintained.

The person resident in India has acquired immovable property outside India as per the above provisions; he may transfer it by way of gift to his relative who is the person resident in India.

## 16.10 ESTABLISHMENT IN INDIA OF BRANCH OR OFFICE OR OTHER PLACE OF BUSINESS

### 16.10.1 Liaison Office

It means a place of business to act as a channel of communication between the principal place of business/H.O. by whatever name called and the entities in India but which does not undertake any commercial/trading/industrial activity directly or indirectly.

No person resident outside India shall without prior approval of the RBI establish in India a branch or liaison office or project office or any other place of business. However, no approval is necessary for the banking company if it has obtained the necessary approval from the RBI.

A citizen of Pakistan, Bangladesh, China, Iran and Sri-Lanka cannot establish branch or liaison office or project office or any other place of business without the permission of the RBI.

The person resident outside India desiring to establish branch/liaison office shall apply to the RBI in FNC-1.

Where a person resident outside India has secured from India a company contract to execute a project in India and the project is funded by bilateral international finance agency shall apply to the RBI in FNC-1 for the permission to establish a project/site office in India.

The person resident outside India and permitted by the RBI may undertake or carry such activities as specified in the regulation.

The person resident outside India permitted by the RBI to establish project/site office in India shall not undertake or carry on any activity other than activity relating to the execution of the project.

The permitted activities of a person resident outside India for a branch in India:

1. Export/import of goods.
2. Rendering professional/consultancy services.
3. Carrying out research work in which perfect company is engaged.
4. Promoting technical/financial collaboration between the Indian company and the overseas company.
5. Representing the parent company in India and acting as buying/selling agent.
6. Rendering services in IT and development of software in India.
7. Rendering technical support to products supplied by parent company.
8. Foreign shipping/Airline company.

The person resident outside India permitted by the RBI to establish a branch/project office in India may remit outside India, the profit of branch or surplus of project on its completion, net applicable to taxes on the production of the prescribed documents and establishing net profits.

## 16.11 ACCEPTANCE OF THE DEPOSIT

The deposit includes deposit of money with bank, company, proprietary concern, firm, trust or any other person.

The funds raised through the ADR/GDR can be held in the deposit in foreign currency accounts with bank outside India, pending its utilization or repatriation in India.

### 16.11.1 Deposits by the India Company and NBFC from NRI/PI on Repatriation Basis

The company incorporated in India, the NBFC registered with the RBI may accept deposits from the NRI on repatriation basis subject to following conditions:

1. Deposits are received under the public deposit scheme.
2. If it is NBFC it should have acquired credit rating.
3. The amount representing the deposit is received by inward remittance from outside India through the normal banking channel or debit to the NRE/FCNR account.

4. The rate of interest payable shall be in conformity with the guidelines of the RBI.
5. Maturity period shall not exceed three years.
6. The company accepting the deposits shall comply with the provisions of any other law regulations as are applicable to in regard to the acceptance of deposits.
7. The amount of aggregate deposits accepted shall not exceed 35% of its NBF.
8. The payment of the interest net of taxes may be made by the company to the depositor by remittance through authorized dealer or credit to the depositors' NRE/FCNR/NRNR/NRO account.
9. The amount of deposits so collected shall not be utilized by the company for re-lending or for undertaking agricultural/plantation activities/real estate business.

### 16.11.2 Deposits by Indian Proprietorship/Film/Company and NBFC on Non-repatriation Basis from NRI/PIO/OCB

Same provisions as above are applicable but repatriation is not permitted.

## 16.12 EXPORT AND IMPORT OF CURRENCY

If the export/import of currency is outside the prescribed norms permission of the RBI will be required.

### 16.12.1 Export and Import of Indian Currency and Currency Notes

Any person resident in India may take outside India (other than to Nepal and Bhutan) currency notes of the Government of India and the RBI notes upto an amount not exceeding ₹ 5000 per person.

The person resident of India who had gone out of India on a temporary visit may bring into India at the time of his return from any place outside India (other than from Nepal and Bhutan), currency notes of the Government of India and the RBI notes upto an amount not exceeding ₹ 5000 per person.

### 16.12.2 Prohibition of Export of Indian Coins

No person shall take or send out of India, the Indian coins which are covered by the Antique and Art Treasure Act, 1972.

### 16.12.3 Import of Foreign Exchange into India

The person may send into India without the limit of Foreign Exchange in any form other than the currency notes, bank notes and traveller cheques.

Any person can bring into India from any place outside India without limit Foreign Exchange (other than un-issued notes) in form of currency notes, bank notes and traveller cheques. He has to make a declaration in form CDF, if (a) the aggregate value of the Foreign Exchange in the form of currency notes, bank notes or traveller cheques brought in by such person at any one time exceeds US $10,000 or its equivalent and/or (b) the aggregate value of the foreign currency notes brought in by such a person at any one time does not exceed US $5000 or its equivalent.

### 16.12.4 Export of Foreign Exchange and Currency Notes

An authorized person may send out of India, foreign currency acquired in the normal course of business.

Any person may take or send out of India (i) Cheques drawn on foreign currency account maintained. (ii) Foreign Exchange obtained by him by drawal from an authorized person in accordance (iii) currency in the safe of vessels or aircrafts which has been taken on board a vessel or aircraft with the permission of the Reserve Bank.

Any person may take out of India—(i) Foreign Exchange possessed by him in accordance with the FEMA Regulations (ii) un-spent Foreign Exchange brought back by him to India while returning from travel abroad and retained in accordance with the FEMA Regulations.

Any person resident outside India may take out of India un-spent Foreign Exchange which he had brought in India. If the amount exceeds the prescribed limit (of 5000/10,000 US $) he should have made a declaration in the CDF form on his arrival in India.

### 16.12.5 Export and Import of Currency to or from Nepal and Bhutan

A person may (i) take or send out of India to Nepal or Bhutan, currency notes of the Government of India and the RBI notes (other than notes of denominations of above ₹ 100), (ii) bring into India from Nepal or Bhutan, currency notes of Government of India and the RBI notes (other than notes of denominations of above ₹ 100 and (iii) take out of India to Nepal or Bhutan or bring into India from Nepal or Bhutan currency notes bring the currency of Nepal or Bhutan.

**Case Study**

Mr. Loma, an Indian national desires to obtain Foreign Exchange for the following purposes:

(a) Payment to be made for securing insurance for health from a company abroad.

(b) Payment of commission on exports under Rupee State Credit Route.

(c) Gift remittance exceeding US $10,000.

Advise him whether he can get Foreign Exchange and if so, under what condition?

## 16.13 POSSESSION AND RETENTION OF FOREIGN CURRENCY

The restrictions are only for the physical possession and retention of foreign currency and not in respect of foreign currency kept in permissible accounts with the authorized dealer's banks.

### 16.13.1 Limit for Possession and Retention of Foreign Currency or Foreign Coins

Foreign currency or foreign coins can be possessed and retained' subject to the following limits:

1. An authorized person within the scope of his authority without any limit.
2. Any person can possess foreign coins without limit.
3. A person, resident in India can retain foreign currency notes, bank notes and foreign currency traveller cheques not exceeding US $2000 or its equivalent in aggregate. Such Foreign Exchange in the form of currency notes, bank notes and traveller cheques should have been acquired by him:
   (i) While on a visit to any place outside India by way of payment for services not arising from any business in or anything done in India; or
   (ii) Acquired by him from any person not resident in India and who is on a visit to India as honorarium or gift or for services rendered or in settlement of any lawful obligation; or

(iii) Was acquired by him by way of honorarium or gift while on a visit to any place outside India; or

(iv) Represents an un-spent amount of Foreign Exchange acquired by him from an authorized person for travel abroad.

4. A person resident in India but not permanently resident therein may possess without limit foreign currency in the form of currency notes or bank notes without limit. Foreign currency was acquired, held or owned by him when him was resident outside India and has been brought into India in accordance with the regulations made under the act.

'Not permanently resident' means a person resident in India for employment of a specified duration (irrespective of length thereof) or for a specific job or assignment the duration of which does not exceed three years.

## 16.14 REALIZATION, REPARTIATION AND SURRENDER OF FOREIGN EXCHANGE

A person who is entitled to obtain Foreign Exchange should surrender it to 'authorized dealer'. He can retain with himself in only as per provisions of the regulations. The provisions of these regulations do not apply to Foreign Exchange in the form of currency of Nepal or Bhutan.

### 16.14.1 Duty of Persons to Realize Foreign Exchange

The person, resident in India to whom any amount of Foreign Exchange is due or has accrued shall take all reasonable steps to realize and repatriate to India such Foreign Exchange.

On realization of the Foreign Exchange due a person shall repatriate the same to India, i.e. bring into or receive in India, and

1. Sell it to an authorized person in India in exchange for rupees.
2. Retain it in account with an authorized dealer in India or EEFC account to the extent specified by the RBI.
3. Use it for discharge of a debt or liability denominated in Foreign Exchange to the extent and in the manner specified by the Reserve Bank.

The person shall be deemed to have repatriated the realized Foreign Exchange to India when he receives in India a payment in rupees from the account of a bank or an exchange house situated in any country outside India maintained with an authorized dealer.

The person shall sell the realized Foreign Exchange to an authorized person within:

1. Seven days if the Foreign Exchange is due or accrued as remuneration for the services rendered or in settlement of any lawful obligation or an income and assets held outside India or as inheritance settlement or gift.
2. Ninety days from the date of receipt in all the other cases.

### 16.14.2 Period for Surrender in Certain Cases

If a person who has acquired or purchased Foreign Exchange for any purpose mentioned in the declaration made by him to an authorized person does not use it for such purpose or for any other purpose for which the purchase or acquisition of Foreign Exchange is permissible he shall surrender such Foreign Exchange or the unused portion thereof to an authorized person within a period a 60 days from the date of its acquisition or purchase by him.

If Foreign Exchange acquired or purchased by any person from an authorized person, is for the purpose of foreign travel then the un-spent balance of such Foreign Exchange shall be surrendered to an authorized person:

1. Within 90 days from the date of return of the traveler to India when the un-spent Foreign Exchange is in the form of currency notes and coins.
2. Within 180 days from the date of return of the traveler to India when the un-spent Foreign Exchange is in the form of traveller cheques.

## 16.15 ENFORCEMENT DIRECTORATE

The directors of enforcement, additional director, special director, deputy director and asst. director of enforcement are appointed by the Central Government. These officers have powers similar to those conferred on the I.T. Act to the income tax authority:

1. Power regarding discovery and production of evidence.
2. Search and seizure.
3. Power to requisition books of accounts.
4. Power to inspect books of accounts.

It may happen that during investigation, draft/cheque/other instrument may come in possession of E.A. That instrument can be given to the RBI/Authorized person for encashment. They will encash the instrument and credit the proceeds realized to separate A/c in name of 'Directorate of Enforcement'.

The RBI/authorized person who encashes cheque/draft/instrument will be identified by the Central Government for any liability that may be incurred by them.

The amount in credit may be returned to the person by the adjudicating authority if it is found that these is no contravention. The Indian currency seized will be returned at the rate 6% interest.

## 16.16 DEPARTMENTAL ADJUDICATION—SECTION 16

The Central Government can authorize certain officers as a adjudicating authority. They can adjudicate cases in respect of violation of the FEMA. These are quasi-judicial authority. They have to follow the principles of natural justice by giving the opportunity of making representation.

The adjudicating authority can hold enquiry only on receiving complaint from the authorized officer. The person can appear either in person or take assistance of the legal practitioner. The adjudicating authority shall dispose off the complaint within one year. If it is not possible he should record the reason for not disposing off the complaint within one year.

A penalty can be imposed, up to thrice the sum involved in such contravention where the amount is quantifiable. If the amount is not quantifiable a penalty up to ₹ 2,00,000 can be imposed.

The adjudicating authority can order the confiscation of any currency, security or any other money property in respect of which contravention has taken place. The authority can direct that the Foreign Exchange holding of any person committing contravention shall be brought back to India.

Right/obligations/proceedings/appeal shall not abate by reason of death or insolvency of the person liable. A proceeding can be continued by or against legal representative.

The person to whom penalty is imposed, is required to make a payment within 90 days of receipt of notice. If such payment is not made he is liable to civil imprisonment up to six months if the demand is for less than ₹ 1 crore if the demand exceeds ₹ 1 crore civil imprisonment can be up to three years. If a person to whom show cause notice is issued does not appear before the adjudicating authority warrant of arrest can be issued.

## 16.17 COMPOUNDING OF OFFENCE

Every application for compounding shall be made along with a fee of ₹ 5000 by way of demand draft in favour of the compounding authority. The application can be made before the commencement of the adjudication or during the process of adjudication but not after the determination of penalty through adjudication.

The offence once compounded, will not be a subject matter of adjudication at any time in future. An application for compounding shall be disposed off by the respective authority within a period of 180 days and the compounding fee so determined shall be paid within a period of 15 days failing which it is presumed that the offence has not been compounded. An offence once compounded and then a similar offence cannot be compounded again within a period of three years. No contravention shall be compounded unless the amount involved in such contravention is quantifiable.

One copy of the order made shall be supplied to the applicant and the adjudicating authority as the case may be.

| Compounding by RBI | Authority | Compounding by Directorate of Enforcement | Authority |
|---|---|---|---|
| Rank | Sum involved in contravention | Rank | Sum involved in contravention |
| Asst. GM | 10 lakhs or less | Deputy Director of Directorate of Enforcement | 5 lakhs or less |
| Dy. General Manager | More than 10 lakhs but less than 40 lakhs | Additional Director of Directorate of Enforcement | more than rupees 5 lakhs but less than rupees 10 lakhs |
| General Manager | 40 lakhs but not more than 100 lakhs | Special Director of Directorate of Enforcement | 10 lakhs or more but less than rupees 50 lakhs |
| Chief General Manager | 100 lakhs or more | Special Director with Deputy Legal Advisor of Directorate of Enforcement | 50 lakhs or more but less than rupees 1 crore |
| | | Director of Enforcement with Special Director of Directorate of Enforcement. | 1 crore or more |

## 16.18 LIBERALIZED REMITTANCE SCHEME FOR RESIDENT INDIVIDUALS

All resident individuals are eligible to avail of the facility under the scheme. The facility is not available to corporate, partnership firms, HUF and Trusts.

This facility is available for making remittance upto $ 2,50,000 per financial year for any current or capital account transactions or a combination of both but including remittances towards gift and donation by a resident individual.

The remittance facility under the scheme is not available for:

1. Remittance for any purpose specifically prohibited under Schedule I of Foreign Exchange Management (Current Account Transactions) Rules, 2000.
2. Remittance for any purpose restricted under Schedule II of Foreign Exchange Management (Current Account Transactions) Rules, 2000.
3. Remittances made directly or indirectly to Bhutan, Nepal, Mauritius or Pakistan.
4. Remittances made directly or indirectly to countries identified by the Financial Action Task Force (FATF) as 'non-co-operative countries and territories' *viz.* Cook Islands, Egypt, Guatemala, Indonesia, Myanmar, Nauru, Nigeria, Philippines and Ukraine.
5. Remittances made directly or indirectly to those individuals and entities identified as posing significant risk of committing acts of terrorism as advised separately by the Reserve Bank to the banks.

## TEST YOUR KNOWLEDGE

1. Bring out the significant differences between the Foreign Exchange Regulation Act, 1973 and Foreign Exchange Management Act, 1999. **(Ref. Para-16.2)**
2. Define the following terms
   a. Currency
   b. Currency note
   c. Foreign currency
   d. Foreign Exchange
   e. Foreign security
   f. Import
   g. Security
   h. Transfer **(Ref. Para-16.3)**
3. Define the term 'person resident in India' and 'person resident outside India'. **(Ref. Para-16.3)**
4. How will you determine whether a particular business unit like a factory or office, is 'person resident in India' under the FEMA? **(Ref. Para-16.3)**
5. What do you mean by the expression 'authorized person'? Explain the provisions relating to the authorized person. **(Ref. Para-16.4)**
6. What are the duties of the authorized person? **(Ref. Para-16.4)**
7. What do you understand by the current account transactions? **(Ref. Para-16.5)**
8. Which are the current account transactions for which drawal of Foreign Exchange is prohibited? **(Ref. Para-16.5)**
9. Which are the current account transactions for which the Foreign Exchange can be drawn subject to the prior approval of the Central Government? **(Ref. Para-16.5)**
10. Which are the current account transactions for which the Foreign Exchange can be drawn subject to the prior approval of the RBI? **(Ref. Para-16.5)**
11. What are the provisions of the FEMA, relating to the export of goods and services? **(Ref. Para-16.6)**
12. In which cases can exports of goods or services be made without furnishing the declaration? **(Ref. Para-16.6)**
13. Explain the meaning of the term 'capital account transaction' under the FEMA? **(Ref. Para-16.7)**
14. Which are the prohibited capital account transactions? **(Ref. Para-16.7)**

15. Explain the provisions for acquiring and transferring immovable property in India by the foreign nationals. **(Ref. Para-16.8)**
16. Explain the provisions for acquiring and transferring immovable property out of India by the Indian citizen or persons of Indian origin. **(Ref. Para-16.9)**
17. What are the provisions for opening and maintaining the branch office or place of business in India by the person resident out of India? **(Ref. Para-16.10)**
18. What are the provisions for acceptance of deposit by Indian company from NRI/PIO? **(Ref. Para-16.11)**
19. Write a short note on import and export of Indian currency. **(Ref. Para-16.12)**
20. What are the provisions in respect of possession and retention of foreign currency? **(Ref. Para-16.13)**
21. What are the provisions relating to realization and repatriation of Foreign Exchange? **(Ref. Para-16.14)**
22. Explain the meaning of the term 'adjudicating authority' under the FEMA. **(Ref. Para-16.16)**
23. What are the penalties provided under the FEMA for the contravention of provisions of Act? **(Ref. Para-16.16)**
24. Explain the provisions relating to the compounding of offence under the act? **(Ref. Para-16.17)**
25. Explain about the liberalized remittance scheme for the resident individual. **(Ref. Para-16.18)**

## MULTIPLE-CHOICE QUESTIONS

1. Foreign Exchange Management Act provides for
   (i) free transactions on current account subject to reasonable restrictions.
   (ii) The RBI control over capital account transactions.
   (iii) either (i) or (ii).
   (iv) both (i) and (ii).
2. Foreign Exchange Management Act provides for
   (i) control over realization of export proceeds.
   (ii) dealing in Foreign Exchange through authorized person.
   (iii) either (i) or (ii).
   (iv) both (i) and (ii).
3. An individual can now open account in ______ can remit upto ______ per calendar year for the purchase of immovable assets and shares abroad.
   (i) Foreign Bank, US $25,000
   (ii) Indian Bank, US $25,000
   (iii) Indian Bank, US $1,00,000
   (iv) Foreign Bank, US $1,00,000
4. A person resident in India means a person who stayed in India for more than ______ during the course of preceding year.
   (i) 180 days
   (ii) 260 days
   (iii) 365 days
   (iv) 182 days
5. Residential status of a person is determined, based upon his stay in ______
   (i) preceding financial year.
   (ii) previous accounting year.
   (iii) current financial year.
   (iv) current accounting year.
6. As per the FEMA, currency includes all
   (i) currency notes.
   (ii) postal notes.
   (iii) postal order.
   (iv) all of the above.

7. As per the FEMA, currency includes all
   (i) money order.
   (ii) cheque and draft.
   (iii) both (i) and (ii).
   (iv) none of the above.
8. As per the FEMA, currency includes all
   (i) travellers' cheque.
   (ii) letter of credit.
   (iii) both (i) and (ii).
   (iv) neither (i) nor (ii).
9. As per the FEMA, currency includes all
   (i) credit cards.
   (ii) ATM cards.
   (iii) debit cards.
   (iv) all of the above.
10. As per the FEMA, Foreign Exchange means
    (i) foreign currency.
    (ii) balance payable in any foreign currency.
    (iii) either (i) or (ii).
    (iv) both (i) and (ii).
11. As per the FEMA, Foreign Exchange means
    (i) draft, cheque, bill of exchange drawn in Indian currency but payable in foreign currency.
    (ii) draft, cheque, bill of exchange drawn in Indian currency but payable in Indian currency.
    (iii) either (i) or (ii).
    (iv) both (i) and (ii).
12. As per the FEMA, Foreign Exchange means
    (i) draft, cheque, bill of exchange drawn in Indian rupee and payable in Indian rupee.
    (ii) draft, cheque, bill of exchange drawn by person outside Indian but payable in Indian currency.
    (iii) either (i) or (ii).
    (iv) none of the above.
13. As per the FEMA, foreign security means
    (i) shares denominated in foreign currency.
    (ii) debenture denominated in foreign currency.
    (iii) bonds denominated in foreign currency.
    (iv) all of the above.
14. As per the FEMA, foreign security means
    (i) shares expressed in foreign currency and dividend is payable in Indian currency.
    (ii) bonds denominated in foreign currency.
    (iii) bonds denominated in foreign currency and redemption will take place in Indian currency.
    (iv) all of the above.
15. As per the FEMA, foreign security means
    (i) stock certificate expressed in Indian rupee.
    (ii) debenture expressed in foreign currency.
    (iii) debenture expressed in foreign currency but redemption will take place in Indian currency.
    (iv) all of the above.
16. Application for permission to extend the period for realization of export period should be made to
    (i) RBI.
    (ii) Central Government.
    (iii) authorized dealer.
    (iv) any one of the above.

17. Which bank account(s) can be opened by NRI/Foreign National in India?
    (i) FCNR
    (ii) NRE
    (iii) NRO
    (iv) Any one of the above
18. Which bank account(s) can be opened by NRI/Foreign National in India maintained in designated foreign currency?
    (i) FCNR
    (ii) NRE
    (iii) NRO
    (iv) Any one of the above
19. Remittance under technical collaboration agreements where payment is in form of royalty is _______ transaction.
    (i) general account
    (ii) current account
    (iii) capital account
    (iv) business
20. Gift remittance exceeding US $5000 per financial year per remitter or donor other than resident individual is permissible with approval of
    (i) Central Government.
    (ii) RBI.
    (iii) authorized dealer.
    (iv) none of the above.
21. Gift remittance upto _______ per financial year per remitter or donor other than resident individual is permissible without approval of any authority.
    (i) US $2,50,000
    (ii) US $2000
    (iii) ₹ 5000
    (iv) ₹ 25,000
22. Out of the following transactions, for which drawals of Foreign Exchange is prohibited?
    (i) Remittance out of lottery winning.
    (ii) Remittance of income from racing.
    (iii) Both (i) and (ii).
    (iv) Neither (i) nor (ii).
23. Out of the following transactions for which drawals of Foreign Exchange is prohibited?
    (i) Remittance for purchase of lottery tickets.
    (ii) Remittance for purchase of banned magazine.
    (iii) Payment for travel to Nepal
    (iv) All of the above.
24. Remittance under technical coloration agreements for payment of royalty is allowed upto _______ % on local sales.
    (i) No limit (freely repatriated)
    (ii) 8
    (iii) 3
    (iv) 1
25. Remittance under technical coloration agreements for payment of royalty is allowed upto _______ % on export sales.
    (i) 5
    (ii) No limit (freely repatriated)
    (iii) 3
    (iv) 1
26. Remittance exceeding 10,00,000 per project for any consultancy services in respect of consultancy project from outside India is allowed with permission of
    (i) Central Government.
    (ii) State Government.
    (iii) RBI.
    (iv) authorized dealer.
27. Release of exchange exceeding US $10,000 or its equivalent in one financial year for one or more private visits to any country is allowed with permission of
    (i) Central Government.
    (ii) State Government.
    (iii) RBI.
    (iv) authorized dealer.

28. Out of following, which are the current account transactions?
    (i) Gift remittance.
    (ii) Release of exchange for studies abroad.
    (iii) Either (i) or (ii).
    (iv) Neither (i) nor (ii).

29. Out of following, which are the current account transactions?
    (i) Release of Foreign Exchange for business travel.
    (ii) Release of Foreign Exchange for meeting expenses for medical treatment abroad.
    (iii) Both (i) and (ii).
    (iv) Neither (i) nor (ii).

30. Which of the following activities are permitted by the RBI for a company engaged in manufacturing and trading activities aboard to set up branch office in India?
    (i) To conduct research work.
    (ii) To render professional or consultancy work.
    (iii) Both (i) and (ii).
    (iv) Neither (i) nor (ii).

31. Which of the following activities are permitted by the RBI for a company engaged in manufacturing and trading activities aboard to set up branch office in India?
    (i) To undertake export and import trading work.
    (ii) To represent the parent company.
    (iii) Both (i) and (ii).
    (iv) Neither (i) nor (ii).

32. Capital account transaction means
    (i) transfer or issue of any foreign security by a person resident in India.
    (ii) transfer or issue of any security by a person resident outside India.
    (iii) both (i) and (ii).
    (iv) neither (i) nor (ii).

33. Capital account transaction means
    (i) any borrowing or lending in Foreign Exchange.
    (ii) deposit between persons resident in India and persons resident outside India.
    (iii) both (i) and (ii).
    (iv) neither (i) nor (ii).

34. Capital account transaction means
    (i) acquisition or transfer of immovable property in India by person resident outside India.
    (ii) export, import or holding of currency of currency note.
    (iii) either (i) or (ii).
    (iv) neither (i) nor (ii).

35. An application for compounding of an offence shall be made by compounding authority in ________ days.
    (i) 15
    (ii) 30
    (iii) 60
    (iv) 180

## ANSWER KEYS

| | | | | | |
|---|---|---|---|---|---|
| **1.** (iv) | **7.** (iii) | **13.** (iv) | **19.** (iii) | **25.** (ii) | **31.** (iii) |
| **2.** (iv) | **8.** (iii) | **14.** (iv) | **20.** (ii) | **26.** (iii) | **32.** (iii) |
| **3.** (i) | **9.** (iv) | **15.** (iv) | **21.** (i) | **27.** (iii) | **33.** (iii) |
| **4.** (iv) | **10.** (iv) | **16.** (i) | **22.** (iii) | **28.** (iii) | **34.** (iii) |
| **5.** (i) | **11.** (iv) | **17.** (iv) | **23.** (iv) | **29.** (iii) | **35.** (iv) |
| **6.** (iv) | **12.** (ii) | **18.** (i) | **24.** (i) | **30.** (iii) | |

# 17

# Information Technology Act, 2000

**Learning Objectives**

*After reading this chapter, you will be able to understand:*

- Scope of the Act
- Electronic records and its validity
- Digital signatures
- Authentication of electronic records
- E-governance
- Electronic offences and penalty

## 17.1 INTRODUCTION

The Information Technology Act is divided into 13 chapters, 94 sections, and 5 schedules.
Chapter 1: Scope and Definitions
Chapter 2: Authentication of Electronic Records Using Digital Signature
Chapter 3: Electronic Governance
Chapter 4: Attribution, Receipt, and Dispatch of Electronic Records
Chapter 5: Secure Electronic Records, and Secure Digital Signature
Chapter 6: Regulation of Certifying Authorities
Chapter 7: Digital Signature Certification
Chapter 8: Duties of Subscriber
Chapter 9: Penalties and Adjudication
Chapter 10: Cyber Regulation Appellate Tribunal

Chapter 11: Offences
Chapter 12: Network Service Provider Not be Liable in certain Cases
chapter 13: Miscellaneous (described the power of various government bodies to make the rules under the IT Act, 2000).

### 17.1.1 Cyber Laws

Businessmen nowadays are increasingly using computers to manage their commercial activities in electronic form instead of traditional paper form. Information kept in electronic form is higly economic, easier to store, retrieve, and speedier to communicate. Now, people are using new communication systems and digital technologies for transacting their business electronically. Although people are aware of advantages which the electronic form of business provides, but they are are reluctant to conduct business or execute transactions in electronic form due to lack of a proper legal framework.

Electronic Commerce eliminates the needs for paper-based transactions. The two principal hurdles which stand in the way of facilitating electronic commerce and electronic governance are requirements of writing and signature for legal recognitions.

At present, many legal provisions assume the existence of paper-based records which should bear the signatures. The law of evidence is traditionally based upon paper-based records and oral testimony.

To facilitate e-commerce, the need for legal changes has become a quintessential requirement. The Government of India realized the need for introducing a new law for making suitable amendments to the existing laws to facilitate e-commerce and to give legal recognitions to electronic records and digital signature. The legal recognitions to electronic records and digital signatures, in turn, will facilitate the conclusions of contract and creations of legal rights and obligations through electronic communications like the internet. The need of legal recognitions to electronic commerce gave birth to the Information Technology Bill, 1999.

In the year 2000, both the houses of parliament passed the Iinformation Technology Bill. The Bill received the assent of the President in August 2000 and came into existence as the Information Technology Act, 2000. This act contains the various aspects of the Cyber Laws.

## 17.2 OBJECTIVE OF ACT

The objectives of the IT Act, 2000 are as follows:

1. To grant legal recognitions for transactions carried out by means of Electronic Data Interchange and other means of communication, commonly referred to as - 'Electronic Commerce' in place of paper-based method of communication.
2. To give legal recognitions to Digital Signature, for authentication of any information or matter that is subjected to authentication under any law.
3. To facilitate Electronic Filing of documents with various government departments.
4. To facilitate electronic storage of data.
5. To facilitate and give legal sanctions to Electronic Fund Transfer between banks and financial institutions.
6. To give legal recognitions for maintaining books of accounts in electronic form by the bankers.
7. To Amend the Indian Penal Code, the Indian Evidence Act of 1872; the Banker's Book Evidence Act of 1891, and the Reserve Bank Of India Act of 1934.

## 17.3 SCOPE OF THE ACT

Information Technology Act, 2000 extend to whole of India. It applies also to any offence or contravention, thereunder committed outside India. However, the act does not apply to the following categories of transactions:

1. A negotiable instrument other than cheque. It means, the IT Act is applicable to Cheque.
2. A power of attorney.
3. A trust as defined in India Trusts Act.
4. A will.
5. Any contract for sale or conveyance of immovable properties.
6. Any such class of documents or transactions as may be notified by the Central Government in the official Gazette.

## 17.4 DEFINITIONS

### 17.4.1 Access—Section 2(1)(a)

'Access' with its grammatical variations and cognate expressions means gaining entry into, instructing or communicating with the logical, arithmetical, or memory function resources of a computer, computer system or computer network.

### 17.4.2 Computer—Section 2(1)(i)

'Computer' means any electronic, magnetic, optical or other high-speed data processing device or system which performs logical, arithmetic, and memory functions by manipulations of electronic, magnetic or optical impulses, and includes all input, output, processing, storage, computer software, or communication facilities which are connected or related to the computer in a computer system or computer network.

### 17.4.3 Computer System—Section 2(1)(l)

'Computer System' means a device or collection of devices, **including** input and output support devices and **excluding** calculators which are not programmable and capable of being used in conjugation with external files, which contain computer programs, electronic instructions, input data, and output data that performs logic, arithmetic, data storage and retrieval, communication control, and other functions

### 17.4.4 Communication Device—Section 2(1)(na)

'Communication Device' means cell phones, personal digital assistance (sic), or combination of both or any other device used for communication, to send or transmit any text, video, audio, or image.

### 17.4.5 Computer Network—Section 2(1)(j)

It means, interconnection of one of more computers using satellite, microwave or other communication channels. It also includes 'computer systems', 'computer devices' and also use of wire or wireless media.

### 17.4.6 Function—Section 2(1)(u)

'Function' in relation to a computer, includes:

- Logic
- Control
- Arithmetical process
- Deletion,
- Storage and retrieval
- Communication, or
- Telecommunication from or within a computer

### 17.4.7 Information—Section 2(1)(v)

'Information' includes:

- Data
- Message
- Text
- Images
- Sound
- Voice
- Codes
- Computer programs
- Software
- Databases
- Micro film, or
- Computer-generated microfiche.

### 17.4.8 Data—Section 2(1)(o)

'Data' means:

- a representation of information, knowledge, facts, concepts or instructions
- which are being prepared or have been prepared in a formalized manner,
- and are intended to be processed, are being processed or have been processed in a computer system or computer network.

It may be in any form including computer printouts, magnetic or optical storage media, punched cards, punched tapes or stored internally in the memory of a computer.

### 17.4.9 Digital Signature

It means authentication of any electronic record by a subscriber through an electronic method. Digital signature has been replace by 'electronic signature' wide Information Technology Amendment Act, 2008.

### 17.4.10 Electronic Signature—Section 2(1)(ta)

'Electronic signature' means authentication of any electronic record by a subscriber by means of the electronic technique specified in the second schedule and includes digital signature.

### 17.4.11 Asymmetric Crypto System—Section 2(1)(f)

It means system consisting of secure key pair, private key and public key.

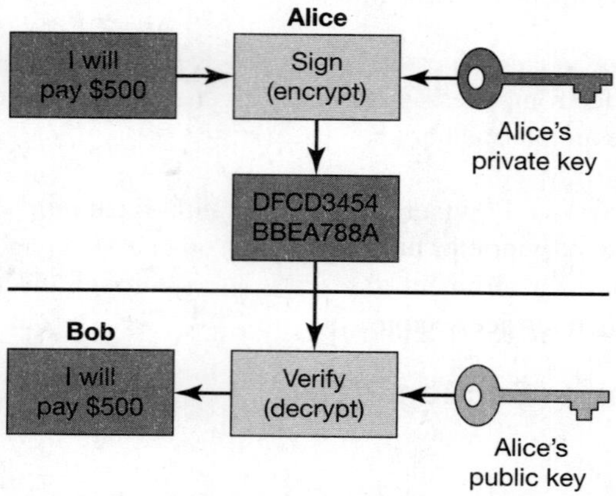


**Figure 17.1** Asymmetric crypto system.

A message that is signed (encrypted) with the private key can be verified (decrypted) with the public key. Since the public key is public, anyone can verify the signature. The public key cannot create such signatures. Validity depends on private key security.

**Key Pair:** It is a private key and corresponding mathematically related public key.

**Private Key:** It means key of key pair used to create digital signature.

**Public Key:** It means key of key pair used to verify digital signature.

### 17.4.12 Secure System—Section 2(1)(ze)

'Secure System' means computer hardware, software, and procedures which:

1. are reasonably secure from unauthorized access and misuse;
2. provide a reasonable level of reliability and correct operation;
3. are reasonably suited to performing the intended functions; and
4. adheres the generally accepted security procedures.;

### 17.4.13 Cyber Security—Section 2(1)(nb)

'Cyber Security' means protecting

| | | |
|---|---|---|
| • information<br>• equipment<br>• devices<br>• computer<br>• computer resource<br>• communication device, and<br>• information stored therein. | from | unauthorized access<br>use<br>disclosure<br>disruption<br>modification, or<br>destruction |

### 17.4.14 Cyber Café— Section 2(1)(na)

'Cyber Café' means any facility from where access to the Internet is offered by any person in the ordinary course of business to the members of the public.

**Originator:** 'Originator' means a person, who sends, generates, stores or transmits any electronic messages or causes any electronic message to be sent, generated, stored or transmitted to any other person, but does not include an intermediary.

**Service Provider:** Service Provider includes any authorized individual, private agency, private company, partnership firm, sole proprietor firm or any such other body or agency which has been granted permission by the appropriate Government to offer services through electronic means in accordance with the policy governing such service sector.

### 17.4.15 Intermediary—Section 2(1)(w)

Intermediary includes:

- Telecom service providers
- Network service providers
- Internet service providers
- Web hosting service providers
- Search engines
- Online payment sites
- Online-auction sites
- Online-market places
- Cyber cafes

## 17.5 DIGITAL SIGNATURE

Digital signature is like a handwritten signature. It should be difficult for the sender to forge and difficult for the receiver to repudiate (reproduce). Generation of Digital Signature uses a technology known as Key Pair (Public Key and Private Key). Users who want to enter into electronic agreement should have key pair. Public key is for distribution, whereas a private key is for the user himself.

For any legal valid electronic document there are two requirements. One is integrity of document, that is, the document has not been changed and authentication, i.e., document is signed.

So, an electronic document to be a legally valid document is two aspects:

1. Hash Function is used for integrity of document
2. Digital signature used for authentication of documents.

### 17.5.1 Hash Function

Hash Function is an algorithm that runs a message or content of agreement. It generates a big alphanumeric number which is known as message digest.

The message digest is an unique value for a single message or content. If anyone changes even a single character in the original message and runs the hash function, it will not generate the same number. This change in value will indicate that the original message has been changed. Always a same number is generated when hash function algorithm is run over the original message.

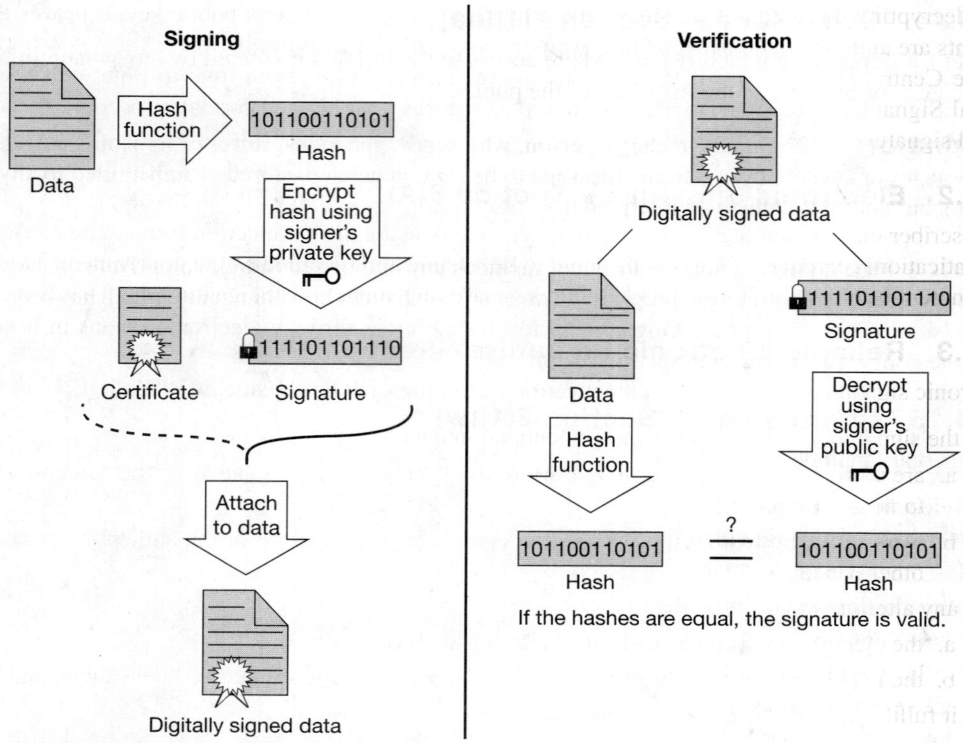


**Figure 17.2** Mechanism of digital signatures.*
* wikipedia.com

The Hash Function technique is used for checking the integrity of a message. After generating the message digest from message with Hash Function, the message digest is encrypted with the private key of its sender. It again generates a value which is known as Digital Signature. This value is transmitted along with the original document in encrypted or direct form. Its receiving authorizes the receiver with the public key of the sender and, therefore, to decrypt the digital signature by generating the message digest. The receiver again generate the message digest by running hash function over the actual message and if it generates the same message digest which the receiver has obtained after decrypting the digital signature, then it will ensure that the message content has not been changed and digital signature belongs to the person who has given the public key to the receiver.

For transmitting a public key safely and providing a proof that the public key with the receiver belongs to the person who has claimed for this, a certificate is obtained from a certifying authority that gives a Digital Certificate and it ensure that the public key actually belongs to a person who has claimed for it. The most popular certifying authority who issues digital certificate is VeriSign.

Message Digest Encrypted with Private Key of the Sender generates digital signatures which are affixed on the agreement document and sent to the receiver. At the receiver's end, digital signatures are decrypted with the sender's public key, and then the Message Digest is generated.

The receiver, again, generates the Message Digest by running the Hash Function Algorithm over the original content of the message. If this Message Digest matches with the Message Digest generated after decrypting the digital signature of the sender by using the sender's public key, it proves that the contents are authentic and the signatures were made by the sender himself.

The Central Government of India has the power to make rules from time to time with respect to Digital Signatures, etc., that is, types of digital signatures, manner and format, procedure for affixing digital signatures, etc.

### 17.5.2 Electronic Signature—Section 3(A)

A subscriber may authenticate any electronic records by using his/her electronic signature or electronic authentication technique which is considered to be reliable and specified by the government. The central government is authorized to fix the procedures for affixing such type of signature.

### 17.5.3 Reliable Electronic Signature—Section 3A(2)

Electronic signature or electronic authentication technique shall be considered reliable if:

1. the signature creation data or the authentication data
   a. are within the context in which they are used, linked to the signatory or the authenticator and to no other person,
   b. were at the time of signing, under the control of the signatory or the authenticator and of no other person,
2. any alteration to
   a. the electronic signature made after affixing such signature, or
   b. the information made after its authentication by electronic signature is detectable, and
3. it fulfils such other prescribed conditions.

### 17.5.4. Secure Electronic Signature—Section 15

An electronic signature shall be deemed to be a secure if the signature creation data –

1. at the time of affixing signature, was under the exclusive control of signatory and no other person; and
2. was stored and affixed in such exclusive manner as may be prescribed.

## 17.6 ELECTRONIC GOVERNANCE

### 17.6.1 What Is Electronic Governance?

Electronic Governance (*i.e.,* E-Governance) means filing of any form, application or other document with government department in electronic form and similarly issue or grant of any license or permit or receipt or payment from government offices and its agencies through electronic means or electronic form.

### 17.6.2 Benefits of Electronic Governance

Electronic Governance helps in low cost, efficient and transparent working of the government departments. Iusses, such as manpower shortage in government organizations and the instances bribery can be easily avoided. Accuracy and record maintenance becomes faster and simplified.

### 17.6.3 Rules of Electronic Governance

The IT Act also provides for legal recognition for Digital Signature. It means any document or data digitally signed will be treated as valid and authenticated electronic records. Filing of any form, application, etc., to government can be done through electronic means, and similarly government department can issue or grant any license, permission, etc., through electronic means.

***Examples***

e-filing of Company incorporation and related documents(www.mca.gov.in)
e-filing related income tax (www.incometaxindiaefiling.gov.in)
e-filing for patent application(www.ipindiaonline.gov.in/on_line)

### 17.6.4 Legal Recognition of Electronic Records—Section 4

Where any act requires that information should be in writing and if such information or form is stored or saved in electronic form, the requirement of the act is satisfied if information or matter is:

1. Rendered or made available in an electronic records; and
2. Accessible, so as to be usable for a subsequent reference.

### 17.6.5 Retention of Electronic Records

If any act provides that documents, records or information shall be retained for any specific period, then requirement of the act is said to be satisfied if such documents, records or information are retained in electronic form:

1. Information contained in electronic form remains accessible and useable for future period of time.
2. Electronic records are retained in the same format in which it was originally sent or received or generated.
3. Details of identification of origin, destination, date and time of dispatch or receipt of records are available.

### 17.6.6 Validity of Electronic Contract—Section 10(A)

Where any contract is made in electronic mode (*i.e.*, communication of proposal, the acceptance of proposals, revocation of proposals and acceptances) or expressed in electronic forms or by means of electronic records, such contract is valid, enforceable and binding the parties involved.

### 17.6.7 Attribution of electronic records—Section 11

An electronic record shall be attributed to the originator:

1. If it was sent by the originator himself;
2. By a person who had the authority to act on behalf of the originator in respect of that electronic record; or
3. By an information system, programmed by or on behalf of the originator, to operate automatically.

### 17.6.8 Acknowledgement of Receipt of Electronic Records—Section 12

Where the originator has not agreed with the addressee that the acknowledgment of receipt of electronic record be given in a particular form or by a particular method, an acknowledgment may be given by:

a. Any communication by the addressee, automated or otherwise; or
b. Any conduct of the addressee, sufficient to indicate to the originator that the electronic record has been received.

Where the originator has stipulated that the electronic record shall be binding only on receipt of an acknowledgment of such electronic record by him, then unless acknowledgment has been so received, the electronic record shall be deemed to have been never sent by the originator.

Where the originator has not stipulated that the electronic record shall be binding only on receipt of such acknowledgment, and the acknowledgment has not been received by the originator within the time specified or agreed or, if no time has been specified or agreed to within a reasonable time, then the originator may give notice to the addressee stating that no acknowledgment has been received by him and specifying a reasonable time by which the acknowledgment must be received by him, and if no acknowledgment is received within the aforesaid time limit, he may after giving notice to the addressee, treat the electronic record as though it has never been sent.

### 17.6.9 Time and Place of Despatch and Receipt of Electronic Record—Section 13

Save as otherwise agreed to between the originator and the addressee, the dispatch of an electronic record occurs when it enters a computer resource outside the control of the originator.

Save as otherwise agreed between the originator and the addressee, the time of receipt of an electronic record shall be determined as follows, namely:

a. If the addressee has designated a computer resource for the purpose of receiving electronic records:
   i. receipt occurs at the time when the electronic, record enters the designated computer resource; or
   ii. if the electronic record is sent to a computer resource of the addressee that is not the designated computer resource, receipt occurs at the time when the electronic record is retrieved by the addressee;
b. if the addressee has not designated a computer resource along with specified timings, if any, receipt occurs when the electronic record enters the computer resource of the addressee.

Save as otherwise agreed to between the originator and the addressee, an electronic record is deemed to be dispatched at the place where the originator has his place of business, and is deemed to be received at the place where the addressee has his place of business.

For the purposes of this section:

a. if the originator or the addressee has more than one place of business, the principal place of business, shall be the place of business;
b. if the originator or the addressee does not have a place of business, his usual place of residence shall be deemed to be the place of business;
c. "usual place of residence", in relation to a body corporate, means the place where it is registered.

## 17.7 DIGITAL SIGNATURE CERTIFICATION

Certifying Authority will issue a Digital Certificate to a Subscriber on payment of certain fees not exceeding ₹ 25000/- after satisfying itself that subscriber hold the private key for corresponding public key to be listed in Digital Certificate, and private key is capable for creating digital signature, etc.

### 17.7.1 Procedure for Obtaining Digital Certificate

A sender sends his public key to the Certification Authority along with information specific to his identification and other relevant information. Application should be accompanied by certificate of practice statement.

The Certification Authority uses this information to verify a sender and his public key, if everything is correct, the Certification Authority returns the sender a Digital Certificate that confirms the validity of the sender's public key.

Actually, a Certifying Authority certifies a public key by digitally signing the sender's public key with an authorized private key. This authorization put the sign on a Digital Certificate. Any user, who wants to use someone's public key, can verify its validity by applying the Certification Authority's public key to the digital signature of the Certifying Authority on the available certificate. In this way, the user gets the actual public key of the sender and can tally this public key with that of the public key available on the digital certificate.

No application can be rejected without giving reasonable opportunities.

### 17.7.2 Suspension of Digital Signature Certificates

A certifying authority may suspend digital signature certificate in public interest, for a period not exceeding 15 days. The certifying authority may suspend a digital signature if a request in this regard is received from the subscriber. On suspension of a digital signature, communication should be made to the respective subscriber.

### 17.7.3 Revocation of Digital Signature Certificates

A certifying authority may revoke a digital signature issued by it:

1. Where the subscriber or any other person, authorized by him, makes a request to that effect.
2. Upon the death of the subscriber.
3. Upon the dissolution of a firm or winding of a company.

The certifying authority may revoke the digital signature if the material fact represented in the digital signature certificate is false or concealed or where the requirement of the digital signature certificate was not satisfied or the subscriber has become insolvent. On revocation of the digital signature, communication should be made to the subscriber.

## 17.8 CYBER APPELLATE TRIBUNAL—SECTION 49

Civil courts have been barred from entering any suit or proceeding in respect of any matter which an adjudicating officer or tribunal is empowered to handle. Provisions relating to tribunal and adjudicating officer are as follows.

### 17.8.1 Appellate Tribunal

The Cyber Appellate Tribunal shall be a appellate body where appeals against the orders passed by the Adjudicating Officers shall be preferred.

The Tribunal shall not be bound by the principle of the code of the civil procedures, but it shall follow the principles of natural justice and it shall have the same powers as those are, vested in a Civil Court.

The Appellate Tribunal shall consist of a single person only. The person is called the Presiding Officer of the Tribunal. He shall be appointed by the Central Government. The presiding officer shall be a person qualified to be a judge of a High Court or has been a member of the Indian Legal Service in the post (Grade I) of that service for at least three years. He shall hold office for a term of five years or up to the maximum age of 65 years, whichever is earlier.

Against an order or decision of the Cyber Appellate Tribunal, an appeal shall be made to the High Court within 60 days.

### 17.8.2 Adjudicating Officer

Affected Party Report for Offences to Cyber Appellate Tribunal shall consist of one person only. The said person is known as the Presiding Officer. He shall be appointed by Central Government. Such a person is equivalent to High court Judge.

An appeal against an Adjudicating Officer's order within 45 days can be made to the Appellate Tribunal. The adjudicating officer pas orders for any reported offence.

### 17.8.3 Powers of Cyber Appellate Tribunal

The jurisdiction, powers and authority of the Cyber Appellate Tribunal may be exercised by the Benches thereof. A Bench may be constituted by the Chairperson with one or two Members of such a Tribunal as he may deem fit.

The Benches shall sit at New Delhi and at such other places as may be specified in notification by the Central Government in consultation with the Chairperson. The Central Government shall, by notification, specify the jurisdiction areas of each Bench. Chairperson may transfer a Member from one Bench to another Bench.

If at any stage of the hearing of any case or matter, it appears to the Chairperson or a Member, that the case or matter is of such a nature that it ought to be heard by a Bench consisting of more Members, then they may be transferred by the Chairperson to such Bench as he may deem fit.

## 17.9 PENALTIES AND ADJUDICATION

An Adjudicating Officer has the power for holding an inquiry in relation to certain computer crimes and for awarding compensation. Penalties can be imposed by adjudicating officer for damage of computer or computer network, for:

1. Copy or extract any data from database without permission.
2. Unauthorized access and downloading.
3. Introduction of virus.
4. Damage to computer system and computer network.
5. Disruption of computer, computer network.
6. Denial to authorized person to access computer.
7. Providing assistance to any person to facilitate unauthorized access to any computer.
8. Charging the service availed by a person to an account of another person by tampering and manipulation of other computers, etc.

Section 43 of this act provides for a penalty of compensation to the affected persons for damage to a computer system, etc. as decided by a Adjudicating Officer.

## 17.10 OFFENCES

Following are the offences and penalties under the IT Act:

### 17.10.1 Offences

1. Tampering with computer source documents.
2. Damaging a computer or computer system.
3. Publishing of information which is obscene in electronic form.
4. Electronic forgery, that is, affixing of false digital signature, making false electronic records.
5. Punishment for cyber terrorism.
6. Electronic forgery for the purpose of cheating.
7. Electronic forgery for the purpose of harming one's reputation.
8. Using as genuine a forged electronic record.
9. Publication of digital signature certificate, for fraudulent purpose.
10. Offences by companies.
11. Breach of confidentiality and privacy.
12. Publishing false Digital Signature Certificate.
13. Misrepresentation or suppressing of material facts.
14. Destroys, deletes or alters any information residing in a computer resource or diminishes its value or utility or affects it injuriously by any means.
15. Steal, conceals, destroys or alters or causes any person to steal, conceal, destroy or alter any computer source code used for a computer resource with an intention to cause damage.

### 17.10.2 Penalty for Offences

Various penalties prescribed under act are shown in below mention table:

| Section | Offence | Penalty |
|---|---|---|
| 65 | Tampering computer source | a. Imprisonment up to three years, or<br>b. Fine upto ₹ 2 lakhs, or<br>c. Both. |
| 66 | Hacking (Computer damage) | |
| 66A | Sending offensive messages through computer Resource | Imprisonment upto three years and Fine. |
| 66B | Punishment for dishonestly receiving stolen computer resource or communication device | Imprisonment for a term up to three years or with fine up to ₹ 1 lakh or both. |
| 66C | Punishment for identity theft | |
| 66D | Punishment for cheating by personating by using computer resource | |
| 66E | Punishment for violation of privacy | Imprisonment for a term up to three years or with fine up to ₹ 2 lakh or both. |
| 66F | Punishment for cyber terrorism | Imprisonment which may extend to imprisonment for life |

| Section | Offence | Penalty |
|---|---|---|
| 67 | Publishing of obscene information in electronic form | First Conviction<br>a. Imprisonment up to three years, or<br>b. Fine up to Rs 5 lakh<br>Subsequent Conviction<br>a. Imprisonment up to five years, or<br>b. Fine up to Rs 10 lakhs. |
| 67A<br><br><br>67B | Punishment for publishing or transmitting of material containing sexually explicit act, in electronic form<br>Punishment for publishing or transmitting of material depicting children in sexually explicit act, etc. in electronic form | First Conviction<br>a. Imprisonment up to five years, or<br>b. Fine up to Rs 10 lakh<br>Subsequent Conviction<br>a. Imprisonment up to seven years, or<br>b. Fine up to Rs 10 lakhs. |
| 68 | Controller's order to cease activities | a. Imprisonment up to two years, or<br>b. Fine upto Rs 1 lakh, or<br>c. Both. |
| 69<br><br>69A | Controller's order to intercept , monitor or decrypt information<br>Directions for blocking for public access of any information through any computer resource | Imprisonment up to seven years with fine |
| 70 | Unauthorized Access of "Protected Systems" | Imprisonment up to 10 years with fine |
| 71<br>72<br>73<br>74 | Misrepresenting or suppressing any material fact<br>Breach of confidentiality<br>Publishing a false Digital Signature Certificate<br>Fraudulent Publication | a. Imprisonment up to two years, or<br>b. Fine upto ₹ 1 lakhs, or<br>c. Both |

Network Service Providers shall not be liable for third parties information or data made available by him if he proves that the offences, was committed without his knowledge or consent.

### 17.10.3 Compounding of an offence—Section 63

The person accused of an offence under this Act may file an application for compounding in the court in which offence is pending for trial and the provisions of sections 265B and 265C of the Code of Criminal Procedure, 1973 shall apply.

### 17.10.4 Cognizable Offence

Any offence punishable with imprisonment of three years and above shall be a cognizable offence. Any offence punishable with imprisonment of three years shall be bailable.

## 17.11 LIABILITY OF BODY CORPORATE

Where a **body corporate**, possessing, dealing or handling any **sensitive personal data or information** in a computer resource which it owns, controls or operates,

1. is negligent in implementing and maintaining **reasonable security practices and procedures,** and
2. thereby causes wrongful loss or wrongful gain to any person,

such a body corporate shall be liable to pay for the damages that it caused by way of compensation to the person so affected.

**Body Corporate** means any company and includes a firm, sole proprietorship or other association of individuals engaged in commercial or professional activities.

**Reasonable security practices and procedures** means security practices and procedures designed to protect such information from unauthorized access, damage, use, modification, disclosure or impairment, as may be specified in an agreement between the parties or as may be specified in any law for the time being in force and in the absence of such agreement or any law, such reasonable security practices and

Procedures, as may be prescribed by the Central Government in consultation with such professional bodies or associations as it may deem fit.

**Sensitive personal data or information** means such personal information as may be prescribed by the Central Government in consultation with such professional bodies or associations as it may deem fit.

## 17.12 DUTIES OF CONTROLLERS OF CERTIFYING AUTHORITY

The duties of controllers of Certifying Authorities can be regarded as functions of controller. A controller may perform all or any of the following functions, namely:

1. Exercise supervision over the activities of the Certifying Authorities.
2. Certifying public keys of the Certifying Authorities.
3. Laying down standards to be maintained by the Certifying Authorities.
4. Specifying the qualifications and experience which employees of the Certifying Authorities should posses.
5. Specifying the conditions, subject to which the Certifying Authorities shall conduct their business.
6. Specify the contents of written or visual material and advertisement that may be distributed or used in respect of a Digital Signature Certificate and the public key.
7. Specifying the form and content of a Digital Signature Certificate.
8. Specifying the form and manner in which accounts shall be maintained by certifying authorities.
9. Specifying the terms and conditions subject to which auditors may be appointed and remuneration paid to them.
10. Facilitating the establishment of any electronic system by Certifying Authority either solely or jointly with other Certifying Authority and regulation of such system.
11. Specifying the manner in which Certifying Authorities shall conduct their dealings with the subscriber.
12. Resolving any conflict of interests between the Certifying authorities and the Subscribers.
13. Laying down duties of the Certifying Authorities.
14. Maintaining a database containing the records of every Certifying Authority like containing such particulars as may be specified by regulations, which shall be accessible to public.

### 17.12.1 Licence to Issue Electronic Signature Certificates

Any person may apply to the controller to obtain license to issue electronic signature certificate. License is granted to issue electronic signature certificates on fulfillment of certain conditions like qualification, expertize, manpower, and financial resourses. License granted is valid for specified period and not transferable or heritable.

Every application for license made shall be accompanied by certificate practice statement and identification of applicant. License can be renewed by application and on payment of prescribed fees.

Controller on receipt of application may grant or reject the application. But, when application is rejected, applicant should be given reasonable opportunity of being heard.

Controller may revoke license on grounds of incorrect or false material information or on ground of contravention of any provisions of act. No license can be revoked without a show cause notice.

A license can be suspended for a period not exceeding 10 days after giving reasonable opportunity of being heard. On suspension, the controller shall publish the notice of suspension or revocation of licenses on the database maintained by him on the website maintained by him.

## 17.13 DUTIES OF THE CERTIFYING AUTHORITIES

Duties of certifying authorities can be summarized as follows:

1. The Certifying Authorities to follow certain rules for providing services of issuance of Digital Certificate to subscribers.
2. Make use of hardware, software and procedures that are secure from intrusion and misuse.
3. Provide a reasonable level of reliability in its services.
4. Adhere to security procedures to ensure that secrecy and privacy of the Digital Signatures are assured.
5. Observe such other standards as may be specified by regulations.
6. Certifying Authority shall ensure the compliance of Act.
7. Certifying Authority shall display its license at the place of business.
8. A Certifying authority, whose license is suspended or revoked, shall immediately surrender the license to the controller.
9. Disclosure: Every Certifying Authority shall disclose its Digital Signature Certificate which contains public key corresponding to its private key, which is used by the Certifying Authority to sign the Digital Signature Certificate of the subscribers.
10. Act in Accordance with the procedure specified in its certification practice statement.

## 17.14 THE DUTIES OF A SUBSCRIBER

In respect of electronic and digital signature, a subscriber has the following duties:

1. Generate Key pair, *i.e.*, public key and private key.
2. Publish Digital Signature Certificate on acceptance of a Digital Signature Certificate.
3. By accepting a Digital Signature Certificate the subscriber certifies to all who reasonably rely on the information contained in the Digital Signature Certificate that
    - The subscriber holds the private key corresponding to the public key listed in the Digital Signature Certificate.
    - All representations made by the subscriber to the Certifying Authority and all material relevant to the information contained in the Digital Signature Certificate are true.
    - All information in the Digital Signature Certificate that is within the knowledge of the subscriber is true.
4. Control private key.

Every subscriber shall exercise reasonable care to retain control of the private key corresponding to the public key listed in his Digital Signature Certificate and take all steps to prevent its disclosure to a person not authorized to affix the digital signature of the subscriber.

If the private key related to Digital Signature Certificate has been compromised, then the subscriber shall communicate the same, without any delay, to the Certifying Authority.

## 17.15 POWER OF THE CENTRAL GOVERNMENT TO MAKE RULES—SECTION 87

The Central Government has power to make rules by notifying in the Official Gazette in respect of certain matters, like:

1. Specify the manner for matter or electronic records which may be authenticated by a digital signature.
2. Specify the format by which electronic records shall be filed or issued.
3. Specify the type of digital signature and the manner, and the format in which it may be affixed.
4. Specify security procedure for the purpose of creating the same electronic records and secure digital signature.
5. Specify the qualifications, experience, and the terms and conditions of the services of the Controller, Deputy Controller and Assistant Controller.
6. Specify the requirements, manner, and the form in which applications is to be made for a license to issue Digital Signature Certificates.
7. Specify the period of validity of the license.
8. Specify the qualifications, experience of an adjudicating officer as well as other officers.
9. Specify salary, allowances, and the terms and conditions of service of the Presiding Officers, etc.

**Note:**

A State Government's rule making powers is limited to the provisions relating to electronic forms and the manner and format of e-records and the fees for their filing.

## 17.16 ISSUE NOT COVERED IN INFORMATION TECHNOLOGY ACT

The Information Technology Act has not addressed the followings areas:

1. Jurisdiction aspects of electronic contracts.
2. Jurisdiction of the Courts and Tax Authorities.
3. Taxation of Goods and services traded through e-commerce.
4. Stamp Duty aspects of the Electronic Contracts.
5. Protection of the Domain Name.
6. Infringement of the copy right law.

## 17.17 EXCLUDING LIABILITY OF INTERMEDIARIES—SECTION 79

1. An intermediary shall not be liable for any third party information, data, or communication link made available or hasted by him.
2. Point 1 shall apply if: –
   a. the function of the intermediary is limited to providing access to a communication system over which information made available by third parties is transmitted or temporarily stored or hasted; or
   b. the intermediary does not: –
      - initiate the transmission,
      - select the receiver of the transmission, and
      - select or modify the information contained in the transmission;
   c. the intermediary observes due diligence while discharging his duties under this Act and also observes such other guidelines as the Central Government may prescribe in this behalf.
3. Point 1 shall not apply if:
   a. the intermediary has conspired or abetted or aided or induced, whether by threats or promise or authorize in the commission of the unlawful act;
   b upon receiving actual knowledge, or on being notified by the appropriate Government or its agency that any information, data or communication link residing in or connected to a computer resource controlled by the intermediary is being used to commit the unlawful act, the intermediary fails to expeditiously remove or disable access to that material on that resource without vitiating the evidence in any manner.

***Note:***

For the purposes of this section, the expression, "third party information" means any information dealt with by an intermediary in his capacity as an intermediary.

## 17.18 NATIONAL NODAL AGENCY—SECTION 70A

The Central Government may, by notification published in the Official Gazette, designate any organisation of the Government as the national nodal agency in respect of Critical Information Infrastructure Protection. National nodal agency is responsible for all measures including Research and Development relating to protection of Critical Information Infrastructure.

## 17.19 INDIAN COMPUTER EMERGENCY RESPONSE TEAM—SECTION 70B

The Central Government shall, by notification in the Official Gazette, appoint an agency of the Government to be called the Indian Computer Emergency Response Team. The Central Government shall provide the agency with a Director General and such other officers and employees as may be prescribed.

The salary and allowances and terms and conditions of the Director General and other officers and employees shall be such as may be prescribed. The Indian Computer Emergency Response Team shall serve as the national agency for performing the following functions in the area of cyber security:

1. collection, analysis and dissemination of information on cyber incidents;
2. forecast and alerts of cyber security incidents;
3. emergency measures for handling cyber security incidents;
4. coordination of cyber incidents response activities;
5. issue guidelines, advisories, vulnerability notes and whitepapers relating to information security practices, procedures, preventation, response and reporting of cyber incidents;
6. such other functions relating to cyber security as may be prescribed.

For carrying out the above functions, the agency may call for information and give direction to the service provides, intermediaries, data centres, body corporate and any other person.

Any service provider, intermediaries, data centres, body corporate or person who fails to provide the information called for or comply with the direction, shall be punishable with imprisonment upto 1 year or with fine upto ₹ 1 lakh or with both. No court shall take cognizance of any offence under this section, except on a complaint made by an officer authorised in this behalf by the agency.

## 17.20 POWER OF A POLICE OFFICER AND OTHER OFFICERS TO ENTER, SEARCH, ETC.—SECTION 80

Notwithstanding anything contained in the Code of Criminal Procedure 1973,

1. Any police officer not below the rank of Inspector, or
2. Any other officer of the Central or State Government, if so authorized by the Central Government.

May enter any public place (includes public conveyance, any hotel, any shop or any other places accessible to the public) and search and arrest without warrant any person found therein who is reasonably suspected of having committed or of committing or is about to commit any offence under this Act.

Where any person is arrested by an officer other than a police officer, such an officer shall immediately send the arrested person to:

1. A magistrate having jurisdiction, or
2. The officer-in-charge of the nearest police station.

## LIST OF LANDMARK JUDGEMENTS

1. ***State vs Amit Prasad***

   *State vs Amit Prasad*, was India's first case of hacking registered under Section 66 of the Information Technology Act, 2000. A case with unique facts this case demonstrated how the provisions of the Indian Information Technology Act could be interpreted in any manner depending on which side of the offence you were on.

2. ***State of Chattisgarh vs Prakash Yadav and Manoj Singhania***

   This was a case registered on the complaint of the State Bank of India Raigarh branch. Clearly a case of Spyware and Malware this case demonstrated in early days how the IT Act could be applicable to constantly different scenarios.

3. ***State of Tamilnadu vs Dr L. Prakash***

   *State of Tamilnadu vs Dr L. Prakash* was the landmark case in which Dr L. Prakash was sentenced to life imprisonment in a case pertaining to online obscenity. This case was also a landmark in a variety of ways since it demonstrated the resolve of the law enforcement and the judiciary not to let off the hook one of the very educated and sophisticated professionals of India.

4. ***NAASCOM vs Ajay Sood and Others (2005)***

   The Delhi High Court declared 'phishing' on the Internet to be an illegal act entailing an injunction and recovery of the damages. It is a form of Internet fraud where a person pretends to be in a legitimate association such as a bank or an insurance company in order to extract personal data from a customer, such as access codes and passwords. The personal data so collected by misrepresenting the identity of the legitimate party is commonly used for the collecting party's advantage. The court held the act of phishing as passing off and tarnishing the plaintiff's image.

5. ***SMC Pneumatics (India) Pvt Ltd vs Jogesh Kwatra***

   The ex-employee of the company had forwarded several emails to the managing director of the company and its other several subsidiary company which are considered by the court as distinctly obscene, vulgar, abusive, intimidating, humiliating and defamatory in nature. The prima facie case of defamation has been observed by the Hon'able Delhi High Court and the restrain order has been issued for not publishing this kind of email in the cyber world.

6. ***State of Tamilnadu vs Suhas Kaati (2004)***

   The case related to posting of the obscene defamatory and annoying message about a divorcee woman in the yahoo message group by Suhas Kaati. The e-mails were also forwarded to the victim for information by the accused through a false e-mail account opened by him in the name of the victim. The posting of the message resulted in annoying phone calls to the lady in the belief that she was soliciting. The court has ordered the imprisonment and fine, under Section 67 of the Information Technology Act, for harassing by using Internet as medium.

## SOME IMPORTANT CASES

### Pune Citibank MphasiS Call Centre Fraud

An amount of USD 3,50,000 from the accounts of four US-based customers was dishonestly transferred to some bogus accounts. This incident caused a lot of ammunition to those lobbying against outsourcing in the United States. Such cases often happen all over the world, but when it happens in India it is a serious matter, and we cannot ignore it. It is a case of sourcing engineering. Some employees gained the confidence of customers and obtained their PIN numbers to commit the fraud. They committed this fraud under the guise of helping the customers to get out of difficult situations.

As per standard business practice, highest level of security measures are practised in the call centers operating from India. If not, they there are fair chances that these organization may lose business. There was not as much of breach of security, but of sourcing engineering. The entire call center employees are checked when they go in and out, so that they cannot note down numbers and, therefore, they could not have noted these down. They must have remembered these numbers, gone out immediately to a cyber café and accessed the customer's Citibank accounts. All those accounts were opened in Pune. The customers complained that the money from their accounts was transferred to those Pune accounts and that's how the criminals were traced. Police has been able to prove the honesty of the call center and has frozen the accounts where the money was transferred. There is need for a strict background check of the call center executives. However, best of background checks cannot eliminate the bad elements from coming in and breaching security. We must still ensure such checks when a person is hired. There is need for a national ID and a national database where a name can be referred to. In this case, preliminary investigations did not reveal that the wrongdoers had any criminal background. Customer education is important to keep them safe from unwanted troubles of this nature. Most banks are guilt of not implanting this.

**sony-sambandh.com Case**

India, recently, has seen its first cybercrime conviction. It all began after a complaint was filed by Sony India Pvt. Ltd, which runs a website, named, www.sony-sambandh.com, targeting the non-resident Indians. The website enables NRIs to send Sony products to their friends and relatives in India after they pay for it online. The company undertakes the job of delivering the products to the concerned recipients. In May 2002, someone logged onto the website under the identity of Barbara Campa and ordered a Sony colour television set and a cordless headphone. She gave her credit card number for payment and requested that the products be delivered to Arif Azim in Noida. The payment was duly cleared by the credit card agency and the transaction processed. After following the relevant procedures of due diligence and verification, the company delivered the items to Arif Azim. At the time of delivery, the company took digital photographs showing the delivery being accepted by Arif Azim. The transaction closed at that point. But after one and a half months, the credit card agency informed the company that this was an unauthorized transaction as the real owner had denied having made the said purchases.

The company lodged a complaint for online cheating with the Central Bureau of Investigation (CBI) which registered a case under the Sections 418, 419 and 420 of the Indian Penal Code. The matter was investigated into and Arif Azim was arrested. The investigation revealed that Arif Azim, while working at a Noida-based call center, illegally gained access to the credit card number of an American national, which he misused on the company's website.

The CBI recovered the colour television set and the cordless headphone. In this matter, the CBI had enough evidences to prove their case, and the accused admitted his guilt. The court convicted Arif Azim under Sections 418, 419 and 420 of the Indian Penal Code. And this was the first time that a cybercrime has been convicted. The court, however, felt that as the accused was a young man of 24-year-old and a first-time offender, a lenient view on his conviction were needed to be taken. The court, therefore, released the accused on probation for one year.

This judgement is of immense significance for the entire nation. Besides being the first conviction in a cybercrime matter, it has shown that the Indian Penal Code can be effectively applied to certain categories of cybercrimes which are not covered under the IT Act, 2000. Secondly, a judgment of this sort sends out a clear message to everyone that law cannot be taken for a ride.

## TEST YOUR KNOWLEDGE

1. What is Cyber Law? **(Ref. Para-17.1)**
2. What are the objectives of the Information Technology Act, 2000. **(Ref. Para-17.2)**
3. What is the scope of Information Technology Act and describe various relevant definitions in it. **(Ref. Para-17.3,17.4)**
4. Explain the computer, computer network and computer system under the Information Technology Act. **(Ref. Para-17.4)**
5. What is digital signature? How is it used for the authentication of electronic record? **(Ref. Para-17.5)**

6. What do you understand by the term 'hash function?' **(Ref. Para-17.5)**
7. What is e-governance? Explain the various provisions for e-governance in Chapter-3 of IT Act. **(Ref. Para-17.6)**
8. Write a short notes on digital signature certificate. **(Ref. Para-17.7)**
9. Write a short note on the Cyber Appellate Tribunal. **(Ref. Para-17.8)**
10. Which activities can be considered as offences under the Information Technology Act and what are the penalties thereof in IT Act? **(Ref. Para-17.9,17.10)**
11. Explain the liabilities of companies in the Information Technology Act. **(Ref. Para-17.11)**
12. Explain the duties of the controller of certifying authorities **(Ref. Para-17.12)**
13. Explain the duties of the certifying authorities. **(Ref. Para-17.13)**
14. What are the duties of a sub scriber? **(Ref. Para-17.14)**
15. What are the powers of Central Government to make rules under the act? **(Ref. Para-17.15)**
16. Explain the various issues covered and not covered in IT Act. **(Ref. Para-17.16)**

## MULTIPLE-CHOICE QUESTIONS

1. The Information Technology Act is popularly known as ______
   (i) Cyber law.
   (ii) Hacking law.
   (iii) Electronic law.
   (iv) Security law.
2. The Information Technology Act is not applicable to
   (i) Whole of India.
   (ii) Whole of India except state of Jammu and Kashmir.
   (iii) Power of attorney.
   (iv) None of the above.
3. The Information Technology Act is not applicable to
   (i) Will.
   (ii) Cheque.
   (iii) Bills of exchange.
   (iv) All of the above.
4. The Information Technology Act consists of ______ chapters.
   (i) 12
   (ii) 13
   (iii) 14
   (iv) 15
5. The Information Technology Act consists of ______ sections.
   (i) 90
   (ii) 99
   (iii) 100
   (iv) 94
6. Out of the following, which are the objectives of the Information Technology Act?
   (i) To give legal recognization of e-commerce transactions.
   (ii) To facilitate electronic storage of data.
   (iii) Both (i) and (ii).
   (iv) None of the above.
7. Out of the following, which are the objectives of the Information Technology Act?
   (i) To give legal recognization to digital signatures.
   (ii) To eliminate signatures.
   (iii) Both (i) and (ii).
   (iv) None of the above.

8. Out of following, which are the objectives of Information Technology Act?
   (i) To facilitate the electronic filing of documents.
   (ii) To facilitate electronic storage of data.
   (iii) To facilitate online crime investigation.
   (iv) None of the above.
9. Out of following, which are the objectives of Information Technology Act?
   (i) To recognize e-commerce transactions.
   (ii) To allow chat between persons.
   (iii) To pay stamp duty online.
   (iv) Both (i) and (iii).
10. _______ is the key of the key pair used to creating digital signature.
   (i) Public key
   (ii) Private key
   (iii) Both (i) and (ii)
   (iv) Pass key
11. _______ is the key of the key pair used to verify digital signature.
   (i) Public key
   (ii) Private key
   (iii) Both (i) and (ii)
   (iv) Pass key
12. Key pair includes
   (i) Public key.
   (ii) Private key.
   (iii) Both (i) and (ii).
   (iv) Pass key.
13. By using _______ any one can verify digital signature.
   (i) Public key
   (ii) Private key
   (iii) Both (i) and (ii)
   (iv) Pass key
14. _______ is the unique value for message or content.
   (i) Hash
   (ii) Message digest
   (iii) Encryption
   (iv) Private key
15. Electronic Governance means and includes
   (i) Filing any form online.
   (ii) Filing any form offline.
   (iii) Make application online.
   (iv) Both (i) and (iii).
16. What are the benefits of electronic governance?
   (i) Low cost
   (ii) Efficient working of government
   (iii) Transparency in working of government
   (iv) All of the above
17. _______ provides legal recognition for electronic records.
   (i) The Indian Contract Act
   (ii) The Companies Act
   (iii) The Evidence Act
   (iv) The Information Technology Act
18. _______ issue digital certificate.
   (i) The Certificate Authority
   (ii) The State Government
   (iii) The Central Government
   (iv) NASCOM
19. An appeal can be made to _______ against the order of an appellate tribunal.
   (i) A Magistrate Court
   (ii) A High Court
   (iii) The Supreme Court
   (iv) Both (i) and (ii)
20. An appeal can be made to high court against the order of appellate tribunal within _______ days.
   (i) 30
   (ii) 45
   (iii) 60
   (iv) 90

21. ______ is an offences under the Information Technology Act.
   (i) Sending offensive message
   (ii) Stealling information
   (iii) Video conference
   (iv) both (i) and (ii)

22. Digital signature can be suspended by the certifying authority in case of ______
   (i) Public interest.
   (ii) Interest of any person.
   (iii) Interest of user.
   (iv) Both (i) and (ii).

23. Digital signature can be suspended by ______
   (i) The Central Government.
   (ii) A State Government.
   (iii) A Certifying authority.
   (iv) The Controller.

24. Digital signature can be issued by ______
   (i) The Central Government.
   (ii) A State Government.
   (iii) A Certifying Authority.
   (iv) The Controller.

25. Digital signature cannot be suspended for period exceeding ______ days.
   (i) 15
   (ii) 30
   (iii) 45
   (iv) 60

26. Certifying authority can be appointed by ______
   (i) The Central Government.
   (ii) A State Government.
   (iii) A Certifying authority.
   (iv) The Controller.

27. An application for licence to issue electronic signature certificates is made along with which document?
   (i) Certificate of practice.
   (ii) PAN.
   (iii) Driving licence.
   (iv) Electricity bill.

28. The controller shall publish notice of ______ of licence in the database maintained by him.
   (i) Suspension
   (ii) Revocation
   (iii) Both (i) and (ii)
   (iv) None of above

29. Controller may revoke a licence on ground of ______ information contained in application.
   (i) False
   (ii) Incorrect
   (iii) Both (i) and (ii)
   (iv) None of above

30. No licence shall be suspended by controller for period exceed than ______ days.
   (i) 10
   (ii) 15
   (iii) 30
   (iv) 45

## ANSWER KEYS

| | | | | | |
|---|---|---|---|---|---|
| **1.** (i) | **6.** (iii) | **11.** (i) | **16.** (iv) | **21.** (iii) | **26.** (iv) |
| **2.** (ii) | **7.** (i) | **12.** (iii) | **17.** (iv) | **22.** (i) | **27.** (i) |
| **3.** (iv) | **8.** (iv) | **13.** (i) | **18.** (i) | **23.** (iii) | **28.** (iii) |
| **4.** (ii) | **9.** (i) | **14.** (ii) | **19.** (ii) | **24.** (iii) | **29.** (iii) |
| **5.** (iv) | **10.** (ii) | **15.** (iv) | **20.** (iii) | **25.** (i) | **30.** (i) |

# 18

# Companies Act, 2013: Types of Companies and Their Characteristics

**Learning Objectives**

*After reading this chapter, you will be able to understand:*

- Company and corporate veil
- Classes of companies under the Companies Act, 2013
- Registration and incorporation of companies
- Contracts entered at the time of incorporation
- Promoters and their duties

## 18.1 DEFINITION OF A COMPANY

### 18.1.1 Literary Meaning

Company is an association of persons formed for the purpose to achieve some common objects.

### 18.1.2 Legal Meaning—Section 2 (20)

Company means a company formed and registered under this act or an existing company. This act means, company registered under the Companies Act, 2013. Existing company means a company formed and registered under any of the previous Companies Act (i.e., Companies Act, 1956 or Indian Companies Act, 1913 or Indian Companies Act, 1882.)

The definition does not bring out clearly the meaning of a company. For a common man, a 'company 'means, an association of persons for certain purpose. But all association of persons cannot be technically called 'companies'.

## 18.2 THE CHARACTERISTICS OF A COMPANY

Company format of business is known for its various unique characteristics which can be understood by one as under:

### 18.2.1 Incorporated Association

A company must be incorporated or registered under the Companies Act. Minimum number required for the purpose is seven in case of a public company,and two in case of a private company, and one person in case of an one person company **(Section 3).**

### 18.2.2 Artificial Person

A company is created with prior sanction of law and is not itself a human being. It is, therefore, called an artificial entity. As such an entity is always clothed with certain legal rights and obligations; hence, it is considered as a person. A company is, accordingly, an artificial person.

### 18.2.3 Separate Legal Entity

Unlike partnership, a company is also distinct from the persons who constitute it. **Section 9** of the Companies Act says that on registration, the association of persons becomes body corporate by the name contained in the memorandum.

In the famous case of **Salomon vs Salomon & Co. Ltd.,** it was observed that a company is at law a different person altogether from the subscribers; although it may be that after incorporation the business is precisely the same as it was before, and the same persons are managers, and the same hands receive the profits, the company is at law not the agent of the subscribers or trustee to them. Nor are the subscribers as members liable in any shape or form, except to the extent and in the manner provided in the Act.

The facts of the famous **Salomon's case** were as follows:

> Salomon carried on business as a leather merchant. He sold his business for a sum of £30,000 to a company formed by him along with his wife, daughter, and four sons. The purchase consideration was satisfied by allotment of 20,000 shares of £1 each and issue of debentures worth £10,000 secured by floating charge on the company's assets in favour of Mr Salomon. All the other shareholders subscribed for one share of £1 each. Mr Salomon was also the managing director of the company. The company almost immediately ran into difficulties and eventually became insolvent and winding up commenced. At the time of winding up, the total assets of the company amounted to £6,050; its liabilities were £10,000 secured by the debentures issued to Mr Salomon and £8,000 owing to unsecured trade creditors. The unsecured sundry creditors claimed the whole of the company's assets, *viz.*, £6,050 on the ground that the company was a mere alias or agent for Mr Salomon.
>
> **It was held that contention of the trade creditors could not be maintained, because the company, being in law a person quite distinct from its members, could not be regarded as an agent or trustee** for Salomon. Also, the company's assets must be applied in payment of the debentures as a secured creditor is entitled to payment out of the assets on which his debt is secured in priority to unsecured creditors.

In **Lee vs Lee Air Farming Limited**, a company was formed for the purpose of manufacturing aerial top-dressing. Lee, a qualified pilot, held majority of shares in the company and by the articles was appointed director of the company and chief pilot. Lee was killed while piloting the company's aircraft and his widow claimed compensation for his death under the Workmen Compensation Act. The company opposed the claim on the ground that Lee was not a 'worker' as the same person could not be employer and the employee.It was held that there was a valid contract of service between Lee and the company, and Lee was, therefore, a worker, Mrs Lee's contention was upheld.

### 18.2.4 Limited Liability Company

The company being a separate person, its members are not as such liable for its debts. In the case of a company **limited by shares**, the liabilities of its members are limited to the **nominal value of shares** held by them. Thus, if the shares are fully paid-up, their liability will be nil.

However, companies may be formed with unlimited liability of members. In case of unlimited liability companies' members shall continue to be liable till each paise has been paid-off.

In case of **companies limited by guarantee**, the liability of each member shall be determined by the **guarantee amount**, *i.e.*, he shall be liable to contribute up to the amount guaranteed by him. But, in case of a guarantee company having share capital, the liability shall be limited to the aggregate of the amount remaining unpaid on the shares held by a member and the amount guaranteed by him unlimited liability of a member of a limited liability company.

### 18.2.5 Transferability of Shares

Since business is separate from its members in a company form of organization, it facilitates transfer of members' interest. The shares of a company are transferable in the **manner provided** in the **Articles** of the company. However, in a private company, certain restrictions have to be placed on such transfer of shares, but the right to transfer is not taken away absolutely.

### 18.2.6 Perpetual Existence

A company being an artificial person cannot be incapacitated by illness and it does not have an allotted lifespan. Situations like death, insolvency, or retirement of its members leaves the company unaffected. Members may come and members may go, but the company goes on forever.

### 18.2.7 Separate Property

Shareholder is not the part owner of the company or its property, he is only given certain rights by law e.g. to vote,to attend meetings, to receive dividends.It was observed that even where a shareholder held almost entire share capital he did not even have an insurable interest in the property of the company.

### 18.2.8 Common Seal

A company being an artificial person is not bestowed with a body of natural being. Therefore, it has to work through its directors, officers and other employees. But, it can be held bound by only those documents which bear its signatures. **Common seal is the official signature of a company.** Now, common seal has been made optional. Following documents require common seal, if company has common seal:

1. Power of Attorney
2. Share Certificate
3. Share warrant

### 18.2.9 Company May Sue and Be Sued in Its Own Name

Another fallout of separate legal entity is that the company, if aggrieved by some wrong done to it may sue or be sued in its own name.

**Case Study**

X is a director who has 20 years of professional experience. On this basis, X Ltd has employed him as a director. Can X Ltd say that the director X's experience is company's experience?

**Case Study**

S & Co. was formed with S, his wife, daughter and four sons as its subscribers and the only members. The company took over the shoe business of S for ₹ 30,000 giving him, as consideration, 20,000 shares of ₹ 1 each and debentures worth ₹ 10,000 with a charge on the company's assets. All members, except S. purchased one share each. S and his two sons constituted the Board of Directors of the company. Due to general trade depression, the company went into liquidation. The assets of the company amounted to ₹ 6,000, whereas its creditors amounted to ₹ 17,000, of which ₹ 10,000 due to S (secured by the charge on company's assets) and ₹ 7,000 due to unsecured creditors. S claimed the assets of the company as his debt is secured by the charge over them. On the other hand, the unsecured creditors are contending that they should be paid in priority over S as the company and S is one and the same person. Who is entitled to assets?

## 18.3 BODY CORPORATE

Body Corporate means, an **association of persons** which has been incorporated under some statute having perpetual succession, a common seal and having a legal entity different from the members constituting it. **Sub-section (11) of Section 2** of the Companies Act, 2013 defines the expression 'body corporate' as follows:

> **'Body corporate' or 'corporation'** includes a company incorporated outside India but does not include: (a) co-operative society registered under any law relating to co-operative societies; (b) any other body corporate not being a company which the Central Government may, by notification in the Official Gazette, specify in this behalf."

It may be noted that Central Government has reserved the right to declare any association of persons as a body corporate. Thus, the words 'body corporate' are not equivalent to the words 'incorporated company'. Incorporated company is a body corporate, but many body corporates are not incorporated companies. **(Madras Central Urban Bank Ltd. vs Corporation of Madras)**. The expression 'corporation' or 'body corporate' is, thus, wider than the term 'company'.

## 18.4 LIFTING OF THE CORPORATE VEIL

The advantages of incorporation are allowed to be enjoyed only by those who want to make an honest use of the company. In case of a dishonest and fraudulent use of the facility of incorporation, the law lifts the corporate veil and identifies the persons who are behind the scene. They are held responsible for the perpetration of fraud.

The circumstances under which the courts may lift the corporate veil may broadly be grouped under the following two heads:

1. Under statutory provisions.
2. Under judicial interpretations.

### 18.4.1 Under Statutory Provisions

The veil of corporate personality may be lifted in certain cases or pierced as express provisions of the Act. In other words, the advantage of 'distinct activity' and limited liability' may not be allowed to be enjoyed in certain circumstances, Such cases are:

**18.4.1.1 Misrepresentation in Prospectus—Section 34 and 35** In case of misrepresentation in a prospectus, every director, promoter, and every other person, who authorizes issue of prospectus which contains misstatement incurs liability towards those who subscribed for shares on the faith of untrue statement.

**18.4.1.2 Failure to Return Application Money—Section 39** In case of issue of security by a company to the public, if minimum subscription as stated in the prospectus has not been received within **30 days** from issue of the prospectus the company must return the application money within 15 days of closure of issue. If money is not paid within such period, directors shall be personally liable to return the money with interest @ 15% per annum.

**18.4.1.3 Misdescription of Name—Section 12** Where an officer of a company signs on behalf of the company, any contract, bill of exchange, hundi, promissory note, cheque or order for money, such person shall be personally liable to the holder if the name of the company is either not mentioned or is not properly mentioned.

***Example***

Director Blum signed the cheques in name of 'Bomore Medial Supplies', instead of 'Bomore Medical Supplies Ltd.' It was held that Blum is personally liable for this misdescription.

**18.4.1.4 For Investigation of Ownership of a Company—Section 216** Under **Section 216, the Central Government** may appoint one or more inspectors to investigate and report on the membership of any company for the purpose of determining the true persons who are financially interested in the company and who control policy or materially influence it.

**18.4.1.5 Fraudulent Conduct—Section 339** Where in the case of winding-up of a company it appears that any business of the company has been carried on with **intent to defraud creditors** of the company or any other person, or for a fraudulent purpose, those who are knowingly parties to such conduct business may, if the Tribunal thinks it proper so to do, be made personally liable without any limitation as to liability for all or any debts or otherliabilities of the company. Liability under this section may be imposed only if it is proved the business of the company has been carried on with a view to defraud its creditors.

**18.4.1.6 Liability for Ultra Vires Acts** Directors and other officers of a corporate will be personally liable for all those acts which they have done on behalf of company if the same are ultra vires the company.

**18.4.1.7 Liability Under Other Statutes** Besides the Companies Act, directors and other officers of the company may be held **personally liable** under the provisions other statutes.

### 18.4.2 Under Judicial Interpretations

Some of the cases where the veil of incorporation was lifted by judicial decisions may be discussed to form an idea as to the kind circumstances under which the facade of corporate personality will be removed.

**18.4.2.1 Protection of Revenue** In **Sir Dinshaw Maneckjee Petit**, the assesses was a millionaire earning huge income by way of dividends and interest. He formed four private companies and transferred his investments to each of these companies in exchange of their shares. The dividends and interest income received by the company was handed back to Sir Dinshaw as a pretended loan. It was held that the company was formed by assesses purely and simply a means of avoiding tax and the company was nothing more than assesses himself. It did no business, but was created simply as a legal entity to ostensibly receive the dividends and interest and to hand them over to the assesses as pretended loans.

**18.4.2.2 Prevention of Fraud or Improper Conduct** Where the medium of a company has been used for committing fraud or improper conduct, courts have lifted the veil and looked at the realities of the situation.

**18.4.2.3 Determination of the Enemy Character of a Company** Company being an artificial person cannot be an enemy or friend. However, during war, it may become necessary to lift the corporate veil and see the persons behind as to whether they are enemies or friends. It is because, though a company enjoys a distinct entity, its affairs are essentially run by individuals.

**18.4.2.4 Formation of Subsidiaries to Act as an Agent** In **Merchandise Transport Limited v. British Transport Commission**, a transport company wanted to obtain licenses for its vehicles, but it could not do so if it made the application in its own name. It, therefore, formed a subsidiary company and the application for licenses was made in the name of the subsidiary. The vehicles were transferred to the subsidiary. Held, the parent and the subsidiary company were one commercial unit and the application for licenses was rejected.

**18.4.2.5 In Case of Economic Offences** In **Santanu Ray v. Union of India**, it was held that in case of economic offences, a court is entitled to lift the corporate entity and pay regard to the economic realities behind facade.

**18.4.2.6 Where Company is Used to Avoid Welfare Legislation** Where it was found that the sole purpose for formation of the new company was to use device to reduce the amount to be paid by way of bonus to workers, the Supreme Court upheld the piercing of the veil to look at the real transactions.

**Case Study**

An English company was formed for selling tyres in England produced by a German company based in Germany. The majority of English company's shares were held by the German company. The overwhelming majority of the shareholders and all directors were German nationals residing in Germany. The English company filed suit during world war-I to recover trade debts. Could the company be allowed to proceed with the action?

**Case Study**

H was appointed as a managing director of X Ltd., on the condition that he shall not entice away the customers of the company during his stay in the company or afterwards. He left his job at X Ltd and formed a new company, V Ltd. which enticed away X's customers. What remedies, if any, are available to X Company?

**Case Study**

A public limited company has only seven shareholders, all the shares being fully paid up. All the shares of one such shareholder are sold by the Court in an auction and purchased by another shareholder. The Company continues to carry on its business thereafter. Discuss the liabilities of the shareholders of the company.

## 18.5 ILLEGAL ASSOCIATION

**Section 464** of the Companies Act, 2013 provides that no company, association or partnership consisting of more than **50 persons** for the purpose of carrying on any business can be formed unless it is registered under the Companies Act or is formed in pursuance of some other Indian laws. Thus, if such an association is formed and not registered under the Companies Act or any other laws, it will be regarded as an 'illegal association' although none of the objects for which it may have been formed is illegal. **Section 464** does not apply to the following cases:

1. Association or partnership, if it is formed by professionals who are governed by special acts.
2. Joint Hindu Family: Section 464 does not apply to a joint family, that is, a joint Hindu family may carry on any business, even for earning profits and with any number without being registered or formed in pursuance of any Indian Law as required by Section 464 of the Companies Act, 2013 and yet it will not be an illegal association.

**Case Study**

The *karta* of a joint Hindu family 'A', consisting of 31 adult members, and the *karta* of another joint Hindu family 'B', consisting of 22 adult members, on behalf of their respective families, enters into a partnership, but without getting registered under the Companies Act. After two years, some disputes arose and they sought the help of the court. Can the court interfere?

## 18.6 EFFECTS OF AN ILLEGAL ASSOCIATION

Every member is personally liable for all liabilities incurred in the business.Members are punishable with fine. Such an association cannot enter into any contract. Such an association **cannot sue** any of its members or any outsiders, not even if the association is subsequently registered as a company.It cannot be sued by a member or an outsider for any debts due to it, because it cannot contract for any debt.It cannot be wound up even under the provisions relating to winding up of unregistered companiesbecause law does not recognize its very existence.

The illegality of an illegal association cannot be cured by subsequent reduction in the number of its members. **(Kumar Swami Chettiar vs M.S.M. Chinnathambi Chettiar)**,The profits made by an illegal association are, however, liable in assessment of incometax **(Gopaji Co. vs C.I.T.A.)**

**Case Study**

Mr P and his other 50 friends carry on business under the name of P. Ltd, but it was not registered under the Companies Act, 2013. Is Mr P. liable under the Act.

**Case Study**

An association of 52 persons starts a banking business without being registered. Four members retire and, thereafter, a suit is instituted by one of the continuing members for the partition of the assets of the business. Is the suit competent?

## 18.7 ADVANTAGES OF INCORPORATION

As compared to other types of associations, an incorporated company has the following advantages:

### 18.7.1 Independent Legal Entity

Unlike a partnership firm which has no existence apart from its members, a company is a distinct legal person independent of its members.

### 18.7.2 Limited Liability

A company can be formed with the liability of its members limited. In the case of limited companies, no member is bound to contribute anything more, than the nominal value of the shares held by him or/and the amount guaranteed by him.

### 18.7.3 Perpetual Succession

An incorporated company has perpetual succession. Notwithstanding, any change in its members, the company will be the same entity with the same privileges and immunities, estate and possessions. This is a distinct advantage over and above a partnership where situations like death, insolvency, insanity or separation of members, *i.e.,* partners will not only have a bearing on its business but may even result in the dissolution of the firm.

### 18.7.4 Transferability of Shares

**Section 44** of the Companies Act, 2013 of the Act provides that the shares of any member in a company shall be movable property, transferable in the manner provided by the articles of the company. The facility of free transferability of shares encourages investment in the shares of the companies.

### 18.7.5 Infinite Membership

Another advantage of incorporation is that there is no limit to the maximum number of members in a public company. Accordingly a very large number of people including the juristic ones, can combine and contribute to the formation and financing of the company.

### 18.7.6 Separate Property

The property of the company is not the property of the shareholders; it is the property of the company. In the case of **Gramophone and Typewriter CL vs Stanley** it was held that no member or director can claim himself to be the owners of such a company's property or use the properties of the company.

### 18.7.7 Control and Management

The company law provides for all the managements of the companies through the elected representatives of the members, known as the directors and therefore, no shareholder is to worry about the management of the company.

## 18.8 DEFINITION OF A PUBLIC COMPANY

**Section 2(71)** of the Companies Act, 2013, defines a public company. Public Company means, a company which:

1. Is not a private company.
2. Has a minimum paid-up capital as may be prescribed;
3. Is a private company, which is a subsidiary of a company, and not a private company.

**Case Study**

Y Pvt Co. is a subsidiary of X Co., which is a public Company? What is type of company Y Pvt Co is?

## 18.9 DEFINITION OF A PRIVATE COMPANY

As per **Section 2(68) of the Companies Act, 2013**, 'Private company' means a company which has minimum paid-up capital as may be prescribed, and by its articles:

1. Restricts the right to transfer its shares;
2. Limits the number of its members to **200**, not including;
   (i) Persons who are in the employment of the company, and
   (ii) Persons who having, been formerly in the employment of the company, were members of the company while in employment and have continued to be members after the employment ceased.Here, it should be noted that joint holders of the shares are treated as single members..
3. Prohibits any invitation to the public to subscribe for any securities of the company.

**Case Study**

In a private company, 199 members are there who were first appointed as a member then joined as an employee, two members holding one share and 15 debenture holders. Did the Company crossed maximum limit?

**Case Study**

In a private limited company, it is discovered that there are, in fact, 204 members. On equity, it is ascertained that six of such members have been employees of the company in the recent past and that they acquired their shares while they were still employees of the company. Is it necessary to convert the company into a public limited company?

## 18.10 DISTINCTION BETWEEN PRIVATE AND PUBLIC COMPANY

'In the case of a private company, minimum number persons to form a company are **two** while it is **seven** in the case of a public company. In case of a private company, the maximum number must not exceed two hundred, whereas there is no such restriction on the maximum number of members in case of a public company.

In a private company, the right to transfer shares is restricted, whereas in case of public company the shares are freely transferable.

A private company cannot issue a prospectus, while a public company may, through prospectus, invite the general public to subscribe for its shares or debentures.

A private company must have at least two directors, whereas a public company must have at least three directors.

A private company cannot accept deposits from public. There is no such restriction for a public company.

## 18.11 LIMITED LIABILITY COMPANIES

The discussion on limited liability companies may be divided under the following three heads:

1. Companies limited by shares;
2. Companies limited by guarantee;
3. Companies limited by a guarantee, having share capital.

### 18.11.1 Companies Limited by Shares

A company having the liability of its members limited by the memorandum, to the amount if any, unpaid on the shares, respectively, held by them is termed as a company limited by shares.

A company of this type is commonly called, 'Limited Liability Company'. Although, the liabilities of the company are never limited, but it is the liabilities of its members are limited. The liabilities of the members can be enforced at any point of time during the existence and, also during the winding-up of such a company.

A company of this nature must have share capital as the extent of liabilities, is determined by the face value of its shares. However, except where the articles, otherwise, provide, there are no liabilities to pay any balance amount due on the shares, except in pursuance of calls duly made in accordance with law and the articles while the company is a going concern or of calls made in the event of winding-up of the company.

### 18.11.2 Companies Limited by Guarantee

A company limited by guarantee, may be defined as a company having liability of its members limited by the memorandum to such an amount that its members may respectively undertake by the memorandum to contribute to the assets of the company in the event of its being wound-up.

The liability of a member in the case of a company limited by guarantee, where the company has no share capital, is limited to the amount which he has undertaken by the memorandum of association to contribute to the assets of the company in the event of its being wound-up.

### 18.11.3 Companies Limited by Guarantee Having Share Capital

The liability of a member of a guarantee company having share capital is not merely limited to the amount guaranteed. he may be called upon to also contribute to the extent of any sums remaining unpaid on the shares held by him.

**Case Study**

Mr. X is holding 500 equity shares of ₹ 10 each on which ₹ 5 on each share is already paid. What amount can the company demand from Mr. X?

## 18.12 UNLIMITED LIABILITY COMPANY

A company having no limit on the liability of its members is an unlimited company. Thus, in the case of an unlimited liability company, the liability of each member extends to the whole amount of the company's debt and liabilities. It may be seen that the liability of members of an unlimited company is similar to that of the partners, but unlike the liability of partners, the members of the company cannot be directly proceeded against. Company being a separate legal entity, the claims can be enforced only against It company. Thus, creditors shall have to institute proceedings for winding up the company for their claims. But the official liquidator may call upon the members to discharge the debts and liabilities without limit.

An unlimited company may or may not have share capital. The articles of association of an unlimited company must state the number of members with which the company is to be registered and, if the company has share capital, the amount of share capital with which the company is to be registered. As the capital, if any, is stated in the articles and not in the memorandum, it may be varied, increased or reduced, by passing a special resolution.

## 18.13 CONVERSION OF A PRIVATE COMPANY INTO A PUBLIC COMPANY

The discussion on conversion of a private company into a public company may be grouped under the following heads:

1. Conversion by default;
2. Conversion by choice.

### 18.13.1 Conversion by Default

Where a private company default in compliance with the statutory requirements as laid down in Section 2(68) of the Companies Act, 2013 (*i.e.*, if its membership exceeds 200 or it invite public to subscribe to security of company), its becomes a public company automatically.

As a consequence, the company shall cease to enjoy the privileges and exemption conferred on a private company and the provisions of the Companies Act apply to it as if it were a public company.

However, Central Government on being satisfied that the failure to comply the conditions was accidental or due to inadvertence or to some other sufficient cause, may grant relief from such consequence as aforesaid. The relief granted on grounds which the central government feels is just and equitable.

### 18.13.2 Conversion by Choice—Section 14

A private company may, of its own choice become a public company. The following steps are necessary for this purpose:

**18.13.2.1 Special Resolution** A private company desiring to become a public company must pass a special resolution deleting from its articles the requirements of Section 2(68). Application in Form No. INC 27 shall be made. A copy of the special resolution so passed must be filed with the Registrar of Companies within 30 days thereof in Form No. MGT 14.

**18.13.2.2 Increase in Membership** If the number of members is less than seven, it must be raised to not less than seven.

**18.13.2.3 Increase in Number of Directors** If the number of directors is less than three, it must be raised to not less than three.

**18.13.2.4 Raising of Paid-up Capital** Where necessary, the paid-up capital must be raised to the minimum limit prescribed for public companies.

**18.13.2.5 Filing of Copy of Prospectus or Statement in Lieu of Prospectus** Within 30 days from the passing of the special resolution, a prospectus or a statement in lieu of prospectus in the prescribed Form must be filed with the Registrar.

## 18.14 GOVERNMENT COMPANIES

**Section 2(45)** defines a Government company to mean any company in which not less than 51% of the paid-up share capital is held by:

1. The Central Government; or
2. Any State Government or Governments; or
3. Partly by the Central Government and partly by one or more State Governments.
4. A subsidiary of a Government company shall also be treated as a Government company.

**Case Study**

The paid up capital of X Ltd is 1,00,000 equity shares of ₹ 10 each. The central government, Government of Gujarat and Government of Tamilnadu are respectively hold 4,00,000, 50,000 and 50,000 equity shares in this company. Can X Ltd be regarded as a Government company?

**Case Study**

40% of the paid-up share capital of company A is held by the Central Government and 11% by public institutions like the Life Insurance Corporation of India and the Unit Trust of India. Is A Ltd a Government Company?

## 18.15 FOREIGN COMPANY—SECTION 2(42)

A foreign company means a company or body corporate incorporated outside India and having a place of business in India. Accordingly, a company which is incorporated outside India and employs agents in India, but has no office or does not establish a place of business in India will not be a foreign company.

A company shall be said to have a place of business in India if it has a specified or identifiable place at which it carries on business such as an office, storehouse, godown, and other premises having some concrete connection between locality and business. Having a share transfer office or share registration office will constitute a place of business.

It may be noted that **Section 2(42)** defines a foreign company in terms of its place of incorporation. If the company is established outside India and has a place of business in India, then only it will be a foreign company under this section.

## 18.16 HOLDING AND SUBSIDIARY COMPANIES

'Holding' and 'subsidiary' companies are **relative terms**. A company is holding company of another if the other is its subsidiary.According to **Section 2(87)** of the Companies Act, 2013, a company shall be deemed to be a subsidiary of another, in the following cases:

1. The other company controls the composition of its Board of Directors;
2. The other company holds more than half of total share capital or control in other company either by itself or by its subsidiary companies.

***Example***

Where Company B is a subsidiary of Company A, and Company C is a subsidiary of Company B, then Company C shall be a subsidiary of Company A. If the Company D is a subsidiary of Company C, then Company D shall also be a subsidiary of Company B, and consequently also of Company A.

### 18.16.1 Control of Composition of Board of Directors

The composition of the Board of Directors of a company shall be deemed to be controlled by the other if the latter has the power, without the consent or concurrence of the other persons to appoint or remove all or majority of the directors.

**Case Study**

The paid-up share capital of XYZ (Private) Company Limited is ₹ 20 Lakh consisting of 2,00,000 Equity shares of ₹10 each fully paid-up. ABC (Private) Limited and DEF (Private) Limited are holding 60,000 and 50,000 shares respectively in XYZ (Private) Limited. Examine with reference to the provisions of the Companies Act, 2013 whether XYZ (Private) Limited is a subsidiary company?

## 18.17 PROMOTER

In layman language, any person, who conceives of the idea of forming a company, and actually put it into existence, can be termed as promoter. As per Section 2 (69) of the Companies Act, 2013, promoter means a person:

1. who has been named as such in a prospectus or is identified by the company in the annual return referred to in section 92; or
2. who has control over the affairs of the company, directly or indirectly whether as a shareholder, director or otherwise; or
3. in accordance with whose advice, directions or instructions the Board of Directors of the company is accustomed to act.

"A promoter is one who undertakes to form a company with reference to a given object and to set it going, and who takes the necessary steps to accomplish purpose," **(Twycross vs Grant)**

A company promoter is a person who originates a scheme for the formation of the company, has the Memorandum and Articles prepared, executed and registered, and finds the first directors, settles the terms of preliminary contracts and prospectus and makes arrangements for advertising and circulating the prospectus and placing the capital. A promoter is a person who does the necessary preliminary work for the formation of a company.

A promoter may be an individual, firm, an association of persons or a body corporate. However, everyone who is connected with the formation of a company may not be a promoter. For instance, under the Companies Act, persons acting in a professional capacity to assist persons engaged in procuring the formation of a company (*e.g.,* Company Secretary, Chartered Accountants, etc.) are not considered as promoters.

## 18.18 LEGAL POSITION OF PROMOTERS

The promoters occupy an important position and have wide powers relating to the formation of a company. His legal position is clear.

It is interesting to note that he is neither an agent nor a trustee of the proposed company. He is not the agent, because there is no company yet in existence and he is not a trustee, because there is no trust in existence. But, it does not mean that the promoter does not have any legal relationship with the proposed company. The correct way to describe his legal position is that he stands in a fiduciary position towards the company about to be formed.

In **Erlanger vs New Sombrero Phosphate Co.,** it was held that "The promoters of a company stand undoubtedly in a fiduciary position. They have in their hands the creation and moulding of the company.

They have the power of defining how and when and in what shape and under what supervision, it shall start into existence and begin to act as a trading corporation."

It was observed in **Lagunas Nitrate Co. vs Langunas Syndicate** that "The Promoters stand in fiduciary position to those persons whom they induce to become shareholders in it."

This fiduciary relationship imposes an obligation on the promoter that he must act honestly and must make a complete disclosure of all material facts relating to the formation of the company. There are two fiduciary duties of a promoter not to make any secret profits and to make a full disclosure to the company. It was held that the disclosure should be made to an independent and competent Board of Directors. Where it is not possible to constitute an independent board of directors, the disclosure should be made to the whole body of persons who are invited to become shareholders and this can be done through the prospectus.

In **Gluckstein vs Barnes**, it was held that making of profit is not forbidden; what is forbidden is non-disclosure of it. Thus, we can conclude by stating that the promoter is neither the agent nor a trustee for the company he promoters, but he stands in a fiduciary relationship with the company.

## 18.19 DUTIES OF PROMOTER OF A COMPANY

### 18.19.1 To Disclose Secret Profits

A promoter must not make any secret profit at the expense of the company that he promotes. If he has made any secret profit, it is his duty to disclose all the money secretly obtained by way of profit. If he fails to do so, the company may recover such profits from him. In the case of **Gluckstein vs Barnes**, it was held that promoter is not forbidden to make profit, but to make secret profit.

### 18.19.2 To Disclose all Material Facts

A promoter should make full disclosure of all the material facts regarding the formation of a company. The promoter is not allowed to derive a profit from the sale of his own property to the company unless all material facts are disclosed.

If a promoter contracts to sell to the company, a property without making a full disclosure, and the property was acquired by him at a time when he stood in a fiduciary position towards the company, the company may either rescind it or affirm the contract and then recover the secret profits from promoters. The material fact may be disclosed to an independent and competent board of directors of the company or in the Articles of Association or in the prospectus or to the whole body of shareholders.

A promoter is required to provide sufficient information and details in notice, agenda papers and explanatory statement attached with notice of general meeting. As per Section 102 of Companies Act, 2013, action can be taken against them if due to non-disclosure or insufficient disclosure, he has obtained any profit or gain.

### 18.19.3 Promoter Must Make Good to the Company What He Has Obtained as a Trustee

A promoter stands in a fiduciary position towards the company. It is duty of the promoter to make good to the company what he has obtained as trustee and not what he may get at any time. **[Jubliee Cotton Mills Ltd. vs Lewis]** Promoter must not make an unfair use of his position. The promoters must make a fair and reasonable use of his powers and position. He must act honestly.

### 18.19.4 To Act Diligently

The promoter is under an obligation to discharge his duties diligently. He must disclose all the private arrangements resulting in profit by the formation of the company.

### 18.19.5 To Use Public Issue Money for Object for Which It was Raised

As per Section 13(8), a company cannot change its object without passing special resolution when it has unutilized amount of public issue. In addition, company shall give an opportunity to dissenting shareholders to exit.

## 18.20 PRELIMINARY CONTRACTS OR PRE-INCORPORATION CONTRACT

Contracts made by promoters with parties to acquire some property or right for and on behalf of a company yet to be formed, are termed as 'pre-incorporation or 'preliminary' contracts. Such contracts are not legally binding on the company even after its incorporation, because two consenting parties are necessary to a contract whereas the company is a non-entity before its incorporation. The company has no legal existence until it is incorporated. Thus, a company cannot sue or be sued for pre-incorporation contracts.

## 18.21 EFFECTS OF PRE-INCORPORATION CONTRACTS

Promoter who start company, require carrying out number of transaction and entering into contract on behalf of company before the company commence its business and acquire legal status. Pre-incorporation contracts have following effects:

### 18.21.1 Not Binding on Company

A company, when registered, is not bound by pre-incorporation contracts, because at the time of making the contract the company was not in to existence. Company is not liable even if it has taken some advantage from contract.

### 18.21.2 Cannot Ratify the Agreement

A company when registered cannot ratify or adopt the pre-incorporation agreements, because a contract can be ratified only when it is made by an agent for principal who is in existence and is competent to contract at the time when the contract is made. Since company was not in existence, therefore, ratification is not possible.

It was held in the case of **Howard vs Patent Ivory Mfg.** that after incorporation, a company may enter into a new contract to carry into effect the contract made by the promoters before the incorporation.

### 18.21.3 Promoter Personal Liability

Promoters would be personally liable for any liability undertaken or aroused out of contract. **(Kelner vs Baxter)**

### 18.21.4 Company Cannot Sue

The company cannot enforce the preliminary agreements nor has any right under it.

**Case Study**

The promoters of a company, before its incorporation, enter into an agreement with P to buy a plot of land on behalf of the company. After incorporation the company refuses to buy the said plot of land. Has P any remedy either against the promoters or against the company?

## 18.22 STEPS TO OBTAIN CERTIFICATE OF INCORPORATION

First of all, the promoters have to decide whether they want to form a public company or a private company. For securing the registration or certificate of incorporation, the following steps are required to be taken:

1. The promoters should ascertain from the Registrar of Companies whether the name by which the company is to be started is available or not.
2. For this purpose, the promoters should decide upon at least three suitable names in the order of preference to afford flexibility to the Registrar. This application should be made to the Registrar of the State where the registered office is to be situated in the prescribed **form No. e-INC-1** along with a fee. Necessary care should be taken while selecting the name that it must not be undesirable or it must not be identical or too nearly resemble the name of an existing company.
3. The Memorandum of Association and articles of association should be prepared. The Memorandum should be signed by seven subscribers in case of a public company and two subscribers in case of a private company. Similarly, the Articles of Association which contains the rules and regulations for the internal management of a company should similarly be signed by subscribers. The memorandum and articles have to be duly stamped.
4. An application in the prescribed form has to be filed online (www.mca.gov.in). The application for registration must be accompanied by the following documents:
   (i) Memorandum and Articles of Association duly stamped, signed and witnessed. The letter from the Registrar regarding the availability of the name should also be attached.
   (ii) As per Section 7 read along with Rule 14 of The Companies (Incorporation) Rules 2014 declaration should be given by an advocate, a Chartered Accountant, Cost accountant or Company Secretary in practice shall be in Form No. INC-8. Declaration is given to effect that all rules and provisions of Companies Act, 2013 have been complied with for registration of company.
   (iii) The affidavit shall be submitted by each of the subscribers to the memorandum and each of the first directors named in the articles in Form No. INC-9 providing that he is not convicted of any offence in connection with the promotion, formation or management of any company, or that he has not been found guilty of any fraud or misfeasance or of any breach of duty to any company under this Act or any previous company law during the preceding five years and that all the documents filed with the Registrar for registration of the company contain information that is correct and complete and true to the best of his knowledge and belief.
   (iv) The agreement, if any, which the company proposes to enter into with any individual for appointment as its managing or whole-time director or manager.
   (v) The particulars of each person mentioned in the articles as first the director of the company and his interest in other firms or bodies corporate along with his consent to act as director of the company shall be filed in Form No. DIR-12 as provided in the Companies (Registration offices and fees) Rules, 2014.
   (vi) Where the location of the registered office is finalized prior to the incorporation of a company by the promoters, the promoters can also file along with the Memorandum and Articles, the verification of its registered office in Form No. INC 22.
5. Once the required documents have been filed and the prescribed amount of fee is paid, the Registrar will scrutinize the documents and if satisfied that all the formalities have been duly complied with, he will issue a certificate of incorporation. The certificate of incorporation is issued by the Registrar in Form No. INC-11. On receiving this certificate, the company becomes a body

corporate. The Registrar shall allot to the company, corporate identity number (CIN) which distinguish one company from another company.

## 18.23 ONE PERSON COMPANY

The concept of One Person Company [OPC] is a new vehicle/form of business, introduced by the Companies Act, 2013, thereby enabling entrepreneur(s) carrying on the business in the sole-proprietor form of business to enter into a corporate framework.

A One Person Company is a hybrid of Sole-Proprietor and Company form of business, and has been provided with relaxed requirements under the Act.

## 18.24 THE FEATURES OF ONE PERSON COMPANY

### 18.24.1 Only One Shareholder

Only a natural person, who is an Indian citizen and resident in India, shall be eligible to incorporate a One Person Company. The term 'Resident in India' means a person who has stayed in India for a period of not less than 182 days during the immediately preceding one calendar year.

### 18.24.2 Nominee for the Shareholder

The Shareholder shall nominate another person who shall become the shareholders in case of death/incapacity of the original shareholder. Such a nominee shall give his/her consent and such consent for being appointed as the nominee for the sole Shareholder. Only a natural person, who is an Indian citizen and resident in India, shall be a nominee for the sole member of a One Person Company.

### 18.24.3 Director

OPC must have a minimum of One Director; the sole shareholder can himself be the sole director. The Company may have a maximum number of 15 directors.

## 18.25 TERMS AND RESTRICTIONS OF ONE PERSON COMPANY

A person shall not be eligible to incorporate more than one One Person Company or become nominee in more than one such company.

A minor cannot become member or nominee of a One Person Company or can hold its shares with beneficial interest.

A One Person Company cannot be incorporated or converted into a company under Section 8 of the act. [Company not for Profit].

A One Person Company cannot carry out non-banking financial investment activities including investment in securities of a body corporate.

An One Person Company cannot convert voluntarily into any kind of company unless two years have expired from the date of incorporation of such a company, except the threshold limit (paid-up share capital) is increased beyond ₹ 50 Lakh or its average annual turnover during the relevant period exceeds ₹ 2 Crores, that is, if the paid-up capital of the company crosses ₹ 50 Lakh or the average annual turnover during the relevant period exceeds ₹ 2 Crores, then the One Person Company has to invariably file forms with the Registrar of Companies, for conversion in to a private or public company, with in a period of six months on breaching the described threshold limits.

## LIST OF LANDMARK JUDGEMENTS

1. ***Soloman vs Solomon and Co. Ltd (1897)***
   The company is a separate legal entity, which is different from its members and creditors.
2. ***Dalmier Co. Ltd vs Continental Tyre and Rubber Co. (1916)***
   The corporate veil of the company could be lifted to ascertain if the company was alien enemy or not.
3. ***Jones vs Lipsman (1962)***
   If the company is formed for some fraudulent of improper purpose, its separate legal entity character can be avoided and the corporate veil can be lifted.
4. ***Hendon vs Adelmann (1973)***
   If the name of the company is not properly used and there is no indication that the acts are done on behalf of the company, then the persons who have actually done the act, will be personally liable.
5. ***Hindustan Lever Ltd vs Bombay Soda Factory (1964)***
   On the conversion of a private company into public company, no new company comes into existence. The legal personality of the company is not affected.
6. ***Turner Morrison and Co. Ltd vs Hungerford Investment Trust Ltd (1969)***
   A holding company and its subsidiary are a separate legal entity.
7. ***State Trading Corporation of India vs CTO (1963)***
   The Government company is not a department of the state.
8. ***Heavy Engg. Mazdoor Union vs State of Bihar (1969)***
   The corporation's entire share capital was contributed by the Central Government and it could not be said that the undertaking carried out by the corporation, is carried out by the Central Government.
9. ***Erlanger vs New Sambrero Phosphate Co. (1878)***
   The promoter stands in fiduciary relation to the company which he promotes.
10. ***Kelner vs Baxter (1866)***
    The promoters are personally liable for pre-incorporation contract they had entered into.
11. ***Natal Land and Colonization Co. vs Pauline Colliery Syndicate (1904)***
    The company cannot sue on pre-incorporation contract.

## TEST YOUR KNOWLEDGE

1. Define a company and explain its characteristics as regards to perpetual succession. **(Ref. Para-18.1,18.2)**
2. A company on incorporation becomes a separate legal entity. Explain with a leading decided case. **(Ref. Para-18.2)**
3. Explain the characteristics of a company, in regards to limited liability and separate property. **(Ref. Para-18.2)**
4. Explain clearly the concept of 'perpetual succession' and 'common seal', in relation to a company incorporated under the Companies Act, 2013. **(Ref. Para-18.2)**
5. A company has a separate legal entity, different from its members. Under what circumstances can this be lifted under the Companies Act? **(Ref. Para-18.4)**
6. What is an 'Illegal Association'? What are the effects of illegal associations? **(Ref. Para-18.5,18.6)**

7. Can the shareholders claim the property of the company as their own property? **(Ref. Para-18.7)**
8. Define a private company. How does it differ from a public company. **(Ref. Para-18.9,18.10)**
9. Define the public company under the Companies Act, 2013. **(Ref. Para-18.8)**
10. Distinguish between a private company and a public company. **(Ref. Para-18.10)**
11. What is a 'Company Limited by shares' and 'Limited by guarantee'? **(Ref. Para-18.11)**
12. Write a short note on unlimited company. **(Ref. Para-18.12)**
13. Is it possible to convert a private company into a public company? Is so, how? **(Ref. Para-18.13)**
14. When can any company be said as a government company? **(Ref. Para-18.14)**
15. Define 'Holding company'. When can you say a company to be a subsidiary company of another company? **(Ref. Para-18.16)**
16. Who is a promoter? Explain in brief, the positions of a promoter relating to his rights and duties in a company. **(Ref. Para-18.17,18.18)**
17. What remedies are available against the promoter, when he makes secret profit? **(Ref. Para-18.19)**
18. What do you understand by a preliminary contract? **(Ref. Para-18.20)**
19. Write short note on 'pre-incorporation contract'. **(Ref. Para-18.20)**
20. Discuss the steps involved for the incorporation of companies in India? **(Ref. Para-18.22)**
21. Write down the steps to start a private company **(Ref. Para-18.22)**
22. Write down the steps required to take to incorporate, the public limited company. **(Ref. Para-18.22)**

## MULTIPLE-CHOICE QUESTIONS

1. The property of a company belongs to the
   (i) Company.
   (ii) Shareholders.
   (iii) Members.
   (iv) Promoters.
2. Which type of company's shares are freely transferable?
   (i) Private company.
   (ii) Public company.
   (iii) Both (i) and (ii).
   (iv) None of the above.
3. The minimum number of members in case of a public company is
   (i) 1.
   (ii) 2.
   (iii) 5.
   (iv) 7.
4. The minimum number of members in case of a private company is
   (i) 1.
   (ii) 2.
   (iii) 3.
   (iv) 7.
5. The maximum number of members in case of a private company is
   (i) 200.
   (ii) 100.
   (iii) 150.
   (iv) 50.

6 The maximum number of members in case of a public company is
   (i) 0.
   (ii) no limit.
   (iii) 50.
   (iv) 100.

7. Minimum subscription should be received within ______ days from the issuance of the prospectus
   (i) 30
   (ii) 60
   (iii) 90
   (iv) 135
8. Liability of a member in case of a private company is
   (i) Limited.
   (ii) Unlimited.
   (iii) Both ((i) or (ii).
   (iv) None of the above.
9. Minimum paid-up share capital in case of a private company is ______
   (i) No limit prescribed by Government.
   (ii) 2 lakhs.
   (iii) 3 lakhs.
   (iv) 4 lakhs.
10. Minimum paid-up share capital in case of a public company is ______
    (i) 1 lakh.
    (ii) 3 lakhs.
    (iii) No limit prescribed by Government.
    (iv) 7 lakhs.
11. The liability of members when a company is limited by guarantee is ______
    (i) The unpaid value of shares.
    (ii) The guarantee amount.
    (iii) Unlimited liability.
    (iv) None of these.
12. The liability of the members when company is limited by shares is ______
    (i) The unpaid value of shares.
    (ii) The guarantee amount.
    (iii) Unlimited liability.
    (iv) None of these.
13. XYZ Company shares are totally held by government. It can be called a government company.
    (i) True
    (ii) False
14. Transfer of shares in the company is
    (i) Restricted.
    (ii) Freely transferable.
    (iii) Prohibited.
    (iv) None of these.
15. Generally, a company's liability is
    (i) Limited.
    (ii) Unlimited.
    (iii) Situation does not arise.
16. X Company is holding majority of shares in Y company. Will X and Y companies will be the same entity?
    (i) Yes
    (ii) No
17. A company is considered as a government company, if it is holds ______% of paid-up share capital.
    (i) More than 30
    (ii) More than 40
    (iii) More than 50
    (iv) None of these
18. The Central Government's permission is required in case of ______ conversion ______.
    (i) Private to public.
    (ii) Public to private.
    (iii) Both (i) or (ii).
    (iv) None of these.
19. ______% of shares should be held by a company in another company in another company in order to become subsidiary.
    (i) More than 50
    (ii) More than 40
    (iii) More than 30
    (iv) More than 20

20. Maximum capital of private company is
    (i) 50 lakhs.
    (ii) 1 crore.
    (iii) 1.5 crore.
    (iv) unlimited
21. While calculating the maximum limit, in case of private company, which of the following will not be included?
    (i) Employee
    (ii) Member + Employee
    (iii) Member
    (iv) None of these
22. Can a private company go for a public issue?
    (i) Yes
    (ii) No
23. Can a private company accept deposits from the public?
    (i) Yes
    (ii) No
24. Invitation to public offering shares or debentures, in case of private company is
    (i) Prohibited.
    (ii) Restricted.
    (iii) Acceptable.
    (iv) None of these.
25. Maximum paid-up capital, in case of public company is.
    (i) 50 lakhs
    (ii) 100 lakhs
    (iii) 125 lakhs
    (iv) No limit

## ANSWER KEYS

| | | | | |
|---|---|---|---|---|
| **1.** (i) | **6.** (ii) | **11.** (ii) | **16.** (ii) | **21.** (i) |
| **2.** (ii) | **7.** (i) | **12.** (i) | **17.** (iii) | **22.** (ii) |
| **3.** (iv) | **8.** (i) | **13.** (ii) | **18.** (ii) | **23.** (ii) |
| **4.** (ii) | **9.** (i) | **14.** (ii) | **19.** (i) | **24.** (i) |
| **5.** (i) | **10.** (iii) | **15.** (i) | **20.** (iv) | **25.** (iv) |

# 19

# Companies Act, 2013: Memorandum, Articles of Association and Prospectus

**Learning Objectives**

*After reading this chapter, you will be able to understand:*

- The Memorandum of Association
- Purpose, format and the contents of the Memorandum and the Articles of Association
- Various clauses of the Memorandum and its alteration procedures
- Doctrine of ultra-vires, indoor management and constructive notice
- Prospectus, its requirements, contents and various offer documents
- Mis-statement in the prospectus and its consequences on the part of a company, promoters, and the directors of company

## 19.1 DEFINE THE MEMORANDUM OF ASSOCIATION

According to **Section 2 (56)** of the Companies Act, 2013, "Memorandum means the Memorandum of Association of a company as originally framed or as altered from time to time".

A Memorandum of Association is the most important document of a company. It contains the fundamental conditions upon which a company can be incorporated. It regulates the relationship of the company with the outside world.

A Memorandum of Association lays down the powers and objects of a company and the scope of operations of the company beyond which its actions cannot go. Any action, outside the scope of the Memorandum of Association, will be *ultra vires* the company and so void.

In **Ashubury Carriage Co. vs Riche,** it was observed that the Memorandum of Association of a company is its charter and define the limitation and powers of a company.

In **Guinness vs Land Corporation of Ireland Bowen,** it was observed that the Memorandum contains the fundamental conditions upon which alone the company is allowed to be incorporated.

It may be noted here that a Memorandum not only defines the powers of the company but also confines them. In fact, it is the foundation on which the structure of a company is based. A company cannot do anything, which is beyond the powers conferred upon the company by the Memorandum of Association.

It is a public document open for inspection to any member of the public. Every person who deals with the company is presumed to have the knowledge of its contents.

A Memorandum shall not be altered except in the manner and to the extent provided in the Act. Even if all the members of the company in the general meeting agree to change this document, they cannot do it without the sanction of the Central Government or the National Company Law Tribunal (NCLT).

## 19.2 PURPOSE OF MEMORANDUM OF ASSOCIATION

The purpose of a Memorandum is to enable the shareholders, creditors and those who deal with the company to know its permitted range of enterprise. Thus, it enables the shareholders to know for what purpose their money is going to be utilized and the risk involved.

## 19.3 PROVISIONS RELATING TO PRINTING AND SIGNATURE OF MEMORANDUM

The Memorandum of Association must be printed, divided into paragraphs, numbered consecutively, and signed by each subscriber in the presence of at least one witness who shall attest the signature **(Sec. 7).** Any natural person, competent to enter into a contract or any artificial person having separate legal entity can be a subscriber to the Memorandum and sign it. One company or body corporate can become a subscriber to the memorandum of another company. A foreigner can be a subscriber to the Memorandum. A minor cannot become a subscriber to the Memorandum.

## 19.4 FORM OF MEMORANDUM OF ASSOCIATION—SECTION 4

The Memorandum of a company shall be in such one of the Forms in Table A, B, C, D, and E in Schedule I as may be applicable to the case of the company. The prescribed Forms are as follows:

| | |
|---|---|
| **Table A** | relates to companies limited by shares |
| **Table B** | relates to companies limited by guarantee and not having a share capital. |
| **Table C** | relates to companies limited by guarantee and having a share capital. |
| **Table D** | relates to unlimited companies not having share capital. |
| **Table E** | Relates to unlimited company having share capital |

## 19.5 CONTENTS OF THE MEMORANDUM OF ASSOCIATION—SECTION 4

Memorandum of Association of every company shall contain the following clauses:

1. The Name Clause
2. The Registered Office Clause
3. The Objects Clause

4. The Liability Clause
5. The Capital Clause
6. The Association Clause

## 19.6 LEGAL REQUIREMENTS AS TO THE NAME CLAUSE

The Memorandum must state the name of the company with 'Limited' as the last word in case of a public limited company and with 'Private Limited' in the case of a private limited company. A company is free to choose any name, but it must not be undesirable or must not resemble the name of any other registered company.

## 19.7 LEGAL REQUIREMENTS AS TO THE REGISTERED OFFICE CLAUSE

The Memorandum of Association must mention the name of the State in which the registered office of the company is to be situated. All communication and notices to be sent to its registered office.

The situation of company's registered office determines the domicile of the company and it is important to determine the jurisdiction of the courts in which the legal action can be taken by or against the company.

All the important documents and books of the company such as Register of Members, Minutes Book, etc., are kept at the registered office.

## 19.8 DISPLAY OF REGISTERED OFFICE ADDRESS

A company's name and address of its registered office must appear prominently outside of all offices or place of business of the company.

Name and address of registered office of the company must be painted or affixed on the outside of every office or place of business in a conspicuous position, in easily legible letters and in the language in general use in the locality. Name of the company must be engraved in legible characters on its seal.

The name and address of registered office must also be mentioned in legible characters in all business letters, bill heads, negotiable instruments, invoices, receipts, etc. of the company.

## 19.9 LEGAL REQUIREMENTS AS TO THE OBJECTS CLAUSE

This is the **most important clause** in the memorandum. It defines the sphere of the company's activities, the specific objectives for the formation of the company. The company cannot do anything, which is not mentioned in the objects clause.

All companies registered under the Companies Act, 2013 must divide the Objects Clause into two parts: (i) Main Objects, and (ii) Objects incidental to achieve the Main Objects.

| | |
|---|---|
| **Main Objects** | This sub-clause contains the main objects of the company to be pursued on its incorporation. |
| **Objects incidental or ancillary to main objects** | It covers the objects which are incidental or ancillary to the attainment of the main object. |

Objects must not be unlawful or against the provisions of Companies Act, 2013, or against the public policy.

## 19.10 LEGAL REQUIREMENTS AS TO THE LIABILITY CLAUSE

This clause states the nature of liability of the members of the company. In the case of a company limited by shares or by guarantee, the fact that the liability of its members is limited must be made absolutely clear. In case of a company limited by shares, the liability of a member is limited to the nominal value of shares held by him. If the shares are fully paid up his liability is nil. But, in case of partly paid-up shares, the liability is limited to the amount which is unpaid.

In case of a company limited by guarantee, the liability clause must state the amount which every member undertakes to contribute to the assets of the company in the event of its winding-up.

## 19.11 CAPITAL CLAUSE

This clause states that amount of the share capital with which the company is to be registered. This clause should also state the number and face value of shares into which the capital of the company is divided.

The capital with which the company is registered is variously described as 'registered' or 'nominal' or 'authorized'.

## 19.12 ASSOCIATION OR SUBSCRIPTION CLAUSE

In this clause, the subscribers declare that they desire to be formed into a company and agree to take shares stated against their names. The names, address, occupation of the subscribers must be given. Each subscriber must sign in the presence of at least one witness who shall attest his signature.

It should be noted that every subscriber must take at least one share. In case of a public company, the Memorandum must be signed by at least seven subscribers, while in case of a private company, two subscribers must sign.

After the registration, no subscriber to the Memorandum can withdraw his subscription on any ground whatsoever.

## 19.13 PROVISIONS FOR CHANGE IN NAME CLAUSE OF MEMORANDUM OF COMPANY OR ALTERATION OF NAME CLAUSE

Company can change its name by own or on the order of central government. Central government will issue order to change name of company when the name of company if found to similar to that of other company's name or registered trade name.

### 19.13.1 Change of Name on Own—Section 13

A company may, by passing a special resolution and with the approval of the Central Government signified in writing, change its name.

But no such approval is required in cases of addition or deletion of the word 'Private' consequent on the conversion of a public company into a private company and vice versa.

### 19.13.2 Rectification of Name on Own or on C.G's Order—Section 16

If, for any reason a company has been registered with a name which is identical with or too closely resembles with the name of an existing company. Company shall change its name within three months from receipt of direction from the Central Government by passing an ordinary resolution. However, a proprietor of a registered trade mark can apply to the central government when name of the company is identical with or too nearly resembles to a registered trade mark within period of three years from the incorporation of the company.

Change of name shall not affect any rights or obligations of the company or render defective any legal proceedings by or against it.

**Case Study**

India Cosmetics Limited was a registered company under the Companies Act, 2013. Later, another company, India Cosmetics and Accessories Limited was formed and registered. Being found similarity in the names of both the Companies, India Cosmetics Limited lodged a complaint against India Cosmetics and Accessories Limited, with the Registrar of Companies, stating that there is sufficient similarity between these two names which may mislead or defraud the public. India Cosmetics and Accessories Limited is intending to alter its name.

Advise India Cosmetics and Accessories Limited to alter the name of the Company according to the provisions of the Companies Act, 2013.

## 19.14 PROCEDURE TO CHANGE REGISTERED OFFICE FROM ONE PLACE TO ANOTHER WITHIN THE SAME CITY

A company can change its registered office from one place to another within the local limits of the same town, village or city, without many difficulties. The Board of Directors is simply required to pass a resolution to that effect. Further, a notice of the change in Form INC 22 should be given to the Registrar of Companies within 15 days.

Necessary changes must also be made in all the records, letterheads, sign boards, etc., and all concerned persons should be informed.

## 19.15 PROCEDURE TO CHANGE REGISTERED OFFICE FROM ONE CITY TO ANOTHER WITHIN JURISDICTION OF THE SAME ROC WITHIN THE SAME STATE

A **meeting of the Board of Directors** is to be called where in the draft **special resolution** is to be passed and general meeting of the company should be called for this purpose and special resolution to this effect must be passed in general meeting. If the shares of the company are listed on the stock exchange(s) a copy of the resolution certifying the change must be sent to the concerned stock exchange(s).

A notice of the change in Form INC 22 should be filled to the Registrar of Companies within 15 days.

The company is also required to file a certified true copy of the resolution along with Form MGT 14 to the Registrar within 15 days of passing of resolution.

## 19.16 PROCEDURE TO CHANGE THE REGISTERED OFFICE FROM THE JURISDICTION OF ONE ROC TO THE JURISDICTION OF ANOTHER ROC WITHIN THE SAME STATE—SECTION 12

No company shall change the place of its registered office from one place to another within a State unless such change is confirmed by the Regional Director.

The company shall make an application in Form INC 23 form to the Regional Director to shift its registered office from one ROC to another ROC within same state.

On application, Regional Director (RD) after hearing party approve or reject application within 30 days from the date of receipt of application for such change. Before making an application to RD, company shall publish a notice in a English newspaper and another notice in a regional language daily newspaper where registered office of company is situated and sent notice to debenture holders, depositors and creditors at least 21 days before making an application to RD.

The company shall file, with the Registrar a certified copy of the confirmation by the RD, for change of its registered office under this section, within 60 days from the date of confirmation, together with a printed copy of the memorandum as altered and the Registrar shall register the same.

**Case Study**

VD Company Ltd. is registered in Tamil Nadu within the jurisdiction of the Registrar of Companies, Chennai. The company proposes to shift its registered office to a place within the jurisdiction of the Registrar of Companies, Coimbatore. State the steps to be taken by the company to give effect to the proposed shifting of its registered office.

## 19.17 PROCEDURE TO CHANGE THE REGISTERED OFFICE FROM ONE STATE TO ANOTHER

If the registered office is to be shifted from one state to another, it can be done by exercising the following the procedures:

1. A special resolution should be passed and a copy thereof filed with the Registrar within 15 days in Form MGT 14.
2. Application is made to the Central Government with a copy of the resolution and other documents after passing a resolution. The list of creditors is also attached to the application.
3. After making an application to central government, advertise the application in Form INC 26 in a English newspaper and another advertisement in a regional daily newspaper should be published. The said advertisement shall be published at least 14 days prior to the hearing.
4. Send notice to creditors and deposit holders who have the right to raise objection. If no objection is raised by any person, the Central Government may order confirming change in the registered office without a hearing.
5. Confirmation order of the Central Government shall be filed with the Registrar of Companies within 30 days in Form INC 28.

## 19.18 PROCEDURE FOR CHANGING THE OBJECTS CLAUSE OF THE MEMORANDUM—SECTION 13

The objects clause of Memorandum is the most important clause. It can be altered by passing a special resolution.

Section 13 lays down that a company, which has raised money from public through prospectus and has any unutilized amount out of the money so raised, shall not change its objects for which it raised the money through prospectus unless a special resolution is passed by the company, and:

1. The details, as may be prescribed, in respect of such resolution shall be published in the newspapers (one in English and one in a vernacular language) which is in circulation at the place where the registered office of the company is situated and shall also be placed on the website of the company, if any, indicating therein, the justification for such change.
2. The dissenting shareholders shall be given an opportunity to exit by the promoters and shareholders having control in accordance with the regulations to be specified by the Securities and Exchange Board.

After passing resolution, Form MGT 14 should be filled with Registrar of Companies. The Registrar shall certify the same within period of 30 days.

For deleting any provision of the object clause, the procedure laid down in Section 13 has to be followed.

## 19.19 ALTERATION OF LIABILITY CLAUSE

A company may increase liability of its member by passing resolution.

A company may, if authorized by its articles, alter its Memorandum to make the liability of its directors, managing director or manager unlimited, by passing a special resolution. This rule applies to future appointees only. This alteration shall be valid only if the officer concerned has given his consent in writing.

## 19.20 DOCTRINE OF *ULTRA VIRES*

The word 'ultra' means 'beyond' and the word 'vires' means 'powers'. Thus, U*ltra Vires* means doing an act beyond the powers. Any activity done contrary to or in excess of the scope of activity of directors, Articles, Memorandum of Companies will be *Ultra Vires*.

The *Ultra Vires* acts can be divided into following categories:

1. An act *Ultra Vires* the directors.
2. An act *Ultra Vires* the Articles of Association.
3. An act *Ultra Vires* the Memorandum of Association.
4. An act *Ultra Vires* the Companies Act.

### 19.20.1 *Ultra Vires* to the Directors

Act *Ultra Vires* to directors means any act beyond the power or authorities granted to the directors by the shareholders of the company. If the act is *Ultra Vires* the directors, it is not altogether void, because this act can be ratified by the general body of shareholders and on such ratification the act becomes binding on the company. But if any unltravires to director act is not ratified, it is not binding to company.

### 19.20.2 *Ultra Vires* to the Article of Association

It means, any act performed or done by the directors beyond the power granted or procedure prescribed under the articles of a company. Acts which are *Ultra Vires* the Articles of Association, but *intra vires* to the memorandum are not altogether void. An act *Ultra Vires* to the articles of the association of a company can be ratified by altering the articles of association of the company.

***Example***

Payment of interest on 'advance calls' at a rate higher than allowed by the article is an *Ultra Vires* act. Such acts can be ratified by the company by altering the articles by passing a special resolution in the general meeting of the company.

### 19.20.3 *Ultra Vires* the Memorandum of Association

The company is formed to carry out or achieve the objects as laid down in the Memorandum. A company cannot do anything which is beyond the purview of the objects clause. If the company does anything which is contrary to the objects clause of Memorandum, it shall be termed as *Ultra Vires* the Memorandum and it shall be wholly void or inoperative. Such an act cannot be subsequently ratified or validated even by a unanimous resolution of all the shareholders.

The purpose of the objects clause of the Memorandum is to see that the company carries on business for objects set out in the Memorandum. The purpose of this doctrine is to protect the interest of shareholders and creditors. The shareholders know the objects for which their money is likely to be used and creditors are protected by ensuring that the funds of the company, which they must look for payment, are not used for unauthorized activities.

The doctrine of *Ultra Vires* was first applied in case of **Ashbury Railway carriage Co. vs Riche.** In this case, the company was formed "to make and sell, or lend or hire, railways carriages and wagons and to carry on the business of the mechanical engineers and general contractors." The company enters into a contract with Riche to finance the construction of railway line in Belgium. Later, the company repudiated the contract on the ground that it was *Ultra Vires*. Riche filed a suit against the company for breach of contract and claimed damages. His plea was that the contract was within the powers of the company as it was covered under the general contractor's business.

The House of Lords held that the contract was *Ultra Vires* the company and, therefore, *void ab initio*. It was, further, held that the contract cannot be made valid by ratification on the part of the shareholders, and so the company was not liable for breach of contract.

In **J. R. Mody vs Shamji Lodha,** the directors of a company, on its behalf, purchased shares of another company. But, this right was not described in the Memorandum of the company. Therefore, the Court held the act as *Ultra Vires*.

Since then, this doctrine has been applied in a number of cases.

The doctrine has been affirmed by the Supreme Court in **Lakshmanaswami Mudaliar vs the LIC of India.** In this case, the directors of a company were authorized to make payments towards any charitable or any general public or useful objects. As per shareholders' resolution, the directors paid ₹ 2 lakhs to a trust formed for the purpose of promoting technical and business knowledge. The court held that the directors could not spend company's money on any such charitable objectives which they might choose. They could spend only for such charitable objects as would be useful for the attainment of company's own objects. The payment was, therefore, *Ultra Vires*.

### 19.20.4 *Ultra Vires* the Companies Act

Any act, which is contrary to or in excess of the scope of activity of the Companies Act, shall be *Ultra Vires* the company. Such an act is void and cannot be ratified by a unanimous resolution of the all the shareholders.

***Example***

Payment of dividend out of capital.

## 19.21 EFFECTS OF *ULTRA VIRES* TRANSACTION

### 19.21.1 Act Null and Void

A contract which is *Ultra Vires* the company is wholly *void ab initio* and of no legal effect. It cannot even be ratified by the whole body of shareholders.

### 19.21.2 Company Cannot Sue or Be Sued

Not only that outsider cannot enforce *Ultra Vires* transactions against the company, but being void, the company can also not enforce such transactions against outsiders. The Memorandum being a public document, it is deemed that persons dealing with the company have the knowledge of the same and if he enters into transactions *Ultra Vires* the company, he cannot enforce it.

### 19.21.3 Injunction

The members of a company are entitled to hold a company to its registered objects. Hence, whenever an *Ultra Vires* act has been committed or is likely to be committed, any member of the company can restrain it by getting an injunction against it.

### 19.21.4 Personal Liability of Directors

It is the duty of directors to see that the funds of the company are used only for legitimate business of the company. If directors make an *Ultra Vires* payment, then he can be compelled to make good the funds used.

### 19.21.5 Personal Liability of Directors to Third Parties

The directors are the agents of the company and should act within its powers. If the directors have induced the third party to make a new contract for which the company has no power, the directors shall be liable to third parties provided the third party was not aware of the lack of authority.

### 19.21.6 *Ultra Vires* Acquired Property

If company's funds were used in acquiring some *Ultra Vires* property, the company has the right to hold the property and protect it against damage by other persons **(National Telephone Co vs St. Peter Constables).**

### 19.21.7 *Ultra Vires* Torts

A company shall not be liable for torts committed outside its objects. The company can be made liable for torts or crimes of its employees, if (a) the tort was committed in the course of an activity which is in the purview of company's Memorandum, and (b) it was committed by the employee within the course of his employment.

## 19.22 ARTICLES OF ASSOCIATION

**Section 2(6)** of the Companies Act, 2013, defines the 'Articles' which means the Articles of Association of a company as originally framed or as altered from time to time in accordance with the Act. The Articles of Association are the rules and regulations or the bye-laws which governs the internal management of the company.

It is the second-most important document to be filed with the Registrar at the time of registration of a company. The various rules and regulations are framed for the purpose of carrying out the objects of the company as stated in the Memorandum of Association. It states the powers of directors, officers and of the shareholders as to voting, etc., the mode and the form in which the business of the company is to be carried out and the mode, and the form in which the changes in the internal regulations can be made.

Thus, Articles of Association are subordinate to the Memorandum of Association of the company. Articles cannot supersede the objects as set out in the Memorandum of Association. The Memorandum lays down what is to be done and the Articles lay down how it is to be done. The Articles must not contain anything which is contrary to Memorandum or Companies Act.

The Articles of Association of a company is contractual force between company and its members as also between the members *inter se* in relation to their rights as such members.

It is not obligatory for public companies limited by shares to have their own Articles **[Section 5].** A public company limited by shares, may either frame its 'Articles' or adopt the rules and regulations contained in Table F of Schedule I of the Companies Act, 2013 **[Section 5].**

An unlimited company must have its Articles of Association which must be registered along with the Memorandum.

## 19.23 DISTINGUISH BETWEEN MEMORANDUM AND ARTICLES OF ASSOCIATION

The Memorandum is the charter of the company which defines its objects and powers. The Articles are the bye-laws of the company, for the internal management of the affairs, for achieving the objects set out in the Memorandum.

The Memorandum is the supreme document of the company, while the Articles are subordinate to the Memorandum. If there is any conflict between the Memorandum and Articles, the Memorandum shall prevail.

Memorandum of Association should not contain any provisions contrary to the Companies Act. Articles must not include any provisions contrary to the Companies Act as well as Memorandum of Association.

Every company must have its own Memorandum. But, a company limited by shares, may or may not have its own Articles. It may adopt Table F of Schedule I of the Act.

The Memorandum defines the relationship between the company and the outsiders, while the Articles define the relationship between the company and its members and among the members themselves.

A new company must prepare its Memorandum and file it with the Registrar before the registration of the company becomes effective. But Articles are not required to be filed for the purpose of registration. A company can adopt Table 'F' if it does not prepare its own Articles.

Any act of the company which is *Ultra Vires* the Memorandum is wholly void and cannot be ratified even by the whole body of shareholders. But, any act which is *Ultra Vires* the Article, but *intra vires* the Memorandum, can be ratified by the shareholders by passing a special resolution.

The Memorandum cannot be altered easily. The procedure laid down in the Act must be followed for altering the various clauses of the Memorandum. In some cases, the approval of the Central Government is required. But, alteration of Articles is not difficult. Articles can be altered by passing a special resolution and the approval from the Central Government is not necessary.

## 19.24 PROVISION RELATED TO PRINTING AND SIGNATURE OF ARTICLES

Articles shall be printed, divided into paragraphs, numbered consecutively and signed by each subscriber of the Memorandum of Association in the presence of at least one witness who shall attest the signatures and shall, likewise, add his address and occupation.

## 19.25 CONTENTS OF THE ARTICLES OF ASSOCIATION

It contains the following matter:

1. The exclusion, whole or in part, of Table F.
2. Share capital.
3. Rights of different classes of shareholders.
4. Allotment of shares.
5. Calls on shares.
6. Lien on shares.
7. Forfeiture of shares.
8. Transfer of shares.
9. Surrender of shares.
10. Share certificate.
11. Issue of share warrants.
12. Increase or decrease of share capital.
13. Conversion of shares into stock.
14. Consolidation and sub-division of shares.
15. Borrowing powers.
16. General meetings, proceedings, thereof, and votes, proxies and polls.
17. Appointment of managerial personnel, *e.g.*, directors, their remuneration, qualifications, powers and proceedings of the Board meetings.
18. Appointment and remuneration of auditors.
19. Dividends and reserves.
20. Accounts and audit.
21. Adoption or execution of preliminary contracts, if any.
22. Capitalization of profits.
23. Notices.
24. Common seal.
25. Winging up.

It should be noted that any provisions of the articles, which is contrary to the provisions of the Companies Act or memorandum, shall be *Ultra Vires* and void.

## 19.26 PROCEDURE FOR THE ALTERATION OF ARTICLES OF ASSOCIATION—SECTION 14

A company has wide powers to alter its Articles to meet the requirements from time to time. Section 8 of the Companies Act, 2013 states that a company cannot alter the Articles of Association without obtaining a prior permission from the Central Government.

A declaration in the meeting of the Board must be taken to change all or any of the regulations of the existing articles, and they shall fix up the day, time, place, and agenda for the general meeting. It should be noted that a company can never replace the existing Articles. It can only change the regulations contained in the Articles.

A proposed alteration conforms to the provisions of the Act and the Memorandum. The change(s) must not increase the liability of any member and must not provide for the expulsion of a member by the company.

A notice calling the general meeting should be sent to every member at least 21 days prior to the meeting wherein the proposed special resolution and the explanation relating to the implications of the proposed change be given.

In case of a listed company, notice shall be send to the respective stock exchange.

A special resolution should be passed by shareholders in the general meeting.

After the Articles have been altered, copy of amended article should be filed with the stock exchange.

A copy of the special resolution along with explanatory statement in Form MGT 14 must be filed with the Registrar.

Necessary changes must be made in all the copies of the Articles.

If the effect of alteration is to convert a public company into a private company, the approval of the tribunal is necessary. Also, a copy of the altered Articles should be filed with the Registrar within 15 days from the date of the receipt of the consent of the tribunal to the alteration.

Once an alteration is made in accordance with provisions, then altered Articles shall be binding on the members in the same way as original Articles.

## 19.27 LIMITATIONS ON ALTERATION OF ARTICLES

A company can alter or add to the Articles of association at any time by passing a **special resolution.** However, the right to alter the Articles is subject to the following limitations or restrictions:

### 19.27.1 Not Inconsistent with Provisions of Any Act

The alteration must not be **inconsistent with any provisions of the Companies Act or any other statute.** For example, where a resolution was passed expelling a member and authorizing the directors to register the transfer of his shares without an instrument of transfer, the resolution was held to be invalid as being against the provision of the Act **(Madhav Ram Chandra Kamath vs Canara Banking Corporation).**

However, Articles may impose on the company conditions stricter than those provided under the law, for example, they may provide that a resolution should be passed by a special majority when the Act requires it to be passed by an ordinary majority.

If the alteration in article will be *Ultra Vires* the memorandum, then it would be void and inoperative. **Allen vs Gold Reefs of West Africa Ltd.**

### 19.27.2 Not Illegal or Against Public Policy

The alteration must not contain anything **illegal or against public policy**.

### 19.27.3 Not inconsistent with the order of a Government or a court

The alteration must not be inconsistent with an order of the Central Government or a Tribunal as the case may be.

### 19.27.4 Must be Bonafide

The alteration must be bonafide for the benefit of the company as a whole. The alteration made shall be valid even if it is likely to affect adversely the interest of some of the members.

### 19.27.5 Must Not Be Fraudulent

If the alteration is for the benefit of majority and it constitutes a fraud on the minority or inflicts hardship on the minority without any corresponding benefit to the company as a whole, it shall be invalid **(Brown vs British Abrasive Wheels Co.).**

### 19.27.6 Must Not Result in Breach of Contract

The alteration must not cause a breach of contract with an outsider. Such an alteration shall be void and the company shall be liable to pay damages to the other party.

### 19.27.7 Must not Increase Liability of the Members

An alteration in the Articles, which has the effect of increasing the liability of the members to contribute to share capital, is not binding on the present members, unless he has given his consent in writing.

An alteration in the Articles which has the effect of converting a public company into a private company shall not be effective unless such an alteration has been approved by the tribunal.

The amended regulation in the Articles of Association cannot operate retrospectively, but only from the date of amendment.

Any alteration made, must be duly incorporated in every copy of the same and every copy of the Articles issued after the date of such alteration must be in accordance with such alteration.

## 19.28 BINDING EFFECTS OF MEMORANDUM AND ARTICLES OF ASSOCIATION

According to Section 10 of the Companies Act, 2013, the Memorandum and Articles of a company, when registered, bind the company and its members as if they, respectively, had been signed by the company and each member. The Memorandum and Articles of Association constitute a binding contract between the company and its each member.

This means that the Articles bind the company to its members and members to the company, members to each other, but do not bind the company or its members to outsiders.

### 19.28.1 Members to the Company

Every member of the company is bound to observe the provisions of the Memorandum and the Articles, as if; each member had signed the same **(Hanuman Prasad Gupta vs Hiralal).** A company can sue its members for the enforcement of these provisions and the members may also be restrained by court from committing the breach of provisions of these documents.

In **Boreland Trustees vs Steel Brothers & Co. Ltd.,** the Articles of the company provided that the shares of any members who became bankrupt should be sold to some other persons at a price to be fixed by the directors. B became bankrupt and his trustee in bankrupt claimed that he was not bound by the Articles of Association and could, therefore, sell the shares as he liked. It was held that the trustee in bankruptcy was bound by the Articles of Association and could not claim the shares against the company.

Each member is not only bound by the covenants of Memorandum and Articles as originally framed but as altered from time to time in accordance with the provisions of the Companies Act.

Shareholders cannot among themselves enter into an agreement which is contrary to or inconsistent with the Articles of Association of the company **[V.B. Rangaraj vs V.b. Gopalakrishana].**

### 19.28.2 Company to the Members

The company is also bound to its members by the provisions of the Articles of Association. Any member is entitled to issue the company or obtain an injunction restraining the company from committing any breach of the Articles or from doing an illegal act. The company is bound to each member in respect of their rights as members. Where a right is conferred by the Articles on a shareholder to record his vote at a company meeting, the chairman of the meeting cannot deprive him of this right.

In **Wood vs Odessa Water Works Co.,** the Articles of Association empowered the company to declare a dividend to be paid to the shareholders with the sanction of the company at general meeting. Instead of paying the dividend in cash, a resolution was passed whereby the dividend was to be paid by issue of debenture bonds. A member filed a suit restraining the company from acting on the resolution. The court granted an injunction restraining the company from acting on the resolution.

These documents bind the company to members in respect of their membership rights and not contractual rights of other kinds.

### 19.28.3 The Members Inter Se

As between the members themselves, they are bound by the provisions of the Articles. The Memorandum and Articles of Association do not constitute express agreement among the members of the company, but each member is bound by these documents on the basis of the implied contract. The Articles regulate their right *inter se*. But such rights can be enforced only through the company.

A shareholder may, however, sue in his own name to restrain another, or others from doing fraudulent or *Ultra Vires* acts. **[Rayfiled vs Hands and Others].** In the Articles provided that every member who intends to transfer shares shall inform the directors who will take the said shares equally between them at a fair value. On their refusal to take the shares, it was held that the directors as members were bound to take shares.

### 19.28.4 Company to Outsiders

Outsider means a person who is not a member of the company. But even a member may be an outsider. **Section 10** creates an obligation binding on the company in its dealings with members in their capacity as members.

The Articles of Association create no contract between the company and outsiders, even though outsiders are named in the Articles in some capacity other than of a member. An outsider is not entitled to enforce the Articles against the company for any breach of right that is conferred on him by the Articles.

In **Browne vs La Trinidad,** the Articles provided that B was to be appointed as director till 1888. But he was removed earlier. The court held that Articles do not constitute a contract between the company and outsider and, therefore, B was not entitled to bring any action against the company.

Even a member cannot enforce provisions of Articles in some capacity other than a member. In **Eley vs the Positive Government Life Assurance Company Ltd.,** the Articles provided that Eley should be the solicitor for life of the company and that he would not be removed from office except for misconduct. He was also a member of the company. Eley acted as solicitor to the company for some years, but he was removed from service without any charge of misconduct. He sued the company for damages for breach of contract. It was held that he had no cause of action, because the Articles did not constitute any contract between the company and himself. Thus, to succeed, the party suing must prove a contract outside and independent of the Articles.

Thus, it can be stated that a company is not bound to outsiders on the basis of Articles. He must prove a contract independent of the Articles of association if he wants to hold the company liable.

**Case Study**

The Articles of a Public Company clearly stated that Mr A will be the solicitor of the company. The Company in its general meeting of the shareholders, resolved unanimously to appoint B in place of Mr A as the solicitor of the company by altering the Articles of Association. Examine, whether the company can do so? State the reasons clearly.

## 19.29 DOCTRINE OF CONSTRUCTIVE NOTICE

The Memorandum and Articles of Association of every company are required to be registered with the Registrar of Companies. And, on registration, documents become public documents. These documents are available for public inspection either in the office of the company or in the office of the Registrar of Companies on payment of fee.

Every person, who deals with the company, is presumed to have read these documents and understood them in their true perspective.

Every person dealing with the company must inspect these documents and make sure that his contract is in conformity with their provisions. Whether he actually reads them or not, he is presumed to have read and understood them.

In **Kotla Venkatswamy v. Ram Murthi,** the Articles provided that all deeds, etc., were to be signed by the managing director, secretary and a working director. A deed signed by the working director and secretary was held to be inoperative and the party was not allowed to seek exemption on the plea that he had not read the Articles.

Accordingly, if a person deals with a company and the transaction turns out to the beyond the powers of the company or its officers as contained in these documents, he cannot enforce it against the company and he shall be personally liable to bear the consequences of such dealings.

***Example***

If the articles provide that a bill of exchange to be effective must be signed by two directors, a person dealing with the company must see that it is so signed; otherwise, he cannot claim under it.

However, the doctrine of constructive notice, discussed here, is subject to one exception, that is, so far as the internal proceedings of the company are concerned, outsiders dealing with the company can assume that everything has been regularly done. This rule is known as the 'doctrine of indoor management'.

## 19.30 DOCTRINE OF INDOOR MANAGEMENT

This rule is based on business convenience and justice. The doctrine of indoor management is an exception to the rule of constructive notice. The doctrine of indoor management imposes an important limitation on the doctrine of constructive notice.

Persons dealing with the company should read these documents and satisfy themselves that the company has the power to enter into the contract, and they are required to do no more. He is not required to examine whether the internal proceedings have been complied with or not. The details of internal procedure are not open for public inspection as the Memorandum and Articles are. Thus, every person dealing with the company is entitled to assume that everything has been done regularly so far as the internal proceedings of the company are concerned. In other words, outsiders can safely assume that provisions of the Articles have been complied with by the company in its internal working. This doctrine seeks to protect the outsiders against the company.

If the Articles of the company give powers to borrow with the sanction of an ordinary resolution in a general meeting, a lender need not enquire whether the general meeting was convened on proper notice, or whether a proper quorum was present at the meeting, or whether the necessary resolution was properly passed. He was entitled to assume that what has been done has been done regularly and can hold the company liable even if internal formalities are found not to have been completed. In other words, if the internal formalities have not been complied with, the contract shall be binding on the company and it shall be liable to outsiders. This rule is known as the doctrine of indoor management.

This rule was first laid down in The **Royal British Bank vs Turquand**. In this case, the directors of a company issued a bond to T. They had the power to issue such bonds, but only subject to the resolution passed at a general meeting of the company. In this case, no such resolution had been passed. It was held that T could recover the amount of the bond from the company on the ground that he was entitled to assume that the resolution had been passed. It was observed that Outsiders are bound to know the external position of the company, but are not bound to know its indoor management.

In the case of **Mahony Vs East Holyford Mining Co.,** article of company suggesting that cheques were to be signed by two named directors and countersigned by the name of a secretary. The secretary of company sent to their banker what purported to be copy of the board resolution naming the directors and secretary. The banker accordingly honoured the cheques accordingly. Subsequently it was found that the directors and the secretary were never appointed. No board meeting was ever held. It was held that bankers were bound to inspect the articles which they did. Beyond that they were neither bound nor entitled to look into the regularity of appointment of the directors and the secretary.

## 19.31 EXCEPTIONS TO THE DOCTRINE OF INDOOR MANAGEMENT

The doctrine of indoor management is subject to the following limitations:

### 19.31.1 Knowledge of Irregularity

The protection under the rule of indoor management cannot be claimed by a person who has the knowledge of the irregularity or constructive notice of irregularity.

In **Howard vs Patent Ivory Manufacturing Co.,** the directors had the power under the Articles to borrow on behalf of the company up to £ 1,000. And for any amount exceeding this sum, the sanction of the shareholders in the general meeting was required. The directors themselves lent £3,500 to the company without the sanction from the shareholders in the general meeting. It was held that the company was liable for £1,000 only.

### 19.31.2 Negligence on the Part of the Outsider

Where the circumstances are of a suspicious nature as to invite further inquiry and the person has failed to enquire into it, he shall not be entitled to protection under this rule.

Similarly, where the transaction is of an unusual nature, the outsider must make detailed inquires.

**Underwood vs Bank of Liverpool:** certain cheques drawn in favour of company were deposited by a director in his personal account. The bank credited the cheques in the account of the directors instead of company's account. The bank argued that they acted on direction of the director of company. The court held that cheque of company could not be given credit to personal account of that director. It is a case of gross negligence on the part of the banker.

### 19.31.3 Forgery

The protection under this doctrine shall not be available where the outsiders have relied upon a forged document, because nothing can validate. A company is not liable for forgeries committed by its officer.

But a company may be held liable for fraudulent acts of its officers acting under their ostensible authority on its behalf.

Share certificate was issued under a common seal of the company. However, signatures of two directors thereon were forged. Shareholders argued that how he can determine forgery, but on the ground of forgery is nullity, certificate was held to be invalid. **(Ruben vs Great Fingall Consolidated Co)**

### 19.31.4 No Knowledge of the Articles

The doctrine of indoor management cannot be invoked in favour of a person who had no knowledge of the Articles of Association of the company.

However, if the contract is within the ostensible authority to bind the company, a company shall be liable for contracts made by him even if he had no knowledge of the articles of company.

### 19.31.5 Acts Outside Apparent Authority

An outsider will not be protected if the act of an officer of a company is one which would not ordinarily be within his powers simply, because under the Articles, power to do the act could have been delegated to him.

In **Anand Bihari Lal vs Dinshaw & Co.,** the plaintiff accepted a transfer of the company's property from its accountant, the transfer was held void. The plaintiff should have seen the power of attorney executed in favour of the accountant by the company.

### 19.31.6 Void or Illegal Transactions

The doctrine of indoor management shall not apply to those transactions, which are void or illegal *ab initio*.

**Case Study**

The secretary of a company issued a share certificate to 'A' under the Company's seal with his own signature and the signature of a director forged by him. 'A' borrowed money from 'B' on the strength of this certificate. 'B' wanted to realise the security and requested the company to register him as a holder of the shares. Explain, whether 'B' will succeed in getting the share registered in his name.

## 19.32 PROSPECTUS

A prospectus, as per **Section 2 (70),** means any documents described or issued as prospectus and includes a red herring prospectus or any notice, circular, advertisement or other document inviting offers from the public for the subscription or purchase of any securities of a body corporate.

A document shall be called a prospectus if it satisfies two conditions:

1. It invites subscriptions to securities; and
2. The aforesaid invitation is made to the public.

As per the Companies Act, 2013, prospectus is required to be issued by a public company when it makes an offer to public to subscribe for securities while public company do not make public offer (*i.e.*, privately placed shares to relatives and friends of the directors), it is not required to prepare prospectus. Therefore, it is necessary to understand what amount as offer to public.

### 19.32.1 What Constitutes an Offer to Public?

**Real test:** It is not who receives offer or the invitation, but who can accept it. If invitation can be accepted by any one whether the prospectus was address to him or not.

An invitation to the public shall include an invitation to any section of the public, whether as members of the company or any other person who is not member as clients of the person.

An invitation shall not be an invitation to the public if it cannot be calculated to result, directly or indirectly, in the shares or debentures becoming available for subscription or purchase by persons other than those receiving the invitation.

**Case Study**

An offer was made by Co. X to the members of Cos. Y and Z to acquire all their shares in these companies in exchange of allotment of shares of Co. X. Whether it could be considered as invitation to public?

**Case Study**

Newspaper advertisement stated, "some shares are still available for sale according to terms of prospectus of a co., which may be obtained on application". Whether newspaper advertisement can be held as prospectus?

## 19.33 CIRCUMSTANCES WHEN THE PROSPECTUS IS NOT REQUIRED TO BE ISSUED

Prospectus is required to be issued only when the public company makes an offer to public to subscribe its shares or debenture. Issue of prospectus by a company is not compulsory in the following cases:

1. It is private company.
2. Public company need not issue a prospectus, if the promoters or directors feel that they can mobilize resources through personal relationship and contracts. Raising capital without issue of prospectus is known as private placement.

3. Where the application form is issued to person to enter into an underwriting agreement with respect to the shares or debentures.
4. Where the application form is issued in relation to shares or debentures not offered to the public.
5. Where the shares or debentures are offered to the existing holders of shares or debentures by way of rights (*i.e.*, rights issue) with or without the right of renunciation in favour of other persons.
6. Where the issue relates to shares or debentures, which are, or to be, uniform in all respects with shares or debentures previously issued and dealt in or quoted on a recognized stock exchange.

## 19.34 ABRIDGED PROSPECTUS—SECTION 33

A prospectus is a very bulky document and, therefore, retail or small investors, generally, do not refer it. Government realized this loophole and, therefore, made provision for abridged prospectus. Section 33 of the Companies Act, 2013, requires that no one shall issue any form of application of shares or debentures of a company unless the same is accompanied by a memorandum containing salient features of prospectus (more commonly known as 'abridged form of prospectus'), as may be prescribed.

It is further required that the abridged prospectus and the share application form should bear the same printed number and the two should be separated by a perforated line. Accordingly, the investor may detach the application form before submitting the same to the company or the designated bankers.

When company has issued abridged prospectus, it is duly bound to furnish prospectus on demand.

## 19.35 STATUTORY REQUIREMENTS IN RELATION TO A PROSPECTUS

A prospectus is, generally, issued after incorporation of the company, and it must contain the matter as specified under the **Companies Act, 2013.**

A prospectus must be **dated** and that date, unless the contrary is proved, be taken as the date of publication of the prospectus. It must be signed by every person who is named therein as a director or proposed director of the company. Where a prospectus is issued in more than one language, a copy of it as issued in each language should be delivered to R.O.C. **Emperor vs Bengal Salt Co.**

Before issue of prospectus to the public, it must be delivered to the registrar for registration. The prospectus must be issued within 90 days after the date on which a copy, thereof, has been delivered for registration.

### 19.35.1 Statement of an Expert

A statement made by an expert shall be included only if expert is or was engaged or interested in the formation or promotion or management of the company and has given his written consent to the issue of the prospectus. Such consent of expert must not be withdrawn by his before the delivery of the prospectus to the Registrar for registration and a statement to that effect, shall be included in the prospectus.

Every prospectus issued shall state that a copy has been delivered to the Registrar and specify attached documents.

The registrar shall not register a prospectus unless all requirements have been complied with and the prospectus is accompanied by the consent in writing of the all person named in the prospectus.

Prospectus shall not be valid if it is issued more than 90 days after the date on which a copy, thereof, delivered to the Registrar.

A prospectus must not include a statement purporting to be made by an expert, unless the expert is a person who is not, and has not been, engaged or interested in the formation or promotion, or in the management, of the company.

Terms of contract mentioned in the prospectus cannot to be varied except subject to the approval in general meeting.

## 19.36 RED HERRING PROSPECTUS—SECTION 32

Provision of 'red herring prospectus' has been made vide Section 32 of Companies Act 2013. Red herring prospectus is used in the book building method of public offer. It is like any other simple prospectus or offer document, but it does not contain information on price of shares and number of securities.

The 'red herring prospectus' means a prospectus which does not have complete particulars on the price of securities offered and the quantum of securities offered. It may give a band or minimum figure of issue size and issue price. Prospective investors bid at different prices at which they would like to subscribe shares. An issue is closed and, then cut-off price is determined. Now, price is fixed. The company is require to file again a prospectus, but with all details of price and number of securities.

## 19.37 THE CONTENTS OF A PROSPECTUS. SECTION 26 AND RULE 3, 5 OF COMPANIES (PROSPECTUS AND ALLOTMENT OF SECURITIES) RULES, 2014

For obtaining a prospectus, a company has to comply with Section 26(1) read with Rule 3 of Companies (Prospectus and Allotment of Securities) Rules, 2014. The following information must be included in a prospectus.

1. Names and addresses of the registered office of the company, company secretary, chief financial officer, auditors, legal advisers, bankers, trustees, if any, underwriters and such other persons as may be prescribed.
2. Dates of the opening and closing of the issue, and declaration about the issue of allotment letters and refunds within the prescribed time.
3. A statement by the Board of Directors about the separate bank account where all mony received out of the issue are to be transferred and disclosure of details of all mony including utilized and unutilized mony out of the previous issue in the prescribed manner.
4. Details about underwriting of the issue.
5. Consent of the directors, auditors, bankers to the issue, expert's opinion, if any, and of such other persons, as may be prescribed.
6. The authority for the issue and the details of the resolution passed therefore.
7. Procedure and time schedule for allotment and issue of securities.
8. Capital structure of the company in the prescribed manner.
9. Main objects of the public offer, terms of the present issue and such other particulars as may be prescribed.
10. Main objects and present business of the company and its location, schedule of implementation of the project;
11. Particulars relating to:
    - management perception of risk factors specific to the project.
    - gestation period of the project.

- extent of progress made in the project.
- deadlines for completion of the project.
- any litigation or legal action pending or taken by a government department or a statutory body during the last five years immediately preceding the year of the issue of prospectus against the promoter of the company.

12. Minimum subscription, amount payable by way of premium, issue of shares otherwise than on cash.
13. Details of the directors including their appointments and remuneration, and such particulars of the nature and extent of their interests in the company as may be prescribed.
14. Disclosures in such a manner as may be prescribed about sources of promoter's contribution.

### 19.37.1 Reports with Prospectus

Every prospectus shall set out the following reports for the purpose of financial information:

1. Reports by the auditors of the company with respect to its profits and losses, and assets and liabilities, and such other matters as may be prescribed.
2. Reports relating to profits and losses for each of the five financial years immediately preceding the financial year of the issue of prospectus including such reports of its subsidiaries and in such manner as may be prescribed. Where company has not completed five financial years than such report for all financial years is required.
3. Reports made in the prescribed manner by the auditors upon the profits and losses of the business of the company, for each of the five financial years immediately preceding the issue and assets and liabilities of its business on the last date to which the accounts of the business were made up, being a date not more than one hundred and eighty days before the issue of the prospectus. Where the company has not completed five financial years than such reports for all financial years is required.
4. Reports about the business or transaction to which the proceeds of the securities are to be applied directly or indirectly.

### 19.37.2 Declaration of Compliance

Every prospectus shall make a declaration about the compliance of the provisions of this Act and a statement to the effect that nothing in the prospectus is contrary to the provisions of this Act, the Securities Contracts (Regulation) Act, 1956 and the Securities and Exchange Board of India Act, 1992 and the rules and regulations made thereunder.

## 19.38 REFUSAL TO REGISTRAR PROSPECTUS BY THE REGISTRAR OF COMPANIES

Section 26 provides that the Registrar shall not register a prospectus, if:

1. It is not dated.
2. It does not comply with the requirements of Section 26 as to the matters and reports to be set out in it.

3. It contains statements or reports of experts engaged or interested in the formation or promotion or management of the company.
4. It includes a statement purported to be made by an expert without a statement that he has given and has not withdrawn his consent to the manner of its inclusion therein.
5. It is not signed by every person who is named therein as a director or proposed director of the company or by his agent authorized in writing.
6. It is not accompanied by the consent in writing of the auditor, legal advisor, attorney, solicitor, banker, or broker of the company or intended company, to act in that capacity.

## 19.39 SHELF PROSPECTUS AND INFORMATION MEMORANDUM—SECTION 31

'Shelf prospectus' is a prospectus in respect of which the securities or class of securities included therein are issued for subscription in one or more issues over a certain period without issue of further prospectus.

A company filing a shelf prospectus with the registrar shall not be required to file prospectus afresh at every stage of offer of securities by it within a period of validity of such a shelf prospectus.

A company filing a shelf prospectus shall be required to file an information memorandum on all material facts relating to new charges created, changes in the financial position as have occurred between the first offer of securities, previous offer of securities and the succeeding offer of securities within such time as may be prescribed by the Central Government, prior to making of a second or subsequent offer of securities under the shelf prospectus.

An information memorandum shall be issued to the public along with shelf prospectus filed at the stage of the first offer of securities and such prospectus shall be valid for a period of one year from the date of opening of the first issue of securities under that prospectus:

Provided that where an update of information memorandum is filed every time an offer of securities is made, such memorandum together with the shelf prospectus shall constitute the prospectus.

The information memorandum and shelf prospectus carry the same obligations as are applicable in the case of a prospectus.

Any variation or changes between the dates of two public issues is highlighted by issing an information memorandum.

## 19.40 MISSTATEMENT IN PROSPECTUS

Misstatement in prospectus means a statement included in a prospectus shall be deemed to be untrue, if the statement is misleading in the form and context in which it is included.

Where the omission from a prospectus of any matter is calculated to mislead, the prospectus shall be deemed, in respect of such omission, to be a prospectus in which an untrue statement is included.

Misleading statement means a statement made by a person who does not care whether the statement is true or false. Fraud means any act committed with the intent to deceive somebody. It includes the deliberate suggestion of an untrue fact by someone, the active concealment of a fact by one having knowledge of the fact, a promise made without any intention of performing it, or any other act intent to deceive.

***Example***

A statement in prospectus says that the share capital has been subscribed when it has only been allotted in fully-paid shares to company's contractor. It was held that it is misstatement in prospectus.

***Example***

A statement says that two leading businessmen of repute have agreed to become directors of a company when they had only expressed their willingness to help the company. It was held that it is misstatement in prospectus.

**Case Study**

A statement in the offer document says that the proceeds from the issue of debentures were to be utilized for improving and developing the business, whereas the actual object of issuing debentures was to pay-off the past liabilities. Can it be considred as a misstatement in the prospectus?

**Case Study**

Statement in the prospectus says that the directors and their friends have subscribed a large portion of capital of a company. Now, they are offering the remaining shares to the public, whereas the fact was that they had only subscribed ten shares each. Is there a misrepresentation in the prospectus?

## 19.41 LIABILITY FOR MISSTATEMENT IN PROSPECTUS—SECTION 34–35

It may be grouped under the following two heads:

1. Civil liability
2. Criminal liability

### 19.41.1 Civil liability—Section 35

Where a person has subscribed for securities of a company acting on any statement included, or the inclusion or omission of any matter, in the prospectus which is misleading and has sustained any loss or damage as a consequences thereof, the company and every person who:

1. Is a director of the company at the time of the issue of the prospectus;
2. Has authorized himself to be named and is named in the prospectus as a director of the company, or has agreed to become such director, either immediately or after an interval of time;
3. Is a promoter of the company;
4. Has authorized issue of prospectus, and
5. Is an expert,

shall, be liable to pay compensation to every person who has sustained such loss or damage.

### 19.41.2 Criminal Liability—Section 34

Where any prospectus is issued or circulated or distributed, which includes any statement which is untrue or misleading in form or context in which it is included or where any inclusion or omission of any matter is likely to mislead, then every person who authorizes the issue of such prospectus shall be liable under Section 447 for fraud.

### 19.41.3 Class Action—Section 37

Complain may be filed under Sections 34 or 35 by group of persons or association of persons who are affected by misleading statement in public issue. When a group of affected parties jointly file a complaint, it is known as class action.

**19.41.3.1 Remedies Available Against the Company to a Person Who Subscribe for securities on faith of misleading prospectus** The injured party may refuse to take securities and get repayment of the amount paid on the securities. But, for this right, he must prove that:

1. The prospectus was issued by or on behalf of the company.
2. There was a material misrepresentation on fact.

However, the right to rescind the contract is lost in the following circumstances:

1. If the allottee does not take steps to set aside the contract within a reasonable time after he comes to know of the misrepresentation.
2. By affirmation of the contract by the allottee after he discovers the misrepresentation.

***Example***

Execution of a transfer for selling shares, voting at a general meeting, accepting dividends, etc.

3. If the company goes into liquidation.

The allottee is also entitled to sue the company for damages. But, in order to succeed, fraudulent misrepresentation must be proved. If the allottee wishes to claim damages, he must surrender the shares to the company. He cannot do the both to retain the securities and claim damages.

**19.41.3.2 Remedies Available Against the Promoters and Directors** The following are some of the remedial measures available to the subscribers who were deceived because of any misleading statements in the prospectus:

1. As per Section 37, a suit may be filed or any other action may be taken under Section 34 or Section 35 or Section 36 by any person, or group of persons, or any association of persons, affected by any misleading statement, or the inclusion, or omission of any matter in the prospectus.
2. He may take proceedings to repudiate the contract and require repayment of his money with interest.
3. He may, in respect of any misleading statement or the inclusion or omission of any matter in the prospectus, bring an action against the directors and promoters, for the recovery of compensation.
4. He may, bring an action for damages against the directors and other persons responsible for failure to disclose matters in a prospectus.
5. He may, in respect of any misleading statement or the inclusion or omission of any matter in the prospectus, bring an action against directors or those who are responsible for the prospectus.

In addition to directors and promoters the liability under the section also attaches to a person who has authorized the issue of the prospectus. However, the words cannot reasonably be held to apply to such persons as bankers, brokers, accountants, solicitors and engineers who merely consent to their names appearing as such in the prospectus.

**Case Study**

Modern Furniture Limited was willing to purchase a teakwood estate in Chhattisgarh State. Its prospectus contained some important extracts from an expert report giving the number of teakwood trees and other relevant information in the estate in the Chhattisgarh State. The report was found inaccurate. Mr 'X' purchased the shares of Modern Furniture Limited on the basis of the above statement given in the prospectus. Will Mr 'X' have any remedy against the company?

## 19.42 DEFENSES AVAILABLE TO DIRECTORS IN CASE OF MISLEADING PROSPECTUS

However, the person other than an expert sought to be made liable may escape his liability, if he proves:

### 19.42.1 Withdrawal of Consent

That he withdraws his consent to become a director before the issue of the prospectus, and that it was issued without his authority or consent.

### 19.42.2 Issue Without Knowledge

That the prospectus was issued without his knowledge or consent and that on becoming aware of its issue, he forthwith gave public notice that it was issued without his knowledge or consent.

### 19.42.3 Ignorance of Untrue Nature of the Statement

That he believed, on reasonable grounds, that the statement was true.

### 19.42.4 Official Documents

That the statement was a correct and fair representation of a public official document.

### 19.42.5 Statement of Expert

A director or promoter may escape from his liabilities where he proves that the statement was made on the authority of an expert who was competent to make it and that person had given the consent and had not withdrawn it.

## 19.43 DEFENSES AVAILABLE TO EXPERTS IN CASE OF MISLEADING PROSPECTUS

An expert can escape liability if he proves that:

1. He withdrew his consent in writing before delivering a copy of the prospectus for registration.
2. After the delivery of the copy of the prospectus for registration, but before allotment thereunder, he, on becoming aware of the untrue statement, withdrew his consent in writing and gave reasonable public notice of the withdrawal and of the reasons therefore.
3. He was competent to make the statement and that he had reasonable ground to believe and did up to the time of the allotment of the shares or debentures, believe that the statement was true.

## LIST OF LANDMARK JUDGEMENTS

1. ***Malahati Tea Syndicate Ltd vs Revenue officer (1973)***

   After change of name has been registered by the Registrar of Companies, a company should commence legal proceeding in its new name.

2. ***Weeek vs Properts (1873)***

   If director of a company act beyond his authority, he is personally liable.

3. ***Brown vs British Abrasive Wheel Co. Ltd (1919)***

   Alteration to article of association must not constitute a fraud on the minority shareholders.

4. ***Sidebottom vs Kershaw Lesse Co. Ltd (1920)***

   Alteration to the article of association must be in good faith and for the benefit of the company as a whole.

5. ***Boreland's Trustee vs Steel Brothers & Co. Ltd (1901)***

   Members of a company are bound to company by provisions of memorandum and articles.

6. ***Wood vs Odessa Water Works Co. (1889)***

   The company is also bound to the members by the provisions of the memorandum and the articles of association.

7. ***Eley vs Positive Govt. Security Life Assn. Co. (1876)***

   Article of association create no contract between a company and outsiders.

8. ***Kotla VenkatSwamy vs Ramamurthi (1934)***

   Every person who is dealing with a company must have knowledge of the memorandum and the articles of association.

9. ***Howard vs Patent Ivory Mfg. Co. (1888)***

   Person cannot take benefit of doctrine of indoor management when he has knowledge of irregularities on the part of a company.

10. ***Ruben vs Great Fingall Ltd (1906)***

    For application of the doctrine of indoor management, transaction should be genuine (i.e., without forgery).

11. ***Forest vs Manchester Etc. Railway Company (1861)***

    Any activity which is incidental for the purpose of achieving the main object of a company is intra-vires.

12. ***Rama Corporation vs Proved Tin and General Investment Co. (1952)***

    Doctrine of indoor management is not applicable when person dealing with a company has no knowledge of the articles of association.

13. ***New Brnswick Co. vs Muggeridge (1860)***

    Nothing should be stated in the prospectus as a fact which is not so, and no fact should be admitted, which might affect the degree of judgment of the investor.

14. ***Peak vs Gurnery (1873)***

    A person who purchase shares in the open market has no remedy against a company or director, even if he has referred the prospectus.

**15.** ***Diwanchand vs Gujranwala Sugar Mills (1937)***

A company is liable for false statement in the prospectus when prospectus is issued by or on behalf of company.

## TEST YOUR KNOWLEDGE

1. What is memorandum of association? What are its different clauses? **(Ref. Para-19.1,19.5)**
2. The memorandum of association is unalterable in character. Explain. **(Ref. Para-19.1)**
3. What are the importance of memorandum? **(Ref. Para-1,19. 2)**
4. Explain the purpose of memorandum. **(Ref. Para-19.2)**
5. Is the memorandum of company required to be printed? if so, explain the relevant rules. **(Ref. Para-19.3)**
6. Write a short note on the form of the memorandum of association. **(Ref. Para-19.4)**
7. What are the legal requirements of the name clause of the memorandum of association? **(Ref. Para-19.6)**
8. Discuss the significance of the registered office clause in the memorandum of association. **(Ref. Para-19.7)**
9. Where to display the address of the registered office? **(Ref. Para-19.8)**
10. The object clause is critical for the business activities of a company. Comment. **(Ref. Para-19.9)**
11. What are the legal requirements as to the liability clause? Can liability of a member be increased? **(Ref. Para-19.10)**
12. What information should be provided under the capital clause of the memorandum? **(Ref. Para-19.11)**
13. What are the requirements of the association clause? Can it be altered? **(Ref. Para-19.12)**
14. How a change can be effected in the name clause? **(Ref. Para-19.13)**
15. Write down steps to change the registered office from one place to another within the same city. **(Ref. Para-19. 14)**
16. State the procedure to be followed by a company for change in registered office from one place to another within same state. **(Ref. Para-19.16)**
17. State the procedure to be followed by a company to shift its registered office from one state to another state. **(Ref. Para-19.17)**
18. What is the procedure to alter the object clause of the memorandum of association? **(Ref. Para-19.18)**
19. How the liability clause can be altered? **(Ref. Para-19.19)**
20. What do you mean by the doctrine of *ultra-vires*? **(Ref. Para-19.20)**
21. Any act which is *ultra-vires* to the directors is void—Comment. **(Ref. Para-19.20)**
22. What are the consequences of the *ultra-vires* act? **(Ref. Para-19.21)**
23. What is an article of association? Does every company require articles ? **(Ref. Para-19.22)**
24. Distinguish between article and memorandum. **(Ref. Para-19.23)**
25. The article of association of a company is subordinate to the company's memorandum of association—Comment. **(Ref. Para-19.23)**
26. Explain the provisions related to printing and signature of article. **(Ref. Para-19.24)**
27. What are the content of the article of association? **(Ref. Para-19.25)**
28. Can company alter article of association? If so, then how? **(Ref. Para-19.26)**

29. The power to alter article is wide yet it is subject to large number of limitations—Comment. **(Ref. Para-19.27)**
30. Explain that article is binding contract between company and its member and member *inter-se*. **(Ref. Para-19.28)**
31. Is the company liable to outsiders by whatever is contained in the article ? **(Ref. Para-19.28)**
32. Write a short note on the doctrine of constructive notice. **(Ref. Para-19.29)**
33. Explain the doctrine laid down in Turquand's case. **(Ref. Para-19.30)**
34. What are the exception to the doctrine of indoor management. **(Ref. Para-19.31)**
35. What is prospectus? Is it compulsory for every company to issue prospectus? **(Ref. Para-19.32)**
36. Explain the term 'invitation to public' with reference to prospectus. **(Ref. Para-19.32)**
37. When a company is not required to issue a prospectus? **(Ref. Para-19.33)**
38. Write a short note on abridged prospectus. **(Ref. Para-19.34)**
39. Steps requirement in relation to prospectus. **(Ref. Para-19.35)**
40. What is red-herring prospectus? What are its unique features? **(Ref. Para-19.36)**
41. What are the contents of a prospectus? **(Ref. Para-19.37)**
42. When registrar of company shall refuse to register the prospectus? **(Ref. Para-19.38)**
43. What is self prospectus? Which company can issue it? **(Ref. Para-19.39)**
44. Write short a note on misstatement in prospectus? **(Ref. Para-19.40)**
45. Who are liable for misstatement in prospectus? **(Ref. Para-19.41)**
46. Explain the remedial measures available to the shareholder, who had applied for shares on the faith of false prospectus. **(Ref. Para-19.41)**
47. Discuss a company's liability for misstatement in prospectus. **(Ref. Para-19.41)**
48. What defenses are available to directors of a company for misstatement in prospectus? **(Ref. Para-19.42)**
49. What defenses are available to promoters of company for misstatement in prospectus? **(Ref. Para-19.42)**
50. What defenses are available to the experts of a company for misstatement in the prospectus? **(Ref. Para-19.43)**

## MULTIPLE-CHOICE QUESTIONS

1. The doctrine of indoor management is an __________ to the doctrine of constructive notice
   (i) Exception
   (ii) Extension
   (iii) Alternative
   (iv) None of these
2. The doctrine of __________ does not apply to acts *void ab-initio.*
   (i) Ultra virus
   (ii) Intra virus
   (iii) Constructive notice
   (iv) Indoor management
3. An act *ultra virus* the directors can be rectified if it is not *ultra-vires*
   (i) The articles
   (ii) The memorandum
   (iii) Company Act
   (iv) Both (ii) and (iii)

4. The lending of funds *ultra-vires*, the company has no rights
   (i) Under the company's act; (iii) under equity;
   (ii) contract act; (iv) none of these.
5. If a new company gets registered with a name which resembles the name of the existing company, then to whom it may apply?
   (i) Central government (iii) ROC
   (ii) SEBI (iv) None of these
6. In case of forgeries, acts done in the name of the company are
   (i) Valid (iii) *Void ab Initio*
   (ii) Void (iv) None of these
7. Signature of memorandum and articles should be done by __________ number of persons in case of a public company
   (i) 7 (iii) 4
   (ii) 5 (iv) None of these
8. Signature of memorandum and articles should be done by __________number of persons in case of private company
   (i) 3 (iii) 2
   (ii) 4 (iv) None of these
9. Can a company sign on behalf of a person in the memorandum and the articles?
   (i) Yes (ii) No
10. Can a minor be a subscriber to the memorandum?
    (i) Yes (ii) No
11. Can foreigners be subscriber to the memorandum?
    (i) Yes (ii) No
12. In the MOA, there are six clauses. We can alter all clauses expect one clause. Which one is that clause?
    (i) Objects Clause; (iii) Association clause;
    (ii) Name clause; (iv) None of these.
13. Address of the registered office is included in ____________
    (i) MOA; (iii) Balance Sheet;
    (ii) AOA; (iv) None of these.
14. Which of the following need not have an MOA?
    (i) Public company; (iii) Government company;
    (ii) Private company; (iv) Statutory Corporation
15. *Ultra-vires* means
    (i) Beyond the power; (iii) Both;
    (ii) Within the power; (iv) None of these
16. *Ultra-vires* loans granted by the company are
    (i) Void; (iii) Valid;
    (ii) Voidable; (iv) None of these.
17. _____ is the charter of a company.
    (i) Memorandum; (iii) Both
    (ii) Articles; (iv) None of these.

18 A private company need not issue prospectus.
(i) Yes (ii) No

19. Prospectus is required to be issued when right issues are made
(i) Yes (ii) No

20. Prospectus is not required to be issued when sweat equity shares are issued to directors and employees
(i) Yes (ii) No

21. Prospectus is required to be issued when issue is for employees under employee stock option scheme
(i) Yes (ii) No

22. When there is an untrue statement in a prospectus, who can sue?
(i) Applicant under IPO; (iii) Purchaser from shareholder;
(ii) Purchaser from stock exchange; (iv) Any person

23. Under which section, the definition of prospectus is given?
(i) 2 (30) (iii) 2 (34)
(ii) 2 (32) (iv) 2 (70)

24. Which of the following are not required for issuing a prospectus?
(i) Private company; (iii) Sweat equity issue;
(ii) In case of right issue; (iv) All these.

25. _______are the prospectus issued instead of full prospectus.
(i) Abridged prospectus; (iii) Shelf prospectus;
(ii) Statement in lieu; (iv) Red herring prospectus.

26. _______includes an engineer, valuer, accountant
(i) Expert; (iii) Auditor;
(ii) Promoter; (iv) Director

27. _________ prospectus were issued in case where securities were issued in stages.
(i) Deemed; (iii) Red herring;
(ii) Shelf; (iv) None of these

28. ________are required to file prior to making second and subsequent issue of securities in case shelf prospectus are filed:
(i) Information memorandum; (iii) Form PAS 3;
(ii) Information articles; (iv) None of these

29. Information memorandum + shelf prospectus together constitutes________________
(i) Memorandum; (iii) Prospectus;
(ii) Articles; (iv) None of these

30. Validity period of shelf prospectus is _______
(i) 1 year; (iii) 3 years;
(ii) 2 years; (iv) 4 years

31. _________ prospectus were issued in order to test the market before finalizing issue size/price.
(i) Deemed; (iii) Red herring;
(ii) Shelf; (iv) None of these

32. When there is an untrue statement in the prospectus. The shareholders who subscribed in the secondary market can sue the company
    (i) Yes (ii) No
33. When there is any untrue statement in the prospectus. The shareholders who were a subscriber to the memorandum can sue the company
    (i) Yes (ii) No
34. Because of misrepresentation in the prospectus, an expert will be criminally liable.
    (i) Yes (ii) No
35. The date of opening of the subscription list means the beginning of the ________from the day of the issue of prospectus.
    (i) 5th; (iii) 10th;
    (ii) 3rd; (iv) 20th
36. Which document is/are alterable in the case of a company?
    (i) Article of Association; (iii) Prospectus;
    (ii) Memorandum of Association; (iv) Both (i) and (ii)

## ANSWER KEYS

| | | | |
|---|---|---|---|
| **1.** (i) | **10.** (ii) | **19.** (i) | **28.** (i) |
| **2.** (i) | **11.** (i) | **20.** (i) | **29.** (iii) |
| **3.** (ii) | **12.** (iii) | **21.** (ii) | **30.** (i) |
| **4.** (i) | **13.** (i) | **22.** (i) | **31.** (iii) |
| **5.** (i) | **14.** (ii) | **23.** (iv) | **32.** (ii) |
| **6.** (iii) | **15.** (i) | **24.** (i) | **33.** (ii) |
| **7.** (i) | **16.** (i) | **25.** (i) | **34.** (ii) |
| **8.** (iii) | **17.** (i) | **26.** (i) | **35.** (i) |
| **9.** (i) | **18.** (i) | **27.** (ii) | **36.** (iv) |

# 20

# Companies Act, 2013: Share Capital and Transfer of Shares

## Learning objectives

*After reading this chapter, you will be able to understand:*

- Share capital and types of shares
- Allotments of shares and rules for allotment
- Voting rights of shareholders
- Issue of shares at par, premium and discount
- Underwriting and brokerage
- Alteration of share capital and reduction of share capital
- Forfeiture, surrender and lien on shares
- Bonus and rights issue
- Calls on share, calls in arrear and calls paid in advance
- Buy-back of shares
- Procedure for acquiring membership of a company
- Termination of membership
- Procedure for transfer of shares
- Transmission of shares
- Nomination of shares

## 20.1 SHARE CAPITAL

The term 'share capital' is used to mean the capital raised by the company through the issue of shares. The shares issued by a company can be either equity shares or preference shares.

The memorandum of the company provides for the 'share capital' clause. Companies limited by guarantee or unlimited companies need not have share capital. Various terms used with reference to capital can be understood as under:

### 20.1.1 Authorized Capital—Section 2(8)

Authorised capitalis the sum stated in the Memorandum of Association as the capital of the company with which it is to be registered. It is also known as nominal or registered capital. The sum so stated is the maximum amount which the company can raise by issuing shares. This amount is divided into shares of fixed denominations.

### 20.1.2 Issued Capital—Section 2(50)

A company may not issue the entire authorised capital at once, i.e., only a part of the authorised capital which the company needs for the time being may be issued. Thus, issued capital is that part of the authorised capital which is offered to the public for subscription in the form of shares,

### 20.1.3 Subscribed Capital—Section 2(86)

Subscribed capital is that part of 'issued capital' for which applications have been received from the public.

### 20.1.4 Called-up Capital—Section 2(15)

Called-up capital is that part of the subscribed capital which has been called up or demanded by the company. Usually the company does not demand the entire amount due on the share at a time, but calls the amount in two or three installments.

### 20.1.5 Paid up Capital—Section 2(64)

Sometimes, subscribers for shares may fail to pay the full amount called up from them. That portion of the called-up capital which is actually paid by shareholders is termed as the paid-up capital.

### 20.1.6 Uncalled Capital

Uncalled capital is the total amount not called up on shares issued. However, the subscribers continue to remain liable for this amount and have to pay it when they are called upon to do so.

***Example***

A company has an authorised capital of ₹ 5,00,000 divided into 50,000 shares of ₹ 10 each; it may decide to issue 20,000 shares of ₹ 10 each. In that case the issued capital shall be ₹ 2,00,000. If the company receivesapplications for 18,000 shares, the subscribed capital shall be ₹ 1,80,000. If the company has calledup ₹ 5 per share, then its called-up capital shall be ₹ 90,000. Against the call money of ₹ 90,000, if company has received ₹ 80,000, then the paid-up capital shall be ₹ 80,000.

### 20.1.7 Reserve Capital

It is that part of the uncalled capital which cannot be called by the company except in the event of winding up. Reserve capital cannot be converted into ordinary capital without the permission of the court.

## 20.2 NATURE OF SHARES

According to Section 2 (84) of the Companies Act, 2013, "a share means a share in the share capital of a company, and includes stock."

In Boreland Trustees vs Steel Bros. & Co., it is defined as the interest of the shareholder in the company measured by a sum of money, for the purpose of liability in the first place, and of dividend in the second but also consisting of a series of mutual covenants entered into by all the shareholder inter se in accordance with the Companies Act.

According to Section 44, the shares, debentures or other interest of any member in a company shall be movable property, transferable in the manner provided by the Articles of the company.

Shares are treated as 'goods' under the Sale of Goods Act and they can be transferred to other persons.

### 20.2.1 Types of Shares

The shares which can be issued by a company are of two types, namely,

1. Equity share capital with a voting right or with differential rights as to dividend, voting or otherwise.
2. Preference shares.

As per Section 43 of the Companies Act, 2013, a company limited by shares can issue only the above two types of shares.

A share signifies the following rights or interest in a company:

1. The interest of a shareholder in the company
2. The right to receive dividend
3. The right to attend and vote at meetings, and receive a share in surplus assets in the event of winding up.
4. The liability of the shareholder to pay calls on share until fully paid up.
5. The right of the shareholder to transfer the share subject to the Articles of Association.
6. Binding covenants on the part of the company as well as the shareholder, as given in the Articles of the company.

## 20.3 EQUITY SHARES

Equity shares are those which are not preference shares. After satisfying the rights of preference shares, the equity shares shall be entitled to a share in the remaining amount of distributable net profits of the company.

The dividend on equity shares is not fixed and may vary from year to year depending upon the amount of profit available. The rate of dividend is decided by the board of the company and approved by shareholders in the annual general meeting.

Equity shareholders have a right to vote on every resolution placed in the meeting and the voting rights shall be in proportion to the paid-up equity capital. Equity shares are also known as ordinary shares.

## 20.4 PREFERENCE SHARES

Preference shares are those shares which have a preferential right in respect of the payment of dividend and with respect to the repayment of the capital. The dividend may consist of a fixed amount or an amount calculated at a fixed rate. They will have a first charge on the distributable amount of profits. A company can issue preference shares by passing a special resolution.

Preference shareholders can vote only on such resolutions which directly affect the rights attached to the preference shares. However, if the preference dividend is not paid fully for more than two years, the preference shareholders shall also get voting right on every resolution placed before the company(as per Section 47, Companies Act, 2013).

## 20.5 KINDS OF PREFERENCE SHARES

Preference shares may be of the following kinds:

### 20.5.1 Cumulative and Non-cumulative Preference Shares

Cumulative preference shares are those which are assured of dividends every year. In the case of cumulative preference share, if in a particular year there are no profits to pay the dividends, the preference dividends shall accumulate and must be paid out of the profits of succeeding years. In subsequent years if there are sufficient profits, the accumulated arrears of dividend will have to be paid along with the dividend for the current year before paying dividend to other shareholders.

All preference shares are *assumed to be cumulative* unless stated to the contrary in the Articles of the company.

On the other hand, in the case of *non-cumulative preference shares, the unpaid preference dividends do not accumulate but lapse*, i.e., the unpaid dividend is not carried forward.

### 20.5.2 Participating and Non-participating Preference Shares

A further preference share can be divided between participating and non-participating preference shares. Participating preference shares are those which, in addition to their preferential dividend, are also entitled to participate in the surplus profits which remain after paying dividend to equity shareholder. If the *articles are silent, all preference shares are deemed to be non-participating*.

Non-participating preference shares are those, which are not entitled to participate in the surplus profits or surplus assets.

### 20.5.3 Redeemable and Irredeemable Preference Shares

Redeemable preference shares are those, the amount of which can be paid back to the holders of such shares. A company limited by shares, if *authorised by its Articles*, may issue preference shares which are to be repaid after a certain fixed period not later than 20 years at the option of company.

Redeemable preference shares may be redeemed:

1. At the fixed time or on happening of particular event;
2. Any time at the company's option; or
3. Any time at the shareholders option.

Irredeemable preference shares are not redeemable except on the winding up of the company.

However companies engaged in the setting up and dealing with infrastructural projects may issue preference shares for a period exceeding 20 years but not exceeding 30 days, subject to the redemption of minimum 10% of such preference shares per year from the 21st year onward or earlier, on proportionate basis, at the option of the preference shareholders.

### 20.5.4 Convertible and Non-convertible Preference Shares

Convertible preference shares are those which can be converted into equity shares within a certain period. The holders of such shares have the right to convert these shares into equity shares. Non-convertible preference shares are those which cannot be converted into equity shares.

## 20.6 REDEMPTION OF REDEEMABLE PREFERENCE SHARES (SECTION 55)

Preference shares, the amount of which can be refunded to the holders of such shares are termed as redeemable preference shares. The paying back of capital is called redemption.

A company limited by shares may, if so authorised by its Articles, issue preference shares which are, at the option of the company, liable to be redeemed.

Such shares can be redeemed only out of the following amounts:

1. The profits of the company, which are available for dividend.
2. The proceeds of fresh issue of shares which are issued for the purpose of redemption.

If any premium is payable on redemption, it must be paid out of the profits or out of the company's securities premium account.If such shares are redeemed out of profits, then the amount equal to the amount paid on redemption must be transferred to a reserve fund to be called 'capital redemption reserve account'.

Redemption of preference shares under Section 55 shall not be taken as reducing the amount of its authorised capital. The redemption of preference shares must be notified to the registrar of companies within 30 days of the date of redemption.

If a company is not in a position to redeem preference shares or pay dividend as per terms of issue, then it may, with the consent of three-fourth of the preference shareholders and with approval of tribunal,issue further redeemable preference shares equal to the amounts due in respect of the unredeemed preference shares.On the issue of such further redeemable preference shares, the unredeemed shares shall be deemed to have been redeemed. The tribunal, at the time of approval, shall order the redemption of preference shares held by such preference shareholders who have not consented to further issue of preference shares.

## 20.7 EQUITY SHARES WITH DIFFERENTIAL RIGHTS OR NON-VOTINGSHARES—RULE 4 OF COMPANIES (SHARE CAPITAL AND DEBENTURES) RULES, 2014

A company can issue equity shares with similar voting rights or differential voting rights. However, not all companies are eligible to issue equity shares with differential voting rights. Equity shares with differential rights are also known as differential equity or non-voting shares. The following conditions shall be fulfilled to issue differential equity shares:

1. The company must have distributable profits for the last three years.
2. The company must not have been defaulted in filing of financial statement and annual returns for the last three financial years.
3. The company must not have failed to pay dividend after its declaration or repay deposit or interest thereon.
4. The Article of the company must authorise issue of such shares.

5. The company must not have defaulted in investors' grievances procedure.
6. The proportion of shares with differential voting rights must not exceed 26% of the post total issued share capital.
7. The company must not have defaulted in repayment of term loan obtained from a public financial institution,a state level financial institution or a scheduled bank.
8. The company must not have defaulted in any dues in respect of statutory dues relating to its employees or defaulted in crediting the amount in investor education and protection fund (IEPF) to the central government.
9. The company should not have been penalised by a court or tribunal during the last three years for any offence under RBI Act, 1934, SEBI Act, 1992, Securities Contract Regulations Act, 1956, Foreign Exchange Management Act, 1999, or any other special act, under which such companies are regulated by sectorial regulators.

### 20.7.1 Procedure

If the company fulfils all conditions as above, it is required to convenea general meeting and pass an ordinary resolution approving the issue of differential equity.In case of listed company, this resolution must be approved by a postal ballot.

## 20.8 VOTING RIGHTS TO SHAREHOLDERS—SECTION 47

Equity shareholders enjoy voting rights for every subject matter while preference shareholders do not have voting right under usual circumstances.

### 20.8.1 Voting Rights of Equity Shareholders

In the case of voting on show of hands, every equity shareholder has one vote irrespective of his holding. In the case of voting on poll, every equity shareholder has votesin proportion to paid-up capital.

### 20.8.2 Voting Rights of Preference Shareholders

Preference shareholders have voting rights on every resolution that directly affects their right. If dividend has been unpaid for any class of preference shares for two years or more, they shall have voting rights on every resolution.

The proportion of voting rights of equity shareholders to the voting rights of preference shareholders shall be in the same proportion as the paid-up capital in respect of the equity shares bears to the paid-up capital in respect of the preference shares.

***Example***

Total paid-up share capital of a company is ₹ 400. It is divided into equity share capital of ₹ 300 and preference share capital of 100. A person holding 20 shares shall have 20% voting rightunder preference share capital but 5% voting rightfor total capital.

### 20.8.3 Voting Rights of Equity Shareholders with Differential Voting Rights

Equity shareholders with differential voting rights have voting rights as per the terms of issue. Non-voting equity shareholders do not have voting right.

## 20.9 ALLOTMENT OF SECURITIES

When a public limited company issues a prospectus inviting the public to subscribe to its securities and people apply for them, this application is an offer to buy the securities and when such applications are accepted by the company, it is termed as 'allotment'.

Allotment results in a binding contract between the company and the prospective security holder. The rules of offer and acceptance are applicable to the application and allotment of securities.

Allotment of shares means the appropriation, by the Board of Directors of a company out of the previously unappropriated capital of the company, of a certain number of shares to persons who have made application for shares.

It is in fact a division of share capital into definite shares of particular value and of different classes and assignment of such shares singly or numerously to different persons.

Allotment is done by resolution of the Board of Directors, as per the Articles of the company. Shares come into existence on allotment. Thus, allotment is the fresh issue of shares. The re-issue of forfeited share cannot be called as allotment; it is simply a sale of shares.

## 20.10 GENERAL PROVISIONS FOR THE ALLOTMENT OF SECURITIES

For an allotment to be valid, it must satisfy the requirement relating to offer and its acceptance. These may briefly summed up as under:

### 20.10.1 By Proper Authority

The allotment of securities must be made by proper authority and the proper authority is the Board of Directors. This authority may, however, be delegated by the Board as per the provisions of Articles of the company. Any allotment of securities made by an improper authority will be void.

### 20.10.2 Within a Reasonable Time

The allotment must be made within a reasonable period of time. What is the reasonable time is a question of fact in each case. As per contract law, the offer must be accepted within a reasonable time. If the application for securities is not accepted within a reasonable time, then the applicant may refuse to take the securities.

### 20.10.3 Must be Communicated

The allotment, to be legally effective and binding, must be communicated to the applicant. Posting a properly addressed and stamped letter of allotment is a sufficient communication even if the letter is delayed or lost in transit.

### 20.10.4 Absolute and Unconditional

The allotment of securities should be absolute and unconditional and must conform to the terms and conditions of the application; otherwise, the applicant shall not be bound to accept them.

Where a person applied for shares in the company on the condition that he would be appointed cashier of a new branch of the company, it was held that he was not bound by allotment unless he was so appointed *[Ramanbhai vs Ghasiram]*.

## 20.11 MODE OF ISSUE OF SECURITIES—SECTION 23

The word 'Securities' is not defined under Companies Act, 2013. However, its meaning is derived from Securities Contract Regulation Act, 1956. It is an inclusive definition and covers shares, debentures, mutual funds and other marketable securities.

A public company may issue securities by the following methods:

1. to the public through prospectus (public offer)
2. through private placement
3. through a rights issue or a bonus issue.

A private company may issue securities by the following methods:

1. by way of rights issue or bonus issue
2. through private placement.

A 'public offer' includes initial public offer or further public offer of securities to the public by a company, or an offer for sale of securities to the public by an existing shareholder, through issue of a prospectus.

As per Section 42(2), 'private placement' means any offer of securities or invitation to subscribe securities to a select group of persons by a company (other than by way of public offer) through issue of a private placement offer letter in Form PAS 4

## 20.12 LEGAL RULES FOR ALLOTMENT—SECTION 39-40

In addition to the general rules as state above, a valid allotment must comply with legal rules contained in the Companies Act. It is also known as restrictions on allotment. Legal rules for allotment of securities are mentioned under Sections 39and40 of the Companies Act, 2013. These provisions may be discussed as under:

1. The prospectus should be filed with the registrar.
2. The application money received on application should be at least 5% of the nominal value of shares. However, as per SEBI guideline, the company should collect 25% of application money at the time of application. The company can collect more money than 25%.
3. The amount of minimum subscription must be received. If the minimum subscription amount is not received, the application money should be refunded within 15 days from closure of issue. If money is not repaid within thistime limit, all directors are jointly liable to repay money with 15% interest per annum.
4. The company should apply to one or more stock exchanges for listing of securities and obtain listing permission. Failure will attract the following punishment:
   - Fine of ₹ 5 to 50 lakhs to the company and
   - Officer in default is liable for imprisonment upto 1 year or a fine of ₹ 50,000 to 1,00,000 or both.
5. The application money received should be kept in a separate bank account (known as escrow account) until allotment. The money should not be utilised except:
   - For adjustment of allotment of securities or
   - For repayment to unsuccessful applicants.

6. The Board of Directors then passes a resolution making the allotment of securities and authorizing the company secretary to issue the letter of allotment.

Section 40 of the Companies Act, 2013, requires that every company offering its securities to the public for subscription by the issue of a prospectus shall, before such issue, make an application to one or more recognised stock exchanges for permission for the shares or debentures to be dealt with in the stock exchange for each such stock exchange. The name of stock exchange where the application is made shall be disclosed in the prospectus.

Where a prospectus states that an application has been made for permission for the shares or debentures to be dealt in one or more stock exchanges, the allotment made under such prospectus shall be void if the permission has not been granted.

However, where an appeal has been preferred against the decision of the stock exchange, the allotment shall not be void until the appeal has been dismissed. An appeal can be preferred against the stock exchange to the SEBI Appellant Tribunal (SAT).

Similarly, where permission has been granted by recognised stock exchanges, all moneys in excess of the application money have to be returned forthwith.

In case the issue is over subscribed, the applications will have to be allotted for a lesser number of shares than applied for. In case shares have been listed on a stock exchange, then the allotment will be made in consultation with the stock exchange.

## 20.13 RETURN OF ALLOTMENT—SECTION 39

Under Section 39 of the Companies Act, 2013, a company, after allotment of its securities must file with the Registrar of Companies, a statement known as 'return of allotment' in the prescribed Form No PAS-3 within 30 days of the allotment. However, no return of allotment is required to be filed with regard to the re-issue of forfeited shares or debenture as it does not amount to allotment but it is the sale of existing securities of the company. In a similar way, no return of allotment is required in the case of re-issue of surrender shares or debenture.

The return of allotment must contain the following particulars:

1. The number and nominal amount of shares allotted.
2. The names, addresses and occupations of the allottees.
3. The amount paid or due and payable on each share.

These details should be certified as correct by signatories to return.

## 20.14 UNDERWRITING AGREEMENT—SECTION 40 (6) READ WITH RULE 13 OF COMPANIES (PROSPECTUS AND ALLOTMENT OF SECURITIES) RULES, 2014

An underwriting agreement is an agreement between the company and an individual, firm or orgnisation, known as underwriter, whereby the latter agrees to take up the whole or part of the securities which may not be subscribed by the public.

This is a sort of insurance covering the shortfall in public response to its securities offered for subscription.

As per Section 40 of the Companies Act, 2013, a company may pay a commission to any person in consideration of his subscribing, or agreeing to subscribe, for any securities of the company, or his procuring, or agreeing to procure subscription for any securities of a company subject to the following conditions:

1. The payment of underwriting commission should be authorised by the Articles of the company.
2. The commission may be paid out of proceeds of the issue or profit of the company or both.
3. The rate of commission must not exceed 5% of the price at which shares are issued, and in the case of debentures 2.5% of the price of debenture. Articles of the company may provide less percentage of underwriting commission.

The prospectus should disclose the names of underwriters, the rate of commission payable to the underwriter and the number of securities which is agreed to be underwritten. A copy of the underwriting contract should be delivered to the Registrar along with the prospectus.Underwriting commission will not be payable on securities which are not offered to the public.

**Case Study**

The Articles of Association of MSW Ltd. contained a provision that upto 4% of issue price of the shares may be paid as underwriting commission to the underwriters. The Board of Directors decided to pay 5% underwriting commission. Can the Board of Directors do so? State the provisions of law in this regard as stated under the Companies Act, 2013.

## 20.15 BROKERAGE

A commission payable to brokers who induce their clients to subscribe for the shares or debentures is termed as 'brokerage'. Brokerage is different from underwriting commission. A broker does not undertake to subscribe for shares if the shares are not taken up by the public. Brokerage is to be paid to a professional person known as broker and who is registered with any recognised stock exchange.

Brokerage payable must be stated in the prospectus. All sums paid on account of commission or brokerage must be disclosed in the balance sheet.

## 20.16 ALTERATION OF SHARE CAPITAL CLAUSE—SECTION 61

A company limited by shares may, if so authorised by its Articles, alter the capital clause of its Memorandum of Associationby passing a resolution in the general meeting. To alter the capital clause, the company may:

1. increase its share capital by issuing new shares;
2. consolidate and divide all or any of its share capital into shares of larger amount than its existing shares;
3. convert all or any of its fully paid-up shares of any denomination;
4. sub-divide its shares, or any of them, into shares of smaller amount than is fixed by the Memorandum; and
5. cancel the shares which have not been taken up by any person and thereby diminish the amount of its share capital.

The powers conferred by this Section can be exercised by a company by passing an ordinary resolution at a general meeting and shall not be required to be confirmed by a court.

A cancellation of shares in pursuance of this Section shall not be deemed to be a reduction of share capital within the meaning of this Act.

The company is required to give a notice to the Registrar of Companies within 30 days of the alteration. The registrar shall then record the notice, make the necessary alterations in the Memorandum or Articles or both.

## 20.17 REDUCTION OF SHARE CAPITAL—SECTION 66

According to Section 66 of Companies Act, 2013, a company limited by shares or a company limited by guarantee and having a share capital may, if so authorised by its Articles, reduce its share capital in any one of the following ways:

1. by extinguishing or reducing the liability on any of its shares in respect of share capital not paid up;
2. by canceling any part of the paid-up capital which is lost as un-represented by available assets;
3. by paying off any part of the paid-up capital which is in excess of the need of the company; and
4. by any other method approved by the tribunal.

## 20.18 PROCEDURE TO THE REDUCTION OF SHARE CAPITAL—SECTION 66

If a company wants to reduce its share capital by any of above method, the company is require to pass a special resolution in the general meeting of the shareholders. This resolution is required to be confirmed by the tribunal. No reduction is allowed if the company is in arrears in repayment of any deposits accepted by it or interest payable on it.

The tribunal shall, before making the order of confirmation, cause to be prepared a list of creditors who are entitled to object and shall cause to be published a notice inviting objections to the reduction. The tribunal should also give notice of application made to it to the central government and Registrar of Companies and consider its objection, if any. In case of listed company, the copy of application is forwarded to SEBI and objections received, if any, should be considered.

The tribunal must also look after the interest of the shareholders. After hearing their objections, if the tribunal is satisfied that every creditor entitled to object has given his consent to the reduction or his debt has been discharged or secured, it may confirm the reduction on such terms and conditions as it thinks fit. The tribunal will not confirm reduction of capital if it is not in conformity with application accounting standards. The company is required to obtain a certificate stating that it has complied with accounting standard from its auditor and submit it to the tribunal.

The tribunal may also order the company to add the words 'and reduced' to its name for a specified time. The tribunal may also order the company to publish the reasons for reduction of capital for public information.

The company is required to file a certified copy of the tribunal order confirming the reduction of capital with the registrar of companies. The resolution for reduction of share capital shall take effect from the date of registration of the tribunal order and minutes. Then the registrar shall issue a certificate to this effect and this certificate shall be the conclusive evidence of the fact that all the requirements of the Act regarding reduction of share capital have been complied with.

In *Tamil Nadu Newsprint and Papers Ltd. vs Registrar of Companies*,the court allowed the company to reduce its capital which was found to be in excess of its needs by permitting it to pay the same partly in cash and partly in the form of non-convertible debentures.

## 20.19 DIMINUTION OF SHARE CAPITAL

When a company reduces its share capital in a certain manner, it is not required to follow the procedure of reduction of capital. This is known as diminution of share capital. Diminution of share capital takes place in the following cases:

1. when the company cancels shares that have not been taken or agreed to be taken;
2. when redeemable preference shares are redeemed;
3. when there is a surrender of shares; and
4. when some shares are forfeited for non-payment of calls.

***Important Note:***

When a company alters its share capital in any manner specified as above or increases the authorised capital or redeems any redeemable preference shares, the notice of such alteration, increase or redemption shall be filed by the company with the registrar in Form No. SH.7 along with the fee, according to Rule 15 of Companies (Share Capital and Debentures) Rules, 2014

## 20.20 ISSUE OF SHARES AT PREMIUM

A company can issue shares either at par or premium or at a discount. The issue of shares at a premium means the issue of shares at a price higher than the nominal value of the share. A company can issue shares at premium at any time. The Companies Act, 2013, does not contain any provision for issue of shares at premium by a company. Any company may issue shares at any premium.

Any offer of shares made to the public at a premium by way of prospectus shall be made in accordance with SEBI guideline.It is not necessary that for issuing shares at premium, powers must be given by the Articles of Association.

## 20.21 UTILISATION OF SECURITIES PREMIUM AMOUNT—SECTION 52

The amount of securities premium account can be utilised for the following purposes specified under Section 52 of the Companies Act, 2013:

1. to issue fully paid bonus shares to the members of the company;
2. to write off the preliminary expenses of the company;
3. to write off the expenses of, or the commission paid or the discount allowed on, any issue of shares or debentures of the company; and
4. to provide for the premium payable on the redemption of preference shares or debentures of the company.
5. for buy-back of shares.

If the amount of securities premium account is used for any other purpose than above specified, it shall be deemed as reduction of capital. The securities premium amount should not be treated as free reserves of the company; they are in the nature of capital reserve. Securities premium account is not treated as issued capital nor reserve capital. Balance in securities premium account cannot be utilised for declaring dividend.

## 20.22 CONDITIONS FOR THE ISSUE OF SHARES AT DISCOUNT—SECTION 53

Company cannot issue any shares at discount. However,it can issue sweat equity shares at discount. If a company issue shares at discount, allotment shall be void and company is liable to pay fine.

## 20.23 STOCK OR STOCK CERTIFICATE

Section 2(84) states that 'share' means share in the share capital of a company, and includes stock, except where a distinction between stock and shares is expressed or implied. Thus, 'stock' is also 'share'.

The term 'stock' may be defined as the aggregate of fully paid-up shares of a member merged into one fund of equal value.

A 'stock' is simply a set of shares put together in a mass, with the peculiarity that they can be dealt with fractionally. Stock is expressed in terms of money and is transferable in units of money. Stock has no nominal value.Stock can be in different denominations.

Only fully paid, shares can be converted into stock. Initially, a company can issue only shares, which can later be converted into stock. The stock can be reconverted into shares. A stockholder has the same rights as that of a shareholder. However, if a stock contains a fraction of share, such fraction is not entitled to voting right at a meeting, but is entitled to dividend and participation of assets in winding up. Stock can be transferred in parts also. Of late, 'stocks' are rarely issued.

## 20.24 DISTINGUISH BETWEEN 'SHARE' AND 'STOCK'

| Share | Stock |
|---|---|
| A share has a nominal value. | A stock has no nominal value. |
| A share has a distinctive number which distinguishes it from other shares. | A stock bears no such number. |
| Shares can be issued originally to the public. | A company cannot make an original issue of stock. Stock can be issued by an existing company by converting its fully paid-up shares. |
| A share may either be fully paid or partly paid. | A stock can never be partly paid; it is always fully paid. |
| A share cannot be transferred in fractions. It is transferred as a whole. | A stock may be transferred in any fractions. |
| All the shares are of equal denomination. | Stock may be different denominations. |
| Shares can be issued by any company, public or private. | Stock can be issued only by a public company limited by shares. |

## 20.25 FORFEITURE OF SHARES

If any member of the company fails to pay a valid call within the stipulated time, the company has two options: it may either sue him for the amount or forfeit the shares for non-payment of the call. Suing the defaulting shareholder to recover the amount is a tedious process and therefore almost all companies prefers to forfeit the shares.

A company can forfeit the shares only if it is authorised by the Articles of Association. As per Regulation 28 of 'Table F', the shares can be forfeited only for non-payment of calls. The power to forfeit the shares must be exercised bonafide.

If the Articles of Association authorise forfeiture of shares, then this power must be exercised strictly in accordance with the rules and procedure laid down in the Articles. If there is any irregularity in the procedure, then the forfeiture may not be valid. Before forfeiture, the board of directors shall issue notice. Notice must state the amount of the call payable, last date for payment and method of payment. Notice must also state that if call money is not paid, shares will be forfeited. If money is not received even after expiry of time period, the board should pass resolution to forfeit shares. The company can reissue forfeited shares.

## 20.26 LEGAL REQUIREMENTS FOR FORFEITURE OF SHARES

The company is required to follow the procedure as per the provisions of the Companies Act and as per the Articles to forfeit the shares. The proper procedure to be followed for the valid forfeiture of shares is as under:

### 20.26.1 In Accordance with Articles

The Articles of Association must empower the company to forfeit the shares. As per *Regulation 28* of 'Table F', shares can be forfeited only for non-payment of calls.

It was held that where shares are once registered in the name of a person, the company has no power to forfeit the shares on the ground of failure of consideration. Its remedy is only to obtain appropriate relief by suit.

Again, where two directors were allotted qualifications shares without any payment and these shares were forfeited by a Board resolution passed at the request of those two directors, the forfeiture was held to be invalid and the directors were held liable to pay the nominal value of the shares–Esparto Trading Co.

### 20.26.2 Proper Notice

*Regulation 29* of Table F provides that a notice requiring payment of the amount due together with any interest accrued must be served mentioning a further day (not less than *14 days* from the date of service of the notice) on or before which the payments is to be made. The notice must also mention that in the event of non-payment, the shares are liable to be forfeited.

The object of the notice is to give the shareholder an opportunity for *payment of the call money, interest and expenses*. A *proper notice* is a condition particular of the amounts due. A proper notice is a condition precedent to the forfeiture, and even the slightest defect in the notice will invalidate the forfeiture—*Public Passenger Services Ltd. vs M.A. Khader.*

Where a notice for the forfeiture was sent by registered AD post and was returned unserved, the forfeiture was held invalid. However, the accidental non-receipt of notice of forfeiture by the defaulter is not a ground for relief against forfeiture.

### 20.26.3 Resolution for Forfeiture

If the defaulting shareholder does not pay the amount within the specified time as required by the notice, the directors may pass a resolution forfeiting the shares (Articles 30 of Table F).

### 20.26.4 Bona Fide and in Good Faith

Power of forfeiture must be exercised bona fide and in good faith. The power cannot be used at the request of the shareholder to relieve him of liability. Such a forfeiture amounts fraud on other shareholders. If shares are forfeited for this reason, the forfeiture is void and the shareholder continues to be responsible for the unpaid part of the issue price.

Even a slight irregularity in forfeiture would be rendering the forfeiture null and void. *The aggrieved shareholder may bring an action for setting aside the forfeiture as well as for damages.* After shares have been forfeited, a further notice intimating forfeiture is not necessary to complete the forfeiture of shares.

**Case Study**

A private limited company issued a certain number of shares as fully paid to a subscriber to the memorandum on the basis of a promissory note executed by him as consideration towards the shares. Since no money was paid towards the allotment, the company after five years from the date of allotment wants to forfeit those shares and re-issue. Can the company do so?

## 20.27 EFFECT OF FORFEITURE OF SHARES

On the valid forfeiture of shares, the original shareholder ceases to be a member of the company and his name must be removed from the register of members.

The original shareholder is free from all liability for past calls. The Articles of the company may, however, make him liable for moneys which were actually due from him. The payment of such amount cannot be enforced as call but may be sued for as a debt. Further, the suit must be filed within three years from the date on which the shares were forfeited.

The name of the original shareholder shall be put on the 'B' list in the event of company going into liquidation within one year of the forfeiture.

In case, the defaulting shareholder approaches the board to cancel the forfeiture, the board is empowered to cancel such forfeiture and claim the due amount with interest.

## 20.28 SURRENDER OF SHARES

Surrender of shares means voluntary return of shares to company for cancellation. There is no provision for the surrender of shares either in the Companies Act, 2013, or in Table F, but the articles of some companies may allow it as a short-cut to the long procedure of forfeiture.

Surrender of shares shall be valid only when there is a provision to this effect in the Articles of Association of the company.Surrender of shares shall be valid only where the forfeiture is otherwise justified. In any other circumstances, surrender of shares cannot be accepted without the sanction of the court, as this would amount to reduction of capital.

Shares are surrendered when the shareholder is unable to make the payment of subsequent calls and wishes to avoid the disgrace of forfeiture. This can happen only in case of partly paid shares. The only exception where fully paid up shares may be accepted is where shares are surrendered in exchange for new shares of the same nominal value (but with different rights). In such a case, the capital is not reduced, but only replaced.Surrendered shares may be *re-issued* in the same way as forfeited shares.

## 20.29 LIEN ON SHARES—RULES 9 TO 12, TABLE 'F' OF COMPANIES ACT, 2013

*Lien* means a right to retain something belonging to another until the claims of the person in possession of the things are satisfied or discharged. It is essentially a right of retention. This right is not conferred by the statute, but is usually provided in the Articles of the company.

The lien on shares means the company's right over the shares until the debts due to it by the shareholder are paid. Regulation 9 of Table F provides for lien on shares which are not fully paid up. Thus, a shareholder cannot transfer his shares unless he pays his debts to the company.

The Articles also authorise the company to sell such shares if the outstanding dues are not paid. Shares can thus be sold by giving 14 days notice to the member. The sale proceeds should be applied towards the payment of outstanding dues, and if there is any surplus, it must be paid to the member.

The company may also have the lien on the dividends payable on shares. The Articles may provide for a lien on fully paid shares for any debt due from the member. But stock exchange regulations generally prohibit the exercise of right of lien on fully paid listed shares.

Where a shareholder pledges his shares to a third party as security for a loan before he incurs any debt to the company and the company has notice of such pledge, then the pledge shall have priority over the lien of the company. Also, when the company registers the transfer of shares which were subject to lien, the company's lien is lost.

In *Bradford Banking Co. vs Briggs Sons & Co.*, some shares were handed over to the bank as security against overdraft. The bank notified the company about the same. The company subsequently was not entitled to any priority because it could not disregard the notice given by the bank.

The death of a shareholder does not terminate the right of lien and it can be exercised against executors also.

## 20.30 BONUS SHARES—SECTION 63

When large amount of reserves are accumulated with the company and the company decides to distribute these past undistributed profits among the shareholders, it may decide to issue shares free of cost to its existing shareholders. Such shares are known as 'bonus shares'.

Bonus shares are issued to the members in proportion to their existing shareholding. On the issue of bonus shares, the issued capital increases while the assets of the company remain intact.

Bonus shares can be issued only where there is a provision to this effect in the Articles of the company. If the Articles do not contain such a provision, the company must pass a special resolution in the general meeting of the shareholders and make such a provision in the Articles.

For issuing bonus shares, a resolution should first be passed by the board of directors and it should then be approved by shareholders in their general meeting. The company should not have defaulted in payment of deposit on maturity or interest thereon. The company should also not have defaulted in payment of statutory dues of employees, such as bonus, gratuity and provident fund. A public listed company issuing bonus shares should ensure that the issue is in conformity with the SEBI guidelines in this respect.

A company may issue bonus shares by utilising the amount available in free reserves, Securities Premium Account and Capital Redemption Reserve Account. No issue of bonus shares shall be made by capitalising on reserves created by the revaluation of assets. It has to ensure that no public or rights issue has been made within 12 months prior to the bonus issue.It also has to ensure that bonus issue is not made in lieu of dividends.

In case the bonus issue appears to result in increase of capital beyond the company's authorised capital, the company has to take steps to increase its authorised capital.

Partly paid shares, if any, should be made fully paid. The stock exchange has to be informed, where the shares are listed, the date of the Board's meeting.

### 20.30.1 Procedure for Bonus Shares

Hold the meeting of the Board of directors to consider the bonus issue proposal including the proportion in which they are to be issued.Intimate the stock exchange the outcome of the Board's meeting. Ensure that the bonus issue is made within sixmonths from the date of the Board meeting.

Hold the general body meeting and get the resolution for issue of bonus shares passed by the members.Forward a copy of the general body resolution to the concerned stock exchange.

If bonus shares are to be issued to non-resident members, obtain consent of the Reserve Bank of India. Fix the date of closure of register of members or record date in consultation with the regional stock exchange.

Issue a public notice, at least seven days before, in respect of closure of register or record date in at least two newspapers—one in English and the other in the vernacular language of the region in which the registered office of the company is situated. Also intimate the concerned stock exchange(s) at least 21 days before the closure of register or record date.

Send the letter of allotment to those members whose names appear in the register of members on a record date.Make necessary entries in the register of members.Prepare share certificates and issue them to the allottees.Within 30 days of the allotment, file a 'Return of Allotment' with the registrar.

Forward a certificate to SEBI duly signed by the issuer company and countersigned by the statutory auditors or by the company secretary in practice that the bonus issue has been made in terms of SEBI guidelines.

## 20.31 PRE-EMPTIVE RIGHT OR RIGHT SHARES—SECTION 62

Companies do not issue the whole of its authorised capital at once. When the directors need more funds for expansion or modernisation, they may issue further shares. However, the directors cannot issue the new shares at their discretion. They have to follow the provisions of Section 62 of the Companies Act, 2013. Certain conditions need to be satisfied for further issue of shares. The further shares shall be offered to existing shareholders. The right to get offer of further shares is known as preemption right.

If the company wants to issue further shares after the expiry of two years from its formation or one year from the first allotment, whichever is earlier, the new shares must be offered to the existing equity shareholders in proportion to the paid-up capital on the shares held by them. The intension behind this provision is that there should be equal distribution of shares.

The right offer should be given by means of a notice specifying the number of shares offered and the time within which this offer is to be accepted. The shareholders must be given time not less than 15 days and not more than 30 days to decide whether to accept the offer or not. Right offer is always made with the price. The notice must clearly state that if the offer is not accepted within the prescribed time, it shall be deemed to have been declined. The notice must also inform the shareholder that he has a right to renounce all or any of the shares offered to him.If the shareholders do not accept the offer or reject the offer, the board of directors may dispose of it in such manner as they think fit.

### 20.31.1 When Further Shares are not Required to be Offered to Existing Shareholders

A company may offer new shares to the outsiders without offering them to the existing shareholders in the following cases:

1. If a special resolution is passed in the general meeting of the company deciding to offer new shares to the outsiders; or
2. If a special resolution is not passed, but the votes cast in favour of the resolution are more than the votes cast against the resolution, and approval of the Central Government is obtained. The Central Government will give its approval, if it is satisfied that the proposal is most beneficial to the company.
3. If the existing shareholders to whom the shares are offered decline to accept the shares.
4. If it is a private company.
5. Where debentures or loans are converted into shares as per terms of issue of debenture or loan agreement.

## 20.32 CALL ON SHARES

Calls on shares means demand by a company on its shareholders to pay the whole or part of the balance remaining unpaid on each share.

When shares are issued to the public, a part of the amount is paid with the application and the remaining part on the allotment of shares. The amount paid on application and allotment is not considered as calls unless the Articles expressly recognize them as call.

The unpaid amount on each share is called by the company in one or two installments. These installments are known as calls.

## 20.33 REQUISITES FOR VALID CALLS

For a call to be valid, the following conditions must be satisfied:

1. It must be made in accordance with the provisions of the Companies Act and Articles of the company.
2. A resolution must be passed by the Board of Directors at a meeting of the directors—Section 179
3. The resolution must specify the amount of call as well as the date and place of payment. All calls should be completed within a period of 12 months from date of allotment.
4. The power to make calls must be exercised bonafide for the benefit of the company.
5. The call must be made on a uniform basis on all shares falling under the same class—Section 49
6. A proper notice must be given to the shareholders.

Regulations 13 to 18 of Schedule F contain following provisions for making call:

1. For each call, at least 14 days' notice must be given to members.
2. An interval of one month is required between two successive calls and not more than one-fourth of the nominal value of shares can be called at one time. However, companies may have their own articles and raise the limit.
3. The board of directors has the power to revoke or postpone a call after it is made.

4. Joint shareholders are jointly and severally liable for payment of calls.
5. If a member fails to pay call money he is liable to pay interest not exceeding the rate specified in the articles or terms of issue or such lower rate, as the board may determine. The directors are free to waive the payment of interest wholly or in part.
6. If any member desires to pay the call money in advance, the directors may, at their discretion, accept and pay interest not exceeding the rate specified in the articles.
7. A defaulting member will not have any voting right till call money is paid by him.

If any of the above condition is not satisfied, the call is said to be invalid. On invalid call, shareholders are not required to pay call money.

**Case Study**

XYZ Company goes for a public issue of each share of face value ₹ 10. The application money is ₹ 2, allotment ₹ 3, first call ₹ 4, final call ₹ 1. Is this valid?

**Case Study**

XYZ Company goes for a public issue application called for on 1st April 2012. The allotment was made on 1st May, 2012, the first call on 1st June 2012, and the second call on 15th June 2012. Can the company do so?

## 20.34 CALLS IN ARREAR

When members fail to pay the call money in time, the amount unpaid on calls is known as 'calls in arrear'.If calls are in arrear interest at 10% p.a. or such lower rate as decided by BOD is paid, the board has the right to waive interest in part or in whole as per Regulation 16 of Table F.

### 20.34.1 Effects of Non-payment of Calls

If a shareholder fails to pay calls within a specified time, the board may forfeit the shares. Article of company may provide that the member who has not paid call on shares shall not exercise voting rights. Non-payment of call by a person for six months will disqualify him from holding office of the directors of the company.

## 20.35 CALLS IN ADVANCE

Sometimes, members may pay the call amounts in advance, i.e., even before amount is called. This is known as calls in advance.Section 50 provides that a company can accept such advance amount, if articles so provide.

However, Section 50 makes it clear that such members who pay advance call amounts shall not be entitled to voting rights in respect of such calls in advance. He will get voting rights only when the amount is called and becomes due.

### 20.35.1 Effects of Calls in Advance

The amount paid in advance by a shareholder is appropriated towards share capital, when the call is actually issued and is due. If a company goes into winding up its operations, the calls in advance aid will be treated as amount payable to unsecured creditors and will be treated accordingly. The amount paid as calls in advance is non-refundable.

## 20.36 BUY-BACK OF SHARES—SECTION 68

The buy-back may be defined as the purchase by a company of its own shares. The legal provisions relating to buy-back may be discussed as under:

### 20.36.1 Sources of Buy-back

A company can purchase its own shares out of:

1. its free reserves; or
2. the securities premium account; or
3. the proceeds of any shares or other specified securities.

However, no buy-back of any kind of shares or other specified securities shall be made out of the proceeds of an earlier issue of the same kind of shares or same kind of other specified securities.

In case shares are bought back out of free reserves, then a sum equal to the nominal value of shares bought back shall be transferred to a reserve account to be called the 'Capital Redemption Reserve Account',the details of which shall be disclosed in the balance sheet. SEBI guidelines stipulate that this account shall be allowed to be used for issue of fully paid bonus shares.

### 20.36.2 Authority of Articles

A company can purchase its shares if buy-back is authorised by its articles.

### 20.36.3 Passing of Resolution

Companies Act has authorised the buy-back by passing a resolution at a meeting of the Board of Directors provided the buy-back does not exceed10% of the total paid-up equity capital and free reserves of the company. However, there cannot be more than one such buy-back in any period of 365 days, although buy-back more than 10% but less than 25% of the total paid-up capital and free reserves is allowed with passing of special resolution.

Buy-back of shares in any financial year must not exceed 25% of its paid-up equity capital in that financial year.

### 20.36.4 Post-Debt Equity Ratio

The post-debt capital ratio of the company is not more than twice the capital and its free reserves after such buy-back. However, the Central Government may prescribe a higher ratio of the debt for a class or classes of companies.

All the shares or other specified securities are fully paid-up.

### 20.36.5 SEBI Guidelines

The buy-back of listed securities should be in accordance with the regulations made by the Securities and Exchange Board of India.

### 20.36.6 Notice

The notice of the meeting where special resolution is proposed to be passed shall be accompanied by an explanatory statement stating and containing the following details:

1. A full and complete disclosure of all material facts.
2. The necessity for the buy-back.
3. The class of security intended to be purchased under the buy-back.
4. The amount to be invested under the buy-back.
5. The time limit for completion of buy-back.
6. The price at which buy-back of shares shall be made.

### 20.36.7 Time Limit

Every buy-back shall be completed within one year of the date of passing the special resolution as above.

### 20.36.8 Buy-back shall be Permissible

The company can buyback shares from the existing shareholders on a proportionate basis through a tender offer or from open market through book-building process. The company may buyback shares from odd-lot holders or securities issued to employees of the company pursuant to a scheme of stock option or sweat equity.

### 20.36.9 Other Paper Work

Where a company has passed a special resolution to buyback its own shares or other securities under this section, it shall, before making such purchases, file with the Registrar and the Securities and Exchange Board of India, a declaration of solvency in the form prescribed, verified by an affidavit to the effect that the Board has made a full inquiry into the affairs of the company as a result of which it is capable of meeting its liabilities and will not be rendered insolvent within a period of one year of the date of declaration adopted by the Board, and signed by at least two directors of the company, one of whom shall be the managing director, if any.

Where a company buys back its own securities, it shall extinguish and physically destroy the securities so bought back within seven days from completion of buy-back.

SEBI guidelines in this regard stipulate that the shares certifications bought back shall be destroyed in the presence of a Registrar or Merchant Banker and the Statutory Auditor. A certificate to his effect shall be furnished to SEBI duly signed by two directors including the managing director and verified by the registrar or merchant banker and statutory auditor.

Where a company completes a buy-back of its shares and other securities under this Section, it shall not make further issue of the same kind of shares including by way of rights or other specified securities within a period of six months except by way of bonus issue or in the discharge of subsisting obligations such as conversion of warrants, stock options schemes, sweat equity or conversion of preference shares or debentures into equity shares.

Where a company buys back its securities under this section, it shall maintain in a register of the securities so bought, the consideration paid for the securities bought back, the date of cancellation of securities, the date of extinguishing and physically destroying of securities and such other particulars as may be prescribed.

A company shall after the completion of the buy-back under this section, file with the Registrar and the Securities and Exchange Board of India, a return containing such particulars relating to the buy-back within thirty days of such completion, as may be prescribed. However, no such return shall be required to be filed with SEBI in case the company buying back is an unlisted company.

**Case Study**

DJA Company Ltd., desirous of buying back of all its equity shares from the existing shareholders of the company, seeks your advice. Examining the provisions of the Companies Act, 2013, advise whether the above buy-back of equity shares by the company is possible. Also state the sources out of which buy-back of shares can be financed.

### 20.36.10 Buy-back of Securities Prohibited

No company shall, directly or indirectly, purchase its own shares or other specified securities:

1. Through any subsidiary company including its own subsidiary companies; or
2. Through any investment company or group of investment companies; or
3. If at default, in repayment of deposit or interest thereon, redemption of debentures or preference shares or payment of dividend or repayment of a term loan or interest thereon to any financial institution or bank;
4. In case it has not complied with provisions of Section 92 (i.e., annual return), Section 127 (i.e., failure to distribute dividends within specified time) and Section 129(i.e., form and contents of financial statements and Compliance with the Accounting Standards).

However, the company is not taken to have purchased its shares in the following cases when it has:

1. Redeemed its redeemable preference shares,
2. Forfeited its shares for non-payment of calls, or
3. Accepted a valid surrender of shares.

## 20.37 MEMBER

Section 2(27) states that a 'member', in relation to a company, does not include the bearer of share warrant. The person whose name is entered into the register of members is known as a member of the company. In the case of company, the terms 'member' and 'shareholder' are used interchangeably.

A person can become a member in the following ways:

### 20.37.1 Subscribers to Memorandum

The subscribers to memorandum are deemed to have agreed to become members. Their names must be entered into the register of members. Practically, they also agree to subscribe to certain shares in the company, while subscribing to the memorandum and hence are also shareholders.

Thus, if the subscribers later do not subscribe to the shares to which they have agreed, they will still be 'members' and will be responsible for payment in respect of shares which they have agreed to subscribe. They will not get voting rights if they do not actually pay for subscription, as voting rights are proportional to the paid-up value of share. A subscriber will cease to be member when he transfers his shares.

### 20.37.2 By Application in Writing

Every other person who has agreed in writing to become a member of the company, and whose name is entered into the register is a member of the company. Thus, a shareholder is not a 'member' unless his name is entered in the register of members of the company. Thus, a shareholder is not a 'member' unless his name is entered in the register of members.

### 20.37.3 By Agreeing to Take Qualification Shares of a Public Company—Director

When a director agrees to take qualification shares, such director is in the same position as if he has signed a memorandum of company for those shares of that number of value. Thus, he is deemed to have agreed to become a member of the company and will be liable in respect of those qualification shares.

### 20.37.4 By Entering His Name in Records of Depository as Beneficiary

In case of demat shares, all shares are in name of depository and the company has no record of persons who hold shares in demat form. Once shares are dematerialised, name of the person is removed from records of the company as a member. However, the person has all rights of a member including that of dividend, voting, bonus shares etc. Hence, it is provided that every person who holds equity share capital of company and whose name is entered as beneficial owner in the records of depository, shall be deemed to be a member of the company. In such case, he does not apply to company 'in writing' but is still a member.

### 20.37.5 By Transfer or Transmission

Shares of a company are freely transferable. It is transferred by executing a transfer deed. When shares are transferred, the purchaser who is also known as transfer or becomes a member of the company when such transfer is registered by the company and his name is recorded in the register of members.

Transmission of shares is transfer of shares by operation of law. Transmission of shares take place on death or insolvency of shareholder. On death of shareholder, his legal representative becomes entitled to shares. The legal representative may apply to the company for registration of shares in his name. On registration of shares, he becomes a member of the company.

### 20.37.6 Other Methods

On surrender of share warrant, the name of the person is entered again into the register of members and he is considered as member of the company.On conversion of debenture into shares, a person becomes member of company.

## 20.38 WHO CAN BECOME A MEMBER OF A COMPANY?

The following personscan be members of a company:

### 20.38.1 Individual

An individual or group of individuals in their joint names can be a member. As per government guidelines, only three persons can be joint members.

### 20.38.2 Body Corporate

Any incorporated body which has a separate legal personality can be a member. Thus, a company registered under Companies Act, Trade Union registered under Trade Union Act or a Cooperative Society registered under Co-operative Societies Act or society registered under Multi-State Co-operative Societies Act, are 'persons' and can become 'members'.

### 20.38.3 Government

The Government of India can become a member and shares are held in name of the President of India. Similarly, as a State Government can hold shares in the name of the Governor.

### 20.38.4 Partnership Firm

A partnership firm cannot be a member of a company. Individual partners can hold shares in their joint names for the benefit of the partnership firm. A partnership firm can be member of 'licensed company' i.e., 'Section 8 company'.

### 20.38.5 Other

A Hindu undivided family(HUF) cannot be member of a company. A trust is not a 'legal person' and therefore cannot be member of a company. A trade union can be member of a company. A society registered under Societies Act cannot be member of a company. However, a society registered under Cooperative Societies Act is a corporate body and can hold shares in its own name.

## 20.39 MINOR AS MEMBER OF COMPANY

A minor cannot apply for shares, as indeed, shares application is a contract between an applicant and the company. A minor cannot subscribe to memorandum of the company. In any case, he cannot incur any liability when he is a minor.

If allotment is made to a minor wrongly, the company can repudiate or cancel the allotment, but must repay all moneys received from such minor.

A minor can be a member through natural guardian. A natural guardian can enter into contract on behalf of the minor for the minor's benefit. Such contract is valid, if it is for benefit of a minor. He can 'apply in writing 'on behalf of the minor. Hence, shares can be registered in the name of the minor indicating the name of guardian representing the minor. Such contract will not be personally binding on the minor, but the minor's property may be held liable.

## 20.40 TERMINATION OF MEMBERSHIP

Membership of a person is terminated, i.e., a person can cease to be a member by one of the following modes:

1. Transfer of shares to another person.
2. Death of member and his heir/legal representative becomes a member or he sells shares to a third person (transmission of shares)
3. Member is adjudged insolvent and shares are transmitted in name of official receiver/official assignee. Until shares are registered in the name of official assignee/receiver or third party, the insolvent continues to be a member.
4. Surrender of shares, which is accepted by company as short-cut to forfeiture
5. Forfeiture of shares.
6. Company exercising lien on shares and selling them.
7. Buy back of shares by company.
8. Redemption of preference shares.
9. Rectification of Register, if ordered by tribunal.
10. Compulsory sale of shares, if ordered by tribunal.
11. Expulsion of member, if permitted by articles.
12. Irregular allotment is avoided by allottee.

## 20.41 RIGHTS OF A MEMBER OF THE COMPANY

The Companies Act, 2013, confers a number of rights on the member of a company. These rights may be summed up as under:

1. To receive the share certificates, on allotment or transfer as the case may be, in due time
2. To have his name entered in the register of members
3. To sell/transfer/gift shares if he desires, subject to articles
4. To receive copies of annual report, financial statement, and the auditor's report
5. To obtain copies of memorandum and articles
6. To receive notice of general meetings with explanatory statement.
7. To vote in postal ballot
8. To participate and vote in general meetings of members either personally or through proxies
9. To inspect record of proxies, register of members, register of directors shareholding auditors' report kept for inspection at AGM
10. To inspect register of charges, copy of instrument creating charges, register of investment in shares and securities not held in company's name, copy of trust deed, register of members, debenture holders and indexes (These rights are also available to debenture holders)
11. To inspect the minute books of the general meetings, register of contracts in which directors are interested, register giving particulars of directors, key managerial personnel and their shareholding, register of loans and investments made by companies (these rights are only to members and not to debenture holders or outsiders)
12. To contest for the post of director of the company or to nominate another person for the post of director
13. To receive dividends in prescribed time once approved in general meetings
14. To receive corporate benefits like rights, bonus etc. once approved

15. To apply to the tribunal to call or direct the Annual General Meeting
16. To proceed against the company by way of civil or criminal proceedings
17. To apply for winding up of the company
18. To receive residual proceeds after completion of winding up
19. To apply to SEBI regarding any grievance.

## 20.42 RIGHTS OF MEMBERS AS A GROUP

Certain rights conferred by the Companies Act can be exercised by a group of members and not an individual member. Following are the rights which may be exercised by a group of members:

1. To requisition an extraordinary general meeting (EOGM)
2. To appoint and remove director or auditors
3. To restrict powers of directors by altering articles
4. To apply to the tribunal to cancel variation or abrogation of rights
5. To demand a poll on any resolution
6. To apply to the Central Government to investigate the affairs of the company.
7. To apply to the tribunal for relief in cases of oppression and/or mismanagement.

## 20.43 TRANSFER OF SHARES—SECTIONS 56 AND 58

Section 56 provides that a company shall not register a transfer of shares of the company unless a proper transfer deed in Form SH 4 as given in Rule 11 of Companies (Share Capital andDebentures) Rules, 2014, duly stamped and executed by or on behalf of the transferor and by or on behalf of the transferee and specifying the name, address and occupation, if any, of the transferee, has been delivered to the company, along with the certificate relating to the shares, or if no such certificate is in existence, along with the letter of allotment of the shares.

### 20.43.1 Time Period for Deposit of Instrument for Transfer

An instrument of transfer of shares, i.e.. Form SH. 4 with the date of its execution specified thereon shall be delivered to the company within sixty (60) days from the date of such execution by or on behalf of the transferor and by or on behalf of the transferee.

### 20.43.2 Value of Share Transfer Stamps to be Affixed on the Transfer Deed

Stamp duty for transfer of shares is 25 paise for every ₹ 100 or part thereof of the value of shares as per notification by the Ministry of Finance, Department of Revenue, New Delhi.

### 20.43.3 Time Limit for Issue of Certificate on Transfer—Section-56(4)

Every company, unless prohibited by any provision of law or of any order of any court, tribunal or other authority, shall, within one month, deliver the certificates of all shares transferred after the application for the registration of the transfer of any such shares, debentures or debenture stock received.

### 20.43.4 Private Company shall Restrict Right to Transfer its Shares

The entire shareholding of a private company may be owned by a family or other private groups. Section 2(58) of the Companies Act, 2013, provides that the articles of a private company shall restrict the right to transfer the company's shares.

### 20.43.5 Restriction on Transfer in Private Company not Applicable in certain cases

Restriction upon transfer of shares in a private company is not applicable in the following cases:

1. The right of a member to transfer his/her shares cannot be applicable in a case where the shares are to be transferred to his representative(s).
2. In the event of death of a shareholder, the legal representatives may require the registration of share in the names of heirs, on whom the shares have been devolved.

### 20.43.6 Time Limit for Refusal of Registration of Transfer

Provisions related to refusal of registration and appeal against refusal is given in Section 58 of the Companies Act, 2013. Power of refusal to register transfer of shares is to be exercised by the company within thirty (30) days from the date on which the instrument of transfer or the intimation of transfer, as the case may be, is delivered to the company.

### 20.43.7 Time Limit for Appeal Against Refusal to Register Transfer by Private Company

As per Section 58(3), a transferee of shares may appeal to the tribunal against the refusal within a period of thirty (30) days from the date of receipt of the notice from the company or in case no notice has been sent by the company, within a period of sixty (60) days from the date on which the instrument of transfer or the intimation of transmission, as the case may be, was delivered to the company.

### 20.43.8 Time Limit for Appeal Against Refusal to Register Transfer by Public Company

As per Section 58(4), a transferee of shares may, within a period of sixty (60) days of such refusal or where no intimation has been received from the company, within ninety (90) days of the delivery of the instrument of transfer or intimation of transmission appeal to the tribunal.

## 20.44 PROCEDURE OF TRANSFER—SECTION 56

### 20.44.1 Procedure for Transfer of Share in a Private Company

Generally, articles contain the detailed provisions as regards the procedure for transfer of shares. The following steps shall be followed by a private company to give effect to the transfer of shares:

1. Transferor should give a notice in writing for his intention to transfer his share to the company.
2. The company, in turn, should notify other members as regards the availability of shares and the price at which such share would be available to them.
3. Such price is generally determined by the directors or the auditors of the company.
4. The company should also intimate to the members, the time limit within which they should communicate their option to purchase shares on transfer.

5. If none of the members comes forward to purchase shares, then the shares can be transferred to an outsider and the company will have no option, other than to accept the transfer.
6. Get the share transfer deed in form SH-4 duly executed both by the transferor and the transferee.
7. The transfer deed should bear stamps according to the Indian Stamp Act. The stamps affixed should be cancelled at the time or before signing of the transfer deed.
8. The signatures of the transferor and the transferee in the share transfer deed must be witnessed by a person giving his signature, name and address.
9. The relevant share certificate or allotment letter should be attached with the share transfer deed and delivered to the company. The share transfer deed should be deposited with the company within sixty (60) days from the date of such execution by or on behalf of the transferor and by or on behalf of the transferee.
10. The board shall consider the received share transfer deed and if the documentation for transfer of share is in order, the board shall register the transfer by passing a resolution.

### 20.44.2 Basic Procedure for Transfer of Share in a Public Company

Section 58(2) provides that the shares or debentures and any interest therein of a public company shall be freely transferable. Usually, the following steps shall be followed by a public company to give effect to the transfer of shares:

1. Get the share transfer deed in form SH-4 duly executed both by the transferor and the transferee.
2. The transfer deed should bear stamps according to the Indian Stamp Act. The stamps affixed should be cancelled at the time or before signing of the transfer deed.
3. The signatures of the transferor and the transferee in the share transfer deed must be witnessed by a person giving his signature, name and address.
4. The relevant share certificate or allotment letter should be attached with the share transfer deed and delivered to the company. The share transfer deed should be deposited with the company within sixty (60) days from the date of such execution by or on behalf of the transferor and by or on behalf of the transferee.
5. The board shall consider the received share transfer deed and if the documentation for transfer of share is in order, the board shall register the transfer by passing a resolution.

**Case Study**

Are the following grounds reasonable for refusal to transfer shares in a private company?

1. Where transferee is a person whose activities are against the interest of the company.
2. The transferee had applied in the past for winding up of the company.
3. The transferee belongs to a rival concern.
4. Where the transferor is indebted to the companyand the article gives authority to the board to refuse the transfers made by an indebted member
5. Where the intended transfer of shares will lead to a change in the management, which would be prejudicial to the interest of company or to public interest.
6. Where the transferee is not financially capable of paying the calls remaining unpaid on the shares
7. The proposed transfer was done without any consideration

**Case Study**

Ramesh, who is a resident of New Delhi, sent a transfer deed for registration of transfer of shares to a company at the address of its Registered Office in Mumbai. He did not receive the shares certificates even after the expiry of four months from the date of dispatch of transfer deed. He lodged a criminal complaint in the court at New Delhi. Decide, under the provisions of the Companies Act, 1956, whether the Court at New Delhi is competent to take action in the said matter.

## 20.45 NOMINATION—SECTION 72

Section72 of Companies Act, 2013, provides for nomination by the security holders. The effect of nomination is that on the death of a security holder, the nominee becomes entitled to the security belonging to the security holder.

Nomination is optional. Every natural holder of security can nominate a nominee at any time. Nomination should be made in the prescribed form, i.e., From No. SH 13. On receipt of signed and valid nomination form, the company should record it in the register of security holder within a period of 2 months.

Only individual persons can be appointed as nominees. A company or body corporate cannot be appointed as nominee. Two or more individuals can be appointed as joint nominees. A minor can also be appointed as nominee but in such case, one major is appointed as guardian of the nominee.

The nominee has following rights on the death of the security holder:

1. Right to dividend, right shares, bonus shares etc.
2. No right to vote.
3. Right to become member.
4. Right to transfer security.

Nomination is overriding to the claim of legal representatives of deceased security holders.

## 20.46 TRANSMISSION OF SECURITIES

The term 'transmission of securities' means the process whereby the ownership of securities is transferred to another person by operation of law and not on account of the will of the security holder.

Transmission of security takes place on the death, lunacy or insolvency of a shareholder. It also takes place where the holder is a company, if it goes into liquidation.

In case of death of the security holder, his security vests in his legal representatives. If they desire, they may ask the company to register them as holders on those security and for this purpose no instrument of transfer is needed. The company can register the security on the basis of will or succession certificate.

The rules regarding transmission of security are given in the Articles of Association of the company. A company may refuse to register a transmission. But this power must be exercised in good faith and in the interest of the company. However, in case of refusal, the aggrieved party can appeal to the tribunal in the same manner as in the case of refusal to register transfer of securities.

In case of transmission of security, there is no instrument of transfer, no stamp duty is required to be paid.

## 20.47 CERTIFICATE OF SECURITY—SECTION 56

A security certificate is a document which specifies the number of the security held by a person. It is issued by the company under its common seal. This document is prima facie evidence of the title of the person to the security mentioned therein.

Every person whose name appears in the register of members is entitled to receive the security certificate from the company. Certificate of security can be issued for partly paid shares also. For issue of security certificate, permission of central government is not required to be obtained. A nominal amount of stamp duty is paid at the time of issue of security certificate.

Share certificate is issued in Form No. SH-1. It has the following contents:

1. name of the company.
2. serial number of the certificate.
3. name and address of the shareholder.
4. number of security held by him.
5. distinctive number of security.
6. type or class of security.
7. revenue stamp.
8. common seal of the company.
9. signatures of two directors and the secretary.

Every company must deliver the certificates of all securities allotted, transferred or transmitted within a period of:

1. two months from the date of incorporation, in the case of subscribers to the memorandum;
2. two months from the date of allotment, in the case of any allotment of any of its shares;
3. one month from the date of receipt by the company of the instrument of transfer or, as the case may be, of the intimation of transmission, in the case of a transfer or transmission of securities;
4. six months from the date of allotment in the case of any allotment of debenture.

## 20.48 DISTINCTION BETWEEN SHARE AND SHARE CERTIFICATE

A share certificate is a prima facie evidence of the shares held by a person. Thus, a 'share certificate' is neither 'goods' nor 'chose in action'. Loss of share certificate does not mean loss of 'share' as a duplicate can always be obtained. The 'share' is considered as 'goods' and 'chose in action', but 'share certificate' is neither goods nor chose in action.

## 20.49 DUPLICATE SHARE CERTIFICATE

A certificate may be renewed or duplicate of a certificate may be issued if such certificate

1. is proved to have been lost or destroyed, or
2. having been defaced, mutilated or torn is surrendered to the company.

Following is the procedure for the issue of duplicate share certificates:

1. In case of loss or destruction of certificate, the board of directors has to give its prior consent. Usually, it is done by passing a resolution after the board obtainsa request to this effect from the shareholder.
2. If mutilated or torn, the share certificate in lieu of which the duplicate is being issued should be surrendered to the company for cancellation.
3. The company can charge a fee for the issue of the duplicate share certificate but it should not be more than ₹ 50 per certificate.
4. In case of lost or stolen certificates, there should be proper evidence of loss as well as indemnity. The expenses of giving a public notice and investigating the case are to be borne by the member.
5. Fact about duplicate certificate must be clearly shown on its stub by way of rubber stamp. Necessary particulars must be recorded in the member register in Form No. SH-2.
6. Duplicate share certificate should be issued within period of 15 days in case of listed company and 3 months in case of unlisted company, from the date of application.
7. Mutilated, defaced or torn certificates surrendered to the company must immediately be defaced by a 'cancellation mark' and may be destroyed after three years on the authority of a board resolution.

If a certificate is renewed or a duplicate certificate is issued with a fraudulent motive, the company shall be punishable with a fine from 5 times to 10 times of face value of shares and every officer who is in default may be liable under Section 447 for fraud.

The issue of duplicate certificates is governed by the rules prescribed by the Government under the Companies (Issue of Share Certificates) Rules, 1960.

## 20.50 DEBENTURE

A 'debenture' is a movable property transferable in the manner provided by the articles of the company.

According to Section 2(13), *a 'debenture' includes debenture stock, bonds and any other instrument of the company*, whether constituting a charge on the assets of the company or not.

Debenture does not become a share capital. Debenture is not 'stock'. Debenture is not 'goods'. A debenture holder is not a member of company but creditor. Debenture and shares convey distinct and separate meaning although they belong to the same genesis. *R. D. Goyal vs Reliance Industries*.

A debenture is a document which either creates debt or acknowledges it [*CIT vs Cochin Refineries Ltd.*] Adebenture may be secured or unsecured. A debenture is, in effect, a debt and acknowledgement of debt. It is one of the ways of raising loans.

The difference between debentures and loans is that while debentures can be issued to the public, loan is taken by a company from an institution or bank. The debenture certificate is an acknowledgement of loan. Debenture carrying voting rights cannot be issued. A 'bond' is also a debenture. Since debentures are freely transferable, a company cannot issue non-transferable bonds. A private company cannot issue debentures to the public. It can make only a private issues of debentures.

Debentures can be issued only by the Board of Directors at a meeting. These powers cannot be delegated to a committee or the resolution for issue of debentures cannot be passed by circulation.

## 20.51 TYPES OF DEBENTURE

Debentures may be of the following kinds:

### 20.51.1 Redeemable or Irredeemable Debenture

Debentures can be redeemable or irredeemable. Normally, irredeemable debentures are never issued although there is no legal ban. As such, SEBI guidelines are on the assumption that only redeemable debenture will be issued.

Perpetual debenture means irredeemable debenture. If perpetual secured debenture is issued, the borrower can never repay the loan and get, the security released. Normally, the mortgagor has the legal right to repay the loan and free the property from the charge.

However, Section 120 specifically allows issue of irredeemable debentures or issue of debentures for a very long period,even up to 100 years. Debentures can also be issued which are redeemable only on happening of a contingency which is very remote. Normally, irredeemable debentures are almost never issued, though legally permitted.

### 20.51.2 Convertible or Non-convertible Debenture

'Convertible debenture' means part or whole of the debenture can be converted into equity shares at a later date at a pre-determined rate per share.

The debentures continue to remain debentures and earn interest until they are converted into equity shares of the company. The debentures may be fully convertible or party convertible. For example,out of a debenture of ₹ 100, ₹ 60 may be converted into one share of ₹ 10 and the balance ₹ 40 canl be treated as non-convertible portion. It means that a share of company of face value of ₹ 10 is issued at a premium of ₹ 50 per share.

### 20.51.3 Secured or Unsecured Debenture

Debentures can be secured or unsecured. The security may be charge on assets. Debentures can be secured against property of the company.

Even if trust deed is not executed, the debenture holder can take action on behalf of himself and other debenture holders of the same class.

## 20.52 RIGHTS OF DEBENTURE HOLDER

Debenture holders have certain rights available to them. They are as follows:

1. To receive interest and/or redemption when due.
2. To receive a copy of trust deed on request.
3. To apply for winding up, if the company fails to pay its debt on maturity.
4. To approach a debenture trustee with grievance, if any.

These rights are, however, not absolute. Theyare subject to provisions of Companies Act and memorandum and articles of the company.

## 20.53 DEBENTURE TRUSTEE—SECTION 71

A debenture trustee is appointed to protect the interest of debenture holders as the latter may hold a nominal number of debentures and they do not have the time to look after their interest in properties charged to them.

Under the trust deed, a charge on the company's property is created in favour of the trustee who acts as supervisory of property charged for the benefit of debenture holders.

The following category of person cannot be appointed a trustee if:

1. he beneficially holds shares in the company.
2. he is beneficially entitled to moneys which are to be paid by the company to the debenture trustees.
3. he has entered into any guarantee in respect of principal debts secured by the debentures or interest thereon.

If the company issues secured debentures, it is not possible to create charge in favour of each individual debenture holder. Hence, the charge is created in favour of debenture trustees. The trustees look after the interests of debenture holders. They supervise creation of charge; ensure that debenture holders are getting interest on due dates and the principal amount after redemption. Normally, a bank or financial institution is appointed as trustee of debenture holders.

Debenture trustees can be appointed for more than five years at a time, even if the trustee is a firm or body corporate. Appointment of one or more debenture trustees is mandatory if a company wants to issue prospectus or letter of offer to public. Such appointment must be made before issue of prospectus or letter of offer. The prospectus or letter of offer must state that the trustees have given their consent to act as trustee.

As per SEBI guidelines, appointment of trustees is mandatory if debenture maturity is 18 months or more. However, now such appointment is mandatory in all the cases.

**Case Study**

Can the following persons be appointed as debenture trustee?

1. A shareholder who has no beneficial interest
2. A creditor,to whom the company owes only ₹ 499.
3. A person who has given a guarantee for repayment of amount of debenture issued by company.

## 20.54 FUNCTIONS OF DEBENTURE TRUSTEES—SECTION 71 READ WITH RULE 18 OF COMPANIES (SHARE CAPITAL AND DEBENTURES) RULES, 2014

The function of trustees is to protect the interest of debenture holders and to redress the grievances of debenture holders effectively. In particular,a debenture trustee may take steps as he may deem fit. The following are the functions of a debenture trustee:

1. To ensure that the assets of the company are sufficient to discharge the principal amount at all times.
2. To ascertain that the prospectus or letter of offer does not contain any matter which is inconsistent with terms of debentures or the trust deed.
3. To ensure that the company does not commit any breach of covenants and provisions of the trust deed.

4. To take steps to call a meeting of debenture holders as and when required.
5. In case of listed companies, to check whether SEBI guidelines are being followed by the company, in respect of debenture redemption reserve and other matters.
6. If company defaults in payment of interest or repayment of debentures, to take action for enforcing the security.
7. To sell or lease the property and to renew the lease.
8. Take a mortgage so that title deeds are transferred to the trustees.
9. To appoint a receiver if the security has to be enforced. If a receiver is appointed, the provisions in respect of receiver as during winding up apply.
10. To obtain periodic report/ information from company.
11. To inspect mortgaged property and related register and books of accounts.
12. To place restrictions on creation of further charge on same property without permission of trustees.
13. To appoint a nominee director on the board of the company in the event of:
    a. Two consecutive defaults in payment of interest to the debenture holders or
    b. Default in creation of security for debenture or
    c. Default in redemption of debenture.

## 20.55 PROVISIONS FOR CREATION OF DEBENTURE REDEPTION RESERVE—SECTION 71 READ WITH RULE 18 OF COMPANIES (SHARE CAPITAL AND DEBENTURES) RULES, 2014.

A company issuing debentures must create a debenture redemption reserve [DRR] for redemption of such debentures. Adequate amounts should be transferred to DRR out of profits of the company every year until such debentures are redeemed.

DRR should be adequate to pay the value of debentures plus accrued interest, if not already paid. Since DRR is to be created out of profits, there is no obligation to create DRR, if there is no profit.

The company shall create a debenture redemption reserve for the purpose of redemption of debentures, in accordance with the conditions given below:

1. It shall be created out of the profits of the company available for payment of dividend.
2. The company shall create debenture redemption reserve equivalent to at least 50% of the amount raised through the debenture issue before debenture redemption commences.
3. Every company required to create debenture redemption reserve shall, on or before the 30th day of April in each year, invest or deposit, as the case may be, a sum which shall not be less than 15% of the amount of its debentures maturing during the year ending on the 31st day of March of the next year, in any one or more of the following methods:
    a. in deposits with any scheduled bank, free from any charge or lien;
    b. in unencumbered securities of the Central Government or of any State Government;
    c. in securities or bonds mentioned in Section 20 of the Indian Trusts Act, 1882.
4. The amount invested or deposited as above shall not be used for any purpose other than for redemption of debentures maturing during the year referred to above. Provided that the amount remaining invested or deposited, as the case may be, shall not at any time fall below 15% of the amount of the debentures maturing during the year ending on the 31st day of March of that year.

5. In case of partly convertible debentures, debenture redemption reserve shall be created in respect of non-convertible portion of debenture.
6. The amount credited to the debenture redemption reserve shall not be utilised by the company except for the purpose of redemption of debentures.

## LIST OF LANDMARK JUDGEMENTS

1. ***LIC vs Escorts Ltd (1986)***
   Interest of shareholders is represented by his shareholding.
2. ***Morgan Stanely Mutual Fund vs Kartik Das (1994)***
   Shares before allotment are not goods, as shares do not exist before allotment is made.
3. ***Killick Nixon Ltd vs Bank of India (1983)***
   A transferee of shares is not a member unless his name is registered in the register of members.
4. ***R. Baliram vs Buckingham & Carnatic Co. Ltd (1969)***
   Minor can be member through natural guardian.
5. ***Diwan Singh vs Minerva Films Ltd (1959)***
   Fully paid shares can be transferred to minor
6. ***Radhey Shayam Gupta vs Kamal Oil (1999)***
   If the name of person appears in the register of member, there is presumption that he is a member.
7. ***Ram Govind Mishra vs Allahabad Theaters (P) Ltd (1997)***
   If one of the joint holders dies, shares are automatically transferred to the name of surviving joint holders. In such case, any question of nomination, will, succession etc. does not arise.
8. ***Smt. Kamalabai vs Vithal Prasad Co. P. Ltd (1993)***
   No stamp duty is payable on transmission of shares.
9. ***Xavier Joseph vs Indo-Scottish Brand (2002)***
   Private company can refuse transmission.
10. ***Bajaj Auto Ltd vs CLB (1998)***
    Power of Board to refuse registration of transfer of shares must be in the interest of company and the general body of shareholders. The board should act bonafide and for the benefit of the company as a whole.
11. ***All Indian bank officers confederation vs Dhanlakshmi Bank Ltd (1977)***
    A trade union registered under trade union act is considered as a person and can become member of a company.
12. ***Claude-lila Paralekar vs Sakal Papers (P) Ltd (2005)***
    If the shares are in joint names, the transfer form must be jointly signed.
13. ***Kaushalya Devi vs National ins. Cable Co. of India Ltd (1977)***
    When shares are transferred by a forged transfer, the transferee does not get any title to shares.
14. ***Barton vs North Staffordshires Railway (1888)***
    If a company transfers securities on the basis of forged transfer deed, the company will still be liable to the original holder of security.

15. ***Worldwide agencies vs Margaret T. Desor (1990)***

    Transmission is instantaneous transfer of ownership to the heirs of the last holder from the moment of death of the last holder and what the company does is only secretarial work of entering the name of the legal heir in records.

16. ***Rishyashringa Jewellery Ltd vs Stock exchange (1996)***

    If a company makes application to more than one stock exchange and even if one of the stock exchanges refuses to list the shares, the entire issue becomes a void and the entire application money must be repaid.

17. ***Bhagwati Developers vs Peerless general finance & investment Co. (2005)***

    Reserve arising from revaluation of assets can be used for issue of bonus shares.

18. ***Head (Henry) & Co. Ltd vs Roper Holding Ltd (1951)***

    If a company issues shares at a premium for consideration other than cash, a sum equal to the amount or value of premium must be transferred to the share (not securities) premium account.

19. ***CIT vs Standard VacuumsOil Co. (1966)***

    There can be no objection to charging of varying rates of premium in respect of block of shares carrying same rights.

20. ***Greaves Cotton & Co. Ltd vs State of Maharasthtra (2005)***

    Issue of debenture certificate in case of fully convertible debenture not required.

21. ***Levy vs Abercorris Slate & Slab Co. (1888)***

    Debenture is a document given by a company as evidence of debt to holder usually arising out of a loan and most commonly secured by charge.

22. ***Herdilia Unimers Ltd vs Renu Jain (1998)***

    The moment the shares are allotted and a shareholder's name is placed on the register of member, the person would become ashare holder of the company irrespective of whether the person had received the share certificate or not.

## TEST YOUR KNOWLEDGE

1. Explain the various terms used in reference of capital under Companies Act, 2013. **(Ref. Para-20.1)**
2. Explain reserve capital. **(Ref. Para-20.1)**
3. Write the difference between called up capital and uncalled capital. **(Ref. Para-20.1)**
4. Define shares. **(Ref. Para-20.2)**
5. What does shares signify in a company? **(Ref. Para-20.2)**
6. Define the term 'share' and explain its characteristics. **(Ref. Para-20.2)**
7. Write a short note on equity shares. **(Ref. Para-20.3)**
8. Explain the term 'equity shares' and 'preference shares' **(Ref. Para-20.3,20.4)**
9. What are the different kinds of share which a company can issue under Companies Act, 2013? **(Ref. Para-20.5)**
10. Preference shares are always presumed to be cumulative. Comment. **(Ref. Para-20.5)**
11. A company can issue irredeemable preference shares. Comment. **(Ref. Para-20.5)**
12. When can a company issue redeemable preference shares? **(Ref. Para-20.6)**
13. Out of which sources can a company redeem preference shares? **(Ref. Para-20.5)**

14. When and which company can issue equity with differential voting right? **(Ref. Para-20.7)**
15. Preference share holders can never have voting right. Comment. **(Ref. Para-20.8)**
16. How are voting rights available to various types of shareholders? **(Ref. Para-20.8)**
17. What is meant by allotment of shares? **(Ref. Para-20.9)**
18. What are the conditions required to be complied with by a public company before allotment of shares? **(Ref. Para-20.10,20.11)**
19. What is return of allotment? When is a company required to file return of allotment? **(Ref. Para-20.13)**
20. Define underwriting. As per Companies Act, what is maximum percentage of underwriting paid by a company? **(Ref. Para-20.14)**
21. Write a short note on brokerage. **(Ref. Para-20.15)**
22. State the legal provisions relating to alteration of share capital of a company. **(Ref. Para-20.16)**
23. Can a company reduce its capital? If so, what are the methods of reduction of capital? **(Ref. Para-20.17)**
24. Explain the procedure for reduction of capital. **(Ref. Para-20.18)**
25. What do you understand by diminution of capital? **(Ref. Para-20.19)**
26. Can a company issue shares at premium? **(Ref. Para-20.20)**
27. The amount of securities premium account can be utilised for any purpose. Comment. **(Ref. Para-20.21)**
28. What are the requirements for issue of shares at discount? **(Ref. Para-20.22)**
29. Write short notes on stock certificate. **(Ref. Para-20.23)**
30. Distinguish between shares and stock. **(Ref. Para-20.24)**
31. When and how shares may be forfeited? **(Ref. Para-20.25,20.26)**
32. What is the effect of forfeiture? **(Ref. Para-20.27)**
33. What do you understand by surrender of shares? **(Ref. Para-20.28)**
34. A company can exercise lien any time. Comment. **(Ref. Para-20.29)**
35. Write down the steps to issue bonus shares. **(Ref. Para-20.30)**
36. What are the provisions regarding further issue of share capital? **(Ref. Para-20.31)**
37. Issue of further share capital should first be made to existing shareholders. Comment. **(Ref. Para-20.31)**
38. What is calls on shares? What are the requirements of valid calls? **(Ref. Para-20.32,20.33)**
39. What will bethe effect of non-payment of calls? **(Ref. Para-20.34)**
40. What are calls in advance? What will be the effect of calls in advance? **(Ref. Para-20.35)**
41. What do you mean by the term 'buy-back'? Explain the legal provisions relating to buy-back. **(Ref. Para-20.36)**
42. A company is not allowed to purchase its own shares. Is it a correct statement? **(Ref. Para-20.36)**
43. Discuss the modes of acquiring membership of a company. **(Ref. Para-20.37)**
44. Who can become member of a company? **(Ref. Para-20.38)**
45. Can a minor become member of a company? **(Ref. Para-20.39)**
46. How does the membership of a person terminate? **(Ref. Para-20.40)**
47. On redemption of preference shares, a person ceases to be a member of a company. Comment. **(Ref. Para-20.40)**
48. Discuss the rights of members. **(Ref. Para-20.41)**
49. Write down any five rights available to a group of members. **(Ref. Para-20.42)**

50. Explain the procedure for transfer of shares. **(Ref. Para-20.44)**
51. What remedies are available to the aggrieved party when the transfer of shares is wrongly refused by a company? **(Ref. Para-20.43)**
52. What is meant by nomination of shares? **(Ref. Para-20.45)**
53. What rights are available to the nominee on death of a shareholder? **(Ref. Para-20.45)**
54. Write short notes on transmission of shares. **(Ref. Para-20.46)**
55. What is a share certificate? **(Ref. Para-20.47)**
56. What should be the content of a share certificate? **(Ref. Para-20.47)**
57. Explain the difference between share and share certificate. **(Ref. Para-20.48)**
58. When can a company issue duplicate share certificate? State the procedure for this purpose. **(Ref. Para-20.49)**
59. What is debenture? **(Ref. Para-20.50)**
60. What are the various kinds of debentures? **(Ref. Para-20.51)**
61. Write down the rights available to debenture holders. **(Ref. Para-20.52)**

## MULTIPLE-CHOICE QUESTIONS

1. The minimum application money should be ______ of nominal value.
   (i) 5% (ii) 3% (iii) 2% (iv) none of these
2. The minimum application money should be ______ of nominal value as per SEBI guidelines.
   (i) 25% (ii) 30% (iii) 40% (iv) none of these
3. A company cannot pay underwriting commission unless it is authorised by its ______.
   (i) Articles (ii) Memorandum (iii) Both (i) & (ii) (iv) None of the above
4. In case of shares,maximum underwriting commission will be
   (i) 2% (ii) 3% (iii) 5% (iv) none of these
5. In case of debentures,maximum underwriting commission will be
   (i) 3% (ii) 4% (iii) 2.5% (iv) none of these
6. If a company wants to place shares to brokers, they should be given a maximum of ______ as brokerage commission.
   (i) 3% (ii) 2% (iii) 1.5% (iv) none of these
7. Which of the following is a right of the members of a company?
   (i) Right to have a share (ii) Right to appoint auditor (iii) Right to appoint director (iv) All the above
8. Which of the following cannot become a member of a company?
   (i) Partnership firm. (ii) Foreigner. (iii) State Government. (iv) Central Government.

9. For calculating the number of members in a private company, joint holders will be treated as ______.
   (i) 1
   (ii) 2
   (iii) 3
   (iv) 4
10. A company must inform the registrar about redemption of preference shares within
   (i) 21 days.
   (ii) 15 days.
   (iii) 30 days.
   (iv) None of the above.
11. Share premium amount is treated as the ______ capital of a company.
   (i) issued
   (ii) reserve
   (iii) subscribe
   (iv) none of the above
12. Capital redemption reserve must be used for the issue of
   (i) fully paid bonus shares.
   (ii) fully paid equity shares.
   (iii) preference shares.
   (iv) none of the above.
13. Part of the issued capital taken by public is called ______.
   (i) Subscribed capital
   (ii) Called-up capital
   (iii) Un-called capital
   (iv) Paid-up capital
14. Part of authorised capital which is offered by the company for subscription is ______.
   (i) subscribed
   (ii) issued
   (iii) un-called
   (iv) called-up
15. Stamp duty on registration of the company is payable based on ______ capital.
   (i) nominal
   (ii) authorised
   (iii) either (i) or (ii)
   (iv) none of these
16. ______ preference shares carry the right to cumulate the dividends.
   (i) Convertible
   (ii) Cumulative
   (iii) Non-converted
   (iv) None of these
17. Paying back of capital is called
   (i) Redemption.
   (ii) Conversion.
   (iii) Participation.
   (iv) None of these.
18. Premium amount on the securities are transferred to ______ account.
   (i) securities premium
   (ii) reserve fund
   (iii) capital reserve
   (iv) none of these
19. ______ are the shares issued by the company to its employees or directors for consideration other than cash.
   (i) Bonus
   (ii) Sweat
   (iii) Right
   (iv) None of the above
20. Cumulative preference shareholders have voting right if dividends are in arrears for ______ years.
   (i) 1
   (ii) 2
   (iii) 3
   (iv) 4
21. ______ is an aggregate of fully paid share that have been legally consolidated.
   (i) Share
   (ii) Stock
   (iii) Both (i) and (ii)
   (iv) None of the above
22. ______ have fixed denomination.
   (i) Share
   (ii) Stock
   (iii) Both (i) and (ii)
   (iv) None of the above

23. ______ should be passed by the company to offer shares to outsiders.
    (i) Special resolution
    (ii) Ordinary resolution
    (iii) C.G
    (iv) None of the above
24. A company must pass ______ for reducing its share capital.
    (i) ordinary resolution
    (ii) special resolution
    (iii) Central Government permission
    (iv) none of the above
25. Which of the following can be used for buy-back of shares?
    (i) Free reserves
    (ii) Securities premium
    (iii) Proceeds of fresh issue of shares
    (iv) All of the above
26. Buy-back by board resolution can only be upto ______% of total paid up capital and free reserve.
    (i) 15
    (ii) 10
    (iii) 25
    (iv) 20
27. Buy-back should be less than or equal to ______% of total paid-up capital and free reserve.
    (i) 25
    (ii) 30
    (iii) 35
    (iv) 40
28. In case of buy-back, post debt equity ratio should not be more than ______.
    (i) 1:2
    (ii) 2:1
    (iii) 3:1
    (iv) 1:3
29. Every buy-back shall be completed within ______ month from the date of passing the Special Resolution.
    (i) 6
    (ii) 8
    (iii) 10
    (iv) 12
30. ______ companies are permitted to buy back its shares.
    (i) Insolvent
    (ii) Solvent
    (iii) Both (i) and (ii)
    (iv) None of the above
31. Buy-back securities should be physically destroyed within ______ days.
    (i) 7
    (ii) 17
    (iii) 21
    (iv) 28
32. After buy-back, a company cannot issue the same kind of shares for ______ months.
    (i) 6
    (ii) 12
    (iii) 18
    (iv) 24
33. Within 30 days of completion of buy-back, the company shall file the details with whom ______.
    (i) Registrar
    (ii) SEBI
    (iii) Both (i) and (ii)
    (iv) None of the above
34. The maximum premium amount that can be charged as per Companies Act is ______.
    (i) 10%
    (ii) 15%
    (iii) 20%
    (iv) None of these
35. A company, to issue sweat equity shares, must pass a ______
    (i) special resolution
    (ii) ordinary resolution
    (iii) unanimous resolution
    (iv) none of these
36. Stamp duty to be paid at the time of issue of share certificate is
    (i) nominal
    (ii) high
    (iii) very high
    (iv) none of these

37. In case of ______, a duplicate can be obtained if it is lost.
(i) share warrant
(ii) share certificate
(iii) dividend coupon
(iv) none of the above

38. For a company to accept calls in advance from shareholders, itshould have permission in
(i) MOA
(ii) AOA
(iii) BOD
(iv) None of these

39. Forfeiture can be made only if it is authorised by ______.
(i) AOA
(ii) MOA
(iii) ROC
(iv) CG

40. Name of the members is struck off from the register in case of ______.
(i) issue of share certificate
(ii) forfeiture
(iii) Both (i) and (ii)
(iv) None of the above

41. ______ days have to be given for payment of call money from the date of service of notice.
(i) 14
(ii) 13
(iii) 12
(iv) 11

42. ______ arises in respect of debt due on shares as well as on other transactions.
(i) Forfeiture
(ii) Lien
(iii) Both (i) and (ii)
(iv) None of the above

43. Return of partly paid shares by the shareholders to the company is ______.
(i) surrender
(ii) forfeiture
(iii) lien
(iv) none of the above

44. ______ is a short-cut to forfeiture
(i) Lien
(ii) Surrender
(iii) Right issue
(iv) None of the above

45. No consideration shall be paid by the company in exchange of ______ shares.
(i) lien
(ii) forfeited
(iii) surrendered
(iv) none of the above

46. The person who transfers his shares is called ______.
(i) transferee
(ii) transferor
(iii) promisor
(iv) promisee

47. The person to whom the shares are transferred is called ______.
(i) transferee
(ii) transferor
(iii) endorser
(iv) endorsee

48. ______ is an instrument of transfer signed by the transferor in which the name and date are not filled.
(i) Forged transfer
(ii) Blank transfer
(iii) Both (i) and (ii)
(iv) None of the above

49. ______ transfer is null and void.
(i) Forged
(ii) Blank
(iii) Both (i) and (ii)
(iv) None of the above

50. If the ownership of shares goes to another by operation of law, it is called as ______.
(i) transfer
(ii) transmission
(iii) Both (i) and (ii)
(iv) None of the above

51. Transfer is effected by ______.
    (i) sales
    (ii) death
    (iii) insolvency
    (iv) none of the above
52. Transmission is effected by ______.
    (i) sale
    (ii) death
    (iii) insolvency
    (iv) Both (ii) and (iii)
53. In which of the following, stamp duty and consideration are not necessary? ______
    (i) Transfer
    (ii) Transmission
    (iii) Both (i) and (ii)
    (iv) None of the above
54. Own funds are called ______.
    (i) debenture capital
    (ii) share capital
    (iii) loan capital
    (iv) None of the above
55. Debenture forms part of ______.
    (i) capital
    (ii) loan
    (iii) fund
    (iv) None of the above
56. Shareholders are ______.
    (i) owners
    (ii) creditors
    (iii) debtors
    (iv) none of the above
57. Debenture holders are ______.
    (i) owners
    (ii) creditors
    (iii) debtors
    (iv) none of the above
58. Return paid on shares is ______.
    (i) interest
    (ii) dividend
    (iii) commission
    (iv) none of the above
59. Return paid on debentures is ______.
    (i) interest
    (ii) dividend
    (iii) commission
    (iv) tax
60. Which of the following have voting rights?
    (i) Shareholders
    (ii) Debenture holder
    (iii) Both (i) and (ii)
    (iv) None of the above
61. ______ on debenture is payable even if there are no profits.
    (i) Interest
    (ii) Dividend
    (iii) Commission
    (iv) None of the above
62. Debentures payable to a holder of certificate is called ______.
    (i) bearer
    (ii) unregistered
    (iii) secured
    (iv) Both (i) and (ii)
63. Debentures payable to person whose name appears both on debenture certificate and company's register is called ______.
    (i) bearer
    (ii) unregistered
    (iii) registered
    (iv) none of the above
64. Debentures which have the charge on the property of the company is ______.
    (i) secured
    (ii) unsecured
    (iii) registered
    (iv) none of the above

65. Debenture which are repayable only on the event of winding up is called
   (i) redeemable
   (ii) irredeemable
   (iii) perpetual
   (iv) Both (ii) and (iii)

66. Which reserve is required to be created for redemption of debentures?
   (i) DRR
   (ii) Free reserve
   (iii) CRR
   (iv) None of these

67. ______ preference shares do not carry the right to accumulate dividends.
   (i) Convertible
   (ii) Cumulative
   (iii) Non-cumulative
   (iv) None of these

68. ______ are the shares issued by the company to its existing shareholders free of cost.
   (i) Bonus
   (ii) Sweat
   (iii) Right
   (iv) None of the above

69. ______ are the shares issued by the company to its existing shareholder as a matter of right with price.
   (i) Bonus
   (ii) Sweat
   (iii) Right
   (iv) None of the above

70. When the shares are transferred to X from Y, Y will be a ______ of the company.
   (i) member
   (ii) shareholder
   (iii) partner
   (iv) None of these

## ANSWER KEYS

| | | | | |
|---|---|---|---|---|
| **1.** (i) | **15.** (iii) | **29.** (iv) | **43.** (i) | **57.** (ii) |
| **2.** (i) | **16.** (ii) | **30.** (ii) | **44.** (ii) | **58.** (ii) |
| **3.** (i) | **17.** (i) | **31.** (i) | **45.** (iii) | **59.** (i) |
| **4.** (iii) | **18.** (i) | **32.** (i) | **46.** (ii) | **60.** (i) |
| **5.** (iii) | **19.** (ii) | **33.** (i) | **47.** (i) | **61.** (i) |
| **6.** (iv) | **20.** (ii) | **34.** (iv) | **48.** (ii) | **62.** (i) |
| **7.** (iv) | **21.** (ii) | **35.** (i) | **49.** (i) | **63.** (iii) |
| **8.** (i) | **22.** (i) | **36.** (i) | **50.** (ii) | **64.** (i) |
| **9.** (i) | **23.** (i) | **37.** (ii) | **51.** (i) | **65.** (i) |
| **10.** (iii) | **24.** (ii) | **38.** (ii) | **52.** (iv) | **66.** (i) |
| **11.** (iv) | **25.** (iv) | **39.** (ii) | **53.** (ii) | **67.** (iii) |
| **12.** (i) | **26.** (ii) | **40.** (ii) | **54.** (ii) | **68.** (i) |
| **13.** (i) | **27.** (i) | **41.** (i) | **55.** (ii) | **69.** (iii) |
| **14.** (ii) | **28.** (ii) | **42.** (ii) | **56.** (iv) | **70.** (i) |

# 21

# Companies Act, 2013: Meeting and Power of Board

## Learning Objectives

*After reading this chapter, you will be able to understand:*

- Types of meetings and its purpose
- Requirement for meeting and provisions for notice
- Extra-ordinary general meeting by shareholders
- Proxy and quorum
- Adjournment of meeting
- Chairman and his power
- Minute of meeting

A company is an association of several persons. Decisions are made in a company according to the view of the majority. Various matters are discussed and decided upon in meetings, which take place between members and between the directors. The Companies Act, 2013, contains several provisions for such meetings. These provisions have to be understood and followed.

For a meeting, there must be *at least two persons*. One member cannot constitute a company meeting even if he holds proxies for other members.

## 21.1 KINDS OF COMPANY MEETINGS

Broadly, meetings in a company are of the following types

1. Meetings of members:
   (a) Statutory general meeting.
   (b) Annual general meeting.
   (c) Extraordinary general meeting.
2. Board meetings: It also includes meetings of the committees of the board.
3. Meetings of creditors:
   (a) For purposes other than winding up, and
   (b) For winding up.
4. Class meeting: Meetings of a particular class of shares.

## 21.2 REQUISITES OF A VALID MEETING

The following conditions must be satisfied for a meeting to be called a valid meeting:

### 21.2.1 By Proper Authority

A meeting must be *properly convened.* The persons calling the meeting must be authorised to do so. If the meeting is called by the person who does not have authority, meeting is said to be invalid.

### 21.2.2 Proper Notice

*Proper and adequate notice* must have been given to all those entitled to attend the meeting. The notice of meeting should have been given well in advance. The provisions regarding serving notice to the members for general meetings are discussed in detail in the next section.

### 21.2.3 Chairman

The meeting must be legally constituted. There must be a *chairperson.* It is not possible to convene a meeting if the chairperson is not present at the time of meeting.

### 21.2.4 Quorum

Quorum stands for the minimum number of members to be present at the meeting to discuss the subject matter at the meeting. The *rules of quorum* must be maintained and the provisions of the Companies Act, 2013 and the articles must be complied with. If the meeting is convened without quorum, the meeting will be invalid.

### 21.2.5 Other Rules

The business at the meeting must be *validly transacted.* The meeting must be conducted in accordance with the regulations governing the meetings. The rules of article of the association in this regard should be followed.

## 21.3 DIFFERENT MANNER OF SERVING NOTICE TO MEMBERS

Notice of general meeting can be given in any manner prescribed in Section 20:

1. By *handing over the notice to the member* personally, or
2. By *post* under a certificate of posting or by *registered post* or *speed post*.
3. By electronic means.

Notice is deemed to have been served on a person to whom the notice is addressed, if the notice is posted to him, by affixing stamps of requisite value at his address registered in India (*Col. Kuldip Singh Dhillon v. Paragon Utility Financiers P Ltd*)

In case of notice by post, notice of meeting is deemed to be served *48 hours* after the time of posting irrespective of actual date of receipt of notice by the member. This is so even when the day after 48 hours happens to be a Sunday or holiday.

### 21.3.1 Notice in Case of Joint Holders

In case of joint holding, notice is necessary only to the *first joint holder* in the register of members, i.e., whose name appears first in the register.

### 21.3.2 Notice by Registered Post or by UPC

As per *Section 20*, a member can inform the company in *advance* that notice should be sent to him under a postal certificate or by registered post or courier with acknowledgement.

A member may request the company for delivery of document through a particular mode. He should *deposit a sum sufficient to defray the expenses* in doing so. If he has done that, and if the notice is not served the way the member wanted it to be served, the notice will not be deemed to have been given.

## 21.4 PROVISIONS REGARDING NOTICE OF GENERAL MEETING

A meeting cannot be held unless a proper notice containing the necessary information has been given at the proper time to all persons entitled to attend the meeting.

A notice convening a general meeting must be given *at least 21 clear days* prior to the date of meeting as per Section 101.

However, an annual general meeting may be called and held at a shorter notice, if consent is given in writing or electronic mode by members holding 95 percent of the total voting power of the company.

Notice of every meeting of the company must be sent to all members entitled to attend and vote at the meeting. Notice of the AGM must be given to the statutory auditor of the company.

The notice may be given to any member either personally or by sending it by post to him at his registered address, or if there is none in India, to any address within India supplied by him for the purpose.

Where notice is sent by post, service is effected by properly addressing, pre-paying and posting the notice.

A notice may be given to joint holders by giving it to the joint holder *first named in the register of members*.

A notice calling a meeting must *state the place, day and hour* of the meeting and must contain the agenda of the meeting.

The notice must describe type of meeting. A statement of the business to be transacted at the general meeting should be given in the notice.

Where any items of special business are to be transacted at the meeting, an explanatory statement setting out all material facts concerning each item of the special business including the concern or interest, if any, therein of every director and manager, if any, must be annexed to the notice. If it is intended to propose any resolution as a special resolution, such intention should be specified.

A notice convening an *AGM must be accompanied by the annual accounts* of the company, the director's report and the auditor's report.

The copies of these documents could, however, be sent less than *21 days* before the date of the meeting if agreed to by all members entitled to vote at the meeting.

As per Section 101(3), notice of general meeting must be in *writing* and should be given to

1. *All members* as per the address available in Register of Members
2. In case of *insolvent members*, to their assignee by post or if the address is not known, to the earlier known address of the insolvent member
3. In case of *deceased member, to his representatives*, and if his address is not known, to earlier address of the deceased member/members.
4. To *auditors*
5. To *preference shareholders*
6. In case of joint holding, noticed is necessary only to first joint holder in the register of members, i.e., to the one whose name appears first in the register.

### 21.4.1 Accidental Omission to give Notice of General Meeting

An accidental omission to give notice to or non-receipt of notice by a member *will not invalidate* the proceedings of the meeting [Section 101(4)].

### 21.4.2 Intentional Omission

An intentional omission to send a notice to even one member will invalidate the meeting.

In *Rajiv Khandelwal vs Amigo Multifilm* it was held that all resolutions passed at an extraordinary general meeting (EOGM) were declared as null and void when it was found that proper notice of meting was not given.

## 21.5 ANNUAL GENERAL MEETING (AGM)—SECTION 96

An annual general meeting must be held by every type of company, public or private, limited by shares or by guarantee, with or without share capital or unlimited company, once in a year.

Every company must in each calendar year hold an annual general meeting. In addition, the gap between two annual general meetings should not be more than 15 months or within a period of six months from closing of the financial year.

However, a company should hold its first annual general meeting within nine months from the closing of the financial year. In such a case, it need not hold any annual general meeting in the year of its incorporation as well as in the following year.

### 21.5.1 Extension of Time for Holding AGM

In case there is any difficulty in holding any annual general meeting (except the first annual meeting), the registrar of companies (ROC) may, for any special reasons shown, grant an extension of time for holding the meeting by a period not exceeding three months, provided the application for the purpose is made before the due date of the annual general meeting.

However, general delay in the completion of the audit of the annual accounts of the company is not treated as 'special reason' for granting extension of time for holding its annual general meeting. Generally, in such circumstances, an AGM is convened and held at the proper time. All matters other than accounts are discussed. All other resolutions are passed and the meeting is adjourned to a later date for discussing the final accounts of the company. However, the adjourned meeting must be held before the last day of holding the AGM.

The AGM must be held on a working day during business hours (i.e. between 9.00 A.M. to 6 P.M.) at the registered office of the company or at some other place within the city, town or village in which the registered office of the company is situated.

Thus, AGM cannot be organised on a Sunday or a public holiday and it cannot be held in the evenings or in the night after business hours. As per Section 2 (38), public holiday means a 'public holiday' declared under 'Negotiable Instruments Act'. Further, all Sundays are 'public holidays'.

**Case Study**

XYZ co., incorporated on 1st January 2013. The AGM should be held on 1st July 2014. The ROC extended that time to 1st September 2014. Is the AGM valid?

**Case Study**

M.M. Ltd is incorporated on 1st January 2014. Which is last date for conveying its first AGM?

## 21.6 REPORT ON AGM—SECTION 121

Every listed public company is required to prepare a report on each annual general meeting including the confirmation to the effect that the meeting was convened, held and conducted as per the provisions of the Act and the rules made thereunder. A copy of the report is to be filed with the Registrar in Form No. MGT—15 within thirty days of the conclusion of annual general meeting, along with the prescribed fee.

According to Rule 31, the report shall be prepared in accordance with the following rules:

1. A report under this section shall be prepared in addition to the minutes of the general meeting.
2. The report shall be signed and dated by the chairman of the meeting or in case of his inability to sign, by any two directors of the company, one of whom shall be the managing director, if there is one.
3. Such report shall contain the details in respect of the following:
    - The day, date, hour and venue of the annual general meeting.
    - Confirmation with respect to appointment of chairman of the meeting.

- Number of members who attended the meeting.
- Confirmation of quorum.
- Confirmation with respect to compliance of the Act and the Rules, secretarial standards made thereunder with respect to calling, convening and conducting the meeting.
- Business transacted at the meeting and result thereof.
- Particulars with respect to any adjournment, postponement of meeting, change in venue.
- Any other points relevant for inclusion in the Report.

4. Such report shall contain a fair and correct summary of the proceedings of the meeting.

## 21.7 NOTICE OF ANNUAL GENERAL MEETING

As per Section 101 of the Companies Act, 2013, a general meeting of a company may be called by giving a clear 21 days' notice in writing.

The notice must state that the meeting is an annual general meeting. The time, date and place of the meeting must be mentioned in the notice.

The notice of the meeting must be accompanied by a copy of the annual accounts of the company, director's report on the position of the company for the year and auditor's report on the accounts. A proxy form should be enclosed with the notice.

Companies having share capital should also state in the notice that a member is entitled to attend and vote at the meeting and is also entitled to appoint proxies in his absence. A proxy need not be a member of that company.

**Case Study**

Articles of the association of ABC Ltd provide 25 clear days' notice for AGM. The company convenes AGM at the end of notice of 21 clear days. Is AGM held by company valid?

## 21.8 DEFAULT IN HOLDING AN ANNUAL GENERAL MEETING—SECTION 97-99

If there is any default in holding an annual general meeting, any member of the company may apply to the tribunal. The tribunal may call, or direct the calling of the meeting, and give such ancillary or consequential directions as it may consider expedient in relation to the calling, holding and conducting of the meeting.

The tribunal may direct that one member present in person or by proxy shall be deemed to constitute the meeting. A meeting held in pursuance of this order will be deemed to be an annual general meeting of the company.

A fine which may extend to ₹ 1,00,000 on the company and every officer of the company who is in default may be levied and for continuing default, a further fine of ₹ 5000 per day during which the default continues may be levied.

## 21.9 USUAL BUSINESS AT AN AGM—SECTION 102

At every AGM, the following matters must be discussed and decided. Since such matters are discussed at every AGM, they are known as ordinary business. All other matters and business to be discussed at the AGM are special business.

The following matters constitute ordinary business at an AGM:

1. Consideration of annual accounts, director's report and the auditor's report.
2. Declaration of dividend, if any.
3. Appointment of directors in the place of those retiring.
4. Appointment of and the fixing of remuneration of the statutory auditors.

In case any other business (special business) has to be discussed and decided upon, an explanatory statement of the special business must also accompany the notice calling the meeting.

The notice must also give the nature and extent of the interest of the directors or manager in the special business, as also the extent of the shareholding interest in the company of every such person.

In case approval of any document has to be done by the members at the meeting, the notice must also state that the document would be available for inspection at the registered office of the company during the specified dates and timings.

## 21.10 EXTRAORDINARY GENERAL MEETING—EGM—SECTION 100

Every general meeting (i.e. meeting of members of the company) other than the annual general meeting is an extraordinary general meeting.

Such meeting is usually called by the board of directors for some urgent business which cannot wait to be decided until the next AGM. Every business transacted at such a meeting is special business.

An explanatory statement of the special business must also accompany the notice calling the meeting. The notice must also give the nature and extent of the interest of the directors or manager in the special business, as also the extent of the shareholding interest in the company of every such person.

In case approval of any document has to be done by the members at the meeting, the notice must also state that the document would be available for inspection at the Registered Office of the company during the specified dates and timings.

The Articles of Association of a Company may contain provisions for convening an extraordinary general meeting. It may provide that 'the board may, whenever it thinks fit, call an extraordinary general meeting' or it may provide that 'if at any time there are not within India, directors capable of acting who are sufficient in number to form a quorum, any director or any two members of the company may call an extraordinary general meeting'.

## 21.11 EXTRAORDINARY GENERAL MEETING ON REQUISITION

The members of a company have the right to require the calling of an extraordinary general meeting by the directors. The board of directors of a company must call an extraordinary general meeting if required to do so by the following members:

1. members of the company, holding on date of receipt of requisition of EGM, not less than one-tenth of such of the voting rights in regard to the matter to be discussed at the meeting ; or
2. if the company has no share capital, the members representing not less than one-tenth of the total voting rights on the date receipt of requisition in regard to the said matter.

The requisition must state the objects of the meetings, be signed by the requisitioning members and deposited at the company's registered office.

When the requisition is deposited at the registered office of the company, the directors should, within 21 days, move to call a meeting. The meeting should be actually be held within 45 days from the date of the lodgement of the requisition.

If the directors fail to call and hold the meeting as aforesaid, the requisitioners or any of them meeting the requirements as above, as the case may be, may themselves proceed to call a meeting within three months from the date of the requisition, and claim the necessary expenses from the company. The company can make good this sum from the directors in default.

At such an EGM, any business which is not covered by the agenda mentioned in the notice of the meeting cannot be voted upon.

## 21.12 EOGM BY TRIBUNAL—SECTION 98

If for any reason, it is *impracticable to call* a meeting of a company other than an annual general meeting, or to hold or conduct the meeting of the company, the tribunal may, either i) on its *own motion*, or ii) on the application of any director of the company, or of any member of the company who would be entitled to vote at the meeting, order a meeting to be called and conducted as the tribunal thinks fit, and may also give such other ancillary and consequential directions as it thinks fit expedient. A meeting so called and conducted shall be deemed to be a meeting of the company duly called and conducted.

## 21.13 PROXY—SECTION 105

In case of a company having a share capital and in the case of any other company, if the articles so authorise, any member of a company entitled to attend and vote at a meeting of the company shall be entitled to appoint another person (whether a member or not) as his proxy to attend and vote instead of himself.

Every notice calling a meeting of the company must contain a statement that a member entitled to attend and vote is entitled to appoint one proxy in the case of a private company and one or more proxies in the case of a public company and that the proxy need not be member of the company. But in case of Section 8 Company, proxy to be appointed should be member of company.

A member may appoint another person to attend and vote at a meeting on his behalf. Such other person is known as 'proxy'.

A member may appoint one or more proxies to vote in respect of the different shares held by him, or he may appoint one or more proxies in the alternative, so that if the first named proxy fails to vote, the second one may do so, and so on. A person appointed as proxy shall not act as proxy on behalf of more than 50 members and members holding the aggregate more than 10% of the total share capital of company carrying voting right.

The member appointing a proxy must deposit with the company a proxy form at the time of the meeting or prior to it giving details of the proxy appointed. However, any provision in the articles which requires a period longer than 48 hours before the meeting, for depositing with the company any proxy form appointing a proxy, shall have the effect as if a period of 48 hours had been specified in such provision.

The proxy form must be in writing and be signed by the member or his authorised attorney duly authorised in writing or if the appointer is a company, the proxy form must be under its seal or be signed by an officer or an attorney duly authorised by it. Proxy form should be in Form MGT-11.

Since proxy is a mere agent, he cannot appoint another proxy unless specifically authorised by the principal.

Right of member to vote in person supersedes rights conferred by grant of proxy. Where a member who has given proxy personally attends and votes and proxy also votes, the vote of member is valid and vote of the proxy is to be rejected. However, mere presence of a member does not imply revocation of proxy appointed by him.

A proxy is not entitled to vote except on a poll. Therefore, a proxy cannot vote on show of hands. A proxy cannot speak at the meeting. He is entitled to vote only at the poll. Since he cannot speak, he cannot ask questions in writing also, for in reality, it is a one-way mode of 'speaking'. However, a proxy can demand a poll or join in demanding a poll.

A proxy can be appointed for general meetings. However, for board meetings, appointment of proxy is not allowed.

## 21.14 REVOCATION OF PROXY AFTER APPOINTMENT

The proxy can be revoked by the member at any time, and is automatically revoked by the death or insolvency of the member.

The member may revoke the proxy by voting himself before the proxy has voted, but once the proxy has exercised the vote, the member cannot recast his vote. Where two proxy forms by the same shareholder are lodged in respect of the same votes, the last proxy form will be treated as the correct proxy form.

## 21.15 QUORUM FOR GENERAL MEETING—SECTION 103

Quorum refers to the minimum number of members who must be present at a meeting in order to constitute a valid meeting.

Unless the articles of a company provide for larger quorum, the following number of members personally present will be quorum for a general meeting:

| Situation | No of members to form quorum |
|---|---|
| Public company—if the number of members present as on date of meeting is not more than 1000 | 5 members |
| Public company—if the number of members present as on date of meeting is more than 1000 but not more than 5000 | 15 members |
| Public company—if the number of members present as on date of meeting is more than 5000 | 30 members |
| Private company | 2 members |

A meeting without the minimum quorum is *invalid* and decisions taken at such a meeting are not binding.

The articles of a company may provide for a quorum, without which a meeting will be construed to be invalid.

### 21.15.1 When Quorum is Required to be Present

It has been held by courts that unless the articles otherwise provide, a quorum needs to be present only when a meeting is commenced, and it is immaterial that there was no quorum at the time when the vote was taken.

Further, unless the articles otherwise provide, if within half-an-hour from the time appointed for holding a meeting of the company, a quorum is not present in person, the meeting :

1. if called upon the requisition of members, shall stand dissolved;
2. in any other case, it shall stand adjourned to the same day in the next week, at the same time and place, or to such other day and time as the Board of Directors may determine.

If at the adjourned meeting also, the quorum is not present within half-an-hour from the time appointed for holding the meeting, the members present shall form a quorum.

In case the tribunal calls or directs the calling of a meeting of the company, when default is made in holding an annual general meeting, the government may give directions regarding the quorum including a direction that even one member of the company present in person, or by proxy shall be deemed to constitute a meeting.

Similarly the tribunal may, direct a meeting of the company (other than an annual general meeting) to be called and hold, where for any reason it is impracticable to call a meeting and direct, that even one member present in person or by proxy shall be deemed to constitute a meeting.

### 21.15.2 Quorum of One Man

The word 'meeting' prima facie means coming together of more than one person. As such, with one man, a meeting cannot be held. However, there are certain exceptional situations when holding of meetings even with one member present in the meeting, as stated below, is held as valid.

If the entire share capital is held by one person, in such case the presence of that person alone shall constitute a quorum for any meeting of the company. In *East v Bennet Bros. Ltd*, it was held that a meeting of preference shareholders attended by the only preference shareholder of the company was proper.

According to Section 97 of the Companies Act, 2013, if default is made in holding the annual general meeting the tribunal may, on application of any member, call or direct calling of the said meeting and in such cases it may direct that one member present in person or by proxy shall be deemed to constitute a quorum for the meeting.

As provided under Section 98 of the Companies Act, 2013, the tribunal may order for holding of any other general meeting and may direct that one member present in person or by proxy shall constitute the quorum for the meeting.

**Case Study**

XYZ is a company conducting an AGM. There are three members personally present and one member present in his individual capacity and as a representative of a body corporate. State whether the AGM is valid?

**Case Study**

XYZ Ltd provided in articles that quorum for the general meeting should be seven members. Is it a valid provision in the article of the association? If articles provide that quorum for the company should be two members, is it as per Companies Act, 2013?

## 21.16 CHAIRMAN OF A GENERAL MEETING—SECTION 104

For fair conduct of a meeting, a person is required to chair the meeting. The chairman of the board of directors generally chairs all the meetings. The articles of association of the company regulate the appointment of chairman of the board.

If there is no chairman or he is not present within 15 minutes after the appointed time of the meeting or is unwilling to act as chairman of the meeting, the directors present may elect one among themselves to be the chairman of the meeting.

If, however no director is willing to act as chairman or if no director is present within *15 minutes* after the appointed time of the meeting, the members present should choose one among themselves to be chairman of the meeting. If, after the election of a chairman on a show of hands, poll is demanded and taken and a different person is elected as chairman, then that person will be the chairman for the rest of the meeting.

## 21.17 POWERS OF THE CHAIRMAN OF A GENERAL MEETING

The Act and the articles of the company provide various powers and duties of the chairman of a company, some of which are given below:

1. Section 107 of the Act empowers the chairman to declare the result of voting by show of hands.
2. As per Section 109 of the Act, a poll may be ordered by the chairman of a meeting and shall be ordered to be taken by him when demanded by members as specified in the said section.
3. Section 109 of the Act empowers the chairman of the meeting to appoint scrutinisers to scrutinise the votes given on the poll and to report to him.
4. The chairman has the power under Section 109 to remove any scrutiniser from office any time before the result of the poll is declared and to fill the vacancy caused by the removal.
5. As per Section 109 of the Act, the chairman of the meeting shall have the power to regulate the manner in which a poll shall be taken
6. As per Section 118 of the Act, the chairman has the power to exclude certain matters from the minutes of the meeting if he is of the opinion that (i) it is or would reasonably be regarded as defamatory of any person (ii) is irrelevant or immaterial to the processing or is detrimental to the interest of the company.
7. The chairman has to regulate the proceedings at the meeting, allow speakers to speak at the meeting and fix their time, check pandemonium at the meeting, and pull out persons using personal reference and irrelevant approaches.
8. The chairman has to see that the provisions of the Companies Act, 2013, articles of the company and any other law are complied with.
9. The chairman has to ensure that proper and correct minutes are prepared and signed within the time specified in the Act.

## 21.18 POLL—SECTION 109

The chairman may order a poll when a resolution proposed by the board is lost on the show of hands or if he is of the opinion that the decision taken on the show of hands is likely to be reversed by poll. When a poll is taken, the decision arrived at by poll is final and the decision on the show of hands has no effect.

A poll is allowed only if the prescribed number of members demand a poll. A poll must be ordered by the chairman if it is demanded:

1. in the case of a company having a share capital, by any member or members present in person or by proxy and holding shares in the company:
   (i) which confer a power to vote on the resolution not being less than one-tenth of the total voting power in respect of the resolution, and
   (ii) on which an aggregate sum of not less than ₹ 5 Lakh has been paid up.
2. in the case of any other company, by any member or members present in person or by proxy and having not less than one-tenth of the total voting power in respect of the resolution.

As per Section 109 of the Companies Act, 2013, poll demanded on a question of adjournment shall be taken immediately. As per Section 104 of the Companies Act, 2013, a poll demanded on election of chairman of the meeting shall be taken forthwith. A poll demanded on any other matter except adjournment or election of chairman shall be taken at such time not being later than 48 hours from the time when the demand was made.

## 21.19 POSTAL BALLOT—SECTION 110

Postal ballot is one method of voting. As per Section 2(65), postal ballot includes voting by shareholders by postal or electronic mode instead of voting personally by presenting for transacting businesses in a general meeting of the company.

Passing of resolution by postal ballot will be mandatory relating to business as may be specified by Central Government under Rule 22 of Companies (Management & Administration) Rules, 2014. The company may get any other resolution passed through postal ballot, if it so desires.

All resolutions which are required to be passed at General Meeting can be got passed through postal ballot. However, holding of AGM is a statutory requirement as per Section 96 and holding of AGM is essential. Passing of resolution by postal ballot will not eliminate the requirement of holding AGM.

## 21.20 PROCEDURE FOR PASSING RESOLUTION BY POSTAL BALLOT

A company which seeks to pass resolution by postal ballot shall take the following steps:

1. Pass necessary board resolution for postal ballot. The board resolution should make the company secretary, along with one of the functional directors, responsible for the entire postal ballot process.
2. The board should also fix the date and time schedule for the various activities and finalise the calendar of events.
3. The board of directors shall appoint one scrutiniser, who is not in employment of the company. He may be a retired judge or any person of repute who, in the opinion of the board can conduct the postal ballot voting process in a fair and transparent manner. Any person, including a retired judge, CA, ICWA or ICSI or advocate can be appointed. However, only an individual can be appointed as scrutiniser by name. A firm or corporate body cannot be appointed as scrutiniser.
4. A 'calendar of events' prescribing dates for various events should be finalised in the same board meeting. The 'calendar of events' contains date of dispatch of notice, last date for receiving ballot, copy of board resolution etc.

5. A copy of board resolution, along with calendar of events, should be dispatched to the Registrar of Companies for information within one week of passing board resolution, for his information.
6. The company should send a notice to all shareholders along with draft resolution, explaining reasons thereof.
7. The company may make a note below the notice of Annual General Meeting, for understanding of members, that the transaction(s) at serial numbers as specified in the notice requires consent of shareholders through postal ballot. The notice should be placed on the website of the company, if any.
8. Postal ballot should be sent by registered post with Acknowledgement Due, along with a postage pre-paid envelope for facilitating communication of assent or dissent by the shareholder to the resolution. Notice can be sent by registered post or under certificate of posting or courier or electronic mode.
9. In addition, an advertisement should be published in a leading newspaper and in one vernacular newspaper circulating in the state in which the registered office of the company is situated, about having dispatched the ballot papers.
10. The assent or dissent must be sent within 30 days from date of posting of the letter.
11. The resolution will be deemed to have been passed if it is assented by the requisite majority of shareholders by means of a postal ballot.
12. Postal ballot should be posted to all members. The ballot should be serially numbered and have distinguishing water mark, to avoid printing of duplicate ballot papers. The ballot should be in the prescribed form.
13. A member can return the ballot in person or through courier at his own cost and it should be accepted.
14. The ballot can be signed by the first named shareholder and in his absence, by the next named shareholder. Unsigned postal ballots will be rejected.
15. Voting right shall be reckoned on the paid-up value of shares registered in the name of shareholder on the date of dispatch of notice.
16. The pre-paid envelope should be addressed to the scrutiniser appointed by the board.
17. The last date by which postal ballot has to reach the company should be specified in the postal ballot sent to members. Ballots received after that date will be strictly treated as reply not received. Ballot papers received after due date are to be ignored
18. The result should be declared on the website of the company along with the scrutiniser's report.

## 21.21 BUSINESS PASSING RESOLUTION THROUGH POSTAL BALLOT

As per Rule 22 of Companies (Management & Administration) Rules, 2014, following businesses shall be passed through postal ballot only in the case of listed company:

1. Alteration in the object clause of memorandum
2. Alteration of articles defining private company
3. Alteration of articles of associations (AOA) in relation to insertion of provisions defining private company.
4. Issue of sweat equity to promoters in case of listed company.

5. Issue of shares with differential voting rights.
6. Variation of shareholders' right.
7. Buy-back of shares.
8. Election of small shareholders' director.
9. Sale of the whole or substantially whole of undertaking of company.
10. Giving loans or extending guarantee or providing security in excess of limit specified under Section 186.

**Case Study**

ABC Ltd, a listed company, passed resolution for alteration in the object clause of memorandum by show of hands. Is it proper?

**Case Study**

In case alteration of AOA to deletion or insertion of provisions defining private company is passed by resolution through postal ballot, is it as per the provisions of Companies Act, 2013?

**Case Study**

ABC Ltd, which is listed at Bombay Stock Exchange passes a resolution for buy-back of own shares through postal ballot. Is the action of ABC Ltd proper?

One-person Company and other companies having members up to 50 are not required to transact any business through postal ballot.

## 21.22 ADJOURNMENT OF MEETING

Adjournment means suspending the proceedings of a meeting for the time being so that the meeting may be continued at a later date and time fixed in that meeting itself at the time of such adjournment or decided later on.

Only the business not finished at the original meeting can be transacted at the adjourned meeting.

The majority of members at a meeting may move an adjournment motion at a meeting. If the chairman adjourns the meeting, ignoring the views of the majority, the remaining members can continue the meeting.

The chairman cannot adjourn the meeting at his own discretion without there being a good cause for such an adjournment. Where the chairman, acting bona fide within his powers, adjourns the meeting as per the view of the majority, the minority members cannot to continue with such meeting and, if they do the proceedings there will be null and void.

Despite provisions in the articles that chairman can adjourn meeting only with the consent of members, in the following cases, he may adjourn the meeting on his own:

1. If there is no quorum within half-an-hour.
2. Short adjournment for unruly behaviour

An adjourned meeting is merely the continuation of the original meeting and therefore, a fresh notice is not necessary, if the time, date and place for holding the adjourned meeting are decided and declared at the time of adjourning it.

If a meeting is adjourned without stipulation as to when it will be continued, fresh notice of the adjourned meeting must be given. If the article of the company provides, a fresh notice is required to be given for the adjourned meeting.

Time for poll is not adjournment; it is only recess. If meeting is stopped for holding a 'poll', it is not 'adjournment' but a 'recess'. Poll is part of meeting and meeting is said to be continuing when poll is being held.

## 21.23 MEETING OF DEBENTURE HOLDERS

A company issuing debentures may provide for the holding of meetings of the debenture holders. At such meetings, generally matters pertaining to the variation in terms of security or to alteration of their rights are discussed. All matters connected with the holding, conduct and proceedings of the meetings of the debenture holders are normally specified in the Debenture Trust Deed. The decisions at the meeting made by the prescribed majority are valid and lawful and binding upon the minority.

## 21.24 MEETING OF CREDITORS

Sometimes, a company, either as a running concern or in the event of winding up, has to make certain arrangements with its creditors. Meetings of creditors may be called for this purpose. A company may enter into arrangements with creditors with the sanction of the court for reconstruction or for any other arrangement.

The court/tribunal, on application, may order the holding of a creditors' meeting. If the scheme of arrangement is agreed to by majority in number of holding debts to a value of three-fourth of the total value of the debts, the court may sanction the scheme. A certified copy of the court's order is then filed with the registrar. The court order is binding on all the creditors and the company only after it is filed with registrar.

Similarly, in case of winding up of a company, a meeting of creditors and of contributories is held to ascertain the total amount due by the company and also to appoint a liquidator to wind up the affairs of the company.

## 21.25 ONE-MAN MEETING

Normally, one person cannot constitute a meeting even if he holds proxies for all members. However, in the following circumstances, one person shall form the quorum for a general meeting:

1. If all the shares of a particular class are held by one person [*East vs Bennet Bros. Ltd*].
2. If there is only one creditor or debenture-holder, he constitutes quorum for the creditors / 'debenture-holders' meeting.
3. Company Law Board may issue directions under Section 97 or Section 98 that one member, present in person or by proxy, shall constitute quorum.

## 21.26 MOTION

Motion means a proposal to be discussed at a meeting by the members. A resolution may be passed accepting the motion, with or without modifications or a motion may be entirely rejected.

A motion, on being passed as a resolution becomes a decision. A motion must be in writing and signed by the mover and put to the vote of the meeting by the chairman.

Only those motions which are mentioned in the agenda to the meeting can be discussed at the meeting. However, motions incidental or ancillary to the matter under discussion may be moved and passed.

Generally, a motion is proposed by one member and seconded by another member.

## 21.27 KINDS OF RESOLUTIONS

Resolutions mean decisions taken at a meeting. A motion, with or without amendments is put to vote at a meeting. Once the motion is passed, it becomes a resolution. A valid resolution can be passed at a properly convened meeting with the required quorum. There are broadly three types of resolutions:

1. Ordinary resolution—Section 114
2. Special resolution—Section 114
3. Resolution requiring special notice—Section 115

### 21.27.1 Ordinary Resolution

An ordinary resolution is one which can be passed by a simple majority, i.e., if the votes (including the casting vote, if any, of the chairman) at a general meeting cast by members entitled to vote in its favour are more than the votes cast against it. Voting may be by way of a show of hands or by a poll, provided 21 days notice has been given for the meeting.

### 21.27.2 Special Resolution

A special resolution is one which is passed by a 75 % majority only, i.e., the number of votes cast in favour of the resolution is at least three times the number of votes cast against it, either by a show of hands or on a poll in person or by proxy. Form MGT-14 is required to be filed with the registrar of companies along with an explanatory statement.

The intention to propose a resolution as a special resolution must be specifically mentioned in the notice of the general meeting. Special resolutions are needed to decide on important matters of the company.

Examples where special resolutions are required are:

1. To alter the domicile clause of the memorandum from one state to another or to alter the objects clause of the memorandum.
2. To alter the articles of association
3. To change the name of the company by omitting 'Limited' or 'Private Limited'.

## 21.28 RESOLUTION REQUIRING SPECIAL NOTICE—SECTION 115

There are certain matters specified in the Companies Act, 2013, which may be discussed at a general meeting only if a special notice is given regarding the proposal to discuss these matters at a meeting.

A special notice enables the members to be prepared on the matter to be discussed and gives them time to indicate their views on the resolution. Special notice is given by any member holding not less than 1% of total voting power or holding shares on which an aggregate sum not exceeding ₹ 5,00,000 has been paid up.

In case special notice of resolution is required by the Companies Act, 2013 or by the articles of a company, the intention to propose such a resolution must be notified to the company at least 14 days before the meeting. The company must, *within seven days* before the meeting, give the notice of the proposed resolution to its members.

Notice of the resolution is required to be given in the same way in which notice of a meeting is given, or if that is not practicable, the company may give notice by advertisement in a newspaper having an appropriate circulation or in any other manner allowed by the articles, not less than seven days before the meeting.

The following matters require Special Notice before they are discussed at the meeting:

1. To appoint, at an annual general meeting appointing an auditor, a person other than a retiring auditor.
2. To resolve at an annual general meeting that a retiring auditor shall not be reappointed.
3. To remove a director before the expiry of his period of office.
4. To appoint another director in place of the removed director.
5. Where the articles of a company provide for the giving of a special notice for a resolution, in respect of any specified matter or matters.

A resolution requiring special notice may be passed either as an ordinary resolution (simple majority) or as a special resolution (75 % majority).

## 21.29 MINUTES OF PROCEEDINGS OF GENERAL MEETING—SECTION 118-119

Every company must keep minutes of the proceedings of general meetings and of the meetings of board of directors and its committees. The minutes are a record of the discussions made at the meeting and the final decisions taken thereat.

Every company must keep minutes containing details of all proceedings at the meetings. The pages of the minute books must be consecutively numbered and the minutes must be recorded therein within 30 days of the meeting. They have to be written directly on the numbered pages. Pasting or attaching of papers is not allowed.

Each page of every such minutes books must be initiated or signed and last page of the record of proceedings of each meeting in such books must be dated and signed by:

1. the chairman of the meeting or that of the succeeding meeting in the case of a meeting of the Board of directors or committee thereof, and
2. the chairman of the meeting within the aforesaid 30 days or in the event of the death or inability of that chairman within the period, by a director duly authorised by the Board of Directors for the purpose, in the case of a general meeting.

The tribunal, however, may not object if minutes are maintained in loose leaf form provided all other procedural requirements are complied with and all possible safeguards against manipulation or interpolation of the minutes are ensured.

The loose leaves must be bound at reasonable intervals. Entering the minutes in a bound minute book by a chemical process, which does not amount to attachment to any book by pasting or otherwise is permissible, provided the original signatures of the chairman are given on each page on the mechanical impression of the minutes,.

All appointments of officers made at any of the meetings must be included in the minutes of the meeting.

In the case of a meeting of the board of directors or its committee, the minutes must also state the names of directors present at the meeting and the names of directors, if any, dissenting from, or not concurring with a resolution passed at the meeting.

The chairman may exclude from the minutes any matters which are defamatory, irrelevant or immaterial or which are detrimental to the interests of the company. The discretion of the chairman with regard to the inclusion or exclusion of any matter is absolute and unfettered.

Where minutes of the proceedings of any meeting have been kept properly, they are, unless the contrary is proved, presumed to be correct, and are valid evidence that the meeting was duly called and held, and all proceedings thereat have actually taken place, and in particular, all appointments of directors or liquidators made at the meeting shall be deemed to be valid.

The minute books of the proceedings of general meetings must be kept in the registered office of the company. It should be kept in custody of the company secretary or director as authorised by passing a resolution.

Any member has a right to inspect, free of cost during business hours at the registered office of the company, the minutes books containing the proceedings of the general meetings of the company. Further, any member shall be entitled to be furnished, within 7 days after he has made a request to the company, with a copy of any minutes on payment of ₹10 for each page or part of page.

If any inspection is refused or copy not furnished within the time specified, the tribunal is empowered to direct immediate inspection or sending of copy and penalise the company and its officer in default with fine. However, the minutes books of the board meetings are not open for inspection of members.

## 21.30 MEANING OF BOARD OF DIRECTORS

Company being an artificial entity, has to act through natural persons and they are named as directors and collectively as board of directors. The management of the affairs of the company is vested in the board of directors and thus they become the working organ of the company.

The board of directors of a company is entitled to exercise all such powers and to do all such acts and things as the company is authorised to exercise and do. The powers of the board can be classified into following categories:

1. Power that could be exercised only at the meeting of the board:
    - Section 179 of Companies Act, 2013
    - Section 182 of Companies Act, 2013
    - Section 183 of Companies Act, 2013

2. Power that could be exercised only with the consent of the company at general meeting:
   - Section 180 of Companies Act, 2013.
   - Section 181 of Companies Act, 2013
   - Section 192 of Companies Act, 2013

The board of directors of a company cannot enter in to the following transactions:

1. Forward dealing in securities of the company—Section 194 of Companies Act, 2013
2. Insider trading—Section 195 of Companies Act, 2013

## 21.31 POWERS OF THE BOARD OF DIRECTORS WHICH CAN BE EXERCISED AT THEIR MEETING—SECTION 179

*Section 179* of the Companies Act, 2013, specifies certain powers which can be exercised by the board only by passing a resolution at a board meeting. However, some of these powers may be delegated by the board in the manner prescribed.

### Powers exercisable only by a resolution at a board meeting as per Act:

As per Section 179 and other various provisions of Companies Act, the board shall exercise the following powers only by means of a resolution passed at a meeting of the board:

1. To make calls on shares.
2. To authorise buy-back up to 10% paid up capital and free reserve in a year.
3. To issue securities including debentures, whether in or outside India.
4. To borrow money
5. To invest funds of the company.
6. To grant loans or give guarantee or provide security in respect of loans.
7. To approve financial statement and the board's report.
8. To diversify the business of the company.
9. To approve amalgamation, merger or reconstruction.
10. To take over a company or acquire a controlling or substantial stake in another company.

***Important Note:***

The resolution in pursuance of powers of the board mentioned above shall be filed with the registrar in form MGT-14 within 30 days of passing such resolution.

Ministry of Corporate Affair (MCA) has vide its General Circular 19/2014, clarified with regard to issue of duplicate share certificates, that a committee of directors may exercise such powers subject to any restrictions imposed by the board in this regard in the light of the provisions of Sections 179, 180 and Regulation 71 of Table 'F' of Schedule I to the Companies Act, 2013.

**Powers exercisable only by a resolution at a board meeting as per rules of Companies Act 2013:**

1. To make political contributions.
2. To appoint or remove key managerial personnel (KMP).
3. To appoint internal auditors and a secretarial auditor.

### 21.31.1 Delegation of Powers

The power to invest, borrow and grant loan or guarantee or security can (Point nos. *d* to *f* as mentioned above) be delegated. Power of board can be delegated to a committee of board or managing director, manager or other principal officer of the company or by branch officer in case of branch by means of a resolution passed by the board. Resolution delegating powers should be passed at a board meeting. Power to make inter-corporate loans and investments cannot be delegated by the company according to Section 186. The company, in a general meeting, may impose any restrictions and conditions on the exercise by the board of any of the powers specified above.

Besides the powers specified in Section 179, there are certain other powers also which can be exercised only at the meeting of the board:

1. The power of filling casual vacancies in the board.
2. The power to make political contributions—as per Section 182 of Companies Act, 2013

For the following matter, the consent of every director entitled to vote and present is required at the board's meeting:

1. The power to appoint a person as managing director or manager who is holding either office in another company—Sections 203 of Companies Act, 2013.
2. The power to give loan to, or invest in any shares of, any other body corporate—Section 186 of Companies Act, 2013

## 21.32 PROHIBITION AND RESTRICTION REGARDING POLITICAL CONTRIBUTIONS BY DIRECTORS—SECTION 182

Contribution means any payment made without consideration. It includes donation, subscription or any other payment. It includes contribution made to a political party or to any person for political purpose.

Section 182 considers political contribution made whether directly or indirectly. Directly means the company has contributed towards the expenses for political party or donation made to political party. Indirect contribution means payment made to any person for benefit which a political party has obtained from that person.

Political contribution also includes any expenditure incurred by a company on advertisement in any publication by or on behalf of a political party or for its advantage.

Government companies and companies which have been in existence for less than three financial years are not allowed to make political contributions. Political contribution may be made by any other company is subject to the following conditions:

1. The aggregate amounts contributed and proposed to be contributed by a company in any financial year shall not exceed 7.5% of its average net profits of preceding last three financial years.
2. Board resolution should be passed.

Following details regarding contribution should be disclosed in profit and loss account:

1. the amount of contributions during the financial year
2. the name of the party or person to which the amount has been contributed.

### 21.32.1 Penalty

If contribution is made in contravention:

1. the company shall be punishable with fine up to 5 times the amount so contributed and
2. the officer who is in default shall be punished with imprisonment up to six months and fine which may extend to five times the amount of contribution.

***Important Note:***

'Political party' means an association or body of individuals registered with the Election Commission of India as a political party.

## 21.33 POWER OF THE BOARD TO MAKE CONTRIBUTION TO NATIONAL DEFENCE FUND—SECTION 183

A company can contribute any amount to national defence fund or any other fund approved by the central government for the purpose of defence fund. The amount can be contributed to national defence fund by the board of directors or any person or authority exercising powers of board or of the company in a general meeting.

The provision of Section 183 is overriding to Sections 180, 181, 182 and anything contained in memorandum or article of association of company. The company should disclose in its profit and loss account the total amount contributed to national defence fund in the financial year.

## 21.34 POWERS THAT CAN ONLY BE EXERCISED BY THE BOARD OF DIRECTORS OF A PUBLIC COMPANY WITH THE CONSENT OF THE COMPANY IN A GENERAL MEETING—SECTION 180

The Companies Act, 2013, imposes certain restrictions on the powers of the Board. As per Section 180(1) of the Act, the Board shall not exercise the following powers without prior consent of the shareholders in a general meeting:

1. Sell, lease or otherwise dispose of the whole, or substantially the whole of undertakings of the company.

***Important Note for Section 180(1)(a):***

The same provision is applicable when a company has more than one undertaking. The company can sell, lease or otherwise dispose of any one of the undertaking.

**Meaning of undertaking:** An undertaking is that in which a company has made investment more than 20% of its net worth or that which generates 20% of the total income as per the last audited balance sheet.

**Net worth:** Net worth is the aggregate value of paid-up capital (+) all reserves created out of profits and securities premium account (–) accumulated losses, deferred expenditure and miscellaneous expenditure not written off as per last audited balance sheet.

**Substantially the whole of undertaking:** This stands for 20% or more value of undertaking as per the last audited balance sheet in any financial year.

This provision is not applicable when the general business of a company is to sell or lease property.

2. Invest, otherwise than in trust securities, the compensation received in respect of the compulsory acquisition of any undertaking of the company as a result of merger or amalgamation.
3. Borrow money, if money already borrowed, together with the money to be borrowed will exceed the aggregate of paid-up capital and free reserves of the company.

***Important Note for Section 180(1)(c)***

Temporary loans obtained from the company's bankers in the ordinary course of business are not considered as borrowings. Temporary loans mean *loans repayable on demand* or loans repayable within *six months* of the date of the loan. Loan for short term, cash credit arrangements, discounting of bills are examples of temporary loans. Loan raised for the purpose of financial expenditure of capital nature is not temporary loan.

Banking companies are granted exemption from provision of this section in the ordinary course of business.

The resolution passed in the general meeting shall specify the total amount up to which money may be borrowed by the Board; otherwise the resolution shall be void.

4. Remit, or give time for the repayment of any debt due by a director. However, advance given in the ordinary course of business to a director may be renewed by a banking company without the approval of the general meeting.

Section 180 is applicable to all companies. Special resolution is required to be passed at general meeting.

***Important Note:***

Section 180 of Companies Act, 2013 came into force with effect from 12th September, 2013, and requires a company to pass a special resolution at its general meeting. Earlier, Section 293 of the Companies Act, 1956, required a company to pass an ordinary resolution at a general meeting. MCA has clarified vide its circular no. 15/2013 that if a company had issued its notice before 12th September, 2013, it will be sufficient if the company has passed ordinary resolution instead of special resolution.

## 21.35 PROHIBITION AND RESTRICTION REGARDING CHARITABLE FUND BY DIRECTORS—SECTION 181

The board of directors of a company may contribute or donate to bona fide charitable and other funds with prior permission obtained at a general meeting when such aggregate amount of contribution, in any financial year, exceeds 5% of its average net profit for three immediately preceding financial years. Any amount spent for the welfare of employees (e.g., a school or a hospital for the benefit of employees) is included within the meaning of charitable contribution.

The resolution passed by shareholders in a general meeting must specify the total amount up to which money may be contributed by the board. This section is applicable to all companies.

***Important Note:***

If a company has obligation to contribute to corporate social responsibility (CSR) fund as per Section 135 of the Companies Act, 2013, or donate to the prime minister's national relief fund, donation to such funds shall not require compliance with Section 181 of Companies Act, 2013

## 21.36 RESTRICTION ON NON-CASH TRANSACTION INVOLVING DIRECTORS—SECTION 192

Section 192 regulates arrangements in respect of acquisition of assets for consideration other than cash between a company and a director of company or holding company or its subsidiary company or its associate or person connected with such director. A company cannot enter into an agreement by which:

1. a director of the company or its holding, subsidiary or associate company or a person connected with him acquires assets for consideration other than cash, from the company; or
2. the company acquires assets for consideration other than cash, from such director or person so connected.

Such arrangements shall require prior approval by resolution in a general meeting. If a director or a connected person is a director of its holding company, approval is also required to be obtained by passing a resolution in a general meeting of the holding company. The notice of special resolution shall include the particulars of the arrangement along with the value of the assets involved in such arrangement duly calculated by a registered valuer. If arrangement is entered into by a company or its holding company in contravention of provisions, it is voidable at the instance of company. The arrangement will be valid if:

1. restitution of any money is not possible and the company has been indemnified by any other person; or
2. any rights are acquired bona fide for value and without notice of the contravention of the provisions of this section by any other person.

***Important Note:***

Associate company means a company in which the other company has a control of 20% of total share capital or business decisions under agreement, but which is not subsidiary of the company and includes a joint venture company

## 21.37 PROHIBITION ON FORWARD DEALINGS IN SECURTIES OF COMPANY—SECTION 194

The director or key managerial personnel (KMP) should not buy in the company or its holding company or subsidiary or associate company:

1. a right to call for delivery or a right to make delivery at a specified price and within a specified time, of a specified number of relevant shares or a specified amount of relevant debentures; or
2. a right, as he may elect, to call for delivery, or to make delivery at a specified price and within a specified time, of a specified number of relevant shares or a specified amount of relevant debentures.

The director or any other KMP of company is punishable with imprisonment for a term which may extend to 2 years or with fine of not less than ₹ 1 lakh but not more than ₹ 5 lakh or with both if he contravenes the above provisions. Securities acquired in contravention are required to be surrendered to the company.

***Important Note:***

'Key managerial personnel', in relation to a company, means—

(i) the chief executive officer or the managing director or the manager
(ii) the company secretary
(iii) the whole-time director
(iv) the chief financial officer and
(v) such other officer as may be prescribed.

## 21.38 PROHIBITION ON INSIDER TRADING—SECTION 195

Section 195 prohibits directors or key managerial personal of a company from dealing in securities of the company or counselling, procuring or communicating, directly or indirectly, about any non-public price sensitive information to any person.

Price sensitive information means any information which relates, directly or indirectly, to a company and which if published is likely to materially affect the price of securities of the company. However, prohibition is not applicable if the director or KMP is required to communicate in ordinary course of business or profession or employment or under any law.

If a person contravenes this provision, he shall be punishable with imprisonment up to 5 years or fine not less than ₹ 5 lakhs but which may extend to ₹ 25 Crore or three times the amount of profits made out of insider trading, whichever is higher or with both.

## 21.39 FREQUENCY OF BOARD MEETINGS—SECTION 173

A company can convene any number of board meetings to discuss business as required. The first board meeting should be held within 30 days from the date of incorporation of the company. Subsequent board meetings shall be held in such a way that:

1. At least four board meetings are held in a calendar year.
2. The maximum gap between two meetings is not be more than 120 days.

A one-person company, small company and dormant company:

1. Should hold at least one board meeting in each half of the calendar year.
2. Should ensure that the minimum gap between two meetings is not less than 90 days.

If a board meeting is called but could not be held due to want to quorum, provision of Section 173 is complied with as per Section 174(4) of the Companies Act, 2013.

**Case Study**

The board of directors of ABC Ltd met three times in the year 2014 and the fourth meeting, though called, could not be held for want of quorum. Examine with reference to the relevant provisions of the Companies Act, 2013, whether any provisions of the Companies Act, 2013 have been contravened.

## 21.40 DAY, TIME AND PLACE OF BOARD MEETING

A board meeting can be held during business hours and on a day which is not a public holiday. However, if the meeting is adjourned for want of quorum and if the articles do not otherwise provide, the meeting will stand adjourned automatically to the same day, in the next week at the same place and time. If that day happens to be a public holiday, then to the meeting is held on the next succeeding day, which is not a public holiday at the same place and time.

The board meeting can be held at any place. It is not necessary to hold board meeting at the registered office. Board meeting can be held by way of video conferencing also. (The provisions for board meeting through video conferencing is explained in detail at a later part of this chapter) Directors can hold a board meeting even outside india. Such board meetings can be held outside business hours.

## 21.41 NOTICE OF BOARD MEETING—SECTION 173

Board meeting should be called by giving 7 days' notice in writing to the directors at their registered addresses, by hand delivery, by post or by electronic means.

### 21.41.1 Meeting at Shorter Notice

Board meeting can be called at shorter notice subject to following conditions:

1. If the company is required to have an independent director:
   - Presence of at least one independent director is required.
   - In case of absence of independent director, the decision taken at such meeting shall be circulated to all the directors, and shall be final only on ratification thereof by at least one independent director.
2. If the company is not required to appoint an independent director, the meeting can be called at a shorter notice without any conditions to be complied with.

As per Regulation 67 of Table F of Companies Act, 2013, a board meeting can be called by any director or manager or secretary on requisition of director.

Notice is also required to be given to every other director at his usual address in India. *Parameshwari Prasad Gupta vs Union of India*, Supreme Court has held that for a board meeting to be effective, it must be duly convened by proper notice to each director and in default, the meeting is irregular.

If the loan agreement with bank or financial institute provides, notice of board meeting should be given to them. If the directors specify a particular method of sending notice, it should be given as per the specified method. Notice should be given to a director even if he has stated that he will not be able to attend. Notice should be given to a director even he cannot participate or vote on the subject to be transacted at the meeting. For adjourned board meeting, fresh notice is not required to be given but if the board meeting is adjourned sine die, fresh notice is required.

No format of notice is prescribed by the act. Notice of the board meeting shall specify that a director can participate either through audio or video means instead of personal presence. Failure to send notice even to a single director would render the resolution passed at the meeting null and void. If there is a default in providing the notice, every officer (company secretary) who is responsible is liable to pay a fine of ₹ 25,000.

**Case Study**

The board of directors of M/s Infotech Consultants Limited, registered in Calcutta, proposes to hold the next board meeting in the month of May, 2015. They seek, your advice in respect of the following matters:

(i) Can the board meeting be held in Chennai, when all directors of the company reside at Calcutta?
(ii) Whether the board meeting can be called on a public holiday and that too after business hours as the majority of the directors of the company have gone to Chennai on vacation?
(iii) Is it necessary that the notice of the board meeting should specify the nature of business to be transacted?

Advise with reference to the relevant provisions of the Companies Act, 2013.

## 21.42 CONTENT OF BOARD MEETING NOTICE

Notice of board meeting contains details regarding place, date and time of the meeting. Agenda is not mandatory for board meeting but it is a good corporate practice. However for the following subject matters, agenda is compulsory:

1. When a public company or a private company which is a subsidiary of a public company would like to appoint a person as its managing director, if he is the managing director or manager of one and not more than one, other company including a private company which is not a subsidiary of a public company (Section 203 of Companies Act, 2013).
2. Where a public company or a private company which is a subsidiary of a public company wants to appoint a person as its manager, if he is the manager or managing director of one and not more than one other company (Section 203 of Companies Act, 2013).
3. When a company grants inter-corporate loan in excess of limit (Section 186 of Companies Act, 2013).

## 21.43 QUORUM FOR BOARD MEETING—SECTION 174

It is necessary for directors to attend board meetings personally. Proxies are not allowed at board meetings. However, any expert can attend a board meeting, if he is invited by the board subject to condition that he cannot vote. If any person is invited as an expert at a board meeting, he is known as special invitee. Special invitees are not counted for quorum.

Quorum means minimum number of directors competent to transact and vote on any business before the meeting. Quorum for board meeting is one-third of the total strength (fraction in that one-third is rounded off as one) or 2 directors whichever is higher.

***Example***

A Ltd has 9 directors on board. Quorum will be 1/3 × 9 = 3 or 2 whichever is higher. So in the given case, the quorum is 3 directors. But if the board has 8 directors, quorum will be 1/3 × 8 = 2.66. Any fraction is rounded off as one. So it will be 3 or 2 (whichever is higher).

Directors whose place is liable to be vacant should not be considered for calculating total strength.

***Example***

A Ltd has 10 directors on board. Before the board meeting, one director resigned. Thus, the total strength will be 9 directors and the quorum will be 1/3 × 9 = 3 or 2 whichever is higher.

The article of association of a company may provide for a higher quorum. If the number of directors is reduced below quorum, then the remaining directors may hold the meeting for the following purposes: to call a general meeting or to increase the number of directors. It was held in the case of *Rajan N. Doshi vs British Burma Petroleum Co. Ltd.* that a single director cannot act for a purpose other than calling general meeting for the appointment of directors.

Quorum is required to be present throughout the meeting. A meeting held without quorum is invalid. Interested directors will not be counted for the purpose of quorum. If, at any time, interested directors exceed or equal to 2/3rd of the total strength, the remaining non-interested shall be the quorum, provided it is not less than two. If quorum is not present, the meeting is adjourned.

***Important Note:***

Directors participating in a meeting through video conferencing or other audio visual means shall be counted for the purpose of quorum, unless he is to be excluded for any items of business under any provisions of the Act or the rules.

Section 174 is not applicable to a One-person Company.

## 21.44 MATTERS WHICH CANNOT BE DEALT AT BOARD MEETING THROUGH VIDEO CONFERENCING

The following matters cannot be dealt at a board meetings held though video conferencing:

1. Approval of the annual financial statements;
2. Approval of the board's report;
3. Approval of the prospectus;
4. Audit committee Meetings for consideration of accounts; and
5. Approval of the matter relating to amalgamation, merger, demerger, acquisition and takeover.

## 21.45 CHAIRMAN OF BOARD MEETING

For a valid board meeting, a proper person should be in the chair. Article of association will normally provide for election of chairman and the period up to which he is to hold office. Regulation 70 of Table F of Companies Act, 2013, prescribes the provision for appointment of chairman of a board meeting.

The board may elect a chairman of its meetings and determine the period of his office. If no chairman is elected or if, at any meeting, the chairman is not present within 5 minutes after the time appointed for holding the meeting, the directors present may select any one of them to be chairman of the meeting. Chairman of board and chairman of meeting are different. Chairman of meeting is the chairman only for one meeting.

In case of equality of votes, the chairman of the board has second or casting vote. Casting vote is available to the chairman of board either on show of hand or on poll. The chairman of meeting also has a casting vote on equality if the article of the company does not restrict it specifically. The chairman has absolute discretion in using casting vote. He may refuse to cast second vote on equality. Only a director can be the chairman of a board meeting.

## 21.46 VOTING AT BOARD MEETING

Matters at a board meeting are decided by a majority of votes. There are three exceptions to the majority rule. In the following matter, unanimous approval of board is required:

1. Appointment of managing director, if the person is already a managing director or manager (Section 203 of Companies Act, 2013).
2. Appointment of manager, if the person is already a manager (Section 203 of Companies Act, 2013).
3. Inter-corporate loan (Section 186 of Companies Act, 2013).

A director cannot participate or vote on the resolutions in which he is interested. Voting at board meeting is by show of hands only. Poll method is not available as each director is entitled for one vote.

## 21.47 MINUTES OF BOARD MEETING—SECTION 118

'Minute' means the official record of the proceeding of a meeting. It should be recorded within 30 days from the conclusion of meeting. However, it is not required to be signed within 30 days. Separate minute books should be prepared for board, general and committee meetings.

Each page of minute book should be numbered consecutively. Each page of the minute book should be initialled or signed and the last page of the minute shall be dated and signed by the Chairman of the said meeting or the Chairman of the next meeting. It is not necessary that chairman of subsequent meeting should have attended meeting. No attachment shall be made to the minute's book by pasting or otherwise. The chairman has the power of inclusion or non-inclusion of any matter in the minutes, if he is of the opinion that such matter is defamatory of any person or it is irrelevant or immaterial or it is detrimental to the interest of the company.

The minutes book must be a bound book. However maintaining minute book in loose leaf is permitted but in such circumstances, the company must get it bounded within a reasonable interval of time (not more than 6 months).

The Companies Act, 2013, does not contain any provision regarding inspection or supply for copy of minute to shareholders. Unless the article of association provides to the contrary, a shareholder has no right of inspection or of obtaining copies of the minutes of its board meetings (MCA View).

A statutory auditor, as part of discharge of his duties, is required to verify the minutes and is entitled to demand extract and preserve them as audit papers. Similarly, a cost auditor or a company secretary in practice, for the purpose of secretarial audit, has the right to verify the minutes of board meeting and demand extracts thereof. MCA has clarified that the minutes book shall be kept at the registered office and that it can be moved only when the board meeting takes place outside the registered office of the company for that purpose. The company shall observe secretarial standard with respect to board meeting.

Where the minutes of the proceeding of the board or a committee thereof have been kept in accordance with Section 118, then until the contrary is proved.

1. The meeting shall be deemed to have been duly called and held
2. All proceedings thereat shall be deemed to have been duly taken place and
3. All appointment of directors/resignation at the meeting shall be deemed to be valid.

**Case Study**

Accurate Arcs Ltd maintains the minutes book of the board meetings in loose-leaf system and gets them bound once in three months. Can it do so? Board meetings were held on 24th March, 2014 and 15th April, 2014. Mr. Rameshwar, who was the chairman of these two Board Meetings died on 1.5.2014, without signing the minutes. How should be the minutes be signed and by whom?

## LIST OF LANDMARK JUDGEMENTS

1. ***Amrit Kaur Puri vs Kapurthala Flour Oil & General Mills Co. (P) Ltd (1984)***
   Company can fix higher quorum for board meeting than what is specified under Companies Act.
2. ***Marshall's Valve Gear Co. vs Manning Wardel & Co. Ltd (1909)***
   Shareholders are competent to intervene in respect of matters delegated to BOD, when directors act for their own personal interest in complete disregard of interest of company.
3. ***B. N. Vishwanathan vs Tiffins B. A. and (P) Ltd (1953)***
   Shareholders may exercise power in general meeting where none of directors was validly appointed.
4. ***Barron vs Potter (1914)***
   When there is deadlock in management, majority shareholders may exercise powers in general meeting.
5. ***P. K. Neangadi vs Malayalee Bank Ltd (1971)***
   Where director has misapplied or misappropriated money or property of company, the court may order him to repay the money or restore property or to pay compensation.
6. ***Ferrucccio Sias vs Jai Manga Ram Mukhi (1998)***
   Notice of board meeting sent by fax is adequate notice.
7. ***R. Khemka vs Decccan Enterprises (P) Ltd (1998)***
   Telephonic invitation or oral invitation cannot amount as notice of board meeting.
8. ***Ernakulaum Financiers vs Joseph Chandy (1998)***
   Once a meeting is requisitioned, the board is under obligation to hold EOGM.

9. ***LIC vs Escorts Ltd (1986)***
   Requisitioners are not required to disclose reason for their proposed resolution for EOGM.
10. ***Radheshyam Tulsian vs Panchmukhi Investment (2002)***
    Meeting without notice and without quorum is invalid.
11. ***NVR Nagappa Chettair vs Madras Race Club (1951)***
    Twenty-one days' notice is mandatory for GM, unless expressly waived by members by giving consent.
12. ***Rajiv Khandelwal vs Amigo Multifilm (1999)***
    Intentional omission to send notice to even one member will invalidate the meeting.
13. ***Palak Kumar vs Cine & Supply (2002)***
    No business can be transacted at GM for which notice was not given.
14. ***T. V. Mathew vs Nadukkara Agro Processing (2002)***
    There is no provision to grant extension for holding first AGM.
15. ***Bejoy Kumar Karkani vs Asst. ROC (1985)***
    If accounts are not ready, the meeting may be adjourned, but even the adjourned meeting must be held within the statutory period including the time extension allowed.
16. ***Young vs South African Etc. (1896)***
    Preference share holder is also member of company.
17. ***Cousins vs International Brick Co. Ltd (1931)***
    A proxy may be described as an agent appointed as a member to act on his behalf at the meeting.
18. ***Maxwell Dyes Chemicals vs Kothari Industrial Corporation (1996)***
    Fresh proxy is not necessary for the adjourned meeting.
19. ***John vs Rees (1969)***
    Chairman can adjourn meeting shortly for unruly behaviours.
20. ***Jackson vs Hamlyn (1953)***
    Time taken for poll is not adjournment, it is only recess.
21. ***Tamal Kumar Majumdar vs UOI (2000)***
    Voting is a basic right of a member.
22. ***Ebrahim Sai vs South Indian Industries Ltd (1938)***
    Director is entitled to notice even if he is out of India and that right to receive notice cannot be waived.
23. ***Parmeshwari Prasad Gupta Vs UOI (1974)***
    Failure to send notice even to one director would render the resolution passed at the meeting null and void.
24. ***Maharani Yogeshwari vs Lake Shore place Hotel (1996)***
    Quorum is required at the adjourned board meeting also.
25. ***Amit Kumar Puri vs Kapurthala Flour Oil Mills (1984)***
    Article of association can provide higher quorum but not lower quorum for board meeting.

**26.** ***Ashish das Gupra vs Satvinder Singh (2000)***

Board meeting is invalid, if there is no quorum and all decisions at such meeting are also invalid.

**27.** ***Pramod Kumar Mittal vs Sourthern Steel (1980)***

Notice of board meeting need not be given unless article provides otherwise.

**28.** ***Nazir Hoosein vs Darajus Bhattena (2000)***

Chairman of board of directors is central figure in holding the meeting and is the controlling factor in the conduct of a meeting.

## TEST YOUR KNOWLEDGE

1. Discuss the different kinds of meeting. **(Ref. Para-21.1)**
2. What are the requisites of a valid general meeting? **(Ref. Para-21.2)**
3. Every general meeting, in order to be valid, must be duly conveyed, properly constituted and conducted. Comment. **(Ref. Para-21.2)**
4. By what different methods notice of general meeting can be served? **(Ref. Para-21.3)**
5. Notice of general meeting must be served by UPC. Comment. **(Ref. Para-21.3)**
6. Explain the provisions regarding notice of a general meeting. **(Ref. Para-21.4)**
7. Omission go give notice of general meeting invalidate meeting. Comment. **(Ref. Para-21.4)**
8. What are the provisions under Companies Act regarding holding annual general meeting? **(Ref. Para-21.5)**
9. Write short note on time limit for holding annual general meeting. **(Ref. Para-21.5)**
10. Annual general meeting should be held within six months from end of the financial year. Comment. **(Ref. Para-21.5)**
11. What remedy is available when a company defaults in holding annual general meeting? **(Ref. Para-21.8)**
12. What is significance of annual general meeting? **(Ref. Para-21.9)**
13. What is extraordinary general meeting? When it is called? **(Ref. Para-21.10)**
14. State the circumstances in which an extra-ordinary general meeting can be called on requisition? **(Ref. Para-21.11)**
15. When can an extraordinary general meeting be called by Tribunal? **(Ref. Para-21.12)**
16. Explain the provisions regarding proxy. **(Ref. Para-21.13)**
17. Any person can be appointed as proxy. Is it correct? **(Ref. Para-21.13)**
18. Proxy, once appointed, is irrevocable. Comment. **(Ref. Para-21.14)**
19. What is the meaning of quorum? What are the provisions of quorum under Companies Act? **(Ref. Para-21.15)**
20. Can one person constitute quorum? **(Ref. Para-21.15)**
21. Write short note on chairman of general meeting. **(Ref. Para-21.16)**
22. When should the chairman order for poll? **(Ref. Para-21.18)**
23. What is postal ballot? Is it mandatory for all business? **(Ref. Para-21.19)**
24. State the procedure for postal ballot. **(Ref. Para-21.20)**
25. Write down any five businesses which can be passed by way of postal ballot. **(Ref. Para-21.21)**

26. Adjourned meetings do not require fresh notice. Comment. **(Ref. Para-21.22)**
27. When and by whom is a meeting of debenture holders called? **(Ref. Para-21.23)**
28. Write short note on meeting of creditors. **(Ref. Para-21.24)**
29. One man can convene a valid meeting. Comment. **(Ref. Para-21.25)**
30. What do you understand by motion? **(Ref. Para-21.26)**
31. Write short note on minutes of general meeting. **(Ref. Para-21.29)**
32. What are the different types of resolution which may be passed by a company? **(Ref. Para-21.27)**
33. When is a company required to pass special resolution? **(Ref. Para-21.27)**
34. Which resolutions require special notice? **(Ref. Para-21.28)**
35. What are the provisions for the minutes of a general meeting? **(Ref. Para-21.29)**
36. Certain powers are to be exercised by the board of directors of company only at the board meeting. What are those powers? **(Ref. Para-21.31)**
37. Explain the powers available to the board of directors only with consent of shareholders. **(Ref. Para-21.34)**
38. At what frequency should board meetings be held? **(Ref. Para-21.39)**
39. Can a company convene a board meeting on a public holiday? **(Ref. Para-21.40)**
40. At which place can a board meeting be convened? **(Ref. Para-21.40)**
41. What is the notice period required for a board meeting? **(Ref. Para-21.41)**
42. No notice of board meeting was sent to one of the directors. Is the meeting valid? **(Ref. Para-21.41)**
43. What should be contents of notice for a board meeting? **(Ref. Para-21.42)**
44. What is the quorum for a board meeting? How is it calculated? **(Ref. Para-21.43)**
45. Who can be the chairman of a board meeting? **(Ref. Para-21.45)**
46. How is voting is carried out at a board meeting? **(Ref. Para-21.46)**
47. State the provisions under Companies Act for preparation and signing of minutes of meetings. **(Ref. Para-21.47)**

## MULTIPLE-CHOICE QUESTIONS

1. The time gap between two AGMs shall not exceed ______.
   (i) 15 months
   (ii) 18 months
   (iii) 16 months
   (iv) None of these
2. The first AGM must be held within ______ from the incorporation of the company.
   (i) 15 months
   (ii) 18 months
   (iii) 12 months
   (iv) None of these
3. Every AGM must be held within ______ from the end of the F.Y.
   (i) 4 months
   (ii) 6 months
   (iii) 9 months
   (iv) None of these
4. Any company cannot hold AGM on a public holiday.
   (i) Yes
   (ii) No

5. AGM should be held
   (i) at the head office.
   (ii) within the same town or city where the registered office is situated.
   (iii) at the corporate office.
   (iv) None of these.
6. Board of directors has the authority to issue notice of the general meeting.
   (i) Yes
   (ii) No
7. Notice of the general meeting should be sent to preference shareholders also.
   (i) Yes
   (ii) No
8. The proxy must be a member of the company. Do you agree with this statement?
   (i) Agree
   (ii) Disagree
9. In case of private company the quorum should be
   (i) two members
   (ii) three members
   (iii) four members
   (iv) None of these
10. Quorum for a general meeting should be present at the
    (i) commencement of meeting.
    (ii) middle of the meeting.
    (iii) end of the meeting.
    (iv) Any time during meeting.
11. Before AGM ______ report is sent by the directors to its members.
    (i) Statutory
    (ii) Audit
    (iii) Annual
    (iv) None of the above
12. ______ company is/are required to hold A.G.M.
    (i) Public company
    (ii) Private company
    (iii) Government company
    (iv) All the three
13. The resolutions passed at AGM are ______
    (i) Valid
    (ii) Void
    (iii) Voidable
    (iv) Void *ab initio*
14. Every business transacted at an EGM is a/an ______ business.
    (i) Ordinary
    (ii) Special
    (iii) Both (i) & (ii)
    (iv) None of the above
15. In the absence of quorum, the proceedings of the meeting will be ______.
    (i) valid
    (ii) void
    (iii) voidable
    (iv) None of the above
16. If quorum is not present within ______ time, the meeting will stand dissolved.
    (i) ½ Hr.
    (ii) 1 Hr.
    (iii) 1½ Hr.
    (iv) 2 Hr.
17. ______ Order is empowered to call an EGM even though one member is present in person or by proxy.
    (i) Tribunal
    (ii) Government
    (iii) ROC
    (iv) None of these

18. Voting right cannot be exercised in case of ______
    (i) calls in advance
    (ii) calls in arrears
    (iii) Both (i) and (ii)
    (iv) None of the above
19. Who can use the casting vote in the case of equality of votes?
    (i) Chairman
    (ii) Director
    (iii) Auditor
    (iv) Manager
20. The chairman, on his own motion, ______ also orders a poll.
    (i) must
    (ii) should
    (iii) may
    (iv) None of the above
21. The chairman conducts the poll within ______ hours from the demand.
    (i) 24
    (ii) 48
    (iii) 72
    (iv) 36
22. Depositing of proxy with the company should be made within how many hours?
    (i) 24
    (ii) 48
    (iii) 36
    (iv) 72
23. If the notice contains a special business, then an ______ statement shall be enclosed.
    (i) explanatory
    (ii) enquiry
    (iii) Both (i) and (ii)
    (iv) None of the above
24. Proxies cannot vote on ______.
    (i) show of hands
    (ii) poll
    (iii) Both (i) & (ii)
    (iv) None of the above
25. ______ is the official recording of the proceedings of a meeting
    (i) Quorum
    (ii) Minutes
    (iii) Both (i) and (ii)
    (iv) None of the above
26. Minutes, in the case of a general meeting, should be recorded within ______ days from the date of conclusion of every meeting.
    (i) 10
    (ii) 20
    (iii) 30
    (iv) 40
27. Loose-leaf minutes are to be bound into books at regular intervals of ______ months.
    (i) 6
    (ii) 7
    (iii) 8
    (iv) 9
28. A special resolution is passed with
    (i) simple majority
    (ii) 60% majority of members present
    (iii) 75% majority of members present
    (iv) None of the above
29. A poll can be demanded by any member present in person or by proxy if he has voting powers at least equal to:
    (i) 1/5th
    (ii) 1/10th
    (iii) 1/20th
    (iv) 1/30th
30. Which of the following meeting can be held more than once in a calendar year?
    (i) E.G.M
    (ii) Creditors' meeting for winding up
    (iii) A.G.M
    (iv) None of the above

31. The expenses of holding an E.G.M by the requisitionists will be ultimately borne by ______.
    (i) company
    (ii) requisitionists
    (iii) all directors in default
    (iv) None of the above

## ANSWER KEYS

**1.** (i)
**2.** (ii)
**3.** (ii)
**4.** (i)
5. (ii)
**6.** (i)
**7.** (i)
**8.** (ii)
**9.** (ii)
**10.** (i)
**11.** (iii)
**12.** (iv)
**13.** (i)
**14.** (ii)
**15.** (ii)
**16.** (i)
**17.** (i)
**18.** (i)
**19.** (i)
**20.** (iii)
**21.** (ii)
**22.** (ii)
**23.** (i)
**24.** (i)
**25.** (ii)
**26.** (iii)
**27.** (i)
**28.** (iii)
**29.** (ii)
**30.** (i)
**31.** (iii)

# 22

# Companies Act, 2013: Management of Company

**Learning objectives**

*After reading this chapter, you will be able to understand:*

- Directors and their position
- Qualification and disqualification for directors
- How directors are appointed
- Resignation and removal of directors
- Managing directors—manager
- Remuneration of directors
- Schedule V

## 22.1 DEFINITION OF DIRECTOR

Section 2(34) of the Companies Act, 2013, defines a 'director' as a person appointed to the board of a company. It means that the person cannot be considered as director unless he is appointed by any method (i.e., either by the board or by shareholders) to the board of company.

## 22.2 DISQUALIFICATION OF DIRECTOR—SECTION 164

Section 164(1) of the Companies Act, 2013, provides that the following persons shall not be capable of being appointed as directors of a company:

1. A person found by a competent court to be of unsound mind and such finding remaining in force.
2. An undischarged insolvent.

3. A person who has applied to be adjudged an insolvent.
4. A person who has been convicted by a court of an offence whether involving moral turpitude or otherwise and sentenced in respect thereof to imprisonment for not less than 6 months, and a period of 5 years has not elapsed from the date of the expiry of the sentence. Court, here, means either an Indian court or a court outside India.
5. If a person has been convicted of any offence and sentenced for period of 7 years or more, he shall not be eligible to be appointed as director in any company.
6. A person who has been disqualified by a court or tribunal, unless permission of the court or tribunal has been obtained for his appointment.
7. A person who has not paid any call in respect of shares of the company held by him, whether alone or jointly with others and 6 months have elapsed from the last date fixed for the payment of the call.
8. A person who has been convicted of offence dealing with related party transactions under Section 188 at any time during the preceding 5 years.
9. A person who has not obtained director identification number.

***Important Note:***

Disqualifications referred to in the above clauses (d), (e) and (g) shall not take effect:

(i) for 30 days from the date of conviction or order of disqualification;
(ii) where an appeal is preferred within 30 days as aforesaid against the conviction resulting in sentence or order, until expiry of 7 days from the date on which such appeal or petition is disposed off; or
(iii) where any further appeal is preferred against order or sentence within 7 days, until such further appeal or petition is disposed off.

As per Section 164 (2), a person who is or has been director of a company shall become disqualified if the company:

1. has not filed the financial statements or annual returns for any continuous 3 financial years; or
2. has failed to repay deposit or interest thereon on due date or redeem its debentures on due date or pay dividend and such failure continues for 1 year or more.

On default of Section 164(2), director of defaulting company becomes disqualified to act as director of any other company for 5 years. He cannot be re-appointed as director in the defaulting company for a period of 5 years. However, he may continue as director in any other company.

A public company cannot add additional disqualification to the director, but an independent private company may add more disqualifications.

**Case Study**

State with reference to the relevant provisions of the Companies Act, 2013, whether the following persons can be appointed as a director of a public company:

(I) Mr. A, who has huge personal liabilities far in excess of his assets and properties, has applied to the court for adjudicating him as an insolvent and such application is pending.

(ii) Mr. B, who was caught red-handed in a shop-lifting case two years ago, was convicted by a court and sentenced to imprisonment for a period of eight weeks.
(iii) Mr. C, a former bank executive, was convicted by a court eight years ago for embezzlement of funds and sentenced to imprisonment for a period of one year.
(iv) Mr. D is a director of DLT Limited, which has not filed its annual returns pertaining to the annual general meetings held in the calendar years 2013, 2014 and 2015.

**Case Study**

Mr. Ram is a director of ABC Limited, XYZ Limited and PQR Limited. ABC Limited was regular in filing annual returns, but it did not file annual accounts for the year ended 31st March, 2015. Further ABC Limited failed to pay interest on loans taken from a public financial institution from 1st January, 2015 onwards and also failed to repay the matured deposits on due date from 1st April, 2015 onwards.

Mr. Ram is proposed to be appointed as additional director of MN Limited on 1st June, 2015. MN Limited has sought a declaration from Mr. Ram to the effect that the disqualification specification Section 164 of the Companies Act, 2013, is not applicable in his case. Mr. Ram seeks your advice on the following:

(i) Whether it is in order for him to give the declaration sought by MN Limited in view of the defaults committed by ABC Limited.
(ii) Whether he can continue as a Director in XYZ Limited and PQR Limited and also seek reappointment when he retires by rotation at the annual general meetings of the respective companies to be held in September, 2015.

Advise explaining the relevant provisions of the Companies Act, 2013. Would your answer be different if Mr. Ram resigned his office of director in ABC Limited on 31st December, 2014?

**Case Study**

Mr. A is a director of ABC Limited, which failed to repay matured deposits from 1st April, 2015 onwards and the default continues. But ABC Limited is regular in filing annual accounts and annual returns Mr. A is also a director of PQR Limited and XYZ Limited.

Answer the following questions with reference to the relevant provisions of the Companies Act, 2013:

(i) Whether Mr. A is disqualified under Section 164 of the Companies Act, 2013 and if so, whether he is required to vacate his office of director in PQR Limited and XYZ Limited.
(ii) Is it possible for the board of directors of DEF Limited to appoint Mr. A as an additional director at the board meeting to be held on 15th May, 2015? Would your answer be different if Mr. A ceased to be a director of ABC Limited by resignation on 1st March, 2015?

## 22.3 LEGAL POSITION OF DIRECTOR

Companies Act does not mention anything on legal position of directors. They have, at various times, been described by judges as agents, trustees or managing partners

### 22.3.1 Directors as Agents

Directors may correctly be described as agents of the company. The ordinary rules of agency will, therefore, apply to any contract or transaction made by them on behalf of the company. Thus, where the directors contract in the name and on behalf of the company, it is the company which is liable on it and not the directors.

However, directors incur a personal liability in the following circumstances:

1. Where they contract in their own names. Where the chief executive of the company executed a promissory note and borrowed an amount for the company's sake, it could not be said that amount was borrowed by him, in his personal capacity.
2. Where they use the company's name incorrectly, e.g., by omitting the word 'Limited'
3. Where the contract is signed in such a way that it is not clear whether it is the principal (the company) or the agent who is signing.
4. Where they exceed their authority—*Weeks vs Propert (1873)*

### 22.3.2 Directors as Trustees

Directors are regarded as trustees of the company's assets and of the powers that vest in them because they administer those assets and perform duties in the interest of the company and not for their own personal advantage.

### 22.3.3 Directors as Employees of the Company

Where a director accepts employment under the company under a separate contract of service, in addition to the directorship, he is also treated as an employee or servant of the company.

## 22.4 DUTIES OF A DIRECTOR—SECTION 166

Section 166 of the Companies Act, 2013, prescribes the duties of a director. The duties provided under Section 166 are applicable to all type of companies and to all directors. It includes:

1. To act in accordance with the articles of the company.
2. To act in good faith to promote the objects of the company for the benefit of its members as a whole, and in the best interests of the company, its employees, the shareholders, the community and for the protection of environment.
3. To exercise his duties with due and reasonable care, skill and diligence and exercise independent judgment.
4. Not to involve in a situation in which he may have a direct or indirect interest that conflicts, or possibly may conflict, with the interest of the company.
5. Not to make or attempt to make any undue gain or advantage either to himself or to his relatives, partners, or associates.
6. Not to assign his office. If any assignment is made, it shall be void.

If a director is found guilty of making any undue gain, he shall be liable to pay an amount equal to that gain to the company. Further, if a director of the company contravenes the provisions of this section such director shall be punishable with fine which shall not be less than one lakh rupees but which may extend to five lakh rupees.

## 22.5 APPOINTMENT OF DIRECTORS

The director of a company may be appointed by any one of the following methods:

Appointment of first directors – By Article Of Association
Appointment at general meeting
Appointment by the board of directors
Appointment by third parties
Appointment by central government.

## 22.6 APPOINTMENT OF FIRST DIRECTORS—SECTION 152

Article of association contains the name of the first directors. As per Regulation 60 of Table F of Companies Act, 2013, the names of first directors are determined in writing by subscribers to the memorandum or their majority. Where the articles do not contain the names of the first directors, the subscribers to the memorandum, who are individuals, shall be the first directors of the company.

The first directors hold office until the directors are appointed as per provisions of Section 152 of Companies Act, 2013. In the case of a One-person Company, an individual being a member shall be deemed to be its first director until the director(s) are duly appointed by the member in accordance with the provisions of Section 152. Section 152 is applicable to all companies.

If all the subscribers to the memorandum are body corporate, the company will have no directors until the first directors are appointed under Section 152.

## 22.7 APPOINTMENT OF DIRECTORS AT GENERAL MEETING OR DIRECTORS RETIREMENT BY ROTATION—SECTION 152

Directors of a *public company* must be appointed in a *general meeting*. Article of public company may provide for the retirement of all directors at every annual general meeting.

If the articles do not provide for the retirement of all directors at every annual general meeting, at least 2/3$^{rd}$ of the total number of directors must be persons whose period of office is liable to determination by rotation. Any fraction, while calculating 2/3$^{rd}$, shall be rounded off to the one. Alternatively, it can be said that only 1/3$^{rd}$ of the total number of directors can be non-rotational directors. Here, total directors mean directors appointed by company.

Independent directors are not included for the calculation of total directors for counting rotational directors. Independent directors are not liable to retire by rotation.

> ***Important Note:***
>
> Rotational directors are liable to retire once in three years. Non-rotational directors are not liable to retire. They will hold office until they resign or disqualified or removed or on the expiry of time for which they are appointed. Non-rotational directors are appointed only at a general meeting.

One-third of rotational directors shall retire at every general meeting. Any fraction in calculation of 1/3rd should be rounded off the nearest of one.

The directors who have been longest in office since their last appointment are liable to retire by rotation at every annual general meeting. If two or more directors were appointed on the same day, retirement by rotation will be decided between persons as under:

1. As per agreement if any or
2. As per mutual consent or
3. By lots.

If AGM is held in time but could not be held for disturbances or unavoidable reason beyond control of company, the retiring director will not be retired on the last day on which AGM should have been held but will retire in the adjourned meeting when held.

The company has following options with respect to director retiring by rotation:

1. To re-appoint the retiring director.
2. To appoint some other person as director in place of the retiring director.
3. Not to re-appoint the retiring director or any other person as director in his place.

Directors of private company are appointed as per provision of its article. If the article is silent, directors are appointed in a general meeting by the shareholders. It is not compulsory under the law for a private company to appoint rotational directors unless the articles of association of the company so required.

**Case Study**

ABC Company Ltd, in its first general meeting appointed six directors whose period of office is liable to be determined by rotation. Briefly explain the procedure and rules regarding retirement of these directors.

## 22.8 DEEMED APPOINTMENT OF RETIRING DIRECTOR—SECTION 152

The vacancy caused by retirement of a director by rotation should be filled up at the same meeting or at an adjourned meeting. If, in the adjourned meeting, the vacancy is not filled in nor it is expressly provided not to fill in the vacancy, then the retiring director shall be deemed to be reappointed. However, in the following cases retiring director will not be deemed to be reappointed:

1. At any previous meeting, a resolution for the appointment of director was put to vote, but was lost.
2. If the retiring director has expressed his unwillingness to continue in writing.
3. If the retiring director is disqualified.

## 22.9 APPOINTMENT OF DIRECTOR OTHER THAN A RETIRING DIRECTOR—SECTION 160

A person who is not a retiring director may give notice to the company to stand for directorship. It means following persons are eligible for appointment of director under Section 160:

1. Additional director
2. Alternate director
3. Nominee director
4. Director appointed to fill casual vacancy
5. Any other person.

Whenever a company wants to appoint any person as regular director, the procedure of Section 160 is applicable. To appoint any person as director (known as regular director) other than a retiring director, the following steps should be taken:

1. Any member of the company or person proposing himself for candidature of director should give at least 14 days' notice to the company before the general meeting.
2. The notice should be deposited at the registered office of the company with a deposit of ₹ 1 lakh. If the candidate is elected as director or gets more than 25% of the total valid votes cast, either on show of hands or on poll on such resolution, the deposit will be refunded.
3. The company must inform the members at least 7 days before the general meeting, either by email or by individual notices where company has no email ids available. If it is not possible to email or issue individual notice, the company shall place an advertisement of this fact in at least two newspapers circulating in the place where its registered office is situated, of which one must be in English and the other in the regional language of that place. Notice is also to be placed on the website of the company, if any.

Section 160 is not applicable to a private company. A private company can appoint a person as director as per the provisions of its article. If the article is silent in this matter, a person can be appointed as director at the general meeting directly and no special notice is required to be given.

## 22.10 CONSENT OF DIRECTOR WITH ROC AND COMPANY—SECTION 152

The consent to act as director is given by the proposed director to the company before he is appointed as director. A person proposed to be appointed as director should file his consent to act as director in Form DIR-2 to company. On receipt of consent to act as director, the company, in turn, is required to file such consent in Form DIR-12 with the registrar within 30 days of appointment of director.

Provisions of consent of director are applicable to all companies and to all types of directors. A person whose name is included as first director in article is also required to file consent to act as director at the time of incorporation of company. However, the consent of the registrar shall not be required to be filed if:

1. a director is re-appointed after retirement by rotation or immediately on the expiry of his term of office.
2. a director appointed by the tribunal.

## 22.11 DIRECTOR IDENTIFICATION NUMBER—SECTION 153–159 AND RULE 9

Every individual, who is to be appointed as director of a company shall make obtained a director identification number (DIN). Person cannot hold more than one DIN. Every person or company is required to quote the DIN in such return, forms or particulars relating to the director while filing forms.

### 22.11.1 Procedure to Obtain DIN

To obtain DIN the following steps are required to be taken:

1. An application for allotment of director identification number to the central government in Form DIR-3.
2. An application is made online.
3. Form DIR-3 shall be signed and submitted electronically by the applicant using his or her own digital. The signature certificate shall be verified digitally by a practicing professional (CA, CS, CWA) or company secretary in whole-time employment or by a director of the existing company.
4. The user is required to get registered on portal of mca.gov.in and obtain a user id and password.
5. Form DIR-3 should be uploaded on the website of mca.gov.in along with fees. The fee is paid online. The system generates a provisional DIN.
6. When provisional DIN has been generated, the central government shall process the application received for allotment of DIN and decide on the approval or rejection. If the central government, on examination, finds any defects or incompleteness, then it may intimate such defects by placing it on the website. In case of defect, the applicant is required to resubmit the application within 15 days.
7. The director is intimated his DIN.
8. The director, on receipt of director identification number, intimates it to all companies that he is a director in Form DIR-3B within one month of intimation.
9. The company shall intimate DIN to the Registrar within 15 days of receipt of Form DIR-3C from the director.
10. If there is any change in the particulars of director, after obtaining DIN, the director should intimate such changes online in DIR-6 within 30 days.

### 22.11.2 Documents to be Attached

The following scanned documents shall be attached with the DIN application form:

1. High resolution photograph of the applicant
2. Proof of identity;
3. Proof of residence;
4. Proof of date of birth
5. Proof of father's name. Proof of father's name is not required in the case of foreign nationals
6. Verification by the applicant in Form DIR-4.
7. Specimen signature duly verified and the digitally signed form.
8. Copy of passport in the case of foreign nationals.
9. Permanent account number.

## 22.12 APPOINTMENT OF DIRECTOR BY BOARD OF DIRECTORS—SECTION 161

The board of a company may appoint:

1. Additional directors—Section 161(1)
2. Director to filling up the casual vacancy—Section 161(4)

3. Alternate directors—Section 161(2).
4. Nominee directors—Section 161(3)

## 22.13 APPOINTMENT OF ADDITIONAL DIRECTOR–SECTION 161(1)

Section 161(1) is applicable to all companies. If the articles authorise, the board may appoint additional directors. Regulation 66 of Table F of Companies Act, 2013 authorises the board to appoint additional directors. Additional directors, together with the directors, should not exceed the maximum number fixed by the articles. A person who fails to get appointed as a director in a general meeting cannot be appointed as an additional director.

Additional directors hold office only up to the date of the next annual general meeting of the company. If the AGM is not held, the additional director is deemed to vacate office on last day on which AGM should have been held. Additional directors will enjoy the same powers and rights as other directors. The appointment of additional directors may be made either at a meeting of the board or by passing a resolution by circulation. If the board is unable to appoint an additional director, he can be appointed through a general meeting.

## 22.14 FILLING UP CASUAL VACANCY–SECTION 161(4)

It means a vacancy in the office of a director appointed by the shareholders in a general meeting and caused by the *death, resignation, insolvency or disqualification*. It does not include vacancy created because of retirement of a director by rotation. If the term of a director reaches expiry, it does not create casual vacancy.

If a director appointed in a general meeting vacates office before the expiry of his term, the board in its meeting can fill in the vacancy. However, if a director appointed by the board vacates before his term, it is not casual vacancy. The person appointed in casual vacancy will hold office until the time the person in whose place he has been appointed could have held office.

Section 161(4) does not apply to a private company. A private company can fill casual vacancies as per provision of its articles or by passing a resolution in a general meeting.

## 22.15 ALTERNATE DIRECTOR–SECTION 161(2)

If any director of a company is absent or is on leave for a period of three or more months from India, the company may appoint any other person as director in his place. Such a director is called as alternate director. The board of directors may appoint an alternate director if authorised by its articles or by resolution at a general meeting. The board can appoint an alternate director either at its meeting or passing resolution by circulation.

A person shall not be appointed as alternate director for an independent director unless he is qualified to be appointed as independent director under Companies Act, 2013. The person appointed as alternate director shall not hold any alternate directorship for any other director in the company. Section 161(2) is applicable to all companies. An alternate director cannot be counted towards maximum number of directorship.

An alternate director is subject to the same liability and supposed to perform the same duties as any other director. He is neither agent nor proxy of the original director. An alternate director appointed as such for the first time shall be required to file his consent with the registrar.

### 22.15.1 Tenure of Alternate Director

An alternate director vacates his office where:

The original director returns to India.
The tenure of the original director is complete.
The original director dies
The original director vacates his office.
The original director resigns from his office.

If the original director is a non-retiring director, an alternate director appointed in his place can continue till the time original director vacates his office or returns to India. If the original director is a rotational director and his term expires before he returns to the state where board meetings are ordinarily held, the provision of automatic reappointment is applicable to the original director and not the alternate director.

**Case Study**

Mr. Q, a Director of PQR Limited proceeding on a long foreign tour, appointed Mr. Y as an alternate director to act for him during his absence. The articles of the company provide for appointment of alternate directors. Mr. Q claims that he has a right to appoint alternate director. Examine the validity of action of Mr. Q.

## 22.16 NOMINEE DIRECTOR—SECTION 161(3)

The board of directors can appoint a director nominated by:

1. Any financial institution in pursuance of any law or agreement or
2. Central government or state government by virtue of its shareholding in a government company.
3. Any other person who represent its interest.

The directors appointed by any private equity investor may be covered in the above third category. The board may appoint a nominee director subject to provisions in its article of association.

## 22.17 WHO IS AN IDEPENDENT DIRECTOR?—SECTION 149(6)

An independent director is someone who does not have any material or pecuniary relationship with the company or directors. The managing director or whole-time director of the company cannot be considered as independent director. Section 149(6) of the Companies Act, 2013, prescribes the criteria for independent directors, which are as follows:

1. Such individuals must possess integrity and relevant industrial expertise;
2. Such individuals must not have any material or pecuniary relationship with the company or its subsidiaries;

3. They or their relatives should not have had any pecuniary relationship with the company or its subsidiaries, amounting to 2% or more of its gross turnover or total income or ₹ 5 lakh, whichever is less, during the two immediately preceding financial years or in the current financial year;
4. Such appointees or their relatives should not have any key managerial position in the company or its subsidiary companies during any of the three preceding financial years;
5. Such persons or their relatives should not have been an employee of the company or its subsidiary companies during any of the three preceding financial years;
6. They or their relatives must not be a chief executive or director of a non-profit organisation which receives 25% or more of its receipts from the company or its subsidiary companies or its promoters or directors or from anyone who holds 2% of voting rights in such companies;
7. Such individuals must not be a promoter of the company or its subsidiaries;
8. They must not hold more than 2% voting rights in the company either by themselves or together with their relatives.

## 22.18 PROVISIONS RELATING TO INDEPENDENT DIRECTOR—SECTION 149

### 22.18.1 Minimum number of independent director—Section 149(4)

The central government may prescribe the minimum number of independent directors for various classes of public companies. A listed public company shall have at least one-third of the total number of directors as independent directors. Rule 4 of Companies (Appointment and Qualification of Directors) Rules, 2014, provides that the following public companies shall have at least two independent directors:

1. Which is having a paid-up share capital of ₹10 crore or more; or
2. Which is having turnover of ₹100 crore or more; or
3. Which have, in aggregate, outstanding loans, debentures and deposits, exceeding ₹ 50 crore.

### 22.18.2 Qualification—Rule 5 of Companies (Appointment and Qualification of Directors) Rules, 2014

An independent director shall possess appropriate skills, experience and knowledge in one or more fields of finance, law, management, sales, marketing, administration, research, corporate governance, technical operations or other disciplines related to the company's business.

As per Section 149(6) the following person can be appointed as independent director:

1. A person who is not a managing director or whole-time director or nominee director.
2. A person of integrity who possesses relevant experience and expertise in the opinion of the board.
3. A person who is not a promoter of the company, its holding, subsidiary or associated company.
4. A person who is not related to the promoter or director of the company, its holding or subsidiary or associate company.
5. A person who or whose relative has pecuniary relationship with company, its holding company or subsidiary company or associate company or their promoters, or directors, amounting to 2% or more of its gross turnover or total income or ₹ 50 lakhs, whichever is lower, during the last two financial years.

6. Who, neither himself nor any of his relatives:
   - holds or has held the position of a key managerial personnel or employee of the company or its holding, subsidiary or associate company in any of the three immediate preceding financial years;
   - is or has been an employee or proprietor or a partner, in any of the three financial years immediately preceding the financial year in which he is proposed to be appointed, of —
     - a firm of auditors or company secretaries in practice or cost auditors of the company or its holding, subsidiary or associate company; or
     - any legal or a consulting firm that has or had any transaction with the company, its holding, subsidiary or associate company amounting to 10% or more of the gross turnover of such firm;
   - holds together with his relatives 2% or more of the total voting power of the company; or
   - is a chief executive or director, by whatever name called, of any non-profit organisation that receives 25% or more of its receipts from the company, any of its promoters, directors or its holding, subsidiary or associate company or that holds 2% or more of the total voting power of the company.

### 22.18.3 Tenure

Independent directors are not required to be retired by rotation. The tenure of the independent directors must not exceed two consecutive periods of 5 years each, and can be extended for a second term only after the board passes a special resolution and discloses such appointment in the board's report. Section 149(11) mandates that reappointment after the expiry of second term can be done only after a cooling period of 3 years. During the cooling-off period of 3 years, independent directors cannot be appointed in or be associated with the company in any other capacity, either directly or indirectly.

### 22.18.4 Remuneration

The Act expressly disallows independent directors from obtaining stock options and remuneration other than sitting fees and reimbursement of travel expenses for attending the board and other meetings. Profit-related commission may be paid to them, but subject to the approval of the shareholders.

## 22.19 MINIMUM AND MAXIMUM NUMBER OF DIRECTORS—SECTION 149

Section 149 of the Companies Act, 2013, provides that every public company must have at least three directors, every private company must have at least two directors and a one-person company (OPC) must have at least one director.

A company can appoint a maximum of 15 directors. A company may appoint more than fifteen directors after passing a special resolution in general meeting and approval of central government is not required.

Rule 3 of Companies (Appointment and Qualification of Directors) Rules, 2014, prescribes the following class of companies shall appoint at least one woman director:

1. every listed company
2. every other public company having:
   a. a paid-up share capital of one hundred crore rupees or more; or
   b. a turn-over of three hundred crore rupees or more .

According to Section 151 of the Act, every listed company may have one director elected by small shareholders (discussed in detail in the next section)

## 22.20 SMALL SHAREHOLDERS' DIRECTORS—SECTION 151 ALONG WITH RULE 7 OF COMPANIES (APPOINTMENT AND QUALIFICATION OF DIRECTORS) RULES, 2014

'Small shareholder' means a shareholder (including a preference shareholder) holding shares of nominal value of twenty thousand rupees or less in a public listed company. Equity or preference shareholder who is satisfying the above requirement will be considered as small shareholder.

The Ministry of Company Affairs, in this regard, has prescribed the Companies (Appointment and qualification of Directors) Rules, 2014. Every listed company may have one director elected by small shareholders. The company may appoint a small shareholder on its own or on application by the small shareholder.

### 22.20.1 Procedure for appointment—Rule 7 of Companies (Appointment and qualification of directors) Rules, 2014

1. The company may appoint a small shareholder director (SSD) if notice in writing is given by at least 1000 small shareholders or $1/10^{th}$ of small shareholders, whichever is less.
2. Notice should be given at least 14 days before the general meeting. Notice should contain the name, address and the number of shares held by the person proposed to be appointed as small shareholders' director.
3. Notice should be accompanied by a statement signed by the person whose name is proposed for post of small directors stating:
    a. his director identification number (DIN)
    b. that he is not disqualified to become director.
    c. his consent to act as director to the company.
4. If the proposer does not hold any shares in the company, the details of shares held and folio number need not be specified in the notice.
5. Listed public companies shall elect the small shareholders' nominee through a postal ballot.
6. Small shareholders' director can be appointed for maximum of 3 years and he need not retire by rotation. The person can be elected for another period of 3 years on expiry of his tenure. He cannot be reappointed more than once.
7. A person shall not hold office as small shareholders' director in more than two companies at same time.
8. A person who is small shareholders' director in one company cannot be appointed as small shareholders' director in a second company if it is in competition business or in conflict with the business of the first company.
9. Small shareholders' director shall directly or indirectly not be appointed or associated in any other capacity with the company for a period of 3 years from the date of his cessation as a small shareholders' director.

***Important Note:***

Small shareholders' director is not eligible for appointment as whole-time director or managing director of the company.

### 22.20.2 Disqualifications of SSD

A person shall not be capable of being appointed as small shareholders' director of a company if he is disqualified. Provision of Section 164 is equally applicable to small shareholders' director.

### 22.20.3 Vacation of Office

A person appointed as small shareholders' director shall have to vacate the office if:

1. He incurs any of the disqualification as per Section 164.
2. The office of directors becomes vacant as per Section 176.
3. He is appointed as independent director and ceases to meet the criteria of independency.
4. Removed under Section 169 by members.

**Case Study**

The board of directors of M/s ABC Limited, an unlisted company having a paid-up capital of ₹ 6 crores consisting of equity share capital of ₹ 5 crores, preference share capital of ₹ 1 crore and 1,100 small shareholders' holding equity shares, seeks your advice on the following:

(i) Is it necessary for the company to appoint a director to represent the small shareholders?

(ii) In case the Company decides to appoint such a director, the procedure to be followed by the company for such appointment and the period for which such appointment can be made.

(iii) Can such a director be removed by the company before the expiry of his period of appointment without the consent of the small shareholders?

Advise explaining the relevant provisions of the Companies Act, 2013 and the rules.

## 22.21 MINIMUM AND MAXIMUM NUMBER OF DIRECTORS—SECTION 149(1)

Section 149(1) of the Companies Act, 2013, provides that every public company must have at least three directors, every private company must have at least two directors and every one-person company (OPC) must have at least one director. A company can appoint more than 15 directors usually. A company may appoint more than 15 directors after passing a special resolution in general meeting and approval of the central government is not required.

***Important Note:***

A period of one year has been provided to enable the company existing on or before the commencement of Companies Act, 2013 to comply with Section 149(1). (i.e., the company has to comply on or before 31st March 2015)

## 22.22 NUMBER OF DIRECTORSHIP—SECTION 165

A person cannot hold office at the same time as a director in more than 20 companies. Further, a person cannot hold directorship at the same time in more than 10 public companies and a private company which is a subsidiary of a public company. While counting 20 directorships of a person, alternate directorship is included. The members of a company may, by special resolution, specify any lesser number of companies in which a director of the company may act as director.

Any person holding office as director in more than 20 companies immediately before the commencement of the Companies Act, 2013, shall within 1 year (i.e., one year from 1-4-2014) from such commencement:

1. select not more than 20 of those companies in which he wishes to continue as director.
2. resign his office as director in the other companies. Here, resignation will take immediate effect on the dispatch.
3. intimate the choice to each of the companies in which he was holding the office of director before such commencement and to the registrar having jurisdiction in respect of each such company.

If a person is already holding directorship in 20 companies and appointed as director in one or more other companies, all new appointments will be not take effect and will be regarded as void.

### 22.22.1 Penalty

If a person acts as director in more than 20 companies at a time, he is liable for a fine which is not less than ₹ 5,000 but which may extend up to ₹ 25,000 for every day.

**Case Study**

Mr. Influential is already a director of 19 companies. He is being appointed as a director of another company named M/s Expensive Remedies Ltd. Advise Mr. Influential in regard to the following:

(i) Restrictions on the number of directorships to be held by an individual and whether he can accept the new appointment in view thereof.

(ii) What are the companies to be excluded for the purpose of calculating the ceiling on the appointment of directors?

**Case Study**

Mr. PMC is Director in 19 public limited companies as on 30th July, 2014. He continues to be so until 4th September, 2014. The following companies appoint Mr. PMC as Director at their respective annual general meetings held on dates mentioned against their names.

(i) PQR Ltd. (AGM held on 29th September, 2014).

(ii) BCD Private Ltd. (AGM held on 25th September, 2014).

(iii) City Traders Association (A company registered under Section 8 of the Companies Act, 2013—AGM held on 26th September, 2014).

(iv) TSP Ltd. (AGM held on 25th September, 2014).

You are required to state with reference to the relevant provisions of the Companies Act, 2013, the options available to Mr. PMC in respect of accepting or not accepting the appointment of Director of the above companies.

## 22.23 VACATION OF OFFICE OF DIRECTOR—SECTION 167

As per Section 167, the office of a director shall become vacant if:

1. If he incurs any disqualification as specified in Section 164.
2. He is convicted by a court of any offence involving moral turpitude or otherwise and sentenced in respect thereof to imprisonment for not less than 6 months. Provided that office shall be vacated by the director even if he has filed an appeal against order of such court.
3. He absents himself from all the meetings of the board of directors held during a period of 12 months with or without seeking leave of absence of the board. Attendance at board meeting may be by physical presence or virtually through the audio-visual mode (as in a conference call).

> ***Important Note:***
>
> The original director will stand vacated if he has not attended any board meeting during a period of 12 months personally. Hence, physical or electronic presence of original director is required at least in one board meeting during the period of 12 months in a financial year even when an alternate director is appointed in place of the original director.

4. He acts in contravention of Section 184 of the Companies Act, 2013.
5. He fails to disclose his interest in any contract or arrangement in which he is directly or indirectly interested.
6. He becomes disqualified by an order of court or tribunal.
7. He is removed as per Section 169 of the Companies Act, 2013.
8. He, having been appointed a director by virtue of his holding any office or other employment in the holding, subsidiary or associate company, ceases to hold such office or other employment in that company.

A private company which is not a subsidiary of a public company may, by its articles, provide that the office of director shall be vacated on any grounds in addition to those specified above. Where all the directors of a company vacate their offices under any of the disqualifications specified above, the promoter or, in his absence, the central government shall appoint the required number of directors who shall hold office until the directors are appointed by the company in the general meeting. Under Section 167, vacating office is automatic. It does not require the issue of any notice on part of company or passing of board resolution.

A director who acts after vacating office is punishable with imprisonment for a term which may extend to one year or with pay which shall not be less than ₹ 1,00,000 but which may extend to ₹ 5,00,00 or, with both.

## 22.24 REMOVAL OF DIRECTOR BY SHAREHOLDER—SECTION 169

Section 169 empowers shareholders to move proposal for removal of director. To remove a director, it is not necessary to prove any kind of breach of trust or misconduct on part of the director. Article of association cannot take away the right of shareholders to remove directors. Right to remove director is a statutory right of shareholders. To remove a director under Section 169, an ordinary resolution should be passed at the general meeting. The following steps should be taken:

1. Special notice must be given by member(s) holding not less than 1% of total voting power or holding shares on which an aggregate sum of not less than ₹ 5,00,000 has been paid as on date of notice.

2. Notice must be given at least 14 days before meeting. The notice must disclose the grounds on which the director is proposed to be removed, and it should be signed by the members.
3. The company should notify to its members about the notice at least 7 days before the meeting and intimate to the concerned director immediately.
4. The director concerned is entitled to make a representation in writing against his removal at the meeting. The company is bound to send a copy of the representation to every member. If the representation is received too late or could not be sent, the concerned director may request the company to read in the general meeting.
5. The representation made by the concerned director is neither required to be sent to members nor need to be read out at a meeting, if on application, the tribunal has permitted waiver. An application for this purpose can be made either by the company or by any other aggrieved party. The tribunal may grant permission if it is satisfied that if right of representation is availed, it can create needless publicity or become defamatory to the company.
6. At the general meeting, the proposal is discussed and an ordinary resolution is passed.

The directors appointed by the tribunal under Section 242 of Companies Act, 2013, cannot be removed by the shareholders in a general meeting.

The shareholders may recommend appointment of any other director in place of the removed director through special notice. Such a director can hold office only for the tenure of removed director. If a new director is not appointed as aforementioned, then board may fill the position through casual vacancy.

**Case Study**

Mr. Stubborn is a director of M/s Doubtful Industries Ltd. He, along with other two directors, has been running the company for the past twenty years without declaring any dividends or giving any benefit to the shareholders. Frustrated by this, some shareholders are desirous of giving notice to pass a resolution with the support of other shareholders for his removal as a director in the Annual General Meeting of the Company to be held in the month of December, 2015. State the procedure to be followed for the removal of Mr. Stubborn as a director and the right of Mr. Stubborn to defend his position.

## 22.25 COMPENSATION FOR LOSS OF OFFICE—SECTION 202

Compensation for loss of office can be paid to the managing director, whole-time director or manager. An ordinary director is not entitled to get compensation under this section. However, in the following situation no compensation is payable to the managing director or whole-time director or manager:

1. Where a director resigns the office due to reconstruction or amalgamation of the company with another company and he is appointed as manager or managing director or whole-time director of the other office in the resulting company.
2. Where a director resigns otherwise than on reconstruction or amalgamation.

3. Where a director vacates office under Section 203 of Companies Act, 2013, or 283 of Companies Act, 1956
4. Where winding up of the company is due to negligence or default of the director in question.
5. Where a director has been guilty of any fraud or breach of trust or gross negligence or mismanagement of the affairs of company.
6. Where a director has taken part in bringing about the termination of his office.

As per Rule 17 of Companies (Meetings of board and its powers) Rules, 2014, a company cannot pay any compensation for loss of office to its managing director, whole-time director or manager, if:

1. The company is in default in repayment of deposit, redemption of debenture or interest on it.
2. The company is in default in repayment of any liability payable to any bank or financial institution.
3. The company is in default in payment of any dues to central government, state government, statutory authority or local authority. (i.e., income tax, sales tax, municipal tax, VAT, or excise duty)
4. There are outstanding statutory dues to employees or workmen other than disputed amount.
5. The company has not paid dividend on preference shares or not redeemed preference shares on due date.

### 22.25.1 Quantum of Compensation

The quantum of compensation is calculated on the remuneration, which he would have earned, if he had been in office for the unexpired residue period or 3 years, whichever is shorter. The amount of compensation is calculated on the basis of average remuneration actually earned during period of 3 years immediately before termination or on the basis of average remuneration actually earned by him during the period he has been in office.

## 22.26 RESIGNATION BY DIRECTOR—SECTION 168 AND RULE 15-16

A director can resign from his office by giving notice in writing. On receipt of resignation, the board shall:

1. intimate the registrar in Form DIR-12 within 30 days and
2. include the fact of resignation in the directors' report of the next general meeting of the company and
3. post the information on its website (if any).

The director should also forward a copy of his resignation along with detailed reasons for the resignation to the registrar in Form DIR-11 within 30 days from the date of resignation. The resignation becomes effective from the date on which the notice is received by the company or the date specified by the director in the notice, whichever is later. Provided that the director who has resigned shall be liable, even after his resignation, for the offences which occurred during his tenure, the resignation shall be effective even when no other director is in office.

Where a director has tendered his resignation, he cannot be held liable for liability incurred by the said company after the date of acceptance of his resignation. For the resignation to be valid, it must be addressed to the company. A director can resign by writing a letter either to the chairman or secretary of the company. Where a director has contracted to act for a fixed period, he may resign subject to payment of damages for premature termination. Once a director has given a notice of resignation, he cannot withdraw it.

If all the directors of a company resign from their office or vacate their office, the promoter or, in his absence, the central government shall appoint the required number of directors to hold office until the directors are appointed by the company in a general meeting.

**Case Study**

Due to internal problems in the working of M/s Infighting Detergents Ltd, Mr. Satyam, the executive director, and Mr. Shivam, a director, have submitted their resignations and decided to dissociate themselves from the working of the company. Mr. Sundaram, the managing director, decides to refuse their resignations. Examine whether the managing director can compel Mr. Satyam and Mr. Shivam to continue as per the provisions of the Companies Act, 2013.

## 22.27 VALIDITY OF THE ACTS OF THE DIRECTOR WHERE HIS APPOINTMENT IS INVALID—SECTION 176

The acts done by a director shall be valid even if his appointment is discovered to be invalid because of any defect or disqualification or where his appointment had been terminated by virtue of any provision contained in the Companies Act or in the articles.

## 22.28 POWER OF BOARD OF DIRECTORS

Companies Act, 2013, provides for general powers of the board of directors. The board of directors of a company shall be entitled to exercise all such powers, and to do all such acts and things, as the company is authorised to exercise and do.

Shareholders, by amending the articles, may restrict the powers of the board. However, such amendment cannot be made retrospectively and a meeting of shareholders cannot therefore invalidate any act validly done by the board.

### 22.28.1 Exception

In the following cases, however, the general meeting of shareholders is competent to intervene and act in respect of a matter delegated to the board of directors:

### 22.28.2 Directors Acting Mala Fide

Where the directors act for their own personal interests in complete disregard to the interests of the company or where the personal interest of the directors clashes with their duties towards the company

### 22.28.3 Directors Themselves Wrong Doers

Where the directors themselves the wrong doers and have acted mala fide.

### 22.28.4 Incompetency of the Board

When the board has become incompetent to act, e.g., where all the directors constituting the board are interested in dealing or where none of the directors was validly appointed, the majority of shareholders may exercise powers in a general meeting of the company.

### 22.28.5 Deadlock in Management

When there is a deadlock in the management such that the directors cannot exercise some of their powers.

It is the collective wisdom of the directors which has been conferred the privilege of managing the affairs of the company. Individual directors do not have any general powers.

## 22.29 RELATED PARTY TRANSACTION—SECTION 188

Section 188 requires a company to obtain approval of the board and of the members in certain situations, prior to any transaction or entering into an agreement with a related party. Section 188 is applicable to all companies.

### 22.29.1 Who is a Related Party?

Section 2(76), read with Rule 3 of Companies (specification of definitions details) Rules, 2014, defines a related party as under:

'Related party', with reference to a company, means:

1. a director or his relative;
2. a key managerial personnel or his relative;
3. a firm, in which a director, manager or his relative is a partner;
4. a private company in which a director or manager is a member or director;
5. a public company in which a director or manager is a director or holds, along with his relatives, more than 2% of its paid-up share capital;
6. any body corporate whose board of directors, managing director or manager is accustomed to act in accordance with the advice, directions or instructions of a director or manager;
7. any person on whose advice, directions or instructions, a director or manager is accustomed to act;
8. any company which is:
    - a holding, subsidiary or an associate company of such company; or
    - a subsidiary of a holding company to which it is also a subsidiary;
9. a director or key managerial personnel of the holding company or his relative.

### 22.29.2 Related Party Transactions

The following transactions between a company and its related party are known as related party transactions:

1. sale, purchase or supply of any goods or material;
2. selling or otherwise disposing of, or buying property of any kind;
3. leasing of property of any kind;
4. availing or rendering of any services;
5. appointment of any agents for purchase or sale of goods, materials, services or property;
6. appointment to any office or place of profit in the company, its subsidiary company or associate company; or
7. under-writing the subscription of any shares in or derivatives thereof.

### 22.29.3 What is 'Office' or 'Place of Profit'?

'Office' or 'place of profit' means any designation or post under a company which carries any remuneration apart from any remuneration a person is getting from the company as director. Remuneration means any salary, fees, commission, perquisites or right to occupy any premises.

Section 188 suggests an office or place of profit in following manner:

1. Office or place of profit held by director: In case of office or place held by the director, it shall be deemed to be an office or place of profit if the director holding it obtains from the company anything by way of remuneration over and above the remuneration to which he is entitled as director.
2. Office or place of profit held by a person other than director: In case of office or place held by any person other than director, it shall be deemed to be an office of place of profit if such person obtains from the company anything by way of remuneration over and above the remuneration, by whatever name called.

### 22.29.4 Exemption or Non-applicability

The above-mentioned provisions will not be applicable in case of transactions entered into by the company in its ordinary course of business, which are on arm's length basis. 'Arm's length transaction' means a transaction between two related parties that is conducted as if they were unrelated, so that there is no conflict of interest.

***Example***

Let us assume a bank whose normal course of business provides 9% interest rate to its customers for placing fixed deposit for a two-year tenure. It offers 9.25% – a higher rate – to all its group employees. One may argue that the higher rate is not at arm's length. Alternatively, one may argue that banks devise different strategies for various categories of customers. Employee population of the entire group provides a significant customer-base for the bank and hence providing higher rate is in accordance with business strategy and meets the criteria of arm's length. The arm's length assessment is a subjective exercise and requires judgment after considering various parameters.

Section 188 is not applicable where transaction is arising out of corporate restructuring or amalgamation etc. as per Ministry of Corporate Affairs (MCA) Circular 30/2014.

### 22.29.5 Approval or Permission

If related party transaction is at arms' length and in the ordinary course of business, it is approved by the audit committee. If a related party transaction is not at arm's length or not in the ordinary course of business or both, the following permissions are needed:

- Audit committee approval
- Prior consent of the board by a resolution at a board meeting irrespective of capital of company or value of transaction.

***Important Note:***

Where any director is interested in any contract or arrangement with a related party, such director shall participate in the board meeting in which the contract or arrangement is discussed. As per Rule 15 of the Companies (Meeting of Board and Its Powers) Rules, 2014, where any director is interested in any contract or arrangement with a related party, such director shall not be present at the meeting during discussions on the subject matter of the resolution relating to such contract or arrangement.

Related party transactions by a company having paid-up capital of ₹ 10 crore or more, or exceeding value of transactions as mentioned below will require prior approval of shareholders by ordinary resolution:

1. Sale, purchase or supply of any goods or materials directly or through appointment of agents exceeding 10% of the annual turnover or ₹ 100 Cr., whichever is lower.
2. Selling or otherwise disposing of, or buying property of any kind, directly or through appointment of agents, exceeding 10% of net worth or ₹ 100 Cr., whichever is lower.
3. Leasing of property of any kind exceeding 10% of the net worth or 10% of turnover or ₹ 100 Cr., whichever is lower.
4. Availing or rendering of any services, directly or through appointment of agents, exceeding 10% of the turnover or ₹ 50 Cr., whichever is lower.
5. Appointment to any office or place of profit in the company, its subsidiary company or associate company, at a monthly remuneration exceeding ₹ 2.5 lakhs.
6. Remuneration for under-writing the subscription of any securities or derivatives thereof of the company exceeding 1% of the net worth.

***Important Note:***

The turnover or net worth shall be on the basis of the audited financial statement of the preceding financial year.

No member of the company shall vote on such special resolution, to approve any contract or arrangement which may be entered into by the company, if such member is a related party.

Even though related party transaction between holding company and its 100% subsidiary company is beyond threshold limit, ordinary resolution is not required to be passed, if 100% subsidiary company's accounts are consolidated with such holding company and placed before shareholders at the general meeting for approval.

## 22.29.6 Disclosure

The notice or agenda of the board meeting at which the resolution of related party transaction is proposed to be moved shall disclose details as per the Act. Every director of a company who is in any way, whether directly or indirectly, concerned or interested in a contract or arrangement or proposed contract or arrangement entered into or to be entered into:

1. with a body corporate in which such director or such director in association with any other director, holds more than 2% shareholding of that body corporate; or
2. with a body corporate in which such director is a promoter, manager, chief executive officer of that body corporate; or
3. with a firm or any other entity in which, such director is a partner, owner or member, as the case may be,

shall disclose the nature of his concern or interest in contract at the meeting of the board in which the contract or arrangement is discussed.

***Important Note:***

Where any director is not interested at the time of entering into such contract or arrangement, but becomes interested after the contract is entered into, he should disclose his interest forthwith when he becomes interested or at the first meeting of the board held after he becomes interested.

Every related party transaction or contract shall be disclosed in the board's report along with the justification for entering into such contract or arrangement. The company shall maintain a register in Form MBP 4 and shall enter therein, the particulars of contracts or arrangements with a related party under Section 188. In addition to the above, in the case of listed company:

1. Details of all materials pertaining to related party transaction are to be disclosed quarterly along with the compliance report on corporate governance.
2. Policy on dealing with related party transaction is to be disclosed on the company's website and annual report

### 22.29.7 Penalty

The company may proceed against a director or employee, who had entered into contract or arrangement in contravention of the provisions, for recovery of any loss sustained by it as a result of such contract or arrangement. Such a director shall be disqualified for a period of 5 years. In case of a listed company, such director or employee may be punishable with imprisonment for a term up to 1 year and/or with fine of ₹ 25,000 to ₹ 5,00,000. In case of any other company, such director or employee may be punishable with fine of ₹ 25,000 to ₹ 5,00,000.

## 22.30 DISCLOSURE OF DIRECTOR'S INTEREST—SECTION 184

Section 184 is applicable to all companies. It specifies the following two types of disclosure:

1. General disclosure
2. Specific disclosure

'Disclosure of interest' means making aware about interest but where all other directors are aware about interest, formal notice of disclosure is not required.

### 22.30.1 General Disclosure—Section 184(1)

General disclosure is given before the first board meeting in which a person participates as director. An existing director should disclose his direct or indirect interest in any contract or arrangement by giving general notice to the board at the first board meeting held after the beginning of the financial year. Notice is given in Form MBP-1. If there is any change in interest, it is required to be disclosed in the next board meeting held after change has taken place. The notice should specify that he:

1. is a director or a member of a specified body corporate or is a member of a specified firm and is to be regarded as concerned or interested in any contract or arrangement entered into with that company or firm.
2. is a promoter, manager, chief executive officer of body corporate or with a firm or any other entity in which such director is a partner, owner or member as the case maybe.

### 22.30.2 Specific Disclosure—Section 184(2)

If the director has not given general notice of his interest, he can give notice before or after board meeting in which such contract has been entered into or is likely to be discussed.

Every director of a company who is in any way, whether directly or indirectly, concerned or interested in a contract or arrangement or proposed contract or arrangement entered into or to be entered into:

1. with a body corporate in which such director or such director in association with any other director, holds more than 2% shareholding of that body corporate, or
2. with a body corporate in which such director is a promoter, manager, chief executive officer of that body corporate; or
3. with a firm or any other entity in which, such director is a partner, owner or member, as the case may be,

shall disclose the nature of his concern or interest at the meeting of the board in which the contract or arrangement is discussed.

Section 184 will not apply to a contract between two companies where one or more directors of one company holds not more than 2% of the paid-up capital of the other company. A limit of 2% is considered at the point of time when the contract is entered in to and not at the time when disclosure is made.

The interested director cannot participate or vote at a board meeting where contract or arrangement is discussed in which he is interested. His presence will not be counted for the purpose of quorum at the time of discussion and at the time of voting. If he casts vote, his vote shall be void.

Such notices are preserved for a period of 8 years at the registered office and are to be kept in custody of the secretary of the company or any other person authorised by the board on his behalf.

### 22.30.3 Penalty

Following are the effects of contravention of Section 184:

1. The director will vacate office under Section 167 of Companies Act, 2013.
2. The contract becomes voidable at the option of the board.
3. The director is punishable with imprisonment up to one year or with fine which shall not be less than ₹ 50,000 but which may extend to ₹ 1 lakh, or with both.
4. Any secret profit made is liable to refunded to company.

## 22.31 LOAN TO DIRECTORS—SECTION 185

Section 185 provides that, a company cannot give, directly or indirectly, any loan to or give any guarantee or provide any security for any loan taken or given by:

1. any director of the lending company or of a company which is its holding company
2. any partner or relative of the director.
3. any firm in which any such director or relative is a partner.
4. any private company in which any such director is a director or member.
5. any body corporate at a general meeting of which 25% or more voting power is controlled by one or more directors collectively.
6. any body corporate where the board of directors, managing director or manager whereof is accustomed to act according to the directions of directors of the lending company.

Section 185 is applicable to public and certain private companies. At the same time, if one company has to lend money to another company, Section 185 is required to be followed by the lending company as well as the borrowing company. Section 185 is applicable to a loan represented by a book debt.

***Important Note:***

The following persons are defined as relatives under Section 2(77) of Companies Act, 2013:

1) Members of HUF
2) Spouse
3) Father, mother, son, son's wife, daughter, daughter's husband, brother and sister.

Section 185 is not applicable to any loan made, guarantee given or security provided by:

1. a banking company during its ordinary course of business(if interest is charged at rate not less than the bank rate declared by RBI).
2. a holding company to its subsidiary company.

Section 185 is not applicable when the advance salary is given as per the policy of the company to the wife of the managing director if the wife of the managing director is an employee of the company. Section 185 is not applicable for giving any loan to a managing director or a whole-time director:

1. As part of the conditions of service extended by the company to all its employees.
2. Pursuant to any scheme approved by the members by special resolution. Such scheme may include housing loan scheme, education loan scheme, employee stock ownership plan (ESOP) etc.

### 22.31.1 Penalty

For contravention of Section 185:

1. The company is liable to pay fine not less than ₹ 5 lakhs but not more than ₹ 25 lacs.
2. The director and every other person who was party to the loan or guarantee is punishable for:
   - imprisonment up to 6 months or
   - fine of not less than ₹ 5 lakhs but not more than ₹ 25 lakhs or
   - both.
3. The person who was party is liable for repayment of loan.

For contravention of Section 185, both lender of loan and receiver are liable for punishment.

**Case Study**

In the light of the conditions laid down by Section 185 of the Companies Act, 2013, examine if the following transactions can be considered as loans to directors:

(i) Advance payment of salary to the employee who is also the spouse of the managing director of the company.
(ii) A sale of flat of the company at the current market rate and price. The director pays 60% cash immediately and contracts to pay the balance in ten monthly instalments.
(iii) A loan to a firm in which the director of the company is a partner.

**Case Study**

Mr. X is a director of M/s ABC Ltd. He has approached M/s Housing Finance Co. Ltd for the purpose of obtaining a loan of ₹ 50 lakhs to be used for the construction of his residential house. The loan was sanctioned subject to the condition that M/s ABC Ltd should provide the guarantee for repayment of loan instalments by Mr. X. Advise Mr. X.

## 22.32 MANAGING DIRECTOR—SECTION 2(54)

Section 2(54) defines 'managing director' as a director who, by virtue of an agreement with the company or of a resolution passed by the company in a general meeting or by its board of directors, or by virtue of its memorandum or articles of association, is entrusted with substantial powers of management which would not otherwise be exercisable by him. The expression includes the director occupying the position of a managing director, by whatever name called.

### 22.32.1 Appointment of Managing Director

A managing director may be appointed either by way of:

1. an agreement with the company
2. a resolution passed by the company in a general meeting
3. a resolution passed by the board of directors
4. a memorandum or articles of association.

If the appointment of MD and whole-time director (WTD) is within Schedule V, no permission of central government is required to be obtained.

A person, who is either the managing director or a manager of one company, cannot be appointed as a managing director of another public company or private company which is a subsidiary of a public company unless such an appointment is approved by unanimous resolution of the BOD of the other company.

A person may be managing director of any number of private companies.

### 22.32.2 Tenure of Appointment—Section 196

The MD or WTD or manager cannot be appointed for more than 5 years at a time. Appointment includes re-appointment. However, he may be re-appointed or re-employed for periods not exceeding 5 years on each occasion. Further, such reappointment or extension shall not be sanctioned earlier than 1 year before the expiry of his term. If re-appointment is not within Schedule V, permission of central government is needed for reappointment. The provisions of Section 196 are applicable to all companies.

## 22.33 DISQUALIFICATION OF MANAGING DIRECTOR OR WHOLE-TIME DIRECTOR OR MANAGER—SECTION 196

A person cannot be appointed or continued to be employed as managing or whole-time director or manager by a company, who:

1. is below age of 21 years or has attained the age of 70 years.

2. is an undischarged insolvent, or has at any time been adjudged an insolvent.
3. suspends, or has at any time suspended, payment to his creditors, or makes or has at any time made a composition with them.
4. has, at any time, been convicted by a court of law for an offence involving moral turpitude and sentenced for a period of more than 6 months.

A person who has attained age of 70 years can be appointed as managing director, whole-time director or manager by passing a special resolution with an explanatory statement that includes justification for appointment of such person. A person who is disqualified to be appointed as a director under Section 164 of Companies Act, 2013, cannot be appointed as managing director or whole-time director. Section 196 is applicable to all companies.

## 22.34 WHOLE-TIME DIRECTOR—SECTION 2(94)

Section 2 (94) of the Companies Act, 2013, defines 'whole-time director' as a director in the whole-time employment of the company. He is required to be a director first. A person cannot act as whole-time director in more than one company. Additional director can be appointed as whole-time director.

## 22.35 DISTINCTON BETWEEN MANAGING DIRECTOR AND WHOLE-TIME DIRECTOR

| Managing Director | Whole-time Director |
|---|---|
| A managing director is entrusted with substantial powers of management which are not otherwise exercisable by a director. | A whole time director means a director in whole-time employment of the company. |
| Managing director is not considered as whole-time employee of company | Whole-time director is considered in whole time employment of the company |

## 22.36 MANAGER—SECTION 2(53) OF COMPANIES ACT 2013

'Manager' means an individual who, subject to the superintendence, control and directions of the board of directors, has the management of the whole or substantially the whole of the affairs of the company, and includes a director or any other person occupying the position of a manager, by whatever name called and whether under a contract of service or not.

## 22.37 DISTINCTION BETWEEN MANAGING DIRECTOR AND MANAGER

A 'managing director' is entrusted with substantial powers of management. A 'manager', on the other hand, has the management of the whole or substantially the whole of the affairs of a company.

A managing director is appointed either under an agreement or by a resolution of the board or general meeting or under the provisions of the memorandum or articles. A manager, on the other hand, is usually appointed either under a contract of service or by the board of directors though the articles may also provide for his appointment.

A managing director must be a director whereas a manger may or may not be a director.

A managing director, on his ceasing to be a director, shall automatically cease to be the managing director as well. A manager–director, however, can continue as a manager even though he creases to be a director.

The grounds of disqualifications of a managing director, as given in Section 267, remain effective for whole life and cannot be waived by the central government. Most of the grounds for disqualification of a manager are only for five years and these can also be waived by the central government.

## 22.38 APPOINTMENT OF KEY MANAGERIAL PERSONNEL—SECTION 203

### 22.38.1 Who is a Key Managerial Perosnnel?

As per Section 2(51), key managerial personnel,(KMP) in relation to a company, means:

1. the chief executive officer or managing director or the manager;
2. the company secretary;
3. the whole-time director;
4. the chief financial officer; and
5. such other officer as may be prescribed.

### 22.38.2 Companies Required to Appoint KMP

Section 203 of the Companies Act, 2013, read with Rule 8 provides the appointment of key managerial personnel and makes it compulsory for a listed company and every other public company having a paid- up share capital of ₹ 10 or more, to appoint following whole-time key managerial personnel:

1. managing director, or chief executive officer or manager and in their absence, a whole-time director;
2. company secretary; and
3. chief financial officer.

***Important Note: Rule 8A—Appointment of company secretaries in companies not covered under Rule 8.***

A company other than a company covered under Rule 8, which has a paid-up share capital of ₹ 5 crore or more shall have a whole-time company secretary.

### 22.38.3 Manner of Appointment

Whole-time key managerial personnel of a company are appointed by board resolution. It should contain and approve the terms and conditions of the appointment including the remuneration. Any vacancy in the office of any whole-time key managerial personnel is filled-up by the board within a period of 6 months from the date of such vacancy.

### 22.38.4 Restrictions Regarding Appointment of KMP

An individual shall not be appointed, at the same time, as the chairman of the company, as well as:

1. the managing director or
2. chief executive officer.

However, in the following circumstances, the above restriction will not apply:

1. the articles of the company contain provision for appointment of the same person, or
2. the company carries only a single business, or
3. the company is engaged in multiple businesses and has appointed one or more chief executive officers for each such business as may be notified by the central government.

A whole-time key managerial personnel shall not hold office in more than one company at the same time, except:

1. in the company's subsidiary company,
2. as a director in any other company with the permission of the board,

A person, who is managing director of one company, may be appointed as a managing director or manager of not more than one another company, if following conditions are satisfied:

1. The appointment is approved by unanimous resolution of board of the other company with consent of all directors present at meeting.
2. Specific notice is given to all directors in India.
3. Specific notice should state that such resolution shall be moved at the board meeting.

A whole-time key managerial personnel holding office in more than one company at the same time, shall, within a period of 6 months from such commencement, choose one company in which he wishes to continue to hold the office of key managerial personnel.

### 22.38.5 Other Provisions Relating to KMP

A KMP is included within the meaning of 'Officer in Default' under the Act. A document or proceeding requiring authentication by a company, or contracts made by or on behalf of a company, may be signed by any key managerial personnel or an officer of the company, duly authorised by the Board, on its behalf. Details regarding KMP, changes therein and the remuneration paid to them are required to be disclosed in the annual return of the company. A person whose relative is employed as a KMP in a company is disqualified to be appointed as auditor in that company.

A person is disqualified to be appointed as an independent director if he either himself or through his relative holds or has held the position of a key managerial personnel of the company or its holding, subsidiary or associate company in any of the three financial years immediately preceding the financial year in which he is proposed to be appointed.

The key managerial personnel shall have a right to be heard in the meetings of the audit committee when it considers the auditor's report but shall not have the right to vote.

## 22.39 MANAGERIAL REMUNERATION

The term 'managerial remuneration' is not defined under Companies Act, 2013. It means remuneration paid to the person holding managerial position. Managing directors, whole-time directors, directors and managers hold managerial positions. Managerial remuneration includes any form of payment made or expenditure incurred by the company. It may be paid in any of following forms:

1. Monthly payments (salary)
2. Specified percentage of net profits
3. Commission.

Remuneration includes any expenditure incurred by company:

1. in providing any rent-free accommodation, or any other benefit in respect of accommodation free of charge
2. in providing any other benefit or amenity free of charge or at a concessional rate
3. to effect any insurance on the life of, or to provide any pension, annuity or gratuity.

If sitting fees is paid to the whole-time director or managing director, then it is also included in the managerial remuneration.

### 22.39.1 Schedule V-Part II-Section IV—Perquisite not Included in Managerial Remuneration

Besides the aforesaid remuneration, managerial personnel of a company having no profits or having inadequate profits shall also be eligible to the following perquisites:

1. Contributions to provident fund, superannuation fund or annuity fund to the extent these, either singly or put together, are not taxable under the Income-tax Act, 1961.
2. Gratuity payable at a rate not exceeding half-a-month salary for each completed year of service.
3. Encashment of leave at the end of the tenure.

In addition to the aforesaid perquisites, an expatriate managerial person (including a non-resident Indian) shall also be eligible to the following perquisites:

1. In case of children studying in or outside India, an allowance limited to a maximum of ₹ 12,000 per month per child or actual expenses incurred, whichever is less. Such allowance is admissible up to a maximum of two children.
2. Return holiday passage once in a year by economy class or once in two years by first class to children and to the members of the family from the place of their study or stay abroad to India if they are not residing in India with the managerial person.
3. Return passage for self and family in accordance with the rules specified by the company where it is proposed that the leave be spent in home country instead of anywhere in India.

***Important Note:***

Where any insurance is taken by the company on behalf of its managing director, whole-time director, manager, chief executive officer, chief financial officer or company secretary for indemnifying any of them against any liability in respect of any negligence, default, misfeasance, breach of duty or breach of trust for which they may be guilty in relation to the company, the premium paid on such insurance is not treated as part of remuneration. However, if such person is proved to be guilty, the premium paid on such insurance shall be treated as part of the remuneration as per Section 197(13)

## 22.40 METHODS OF DETERMINATION OF REMUNERATION

The company may determine managerial remuneration payable to its managing director or whole-time director or manager in any of the following ways:

1. By *article of association* of company
2. By passing an *ordinary resolution*
3. By passing *special resolution*, if the article provides so.

The board has not power to fix the remuneration unless authorised by shareholders at a general meeting or as per the provisions of the article.

## 22.41 OVERALL LIMITS ON MANAGERIAL REMUNERATION

Managerial remuneration which a company can pay to its managerial personal can be discussed under the following two heads:

1. Where the company *has profit*
2. Where the company *has no profit or inadequate profit.*

## 22.42 MANAGERIAL REMUNERATION WHERE THE COMPANY HAS PROFIT

A public company and its subsidiary company cannot pay remuneration exceeding 11% net profit to its managerial personnel in any financial year. Net profit is calculated as per Section 198. Net profit is arrived at after charging depreciation.

A director who is neither in the whole time employment of the company nor a managing director may be paid remuneration subject to the following:

1. 1% of the net profits of the company, if the company has a managing, or a whole-time director or a manager.
2. 3% of the net profits of the company in any other case.

However, the company may, in a general meeting, with the approval of the central government authorise the payment of such remuneration at a rate exceeding 1% or, as the case may be, 3% of its net profits.

If the company has one managing director or whole-time director or manager, the remuneration payable shall not exceed 5% of net profit. However, if the company has more than one executive director (MD, WTD), the overall remuneration limit is 10% of net profit.

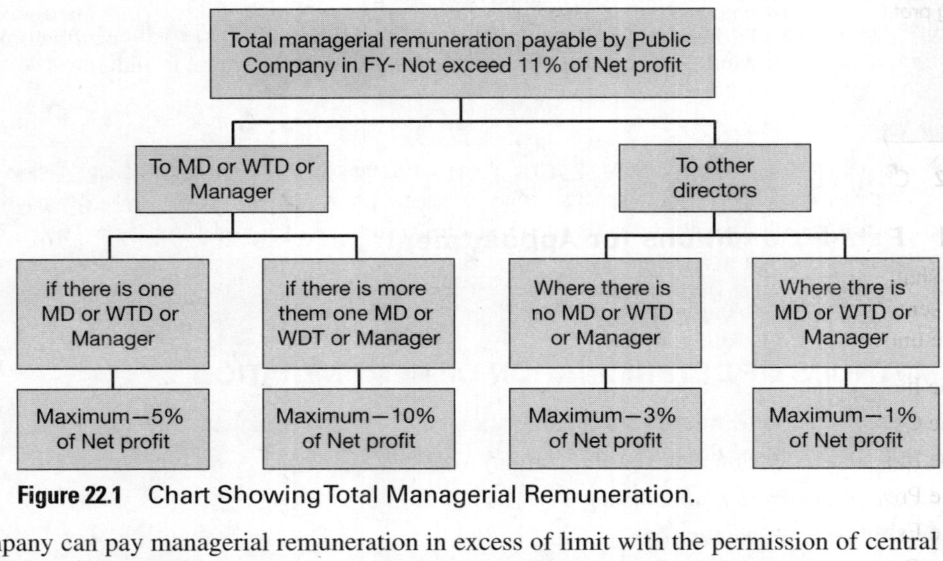


**Figure 22.1** Chart Showing Total Managerial Remuneration.

A company can pay managerial remuneration in excess of limit with the permission of central government. There is no restriction relating to managerial remuneration for a private company.

## 22.43 MANAGERIAL REMUNERATION WHERE COMPANY HAS NO PROFIT OR INADEQUATE PROFIT

If a company has no profit or inadequate profit for any financial year, it may pay managerial remuneration as per Schedule V of Companies Act, 2013.

Every public company and its subsidiary company shall follow Schedule V of Companies Act, 2013. If company can pay managerial remuneration beyond that stipulated in Schedule V, it can do so with the permission of central government.

## 22.44 SALIENT FEATURES OF SCHEDULE-V OF COMPANIES ACT, 2013

If the appointment of managing director or whole-time director or manager satisfies the conditions specified in Schedule V, no permission of central government is required. Schedule V is divided into four parts. The following chart shows framework of Schedule V:

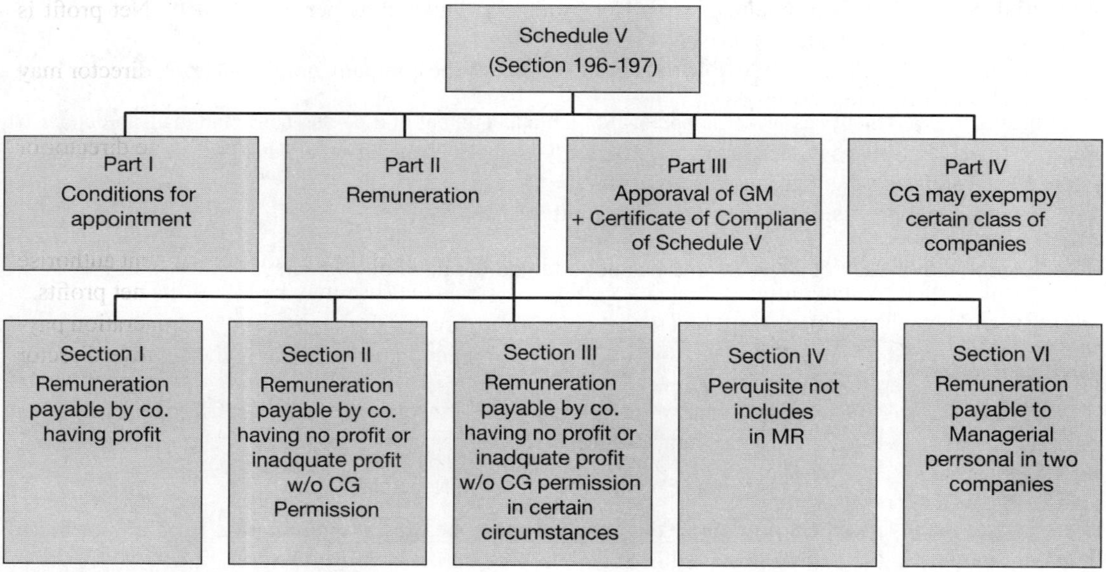


**Figure 22.2** Chart Showing Provision of Schedule V

### 22.44.1 Part-I–Conditions for Appointment

A person shall not be eligible for appointment as a managing or whole-time director or a manager, if he had been sentenced to imprisonment for any period, or to a fine exceeding ₹ 1,000, for the conviction of an offence under any of the following Acts:

1. The Indian Stamp Act, 1899
2. The Central Excises Act, 1944
3. The Industrial (Development and Regulation) Act, 1951
4. The Prevention of food Adulteration Act, 1954
5. The Essential Commodities Act, 1955
6. The Companies Act, 2013

7. The Securities Contracts (Regulation) Act, 1956
8. The Wealth-tax Act, 1957
9. The Income-tax Act, 1961
10. The Customs Act, 1962
11. The Competition Act, 2002
12. The Foreign Exchange Management Act, 1999
13. The Sick Industrial Companies (Special Provisions) Act, 1985
14. The Securities and Exchange Board of India Act, 1992
15. The Foreign Trade (Development and regulation) Act, 1992
16. The Prevention of Money Laundering Act, 2002

He had not been detained for any period under the Conservation of Foreign Exchange and Prevention of Smuggling Activities (COFEPOSA) Act, 1974.

***Important Note:***

Where central government has given its approval to the appointment of a person convicted (as listed under no. 1 to 16) or detained, no further approval is necessary for the subsequent appointment unless he has been so convicted or detained subsequent to such approval.

He has completed the age of 21 years and has not attained the aged of 70 years.

***Important Note:***

Where he has attained the age of 70 years and where his appointment is approved by a special resolution passed by the company in general meeting, no further approval of the central government shall be necessary for such appointment.

Where he is a managerial person in more than one company he draws remuneration from one or more companies subject to the ceiling provided in Schedule V of Part II.

He is resident of India.

***Important Note:***

Not applicable to the companies in Special Economic Zones (SEZ) as notified by Department of Commerce from time to time.

### 22.44.2 PART II-Section I—Remuneration Payable by Companies having Profits

A company having profits in a financial year may pay any remuneration, by way of salary, dearness allowance, perquisites, commission and other allowances, which shall not exceed *5%* of its net profits for one such managerial person, and if there is more than one such managerial person, *11%* for all of them together.

### 22.44.3 PART II-Section II—Remuneration Payable by Companies having no Profits or Inadequate Profits without Approval of Central Government

In any financial year where a company has no profits or its profits are inadequate, it may pay higher of following two options (either A or B) as remuneration to a managerial person:

#### 22.44.3.1 Option—(A)

The company can pay remuneration as per limits shown in the following table by passing an ordinary resolution:

| Where effective capital of company is | Yearly remuneration (in ₹) |
|---|---|
| Negative or Less than ₹ 5 cr. | 60,00,000 |
| ₹ 5 Cr or more but less than 100 Cr. | 84,00,000 |
| ₹ 100 Cr or more but less than 250 Cr. | 1,20,00,000 |
| ₹ 250 Cr and more | 1,20,00,000 plus 0.01% of the effective capital in excess of ₹ 250 crore. |

If special resolution is passed instead of ordinary resolution by the shareholders, the above limits can be doubled for payment of managerial remuneration.

#### 22.44.3.2 Option—(B)

Approval of Central Government is not required in case of managerial person who is functioning in a professional capacity, if he is not having any:

1. Direct or indirect interest in capital of company or its holding company or its subsidiary company or through statutory structure
2. Director or indirect interest or related to directors or promoters of company or its holding company or its subsidiary company,

at any time during last 2 years from appointment, on date of appointment and during appointment

Statutory structure refers to any kind of entity, which is entitle to hold shares in any company formed under any statute. He should possess minimum graduate qualification with expertise and specialized knowledge in the field in which company operates.

> ***Important Note:***
>
> Employee of company holding shares of company not exceeding 0.5% of its paid up capital under Employees Stock Option or by way of qualification shares shall not be considered as person interested in company.

#### 22.44.3.3 Procedure or Conditions for Payment of Remuneration for Part II-Section II

Managerial remuneration should be approved by a resolution of the board of directors and also by the nomination and remuneration committee, if applicable.

The remuneration shall be approved by a resolution of shareholders in a general meeting.

The company has not made any default in repayment of its debt or debenture or interest thereon for a continuous period of 30 days in preceding financial year.

The approval of remuneration by special resolution (SR) should be for not more than 3 years. (SR is required only when the remuneration given is double the limit mentioned.)

The statement, along with the notice of this resolution, should provide information mentioned in the schedule.

The auditor or company secretary of company or company secretary in practice should certify that the requirement of the schedule has been complied with and such certificate shall be incorporated in the return filed with the registrar.

### 22.44.4 PART II-Section III—Remuneration Payable by Companies having no Profits or Inadequate Profits without Central Government Approval in Certain Special Circumstances

In the following circumstances a company may, without central government approval, pay remuneration to a managerial person in excess of the amount specified in Part II:

1. It is a foreign company or any other company which has got approval for such payment by passing a special resolution and total managerial remuneration payable to such other company is within limit specified under Section 197; or
2. The managerial person of the company is not receiving remuneration from any other company, and:
    - the company is a newly incorporated company within a period of 7 years from the date of its incorporation or
    - the company is declared a sick company within 5 years from sanction of scheme of revival.
    - where remuneration is fixed by BIFR and NCLT.
3. An unlisted company in SEZ may pay up to ₹ 240 Lakh yearly if, the company has not raised any money by public issue of shares or debenture in India or has not made any default in repayment of any of its debt or debenture or interest payable thereon for a continuous period of 30 days.

#### 22.44.4.1 Procedure or Conditions for Payment of Remuneration for Part II-Section III

An auditor or company secretary of the company or company secretary in practice certifies that:

1. All secured creditors and term lenders have stated in writing that they have no objection for the appointment of the managerial person as well as the quantum of remuneration and such certificate is filed along with the return as prescribed
2. There is no default on payments to any creditors, and all dues to deposit holders are being settled on time.

### 22.44.5 Part II-Section IV—Perquisite not Included in Managerial Remuneration.

Besides the remuneration, managerial personnel of a company having no profits or having inadequate profits shall also be eligible to the following perquisites:

1. Contribution to provident fund, superannuation fund or annuity fund to the extent these either singly or put together are not taxable under the Income-tax Act, 1961.
2. Gratuity payable at a rate not exceeding half a month salary for each, completed year of service.
3. Encashment of leave at the end of the tenure.

### 22.44.6 Part II-Section V—Remuneration Payable to Managerial Personnel from two Companies

A person who is a managerial person in more than one company shall be able to draw remuneration from one or more of those companies provided that the total remu-neration drawn from the companies does not exceed the higher maximum limit admissible from any one of the companies of which he is a managerial person.

### 22.44.7 Companies Exempted

The restrictions with regard to managerial remuneration contemplated under Sections 197 (including Schedule V) do not apply to independent private companies. Directors of private companies can be paid remuneration as per their provisions of article.

## 22.45 EFFECTIVE CAPITAL

Remuneration to the managerial personnel under Schedule V is paid according to the effective capital of the company. Effective capital is calculated as under:

| Particular | Amount |
|---|---|
| Paid-up share capital (excluding share application money or advances against shares) | |
| Add: Reserve and surplus (Excluding revaluation reserve) | |
| Add: Securities premium account | |
| Add: Long-term loans | |
| Add: Deposits repayable after one year (excluding working capital loan, overdraft, interest due on loan, bank guarantee) | |
| Less: Investments | |
| Less: Accumulated loss and preliminary expenses not written off | |
| Total | |

Negative effective capital means effective capital less than zero.

### 22.45.1 Time when Effective Capital shall be Calculated

Where the appointment of the managerial person is made in the year in which company has been incorporated, the effective capital shall be calculated as on the date of such appointment. In any other case, the effective capital is calculated as on the last date of the financial year preceding the financial year in which the appointment of the managerial person is made.

**Case Study**

Advise M/s Super Specialities Ltd in respect of the following proposals under consideration of its board of directors:

(i) Appointment of managing director who is more than 70 years of age;
(ii) Payment of commission of 4% of the net profits per annum to the ordinary directors of the company;
(iii) Payment of remuneration to an ordinary director for rendering professional services; and
(iv) Payment of remuneration of ₹ 40,000 per month to the whole-time director of the company running in loss and having an effective capital of ₹ 95.00 lakhs.

**Case Study**

M/s Supreme Technologies Ltd propose to appoint Mr. E and Mr. F as whole-time directors for a period of three years with effect from 1st June, 2015. The company proposes to pay a consolidated salary of ₹ 80,000 per month to each of them.

Mr. D, the managing director of the company, has been appointed for a period of five years with effect from 1st January, 2015 on a remuneration payable in the form of commission at the rate of 5% of net profit subject to a minimum remuneration of ₹ 80,000 per month.

The effective capital of the company at the end of the financial year ending 31st December, 2014 is ₹ 4.5 crores and it has been increased to ₹ 5.5 crores on 1st April, 2015 by way of right issue of equity shares. The company did not repay public deposits on the date of maturity from 1st January, 2014 onwards, but the default was made good on 1st April, 2013.

The company seeks your advice on the steps to be taken to comply with the requirements of Section 196 read with Schedule V to the Companies Act, 2013, with regard to the proposed appointment of Mr. E and Mr. F as whole-time directors. Advise, explaining the relevant provisions.

## LIST OF LANDMARK JUDGEMENTS

1. ***Oriental Metal Pressing (p) Ltd. vs B. K. Thakoor (1961)***
   Only an individual can be appointed as director of a company.
2. ***Dean Dayal vs Sri. B. P. Reddy (1984)***
   A manager or any other managerial person is however not a director.
3. ***R. R. Kothandarnan vs CIT (1957)***
   Generally, directors are not employees or servants of a company but there is nothing in law to prevent a director from accepting employment under company by special contract.
4. ***Swapan Dasgupta vs Navin Chand Suchanti (1988)***
   If the article of a private company is silent about appointment of director, then directors are to be appointed by shareholders at a general meeting.
5. ***Vineent Kumar Mathur vs UOI (1996)***
   Directors, as agents, can make a company liable even for contempt of court.
6. ***Rolta India Ltd vs Venire Industries Ltd (2000)***
   A company cannot be restrained from appointing a new director because of an agreement between some groups of shareholders.
7. ***Vijay Krishan Jaidka vs Jaidka Motor Co. Ltd (1996)***
   Where there is no proof that notices of board meeting were served on a director, the director could not be removed on the ground that he abstained from attending meetings.
8. ***Krisna Prasad Pilani vs Colaba Land and mills Co. (1959)***
   The additional director vacates office either on the day on which the next AGM is held or on the last day on which meeting should have been held in accordance with the provisions of the Act, whichever is earlier.
9. ***Namita Gupta vs Cachar Native Joint Stock Co. Ltd (1999)***
   Normally, there should be an individual resolution relating to rejection of election of a retiring director and a separate resolution for election of a new director in that place.
10. ***Cricket Club of India vs Madhav L. Apte (1975)***
    A public company cannot provide for any additional disqualification for the appointment of director
11. ***Needle Industries (P) Ltd vs Needle Industries Neway (i) Holding Ltd (1981)***
    Unless the article authorises, the board of directors cannot appoint an additional director.

12. ***M. K. Srinavasam vs W. S. Subrahamanya Ayyar (1932)***

No casual vacancy arises if a director appointed by the company in a general meeting does not assume office.

13. ***Madhvan Nambiar vs ROC (2000)***

There is no distinction between whole-time director, part-time director and nominee director and liability for acts of omission or commission is equal under the companies act.

14. ***Queen Kuries and Loans (P) Ltd vs Sheena Jose (1993)***

For removal of a director under Section 169 (Similar to Section 285 of Companies Act, 1956), special notice has to be given of a resolution seeking to remove a director. The notice must disclose the ground on which the director is proposed to be removed.

15. ***Labh Singh vs Panaser Mech. Works (P) Ltd (1987)***

In absence of any provisions in the article of association, the director of an independent private company is entitled to continue until removed by general body.

16. ***Chaterbridge Corpration Ltd vs Loyds Banks Ltd (1970)***

If irregularities constituting invalidity is brought to the notice of the director, any act done by the director shall not be valid.

17. ***Ador Samia Ltd vs Indocom Engineering Sys Ltd (1999)***

A director due to retire by rotation must vacate office at the last day on which AGM ought to have been held.

18. ***Registrar vs Orissa Paper Products Ltd (1988)***

Resignation must be submitted either to the company or to the board of directors. A resignation sent to a third party is not effective.

19. ***Tarlok Chand Khanna vs Rajkumar Kapoor (1983)***

A permanent director can be removed by members from the office.

20. ***Venkatachalpati vs Guntur Mills (1929)***

Where the whole body of directors is aware of interest of directors, a formal disclosure is not necessary.

21. ***Sussen Textiles bearing Ltd vs Union of India (1984)***

Guarantee commission paid to a director is not managerial remuneration

22. ***Hannibal (E) and Co. vs Frost (1988)***

The MD of a company used the funds of the company for paying bribes; the court held that he had no authority to use company's fund for an illegal purpose. The company can recover the money from the MD.

23. ***D. Ross Porter vs Pioneer Seed Co. Ltd (1989)***

Company cannot refuse to appoint an alternate director for malafide reasons.

## TEST YOUR KNOWLEDGE

1. Explain the term 'director'. **(Ref. Para-22.1)**
2. What are the disqualifications of directors? **(Ref. Para-22.2)**
3. State the legal position of directors. **(Ref. Para-22.3)**
4. Explain, in brief, about the various methods of appointment of directors of a company. **(Ref. Para-22.5)**
5. How are the first directors of a company appointed? **(Ref. Para-22.6)**

6. Explain the circumstances under which a director retiring at an annual general meeting shall be deemed to have been reappointed even though no such appointment has been made. **(Ref. Para-22.8)**
7. Can a person who is not a member of the company become its director? State the procedure in this regard. **(Ref. Para-22.9)**
8. Which directors are not required to file consent with ROC? **(Ref. Para-22.10)**
9. Write short note on Director Identification Number. **(Ref. Para-22.11)**
10. Can a company appoint additional directors? How? **(Ref. Para-22.13)**
11. Additional directors appointed hold office for their life-time. Comment. **(Ref. Para-22.13)**
12. How is casual vacancy filled if it arises in the office of directors? **(Ref. Para-22.14)**
13. A director filling a casual vacancy is not a retiring director. Comment. **(Ref. Para-22.14)**
14. Explain in detail the provisions relating to appointment of an alternate director. **(Ref. Para-22.15)**
15. State the provisions relating to minimum and maximum number of directors. **(Ref. Para-22.19)**
16. Explain, in detail, the provisions relating to the appointment of small shareholders' directors. **(Ref. Para-22.20)**
17. How can the number of directors be increased? **(Ref. Para-22.21)**
18. How can the number of directors be decreased? **(Ref. Para-22.21)**
19. One person can be a director in any number of companies. Comment. **(Ref. Para-22.22)**
20. State the provisions and restrictions on the number of directorship that a person can hold. **(Ref. Para-22.22)**
21. When shall a director vacant his office? **(Ref. Para-22.23)**
22. Who can remove a director? **(Ref. Para-22.24)**
23. Explain briefly the provisions of the Companies Act, relating to the removal of a director in case of receipt of an appropriate special notice by the company for this purpose. **(Ref. Para-22.24)**
24. Can a company pay compensation to its directors for loss of office? Explain briefly the provisions in this regard. **(Ref. Para-22.25)**
25. State the circumstances in which a director can resign from his office. **(Ref. Para-22.26)**
26. When does the resignation of a director become effective? **(Ref. Para-22.26)**
27. Can a managing director be relieved immediately on tendering resignation? **(Ref. Para-22.26)**
28. State the provisions relating to approval of contracts in which a director is interested. **(Ref. Para-22.29)**
29. Outline the provisions with regard to disclosure of interest by directors. What are the consequences of non-disclosure? **(Ref. Para-22.30)**
30. An interested director cannot attend the board meeting. Comment. **(Ref. Para-22.31)**
31. State the provisions relating to making loans to directors. **(Ref. Para-22.31)**
32. Define managing director. **(Ref. Para-22.32)**
33. State the provisions relating to managing director. **(Ref. Para-22.32)**
34. Can a person be appointed as managing director of two companies? **(Ref. Para-22.32)**
35. Is it necessary to appoint a managing director for every company? **(Ref. Para-22.32)**
36. What are the disqualifications for managing director? **(Ref. Para-22.33)**
37. Define manager. **(Ref. Para-22.36)**
38. What are the disqualifications for vacation of office of a manager? **(Ref. Para-22.33)**
39. Distinguish between managing director and manager. **(Ref. Para-22.37)**
40. Explain, in detail, the remuneration to which directors and managers are entitled under the Companies Act, 2013. **(Ref. Para-22.39)**
41. Explain Schedule V of the Companies Act, 2013 . **(Ref. Para-22.44)**

## MULTIPLE-CHOICE QUESTIONS

1. Private company must have at least ______ directors.
   (i) 3 (iii) 5
   (ii) 2 (iv) 7
2. A private company must have at least ______ directors.
   (i) 3 (iii) 5
   (ii) 2 (iv) 7
3. Until the directors are duly appointed, all signatories to the ______ of the company are deemed to be directors of company.
   (i) prospectus (iii) appointment letter
   (ii) memorandum (iv) consent letter
4. Directors liable to retire by rotation to retire every ______ years.
   (i) one (iii) three
   (ii) two (iv) four
5. Proposal for appointment of a person who is not a retiring director, can be made by ______.
   (i) any person interested in his appointment (iii) Either (a) or (b)
   (ii) any member (iv) Neither (a) nor (b)
6. Appointment of additional director can be made by ______.
   (i) any other director (iii) shareholders
   (ii) board of directors (iv) general meeting
7. The managing director shall be necessary to be a ______.
   (i) director (iii) shareholder
   (ii) member of company (iv) all of the above
8. Any director may be removed by ______.
   (i) board resolution (iii) resolution by circulation
   (ii) special resolution (iv) ordinary resolution
9. Director appointed by which authority can be removed by an ordinary resolution?
   (i) Director appointed by the board (iii) Either (a) or (b)
   (ii) Director appointed by the company at a general meeting (iv) Neither (a) nor (b)
10. The office of the director shall become vacant immediately when ______.
    (i) the director adjudged insolvent
    (ii) the director is convicted in an offence involving moral turpitude
    (iii) the director disqualified by an order of court/tribunal
    (iv) all of the above
11. Disclosure of interest by director does not apply to ______.
    (i) private company (iii) government company
    (ii) public company (iv) None of the above
12. A managing director cannot be appointed at a time for a term exceeding ______.
    (i) 10 years (iii) 3 years
    (ii) 5 years (iv) 1 year

13. Simultaneous appointment of ______ and ______ is prohibited.
    (i) director and managing director
    (ii) managing director and whole-time director
    (iii) managing director and manager
    (iv) All of the above.
14. A managing director must be a ______ first.
    (i) director
    (ii) shareholder
    (iii) all of the above
    (iv) none of the above
15. Out of the following, which power can be exercised by directors only at the board meeting?
    (i) Power to issue debenture
    (ii) Power to borrow money otherwise than on debenture
    (iii) Either (a) or (b)
    (iv) Neither (a) nor (b)
16. Out of the following, which power can be exercised by directors only at the board meeting?
    (i) Power to invest fund of company
    (ii) Power to make loan
    (iii) Power to make calls on shares
    (iv) All of the above
17. Out of following, which power of the board can be exercised with approval in a general meeting?
    (i) Sell or lease undertaking of company
    (ii) Borrow money in excess of its paid-up capital and free reserve
    (iii) Either (a) or (b)
    (iv) Neither (a) nor (b)
18. Consent of ______ is required for certain contracts in which particular directors are interested.
    (i) board of directors
    (ii) shareholders
    (iii) state government
    (iv) central government
19. An interested director is not allowed to ______
    (i) participate in the discussion
    (ii) vote
    (iii) both (a) and (b)
    (iv) None of above
20. No person shall be appointed manager of a company if ______.
    (i) he is an undischarged insolvent
    (ii) he has been convicted of any offence involving moral turpitude in the last 5 years
    (iii) he has suspended payment to creditors in the last 5 years
    (iv) All of the above
21. ______ provides guidelines for remuneration of managing personnel.
    (i) Schedule V
    (ii) Schedule II
    (iii) Schedule VI
    (iv) Schedule III
22. Approval of the central government is required in case the remuneration payable to the managing director or whole-time director exceeds ______ % of net profit for one such director.
    (i) 1%
    (ii) 5%
    (iii) 3%
    (iv) 11%

## ANSWER KEYS

| | | | | | |
|---|---|---|---|---|---|
| **1.** (i) | **5.** (iii) | **9.** (iii) | **13.** (iii) | **17.** (iii) | **21.** (i) |
| **2.** (ii) | **6.** (ii) | **10.** (iv) | **14.** (i) | **18.** (i) | **22.** (ii) |
| **3.** (ii) | **7.** (i) | **11.** (iv) | **15.** (iii) | **19.** (iii) | |
| **4.** (iii) | **8.** (iv) | **12.** (iii) | **16.** (iv) | **20.** (iv) | |

# 23

# Payment of Bonus Act, 1965

**Learning objectives**

*After reading this chapter, you will be able to understand:*

- Application of Bonus Act
- Allocable surplus and available surplus
- Eligibility for bonus and calculation of days
- Minimum and maximum bonus
- Set on and set off of allocable surplus

## 23.1 INTRODUCTION

The practice of paying bonus in India appears to have originated during the First World War when certain textile mills granted 10% of the wages as war bonus to their workers in 1917.

In 1950, the Full Bench of the Labour Appellate evolved a formula for the determination of the bonus. A plea was made to raise that formula in 1959. At the second and the third meetings of the Eighteenth Session of the Standing Labour Committee held in New Delhi in March/April 1960, it was agreed that a Commission be appointed to go into the question of bonus and evolve suitable norms. A Tripartite Commission was set up by the Government of India to consider in a comprehensive manner the question of the payment of bonus based on the profits to the employees employed in establishments and to make recommendations to the Government. The Government of India accepted the recommendations of the Commission subject to certain modifications. To implement these recommendations, the Payment of Bonus Bill was introduced in the Parliament.

In *Jalan Trading Co. (P) Ltd vs Mills Mazdoor Union,* Honourable Supreme Court has held that the object of the Payment of Bonus Act is to maintain peace and harmony between the labour and the management by allowing the employees to share the prosperity of the establishment.

## 23.2 APPLICATION OF THE ACT

The Payment of Bonus Act is applicable to:

1. Every factory.
2. Every establishment in which 20 or more persons are employed on any day during an accounting year.

The Payment of Bonus Act is applicable to the whole of India. A factory or establishment located anywhere in India is subject to the provisions of Bonus Act. An establishment to which this Act applies shall continue to be governed by this Act, notwithstanding that the number of persons employed therein falls below 20.

The appropriate government may, by notification in the Official Gazette, apply the provisions of this act to any establishment, employing less than 20 but not less than 10 persons. The appropriate government can do so after giving notice of two months in advance.

**Case Study**

Examine whether the Payment of Bonus Act, 1965 will be applicable to the following cases:

(i) J who is working in a social welfare organization.

(ii) D, an employee, employed by an establishment, engaged in an industry carried on by a department of the Central Government.

**Case Study**

A workshop is employing 50 workmen. A shop-supervisor is drawing monthly wages of ₹ 9000. The HRD paid annual bonus to all the employees except the supervisor. The supervisor contends that he is also entitled to the bonus. Referring to the provisions of the Payment of Bonus Act, 1965 decide whether the HRD's action is correct.

## 23.3 ACT NOT TO APPLY TO CERTAIN CLASSES OF EMPLOYEES—SECTION 32

The Payment of Bonus Act shall not apply to the following categories of persons:

1. The employees of Life Insurance Company (LIC), Reserve Bank of India (RBI), Red Cross Society, universities and other educational institutions, institutions including hospitals, chambers of commerce and social welfare institutions established not for the purposes of profit.
2. The seamen.
3. The employees registered or listed under any scheme, made under the Dock Workers (Regulation of Employment) Act, 1948 and employed by the registered or listed employees.

4. The employees employed by an establishment engaged in industry carried on by or under the authority of any department of the Central Government or a State Government or a local authority.
5. The employees employed through the contractors on building operations.
6. The employees employed by the Industrial Finance Corporation of India (IFCI), any financial corporation established under Section 3 or any joint financial corporation established under Section 3(A) of the State Financial Corporations Act, 1951, The Deposit Insurance Corporation, The Agricultural Refinance Corporation, UTI and IDBI.
7. Any other financial institution (other than a banking company) being an establishment in a public sector which the Central Government may by notification in the Official Gazette specify having regard to:
   (i) Its capital structure.
   (ii) Its objective and nature of its activities.
   (iii) The nature and extent of financial assistance or any concession given to it by the government.
   (iv) Any other relevant factor.
8. The employees employed by the inland water transport establishments, operating on routes passing through any other country.

**Case Study**

Decide with reasons in the light of the Payment of Bonus Act, 1965 whether the following persons are entitled for bonus:

(i) A University teacher.
(ii) An employee of the 'NABARD'.
(iii) A reinstated employee without wages for the period of dismissal.
(iv) A retrenched employee who worked for 45 days in a year on a salary of ₹ 4000 per month.
(v) An apprentice.

## 23.4 DEFINITION

### 23.4.1 Accounting Year—Section 2(1)

The accounting year means in relation to a corporation, the year ending on the day on which the books of the account of the corporation are closed and balanced.

In relation to a company, this term means a period in respect of which any profit or loss account of the company, laid before it in an annual general meeting (AGM) is made up whether that period is a year or not.

In any other case, the term 'accounting year' means either the year commencing on the first day of April or if the accounts of an establishment maintained by the employer thereof are closed and balanced on any other day other than the 31st day of March, then at the option of the employer the year ending on the day on which its accounts are so closed and balanced. If however, the said option is once exercised by the employer, it cannot be exercised once again except with the permission in writing of the prescribed authority and upon such conditions as that authority may think fit. In other words, the exercise of the said option can only take place on obtaining the previous written permission of the prescribed authority and the prescribed authority may impose such conditions as it may think fit.

### 23.4.2 Establishment in a Private Section—Section 2(15)

The establishment may be in a private sector or public sector. When it is in the private sector, it means any establishment other than the establishment in the public sector.

### 23.4.3 Establishment in a Public Section—Section 2(16)

The establishment in the public sector means an establishment owned, controlled or managed by:

1. A government company.
2. A corporation in which not less than 40% of its capital is held whether singly or taken together by the government or the RBI or a corporation owned by the government or the RBI.

### 23.4.4 Employer—Section 2(14)

In relation to the establishment which is a factory employer means the following persons:

1. The owner or occupier of the factory.
2. The agent of such owner or such occupier.
3. The legal representative of a deceased owner or occupier of factory.
4. Where a person has been named as a manager of a factory under the Factories Act, 1948.

In relation to any other establishment which is not a factory employer means the following persons:

1. The person who has the ultimate control over the affairs of the establishment.
2. If the said affairs are entrusted to a managing director then such manager or managing director.

### 23.4.5 Employee—Section 2(13)

An employee means any person, other than an apprentice employed on a salary or wages not exceeding ₹ 21,000 per month in any industry to do any skilled or unskilled, manual, supervisory, managerial, administrative, technical or clerical work for hire or reward whether the terms of employment are express or implied.

### 23.4.6 Available Surplus

The available surplus under the Payment of Bonus Act, 1965 means the available surplus computed under Section 5 after deducting certain prior charges from the 'gross profits'.

### 23.4.7 Allocable Surplus—Section 2(4)

Allocable surplus means:

1. 67% of the available surplus for companies other than the banking companies which comply with Section 194 of the Income Tax Act.
2. 60% of the available surplus in all the other cases.

Thus, the allocable surplus is in fact an appropriation out of the 'Available surplus' for the payment of bonus to the employees subject to the maximum and minimum bonus limits.

### 23.4.8 Salary or Wages—Section 2(21)

The salary or wages means all remuneration payable to an employee in respect of his employment or work done in such employment. It includes the dearness allowance and free food allowance. However, the allowances not included in the salary or wages are following:

1. Over time allowance.
2. Value of any house accommodation or supply of water, medical attendance or any concessional supply of food.
3. Travelling concession.
4. Bonus.
5. Contribution paid or payable to provident fund.
6. Any retrenchment, compensation or gratuity or any retirement benefits.
7. Any commission.

**Case Study**

Prakash Chandra is working as a salesman in a company on salary basis. The following payments were made to him by the company during the previous financial year:

(i) Overtime allowance.
(ii) Dearness allowance.
(iii) Commission on sales.
(iv) Employer's contribution towards the pension fund.
(v) Value of food.

Examine, as to which of the above payments form a part of the 'salary' of Prakash Chandra under the provisions of the Payment of Bonus Act, 1965.

## 23.5 WHO IS ENTITLED TO BONUS?

As per Section 8 of the Payment of Bonus Act, every employee of an establishment is entitled to bonus in an accounting year, provided he has worked in that establishment, for not less than 30 working days in the year on a salary less than ₹ 21,000 per month.

An employee is entitled to bonus in the following cases:

1. A temporary workman is entitled to bonus on the basis of the total number of days worked by him.
2. An employee of a seasonal factory is entitled to proportionate bonus and not the minimum bonus as prescribed under Section 10 of the Act.
3. A part-time employee as a sweeper engaged on a regular basis is entitled to bonus.
4. A retrenched employee is eligible to get bonus, provided he has worked for a minimum qualifying period.
5. A probationer is an employee and as such is entitled to bonus.
6. A dismissed employee, reinstated with back wages, is entitled to bonus.
7. A piece-rated worker is entitled to bonus.

It may be noted that if an employee is prevented from working by an act of the employer, which is declared illegal by a competent court then the employee's statutory eligibility for bonus within the meaning of Section 8 cannot be lost. The word 'worked' in the section means ready and willing to work.

**Case Study**

Referring to the provisions of the Payment of Bonus Act, 1965 state, whether the persons entitled to bonus under the Act are following:

(i) An apprentice.
(ii) An employee, dismissed on the ground of misconduct.
(iii) A temporary workman.
(iv) A piece-rated worker.

## 23.6 DISQUALIFICATION FOR BONUS—SECTION 9

An employee shall be disqualified from receiving bonus under the Act, if he is dismissed from service for

1. Fraud.
2. Riotous or violent behaviour while on the premises of the establishment.
3. Theft, misappropriation or sabotage of any property of the establishment.

In any of above circumstances, the employee's right to bonus shall lapse. The Madras High Court has held in the case of *Pandian Roadways Corporation Ltd vs Presiding officer* that an employee who is dismissed from service on the ground of misconduct is disqualified from any bonus and not merely for the bonus of the accounting year in which he is dismissed.

In the following cases, an employee is not entitled to bonus:

1. An apprentice is not entitled to bonus.
2. An employee employed through contractors on the building operation.
3. An employee, employed by the inland water transport establishment, operating on routers passing through any other country.

**Case Study**

A is an employee of a company. The amount of the bonus, payable to A during the year 2006–07 is ₹ 10,000 but the company paid him ₹ 7000 only and a sum of ₹ 3000 was deducted from the bonus, against the loss suffered by the company due to misconduct of A during the same accounting year. A files a suit against the company for the recovery of the deducted amount. Decide whether A would be given any relief by the court under the provisions of the Payment of Bonus Act, 1956? What will be your answer, if the losses are related to the accounting year 2005–06?

## 23.7 COMPUTATION OF THE NUMBER OF WORKING DAYS

The qualifying period of service which entitles an employee to claim the minimum bonus is 30 working days. Section 13 authorizes the employer to proportionately reduce the bonus if the employee has not worked for all the working days in an 'accounting year'.

Section 14 provides that the following days shall be deemed to be the working days of an employee and shall be counted while calculating the total working days for the purpose of a bonus:

1. The days when he has been laid off under an agreement or as permitted by standing orders under the Industrial Disputes Act, 1947 or the Industrial Employment Standing Orders Act or under any other law applicable to the establishment.
2. The days when he has been on leave with salary or wage.
3. The days when he has been absent due to a temporary disablement caused by an accident arising out of and in the course of his employment.
4. The days on which the employee has been on maternity leave with salary or wage (i.e., maternity leaves allowed as per the law) during the accounting year.

**Case Study**

X, a temporary employee drawing a salary of ₹ 3000 per month in an establishment to which the Payment of Bonus Act, 1965 applies was prevented by the employers from working in the establishment for 2 months during the financial year 2001–02, pending certain inquiry. Since there were no adverse findings, 'X' was re-instated in service later, when the bonus was to be paid to other employees, the employers refuse to pay bonus to 'X' even though he has worked for the remaining 10 months in the year. Referring to the provisions of the Payment of Bonus Act, 1965 examine the validity of the employer's refusal to pay bonus to 'X'.

**Case Study**

ABC Textiles Ltd employed 20 full-time and five part-time employees who were drawing a salary of less than ₹ 10,000 per month. After completing service of 28 days in an accounting year, 10 full-time employees submitted their resignations and left the service of the company. The Board of Directors of this company decided not to give the bonus to the employees who resigned to the remaining full-time employees and to the part-time employees. Against the decision, all the employees applied to the authorities for relief.

Decide, stating the provisions of the Payment of Bonus Act, 1956 whether the employees who resigned the remaining full-time employees and part-time employees will get relief.

**Case Study**

Mr. 'E' joined as a supervisor on a monthly salary of ₹ 3400 on 1 February 2007 and resigned from his job on 28 February 2007. The company declared a bonus of 20% to all the eligible employees and paid it on time. Mr. 'E', knowing the facts, made a claim to the HRD, which in turn rejected the claim. Examine the validity in the light of the provisions of the Payment of Bonus Act, 1965.

## 23.8 WHO IS LIABLE TO PAY BONUS?

An owner, occupier or controller of every factory or establishment in which 20 or more persons are employed on any day during an accounting year is liable to pay bonus.

The controller of public sector establishments is also liable to pay bonus if the establishment is selling any goods in competition with an establishment in the private sector and the income from such sale is not less than 20% of its gross income.

## 23.9 PAYMENT OF MINIMUM BONUS—SECTION 10

The employer is bound to pay every employee in respect of every accounting year, a minimum bonus which shall be 8.33% of the salary or wage earned by the employee during the accounting year or ₹ 100 whichever is higher, whether or not the employer has any allocable surplus in the accounting year.

But if the employee has not completed 15 years of age at the beginning of the accounting year, he will be entitled to the minimum bonus which shall be 8.33% of the salary or wage during the accounting year or ₹ 60 whichever is higher. The minimum bonus is payable even in case of loss.

## 23.10 PAYMENT OF MAXIMUM BONUS—SECTION 11

The bonus at higher rate than the minimum is payable only when allocable surplus in any accounting year exceeds the amount of the minimum bonus, payable to the employees. The maximum limit of the bonus payable to an employee is 20% of the salary or wages earned by the employee during that year.

While calculating the allocable surplus, the amount set on or the amount set off shall be taken into account as per the provisions of set on and set off.

## 23.11 CALCULATION OF BONUS WITH RESPECT TO CERTAIN EMPLOYEES—SECTION 12

The employee drawing a salary up to ₹ 21,000 per month is eligible for bonus. Where the salary or wage of an employee exceeds ₹ 7,000 per month, the bonus shall be calculated as if his salary or wage were ₹ 7,000.

*Example*

| Salary of Employee (per month) | Calculation of Bonus @ 9% | Amount of Bonus Payable |
|---|---|---|
| ₹ 2500 | $2500 \times \frac{9}{100} \times 12$ | ₹ 2700 |
| ₹ 3500 | $3500 \times \frac{9}{100} \times 12$ | ₹ 3780 |
| ₹ 9000 | $7000 \times \frac{9}{100} \times 12$ | ₹ 7560 |

Section 13 suggests that the bonus where the employee has not worked for all working days in an accounting year then the minimum bonus if higher than 8.33% can be reduced proportionately.

## 23.12 ADJUSTMENT OF CUSTOMARY OR INTERIM BONUS—SECTION 17

In any accounting year, an employer has paid any Puja bonus or other customary bonus to an employee, than the former shall be entitled to deduct the amount of bonus so paid from the amount of bonus payable by him to the employee under this Act in respect of that accounting year. The employee shall be entitled to receive only the balance.

The employer can do the same thing where he has paid a part of the bonus payable under this Act, to an employee in advance.

As per Section 18 if in any accounting year, an employee is found guilty of misconduct, creating a financial loss to the employer then the employer can lawfully deduct the amount of loss from the amount of bonus payable by him to the employee in respect of that accounting year only. In this case, the employee shall get only the balance if there be any.

**Case Study**

X is an employee in a company. The amount of bonus payable to him during the year 2007–08 is ₹ 14,000. The company deducted a sum of ₹ 4000 against the 'Puja Bonus' already paid to him during the said year and paid the remaining amount. X files a suit against the company for the recovery of the deducted amount. Decide under the Payment of Bonus Act, 1965 whether X would be given any relief by the court?

**Case Study**

Skypark Wooden Toys Limited was established at Kolkata in the year 2005, employing 100 workmen. Since then, the company suffered losses but the minimum bonus was paid in the accounting years of 2006 and 2007. In the accounting year 2008, the company earned huge profits. After mitigating the previous losses, the company is having surplus profits and wants to pay the bonus to its workmen. Skypark Wooden Toys Limited wants legal advice on the following issues:

(a) How much minimum and maximum bonus may be paid to the workmen?

(b) Whether the company may adjust the Puja bonus already paid to the workmen while calculating the amount of the bonus payable to the workmen for that accounting year or

(c) The company wants to give wooden toys as bonus, instead of cash. Whether the company can do so?

Advise Skypark Wooden Toys Limited, stating the provisions of the Payment of Bonus Act, 1965.

## 23.13 SET ON AND SET OFF OF ALLOCABLE SURPLUS—SECTION 15

The provisions relating to 'set on' and 'set off' of the allocable surplus are stated as under:

### 23.13.1 Set On of Allocable Surplus

Where for any accounting year, the allocable surplus exceeds the amount of the maximum bonus payable to the employees in the establishment under Section 11 then the excess shall subject to a limit of 20% of the total salary or wage of the employees employed in the establishment in that accounting year be carried forward for being set on in the succeeding accounting year and so on up and inclusive of the Fourth Accounting Year. This excess amount can be utilized for the payment of bonus for the forthcoming years.

### 23.13.2 Set Off of Allocable Surplus

In cases where there is no allocable surplus or where the allocable surplus falls short of the amount of the minimum bonus payable to the employees under Section 10 and there is no amount or sufficient amount carried forward and set on under the aforesaid provisions which could be utilized for paying minimum bonus minimum amount of bonus or deficiency in bonus shall be carried forward for being set off in the succeeding accounting year and so on upto and inclusive of the Fourth Accounting Year.

### 23.13.3 Utilization of Carried Forward Amount

Where in any accounting year, any amount has been carried forward and set on or set off under this Section 15 then in the calculating bonus for the succeeding accounting year, the amount of set on or set off, carried forward from the earliest accounting year shall first be taken into account.

## 23.14 LIABILITY OF THE NEW FIRM TO PAY BONUS—SECTION 16

The new establishment is exempted from the liability to pay bonus for the initial five accounting years. However, if the employer earns profits in any accounting year during this period of five years then the bonus shall be payable in respect of that accounting year. It may be noted, that an establishment shall not be deemed to be newly set up merely by reason of a change in its location, management, name or ownership.

### 23.14.1 First Five Accounting Years

In case of a new establishment in the first five accounting years following the accounting year in which the employer sells the goods produced or manufactured by him or renders services as the case may be the bonus shall be payable only in respect of the accounting year in which the employer derives profits from such an establishment. Such bonus shall be calculated in accordance with the provisions of the Act relating to that year but without applying the provisions for set on and set off.

It may be noted that an employer shall not be deemed to have derived profit in the accounting year unless:

1. He has made a provision for the depreciation under the Income Tax Act.
2. The arrears of such depreciation and losses for the previous accounting years have been fully set off against his profits.

### 23.14.2 Sixth and Seventh Accounting Year

But in the sixth and seventh accounting years, the provisions of Section 15 shall apply subject to the following modifications, *viz.*,

1. For the sixth accounting year, set on or set off shall be made in the manner illustrated in the fourth schedule, taking into account the excess or deficiency if any, as the case may be of the allocable surplus set on or set off in respect of the fifth and sixth accounting years.
2. For the seventh accounting year, the same principle is to be followed but the excess or deficiency of the allocable surplus set on or set off in respect of the fifth and sixth and seventh accounting year has to be taken into account.

### 23.14.3 From the Eighth Accounting Year

From the eighth accounting year, following the accounting year in which the employer sells the goods, produced or manufactured by him or renders services, the provisions of Section 15 shall apply in relation to such an establishment as they apply in relation to any other establishment.

## 23.15 PRESUMPTIONS ABOUT THE ACCURACY OF BALANCE SHEET AND PROFIT AND LOSS ACCOUNT OF THE COMPANY—SECTION 23

When a dispute arises before any arbitrator or industrial tribunal between an employer and his employees regarding the bonus payable under the Payment of Bonus Act and the pending amount.

During the course of such a proceeding, the balance sheet and the profit and loss account of an employer being a corporation or a company other than a banking company may be produced. If these statements of accounts are audited by the Comptroller and Auditor General of India or by the auditors qualified under Section 226 of the Companies Act then as specifically provided in Section 23 of the Payment of Bonus Act the said authority may presume that those are accurate. In view of this presumption, the corporation or company need not prove the accuracy of such statements by affidavit or any other mode.

But if the said authority is satisfied that those statements are not accurate it may take such steps as it thinks necessary to find out the accuracy thereof. Further the trade union and if there is no trade union, the employees being a party to the dispute may apply to the specified authority, seeking a clarification relating to any item in the balance sheet or profit and loss account. On the receipt of such an application the specified authority is to satisfy itself as to the necessity of such clarification. On being thus satisfied the specified authority may direct the corporation or the company to furnish to the trade union or the employees such clarifications within such time as may be specified in the direction.

## 23.16 PROCEDURE AS REGARDS THE RECOVERY OF BONUS—SECTION 21

Section 21 of the payment of Bonus Act, 1965 lays down one of the modes for the recovery of money due as bonus under a settlement or agreement or an award.

1. The employee makes an application for the recovery of the amount to the appropriate government.
2. Application is to be made within one year from the date on which the money is due but it may be entertained even after the expiry of the said period of one year if the appropriate government is satisfied, that the applicant had sufficient cause for not making the application within the said period.
3. The application can be made by an employee or any person authorized on his death assignee or heir(s).
4. The appropriate government on being satisfied, issues a certificate to the collector for the amount so due. Thereupon the collector shall proceed to recover the same in the same manner as an arrear of the land revenue.

## 21.17 TIME LIMIT FOR THE PAYMENT OF BONUS—SECTION 22

All amounts payable to an employee by way of bonus under the Payment of Bonus Act shall be paid in cash by his employer:

1. Where there is a dispute regarding payment of bonus, pending before any authority under Section 22 within a month from the date on which the award becomes enforceable or the settlement comes into operation in respect of such dispute.
2. In any other case, within a period of eight months from the close of the accounting year. But this period of eight months may be extended up to a maximum of two years by the appropriate government. This extension is to be granted on the application of the employer and only for sufficient reasons (Section 19).

## 23.18 POWERS OF INSPECTORS—SECTION 27

The appropriate government may by a notification in the Official Gazette appoints such persons as it thinks fit to be the inspectors for the purposes of the Payment of Bonus Act and may define the limits, within which they shall exercise jurisdiction.

An inspector thus appointed has to ascertain whether any of the provisions of this Act has been complied with and for this purpose he may:

1. Require an employer to furnish such information as he may consider necessary.
2. At any reasonable time, enter into any establishment connected therewith and require anyone found in charge thereof to produce before him for examination any account books, registers and other documents relating to the employment of persons or the payment of salary or wage or bonus in the establishment.
3. Examine, with respect to any matter relevant to any of the purpose aforesaid, the employer, his agent or servant or any other person when the inspector has a reasonable cause to believe to be or have been an employee in the establishment.
4. Make copies of or take extracts from any books register or other document maintained in relation to the establishment.
5. Exercise such other powers as may be prescribed (Section 27).

The inspector appointed as aforesaid is deemed to be a public servant under the Indian Penal Code. Any person whom the Inspector calls upon to produce any account book, register or other document or to give information shall be legally bound to do so.

The provisions of Section 27 do not empower the inspector to require a banking company to furnish or disclose any statement or information or to produce or give inspection of any of its books of account or other documents which a banking company cannot be compelled to furnish or disclose.

## 23.19 APPLICATION OF THE ACT TO ESTABLISHMENT IN PUBLIC SECTOR—SECTION 20

The provision of the Payment of Bonus Act shall also apply to the establishment in a public sector if the following conditions are satisfied:

1. An establishment in the public sector sells any goods produced or manufactured by it or render any services in competition with the establishment in the private sector.
2. And income from such sale or service or both is not less than 20% of the gross income of the establishment in the public sector.

## 23.20 BONUS LINKED WITH PRODUCTION OR PRODUCTIVITY—SECTION 31 A

There may be an agreement or settlement by the employees with their employer for the payment of an annual bonus, linked with production or productivity in lieu of the bonus paid on profit as is payable under Section 31 A, of the Payment of Bonus Act.

Accordingly, when such an agreement has been entered into, the employees are entitled to receive bonus, as per the terms of the agreement or settlement subject to the following restrictions imposed by Section 31 A, which are as follows:

1. Any such agreement or settlement whereby the employees extinguish their right to receive the minimum bonus, under Section 10 shall be null and void in so far as it purports to deprive the employees the right of receiving the minimum bonus.
2. If the bonus payable under such an agreement exceeds 20% of the salary or wages earned by the employees during the relevant accounting year such employees are not entitled to the excess over 20% of salary or wages.

**Case Study**

The management of Shakthi Mills Ltd, entered into an agreement with their employees to pay them a bonus based on the production in lieu of the bonus based on the profits from the Accounting Year 2007. The employees further agreed to forego their right to receive the minimum bonus and instead accept 25% of their salary/wage as the bonus based on productivity. Is such an agreement valid? Examine in the light of the provisions of the Payment of Bonus Act, 1965.

**Case Study**

On 1 January 2002, the Aryan Textiles Ltd agreed with the employees for the payment of an annual bonus, linked with the production or productivity instead of the bonus based on profits subject to the limit of 30% of their salary wages during the relevant accounting year. It was also agreed by the employees that they will not claim the minimum bonus stated under Section 10 of the Payment of Bonus Act, 1965. As per the agreement, the employees of the Aryan Textiles Ltd claimed the annual bonus, linked with the production or productivity in the relevant accounting year. On the refusal of the company the employees of the company moved to the court for relief.

Decide in reference to the provisions of the Payment of Bonus Act, 1965 whether the employees will get the relief? In spite of the aforesaid agreement whether the employees are still entitled to receive the minimum bonus.

## 23.21 POWER OF EXEMPTION—SECTION 36

Section 36 lays down that the appropriate government by notification in the Official Gazette, exempt for such period as may be specified therein and subject to such conditions as may think fit to impose, such establishment or class of establishments from all or any of the provisions of this Act. To provide such exemptions the following aspects must be considered:

1. The appropriate government shall consider, the financial position and other relevant circumstances of an establishment or class of establishment.
2. It should be of the opinion that it would not be in the public interest to apply all or any of the provisions of the Act.
3. If the bonus liability is negligible compared to the loss suffered, a company should not be relieved of the liability to pay the minimum bonus.
4. If the losses sustained by the employer are not due to any misconduct on the part of the employees, the employer is liable to pay statutory minimum bonus.

**Case Study**

In an accounting year, a company to which the Payment of Bonus Act, 1965 applies suffered heavy losses. The Board of Directors of the said company decided not to give bonus to the employees. The employees of the company moved to the court for relief. Decide in the light of the provisions of the said Act whether the employees will get relief?

## LIST OF LANDMARK JUDGEMENTS

1. ***ONGC vs Shyam Kumar Sahegal (1995)***
   Every employee reinstated in service and otherwise qualified is eligible for bonus. The employers' statutory liability for bonus cannot be said to have been lost and the employees concerned shall be entitled to the bonus if he is reinstated in service.

2. ***Upendra Chandra vs United Bank of India***
If the customary bonus does not relate to profits but is merely an outcome of negotiations between the employers and employees. It is not deductible.
3. ***Gopalan vs Angamali Chit Fund (1977)***
The statutory bonus of 8.33% shall be payable, whether there are profits in the accounting year or not. The bonus is implied term of employment and does not depend upon the projects.
4. ***Workman of Associated Rubber Industries Ltd vs Associated Rubber Industries Ltd (1986)***
Where a subsidiary company, wholly owned by the principal company, is amalgamated with the principal company, the workmen of the principal company are entitled to the bonus by including the income of the subsidiary company, along with the gross profits of the principal company.
5. ***Binny Ltd vs Workman (1973)***
The claim for bonus can be made only after the close of the accounting year, the gross profit is calculated only at the end of accounting year and the available and allocable surplus can also be worked out only at the end of the accounting year.
6. ***Bank of Madura Ltd vs Employee's Union (1970)***
The probationer is an employee and as such is entitled to bonus.
7. ***Automobile Karmchari Sangh vs Industrial Tribunal (1970)***
The part time employee as a sweeper engaged on regular basis is entitled to bonus.
8. ***Mathuradas Kani vs Labour appallent Tribunal (1958)***
The piece rated worker is entitled to bonus.
9. ***East Asiatic Co. (P) Ltd vs Industrial Tribunal (1961)***
The retrenched employee is eligible to get bonus, provided he has worked for the minimum qualifying period.
10. ***UOI vs R. C. Jain (1981)***
The Delhi Development Authority is a local authority and hence its employees are not entitled to the payment of bonus.
11. ***KLJ Plastics vs Labour Court (2002)***
If an employee is guilty of riotous and disorderly behaviour for assaulting the managers and is dismissed, he is disqualified for bonus.
12. ***State of Tamil Nadu vs K. Subansyamam (1989)***
The employees should be heard before granting exemption. The exemption cannot be granted retrospectively.
13. ***Associated Publishers Madras vs Govt. of Tamil Nadu (1985)***
If the bonus liability is negligible, compared to the total loss granting exemption may not be advisable.

## TEST YOUR KNOWLEDGE

1. Discuss the categories of employees who are not entitled to claim bonus, under the Payment of Bonus Act. **(Ref. Para-23.3)**
2. What do you understand by the term 'allocable surplus'? **(Ref. Para-23.4)**
3. What do you understand by the term 'available surplus'? **(Ref. Para-23.4)**
4. Specify the any five kinds of establishments which are not covered under the Payment of Bonus Act. **(Ref. Para-23.3)**

5. Explain the meaning of salary and wages under the Payment of Bonus Act, 1965. **(Ref. Para-23.4)**
6. Explain the meaning of employer and employee under the Payment of Bonus Act. **(Ref. Para-23.4)**
7. Explain the meaning of accounting year under the Payment of Bonus Act, 1965. **(Ref. Para-23.4)**
8. Who is entitled to bonus? **(Ref. Para-23.5)**
9. An employee found guilty of misconduct, causing a financial loss to the employer is entitled for bonus. Decide. **(Ref. Para-23.6)**
10. Explain the procedure relating to the computation of working days for the purpose of payment of bonus under the Payment of Bonus Act. **(Ref. Para-23.7)**
11. Can there be a deduction in the amount of bonus, on the ground that the employee has not worked for all working days in an accounting year? **(Ref. Para-23.7)**
12. Who is liable to pay bonus? **(Ref. Para-23.8)**
13. Explain the provisions relating to the minimum and maximum amount of bonus payment to an employee for an accounting year. **(Ref. Para-23.9)**
14. Explain the provisions of the Payment of Bonus Act, 1965 relating to the adjustment of customary bonus against the bonus payable under act. **(Ref. Para-12)**
15. Explain the rules of set on and set off of allocable surplus under the Payment of Bonus Act. **(Ref. Para-23.13)**
16. Explain the provisions of the Payment of Bonus Act, 1965 regulating the payment of bonus by new establishment. **(Ref. Para-23.14)**
17. A company calculates the bonus from the accounting position, as per the balance sheet and profit and loss account. Can a worker rely on the correctness of the balance sheet and profit and loss account? **(Ref. Para-23.15)**
18. Explain the procedure to recover the bonus. **(Ref. Para-23.16)**
19. What is the time limit within which the payment of bonus due to an employee under the act be paid? **(Ref. Para-23.17)**
20. What are the powers of an inspector under the Payment of Bonus Act? **(Ref. Para-23.18)**
21. Is the provision of act applicable to public sector undertaking? **(Ref. Para-23.19)**
22. Explain the special provisions with respect to bonus linked with production. **(Ref. Para-23.20)**
23. Examine the power of the government to grant exemption to an establishment from the Payment of Bonus Act, 1965. **(Ref. Para-23.21)**

## MULTIPLE-CHOICE QUESTIONS

1. Employees of LIC will not cover under the Payment of Bonus Act, 1965.
   (i) Yes
   (ii) No
2. Employees of the RBI will not cover under the Payment of Bonus Act, 1965.
   (i) Yes
   (ii) No

3. Employees employed through contractors on building operations, will cover under Payment of Bonus Act, 1956.
   (i) Yes
   (ii) No
4. Employees employed under the Indian Red Cross Society will cover under the Payment of Bonus Act, 1956.
   (i) Yes
   (ii) No
5. Employees employed under the educational institutions, will cover under the Payment of Bonus Act.
   (i) Yes
   (ii) No
6. Employees employed under any financial corporation established under the state financial corporation Act, will not cover under the Payment of Bonus Act.
   (i) Yes
   (ii) No
7. Every other establishment, other than the factory in which there are more than __________ employees, must be to come under the Payment of Bonus Act.
   (i) 15
   (ii) 20
   (iii) 25
   (iv) 30
8. In an establishment 15 employees were working with a salary below than ₹ 3500 and seven employees, working with a salary more than ₹ 3500. Is the establishment covered under the Payment of Bonus Act, 1956?
   (i) Covered
   (ii) Not covered
9. If an establishment in the previous year, was covered under the Payment of Bonus Act. But in this year the employees had reduced to below 20. Is that establishment covered under the Payment of Bonus Act.
   (i) Covered
   (ii) Not covered
10. Where any employee, committed any fraud, in that accounting year. Mention whether he is eligible for bonus. Who has been dismissed from service?
    (i) Yes
    (ii) No
11. Where any employee was dismissed because of Riotous/Violent behaviour in the premises, whether he is eligible for bonus.
    (i) Yes
    (ii) No
12. Where an employee dismissed but reinstated with back wages, will be entitled to bonus.
    (i) Yes
    (ii) No

13. A temporary workman is entitled to bonus on the basis of
    (i) total no. of days worked.
    (ii) all working days.
    (iii) no bonus will be allowable.
    (iv) none of the above.
14. An employee of a seasonal factory will be given minimum bonus, if he had not worked for sufficient days.
    (i) Yes
    (ii) No
15. Gross profit of an employer, in the case of banking company, will be calculated as per ________ under the Payment of Bonus Act.
    (i) Schedule I (iii) Schedule III
    (ii) Schedule IV (iv) none of these
16. Gross profit of an employer in case of any other company other than the banking company will be calculated as per ________ under Payment of Bonus Act.
    (i) Schedule I (iii) Schedule III
    (ii) Schedule II (iv) none of these
17. The allocable surplus in case of the employer is company other than banking company ________ of available surplus.
    (i) 60 per cent (iii) 20 per cent
    (ii) 67 per cent (iv) 8.33 per cent
18. The allocable surplus, in case of the employer is a banking company ________ of available surplus.
    (i) 60 per cent (iii) 20 per cent
    (ii) 67 per cent (iv) 8.33 per cent
19. While calculating the direct tax payable u/s 7 of the Payment of Bonus Act which of the following should not be considered?
    (i) Profits (iii) Speculation loss
    (ii) Capital gains (iv) Unabsorbed depreciation
20. What is the minimum bonus u/s 10 of the Payment of Bonus Act.
    (i) 8.3% or ₹ 100 ↑ (iii) 8.33% or ₹ 60 ↓
    (ii) 8.33% or ₹ 100 ↓ (iv) none of the above
21. What is the minimum bonus u/s 10 of the Payment of Bonus Act if employee has not completed 15 years of age?
    (i) 8.33% or ₹ 60 ↑
    (ii) 8.33% or ₹ 60 ↓
    (iii) 8.33% or ₹ 100 ↓
    (iv) 8.33% or ₹ 100 ↓
22. What is the maximum bonus u/s 11 of the Payment of Bonus Act.
    (i) 20% of wages (iii) 17.5% of wages
    (ii) 15% of wages (iv) None of the above
23. Set on can be done for the next ________ accounting years.
    (i) 5 (iii) 4
    (ii) 6 (iv) none of these

24. The bonus shall be paid by the employer in cash. If there is any dispute and settlement has been done, then the employer should pay bonus within
    (i) Two months.
    (ii) One month.
    (iii) Three months.
    (iv) None of these.
25. In general cases, bonus shall be paid within
    (i) Six months.
    (ii) Seven months.
    (iii) Eight months.
    (iv) None of these.

## ANSWER KEYS

| | | | | |
|---|---|---|---|---|
| **1.** (i) | **6.** (i) | **11.** (ii) | **16.** (ii) | **21.** (i) |
| **2.** (i) | **7.** (ii) | **12.** (i) | **17.** (ii) | **22.** (i) |
| **3.** (ii) | **8.** (i) | **13.** (i) | **18.** (i) | **23.** (iii) |
| **4.** (ii) | **9.** (i) | **14.** (ii) | **19.** (iv) | **24.** (ii) |
| **5.** (ii) | **10.** (ii) | **15.** (i) | **20.** (i) | **25.** (iii) |

# 24

# The Payment of Gratuity Act, 1972

**Learning Objectives**

*After reading this chapter, you will be able to understand:*

- To whom gratuity is payable
- How to calculate the amount of gratuity payable?
- When gratuity will be forfeited
- Procedure for nomination in respect of gratuity payment

## 24.1 WHAT IS GRATUITY?

A gratuity is a reward to an employee, for his long and meritorious service with his present employer. It is just like the other retirement benefits, like provident fund and pension intended to help the worker after his retirement from service, either due to superannuation or some physical disability. The Payment of Gratuity Act, 1972 came into force on 16 September 1972. It is a social security measure and was passed to:

1. Ensure the uniform pattern of the payment of gratuity to industrial workers throughout the country.
2. Avoid different treatment to the industrial workers engaged in the establishment, having their branches and places of business throughout the county in different states and under the service conditions, the employees are liable to be transferred from one state to another.

## 24.2 SCOPE OF PAYMENT OF GRATUITY ACT, 1972

The Payment of Gratuity Act, 1972 extends to the whole of India. But in so far as it relates to the plantations or ports it shall not extend to the State of Jammu and Kashmir—Section 1(2).

### 24.2.1 The Act Applies to the Persons Employed in the Following Establishments

The provision of Payment of Gratuity Act is applicable to:

1. Every factory, mine, oilfield, plantation, port and railway company.
2. Every shop and establishment within the meaning of any law in which 10 or more persons are employed or were employed on any day of the preceding 12 months.
3. Such other establishments or class of establishments in which the Central Government may by notification, specify in this behalf and in which 10 persons were employed during the preceding 12 months—Section 1(3).

### 24.2.2 The Act Does Not Apply to the Following Persons

The provision of Payment of Gratuity Act is not applicable to:

1. The Act is not applicable to apprentices.
2. A person who hold civil posts under the Central Government or a State Government and are governed by any other Act or rules, providing for the Payment of Gratuity—Section 2(e).
3. The government may exempt any establishment from the provisions of the Act if its employees are in receipt of gratuity not less favourable than the benefits provided in the Act—Section 5(1).

## 24.3 DEFINITION

### 24.3.1 Appropriate Government—Section 2(a)

In relation to any of the following establishments, the appropriate government means the Central Government which is:

1. An establishment belonging to or under the control of the Central Government.
2. An establishment having branches in more than one state.
3. An establishment of a factory belonging to or under the control of the Central Government.
4. An establishment of a major port, mine, oilfield or Railway Company.

In any other case, 'Appropriate Government' means the State Government.

### 24.3.2 Continuous Service—Section 2-A

An employee shall be said to be in continuous service for a period if he has for the period been in an uninterrupted service, including the service which may be interrupted on account of (a) sickness, (b) accident, (c) leave, (d) absence from duty without leave (not being an absence in respective of which an order treating the absence as a break in service has been passed in accordance with the standing order, rules or regulations, governing the employees of the establishment), (e) layoff, (f) strike, (g) lockout or (h) cessation of work, not due to any fault of the employee whether such uninterrupted or interrupted service was rendered by an employee before or after the enactment of the Amendment Act, 1984.

### 24.3.3 Deemed Continuous Service

Where an employee (not being an employee in seasonal establishment) is not in a continuous service for a period of one year, he shall be deemed to be in a continuous service for a period of one year under the employer if the employee during the period of 12 calendar months preceding the date with reference to which the calculation of gratuity is to be made, has actually worked under the employer for not less than:

(i) 190 days in the case, an employee is employed in a mine below the ground level or in an establishment which works for less than six days in a week and
(ii) 240 days in any other case.

For determining the service for a period of six months for the payment of gratuity, the number of days the employee should have actually worked should be half the number of days which constitute a continuous service for a period of one year (i.e., 95 days, or 120 days, respectively as the case may be—Section 2 A(2).

In the case of a seasonal establishment if the employee, employed in that establishment is not in continuous service for a period of 12 months or 6 months, he shall be deemed to be in continuous service if he has actually worked for not less than 75% of the number of days on which the establishment has actually been in operation during such period—Section 2 A(3).

### 24.3.4 Wages—Section 2(s)

Wages means all emoluments which are earned by an employee while on duty or on leave in accordance with the terms and cash. It includes dearness allowance but it does not include any bonus, commission, house rent allowance, overtime wages and any other allowance.

### 24.3.5 Employee—Section 2(e)

An employee means any person (other than an apprentice) employed on wages in any establishment, factory, mine, oilfield, plantation, port, railway company or shop. He may be employed to do skilled, unskilled, semi-skilled, manual, supervisory, technical or clerical work. The terms of his employment may be expressed or implied. He may be employed in a managerial or administrative capacity. The term 'employee' does not, however include any such person who holds a post under the Central Government or a State Government and is governed by any other act or by any rules providing for payment of gratuity.

### 24.3.6 Employer—Section 2(f)

In relation to any establishment, factory, mine, oilfield, plantation, port, railway company or shop belonging to or under the control of the Central Government or a State Government.

An employer means a person or authority appointed by an appropriate government for the supervision and control of employees. Where to such person or authority has been so appointed, the employer means the head of the ministry of the department concerned belonging to or under the control of any local authority, the employer means the person appointed by such authority for the supervision and control of the employees or where no such person has been so appointed, the chief executive officer of the local authority.

In any other case, the 'employer' means the person who or the authority that has the ultimate control over the affairs of any of the above establishments. Where the said affairs have been entrusted to any other person, the employer means such other person whether called a manager, managing director or by any other name.

### 24.3.7 Family—Section 2(h)

The Act defines the family separately for the male and female employee.

In case of a male employee—the family of the employee shall be deemed to consist of the employee himself, his wife, his children, whether married or unmarried, his dependent parents and the dependent parents of his wife and the widow and children of his predeceased son if any.

In case of a female employee—the family of the employee shall be deemed to consist of the employee herself, her husband, her children, whether married or unmarried, her dependent parents and the dependent parents of her husband and the widow and children of her predeceased son if any.

A lawfully adopted child shall be deemed to be a part of the family of an employee.

## 24.4 CIRCUMSTANCES IN WHICH THE GRATUITY BECOMES PAYABLE

Section 4 of the Act explains the circumstances in which the gratuity becomes payable to an employee.

### 24.4.1 Continuous Service of Five Years

The employee has a right to claim gratuity from his employer on the termination of his employment provided, that he has rendered continuous service with his present employer, for not less than five years:

1. On his superannuation.
2. On his retirement or resignation.
3. On his death or disablement due to accident or disease (In this case, a continuous service of five years is not applicable).

A disablement means such disablement as incapacitates an employee for the work which he was capable of performing before the accident or disease, resulting in such disablement. If a disabled employee is employed after his disablement on reduced wages, his wages for the purpose of calculating the gratuity payable to him on the termination of his employment for the period preceding his disablement shall be taken to be the wages received by him during that period and for the period subsequent to his disablement shall be taken to be the wages as so reduced [Section 4(4)].

**Case Study**

E was an employee of Tea Estate Ltd. The whole of the undertaking of Tea Estate Ltd was taken over by a new company—Asia Tea Estate Ltd. The services of E remained continuous in the new company. After serving for 1 year, E met with an accident and became permanently disabled. E applied to the new company for the payment of gratuity. The company refused to pay gratuity on the ground that E has served only for a year in the company. Examine the validity of the refusal of the directors in the light of the provisions of the Payment of Gratuity Act, 1972.

## 24.5 TO WHOM IS THE GRATUITY PAYABLE?

| Circumstances | Payable to |
|---|---|
| 1. Normal case | Employee |
| 2. In case of death of employee | |
| (a) Nomination has been done | Nominee |
| (b) Nomination has not been done | Legal Heir |
| (c) When nominee(s) or legal heir(s) is minor | The share of such minor shall be deposited with the controlling authority who shall invest the same for the benefit of such minor in such bank or other financial institution as may be prescribed until such minor attains majority. |

## 24.6 CALCULATION OF THE AMOUNT OF GRATUITY PAYABLE

### 24.6.1 Rate of Gratuity

The amount of gratuity payable to an employee shall be at the rate of 15 days' wages for each completed year of service or part thereof in excess of 6 months based on the rate of the basic wages rated employee by the employee concerned [Section 4(2)]. In the case of a monthly rated employee, 15 days' wages shall be calculated by dividing the monthly rate of wages last drawn (including D.A.) by 26 and multiplying the quotient by 15.

### 24.6.2 Rate of Gratuity for Piece Rate Employee

If the employee is a piece rated employee, daily wages shall be computed on the average of the total wages received by him for a period of three months, immediately preceding the termination of his employment. The wages paid to him for any overtime work shall not be taken into account.

### 24.6.3 Rate of Gratuity for Employees Is Seasonal Establishment

In the case of employees employed in a seasonal establishment and who is not so employed throughout the year, the gratuity payable to him shall be at the rate of seven days wages for each season.

### 24.6.4 Maximum Amount of Gratuity—Section 4(3)

The amount of gratuity payable to an employee shall not exceed ₹ 10,00,000. Earlier this limit was ₹ 3,50,000.

### 24.6.5 Mode of Payment of Gratuity

The gratuity payable under the Act shall be paid in cash or if so desired by the payee in demand draft or cheque to the employee or his nominee or legal heir as the case may be.

### 24.6.6 Better Terms of Gratuity—Section 4(5)

The employee may sometimes be entitled to receive better of gratuity under any award or agreement or contract with the employer. In such a case, nothing in Section 4 shall affect the right of the employee to receive better terms.

**Case Study**

An employee is employed in a seasonal establishment. The establishment was in operation for four months only during the accounting year 2010. The employee is not in a continuous service during this period. However, he has worked only for eight days, giving a reason for your answer decide (i) Whether the employer is entitled to gratuity payable under the Payment of Gratuity Act, 1972 and (ii) Would your answer be different in case the employee worked for 100 days?

**Case Study**

Calculate the gratuity payable, if the last drawn wages of an employee who has served for 30 years is (a) ₹ 2000 per month, (b) ₹ 3000 per month, (c) ₹ 36,000 per month and (d) ₹ 30,000 per annum.

**Case Study**

Mr. Ram joined the company on 26 November 1980 and superannuated on 31 May 2006. At the time of joining the job, his monthly salary was ₹ 13,000. On the date of retirement, his monthly salary was ₹ 24,000. He also received overtime of ₹ 2000. Calculate the amount of gratuity.

## 24.7 FORFEITURE OF GRATUITY—SECTION 4(B)

The gratuity of the employee shall be forfeited, to the extent of such damage or loss caused to the employer, in the following circumstances:

1. Where the services of an employee have been terminated for any act, willful omission or negligence causing any damage or loss to or destruction of property belonging to the employer.
2. Where the services of an employee have been terminated for his riotous or disorderly conduct or any other act of violence on his part.
3. Any act which constitutes an offence involving moral turpitude in the course of his employment.

The right of the employee to forfeit the gratuity is available in the above circumstances specified in point no. 1 to 3 and is not available in any other circumstances.

### 24.7.1 No Gratuity Attached in the Execution of a Decree—Section 13

The Act protects the amount of gratuity payable to an employee from the attachment in execution of any decree of any civil revenue of criminal court.

**Case Study**

An employee who is governed by the Payment of Gratuity Act, 1972 committed a theft in the course of his employment. And consequently, his service was terminated. State in this connection, whether the gratuity payable to him shall be wholly or partly forfeited.

**Case Study**

Rajesh was occupying a service quarter of the company. After his retirement, he did not vacate the quarters. In retaliation, the company withheld the gratuity payable to him. Is the action of the company justified?

**Case Study**

National Steels Ltd decided to forfeit the amount of gratuity of its employees A, B and C on account of disorderly conduct and other acts which caused a loss to the property, belonging to the company. A, B and C committed the following acts:

(i) A refused to surrender the occupied land, belonging to the company.

(ii) B committed theft under the law involving offence of moral turpitude.

(iii) C after superannuation, continued to occupy the quarter of the company for six months.

Against the decision of the company, A, B and C applied to the appropriate authorities for relief. The company contented, that the right to gratuity is not a statutory right and the forfeiture of the amount of gratuity was within the law.

Examine the contention of the company and the decision taken by the company to forfeit the amount of gratuity in the light of the Payment of Gratuity Act, 1972.

## 24.8 RULES FOR THE NOMINATION OF GRATUITY

### 24.8.1 Nomination to be Made with a Fixed Time—Section 6(1)

Each employee who has completed one year of service is authorized to make a nomination within 30 days from the date of completion of one year service.

### 24.8.2 Distribution of Gratuity—Section 6(2)

The employee may nominate one or more persons to be as nominees and distribute the amount of gratuity payable to him under the Act amongst more than one nominee.

### 24.8.3 Nomination in Favour of Family—Section 6(3)

If an employee has a family at the time of making a nomination, the nomination shall be made only in the favour of a family member and the nomination already made in favour of any other person (who is not a member of the family) shall be void. But if at the time of making the nomination, the employee has no family, the nomination may be made in favour of any person. If the employee subsequently acquires a family, the nomination already made shall become invalid and the employee shall make within 90 days from the date of acquiring a family, a fresh nomination in favour of a family member.

### 24.8.4 Modification of a Nomination

The employee can modify a nomination made by him earlier at any time by giving a written notice to his employer.

### 24.8.5 Death of the Nominee

In case of the death of the nominee before the death of the employee, the interest of the nominee shall revert to the employee. The employee in such cases, shall make a fresh nomination in respect of such interest.

### 24.8.6 Safe-custody of Nomination—Section 6(7)

Every nomination, fresh nomination or alteration of nomination as the case may be shall be sent by the employee who shall keep the same in his safe custody. The nomination shall be effective from the date of receipt of the same by the employer.

## 24.9 RULES AS TO DETERMINATION OF THE AMOUNT OF GRATUITY

The employee who is eligible for the payment of gratuity under the Act or any person authorized by him in writing to act on his behalf, shall apply to the employer for the payment of gratuity within 30 days from the date the gratuity becomes payable. But where the date of superannuation is known, the employee himself may apply to the employer before 30 days from the date of his superannuation or retirement.

The application for gratuity may be sent to the employer by:

1. A nominee of an employee within 30 days from the date of the gratuity becomes payable to him.
2. A legal heir of the employee shall apply ordinarily within one year from the date of gratuity becomes payable to him by the employer.

The application for the payment of gratuity filled after the expiry of the specified time limit shall be entertained by the employer if the applicant adduces sufficient cause for the delay.

### 24.9.1 Determination of Gratuity

The amount of gratuity as soon as it becomes payable, shall be determined by the employer according to the provisions of the Act.

The employer shall give a notice in writing to the person to whom the gratuity is payable (i.e., employee, nominee or heir of the employee). Notice shall also be given to the controlling authority, specifying the amount of gratuity so determined to be payable. This exercise is to be done by the employer, irrespective of the fact whether an application for the payment of gratuity has been made or not by the person concerned.

### 24.9.2 Payment of Gratuity

The employer shall arrange for the payment of gratuity within 30 days from the date it becomes payable to the person to whom it is payable.

### 24.9.3 Payment of Interest—Section 7(3A)

If the amount of gratuity, payable by the employer is not paid within 30 days, the amount shall pay simple interest at such rate not exceeding the rate notified by the Central Government from time to time for the payment of long term deposits. The interest shall be payable up to the date, until the gratuity is actually paid. If there is a delay in paying the amount of the gratuity due to a fault in the past activity of the employee, no interest shall be payable provided the employer has obtained permission from the controlling authority.

## 24.10 PAYMENT OF GRATUITY IN CASE OF A DISPUTE—SECTION 7(4)

If there is any dispute as to (a) the amount of gratuity payable to the employee (b) the admissibility of any claim of or in relation to an employee for the payment of gratuity or (c) the person entitled to receive the amount of gratuity, the employer shall deposit the amount of gratuity as he admits to be payable with the controlling authority.

Where there is a dispute with regard to any matter or matters specified above, the employer or the employee or any other person, raising the dispute can make an application to the controlling authority for deciding the dispute [Section 7 (4)(b)]. On application, the controlling authority may determine the matter after giving an opportunity of being heard to both the parties. If as a result of such an enquiry it is found that any amount is payable to the employee, the controlling authority shall direct the employer to pay such amount or as the case may be such amount as reduced by the amount deposited, with the controlling authority by him [Section 7 (4)(c)]. The controlling authority shall pay the amount deposited with him by the employer including the excess amount, if any deposited by the employer to the applicant i.e., the employee or the nominee or the heir of the employee. As soon as may be after the deposit is made by the employer, the controlling authority shall pay the amount of deposit—

1. To the employee if the application is made by the employee.
2. To the nominee, guardian of the nominee, the heirs if the applicant is not an employee.

## 24.11 RULES FOR THE RECOVERY OF GRATUITY—SECTION 8

If the amount of gratuity is not paid within the prescribed time, the aggrieved person shall make an application to the controlling authority. On the receipt of the application, the controlling authority shall issue a certificate for that amount to the collector. On the basis of the certificate, the collector shall recover the amount due along with compound interest thereon at such rate as the Central Government may by notification specify from the date of expiry of the prescribed time as arises or the land revenue and pay the same to the person entitled thereto. The controlling authority shall, before issuing a certificate to the collector give the employee a reasonable opportunity of showing the cause against the issue of such certificate. It is provided further that the amount of interest shall in no case exceed the amount of gratuity payable under the Act.

**Case Study**

Mr. X was an employee of Mutual Developers Ltd. He retired from the company after completing 30 years of continuous service. He applied to the company for the payment of gratuity within the prescribed time. The company refused to pay the gratuity and contended that due to stringent financial condition, the company is unable to pay the Gratuity. Mr. X applied to the appropriate authority, for the recovery of the amount of gratuity. Examine the validity of the contention of the company and also state the provisions of law to recover the gratuity under the Payment of Gratuity Act, 1972.

## 24.12 COMPULSORY INSURANCE OF THE EMPLOYEE

The provision for compulsory insurance cover has been introduced to provide an insurance cover to the employer who is under duty to pay gratuity to the employees. The provisions relating to compulsory insurance can be summed up as under:

1. Every employer other than the establishment belonging to or under the control of Central Government or State Government shall obtain insurance in the prescribed manner for his liability for payment towards the gratuity under the Act, from the Life Insurance Company (LIC) or any other prescribed insurer with effect from the date as notified by the Central Government.
2. The appropriate government may subject to the conditions as it thinks fit, exempt any employer who had already established an approved gratuity fund in respect of his employees and who desires to continue such arrangement from the liability of compulsory insurance.
3. Where an employer fails to make any payment by way of premium to the insurance or by way of contribution to an approved gratuity fund, he shall be liable to pay the amount of gratuity due under this Act forthwith to controlling authority.
4. Any person who contravenes the above provisions shall be punishable with a fine upto ₹ 10,000 and in the case of a continuing offence with a further fine of ₹ 1000 per day for each day during which the offence continues.

## 24.13 RULES REGARDING APPOINTMENT OF AN INSPECTOR UNDER THE ACT

The Payment of Gratuity (Amendment) Act, 1984 has added two new Sections i.e. 7 A to the original Act dealing with the appointment of an inspector for the purpose of the Act and their powers.

### 24.13.1 Appointment of Inspectors—Section 7(A)

The appropriate government may by notification, appoint as many inspectors as it deems fit for the purpose of the Act. The appropriate government may by general or special order, define the areas to which the authority of an inspector so appointed shall extend. Where two or more inspectors are appointed for the same area it may also define by such order, the distribution or allocation of the work to be performed by them under the Act. Every inspector appointed under the Act shall be deemed to be a public servant within the meaning of the Indian Penal Code (IPC).

## 24.14 POWERS OF INSPECTORS

Subject to any rules made by the appropriate government under the Act, an Inspector may for the purpose of ascertaining, whether any of the provisions of the Act or the conditions. If any of the exemptions granted there under, have been complied with, exercise all or any of the powers given below:

1. Require an employer to furnish any information as he may consider necessary.
2. Enter and inspect at all reasonable hours with such assistants being person in service of the government or local or any public authority as he think fits any premises or place in the factory, mine, oilfield, plantation, port, railway company, shop and other establishments to which this Act applies for the purpose of examining any register, record or notice or other documents required to be kept or exhibited in relation to the rules made there under or otherwise kept or exhibited in relation to the employment of any person or the payment of gratuity to the employees. He may require the production of any register record or notice for inspection.
3. Examine with respect to any matter relevant to any of the purposes mentioned above, the employer of any person whom he finds in such premises or place and who he has sufficient cause to believe is an employee employed therein.
4. Make copies of or take extracts from any register, record, notice or other relevant documents, where he has reason to believe that any offence under the Act has been committed by the employer, search or seizure under this Act as they apply to any search and seize with the assistant as he thinks fit any register, notice, document as he considers relevant in respect of that offence.
5. Exercise such other powers as may be prescribed. Any person required by the inspector to produce any register, record, notice or other documents or to give any information, he shall be legally bound to do so within the meaning of Sections 175 and 176 of the IPC. The provisions of the Code of Criminal Procedure so far as may be shall apply to any search and seizure made under the authority of a warrant issued under Section 94 of that code.

## 24.15 PROVISIONS RELATING TO PENALTIES—SECTIONS 9–12

The following Act, committed by any person shall be deemed to be an offence under the Act and such person shall be punishable with imprisonment or fine or both, as specified in the act:

### 24.15.1 False Statement or False Representation

If any person, knowingly makes or causes to be made any false statement or false representation for the purpose of avoiding any payment to be made by him, under the Act or enabling any other person to avoiding such payment, he shall be punishable with imprisonment for a term which may extend to 6 months or with a fine which extends to ₹ 10,000 or with both.

### 24.15.2 For Contravention of the Act

The employer who contravenes or makes default in complying with any of the provisions of the Act or rules or order made thereunder, shall be punishable with imprisonment for a term which shall not be less than three months but which may extend to one year or with fine which shall not be less than ₹ 10,000 but which may extend to ₹ 20,000 or with both.

If the offence relates to the non-payment of gratuity, the employer shall be punishable with imprisonment for a term which shall not be less than six months but which may extend to two years. But if the court trying the offence for reason to be recorded in writing is of the opinion, that lesser term of imprisonment or the imposition of fine would meet the requirement of justice, the court may reduce the punishment.

## 24.16 APPEAL FOR PAYMENT OF GRATUITY

Any person aggrieved by an order of the controlling authority may, within 60 days from the date of the receipt of the order, prefer an appeal to the appropriate government or such other authority as may be specified in this behalf by the appropriate government. The appropriate government or the appellate authority may, if it is satisfied that the aggrieved party has been prevented by sufficient cause for preferring the appeal within the specified period of 60 days, extend the said period by a further period of 60 days.

But no appeal by an employer shall be admitted if at the time of preferring the appeal, he does not either produce a certificate from the controlling authority to the effect, that he has deposited the amount equal to the amount of gratuity to be payable to an employee with the controlling authority as required to be deposited or deposits such amount with the appellate authority.

The appropriate government or the appellant authority as the case may be after giving the parties to appeal an for opportunity of being heard, confirm, modify or reserve the decision of the controlling authority.

### LIST OF LANDMARK JUDGEMENTS

1. ***Bharat Gold Mines Ltd vs Regional Labour Commissioner (1987)***
   It was held, that any decision to forfeit the gratuity can be taken only after affording an opportunity to the employee concerned.
2. ***KC Mathew vs Plantation Corporation of Kerala Ltd (2001)***
   The right of gratuity is a statutory right.
3. ***State of Punjab vs Labour Court (1980)***
   The retrenched employee is entitled to gratuity.
4. ***Jeevan Lal Ltd vs Controlling Authority (1982)***
   The employee who is re-employed without any break in service, will be eligible for gratuity.
5. ***Permali Wallance Ltd vs State of M. P.(1996)***
   The right of an employer to forfeit the amount of earned gratuity of an employee whose services were terminated for any act, willful omission or negligence causing a damage to the employer is limited to the extent of the damage and the proof of such damage.
6. ***Ambika Saw Mills vs Asst. Lab. Commissioner (1986)***
   The supply of free food by the employer–company is merely an amenity and as such its money equivalent cannot form part of and be added to the cash salary paid to the employee to form his total wages for computing the amount of gratuity payable to him.
7. ***K. Gangadhar vs The Appellate Authority***
   The provisions of the Act are applicable to commercial and non-commercial organization.
8. ***Muncipal Board vs UOI (1993)***
   The Gratuity Act is applicable to municipal board also.
9. ***Pattathurik K. Damodaran vs M. Kassim Kanju (1993)***
   The gratuity to the employee is his right, as well as the obligation of the employer. By the change in ownership, the relationship of the employer and the employee is not changed. A new employer cannot escape from the liability of the payment of gratuity to the employee.

10. ***Texmaco Ltd vs Sri Ram Dham (1992)***
The employee resigning from service is also entitled to gratuity.
11. ***Mettur Splinning Mills vs Deputy Commissioner of Labour (1983)***
The non-acceptance of the resignation is no hurdle in the way of an employee to claim gratuity.
12. ***Adminstrator, Shree Jagannath Temple (1992)***
An employee, employed in a temple is entitled to a gratuity.
13. ***Champaran Sugar Co. Ltd vs Jt. Labour Commissioner and Appellate Authority (1987)***
The employee's right to interest on delayed payment is statutory.
14. ***Travancore Plywood Industries Ltd vs Regional Joint Labour Commissioner (1966)***
The refusal of an employee to surrender the occupied land belonging to the company is not sufficient ground to withhold gratuity.
15. ***Wazir Chand vs Union of India (2001)***
If the employer has to be paid any amount regarding any type of charge by the employee and if he has not paid for the same during the course of his service then the employer can adjust the amount from the gratuity of the employee.

## TEST YOUR KNOWLEDGE

1. State the kind of establishments which are covered under the Payment of Gratuity Act, 1972. **(Ref. Para-24.2)**
2. List out the establishments that shall be exempted from the Payment of Gratuity. **(Ref. Para-24.2)**
3. Define the term 'super annuation'. **(Ref. Para-24.3)**
4. Explain the term 'family' in connection with the Payment of Gratuity Act, 1972. **(Ref. Para-24.3)**
5. Define the term 'retirement'. **(Ref. Para-24.3)**
6. Explain the continuous service under the Payment of Gratuity Act, 1972 **(Ref. Para-24.3)**
7. Define the term 'wages'. **(Ref. Para-24.3)**
8. When does gratuity become payable? How is it calculated for different types of employees? **(Ref. Para-24.4)**
9. State the provisions of law, relating to the determination and payment of the amount of gratuity. **(Ref. Para-24.6)**
10. An employee was terminated for disorderly conduct, during the course of his employment. To what extent shall gratuity be forfeited? **(Ref. Para-24.7)**
11. Can a gratuity be attached under any order of a criminal court? **(Ref. Para-24.7)**
12. State the procedure for appointing a nominee under different situations, in respect of gratuity payment. **(Ref. Para-24.8)**
13. There was a dispute regarding the amount of gratuity, payable to an employee. How would you resolve the situation? What procedure would you suggest? **(Ref. Para-24.10)**
14. Explain the provisions of the Payment of Gratuity Act, 1972 with regard to the compulsory insurance of the employer's liabilities to pay gratuity. **(Ref. Para-24.12)**
15. Who can appoint inspectors under the Payment of Gratuity Act, 1972? **(Ref. Para-24.13)**
16. Explain the powers of inspectors under the Payment of Gratuity Act, 1972. **(Ref. Para-24.14)**

## MULTIPLE-CHOICE QUESTIONS

1. Completed year of service
   (i) service for one year.
   (ii) continuous service.
   (iii) continuous service for one year.
   (iv) number of years of service.
2. The superannuation means
   (i) the attainment of age of 58 years.
   (ii) the attainment of age of 60 years.
   (iii) attainment of age as fixed in the contract or condition of services.
   (iv) such age certified medically to be fit.
3. The gratuity shall be paid to an employee after he has surrendered continuous service for
   (i) not less than three years.
   (ii) not less than five years.
   (iii) not less than seven years.
   (iv) none of the above.
4. For calculation of gratuity under the Payment of Gratuity Act, 1972 the number of days in a month is to be taken as
   (i) actual number of days on employment.
   (ii) 26 days.
   (iii) 15 days.
   (iv) 30 days.
5. The Payment of Gratuity come into force on
   (i) 23 October 1971.
   (ii) 16 September 1972.
   (iii) 16th September 1971.
   (iv) 23rd October 1972.
6. The gratuity is a benefit which an employee gets at the time of only retirement.
   (i) True
   (ii) False
7. The forfeiture of gratuity is possible under certain circumstances.
   (i) True
   (ii) False
8. The gratuity is benefit which an employee gets at the time of
   (i) festival.
   (ii) new year.
   (iii) retirement.
   (iv) promotion.
9. The Payment of Gratuity Act, 1972 applies to establishment where
   (i) 100 or more employees are employed.
   (ii) 10 or more employees are employed.
   (iii) 20 or more employees are employed.
   (iv) 15 or more employees are employed.
10. The term 'family' under the Payment of Gratuity Act means
    (i) an employee, his wife and his married children.
    (ii) an employee, his wife and his children.
    (iii) an employee and his wife.
    (iv) an employee, his wife, his children, his dependent parents and children of his predeceased son.
11. In the case of death of employee, gratuity shall be paid to his
    (i) wife.
    (ii) legal heir.
    (iii) nominee.
    (iv) children.

12. Choose the incorrect one
    (i) Gratuity is payable to an employee on his retirement.
    (ii) An employee resigning from his service is not entitled to gratuity.
    (iii) A retrenched employee is also entitle to gratuity.
    (iv) All of the above.
13. For each completed year of services or part thereof, an employer shall pay gratuity at the rate of
    (i) 12 days. (iii) 15 days.
    (ii) 10 days. (iv) 7 days.
14. In case of seasonal establishment an employer shall pay gratuity at the rate of ____ for each season.
    (i) 12 days (iii) 15 days
    (ii) 10 days (iv) 7 days
15. The gratuity payable to an employee whose services have been terminated by any and act, willful omission shall be forfeited
    (i) up to 50% of total gratuity. (iii) either (i) or (ii) whichever is less.
    (ii) to the extent of damage or loss caused. (iv) neither (i) nor (ii).
16. Choose the incorrect one
    (i) An employee may make more than one nominee for gratuity.
    (ii) Nomination shall be made in favour of one or more members of family.
    (iii) Nomination in favour of person who is not a member of family shall also be valid.
    (iv) None of the above.
17. An employee who is eligible for payment of gratuity shall apply within _____ from the date of gratuity become payable.
    (i) 30 days (iii) 15 days
    (ii) 60 days (iv) 45 days
18. In case of delay of payment of gratuity, the employer shall pay
    (i) no interest. (iii) compound interest.
    (ii) simple interest. (iv) fine of twice amount levied.
19. In case of dispute regarding the amount of gratuity payable an application shall be made to
    (i) employer. (iii) controlling authority.
    (ii) police. (iv) court.
20. The Payment of Gratuity Act shall be applicable to
    (i) every factory, shop, mine and railway company.
    (ii) every establishment.
    (iii) every mine and rail company.
    (iv) all of the above.

## ANSWER KEYS

| | | | |
|---|---|---|---|
| **1.** (iii) | **6.** (ii) | **11.** (iii) | **16.** (iii) |
| **2.** (iii) | **7.** (i) | **12.** (ii) | **17.** (i) |
| **3.** (ii) | **8.** (iii) | **13.** (iii) | **18.** (ii) |
| **4.** (ii) | **9.** (iii) | **14.** (iv) | **19.** (iii) |
| **5.** (ii) | **10.** (iv) | **15.** (ii) | **20.** (iv) |

# 25

# Employees Provident Fund and Miscellaneous Provisions Act, 1952

**Learning objectives**

*After reading this chapter, you will be able to understand:*

- Basic
- The Employees' Provident Fund Schemes, 1952
- The Employees' Pension Scheme, 1995
- The Employees' Deposit-linked Insurance Scheme, 1976
- Transfer of account and undertaking

## 25.1 BASIC

Employees Provident Fund and Miscellaneous Provisions Act, 1952(EPF Act) provides social security to employees and their dependents under the following schemes:

1. The Employees' Provident Fund Schemes, 1952
2. The Employees' Pension Scheme, 1995
3. The Employees' Deposit-linked Insurance Scheme, 1976.

## 25.2 APPLICABILITY OF THE ACT

### 25.2.1 Applicability

EPF Act is applicable to an establishment which is a factory engaged in industry specified in Schedule I and employing 20 or more persons. The Act is applicable to other establishments which are not factories but engage 20 or more employees on notification of central government. The central government may apply provisions of the Act to any establishment which has engaged less than 20 employees after giving 2 months' notice and publication in official gazette. The Act is applicable to mines other than coal mine. The Act is applicable to the whole of India except to the state of Jammu & Kashmir.

### 25.2.2 Non-applicability

EPF Act is not applicable to societies registered under the Co-operative Societies Act, 1912, if it is employing less than 50 persons and it works without the aid of power. EPF Act is not applicable to establishments under the control of the central government or a state government and whose employees are entitled to the benefit of contributory provident fund or old age pension. An establishment set up under any central or state Act and whose employees are entitled to the benefits of contributory provident fund or old age pension are also outside purview of EPF Act. The central government, on receipt of an application, may exempt any establishment from provisions of the Act on ground of financial position. The central government shall publish notification to this effect.

### 25.2.3 Once Applicable Always Applicable

If provisions of EPF Act becomes applicable once, it is continue to be applicable even if subsequently the number of employees fall below 20.

**Case Study**

An establishment discounted deduction towards contribution to provident fund from its employees' salary and stopped remitting contribution of its share of provident fund when the number of its employees on rolls fell to 15. Do the provisions of the Employees' Provident Funds and Miscellaneous Provision Act, 1952, cease to be applicable to the establishment under such circumstances?

## 25.3 DEFINITIONS

### 25.3.1 Appropriate Government—Section 2(a)

'Appropriate Government' means:

1. in relation to those establishments belonging to or under the control of the Central Government or in relation to an establishment connected with a railway company, a major port, a mine or an oil field or a controlled industry, or in relation to an establishment having departments or branches in more than one state, the central government; and
2. in relation to any other establishment, the State Government.

### 25.3.2 Authorised Officer—Section 2(aa)

As per the EPF Act, 'authorised officer' means any of the following persons:

1. Central provident fund commissioner
2. Additional provident fund commissioner
3. Deputy provident fund commissioner

4. Regional provident fund commissioner
5. Any other officer authorised by the central government by notification.

### 25.3.3 Basic Wages—Section 2(b)

It means all emoluments earned by an employee either on duty or on leave. But it does not include:

1. cash value of food concession
2. dearness allowance
3. house-rent allowance
4. overtime allowance
5. bonus, commission
6. any present or gift

### 25.3.4 Employer—Section 2(e)

For an establishment which is factory, 'employer' means:

1. owner or occupier of factory or his agent or
2. legal representative of deceased owner or occupier or
3. manager appointed under Factories Act, 1948

For any other establishment, 'employer' means:

1. person having ultimate control over the affairs of the establishment
2. manager or managing director to whom affairs are entrusted.

### 25.3.5 Employee—Section 2(f)

'Employee' means any person employed to do any kind of work and includes:

1. Person employed through contractor
2. Person engaged as apprentice not being apprentice engaged under the Apprentices Act, 1961.

The definition of employee is inclusive. It includes part-time employee and sweepers working on few days in month. However, partners of a firm working and drawing salary are not employees.

### 25.3.6 Excluded Employee—Section 2(f)

'Excluded employee' means an employee who, having been member, has withdrawn his accumulated full amount. An employee whose pay exceeds ₹ 15000 p.m. is also considered as excluded employee.

### 25.3.7 Exempted establishment—Section 2(fff)

It means an establishment exempted under Section 17 from all or any provisions of the scheme.

### 25.3.8 Factory—Section 2(g)

'Factory' means any premises, including the precincts thereof, in any part of which a manufacturing process is being carried on or is ordinarily so carried on, whether with the aid of power or without the aid of power. The definition is very wide and includes workshop for repairing and servicing of cars.

'Manufacturing process' means any process for making, altering, repairing, ornamenting, finishing, packing, oiling, washing, cleaning, breaking up, demolishing or otherwise treating or adapting any article or substance with a view to its use, sale, transport, delivery or disposal.

### 25.3.9 Superannuation—Section 2(II)

Superannuation means attaining age of 58 years by an employee member.

**Case Study**

Vimal is an employee in a company. The following payments were made to him during the previous year:

(i) Piece rate wages
(ii) Productivity bonus
(iii) Additional dearness allowance
(iv) Value of Puja gift.

Examine as to which of the above payments form part of basic wage of Vimal under the Employees Provident Fund and Miscellaneous Provisions Act, 1952.

## 25.4 CENTRAL BOARD—SECTION 5

Central government constitutes the central board by notification. It is a body corporate and consists of the following persons as members:

1. Chairman and vice-chairman—2
2. Central PF commissioner, ex-officio—1
3. Central government officials—5
4. Persons representing state governments—15
5. Persons representing employees—10
6. Persons representing employers—10

Thus, the central board consists of total 43 members. Fund is administered and vested by the board. The central board shall maintain accounts of its income and expenditure. Its accounts are audited by the Comptroller and Auditor General. The board is required to submit its working report to the central government.

## 25.5 EMPLOYEE'S PENSION FUND SCHEME—SECTION 6

Employees' pension fund is vested in and administrated by the central board. The board of trustees or central board is constituted by the central government by notification in official gazette. Every employee other than excluded employee is required to join the scheme.

As per Section 6, an employer should make a contribution of 10% of the basic wages, dearness allowance and retaining allowance for each employee. The central government is empowered to increase contribution to 12% after notification in official gazette. The employee is required to make contribution of 10% of pay. He may voluntarily contribute a higher amount. Out of 10 or 12% of contribution, 8.33% is diverted to employees' pension fund.

Contribution made to the fund is invested by a board of trustees. A member (employee) gets interest in his provident fund account as per the rate decided by the government. Non-refundable advances can be granted to a member for:

1. Payment of LIC premium of member
2. Temporary closure of factory for a period more than 15 days.
3. Hospitalisation of employee for one month or more or major surgical operation.
4. Hospitalisation of his family member for one month or more for major surgical operation.
5. Marriage of self or marriage of daughter, sons, sister or brother.
6. Post matriculation education of son or daughter
7. Relief in case of damage to property by a calamity of exceptional nature such as floods, earthquakes or riots.

A member can withdraw the amount accumulated with interest in the following situations:

1. Death
2. Permanent disability
3. Superannuation,
4. Retrenchment
5. Migration from India for permanent settlement abroad
6. Voluntary retirement
7. Certain discharges from employment under Industrial Disputes Act, 1947
8. Transfer to an establishment not covered under the PF Act.

## 25.6 EMPLOYEES' PENSION SCHEME—SECTION 6A

In 1995, Employees' Pension Scheme was introduced and it replaced the earlier Family Pension Scheme, 1971. The Employees' Pension Scheme is compulsory for

1. all persons who were members of the Family Pension Scheme, 1971.
2. persons who become members of the Provident Fund from 16.11.1995

The PF subscribers who were not members of the Family Pension Scheme have an option to join this pension scheme in which the employer's contribution of 8.33% is diverted to Employees' Pension Fund. The central government contributes as approved by the parliament. A member is required to have minimum 10 years' contributory service for entitlement to pension under this scheme. The member is granted monthly pension in following situations:

1. Superannuation on attaining 58 years
2. Retirement
3. Permanent total disablement
4. Death during service
5. Death after retirement or superannuation or permanent total disablement

6. Children pension
7. Orphan pension.

As per the Employees' Pension scheme, pension is paid to:

1. Widow of member for life or until she remarries.
2. Children up to 25 years (maximum 2 children)
3. Orphans, at an enhanced rate

Pension is calculated as per the following formula:

$$\text{Pension} = \text{Pensionable Salary} \times (\text{Pensionable Service} + 2) / 70$$

## 25.7 EMPLOYEES DEPOSIT LINK INSURANCE SCHEME—SECTION 6B

Employees' deposit link scheme is applicable to all establishments to which PF Act is applicable. According to this scheme, contribution to insurance fund by an employer is at the rate of 1% of Basic Wage + Dearness Allowance + Cash value of food concession + Retaining allowance AND administrative expenses @ 0.01% of pay of employee. The employee is not required to contribute any amount towards insurance fund.

The Scheme provides following benefits:

1. On death of the member, an amount equal to the average balance in the account of the deceased during the last 12 months or period of membership, whichever is less, shall be paid to the persons eligible to receive the amount or the Provident Fund accumulations.
2. In case the average balance exceeds ₹ 50,000, the amount payable shall be ₹ 50,000 plus 40% of the amount of such excess subject to a ceiling of ₹ 1 lakh.

## 25.8 RECOVERY OF MONEY DUE FROM EMPLOYER—SECTION 8B

To recover money due from employer, the authorised officer issues a certificate to the recovery officer. The recovery officer may:

1. Attach and sell movable or immovable property of establishment. If immovable property is insufficient, the property of employer may be sold.
2. Arrest the employer and send him to prison
3. Appoint a receiver to manage the property of establishment of the employer.

## 25.9 TRANSFER OF ACCOUNTS—SECTION 17A

When any person leaves one establishment and joins another establishment, any one of the following possible alternatives are available to him with reference to his provident fund account.

### 25.9.1 If the New Establishment is Covered Under PF Act

An employee who is a member of Provident Fund may leave an establishment and obtain employment in another establishment which may be covered under the Act. In such a case, the amount standing to his credit shall be transferred to his account in the new establishment (i.e., the establishment where he is re-employed)

### 25.9.2 If the New Establishment is not Covered Under PF Act

An employee who is a member of Provident Fund may leave an establishment and obtain employment in another establishment which may not be covered under the Act, but which may have a Provident Fund of its own. In such a case, at the request of employee, the amount standing to his credit shall be transferred to his account in the new establishment if the rules of such provident fund permit such transfer. The transfer shall be made within such time as may be specified by the central government.

### 25.9.3 If the Old Establishment was not Covered Under PF Act

An employee may be employed in an establishment to which the provisions of the Act do not apply, but such establishment may have its own Provident Fund. If the employee leaves such establishment and obtains employment in any other establishment which is covered under the Act, then at the request of the employee, the amount standing to his credit will be transferred to his account in the new establishment.

Recently PF office has launched a Universal Account Number (UAN) for provident fund members. This number will enable employee to link his PF account to this number and allow easier portability as well as ease of transfer directly to your bank accounts.

## 25.10 TRANSFER OF ESTABLISHMENT—SECTION 17B

1. On transfer of establishment by sale, gift, lease or license or in any other manner, the employer and transferee are jointly and severally liable to pay contribution and other sums due under PF Act for a period up to the date of transfer.
2. Liability of transferee is limited up to value of assets obtained by him.

## 25.11 PROTECTION OF FUND OF EMPLOYEE FROM ATTACHMENT—SECTION 10

As per Section 10 of EPF Act, 1952, the amount standing to the credit of provident fund account of employee shall not, in any way, be capable of being attached under insolvency proceedings. This protection is available in case of provident fund, pension and insurance amount receivable by the employee under the scheme.

The amount standing to the credit of any member in the Fund:

1. Cannot be assigned or changed.
2. Cannot be liable to attachment under any decree or order of any court in respect of any debt or liability.
3. Cannot be claimed by official receiver.
4. Shall be free from any debt or other liability incurred by the deceased member

However, the employee cannot claim any protection in respect of the money which has been withdrawn by him from the PF account.

## LIST OF LANDMARK JUDGEMENTS

**1. *P.F. Inspector vs Hariharan, (1971)***

Casual workers are not covered to ascertain total strength of establishment.

2. ***Railway Employees Co-operative Banking Society Ltd. vs The Union of India (1980)***
   The definition of 'employee' includes a part-time employee, who is engaged for any work in the establishment, a sweeper working twice or three times in a week, a night watchman keeping watch on the shops in the locality, a gardener working for ten days in a month, etc.
3. ***Hindustan Levers Employees Union vs RPF Commissioner (1995)***
   The encashment of leave would be covered by basic wages for contribution towards provident funds.
4. ***RPF Commissioner vs Management, Hotel Highways Ltd (1992)***
   An apprentice engaged under the Apprentice Act, 1961, or under the standing orders of the establishment is not an employee under Sec 2(f) of PF Act.
5. ***B. T. Mfg. Co. vs T L Association (1960)***
   All or any of the schemes may be exempted if the appropriate government is of the opinion that the benefits already provided to the employees are not less favourable than the statutory benefits provided under the schemes on application.
6. ***Lawly Sen vs RPFC (1959)***
   Workshop for repairing and servicing cars is included within the meaning of definition of factory.
7. ***Burmah Shell Oil Storage and Distributing Co. of India Ltd vs RPF (1980)***
   Ad-hoc payment in terms of settlement is not basic wages.
8. ***P. G. Textile Mills vs UOI (1976)***
   A mere change in the partnership deed does not mean that a new business has come into existence for the purpose of Section 16.
9. ***State vs S. P. Chandani (1959)***
   Provident fund scheme has made the payment of contribution mandatory and the Act provides for no exception under which a specified employer can avoid his mandatory liability.
10. ***Railway Employees Co-operative Banking Society Ltd vs UOI (1980)***
    An employee includes a part-time employee.

## TEST YOUR KNOWLEDGE

1. State the establishments to which the Employees'' Provident Funds and Miscellaneous Provisions Act, 1952, applies. **(Ref. Para-25.1)**
2. Explain 'establishments' to which the Employees' Provident Funds and Miscellaneous Provisions Act, 1952 do not apply. **(Ref. Para-25.1)**
3. State the emoluments paid to employees, which do not come within the purview of 'basic wages' under the Employees' Provident Funds and Miscellaneous Provisions Act, 1952. **(Ref. Para-25.3)**
4. Explain 'Employer' under the Employees' Provident Funds and Miscellaneous Provisions Act, 1952. **(Ref. Para-25.3)**
5. Explain the meaning of 'Factory' under the Employees' Provident Funds and Miscellaneous Provisions Act, 1952. **(Ref. Para-25.3)**
6. Write a note on the composition of Central Board of Trustees under the EPF and MP Act, 1952. **(Ref. Para-25.4)**

7. Explain the law relating to the extent of contribution by an employee to his provident fund under the Employees Provident Fund and Miscellaneous Provisions Act, 1952. Can the amount of contribution be increased by the employee? **(Ref. Para-25.5)**
8. What kind of protection is available to fund lying under Pension Fund? **(Ref. Para-25.11)**
9. An employee leaves the establishment in which he was employed and gets re-employment in another establishment. He desires that his provident fund account be transferred to the establishment wherein he has been employed. Explain the procedure laid down in the Employees' Provident Fund and Miscellaneous Provisions Act, 1952, in this relation. **(Ref. Para-25.10)**
10. Explain the provisions of the Employees' Provident Funds and Miscellaneous Provisions Act, 1952 relating to the liability of an employer in case of transfer of the establishment to another person. **(Ref. Para-25.10)**

## MULTIPLE-CHOICE QUESTIONS

1. PF and Miscellaneous Provisions Act, 1952, covers ______ schemes.
   (i) two
   (ii) three
   (iii) four
   (iv) all
2. PF and Miscellaneous Provisions Act, 1952, is applicable to ______.
   (i) factory employs 20 or more persons
   (ii) factory engaged in any industry specified in Schedule I and employs 20 or more persons
   (iii) establishment employs 20 or more persons
   (iv) Both (ii) and (iii)
3. Applicability of PF and Miscellaneous Provisions Act, 1952 also extends to ______.
   (i) mines
   (ii) only coal mines
   (iii) mine other than coal mines
   (iv) None of the above
4. Applicability of PF and Miscellaneous Provisions Act, 1952, also extends to ______.
   (i) hospitals
   (ii) travel agencies
   (iii) banks
   (iv) All of the above
5. Under PF Act, 'employer' means ______.
   (i) owner of factory
   (ii) occupier of factory
   (iii) Either (i) or (ii)
   (iv) Neither (i) nor (ii)
6. Which of the following statement(s) is/are not correct as per PF Act, 1952?
   (i) Definition of employee is inclusive.
   (ii) Partner of a firm working and drawing salary is employee.
   (iii) Both of the above
   (iv) None of the above
7. Under PF Act, 'employer' is defined under ______.
   (i) Section 1
   (ii) Section 2(a)
   (iii) Section 2(e)
   (iv) Section 2(f)
8. 'Excluded employee' means an employee whose pay exceeds ₹ ______ per month.
   (i) 1500
   (ii) 6000
   (iii) 3500
   (iv) 10000
9. Under PF Act, basic wages includes ______.
   (i) cash value of any food concession
   (ii) DA
   (iii) Both of the above
   (iv) None of the above

10. Under PF Act, basic wages includes ______.
    (i) HRA
    (ii) overtime allowance
    (iii) Both of the above
    (iv) None of the above
11. Under PF Act, basic wages does not include ______.
    (i) bonus
    (ii) commission
    (iii) gifts from employer
    (iv) All of the above
12. Vimal is an employee of a company. He has been paid piece-rate wages, productivity bonus, additional dearness allowance and value of puja gift during a year. Which of the above payment(s) form part of 'basic wage' of Vimal under PF Act, 1952?
    (i) Piece-rate wages and additional dearness allowance
    (ii) Piece-rate wages and productivity bonus
    (iii) Piece-rate wages only
    (iv) Piece-rate wages, productivity bonus and additional dearness allowance
13. Which of the following statement(s) is/are not incorrect as per PF Act, 1952?
    (i) An employee who, having been member, withdraws his accumulated full amount is an exempted employee
    (ii) If an employee who, having been member, withdraws his accumulated full amount from an establishment, such establishment is known as exempted establishment.
    (iii) Exempted employee and exempted establishment are one and the same thing.
    (iv) All of the above.
14. Central Board administer s ______.
    (i) Employees' Provident Fund Scheme
    (ii) Employees' Family Pension Fund Scheme
    (iii) Employees Deposit Linked Insurance Scheme
    (iv) All of the above
15. As per Employees' Provident Fund Scheme, employer's contribution is ______ % of pay.
    (i) 10
    (ii) 11
    (iii) 12
    (iv) 12.5
16. As per Employees' Provident Fund Scheme, employee contribution is ______ % of pay.
    (i) 10
    (ii) 11
    (iii) 12
    (iv) 8.33
17. As per Employees Provident Fund Scheme, employer's contribution is 10 % of ______.
    (i) basic wages, dearness allowance and bonus
    (ii) basic wages, retaining allowance and bonus
    (iii) basic wages, dearness allowance and retaining allowance
    (iv) basic wages, dearness allowance and overtime.
18. As per Employees Provident Fund Scheme, employer's contribution is 10 % of basic wages, dearness allowance and retaining allowance. However it can be increased to ______% by CG.
    (i) 10.75
    (ii) 11
    (iii) 12
    (iv) 20
19. As per Employees Provident Fund Scheme, employer's contribution is 10 % of basic wages, dearness allowance and retaining allowance. Out of the 10 % contribution, ______% is diverted to Employees' Pension Fund.
    (i) 10
    (ii) 11
    (iii) 12
    (iv) 8.33

20. For which of the following purpose an employee who is member of Employees' Provident Fund Scheme is granted non-refundable advances?
    (i) Payment of LIC premium of member.
    (ii) Temporary closure of factory for a period more than one week.
    (iii) Both of the above.
    (iv) None of the above.
21. As per Employees' Pension Scheme, minimum ______ contributory service is required for entitlement to pension.
    (i) 10 months
    (ii) 10 years
    (iii) 240 days in the preceding year
    (iv) 5 years
22. As per Employees' Pension Scheme, pension is paid to:
    (i) Widow for life or until she remarries.
    (ii) Children of deceased employee
    (iii) Orphans gets pension at an enhanced rate
    (iv) All of the above
23. As per Employees' Pension Scheme, pension is paid to maximum ______ children up to age of ______
    (i) 3; 18
    (ii) 2; 20
    (iii) 3; 25
    (iv) 2; 25
24. Employee's Pension Scheme was introduced in the year ______.
    (i) 1990
    (ii) 1995
    (iii) 1971
    (iv) 1952
25. What should be the contribution to insurance fund by an employer as per Employees' Deposit Link Insurance Scheme?
    (i) 1% of basic wage + DA + Cash value of food concession + Retaining allowance AND Administrative expenses @ 0.01% of pay of employee.
    (ii) 2% of Basic wage + DA AND Administrative expenses @ 0.01% of pay of employee.
    (iii) 1% of Basic wage + DA + Cash value of food concession + Retaining allowance AND Administrative expenses @ 0.001% of pay of employee.
    (iv) 1% of Basic wage AND Administrative expenses @ 0.01% of pay of employee.
26. What should be the contribution to insurance fund by an employee as per Employees Deposit Link Insurance Scheme?
    (i) 1% of Basic wage + DA + Cash value of food concession + Retaining allowance AND Administrative expenses @ 0.01% of pay of employee.
    (ii) 8.33% of basic wages or salary
    (iii) Nil
    (iv) Up to value of insurance premium
27. S retires from the services of PQR Ltd, on 31st March, 2009. He had a sum of ₹ $x$ lakhs in his PF Account. It became due for payment to S on 30th April, 2009, but the company made payment of the said amount after one year. Which is most appropriate as per EPF Act, 1952?
    (i) S can claim interest at rate of 12% p.a. for one year.
    (ii) S can claim interest at rate of 15% p.m. for one year.
    (iii) S can claim interest at rate of 12% p.m. for one year.
    (iv) S cannot claim interest.

28. If, in the above question, the scheme provide payment of interest @ 15%, which position will be most suitable as per EPF Act, 1952?
   (i) S can claim interest at rate of 12% p.a. for one year.
   (ii) S can claim interest at rate of 15% p.a. for one year.
   (iii) S cannot claim interest.
   (iv) Scheme will not be valid and interest at bank rate will be paid
29. Mr. A has a contributory service of 30 years and his pensionable salary is ₹ 5000 per month. His pension per month as per PF and MP Act will be ₹ ______.
   (i) 2280
   (ii) 2285
   (iii) 2290
   (iv) 2300
30. Who is liable to pay contribution and other sums due under EPF Act, on transfer of establishment by sale, gift, lease or licence or in any other manner?
   (i) Transferor
   (ii) Transferee
   (iii) Transferor and employee
   (iv) Both (i) and (ii) jointly and severally

## ANSWER KEYS

| | | | | |
|---|---|---|---|---|
| **1.** (ii) | **7.** (iii) | **13.** (i) | **19.** (i) | **25.** (i) |
| **2.** (iv) | **8.** (i) | **14.** (iv) | **20.** (i) | **26.** (i) |
| **3.** (iii) | **9.** (iv) | **15.** (i) | **21.** (ii) | **27.** (i) |
| **4.** (iv) | **10.** (iv) | **16.** (i) | **22.** (iv) | **28.** (ii) |
| **5.** (iii) | **11.** (iv) | **17.** (iii) | **23.** (iv) | **29.** (ii) |
| **6.** (ii) | **12.** (iii) | **18.** (iii) | **24.** (ii) | **30.** (iv) |

# 26

# Limited Liability Partnership Act, 2008

**Learning objectives**

*After reading this chapter, you will be able to understand:*

- Salient features and nature of LLP
- Difference between LLP and other forms of business
- Partners, designated partner and their rights and duties
- Process of incorporation and conversion of a firm or private company into LLP
- Provisions relating to registered office and name
- Financial disclosure, annual return and taxation of LLP
- Winding up and dissolution of LLP

The LLP structure is practised in countries like United Kingdom, United States of America, various Gulf countries, Australia and Singapore. In India, the LLP Act was drafted based on the advice of experts who studied LLP legislations in various countries. The Act is broadly based on UK LLP Act, 2000, and Singapore LLP Act, 2005. Both these Acts allow creation of LLPs in a body corporate form, i.e., as a legal entity, separate from its partners. On the recommendation of various committees, the government introduced the LLP Act in 2009. The Act is applicable all over India.

## 26.1 FEATURES OF LLP

LLP is governed by the Limited Liability Partnership Act, 2008, with effect from April 1, 2009. It combines the advantages of separate legal entity status and limited liability aspect of a company when running a partnership.

Here are some of the main features of LLP:

- LLP is a legal entity, which is separate from its partners. It can own assets in its name, sue and be sued.
- Unlike corporate shareholders, the partners of LLP have the right to manage the business directly.
- One partner is not responsible or liable for another partner's misconduct or negligence.
- There should be a minimum of 2 partners. There is no maximum limit.
- It should be a 'for profit' business.
- It has perpetual succession.
- The rights and duties of partners in LLP will be governed by the agreement between the partners. The partners have the flexibility to devise the agreement according to their choice. The duties and obligations of the designated partners shall be as provided in the law.
- Liability of partners is limited to the extent of his contribution to the LLP. There is no exposure of personal assets of the partner, except in cases of fraud.
- LLP shall maintain annual accounts. However, audit of the accounts is required only if the contribution exceeds Rs. 25 lakhs or annual turnover exceeds Rs. 40 lakhs.
- Partnership Act is not applicable to LLP.

## 26.2 DIFFERENCE BETWEEN PARTNERSHIP AND LLP

| Category | Partnership | LLP |
|---|---|---|
| **Applicable act** | The Indian Partnership Act, 1932. | The Limited Liability Partnership Act, 2008 and LLP Rules 2009. |
| **Registration** | Registration is optional. If partners want to register, they can register with Registrar of the firm. | Registration with Registrar of Companies is required. |
| **Creation** | Created by agreement or contract. | Created by law |
| **Separate legal entity** | It is not a separate legal entity. | It is a separate legal entity. |
| **Name of entity** | Any name as per choice | Name to contain 'Limited Liability Partnership' or 'LLP' as suffix. |
| **Perpetual succession** | It does not have perpetual succession. | It has perpetual succession and partners may come and go |
| **Charter document** | Partnership deed is a charter of the firm. It denotes scope of operation and rights and duties of the partners. | LLP agreement is a charter of the LLP, which denotes its scope of operation and rights and duties of the partners vis-à-vis LLP. |
| **Common seal** | There is no concept of common seal in partnership | It denotes the signature and LLP may have its own common seal, depending upon the terms of the Agreement |
| **Registration process** | Partnership is registered by filing Partnership Deed along with form / affidavit required to be filled with Registrar of Firms along with requisite filing fee | Various e-forms and the LLP Agreement are filed with the Registrar of LLP along with the prescribed fee. |

| Category | Partnership | LLP |
|---|---|---|
| **Right to sue** | Only registered partnership can sue third party | LLP, as a legal entity, can sue and be sued |
| **Number of members** | Minimum 2 and Maximum 20 | Minimum 2 partners and no limit to maximum number of partners. |
| **Ownership of assets** | Partners have joint ownership of all assets belonging to the partnership firm | The LLP is independent of the partners and has ownership of assets |
| **Rights and duties of the partners or designated partners** | It is governed by Partnership Deed. | It is governed by LLP Agreement. |
| **Liability of partners** | Unlimited. Partners are severally and jointly liable for actions of other partners and the firm and liability extends to their personal assets. | Limited to the extent of their contribution towards LLP, except in case of intentional fraud or wrongful act of omission or commission by the partner. |
| **Whether agent?** | Partners are agents of the firm and other partners. | Partners act as agents of LLP and not of the other partners. |
| **Transfer of rights** | Not transferable. In case of death the legal heir receives the financial value of share. | Regulations relating to transfer are governed by the LLP Agreement. |
| **Transfer of share / Partnership rights in case of death** | In case of death of a partner, the legal heirs have the right to get a refund of the capital contribution and a share in accumulated profits, if any. Legal heirs will not become partners | In case of death of a partner, the legal heirs have the right to get the refund of the capital contribution + share in accumulated profits, if any. Legal heirs will not become partners |
| **Director Identification Number(DIN)** | The partners are not required to obtain any identification number | Each designated partner is required to have a DIN before being appointed as Designated Partner of LLP. |
| **Digital signature** | There is no requirement of obtaining digital signature | As e-forms are filled electronically, at least one Designated Partner should have Digital Signatures. |
| **Dissolution** | Firm can be dissolved by agreement, mutual consent, insolvency, certain contingencies, and by court order. | Voluntary or by order of National Company Law Tribunal. |
| **Transferability of interest** | A partner can transfer his interest subject to the Partnership Agreement | A partner can transfer his interest subject to the LLP Agreement |

(*continued*)

| Category | Partnership | LLP |
|---|---|---|
| **Admission as partner** | A person can be admitted as a partner as per the Partnership Agreement | A person can be admitted as a partner as per the LLP Agreement |
| **Cessation as partner** | A person can cease to be a partner as per the agreement | A person can cease to be a partner as per the LLP Agreement or in absence of the same by giving 30 days prior notice to the LLP. |
| **Who is responsible for day-to-day affair?** | Any partner can manage day- to-day business. | Designated partners are responsible for managing the day to day business and other statutory compliances. |
| **Maintenance of minutes** | There is no concept of any meeting of minutes | LLP, by agreement, may decide to record the proceedings of meetings of the partners. |
| **Voting rights** | It depends upon the partnership agreement | Voting rights shall be as decided as per the terms of LLP Agreement. |
| **Annual filing** | No return is required to be filed with Registrar of Firms | Annual statement of accounts and solvency and annual return is required to be filed with Registrar of LLP every year. |
| **Audit of accounts** | Partnership firms are only required to have a tax audit of their accounts as per the provisions of the Income Tax Act | All LLP except for those having turnover less than Rs.40 lakhs or Rs.25 lakhs contribution in any financial year are required to get their accounts audited annually as per the provisions of LLP Act, 2008. |
| **Accounting standards** | Accounting standards are not applicable. | The necessary rules in regard to the application of accounting standards are not yet issued. |

## 26.3 DIFFERENCE BETWEEN COMPANY AND LLP

| Category | Company | LLP |
|---|---|---|
| **Applicable law** | Companies Act, 2013, is applicable. | Limited liability partnership is governed by 'The Limited Liability Partnership Act, 2008' and LLP Rules, 2009. |
| **Name of entity** | Name to contain 'Limited' in case of public company or 'Private Limited' in case of private company as suffix. | Name to contain 'Limited Liability Partnership' or 'LLP' as suffix. |

| Category | Company | LLP |
|---|---|---|
| **Charter document** | Memorandum and Article of association is the charter of the company which defines its scope of operation. | LLP agreement is the charter of the LLP which denotes its scope of operation and rights and duties of the partners vis-à-vis LLP. |
| **Formalities of incorporation** | Various e-forms along with the Memorandum and Articles of association are filed with the registrar of companies with prescribed fee | Various e-forms and the LLP agreement are filed with the registrar of LLP along with the prescribed fee. |
| **Number of members** | In case of private company, 2 to 200 members and minimum 7 members in case of public company. | There should be a minimum of 2 partners. There is no limit to the maximum number of partners. |
| **Rights and duties of the partners or directors** | Rights and duties of the directors are governed by Article of association and resolution passed by shareholders or directors. | Rights and duties of the partners are governed by LLP agreement. |
| **Liability of partners/ members** | Generally limited to the amount required to be paid up on each share. | Limited to the extent of their contribution towards LLP, except in case of intentional fraud or wrongful act of omission or commission by the partner. |
| **Principal-Agent relationship** | The directors act as agents of the company and not of the members | Partners act as agents of LLP and not of the other partners. |
| **Transfer of ownership rights** | Ownership is easily transferable. | Regulations relating to transfer are governed by the LLP agreement. |
| **Transfer of share / partnership rights in case of death** | In case of death of member, shares are transmitted to the legal heirs. | In case of death of a partner, the legal heirs have the right to get the refund of the capital contribution and the share in accumulated profits, if any. Legal heirs will not become partners |
| **Transferability of interest** | A member can freely transfer his interest | A partner can transfer his interest subject to the LLP agreement |
| **Admission as partner / member** | A person can become member by buying shares of a company. | A person can be admitted as a partner as per the LLP agreement |
| **Cessation as partner / member** | A member or shareholder can cease to be a member by selling his shares. | A person can cease to be a partner as per the LLP agreement or in absence of the same by giving 30 days prior notice to the LLP. |

*(continued)*

| Category | Company | LLP |
|---|---|---|
| **Management of day-to-day administration** | Directors are appointed to manage the business and other statutory compliances on behalf of the members. | Designated partners are responsible for managing the day-to-day business and other statutory compliances. |
| **Statutory meetings** | Board meetings and general meetings are required to be conducted as per provisions of the Companies Act. | There is no provision in regard to holding of any meeting. |
| **Voting rights** | Voting rights are decided as per the number of shares held by the members. | Voting rights shall be as decided as per the terms of LLP agreement. |
| **Remuneration to director/partner** | Company can pay remuneration to its directors subject to provisions of Companies Act. | Remuneration to partner will depend upon LLP Agreement. |
| **Contracts with Partners/Director** | Restrictions on board regarding some specified contracts, in which directors are interested. | Partners are free to enter into any contract. |
| **Maintenance of statutory records** | Required to maintain books of accounts, statutory registers, minutes etc. | Required to maintain books of accounts. |
| **Annual filing** | Annual financial statement and annual return are required to be filed with the Registrar of Companies every year. | Annual statement of accounts and solvency and annual Return is required to be filed with Registrar of LLP every year. |
| **Audit of accounts** | Companies are required to get their accounts audited annually as per the provisions of the Companies Act, 2013, | All LLP except those having turnover less than Rs. 40 lakhs or Rs. 25 lakhs contribution in any financial year are required to get their accounts audited annually as per the provisions of LLP Act, 2008. |

## 26.4 LLP AGREEMENT

The mutual rights and duties of partners inter se and those of the LLP and its partners shall be governed by the agreement between partners or between the LLP and the partners. This agreement is known as LLP agreement.

In the absence of any LLP agreement, the mutual rights and liabilities of partners are determined as provided under Schedule I to the Act. LLP may exclude the provisions of Schedule-I by entering into LLP agreement.

In order to ensure better governance, it is always advisable to enter into a well-drafted legal agreement.

### 26.4.1 Stamp duty

Stamp Act provides different amount of stamp duty payable in different states. At present, stamp duty payable on LLP Agreement is same as it is payable on partnership deed.

## 26.5 INCORPORATION DOCUMENT—SECTION 11

For a limited liability partnership to be incorporated,

- two or more persons associated for carrying on a lawful business with a view to profit shall subscribe their names to an incorporation document;
- the incorporation document, along with fees, shall be filed with the registrar of the state in which the registered office of the limited liability partnership is to be situated; and
- Statement declaring by either an advocate, or a company secretary or a chartered accountant or a cost accountant, who is engaged in the formation of the limited liability partnership and by anyone who subscribed his name to the incorporation document, that all the requirements of this Act and the rules made thereunder have been complied with, in respect of incorporation and matters precedent and incidental thereto.

The incorporation document shall—

- be in a form as may be prescribed;
- state the name of the LLP;
- state the proposed business of the LLP;
- state the address of the registered office of the LLP;
- state the name and address of each of the persons who are to be partners of the LLP on incorporation;
- state the name and address of the persons who are to be designated partners of the LLP on incorporation;
- contain such other information concerning the proposed LLP as may be prescribed.

If a person makes statement on above subject matter which he:

- knows to be false; or
- does not believe to be true,

he shall be punishable with imprisonment for a term which may extend to two years with fine which shall not be less than ten thousand rupees but which may extend to five lakh rupees.

**Case Study**

State whether an entity which has objectives such as 'charitable or other not for profit objectives' can be set up under LLP Act?

## 26.6 INCORPORATION BY REGISTRATION

When the requirements of Section 11 have been complied with, the registrar shall within a period of fourteen days-

- register the incorporation document; and
- give a certificate that the LLP is incorporated by the name specified therein.

The certificate issued shall be signed by the registrar and authenticated by his official seal. The certificate shall be conclusive evidence that the limited liability partnership is incorporated by the name specified therein.

## 26.7 PARTNER—SECTION 5–6

LLP should have at least two partners. Any individual or body corporate can be partner of LLP. LLP Act does not provide any qualification to be a partner for LLP but the person should be competent to enter into contract. However, the Act provides a few disqualifications. The following individuals cannot be partner in LLP:

- a person found to be of unsound mind
- a person who is an undischarged insolvent
- a person who has applied for being declared as insolvent and whose application is pending.

### 26.7.1 What if the Number of Partners Reduces Below Minimum?

LLP should have at least two partners. If at any point of time, the number of partners reduces below two and the remaining partner carries on business with knowledge of this fact for a period of more than six months, he is liable in unlimited manner for all liabilities undertaken by the LLP, after 6 months.

**Case Study**

Amar LLP and Ujala LLP want to start another LLP, namely, AMARUJALA LLP. Is it possible?

## 26.8 DESIGNATED PARTNER—SECTION 7–9

'Designated partner', in reference to Limited Liability Partnership, means any partner designated as such pursuant to Section 7 of Limited Liability Partnership Act, 2008.

LLP shall have at least two 'designated partners' who are individuals and at least one of them shall be 'resident in India'. In case one or more of the partners of the LLP are bodies corporate, at least two individuals who are partners of such LLP or nominees of such bodies corporate shall act as 'designated partners'.

'Resident in India' means a person who has stayed in India for minimum 182 days during the immediately preceding 1 year.

If the incorporation document specifies the names of designated partners, such persons shall be designated partners on incorporation.

In case if no partner is designated as such, or if at any time there is only one designated partner, each partner shall be deemed to be a designated partner of the LLP.

An individual can become a designated partner in any LLP if:

- he has given his prior consent to act as such to the LLP in such form and manner as may be prescribed
- he has obtained a Director Identification Number.

LLP is required to file with the registrar, particulars of every individual who has given his consent to act as designated partner in the prescribed form.

The role of designated partners in case of LLP is on the same footage as of Directors in case of a Company. The designated partners are directly responsible for the compliances of all provisions provided under LLP Act, 2008, and the provisions specified in the LLP Agreement.

Rights of designated partner are same as those of other partners. Alike other partners, they are not entitled to any remuneration for their participation in management of LLP unless otherwise specifically provided in the LLP Agreement; yet they have additional responsibilities to comply with.

A designated partner shall be

- responsible for the doing of all acts, matters and things as are required to be done by the limited liability partnership in respect of compliance of the provisions of this Act including filing of any document, return, statement and the like report pursuant to the provisions of this Act and as may be specified in the limited liability partnership agreement; and
- liable to all penalties imposed on the limited liability partnership for any contravention of those provisions.

**Case Study**

Five persons who are willing to incorporate Excel LLP have prepared its LLP agreement which suggest that each partner will be designated partner. Is it as per LLP Act?

### 26.8.1 Designated vs Managing Partner

Designated partners are partners who are responsible for managing the compliance under the LLP Act and managing partners are partners, who are managing the business of the Firm and therefore it is not necessary that a designated partner is also a managing partner and vice versa.

## 26.9 MAJOR DUTIES OF A DESIGNATED PARTNER

Designated partners have a duty to comply with the provisions of LLP Act. Following are the major duties of designated partners:

- Notify any changes in the LLPs to Registrar of Companies.
- Notify any changes in the partners' names and residential addresses to Registrar of Companies.
- Notify any change in Registered Office address to Registrar of Companies.

- File annual return, statement of accounts and other documents specified under the provisions of LLP Act with the Registrar of Companies.
- Sign statement of accounts and solvency
- Preserve and produce before an inspector or any person authorised by him on this behalf with the previous approval of the Central Government, all books and papers of, or relating to, the limited liability partnership or, as the case may be, the other entity, which are in their custody or power
- Sign all e-forms filed with the Registrar of Companies.

Any vacancy arising in the office of the designated partner shall be filled within 30 days and the change shall be intimated to the Registrar of Companies. The partner may cease to be designated partner in accordance with LLP agreement, as per Section 9.

**Case Study**

Mr. A, Mr. B, Mr. C and Mr. D are four partners of EXCEL LLP. Mr. A and Mr. C are appointed as designated partner as per the LLP Agreement. In a motor accident, Mr. A and Mr. C die and the other remaining partners are aware of this fact. The LLP agreement does not provide any provision regarding filling vacancy of designated partner. The remaining partners have not appointed any one of themselves as designated partner. What will be the consequences in the given situation? Who can be regarded as designated partner?

## 26.10 REGISTERED OFFICE

A document may be served on the LLP or a partner or designated partner by sending it by post or by any other mode (to be prescribed under Rules) to the registered office or any other address specifically declared by the LLP.

The LLP shall file Form 12 with the Registrar of LLP for intimating other addresses for service of documents.

### 26.10.1 Procedure for Change of Registered Office

The registered office can be changed as per the LLP agreement or by obtaining consent of all the partners of the LLP. Further consent of the secured creditors of the LLP should also be obtained and a general notice published, not less than 21 days before filing any notice with the Registrar of Companies, in a daily newspaper published in English and in the principal language of the district in which the registered office of the limited liability partnership is situated and circulating in that district giving notice of change of registered office. The notice of shifting of registered office shall be given to the registrar within 30 days of publication of the notice in the newspaper.

## 26.11 NAME OF LLP—SECTIONS 11–21

The proposed partners of LLP should select the name for the LLP before they proceed to register it. The selected name may or may not be available for registration. Therefore, an application should be made to the registrar to check whether the selected name is available for registration. On approval of the selected name, the proposed partners can proceed to file other incorporation documents.

A name which is not rejected on the ground of being undesirable or identical or too nearly resembling that of any other partnership firm or limited liability partnership or body corporate or a registered trade mark, or a trade mark which is subject of an application for registration, of any other person under the Trade Marks Act, 1999, can be reserved for a period of three months from the date of intimation by the Registrar.

Foreign LLP or Companies have an option to reserve their existing names under which they are operating outside India, for a period of 3 years in India, which can be further renewed

A person cannot choose any name for LLP. The LLP Act prescribes guidelines for choosing the name of LLP; under the said guidelines, any name of the LLP should pass the following test:

- The name of the LLP should not be identical with an already registered name.
- The name should not be prohibited.

In case the name requires the consent of any regulatory authority, the consent has to be obtained.

Every LLP is required to write its name, address of registered office and registration number of LLP on its invoices, official correspondence and publications, as per Section 21

### 26.11.1 Change in name of LLP—Section 17

The name of LLP can be changed as per the procedure prescribed in the LLP Agreement. In case the agreement is silent, consent of all the members will be required.

The terms 'same as' or 'identical' signifies that the proposed name of LLP should not be similar or identical to an already registered name. Normally, a name is considered as identical, if the first two starting words of any name matches with an already registered name.

**Case Study**

Oasis Water Products LLP is an already registered LLP. Can businessmen with intent to start a distilled water business, register LLP with the name "Oasis Water India LLP"?

The registrar can reject the proposed name of LLP if it fulfils any of the below conditions:

1. It is identical with an already registered name
2. It contains any prohibited word
3. It does not have the required permission from any regulatory authority.

## 26.12 NAME GUIDELINE—RULE 18 OF LLP RULES, 2009

Rule 18 of the Limited Liability Partnership Rules, 2009, prescribes the guidelines to be kept in mind, while deciding the name of the LLP. Following are main points of the guidelines:

- The name of the limited liability partnership shall not be one prohibited under the Emblems and Names (Prevention of Improper Use) Act, 1950.
- A name shall not generally be reserved, if
  - It includes any words which are offensive to any section of the people;
  - The proposed name is the exact Hindi or English translation of the name of an existing LLP in English or Hindi, as the case may be;
  - The proposed name has a close phonetic resemblance to the name of an LLP in existence;

- It includes the word 'co-operative', 'sahakari' or an equivalent of the word 'co-operative' in the regional languages of the country;
- It connotes the participation or patronage of the Central or State Government;
- The proposed name contains the words 'British India';
- The proposed name implies association or connection with any Embassy or Consulate or of a foreign government or connection with local authorities such as Municipal, Panchayat, Zila Parishad or any other body connected with the Union or State Government;
- The proposed name is vague;
- Provided the name shall be reserved, in case 'No Objection Certificate' is granted by the registered LLP or the Company as the case may be;
- It includes names of registered trade mark, unless the consent of the owner of the trade mark has been produced;
- The proposed name is identical with or too nearly resembles the name of a firm or LLP or company incorporated outside India and reserved by such firm, LLP or company with the registrar in accordance with these rules;
- It is identical with or too nearly resembles the name of the limited liability partnership or a company in liquidation or it is identical with or too nearly resembles names of the LLP or a company which is struck off, up to the period of 5 years;
- It includes words like 'bank', 'insurance' and 'banking', 'venture capital' or 'mutual fund' or such similar names without the approval of the regulatory authority;
- It is intended to or likely to produce a misleading impression regarding the scope or scale of its activities which would be beyond the resources at its disposal;
- The proposed name includes words like French, British, German etc., unless the partners satisfy that there is some form of collaboration and connection with the foreigners of that particular country or place, the name of which is incorporated in the name;
- The proposed name of LLP includes the words 'company secretary', 'chartered accountant', 'advocates' or such similar words as indicative of a profession, as part of the proposed name, the same shall be allowed only after obtaining approval from the Council governing such profession or such authority as may be nominated by the Central Government, on its behalf.

### Case Study

State whether an LLP can be registered with the following names.

1. J.K. LLP, where Jay kay is an already registered LLP
2. Farmer Co-operative LLP
3. Farmer Sahkari LLP
4. Uco Federal LLP
5. Union Carbide LLP
6. Microsoft British India LLP
7. D.I.M.O LLP
8. S.V.R.P LLP
9. Steel Bank LLP
10. SSI LLP

## 26.13 PARTNERS AND THEIR RELATIONS AND EXTENT OF LIABILITY—SECTIONS 22–31

Mutual rights and duties of partners of an LLP inter se and those of the LLP and its partners shall be governed by an agreement between the partners, or agreement between the LLP and its partners. In absence of any such agreements, the mutual rights and duties shall be governed by the LLP Act.

Every partner of an LLP is an agent of LLP for the purpose of the business of LLP but the partner is not an agent of other partner of LLP. LLP, being a separate legal entity, shall be liable to the full extent of its assets whereas the liability of the partners of LLP shall be limited to their agreed contribution in the LLP. LLP is not bound by the act of a partner in dealing with a person if –

- the partner, in fact, has no authority to act for the LLP in doing a particular act; and
- the person knows that he has no authority or does not know or believe him to be a partner of the LLP

The LLP is liable if a partner of the LLP is liable to any person for wrongful act or omission on his part in the course of business of LLP if the said act is within his authority. Obligation of LLP, whether arising in contract or otherwise, shall solely be the obligation of LLP. Liabilities of LLP shall be met out of properties of LLP. A partner is not personally liable for the obligations of LLP solely by reason of being a partner of LLP.

No partner is liable for the wrongful act or omission of any other partner of LLP, but the partner will be personally liable for his own wrongful act or omission. The liability of the LLP and partners who are found to have acted with intent to defraud creditors or for any fraudulent purpose shall be unlimited for all or any of the debts or other liabilities of the LLP.

### 26.13.1 Cessation of Partner

Cessation of a partner on grounds like resignation, death, dissolution of LLP, declaration that a person is of unsound mind, declared or applied to be adjudged as insolvent etc. will not be effective unless:

- the person has notice that the partner has ceased to be so; or
- the notice of cessation has been delivered to ROC.

A person may cease to be a partner of LLP under the following circumstances:

- According to an agreement with the other partners.
- In case of absence of such agreement, by giving a notice in writing of not less than 30 days to the other partners of his intention to resign as partner (as per Section 24(1)).

### 26.13.2 Notice of Cessation

The notice of cessation may be filed by the outgoing partner if he has reasonable cause to believe that LLP has not filed the said notice.

The former partner can be regarded as still being a partner of the LLP unless:

- the person has notice that the former partner has ceased to be a partner of the LLP;

or

- the notice that the former partner has ceased to be a partner of the LLP has been delivered to the Registrar.

### 26.13.3 Liability on Cessation

The cessation of a partner does not, by itself, discharge the partner from any obligation to the LLP or to the other partners or to any other person, which he incurred while being a partner.

### 26.13.4 Right on Cessation

On cessation of the partnership, the former partner or a person entitled to his share in consequence of the death or insolvency of the former partner, shall be entitled to receive from the LLP, unless otherwise provided in the LLP agreement:

- an amount equal to the capital contribution of the former partner actually made to the LLP; and
- his right to share in the accumulated profits of the LLP.

after deduction of accumulated losses of the LLP determined as at the date the former partner ceased to be a partner, in accordance with Section 24(5).

## 26.14 WHISTLE BLOWING—SECTION 31

The court or tribunal may reduce or waive any penalty leviable against any partner or employee of a limited liability partnership, if it is satisfied that:

- such person has provided useful information during investigation of the LLP or
- when any information given by any partner or employee (whether or not during investigation) leads to the limited liability partnership or any partner or employee of such limited liability partnership being convicted under this Act or any other Act.

The partner or employee of any LLP cannot be discharged, demoted, suspended, threatened, harassed or, in any other manner, discriminated against the terms and conditions of his limited liability partnership or employment merely because of his providing information or causing information to be provided about any offence of violation.

## 26.15 CONTRIBUTION BY PARTNER—SECTION 32–33

A contribution of a partner to the capital of LLP may consist of any of the –

- tangible, intangible, movable or immovable property
- other benefits to the LLP including money, promissory notes, contracts for services performed or to be performed.

The obligation of a partner for the contribution shall be as per the LLP agreement. A creditor who extends credit or acts in reliance on an obligation described in the LLP agreement, without the notice of any compromise made between the partners, may enforce the original obligation against such partner.

### 26.15.1 Increase in Contribution

The LLP Act, 2008, or the LLP Rules, 2009, do not contain any specific provisions regarding the procedure for increase in contribution of an LLP. Hence, the procedure for increase in contribution of an LLP shall be governed by the provisions of the LLP Agreement. For indicating an increase in the contribution of an LLP, Form 3 is required to be filed with the registrar within 30 days from the date of alteration. At the time of increase in contribution, stamp duty is payable as per Stamp Act in the same manner as stamp duty is applicable for partnership agreement.

### 26.15.2 Steps for Increase in Contribution by Way of Introduction of New Partner

For increase in contribution by way of introduction of new partner(s), the following steps are involved:

- To check whether the LLP Agreement specifies the procedure for modification of the LLP Agreement for introduction of a new partner.
- If yes, to modify the LLP Agreement, by following the procedure prescribed in the LLP Agreement for modification of the agreement for introduction of a new partner.
- If the LLP Agreement is silent about the procedure to be followed for modification of the Agreement for introduction of a new partner, to pass a resolution by taking consent of all the partners for modification of the Agreement for introduction of a new partner and increase in contribution which is brought in by the new partner.
- If the new partner shall also be a designated partner of the LLP, such person shall obtain Designated Partner's Identification Number (DPIN) from the Central Government by making an application electronically in Form 7 to the Central Government.
- The proposed Designated Partner shall give his prior consent to act as a designated partner and intimate his DPIN, in Form 9, to the LLP.
- Filing of Form 4 by the LLP with the Registrar, within 30 days from the date of appointment of the designated partner or partner, along with the requisite fees.
- Filing of Form 3 by the LLP with the Registrar, within 30 days from the date of modification of the Agreement along with the requisite fees.

## 26.16 VOTING RIGHT

Voting rights of partners is not determined by the contribution brought in by partners and can be specified in the LLP Agreement. If the LLP Agreement is silent about the voting rights of partners, each partner shall be entitled to one vote, irrespective of the capital brought in by him.

**Case Study**

Mr. A, Mr. B, Mr. C and Mr. D are partners of an LLP. Mr. A and Mr. B are designated partners. The LLP agreement provides that Mr. A has double the voting right as compare to Mr. B and Mr. C, while Mr. D has no voting right. Decide the validity of the agreement.

## 26.17 AUDIT AND FINANCIAL DISCLOSURES—SECTION 34–35

An LLP shall maintain the prescribed books of accounts relating to its affairs on cash or accrual basis and according to the double entry system of accounting. Schedule III of the Companies Act, 2013, is not applicable to an LLP. It applies to all companies registered under Companies Act but LLP is a body corporate and not a company. Annual accounts of LLP should reflect true and fair view of its state of affairs.

The accounts of every LLP are required to be audited, except in following situations:

- Turnover does not exceed Rs. 40,00,000 in any financial year; or
- Contribution does not exceed Rs. 25,00,000

The Central Government has powers to exempt certain class of LLP from requirement of compulsory audit.

An LLP is required to file the following documents with the Registrar of Companies:

- Statement of account and solvency, within 30 days from the end of 6 months of the financial year.
- Annual return within 60 days from the end of the financial year. Annual return is filed in Form 11.

### 26.17.1 Appointment of Auditor

The designated partners annually appoint the auditor of the LLP. The first auditor must be appointed before the end of the financial year for which they are appointed. Thereafter, the appointment or reappointment of the auditors must be made one month before the closing of the financial year by the designated partners

In case of failure of the designated partners to appoint the first auditors within the prescribed time, the partners may appoint the first auditors. In case of failure of designated partners to appoint any subsequent auditor within the prescribed time, the partners may appoint such subsequent auditors.

Where no new auditor has been appointed before 30 days prior to the end of financial year, any auditor holding office shall be deemed to be re-appointed unless

- the LLP Agreement requires actual re-appointment; or
- a majority of partners have determined that he should not be re-appointed and have given a notice to this effect to the LLP.

**Case Study**

If an LLP is incorporated on 1st January 2009 and the first quarter of the financial year is from 1st January 2009 to 31st March 2009, then what is time limit for appointment of the first auditor? How is the first auditor appointed in case of failure by designated partners?

**Case Study**

If a subsequent financial year of the LLP is from 1st April 2009 to 31st March 2009, then the first auditor may be appointed by the designated partner at any time before 28th February 2010. In case of failure of designated partners to appoint the first auditors before 28th February 2010, then the first auditors may be appointed by the partners of the LLP.

The designated partners may fill the casual vacancy arisen by removal of an auditor. No time limit has been specified for filling the casual vacancy.

### 26.17.2 Who can be Appointed as Auditor?

An auditor must be independent of the LLP. Member of ICAI holding certificate of practice can be appointed as auditor to conduct audit of LLP. However, the following persons cannot be appointed as auditor of LLP:

- A partner of LLP.
- An employee of the LLP.
- A partner of employee of an associated undertaking.
- A partner or employee of such a person, or a partnership of which such a person is a partner.

### 26.17.3 Exemption from Audit

The Central Government may, by a notification in the official gazette, exempt any class or classes of LLPs from the requirements of audit. However, the exempted LLPs may get their accounts audited voluntarily.

In case of LLPs which avail the audit exemption, the following obligations are prescribed:

- A statement by the partners to the effect that the partners acknowledge their responsibilities for complying with the provisions of this Act and Rules with respect to preparation of accounts is required to be included in the Statement of Account and Solvency.
- A certificate needs to be attached in Form 8 to be filed with the Ministry of Corporate Affair (MCA), along with the Statement of Account and Solvency.

Auditor's report is not required to be filed with Ministry of Corporate Affairs (MCA). The Designated Partners are authorised to fix the remuneration of auditors, unless the LLP Agreement prescribes otherwise.

### 26.17.4 Removal of Auditors

The partners of LLP can remove the auditors by following the procedure as may be laid down in the LLP agreement. If the LLP Agreement is silent about the procedure of removal of auditors, then the auditors can be removed with the consent of all the partners.

## 26.18 ASSIGNMENT AND TRANSFER OF PARTNERSHIP RIGHTS—SECTION 42

The rights of a partner to a share of the profits and losses of the LLP and to receive distribution in accordance with the LLP agreement are transferable, either wholly or in part. However, such transfer of rights does not cause either disassociation of the partner or a dissolution and winding up of the LLP.

Such transfer of right, shall not, by itself, entitle the assignee or the transferee to participate in the management or conduct of the activities of the LLP or access information concerning the transactions of the LLP.

## 26.19 INVESTIGATION—SECTIONS 43–46

The Central Government may appoint one or more competent person as inspector to investigate the affairs of an LLP and to report on it if:

- The Company Law Tribunal (CLB)/Tribunal has declared that affairs of the LLP ought to be investigated. Such declaration can be made by the CLB/Tribunal either suo moto or based on an application received from not less than $1/5^{th}$ of the total number of partners of LLP.
- Court has declared by order that affairs of LLP ought to be investigated.

The Central Government may appoint an inspector to investigate the affairs of an LLP when not less than 1/5th of total number of partners make an application in writing along with supporting evidence. The Central Government may appoint an inspector to investigate the affairs of an LLP where the LLP makes an application to this effect.

The Central Government may appoint an inspector to investigate the affairs of an LLP if, in the opinion of the Central Government, circumstances suggest:

- That the business of the LLP is being or has been conducted with intent to defraud creditors, partners or any other person.
- That the business of the LLP is being or has been conducted for fraudulent or unlawful purpose or in an oppressive manner.
- That the affair of the LLP is not being conducted in accordance with the provisions of this Act.
- That, on receipt of report of registrar, there are sufficient reasons that affairs of the LLP ought to be investigated.

The inspector appointed by the Central Government has the power to investigate the affairs of related entities, whether associated, in past or in present, including past and present designated partners subject to the specified rules and with the permission of the Central Government.

Only an individual person can be appointed as inspector to investigate the affairs of the LLP. Firm, body corporate or association cannot be appointed as inspector to investigate affairs of the LLP.

### 26.19.1 Documents to be Kept Open for Inspection

The LLP shall keep open the following documents for inspection:

- Incorporation document
- Name of partners and changes, if any, made therein.
- Statement of account and solvency.
- Annual return filed by each limited liability partnership with the registrar.

The said documents shall be available for inspection by any person in such manner and on payment of such fee, as may be prescribed.

## 26.20 FOREIGN LLP—SECTION 59 AND RULE 34

On establishment of a place of business in India, a foreign LLP is required to file the prescribed documents for registration with ROC within 30 days of its establishment in India.

Any alteration in the constitution documents, overseas principal office address and partner of foreign LLP is required to be filed with the ROC in the prescribed form within 60 days of the close of the financial year.

Any alteration in the certificate of registration of the foreign LLP, its authorised representative in India and principal place of business in India are required to be filed with the ROC in the prescribed form within 30 days of alteration.

A foreign LLP ceasing to have a place of business in India, is required to give notice to ROC in the prescribed form within 30 days of its intention to close the place of business and from the date of such notice, the obligation of the Foreign LLP to file any document with the ROC shall cease, provided it has no other place of business in India and it has filed all the documents due for filing as on the date of the notice.

## 26.21 TAXATION OF LLP

Since taxation-related matters in India are provided under tax Laws, the taxation of LLPs has not been provided in the LLP Act. Income Tax Act, 1961, contains following provisions regarding taxation of LLPs:

- LLPs are to be taxed on the lines similar to general partnerships under Indian Partnership Act, 1932, i.e., taxation in the hands of the entity and exemption from tax in the hands of its partners.
- The designated partner shall sign the income tax return of an LLP, or where for any unavoidable reason such designated partner is not able to sign the return or where there is no designated partner as such, any partner shall sign the return.
- In case of liquidation of an LLP, every partner will be jointly and severally liable for payment of tax unless he proves that non-recovery cannot be attributed to any gross neglect, misfeasance or breach of duty on his part.

The following points are also worthy of note with reference to income tax of LLP:

- Surcharge is not applicable in the case of LLP.
- Dividend distributable tax is not applicable in case when LLP declares dividend, while it is applicable to a company.
- Loan to director in the case of a company is treated as deemed dividend in hand of the director under Section 2(22) of Income Tax Act, while loan to partner is not treated as deemed dividend in hand of the partner.
- LLP can claim expenses incurred by it for family planning for the benefit of employees.
- Rate of MAT (minimum alternate tax) applicable is 19.055% in case when taxable income of LLP exceeds Rs. 1 crore.
- Section 79 of Income Tax Act, 1961, regarding carry forward and set-off losses cannot be exercised by any LLP.

## 26.22 CONVERSION OF PARTNERSHIP FIRM OR PRIVATE COMPANY OR UNLISTED PUBLIC COMPANY INTO LLP—SECTIONS 55–58

The following forms of businesses can be converted into LLP by complying with the provisions of conversion under LLP Act:

- a partnership firm into LLP.
- a private limited company into LLP.
- an unlisted public company into LLP.

The second, third and fourth schedules to the LLP Act contain provisions relating to conversion of a partnership firm into LLP, a private limited company into LLP and unlisted public company into LLP, respectively.

### 26.22.1 Eligibility for Conversion

***Firm into LLP:*** A firm can be converted into LLP if all the partners of the firm become partners of the LLP and no one else.

***Company into LLP:*** Private limited company and unlisted public company can be converted if and only if:

- there is no security interest in its assets subsisting or in force at the time of application for conversion; and
- all shareholders of the company become partners of LLP and no one else.

### 26.22.2 Procedure and Effect of Conversion

For conversion of firm or private limited company or unlisted public company into LLP, the partners of the firm or shareholders of the company are required to file a statement and incorporation documents in the prescribed form with the ROC.

On receiving the documents for conversion, the ROC shall register the documents and issue a certificate of registration specifying the date of registration as LLP. Upon registration by ROC, the LLP shall intimate Registrar of Firm or Registrar of Companies, as the case may be, about conversion within 15 days of registration.

On and from the date specified in the certificate of registration issued by ROC –

- all property (tangible, intangible, movable and immovable property), liabilities, interest, obligation etc. relating to the firm or private limited company or unlisted public company and the whole of the undertaking of the firm or private limited company or unlisted public company, shall be transferred to and shall vest in the LLP without further assurance, act or deed.
- The firm or private limited company or unlisted public company shall be deemed to be dissolved and removed from the records of Registrar of Firm or Registrar of Companies, as the case may be.

If any property or rights, etc. of the partnership firm or private limited company or unlisted public company is registered with any authority, the LLP shall take steps to notify the authority of the conversion.

Upon conversion, following things/events in favour of or against the firm or private limited company or unlisted public company on the date of registration may be continued, completed and enforced by or against the LLP:

- all proceedings, conviction, ruling, order or judgment of any court, tribunal or other authority pending in any court or tribunal or before any authority on the date of registration.
- every agreement irrespective of whether or not the rights and liabilities thereunder could be assigned.
- deeds, contracts, schemes, bonds, agreements, applications, instruments and arrangements.
- every contract of employment.
- appointment in any role or capacity.
- any approval, permit or licence issued under any other Act, etc.

In case of a firm, every partner of a firm which is converted into an LLP shall continue to be personally liable (jointly and severally with the LLP) for the liabilities and obligations of the firm incurred prior to the conversion or which arose from any contract entered into prior to the conversion. In case any such partner discharges any such liability or obligation he shall be entitled (subject to any agreement with the LLP to the contrary) to be fully indemnified by the LLP in respect of such liability or obligation.

For a period of 12 months commencing on or before 14 days from the date of registration, the LLP shall ensure that every official correspondence of the LLP bears the following:

- a statement that it was, as from the date of registration, converted from a firm or private limited company or unlisted public company into a LLP; and
- the name and registration number, if applicable, of the firm or private limited company or unlisted public company from which it was converted.

**Case Study**

Mr. A and Mr. B are partners of registered partnership firm. Mr. B has been declared as insolvent by court. Now, Mr. A wants to convert partnership into LLP. Is it possible? How?

## 26.23 STEPS FOR CONVERSION OF PARTNERSHIP INTO LLP

To convert an existing partnership into LLP, the following steps should be taken:

### 26.23.1 Step 1—Deciding Partners and Designated Partners

A partnership which desires to convert its status to LLP Form shall decide the designated partners of the proposed LLP. When a partnership firm is proposed to be converted to LLP, only the partners of the partnership firm can be the partners of the converted LLP. The person who is not a partner of the firm cannot be partner of the LLP. To convert a firm into LLP, at least two partners are required. At least two partners have to be designated partners; of them one shall have to be a resident Indian.

### 26.23.2 Step 2—Obtain DIN and Digital Signature

Every designated partner is required to obtain a DPIN (*Designated Partner Identification Number*) from the Central Government.

DPIN is an 8-digit numeric number allotted by the Central Government in order to identify a particular partner and can be obtained by making an online application to the Central Government along with the prescribed fees.

All the forms required for the purpose of incorporating an LLP are filed online; it is not possible to sign them manually. Moreover the DPIN Form is to be signed by the concerned designated partner himself. Therefore, for the purpose of signing these forms, all designated partners of the proposed LLP need to obtain a digital signature certificate (DSC).

### 26.23.3 Step 3—Checking Name Availability for LLP

The name selected may not be available for registration; therefore, an application for reservation of the desired name of the LLP should be made along with the prescribed fees.

### 26.23.4 Step 4—Drafting of LLP Agreement

Once the desired name is available and prima facie permitted, a limited liability partnership agreement should be drafted. The basic contents of the Agreement are:

- Name of LLP
- Name of partners and designated partners
- Form of contribution
- Profit sharing ratio
- Rights and duties of partners
- Proposed business
- Rules for governing the LLP

It is not necessary to have the LLP Agreement signed at the time of incorporation, as the details of the agreement need to be filed in e-Form 3 within 30 days of incorporation but in order to avoid any dispute between the partners as to the terms and conditions of the agreement after the conversion into LLP, it is always beneficial to have the LLP Agreement drafted and executed before the incorporation of the LLP.

### 26.23.5 Step 5—Filing Incorporation Documents

Incorporation documents in e-Form No. 2 and declaration should be filed online at the Website www.llp.gov.in along with the prescribed fees. The fee is based on the total monetary value of contribution of the partners in the proposed LLP. For filing e-forms, digital signature is required of all the designated partners.

Incorporation document (i.e., e-Form No. 2) is an informative document setting down the details of LLP, its partners including designated partners along with their amount of contribution and consent for forming a limited liability partnership to carry on a lawful business with profit motive along with declaration stating that all the requirements of Limited Liability Partnership Act, 2008, regarding incorporation of LLP in India have been complied with.

The partners are required to subscribe their names along with signatures to the subscription sheet, which shall be witnessed by any chartered accountant or company secretary or advocate in practice. In case the subscription sheet is executed outside India, then it must be notarised and consularised.

### 26.23.6 Step 6—Filing Conversion Application

Application for conversion of firm into LLP is submitted in e-Form 17 by the partners of the partnership name covering name, details of address and registration (if any) consent of all partners of the firm along with following details:

- Whether up to date income-tax return is filed under the Income-tax Act, 1961.
- Whether any proceeding by or against the firm is pending in any court or tribunal or any other authority.
- Whether any conviction, ruling, order, judgment of any court, tribunal or other authority in favour of or against the firm is subsisting.
- Whether any clearance, approval or permission for conversion of the firm into limited liability partnership is required from anybody or authority.

All the e-forms will be digitally signed by any designated partner and shall be certified by an advocate or company secretary or chartered accountant or cost accountant in practice engaged in the formation of LLP.

### 26.23.7 Step 7—Certificate of Registration

On completion of the above formalities and filings been complied with by the applicants and approved by the ministry, the registrar will issue a certificate of registration as to conversion of the LLP. The certificate of registration issued is conclusive evidence of conversion of the LLP.

If the registrar refused the registration, the applicant company may apply to the tribunal within sixty days from the date of receipt of such intimation of refusal.

### 26.23.8 Step 8—Information for Conversion to the Register of Firm

In case the partnership firm is registered, than the converted limited liability partnership shall, within fifteen days of the date of conversion, inform the concerned Registrar of Firm with which it was registered under the provisions of the Indian Partnership Act, 1932, about the conversion and of the particulars of the limited liability partnership in:

**List of Documents Required**

- eForm 1-Name availability application
- eForm 7-Application for designated partners identification number
- eForm 2-Incorporation document
- eForm 17-Application for conversion
- eForm 3- Details of LLP agreement
- eForm 4-Consent of partners
- eForm 14- Intimation of conversion to Registrar of Firms
- Subscription sheet
- LLP Agreement duly stamped as per relevant Stamp Act of the State.
- Proof of address of registered office
- Consent of partners
- Statement of partners
- Statement of assets and liabilities of the company duly certified as true and correct by the auditor
- List of all the unsecured creditors along with their consent.
- Approval from any other body/authority, if any required

## 26.24 CONVERSION OF PRIVATE COMPANY IN TO LLP

To convert an existing private company into LLP, the following steps should be taken:

### 26.24.1 Step 1—Deciding Partners and Designated Partners

A private company which desires to convert its status to LLP Form shall foremost decide the designated partners of the proposed LLP, as only the members can be partners of the converted LLP and of these members of the company, at least two partners shall be the designated partners. If a body corporate which was a member of the company desires to act as designated partner of LLP, their nominee can be appointed as the designated partner.

#### 26.24.1.1 Parameters for Deciding Designated Partners

- Minimum two individuals of the total number of partners should be designated partners.
- At least one designated partner should be a resident Indian.

In case of conversion of Private Limited Company into LLP, all the shareholders of the company should be partners in the LLP and no one else; there will also be no security interest subsisting or in force at the time of application in the assets of the company.

### 26.24.2 Step 2—Obtain DIN and Digital Signature

Every designated partner is required to obtain a DIN from the Central Government. If a person already has a DIN, the same can be used for forming LLP. Generally, the DIN and digital signature of a director of a private company shall be valid for LLP too.

### 26.24.3 Step 3—Checking Name Availability for LLP

The next step is to make an application in e-Form 1 of Rule 18(5) of the Limited Liability Partnership Act, 2008, for reservation of the desired name of the LLP on payment of the prescribed fees.

A board resolution passed by the company approving the conversion into LLP shall be attached with the aforesaid form. It is not necessary to file the LLP Agreement at the time of incorporation; it can also be filed within 30 days of the incorporation

### 26.24.4 Step 4—Drafting of LLP Agreement

On availability of the desired name the LLP Agreement should be drafted. The same provisions as indicated in Step 4 for conversion of partnership into LLP (as discussed on Page 682) are applicable here.

### 26.24.5 Step 5—Filing Incorporation Documents

Incorporation documents are prepared and filled online. The same provisions as indicated at Step 5 for conversion of partnership into LLP (as discussed on Page 682) are applicable here.

### 26.24.6 Step 6—Filing Conversion Application

Application for conversion, in e-Form 18, has to be submitted by the shareholder of the company covering name, registration number and date of incorporation of the company, and consent of all shareholders of the company along with following details:

- Whether any security interest in the assets of the company is subsisting or in force
- Whether up-to-date income-tax return is filed under the Income-tax Act, 1961.
- Whether any prosecution has been initiated against or show cause notice received by the company for alleged offences under the Companies Act, 1956.
- Whether any proceeding by or against the company is pending in any court or tribunal or any other authority.
- Whether any conviction, ruling, order, judgment of any court, tribunal or other authority in favour of or against the company, is subsisting.
- Whether any clearance, approval or permission for conversion of the company into limited liability partnership is required from any authority.

All e-forms will be digitally signed by any a designated partner and be certified by an advocate or company secretary or chartered accountant or cost accountant in practice engaged in the formation of LLP.

### 26.24.7 Step 7—Certificate of Registration

On all formalities and filings being complied with by the applicants and approved by the Ministry, the Registrar of LLP issues a Certificate of Registration as to conversion of the LLP. The certificate of registration issued shall be the conclusive evidence of conversion of the LLP.

In the event of the Registrar having refused the registration, the applicant company may apply to the tribunal within 60 days from the date of receipt of such intimation of refusal.

***e-Form 3: Details of LLP Agreement*** This form provides for the necessary information in respect of the LLP Agreement entered into between the partners.

***e-Form 4: Consent of Partners*** Consent of each partner to become a partner of limited liability partnership has to be filed with the Registrar of LLP

### 26.24.8 Step 8—Information for conversion to the register of companies

The converted limited liability partnership has to file, within 15 days of the date of registration, information to the concerned Registrar of Companies with which it was registered under the provisions of the Companies Act, 1956, about the conversion and of the particulars of the limited liability partnership in *e-Form 14*.

## 26.25 COMPROMISE, ARRANGEMENT OR RECONSTRUCTION OF LLPS—SECTION 60

Provisions have been made in the LLP Act for allowing a compromise and arrangement including mergers and amalgamations. Compromise and arrangement can be between LLP and its creditors or between LLP and its partners.

### 26.25.1 Procedure

If a majority representing 3/4th in value of creditors or partners, at the meeting, agree to compromise or arrangement, it shall, if sanctioned by National Company Law Tribunal [NCLT], be binding on all creditors, all the partners and the LLP. NCLT shall pass an order subject to disclosure of all material facts/latest financial position and pendency of the investigation proceedings.

- NCLT order shall be filed with the ROC within 30 days, in order to be effective.
- In case of scheme of the amalgamation, NCLT shall pass order only on receipt of report from the ROC that the affairs of the LLP (transferor LLP) have not been conducted in a manner prejudicial to the interest of the partner/public.

## 26.26 WINDING-UP OF LLP—SECTIONS 63 AND 64

LLPs may be wound up, either voluntarily or by NCLT. LLP may be wound up by NCLT if:

- The LLP decides to be wound up by NCLT;
- The number of partners reduces below 2 for a period of more than 6 months;
- The LLP is unable to pay its debts;
- The LLP has acted against the interests of the sovereignty and integrity of India, the security of the State or public order;
- The LLP has defaulted in filing Statement of Account and Solvency or annual return with the ROC for five consecutive financial years; or
- NCLT is of the opinion that it is just and equitable that the LLP be wound up

On 30th March 2010, MCA has issued Limited Liability Partnership (Winding up and Dissolution) Rules, 2010.

## 26.27 ADVANTAGES OF LLP

LLP form of business is well recognised and offers the following advantages:

- Renowned and accepted form of business worldwide in comparison to Company.
- Low cost of formation.
- Easy to establish.
- Easy to manage and run.

- No requirement of any minimum capital contribution.
- No restrictions on the maximum number of partners.
- LLP and its partners are distinct from each other.
- Partners are not liable for Act of partners.
- Less compliance level.
- No exposure to personal assets of the partners except in case of fraud.
- Less requirement of maintenance of statutory records.
- Less government intervention.
- Easy to dissolve or wind up.
- Professionals can form multi-disciplinary professional LLP, which was not allowed earlier.
- Audit is required only for contributions exceeding Rs. 25 lakh or turnover exceeding Rs. 40 lakh.

## 26.28 DISADVANTAGES OF LLP

LLP form of business is not without disadvantages. Following are the limitations of LLP format of business:

- Any act of the partner without the other partner, may bind the LLP.
- Under some cases, liability may extend to personal assets of partners.
- It cannot raise money from the Public.

## TEST YOUR KNOWLEDGE

1. A limited liability partnership is a body corporate. Comment. **(Ref. Para-26.1)**
2. Provisions of Indian Partnership Act, 1932, are applicable to LLPs and body corporate may be partner of LLP. Comment. **(Ref. Para-26.1)**
3. What are the salient features of limited liability partnership? **(Ref. Para-26.1)**
4. Write the main points of difference between Partnership and LLP. **(Ref. Para-26.2)**
5. There are no shareholders in a limited liability partnership; instead, there are partners. Comment. **(Ref. Para-26.3)**
6. Distinguish between Company and LLP. **(Ref. Para-26.3)**
7. State whether stamp duty is payable on LLP agreement. Is so, how is the amount of stamp duty calculated? **(Ref. Para-26.4)**
8. What governs the mutual rights and duties of the partners of an LLP and that of the LLP with its partners? **(Ref. Para-26.4)**
9. State whether LLP Agreement would be mandatory for all LLPs. **(Ref. Para-26.4)**
10. How are the mutual rights and duties of the partners of an LLP and that of the LLP with its partners determined in the absence of any agreement about the matter? **(Ref. Para-26.4)**
11. What are the requirements of incorporation document to incorporate an LLP? **(Ref. Para-26.5)**
12. What are the registration formalities relating to LLPs? **(Ref. Para-26.6)**
13. When is an individual disqualified from being appointed as a partner of LLP? **(Ref. Para-26.7)**
14. Can an LLP have less than two partners? **(Ref. Para-26.7)**
15. Can any person other than subscriber to an LLP become a partner? **(Ref. Para-26.7)**
16. What is the liability of a partner if the number of members in an LLP reduces to less the minimum permitted? **(Ref. Para-26.7)**
17. All members of a limited partnership firm are 'designated members'. Comment. **(Ref. Para-26.8)**

18. Can partners act as designated partners? **(Ref. Para-26.8)**
19. Who can be a designated partner? **(Ref. Para-26.8)**
20. How can a designated partner be nominated? **(Ref. Para-26.8)**
21. Is there any difference between managing partner and designated partner? **(Ref. Para-26.8)**
22. What are the major duties of a designated partner? **(Ref. Para-26.9)**
23. What is the manner of service of documents on the partner? **(Ref. Para-26.10)**
24. Is it possible to change the registered office of an LLP from one state to another? What is the procedure in this regard? **(Ref. Para-26.10)**
25. An LLP wants to give an other address apart from its registered office for the purpose of receiving communication. What would be your advice? **(Ref. Para-26.10)**
26. What are the broad provisions of the Act in respect of names of LLPs? **(Ref. Para-26.11)**
27. Explain the name guideline prescribed by the government for selection of name of an LLP **(Ref. Para-26.12)**
28. Which names are not allowed to be registered for LLP? **(Ref. Para-26.12)**
29. Does any change in the partners of an LLP affect its existence, rights or liabilities? **(Ref. Para-26.13)**
30. Who can act as partners of an LLP? **(Ref. Para-26.13)**
31. When shall a person cease to be partner of an LLP? **(Ref. Para-26.13)**
32. What results in cessation of partnership interest? **(Ref. Para-26.13)**
33. On cessation of a partner from an LLP, does he get discharged of obligations to the LLP or to the other partners or to any other person? **(Ref. Para-26.13)**
34. Is the partner, on cessation of the partnership, entitled to receive anything from the LLP? **(Ref. Para-26.13)**
35. Write short note on whistle blowing. **(Ref. Para-26.14)**
36. What are the different forms of contribution? **(Ref. Para-26.15)**
37. Can there be an increase in the contribution of an LLP? **(Ref. Para-26.15)**
38. What are the steps for increase in contribution by way of introduction of new partner(s)? **(Ref. Para-26.15)**
39. What are the provisions in the LLP Act regarding voting right of partners? How shall voting rights of partners be determined, if the LLP Agreement is silent on this matter? **(Ref. Para-26.16)**
40. Is every LLP required to maintain and file accounts? **(Ref. Para-26.17)**
41. State whether audit of all LLPs is mandatory. **(Ref. Para-26.17)**
42. Are there any criteria based on which an LLP can claim exemption audit? If so, what are the obligations prescribed on LLPs which avail the audit exemption? **(Ref. Para-26.17)**
43. Can a chartered accountant who is related to the partners of an LLP, be appointed as an auditor of the LLP? **(Ref. Para-26.17)**
44. Who can appoint the first auditors of an LLP? **(Ref. Para-26.17)**
45. What is the time limit for appointment of first auditors of an LLP? **(Ref. Para-26.17)**
46. In case of failure of designated partners to appoint the first auditors within the prescribed period, who can appoint the first auditors? **(Ref. Para-26.17)**
47. What is the time limit for appointment of subsequent auditors of an LLP? **(Ref. Para-26.17)**
48. What will be the position of auditors if he is not re-appointed within 30 days prior to the end of the financial year? **(Ref. Para-26.17)**
49. What is the procedure for removal of auditors? **(Ref. Para-26.17)**
50. Is the partner's interest in the LLP transferable? **(Ref. Para-26.18)**

51. Does the transfer of any right by the partner result in disassociation of the partner or a dissolution and winding up of the LLP? **(Ref. Para-26.18)**
52. Do the partners of an LLP have a right to make an application to the tribunal for carrying out an investigation of the LLP? **(Ref. Para-26.19)**
53. Can the inspector investigating the affairs of related entities, etc. investigate the affairs of present or former partners? **(Ref. Para-26.19)**
54. Which documents will be available for public inspection in the office of the registrar? **(Ref. Para-26.19)**
55. Can foreigners incorporate LLP? **(Ref. Para-26.18,26.20)**
56. How is the profit of a limited liability partnership treated for the purpose of Tax Acts? **(Ref. Para-26.21)**
57. What is the tax treatment being provided for LLPs? **(Ref. Para-26.21)**
58. Who shall be the partners in case of conversion of a private company into LLP or unlisted public company into LLP? **(Ref. Para-26.22)**
59. What are the steps to be taken for conversion of a partnership into LLP? **(Ref. Para-26.23**
60. List the documents that are to be prepared and filled for incorporation of an LLP. **(Ref. Para-26.24)**
61. Can a compromise or arrangement be entered into between the partners and the LLP? If so, what is procedure to be followed in this regard? **(Ref. Para-26.25)**
62. When is the compromise or arrangement binding on all the partners? **(Ref. Para-26.25)**
63. Can an LLP be wound up? How? **(Ref. Para-26.26)**
64. What are the reasons for which an LLP can be wound up? **(Ref. Para-26.26)**
65. Explain any five advantages of LLP. **(Ref. Para-26.27)**
66. What are the advantages and disadvantages of LLP? **(Ref. Para-26.27,26.28)**

## MULTIPLE-CHOICE QUESTIONS

1. LLP Act of India is broadly based on ______.
   (i) UK LLP Act, 2000
   (ii) Singapore LLP Act, 2005
   (iii) Both of the above.
   (iv) None of the above.
2. LLP Act is applicable to ______.
   (i) a few states of India
   (ii) the whole of India
   (iii) the whole of India except Jammu and Kashmir
   (iv) the whole of India and any branches located outside India
3. LLP combines the advantages of ______.
   (i) Partnership and HUF
   (ii) HUF and Company
   (iii) Partnership and Company
   (iv) Partnership and association
4. Which of the following is/are feature(s) of an LLP?
   (i) It is a separate legal entity.
   (ii) It is separate from its partners.
   (iii) It can own assets in its name, sue and be sued.
   (iv) All of the above.
5. Who manages the business of an LLP?
   (i) Shareholders
   (ii) Partners
   (iii) Partners and registrar
   (iv) Both (a) and (b)

6. LLP Act requires a minimum of ______ partners.
   (i) 2 (iii) 5
   (ii) 3 (iv) 7
7. LLP Act requires a maximum of ______ partners.
   (i) 5 (iii) 12
   (ii) 10 (iv) No limit
8. Which of the following statement(s) is/are not correct?
   (i) LLP should be for profit or charitable business.
   (ii) LLP has perpetual succession.
   (iii) Both of the above
   (iv) None of the above
9. Which of the following statement(s) is/are not incorrect?
   (i) LLP shall maintain annual accounts. (iii) Both of the above
   (ii) Partnership Act is not applicable to LLP. (iv) None of the above
10. Which of the following statement(s) is/are not correct?
   (i) The rights and duties of partners in LLP will be governed by the agreement between partners.
   (ii) The duties and obligations of designated partners shall be as provided in LLP Agreement.
   (iii) Both of the above
   (iv) None of the above
11. Liability of the partner is limited to the extent of his ______ in the LLP.
   (i) contribution (iii) as per LLP Act
   (ii) profit sharing ratio (iv) as per Government norms
12. Audit of the accounts of LLP is required only if the contribution exceeds Rs. ______ lakhs or annual turnover exceeds Rs. ______ lakhs.
   (i) 25; 40 (iii) Any amount; any amount
   (ii) 40; 25 (iv) 50; 100
13. Partnership Act is ______ to LLP
   (i) applicable (iii) applicable to certain extent
   (ii) not applicable (iv) not applicable to certain extent
14. Which of the following statement(s) is/are correct?
   (i) In the case of LLP, registration is optional.
   (ii) LLP is required to be registered with Registrar of firm.
   (iii) LLP is required to be registered with Registrar of companies.
   (iv) None of the above.
15. Which of the following statement(s) is/are incorrect?
   (i) Partnership firm can be converted into LLP (iii) Company cannot be converted into LLP
   (ii) LLP can be converted into partnership (iv) None of the above.
16. Which of the following statement(s) is/are incorrect?
   (i) LLP can be converted into company
   (ii) Only a private company can be converted into LLP
   (iii) Only unlisted public company can be converted into LLP
   (iv) All of the above.

17. Which one of the following is most correct?
    (i) LLP is not body corporate
    (ii) LLP is an entity
    (iii) LLP is a legal entity
    (iv) LLP is a separate legal entity.
18. LLP is created by ______.
    (i) Agreement
    (ii) Law
    (iii) Parties
    (iv) Registrar
19. LLP can be wound up ______.
    (i) voluntarily
    (ii) Either (a) or (b)
    (iii) by order of National Company Law Tribunal.
    (iv) Neither (a) nor (b)
20. Who can be partner of LLP?
    (i) Any individual
    (ii) Body corporate
    (iii) Both of the above.
    (iv) None of the above.
21. Who cannot be partner in LLP?
    (i) Person found to be of unsound mind.
    (ii) Person who is an undercharged insolvent
    (iii) Person who has applied for declaring as insolvent and his application is pending.
    (iv) Any of the above
22. LLP shall have at least two designated partners who should be ______.
    (i) individuals
    (ii) a resident in India
    (iii) Both of the above.
    (iv) None of the above.
23. An individual can become a designated partner in any LLP if
    (i) he has given his prior consent
    (ii) he has obtained a Director Identification Number.
    (iii) Either (a) or (b).
    (iv) Both (a) and (b).
24. Who is required to file with the registrar, particulars of every individual who has given his consent to act as designated partner in prescribed form?
    (i) Partner
    (ii) Designated partner
    (iii) LLP
    (iv) Managing partner.
25. Any vacancy arising in the office of designated PArtner shall be filled within ______ and the change shall be intimated to the registrar of companies.
    (i) One month
    (ii) 30 days
    (iii) 60 days
    (iv) 14 days
26. A contribution of a partner to the capital of LLP may be
    (i) tangible or intangible
    (ii) movable or immovable property
    (iii) Both of the above.
    (iv) None of the above.

## ANSWER KEYS

| | | | | |
|---|---|---|---|---|
| **1.** (iii) | **7.** (iv) | **13.** (ii) | **19.** (iii) | **25.** (ii) |
| **2.** (ii) | **8.** (i) | **14.** (iii) | **20.** (iii) | **26.** (iii) |
| **3.** (iii) | **9.** (iii) | **15.** (ii) | **21.** (iv) | |
| **4.** (iv) | **10.** (ii) | **16.** (iv) | **22.** (i) | |
| **5.** (ii) | **11.** (i) | **17.** (iv) | **23.** (iv) | |
| **6.** (i) | **12.** (i) | **18.** (ii) | **24.** (iii) | |

# 27

# Employees' State Insurance Act, 1948

**Learning objectives**

*After reading this chapter, you will be able to understand:*

- What ESI is
- Coverage of ESI
- Provisions of contribution
- Benefits available to insured employee
- ESI court

## 27.1 INTRODUCTION

### 27.1.1 Objectives

The Employees' State Insurance Act, 1948, aims at securing maximum labour welfare through various welfare schemes like providing certain benefits to employees in case of sickness, maternity and employment injury and to make provisions for certain other matters in relation thereto.

### 27.1.2 Applicability

The Act is applicable all over India including Jammu and Kashmir. It is applicable to all factories (including factories belonging to the government) other than seasonal factories. The Act is not applicable to factory or establishment belonging to or under the control of the government whose employees are otherwise in receipt of benefits substantially similar or superior to the benefits provided under this Act.

## 27.2 DEFINITIONS

### 27.2.1 Appropriate Government

In the case of establishment which is under control of the Central Government or a railway administration or a major port or a mine or oilfield, Central Government is the appropriate government. In all other cases, State Government is the appropriate government.

### 27.2.2 Factory

Factory is defined as any premises including the precincts thereof wherein 10 or more persons are or were employed on any day of the preceding 12 months in any part of manufacturing process. The definition does not include mines or railway running shed

### 27.2.3 Employment Injury—Section 2(8)

Employment injury, under this Act, has the same definition as applicable in the case of Workmen Compensation Act, 1923.

### 27.2.4 Employee

Any person employed for wages, directly employed by the principal employer or employed by or through an immediate employer

1. on the premises of the factory or establishment or
2. under the supervision of the principal employer or his agent
3. whose services are temporarily lent or let on hire to the principal employer
4. by the person with whom the person whose services are so lent or let on hire has entered into contract of service

Employee does not include:

1. any member of the Indian naval, military or air forces
2. any person so employed whose wages (excluding remuneration for overtime work) exceed such wages as may be prescribed by the Central Government

### 27.2.5 Principal Employer

In case of factory, owner or occupier of the factory is principal employer. The managing agent of owner or occupier is considered as principal employer. The legal representative of a deceased owner or occupier is principal employer on death of the owner or occupier. The manager of factory is also considered as principal employer.

In an establishment under the control of any department of any government in India, an authority appointed by such government in this behalf or where no authority is so appointed, the head of the department is considered as principal employer.

In any other establishment, any person responsible for the supervision and control of the establishment is principal employer.

### 27.2.6 Seasonal Factory

A seasonal factory is a factory which is exclusively engaged in one or more of the following manufacturing processes, namely,

1. cotton ginning, cotton or jute pressing, decortications of groundnuts, the manufacture of coffee, indigo, lac, rubber, sugar (including gur) or tea or
2. any manufacturing process which is incidental to or connected with any of the aforesaid processes

It also includes a factory which is engaged for a period not exceeding seven months in a year:

1. In any process of blending, packing or repacking of tea or coffee or
2. In such other manufacturing process as the Central Government may, by notification in the Official Gazette, specify

### 27.2.7 Wages

Wages are all remuneration paid or payable, in cash to an employee, if the terms of the contract of employment, express or implied, were fulfilled. It includes any payment to an employee in respect of:

1. Any period of authorised leave
2. Lock-out
3. Strike which is not illegal
4. Lay-off and other additional remuneration, paid at intervals not exceeding two months

Wages do not include any of following amounts:

1. Provident fund or pension fund contribution by the employer
2. Leave travel concession
3. Reimbursement of expenses
4. Gratuity

## 27.3 INSURABLE EMPLOYEE

All employees in factories or establishments to which this Act applies shall be insured. The following persons are not regarded as insurable employees:

1. Workers in mines subject to Mines Act, 1952
2. Workers in a railway running shed
3. Any member of the Indian naval, military or air forces
4. Any person so employed whose wages excluding remuneration for overtime work exceed such wages as may be prescribed by the Central Government

## 27.4 CONTRIBUTION

As per Section 39, both employer and employee both are required to make contribution to the ESI scheme.

The employee's contribution shall be at the rate of 1.75% of wages whereas employer's contribution shall be at the rate of 4.75% of wages. Contributions fall due on the last day of the wage period.

If an employer make default in payment of contribution on due date, he is liable to pay interest at the rate of 12% p.a. If higher interest rate is prescribed by regulations, such higher interest specified shall not exceed the lending rate of interest charged by any scheduled bank. Responsibility of payment of employee and employer's contribution to the ESI Corporation lies with the principal employer. The principal employer may deduct the employee's contribution from wages of employees who are directly employed by him. Employer's contribution is not to be deducted from wages.

Principal employer shall bear the expenses of remitting the contributions to the Corporation. A principal employer, who has paid employer's and employee's contribution on behalf of immediate employer, can recover the amount so paid from immediate employer. The immediate employer is entitled to recover employee's contribution as deduction from wages from the employees employed by or through him. Employee's contribution shall not be paid if his average daily wages are below the prescribed limits. Principal employer and immediate employer are responsible for submission of returns to the ESI Corporation and maintenance of registers. Any contribution payable under the Act may be recovered as arrear of land revenue.

Employees in respect of average daily wages up to ₹ 100/- are exempted from payment of contribution. However, employers will contribute their own share.

## 27.5 ESI BENEFITS—SECTION 46

### 27.5.1 Medical Benefits

Medical benefits include expenses incurred for medical attendance, treatment, drugs and hospitalisation. It is available to the insured person and his family members.

### 27.5.2 Sickness Benefit

To avail sickness benefit, the sickness must be certified by a medical practitioner. It is paid in cash and is available only to the insured person.

### 27.5.3 Maternity Benefit

Maternity benefit is a periodic payment to an insured workman in case of confinement or miscarriage or sickness arising out of pregnancy. Illegal abortion is not covered under the maternity benefit.

### 27.5.4 Disablement Benefit

Disablement may be either temporary disablement benefit or permanent disablement benefit. A medical board or special medical board assesses injury and loss of earning capacity.

### 27.5.5 Other Benefits

Other benefits include funeral expenses in case of death – ₹ 10,000 to eldest member of the family. These benefits are not transferable. They cannot be assigned. An insured person is not entitled for sickness benefit and medical benefit at the same time. Likewise, maternity benefit and temporary disablement benefit are not available to the insured person at the same time. An employer should not dismiss or punish an employee during his period of sickness.

## 27.6 ESI COURT—SECTIONS 74–75

The State government constitutes ESI Court. ESI Court deals with:

1. Adjudication of disputes under the Act
2. Adjudication of claim

Civil court has no jurisdiction to entertain matters related to ESI. Matters related to ESI are dealt with by ESI court.

### LIST OF LANDMARK JUDGEMENTS

1. ***Shaymdevi vs ESIC (1964)***

   The word 'injury' does not mean only visible injury in the form of some wound.

2. ***Hyderabad Asbestos Cement Products, etc. vs ESIC (1978).***

   The word 'employee' would include not only persons employed in a factory but also persons connected with the work of the factory.

3. ***ESIC vs Apex Engg. Pvt. Ltd (1997)***

   Managing director could be an employee of the company. There could be dual capacity, i.e., as managing director as well as a servant of the company.

4. ***Sindhi Sehiti, M.P. Transport Coop. Society Ltd., Bhopal vs Regional Director, Employees' State Insurance Corporation, Indore. (1997)***

   ESI Act will be applicable to a co-operative society having more than 20 employees.

5. ***Narashimha Mills Ltd, Coimbatore vs Regional Director, Employees' State Insurance Corporation, Madras (2000).***

   A godown away from the factory will come within the expression "premises of the factory" for applicability and coverage under the ESI Act. .

6. ***Transport Corporation of India vs Employees' State Insurance Corporation (2000)***

   A notification issued by a State Government under the ESI Act will extend to all branches of the said establishment situated even outside the State.

7. ***Employees' State Insurance Corporation, Bangalore vs Bhagatram & Sons, Bangalore (2001)***

   Use of LPG for manufacture of sweets will be treated as power for applicability of ESI Act.

8. ***Vellipalaym Co-operative Milk Supply Society vs Regional Director, Employees' State Insurance Corporation, Madras, (2004).***

   Storing milk in the cold storage collected by a cooperative society will be the 'manufacturing process' for coverage under the ESI Act.

9. ***Employees' State Insurance Corporation vs Duncan Gleneagles Hospital Ltd., (2005)***

   Pathological tests carried on by a laboratory attached to a hospital would not come within the purview of 'manufacturing process' to attract its coverage under ESI Act.

10. ***Employees' State Insurance Corporation vs M/s. Jaiswal Rolling Mill (2008)***

    Non-deposit of ESI contributions since Code Number was not allotted will not be justified.

11. ***Employees' State Insurance Corporation, Bangalore vs Dharwad Cooperation Milk Producers Societies Union Ltd., Dharwad (2000)***

    Primary liability to pay ESI's contribution is of the principal employer and not the contractor.

12. ***Deputy Director, Employees State Insurance Corporation, Bangalore vs Proprietor, M/s. Summer Palace Restaurant, Ullal, Mangalore (2007)***
    Security guards through Agency will be included for coverage under ESI Act.
13. ***Employees' State Insurance Corporation, Kanpur vs M/s. Tops Food Products (2008)***
    Two firms functioning separately having one sales tax number and electricity connections are not to be clubbed for coverage under ESI Act.
14. ***ESIC vs Ved Parkash Gupta (2008)***
    When father allows his son to use the premises for different type of business, their establishments cannot be clubbed for coverage under ESI Act.
15. ***Managing Director, Orissa Textile Mills Ltd. vs Mandardlulr Naik (1996)***
    Municipal corporation employees are not to be covered by the Act.
16. ***Kirloskar Consultants Ltd. vs Employees' State Insurance Corporation (2001)***
    An establishment providing consultancy services will be deemed as a 'shop' for coverage under the ESI Act.
17. ***Employees' State Insurance Corporation vs K .N. Premanandan (2007)***
    Employees' Insurance Court is empowered to waive or reduce the damages for late remittance of ESI contributions.

## TEST YOUR KNOWLEDGE

1. Explain about applicability about ESI Act. **(Ref. Para-27.1)**
2. Who is principal employer? **(Ref. Para-27.2)**
3. Which establishment can be considered as seasonal factory under ESI Act? **(Ref. Para-27.2)**
4. Define 'employee'. **(Ref. Para-27.2)**
5. Define 'wages'. **(Ref. Para-27.2)**
6. Who is an insurable employee as per ESI Act? **(Ref. Para-27.3)**
7. Who are required to make contribution under ESI Act? **(Ref. Para-27.4)**
8. Which benefits are available to an insured person under ESI Act? **(Ref. Para-27.5)**
9. Explain about maternity benefit available to a woman employee under ESI Act. **(Ref. Para-27.5)**
10. What is an ESI Court? **(Ref. Para-27.6)**

## MULTIPLE-CHOICE QUESTIONS

1. The Employees State Insurance Act is a ______ legislation.
   (i) corporate welfare
   (ii) social welfare
   (iii) insurance oriented
   (iv) None of the above
2. Employees′ State Insurance Act requires contribution by ______.
   (i) employer
   (ii) employee
   (iii) Either (i) or (ii).
   (iv) Both (i) and (ii).
3. ESI Act is not applicable to
   (i) small factories where less than 20 workers are employed
   (ii) seasonable factories
   (iii) factories located in village
   (iv) None of the above.

4. Who has power to make law on the subject matter of 'employees' insurance'?
   (i) Central Government
   (ii) State Government
   (iii) Insurance department of government
   (iv) Both (i) and (ii).
5. What happens when the number of employees falls below 10? Can the factory or establishment escape from the application of the ESI Act, 1948?
   (i) The establishment does not have to apply the provisions of ESI Act, 1948
   (ii) The factory does not have to apply the provisions of ESI Act, 1948
   (iii) The factory and establishment both do not have to apply the provisions of ESI Act, 1948
   (iv) No, the provision of the ESI Act, 1948 continues to apply.
6. Who is considered dependent of the deceased person under the ESI Act, 1948?
   (i) A widow of the deceased person
   (ii) A legitimate or adopted son of the deceased person who has not attained the age of 25 years
   (iii) Unmarried legitimate or adopted daughter
   (iv) All of the above.
7. ______ means an employee who is not liable under this Act to pay the employee's contribution.
   (i) Active employee
   (ii) Exempted employee
   (iii) Passive employee
   (iv) Dormant employee
8. Definition of word 'factory' under ESI Act, does not include ______.
   (i) Mine
   (ii) Railway running shed
   (iii) Both of the above.
   (iv) None of the above.
9. Principal employer under the ESI Act, 1948, includes ______.
   (i) Owner of the factory or establishment
   (ii) Occupier of the factory or establishment
   (iii) Managing agent of the occupier
   (iv) All of the above.
10. Principal employer under the ESI Act, 1948, includes ______.
   (i) Owner or occupier of the factory or establishment
   (ii) Legal representative of a deceased owner or occupier
   (iii) Named manager of the factory or establishment
   (iv) All of the above
11. The definition of 'wages' under the ESI Act, 1948, does not include ______.
   (i) cash remuneration paid by the employer
   (ii) payment for a lockout or strike which is not illegal
   (iii) payment for additional remuneration not exceeding two months
   (iv) Contribution paid by the employer to any pension fund or provident fund
1.2 The ESI Act, 1948, provides certain benefits to the employees in case of ______.
   (i) employment injury
   (ii) sickness
   (iii) maternity
   (iv) All the three.
13. Who has the primary liability/responsibility to deposit (pay) the contribution of employee as well as employer to the ESI Corporation?
   (i) The principal employer
   (ii) The immediate employer
   (iii) The employee
   (iv) The permanent employee

14. Under the ESI Act, 1948, what is the employee's contribution rate in every wage period?
    (i) 1.75%
    (ii) 4.75%
    (iii) 7.15%
    (iv) 7.45%
15. Under the ESI Act, 1948, what is the employer's contribution rate in every wage period?
    (i) 1.75%
    (ii) 4.75%
    (iii) 7.15%
    (iv) 7.45%
16. Employees in receipt of a daily average wage up to ______ are exempted from payment of contribution under the ESI Act, 1948.
    (i) ₹ 100/-
    (ii) ₹ 500/-
    (iii) ₹ 1,000/-
    (iv) ₹ 1,200/-
17. Under the ESI Act, 1948, sickness benefit is paid for a maximum period of up to ______ in a year.
    (i) 45 days
    (ii) 91 days
    (iii) 60 days
    (iv) 78 days
18. Under the ESI Act, 1948, maternity benefit is payable for a period of ______.
    (i) 15 days
    (ii) 3 months
    (iii) 6 months
    (iv) 2 years
19. Under the ESI Act, 1948, temporary disablement benefit at the rate of ______ of wage is payable, as long as the disability continues.
    (i) 70%
    (ii) 80%
    (iii) 90%
    (iv) 100%
20. According to ESI Act, 1948, an amount of ______ is payable to the dependents or to the person who performs the last rites from day one of entering insurable employment.
    (i) ₹ 5,000/-
    (ii) ₹ 10,000/-
    (iii) ₹ 15,000/-
    (iv) ₹ 25,000/-

## ANSWER KEYS

| | | | | |
|---|---|---|---|---|
| **1.** (ii) | **5.** (iv) | **9.** (iv) | **13.** (i) | **17.** (ii) |
| **2.** (iv) | **6.** (iv) | **10.** (iv) | **14.** (i) | **18.** (ii) |
| **3.** (ii) | **7.** (ii) | **11.** (iv) | **15.** (ii) | **19.** (iii) |
| **4.** (iv) | **8.** (iii) | **12.** (iv) | **16.** (i) | **20.** (ii) |

# INDEX